QUI TAM ACTIONS

CONTEMPORARY DECISIONS

Volume 2

* * *

A LandMark Publication

Litigator Series

Qui Tam Actions
Contemporary Decisions
Volume 2

Published in the United States of America
by LandMark Publications.
www.landmark-publications.org

Publication Date: January 2023;
Subject Heading: Administrative Law;
Audience: Law Professionals.

Character Set: ISO 8859-1 (Latin-1);
Language Code: EN;
Interior Type: Text; Monochrome.

Help us serve you better.
Write to landmarkpx@live.com with
your requests, comments and suggestions.

ISBN: 979-8362923914

SUMMARY OF CONTENTS

PROLOGUE

In 1863, "a series of sensational congressional investigations" revealed that war-profiteering military contractors had billed the federal government for "nonexistent or worthless goods, charged exorbitant prices for goods delivered, and generally robbed" the government's procurement efforts. *United States v. McNinch,* 356 U.S. 595, 599, 78 S.Ct. 950, 2 L.Ed.2d 1001 (1958). In response, Congress passed the False Claims Act, now codified at 31 U.S.C. §§ 3729-3733. The Act authorizes a private person, called a relator, to enforce its terms by filing suit "for the person and for the United States Government." § 3730(b)(1). Suits of this type were once so common that "[a]lmost every" penal statute could be enforced by them. *Adams v. Woods,* 6 U.S. (2 Cranch) 336, 341, 2 L.Ed. 297 (1805). Such suits are called "qui tam" suits, from a Latin tag meaning, "who as well for the lord king as for himself sues in this matter." If the relator's qui tam action is successful, she receives a portion of the recovery as a bounty; the lion's share goes to the government. § 3730(d).

The False Claims Act prohibits, among other acts, presenting to the government "a false or fraudulent claim for payment or approval." § 3729(a)(1)(A). One way to present a false claim is to present to a federal healthcare program a claim for payment that violates the Anti-Kickback Statute, 42 U.S.C. § 1320a-7b(b), which prohibits giving or receiving "remuneration" in return for such programs' business. See 42 U.S.C. § 1320a-7b(g) (violations of the Anti-Kickback Statute also violate the False Claims Act).

US v. UCB, Inc., 970 F. 3d 835 (7th Cir. 2020)

FOREWORD

THIS CASEBOOK contains a selection of U. S. Court of Appeals decisions that analyze and discuss issues surrounding *qui tam* claims. Volume 2 of the casebook covers the Sixth through the Eleventh Circuit Court of Appeals.

The Relators in *Cho on Behalf of States v. Surgery Partners, Inc.* filed a second amended complaint that brought causes of action against H.I.G. entities for violation of the False Claims Act, 31 U.S.C. § 3729(a)(1)(A) and (B), and for conspiracy to violate the FCA, 31 U.S.C. § 3729(a)(1)(C). H.I.G. moved for dismissal on several grounds, including that the FCA's first-to-file rule barred the claim. 30 F. 4th 1035 (11th Cir. 2022).

The district court granted the motion, finding that the second amended complaint was barred by the FCA's first-to-file rule. Although the Relators filed the second amended complaint at a time when a prior claim, "the Ashton Action" was no longer pending, the district court held that the relevant question was whether the Ashton Action was pending at the time the Relators filed their *initial* complaint. Because the Ashton Action was pending at that time, the district court concluded that it barred the Relators' action so long as the two actions were related. The district court held next that the two actions were related because "they allege the same essential facts regarding the fraud against the Government committed by Surgery Partners and Logan Labs." Accordingly, the district court dismissed the claim without prejudice. The Relators appeal the district court's grant of the motion to dismiss.

Affirmed—When relators file a qui tam action that is related to an already-pending action, that claim is incurably flawed from the moment it is filed. Here, the Relators' claims focus on the same fraudulent scheme at issue in the Ashton Action, which was pending when the Relators brought this action. Therefore, the Relators' claim is barred under the FCA's first-to-file rule.

* * *

We split our discussion into two parts. First, we address whether the FCA bars a complaint that is (a) filed while a related action is pending, but (b) amended after the related action is dismissed. Second, we determine the proper standard for analyzing whether a claim is related to a previously-filed action, and we apply that standard to the facts before us.

A.

The Relators' first argument on appeal is that the FCA's first-to-file bar is inapplicable because the Ashton Action was no longer pending at the time the Relators filed the second amended complaint. Under the first-to-file bar, "[w]hen a person brings an action under [the FCA], no person other than the Government may

intervene or bring a related action based on the facts underlying the pending action."
31 U.S.C. § 3730(b)(5). As other courts have observed, the first-to-file bar serves two
related purposes: "to eliminate parasitic plaintiffs who piggyback off the claims of a
prior relator, and to encourage legitimate relators to file quickly by protecting the
spoils of the first to bring a claim." *In re Nat. Gas Royalties Qui Tam Litig. (CO2
Appeals),* 566 F.3d 956, 961 (10th Cir. 2009); *see also United States ex rel. Wood v. Allergan,
Inc.,* 899 F.3d 163, 169-70 (2d Cir. 2018).

Here, there is no dispute that the Ashton Action was still pending when the
Relators filed their original complaint. But when the Relators filed their second
amended complaint, the Ashton Action had settled, and therefore was no longer
"pending." *See Kellogg Brown & Root Servs., Inc. v. United States, ex rel. Carter,* 575 U.S.
650, 664 (2015). The core issue, then, is whether it is the filing of a relator's original
complaint or his amended complaint that informs our analysis of the first-to-file bar.
Or, to frame the question another way: Can a first-to-file defect be cured by the filing
of an amended complaint?

We begin our analysis, as always, with the statutory text. In this case, it happens
to be fairly straightforward: a person may not "bring a related action" while the first-
filed action is pending. 31 U.S.C. § 3730(b)(5). We have held several times that the
key phrase—to "bring" an "action"—"has a settled customary meaning at law, and
refers to the initiation of legal proceedings in a suit." *Harris v. Garner,* 216 F.3d 970,
973 (11th Cir. 2000) (en banc) (quoting Black's Law Dictionary 192 (6th ed. 1990)).
Absent any indication to the contrary, "we readily presume that Congress knows the
settled legal definition of the words it uses, and uses them in the settled sense." *Id.* at
974.

Applying that settled definition here, the statutory prohibition turns on the
moment the Relators *initiated* legal proceedings—not on the moment the Relators
amended their complaint. As other circuits have recognized, "an amended . . .
pleading cannot change the fact that [the relator] *brought* an action while another
related action was pending." *Wood,* 899 F.3d at 172 (citing *United States ex rel. Shea v.
Cellco P'ship,* 863 F.3d 923 (D.C. Cir. 2017)). Here, the Relators brought this suit while
the Ashton Action was pending. Therefore, we hold that the first-to-file bar applies.

The Relators offer two counterarguments. First, they argue that the purpose of
the FCA is to encourage more private enforcement, and that we should interpret the
first-to-file bar narrowly in furtherance of that purpose. As we have explained,
however, "[w]e interpret and apply statutes, not congressional purposes." *In re
Hedrick,* 524 F.3d 1175, 1188 (11th Cir. 2008). And in any event, the FCA does not
pursue a singular purpose. It pursues the "twin goals" of rewarding whistleblowers
for bringing fraud to the government's attention, while seeking to discourage
opportunists who would enrich themselves by pursuing fraud the government
already knows about. *See United States ex rel. Springfield Terminal Ry. v. Quinn,* 14 F.3d
645, 649-51 (D.C. Cir. 1994). How best to mediate those competing interests is for
Congress to decide, and Congress has spoken clearly here.

Second, the Relators argue that their interpretation of the first-to-file bar finds
support in Supreme Court precedent and our own precedent. At the Supreme Court
level, the Relators point to *Rockwell International Corp. v. United States,* 549 U.S. 457
(2007), a case that involved the FCA's public-disclosure bar and its original-source
exception. Under the then-applicable version of the statute, courts lacked jurisdiction

over qui tam suits that were "based upon the public disclosure of allegations or transactions 'unless . . . the person bringing the action [was] an original source of the information.'" *Id.* at 460 (quoting 31 U.S.C. § 3730(e)(4)(A) (1994)). The relator in *Rockwell* amended his complaint but asked the Court to consider only his initial complaint in determining whether he was an original source. *Id.* at 473. The Supreme Court rejected that argument, holding that the word "allegations," as used in the public-disclosure bar, "includes (at a minimum) the allegations in the original complaint *as amended.*" *Id.* (emphasis in original). The Court emphasized that a "demonstration that the original allegations were false will defeat jurisdiction." *Id.*

What we can take from *Rockwell* is that where the analysis turns on the *substance* of a relator's allegations in the public-disclosure context, courts cannot ignore new, relevant allegations that reveal a jurisdictional defect. But the crux of the issue here is *timing*. The temporal question of when an action was brought (i.e., filed) remains unaffected by whatever new allegations a relator brings forward. *See Wood,* 899 F.3d at 172. Therefore, *Rockwell* does not help the Relators.

As to our own precedent, the Relators cite to *Makro Capital of America, Inc. v. UBS AG,* 543 F.3d 1254 (11th Cir. 2008), but that decision too is distinguishable. In *Makro,* the original complaint was not a qui tam action under the FCA; it alleged non-FCA fraud and tort claims. *Id.* at 1256. After the plaintiff amended its complaint, restyling it as an FCA qui tam action, the district court granted dismissal based on the then-applicable government knowledge bar, 31 U.S.C. § 3730(b)(4) (1982) (repealed 1986), finding that the suit was based on information that was publicly available at the time of the amended complaint. *Makro,* 543 F.3d at 1256-57. On appeal, we agreed that the filing of the amended complaint was the proper reference point—but only because the original complaint had not been a qui tam action. *Id.* at 1259. We stressed the "disjunction" between the plaintiff's "original claim seeking personal recovery for fraud (and other torts)," and "its *qui tam* claim seeking recovery for fraud committed against the United States." *Id.* at 1259-60. Without that sort of disjunction here, our holding that the Relators first brought an FCA action when they filed their original complaint is not in tension with *Makro.*

As a result, we conclude that the FCA's plain text tethers our analysis to the moment a qui tam action is filed. When the Relators filed this qui tam suit, the Ashton Action was pending. Therefore, the Relators cannot evade the first-to-file bar by amending their pleading after the Ashton Action was dismissed.

B.

Having determined that the first-to-file bar applies to the filing of the original complaint, we now address the Relators' argument that, in any event, their complaint is unrelated to the Ashton Action.

We have not yet adopted a test for determining whether two qui tam actions are related. Both parties suggest that we follow our sister circuits in adopting the "same material elements" test, also called the "same essential elements" test, which the district court applied below. *See United States ex rel. Chovanec v. Apria Healthcare Grp. Inc.,* 606 F.3d 361, 363 (7th Cir. 2010) (collecting cases). Under this test, two actions are related if they "incorporate 'the same material elements of fraud.'" *Wood,* 899 F.3d at 169. That is, "to be related, the cases must rely on the same 'essential facts.'" *Id.* In applying this test, several circuits have compared the two complaints "side-by-side" and asked "whether the later complaint 'alleges a fraudulent scheme the government already would be equipped to investigate based on the first complaint.'" *United States ex rel. Heath v. AT&T, Inc.,* 791 F.3d 112, 121 (D.C. Cir. 2015) (alterations adopted); *see also Wood,* 899 F.3d at 169; *United States ex rel. Carson v. Manor Care, Inc.,* 851 F.3d 293, 303 (4th Cir. 2017).

As these courts have emphasized, this test finds support in the text of the FCA. Under 31 U.S.C. § 3730(b)(5), the first-filed and later-filed claims need not be identical; they need only be "related." Drawing upon this distinction, the same material elements test creates a framework under which § 3730(b)(5) can still bar a later claim, "even if the allegations 'incorporate somewhat different details.'" *Heath,* 791 F.3d at 116. Finding that this test aligns with the FCA's plain text, we adopt it here.

Our next task is to determine whether the district court correctly applied this test to conclude that the Relators' original complaint alleged the same essential facts as did the original complaint in the Ashton Action, which was pending at the time. The Relators contend that it did not for two reasons. First, the Relators named the H.I.G. entities as defendants, whereas the Ashton Action did not. Second, in addition to the Relators' substantive FCA claim, they alleged a conspiracy, which the Ashton relators did not allege.

Beginning with the Relators' first contention, we disagree that the first-to-file bar requires a necessarily defendant-specific approach. Though we have no binding precedent on point, we find instructive the view of our sister circuits that adding a new defendant to the mix does not *necessarily* allow a later-filed action to evade the first-to-file bar, particularly where the new defendant is a corporate relative or affiliate of the earlier-named defendants. *See, e.g., Nat. Gas Royalties,* 566 F.3d at 962; *United States ex rel. Hampton v. Columbia/HCA Healthcare Corp.,* 318 F.3d 214, 218 (D.C. Cir. 2003). What we must determine is whether the addition of a new defendant put the government on notice of a broader, more pervasive, or distinct scheme. Two cases from the D.C. Circuit, *Hampton* and *Heath,* serve as useful bookends for this analysis.

In *Hampton,* the earlier-filed action was brought against one corporate entity, HCA, alleging a "corporate-wide" fraudulent scheme that HCA carried out through its subsidiaries in thirty-seven states. 318 F.3d at 218. A later-filed action alleged that an additional HCA subsidiary perpetrated the same fraudulent scheme in six other states. *Id.* The court held that merely adding another corporate subsidiary did not amount to a difference in the material elements of the alleged fraud. *Id.* Therefore, the later-filed action was barred. At the other end of the spectrum is *Heath.* In that case, the earlier-filed action alleged that Wisconsin Bell, Inc., a subsidiary of AT&T, Inc., engaged in a scheme to defraud the government. *Heath,* 791 F.3d at 118. That scheme, according to the earlier-filed action, was "limited" in scope and did not extend beyond Wisconsin. *Id.* at 121-122. The later-filed action, in contrast, "allege[d] a different and more far-reaching scheme to de-fraud the federal government through service contracts entered into across the Nation." *Id.* at 121. On these facts, the court held that the later-filed action alleged different material elements of fraud. *Id.* at 122-23.

These cases help illustrate that there is no bright-line rule as to whether naming an additional defendant states a different essential claim. We must determine whether the introduction of a new defendant amounts to allegations of a "different" or "more far-reaching scheme" than was alleged in the earlier-filed action. *See id.*

* * *

Taken as a whole, both complaints allege the same essential [ ] scheme carried out by Surgery Partners and Logan Labs. Based on the Ashton Action, the government was already alerted to that scheme, and would have been equipped to investigate whether any corporate affiliates or investors connected to Surgery Partners and Logan Labs were participants. The Relators did not allege different material facts by naming H.I.G. as a defendant without making any allegations that would meaningfully magnify the scope or pervasiveness of the scheme.

In urging that we reach the contrary conclusion, the Relators analogize a case in the public-disclosure context: *Cooper v. Blue Cross & Blue Shield of Florida, Inc.,* 19 F.3d 562 (11th Cir. 1994) (per curiam). In *Cooper,* the question was whether public disclosure of industry-wide insurance fraud, as well as allegations against Blue Cross Blue Shield of Georgia (BCBSG) amounted to public disclosure of fraud by BCBSG's sister corporation—Blue Cross Blue Shield of Florida. *Id.* at 566-67. We held that it did not, reasoning in part that "[r]equiring that allegations specific to a particular defendant be publically disclosed before finding the action potentially barred encourages private citizen involvement and increases the chances that every instance of specific fraud will be revealed." *Id.* at 566.

We find, however, that *Cooper* is distinguishable. To be sure, a public disclosure that one of a company's subsidiaries engaged in fraud may not alert the government to a parallel, distinct scheme by another subsidiary. But our facts are different. A comparison of the two complaints at issue here belies any notion that the Relators are alleging a fraudulent scheme distinct from the one alleged in the Ashton Action. The Relators allege that an additional player who was affiliated with Surgery Partners and Logan Labs had its hands in the same fraudulent scheme. The government would have been equipped, based on the Ashton Action, to investigate this matter. Therefore, the Relators' claim is related to the Ashton Action for purposes of the first-to-file bar.

Finally, the Relators' raise a separate argument that their FCA conspiracy claim under 31 U.S.C. § 3729(a)(1)(C) is unrelated to the Ashton Action, which alleged only substantive FCA violations. That argument can be dealt with in short order. Because the Relators' conspiracy claim is based on the same fraudulent scheme that was alleged in the Ashton Action, the government would have been equipped to investigate both substantive FCA violations and any conspiracies stemming from, or derivative to, the same scheme. *See Heath,* 791 F.3d at 121. Therefore, the Relators' conspiracy claim is related to the Ashton Action and is barred by § 3730(b)(5).

* * *

SIXTH CIRCUIT DECISIONS
Qui Tam Actions

3 F.4th 813 (2021)

UNITED STATES of America ex rel. Azam RAHIMI, Relator-Appellant,
v.
RITE AID CORPORATION, Defendant-Appellee.

No. 20-1063.

United States Court of Appeals, Sixth Circuit.

Argued: January 26, 2021.
Decided and Filed: June 29, 2021.

US ex rel. Rahimi v. Rite Aid Corp., 3 F. 4th 813 (6th Cir. 2021)

Appeal from the United States District Court for the Eastern District of Michigan at Detroit, No. 2:11-cv-11940—Stephen J. Murphy, Iii, District Judge.

ARGUED: Peter A. Patterson, COOPER & KIRK, PLLC, Washington, D.C., for Appellant. William R. Peterson, MORGAN, LEWIS & BOCKIUS LLP, Houston, Texas, for Appellee. ON BRIEF: Peter A. Patterson, Charles J. Cooper, Vincent J. Colatriano, COOPER & KIRK, PLLC, Washington, D.C., Arun Subramanian, William D. O'Connell, SUSMAN GODFREY LLP, New York, New York, for Appellant. William R. Peterson, MORGAN, LEWIS & BOCKIUS LLP, Houston, Texas, Kevin J. Biron, Michael J. Ableson, MORGAN, LEWIS & BOCKIUS LLP, New York, New York, for Appellee. Frederick M. Morgan, Jr., MORGAN VERKAMP, LLC, CINCINNATI, Ohio, for Amicus Curiae.

Before: BATCHELDER, GRIFFIN, and STRANCH, Circuit Judges.

p.819 OPINION

GRIFFIN, Circuit Judge.

Azam Rahimi believes Rite Aid Corporation defrauded the federal government of hundreds of millions of dollars by overcharging it for generic prescription drugs, so he filed suit under the False Claims Act (FCA) and several state-law analogues. The district court dismissed Rahimi's FCA claim under the Act's public-disclosure bar and declined to exercise supplemental jurisdiction over his remaining claims. We agree and affirm.

I.

A.

Defendant Rite Aid Corporation operates a nationwide chain of pharmacies. Like many of its competitors, Rite Aid p.820 offers a discount program—which it calls the "Rx Savings Program"—that provides its members hundreds of generic prescription drugs at reduced prices. The program is free and widely available but excludes customers whose prescriptions are paid in full or in part by publicly funded healthcare programs like Medicare Part D, state-administered Medicaid programs, or TRICARE.

Federal regulations require pharmacies such as Rite Aid to dispense prescriptions for beneficiaries of these healthcare programs at their "usual and customary charge to the general public"— which is often referred to as the "U&C" rate. *See* 42 C.F.R. § 447.512(b)(2). In general terms, this means that pharmacies cannot charge the government more than the "cash price" offered to the public to fill such prescriptions. *See United States ex rel. Garbe v. Kmart Corp.,* 824 F.3d 632, 636 (7th Cir. 2016).

Relator Azam Rahimi alleges that Rite Aid routinely overbilled these government programs because the amounts it charged did not "take into account either the lower Rx Savings Program prices or any lower prices that Rite Aid makes available to other payers." In other words, while everyone agrees that Rite Aid was not required to allow beneficiaries of publicly funded healthcare plans to *participate* in the Rx Savings Program, Rahimi's theory is that Rite Aid was required to offer the government programs an equivalent-or-better discount because of its obligation to provide the U&C rate.

Rahimi, who is a pharmacist, says he first suspected Rite Aid of overbilling the government when he saw Rite Aid's advertisements for the Rx Savings Program that announced publicly funded healthcare programs were specifically excluded from participating. He then called a former classmate and current Rite Aid pharmacist in New York, John Doe, to discuss his suspicions. Doe told Rahimi that at his pharmacy, ninety to ninety-five percent of Rite Aid's non-insured customers were enrolled in the Rx Savings Program and that Rite Aid's billing software "will only generate the 'Rx Savings price' for a customer if the pharmacy has enrolled a customer in the program," and would not generate the price for beneficiaries of government-funded healthcare plans. But when Rite Aid generated bills for those covered by publicly funded health insurance, it still represented the price to be the U&C rate, even though it "did not include the discounts offered to cash-paying customers through the Rx Savings Program."

Doe also obtained specific examples of the alleged fraud from his cousin, a Rite Aid customer whom he knew to be a New York Medicaid beneficiary. By reviewing his cousin's receipts, Doe confirmed that Rite Aid had charged his cousin more for prescriptions than it would members of the Rx Savings Program. Doe relayed this information to Rahimi, who further investigated by calling Rite Aid pharmacies in eight other states, inquiring as to the prices Medicaid beneficiaries would pay for certain generic medications. "In every single instance, [he] learned that the Rite Aid pharmacy was charging Medicaid significantly higher prices for the generic medications than the prices made available to their Rx Savings Program members." Rahimi also obtained examples involving Medicare Part D and TRICARE.

B.

Rahimi contends this practice violates the False Claims Act, 31 U.S.C. § 3729(a), and other state-law analogues because Rite Aid knowingly caused claims to be submitted for reimbursement by the government "that are materially false because they misrepresented Defendant's 'usual and customary charge' to the general public."[1] p.821 This is because, Rahimi says, "Rite Aid consistently charged government health programs higher amounts for the generic medications on the Rx Savings Program list than the amounts Rite Aid charged its cash-paying customers for the same medications." So, he commenced this litigation on May 3, 2011.

A few more pre-litigation facts are in order. First, as required by the FCA, Rahimi disclosed the alleged fraud to the government on May 2, 2011. He explained that he learned in September 2010 that Rite Aid advertised a savings program, and that "it was possible that Rite Aid was not passing on these discounts to Medicaid, as required by many states' 'usual and customary charge' billing rules." But he was uncertain of his theory because he did not know "i) the percentage of Rite Aid's non-insured customers enrolling in the program; or ii) whether Rite Aid might be charging Medicaid a similar or even lower charge compared to the Rx Savings Program charge." Rahimi thus recounted the steps he took to investigate his theory, including his interactions with John Doe.

But his disclosure about the program was far from the only one.

First, from the beginning of Rite Aid's Rx Savings Program (and before Rahimi's disclosures), Rite Aid had clearly stated in its advertisements and announcements that "[p]rescriptions paid for in whole or in part by publicly funded health care programs [were] ineligible" for the discounted drug prices.

Second, the State of Connecticut learned in 2010 (again before Rahimi's disclosures) that several pharmacies were charging Connecticut Medicaid recipients more than their membership discount prices, which authorities believed to violate *existing* law. Nevertheless, Connecticut then *amended* its law to *require* that pharmacies account for any membership discount program when establishing its U&C price for government billing. But rather than reduce the rate it charged the government to match the Rx Savings price, Rite Aid *raised* the prices charged under the Rx Savings Program, in Connecticut only. Other major pharmacies threatened to discontinue their membership discount plans in Connecticut entirely. The Connecticut Attorney General issued a press release concerning Rite Aid on August 25, 2010 to declare that it was subpoenaing Rite Aid for information about changes to its discount drug pricing, which it "falsely blamed on a new state law." The press release summarized the events surrounding the newly enacted law as follows:

> The law requires pharmacies to provide Medicaid and other state programs the same prescription drug discounts they offer consumers. Apparently in response, Rite Aid increased prices and made other changes to its Rx Savings discount drug program in Connecticut. The drug store chain posted signs that falsely blamed the higher prices and program changes on the new law. . . . All . . . benefits remain unchanged for consumers outside Connecticut.

p.822 This development was widely reported in the United States by national and local media.

Third, the Inspector General of the U.S. Department of Health and Human Services announced in October 2009 and October 2010 (yet again before Rahimi's disclosures) that it would be "review[ing] Medicaid claims for generic drugs to determine the extent to which large chain pharmacies are billing Medicaid the usual and customary charges for drugs provided under their retail discount generic programs."

Fourth, a *qui tam* action was unsealed by the United States District Court for the Central District of California the month prior to Rahimi's complaint being filed, which alleged that Kmart Pharmacies were engaging in an identical scheme to overcharge the government for prescriptions dispensed to beneficiaries of Medicaid and Medicare Part D by failing to apply a discount equal to their membership discount program rate when calculating the U&C charge.

With this in mind, we turn back to Rahimi's lawsuit. After he filed his complaint, the district court administratively closed the action while the federal government investigated his allegations and determined whether to intervene in the suit. More than five years later, the government formally declined to intervene in the suit, and the district court lifted the seal and authorized Rahimi to serve Rite Aid with the complaint. Rite Aid then moved for judgment on the pleadings under Federal Rule of Civil Procedure 12(c), contending the pre-filing facts set forth above, "[t]aken together," demonstrated Rahimi could not overcome the Act's prohibition on complaints based on publicly disclosed information, known as the "public disclosure bar." The district court agreed, granted Rite Aid's motion for judgment on the pleadings on Rahimi's federal claim and declined supplemental jurisdiction over Rahimi's eighteen state-law claims. Rahimi then sought reconsideration, which the court denied. Rahimi timely appealed.

II.

The False Claims Act "prohibits submitting false or fraudulent claims for payment to the United States, and authorizes *qui tam* suits, in which private parties bring civil actions in the Government's name." *Schindler Elevator Corp. v. United States ex rel. Kirk,* 563 U.S. 401, 404, 131 S.Ct. 1885, 179 L.Ed.2d 825 (2011) (internal citations omitted). The Act encourages relators "to act as private attorneys-general in bringing suits for the common good," *United States ex rel. Poteet v. Medtronic, Inc.,* 552 F.3d 503, 507 (6th Cir. 2009) (internal quotation marks omitted), and provides lucrative incentives to those who do so, *see* 31 U.S.C. § 3730(d)(1)-(2). However, "[t]o guard against potential 'parasitic lawsuits' and 'opportunistic plaintiffs,' Congress included a public-disclosure bar in the FCA." *United States ex rel. Maur v. Hage-Korban,* 981 F.3d 516, 521-22 (6th Cir. 2020) (quoting *Poteet,* 552 F.3d at 507). That provision "bars *qui tam* actions that merely feed off prior public disclosures of fraud." *United States ex rel. Holloway v. Heartland Hospice, Inc.,* 960 F.3d 836, 843 (6th Cir. 2020). As most recently amended in 2010, the FCA's public-disclosure bar directs that:

> The court shall dismiss an action or claim under [the FCA], unless opposed by the Government, if substantially the same allegations or transactions as alleged in the action or claim were publicly disclosed—
>
> (i) in a Federal criminal, civil, or administrative hearing in which the Government or its agent is a party;
>
> (ii) in a congressional, Government Accountability Office, or other Federal p.823 report, hearing, audit, or investigation; or
>
> (iii) from the news media, unless the . . . person bringing the action is an original source of the information.

31 U.S.C. § 3730(e)(4)(A) (2010).

We generally apply a three-part test to determine whether the public-disclosure bar precludes an otherwise valid FCA claim. "First, we ask whether, before the filing of the *qui tam* complaint, there had been any public disclosures from which fraud might be inferred." *Maur,* 981 F.3d at 522. Second, we assess how closely related the allegations in the complaint are to those in the public disclosures. *Id.* "And third, we ask whether the *qui tam* plaintiff is nevertheless an original source of the information." *Id.* (internal quotation marks omitted). We review de novo a district court's dismissal of a complaint under Rule 12 by way of the public-disclosure bar. *United States ex rel. Harper v. Muskingum Watershed Conserv. Dist.,* 842 F.3d 430, 435 (6th Cir. 2016).

We face one additional complication here. While Rahimi has only one claim under the False Claims Act, the alleged fraud occurred both before and after the FCA was amended in 2010. Because those amendments made substantive changes to the law, which are not retroactive, there are similar but distinct legal tests for pre- and post-amendment conduct. *See Holloway,* 960 F.3d at 843-44. Accordingly, while we retain our usual three-step framework, we will identify areas where the legal tests diverge. But "[u]nder either version of the public-disclosure bar, [a relator] must demonstrate '(1) that the factual premise of [his] claim was not publicly disclosed before [he] filed the lawsuit, or (2) even if it was, that [he] was the original source of the information.'" *Holloway,* 960 F.3d at 843 (quoting *United States ex rel. Advocates for Basic Legal Equal., Inc. v. U.S. Bank, N.A.,* 816 F.3d 428, 430 (6th Cir. 2016) (*ABLE*)).

A.

Under either version of the public-disclosure bar, we must first determine whether "there had been any public disclosures from which fraud might be inferred" before the filing of the *qui tam* complaint. *Maur,* 981 F.3d at 522; *Poteet,* 552 F.3d at 511 (pre-amendment framework). A disclosure is public "if it appears in 'the news media' or is made 'in a criminal, civil, or administrative hearing, [or] in a congressional, administrative, or Government Accounting Office report, audit, or investigation.'" *Poteet,* 552 F.3d at 512 (quoting § 3730(e)(4)(A) (1986)).[2] And a statement or allegation satisfies the inference-of-fraud element if "the information is sufficient to put the government on notice of the likelihood of related fraudulent activity." *Id.* (citation and internal quotation marks omitted). In other words, the "publicly disclosed documents need not use the word 'fraud,' but need merely to disclose information which creates 'an inference of impropriety.'" *United States ex rel. Burns v. A.D. Roe Co. Inc.,* 186 F.3d 717, 724 (6th Cir. 1999) (quoting *United States ex rel. Jones v. Horizon Healthcare Corp.,* 160 F.3d 326, 332 (6th Cir. 1998)).

Disclosures of fraud generally fall into two categories:

> First, if the information about both a false state of facts and the true state of facts has been disclosed, we [will] find that there has been an adequate public p.824 disclosure because fraud is implied. . . . Second, if there has been a direct allegation of fraud, we will find a public disclosure because such an allegation, regardless of its specificity, is sufficient to put the government on notice of the potential existence of fraud.

Poteet, 552 F.3d at 512-13 (internal citations and quotation marks omitted; first alteration in original). However, a public disclosure can also be piecemeal so long as the multiple sources of information reveal the allegation of fraud and its essential elements. "Courts use the following formula to explain that concept: If X + Y = Z, Z represents the *allegation* of fraud and X and Y represent its essential elements." *Holloway,* 960 F.3d at 844 (quoting *Jones,* 160 F.3d at 331) (internal quotation marks and brackets omitted). "In order to disclose the fraudulent *transaction* publicly, the combination of X and Y must be revealed, from which readers or listeners may infer Z, *i.e.,* the conclusion that fraud has been committed." *Id.* (quoting *Jones,* 160 F.3d at 331).

Turning to the facts of this case, the district court found a public disclosure of fraud for two reasons. It first observed that,

> the Connecticut Attorney General's Office issued a press release on August 25, 2010, recounted in the news media, announcing an investigation of [Rite Aid]. The press release stated that Defendant increased its Rx Savings discount program prices in Connecticut "[a]pparently in response" to a new Connecticut law "requir[ing] pharmacies to provide Medicaid and other state programs the same prescription drug discounts they offer consumers." The press release further stated that Defendant "posted signs that falsely blamed the higher prices and program changes on the new law" by claiming that the law required defendant to "impose these drug prices increases on Connecticut consumers."

Second, it found "impossible to ignore" similarities to *United States ex rel. Winkelman v. CVS Caremark Corporation,* 827 F.3d 201 (1st Cir. 2016), which concluded that the public-disclosure bar foreclosed a nearly identical claim brought by a relator against CVS Pharmacy. In the words of that court, the press release and coverage "dwelt, with conspicuous clarity, upon CVS's persistent practice of not giving Medicaid the [membership discount program] price. Indeed, once the Connecticut legislature amended its Medicaid statutes to mandate that CVS provide the [discount rate] to the state's Medicaid program, CVS threatened to end [the program] entirely." *Id.* at 209 (emphasis omitted). The district court thus took its cue from *Winkelman* and concluded that "[t]he revelation that, immediately after Connecticut passed its 2010 law, Defendant raised the prices for its discount program only in Connecticut and publicly blamed the 2010 law for the price increases—just as CVS threatened to terminate its discount program in response to the same law" disclosed a fraud.

Rahimi challenges this conclusion on appeal, reasoning that the whole of the Connecticut Attorney General's press release and surrounding news coverage (the Connecticut Publicity) did not adequately disclose the essential elements of any fraud. He says that unlike the similar press release involving CVS, which specifically alleged that CVS's billings to the government violated the law, "[t]he issue with Rite Aid was . . . that it had raised prices to its Rx Savings Program customers in the state, but was falsely claiming to the public that Connecticut's new law required it do so." In other words, Rahimi says that the Rite Aid press release was only about "the pharmacy's pretextual use of the new Connecticut law to justify raising prices to customers." Thus, he claims that "[t]here was no suggestion of billing fraud against Rite Aid, let alone any disclosure of the p.825 'essential elements' underpinning the present lawsuit."

We are not persuaded by this view of the facts. The following information was disclosed to the public and can be considered together for determining whether there was a public disclosure of the essential elements of a fraud:

- Rite Aid excluded Medicare and Medicaid beneficiaries from participating in its Rx Savings Program.

- Connecticut believed that its pre-existing rules required pharmacies to bill its Medicaid program at the lowest drug price they offered consumers, including their membership discount programs, and passed the new law when some pharmacies disagreed.

- In 2010, directly in response to Connecticut's mandating that pharmacies' U&C price track membership discount prices, Rite Aid *raised* its Rx Savings Program prices in Connecticut *only*.

As the First Circuit concluded in *Winkelman,* these facts were sufficient to publicly disclose a fraud:

> [I]t requires hardly an inferential step to connect the allegedly true and allegedly misrepresented facts. The publicly disclosed materials revealed, quite plainly, that CVS was not providing its [membership discount] price as its U&C price to Connecticut's Medicaid program. That is precisely why the Connecticut legislature essayed a statutory fix. So, too, those materials revealed Connecticut's belief that the [membership discount] prices should have been provided to the state's Medicaid program even before the statutory change. The allegations and transactions that comprised the essential elements of the claimed fraud were in plain sight after these disclosures.

Id. at 209 (internal citation omitted).

Notwithstanding the minor differences between the CVS and Rite Aid press releases, we agree with our sister circuit that the essential elements of the alleged fraud were in plain sight after the Connecticut Publicity. The press release and surrounding national news coverage disclosed that pharmacies doing business in Connecticut were more explicitly required by the newly amended law to charge to the government a price equal to or lower than the discounted price paid by participants of the Rx Savings Program. Accordingly, unless Rite Aid had already matched its Rx Savings Program price to the U&C price (as Rahimi alleges it had always been required to do), it was forced down one of two paths: It either had to lower the U&C rate charged to government healthcare plans to match the Rx Savings rate, or it could raise its discount rate, so that members of the Rx Savings Program paid an amount equal to the government rate. The Connecticut Publicity establishes that Rite Aid took the latter path and falsely blamed the change in law for forcing it to raise prices for the Rx Savings Program. But in *either* circumstance, a change in how Rite Aid priced its generic prescription drugs would reveal both the misrepresented facts (that Rite Aid was billing the government at its real U&C rate) and the true state of facts (that Rite Aid was charging less for the same drugs when dispensed to members of the Rx Savings Program). So even if the Connecticut Publicity did not put a numerical value on the difference between the U&C rate charged to the government programs and the lower rate Rite Aid charged to members of the Rx Savings Program, it sufficiently disclosed the fraud by allowing readers to infer that Rite Aid requested reimbursement from the government for p.826 prescription drugs at higher prices than it offered through the Rx Savings Program.

B.

The second step in the public-disclosure framework is determining whether the public disclosures were sufficiently related to the allegations of fraud contained in the *qui tam* complaint. *Maur,* 981 F.3d at 522.

Under the pre-amendment FCA, this means the *qui tam* claim is "supported by the previously disclosed information" such that a "substantial identity exists between the publicly disclosed allegations or transaction and the *qui tam* complaint." *Poteet,* 552 F.3d at 514. "In applying the substantial-identity test, we held that the relator's claims are based on prior public disclosures where 'essentially the same . . . scheme' was 'the primary focus' of the prior disclosure and the complaint." *Holloway,* 960 F.3d at 847 (quoting *United States ex rel. McKenzie v. Bell-South Telecomm.,* 123 F.3d 935, 940 (6th Cir. 1997)). Pre-amendment *qui tam* actions are barred if they are "based *even partly* upon public disclosures." *Id.* (quoting *McKenzie,* 123 F.3d at 940). Under the updated FCA, we assess "whether the allegations in the complaint are 'substantially the same' as those contained in the public disclosures." *Maur,* 981 F.3d at 522. (quoting *Holloway,* 960 F.3d at 849). Thus, we have recognized that the post-amendment bar is "more lenient" to relators because it requires more similarity between the public disclosures and the *qui tam* allegations. *Holloway,* 960 F.3d at 849-51.

1.

Rahimi contends his *qui tam* claim was not sufficiently related to the publicly disclosed allegations to fall within the ambit of the public-disclosure bar under either version of the FCA. In his view, the district court "wrongly extended its public-disclosure ruling about U&C fraud on Connecticut's Medicaid Program to every single Medicaid program alleged in the complaint . . . *and* federally administered programs[.]" He posits that if "a single news article about a single investigation by a single state attorney general constitutes a 'public disclosure' of any fraud that could be committed by that company *in any state in the country*—under any state's rules, even if significantly different—the purpose of the FCA is defeated, and relators will have no incentive to report fraud in other jurisdictions." In short, Rahimi emphasizes the breadth of his allegations —he says Rite Aid was defrauding the federal government and 18 states, but the Connecticut Publicity involved only one of those states and only one of the three healthcare programs (Medicaid, and not Medicare Part D or TRICARE). Therefore, in his view, the Connecticut Publicity was too narrow to be sufficiently related to the fraud he alleged, so the public-disclosure bar does not apply.

But circuit precedent and the First Circuit's persuasive opinion in *Winkelman* foreclose this argument. In *Holloway,* we concluded, as here, that a relator's claims could not survive the public-disclosure bar because his "allegations add[ed] some new details to describe essentially the same scheme by the same corporate actor" as the publicly disclosed fraud. 960 F.3d at 851-52. We are compelled to reach the same result here.

And even if not bound by *Holloway*, *Winkelman* persuasively explains that once "the same fraudulent scheme [] was laid bare in the Connecticut disclosures, the identification of additional government programs does nothing more than add a level of detail to knowledge that was already in the public domain." 827 F.3d at 210. It further explained:

> The relators labor to distinguish their complaint from the public disclosures by p.827 emphasizing its breadth: the Medicare Part D program was never mentioned in the Connecticut disclosures, nor did those disclosures aver that CVS was allegedly playing fast and loose with the Medicaid program in other states. This argument elevates form over substance. When it is already clear from the public disclosures that a given requirement common to multiple programs is being violated and that the same potentially fraudulent arrangement operates in other states where the defendant does business, memorializing those easily inferable deductions in a complaint does not suffice to distinguish the relators' action from the public disclosures.

Id. We see no reason to disagree.

2.

Rahimi adds an additional reason to reject the district court's conclusion on this issue, claiming that variations in the way administering agencies define their U&C rate put his claim outside the reach of the public-disclosure bar. But before we can consider the merits of that contention, Rahimi has a procedural hurdle—whether he forfeited our consideration of this new position by making it for the first time in his motion for reconsideration before the district court. *See Evanston Ins. Co. v. Cogswell Prop., LLC,* 683 F.3d 684, 692 (6th Cir. 2012) ("Arguments raised for the first time in a motion for reconsideration are untimely and forfeited on appeal.").

Rahimi first says there is no forfeiture because "Rite Aid . . . did not clearly advance the rationale on which the district court relied, [and] did not clearly argue that the Connecticut disclosure was itself sufficient to defeat all of those other claims." We are not persuaded. Once Rite Aid raised the public-disclosure bar and pointed to the disclosures it thought were related to the fraud Rahimi alleged, he had an opportunity to explain why the court should conclude that his claim was not related—for instance, by explaining that each program applied unique U&C rules.

Next, Rahimi claims that he raised this argument in his response to Rite Aid's motion for judgment on the pleadings. But neither of Rahimi's cited examples explained that the existence of various formulations of a U&C price meant that the Connecticut Publicity did not reach the fraud he alleged. In his response to the motion for judgment on the pleadings, he argued that the Connecticut Publicity was insufficient to "lead[] to an inference that Rite Aid overbilled Connecticut Medicaid or other government programs." In other words, he argued that the Connecticut Publicity did not meet the first step of the framework by disclosing *any* fraud—not that the allegations of his *qui tam* complaint were unrelated to the fraud in the public view. And in a court-authorized sur-reply, Rahimi referenced how some state's

Medicaid rules defined "usual and customary" to mean "a pharmacy's lowest charge or require the charge to the government to reflect *all* discounts and special pricing." But he went no further in explaining how any of these differences affected the public disclosure analysis. That is insufficient to preserve the argument for review. *See FTC v. E.M.A. Nationwide, Inc.,* 767 F.3d 611, 630 (6th Cir. 2014).

Finally, Rahimi points to the district court's reasoning in denying his motion for reconsideration. In his view, "when the district court denied reconsideration, it held that it was doing so because, in ruling on Rite Aid's motion, it had *already* 'explicitly considered in detail' the argument based on differences in program billing requirements." But this mischaracterizes what the district court said:

> [T]he motion raises two issues, both of which were explicitly considered in detail and resolved in the Court's initial order.
>
> p.828 First, Relator took issue with the Court's analysis of his claims in light of [*Winkelman*]. . . .
>
> Second, Relator disagreed with the court's discretionary decision not to exercise supplemental jurisdiction over state law claims under the laws of numerous states in a case in which there are no remaining federal claims."

The court did *not* say that it had "explicitly considered in detail" anything relating to the differing U&C definitions.

We therefore conclude that Rahimi forfeited the argument that the public-disclosure bar does not apply because the unique application of varying U&C definitions meant that the fraud he alleged was not sufficiently related to the information in the public domain. Further, we decline Rahimi's invitation to excuse the forfeiture because failing to consider his argument will not result in "a plain miscarriage of justice." *Scottsdale Ins. Co. v. Flowers,* 513 F.3d 546, 552 (6th Cir. 2008) (citation and internal quotation marks omitted).

C.

Having concluded Rahimi's claim alleges fraud that is sufficiently close to transactions already in the public domain, the final step in the analysis is determining whether he may nonetheless pursue his claim as an original source. *See* 31 U.S.C. § 3730(e)(4)(A)-(B).

1.

We must first address an apparent conflict between the Supreme Court's interpretation of the pre-amendment original-source exception and our caselaw. The text of the 1986 version of the FCA provided that an original source is an individual: (1) with "direct and independent knowledge of the information on which the allegations are based;" and (2) who has "voluntarily provided the information to the government before filing an action under [the FCA] which is based upon the information." 31 U.S.C. § 3730(e)(4)(B) (1986). Our court has understood this provision to require an original source to disclose his information to the government before *any* public disclosure of the allegations, *McKenzie,* 123 F.3d at 942, an interpretation that we adopted after consideration of the D.C. Circuit's opinion in

United States ex rel. Findley v. FPC-Boron Employees' Club, 105 F.3d 675 (D.C. Cir. 1997). And it appears we are the only two circuits to read the 1986 version of the Act this way. *See McKenzie,* 123 F.3d at 941-42 (noting circuit split).

Subsequently, in *Rockwell International Corporation v. United States,* 549 U.S. 457, 127 S.Ct. 1397, 167 L.Ed.2d 190 (2007), the Supreme Court interpreted § 3730(e)(4) in a manner that was plainly inconsistent with *McKenzie's* view of the text. *Rockwell* held that the original-source exception applies to "information upon which the relators' allegations are based" rather than "information underlying the public disclosure." *Id.* at 470-71, 127 S.Ct. 1397. In so reasoning, the Court compared § 3730(e)(4)(A)'s bar on actions based on "the public disclosure of allegations or transactions" with subparagraph (B)'s original-source exception for persons having "direct and independent knowledge of the information on which the allegations are based." § 3730(e)(4)(B). The Court first explained that subparagraph (B)'s "information on which the allegations are based" must mean the facts underlying the relator's alleged fraud. *Id.* at 470-71, 127 S.Ct. 1397. Second, it rejected the reading that the "allegations or transactions" referenced in subparagraph (A) must be the same as the "allegations" referenced in subparagraph (B), a reading which would make "original-source status [dependent] on knowledge of information underlying the publicly disclosed allegations." *Id.* at 471, 127 S.Ct. 1397. It reasoned that Congress p.829 would have used the identical phrase in subparagraph (B) if it had "wanted to link original-source status to information underlying the public disclosure." *Id.* Thus, the Court drew a distinction between public allegations and the information *underlying* the public allegations. *Id.* at 471-72, 127 S.Ct. 1397. In sum, the Court held a relator may make the same allegations as disclosed in a prior public disclosure and still qualify for original source status, so long as the relator had direct and independent knowledge of the information underlying his allegations. *See id.* at 472, 127 S.Ct. 1397 ("To bar a relator with direct and independent knowledge of information underlying his allegations just because no one can know what information underlies the similar allegations of some other person simply makes no sense.").

Although the D.C. Circuit has subsequently recognized that requiring a relator to furnish his information to the government before any public disclosure is contrary to *Rockwell* (and therefore no longer follows its *Findley* decision), *see United States ex rel. Davis v. District of Columbia,* 679 F.3d 832, 838-39 (D.C. Cir. 2012), we have continued to apply the *Findley/McKenzie* rule. *See United States v. Garman,* 719 F. App'x 459, 463-64 (6th Cir. 2017); *United States ex rel. Antoon v. Cleveland Clinic Found.,* 788 F.3d 605, 617 (6th Cir. 2015); *Poteet,* 552 F.3d at 515.[3] So the district court considered itself bound to follow that precedent and concluded that Rahimi could not qualify as an original source under the 1986 version of the Act.

We agree with the D.C. Circuit's conclusion in *Davis* and now hold *McKenzie's* interpretation of the original-source exception is incompatible with *Rockwell.* And although we have applied *McKenzie* post-*Rockwell,* we are not bound by our continued, uncritical application of the *Findley/McKenzie* rule because intervening Supreme Court decisions allow a panel of our court to revisit prior precedent, "even in the unusual situation where binding circuit precedent overlooked earlier Supreme Court authority." *Ne. OH. Coal. for the Homeless v. Husted,* 831 F.3d 686, 720 (6th Cir. 2016). This is one of those unusual cases. Accordingly, when applying the 1986 version of the Act, we will no longer require that a relator provide information to the government prior to any public disclosure to qualify as an original source.

2.

While the district court relied on *McKenzie* to conclude that Rahimi could not qualify as an original source under the pre-amendment FCA, we affirm on the alternative grounds that Rahimi did not have direct knowledge of the information on which his allegations were based. *See* § 3730(e)(4)(B) (1986).

We have explained that "direct" knowledge does not require that the relator be a corporate insider because "first-hand knowledge is not a necessary component of direct knowledge." *Antoon,* 788 F.3d at 618 (emphasis omitted). "For instance, a relator may have direct (but not first-hand) knowledge of the billing practices of an institution, and uncover fraud only after consulting a public document that reveals those practices are fraudulent." *Id.* at 618-19. We thus interpret § 3730(e)(4)(B) to mean "direct knowledge is knowledge gained by the relator's own efforts and not acquired from the labor of other people," *id.* at 619 (internal quotation marks omitted), and a relator's knowledge is "independent" if it "does not p.830 depend or rely upon the public disclosure." *Id.* at 617 (internal citation marks and citation omitted). Finally, we are mindful that "[e]ach case is different and must be analyzed to assess the degree of the relator's original input into the facts disclosed to the government." *Id.* at 619.

We conclude that the majority of Rahimi's information was not gained by his own efforts and instead came from John Doe (and Doe's cousin) and therefore cannot itself be considered "direct." On this record, this information—including that a particular Rite Aid pharmacy in New York was charging Medicaid beneficiaries more than the Rx Savings Program rate and that the overwhelmingly majority of cash purchasers at the same pharmacy were members of the Rx Savings Program—was not the fruit of Rahimi's labor. *Id.; see also United States ex rel. Reagan v. E. Tex. Med. Ctr. Reg'l Healthcare Sys.,* 384 F.3d 168, 177 (5th Cir. 2004) ("The plain meaning of the term 'direct' requires knowledge derived from the source without interruption or gained by the relator's own efforts rather than learned second-hand through the efforts of others.").

Beyond this second-hand information, Rahimi's own investigation boiled down to calling various Rite Aid pharmacies and inquiring about particular drug prices charged to customers, not the prices submitted to the government for reimbursement. We have explained that "[t]he purposes of the Act would not be served by allowing a relator to maintain a qui tam suit based on pure speculation or conjecture." *Antoon,* 788 F.3d at 620 (quoting *United States ex rel. Aflatooni v. Kitsap Physicians Servs.,* 163 F.3d 516, 526 (9th Cir. 1999)). In *Antoon,* this principle meant that a patient did not qualify as an original source where he suspected that his doctor had not actually performed a medical procedure based on his own pre- and post-operation observations and medical records but had no further information to establish whether the doctor was personally involved with the surgery. *Id.* at 619-20. We said that, although the relator "*suspects* that [his doctor] submitted a false claim, mere suspicion is insufficient to qualify" that relator as an original source. *Id.* at 620.

The same holds true here. Until Rahimi obtained evidence of individual claims that Rite Aid submitted to state Medicaid programs (included in his Third Amended Complaint), Rahimi could only *suspect* that Rite Aid was submitting false claims to the government based on the rates quoted to him by Rite Aid pharmacists for the prices *beneficiaries* of publicly funded insurance would pay. And because that further evidence was not part of Rahimi's disclosures to the government, it cannot be considered for determining whether he was an original source at the time he filed suit. *See* 31 U.S.C. § 3730(e)(B)(4)(B).

While mere reference to public documents is not an automatic bar to original-source status, the inquiry is fact-dependent and must be analyzed as to the degree of the relator's original input into the facts disclosed to the government. *Antoon,* 788 F.3d at 618 (collecting cases). Here, Rahimi's original input consists solely of putting more flesh on the fraud scheme, of which the bones were already public. It would be contrary to the purpose of the Act to extend the original source exception to such activities. Accordingly, we hold that Rahimi does not qualify as an original source under the 1986 version of the Act.

3.

The FCA now provides:

> For purposes of this paragraph, "original source" means an individual who either (i) prior to a public disclosure under p.831 subsection (e)(4)(A), has voluntarily disclosed to the Government the information on which allegations or transactions in a claim are based, or (2) who has knowledge that is independent of and materially adds to the publicly disclosed allegations or transactions, and who has voluntarily provided the information to the Government before filing an action under this section.

31 U.S.C. 3730(e)(4)(B) (2010). Therefore, the original source exception is now explicitly tied to public disclosures, but Congress also provided a safety valve for relators who do not furnish the information to the government before a public disclosure but have "knowledge that is independent of and materially adds to the publicly disclosed allegations." *Id.* "Materiality in this setting requires the claimant to show it had information '[o]f such a nature that knowledge of the item would affect a person's decision-making,' is 'significant,' or is 'essential.'" *ABLE,* 816 F.3d at 431 (quoting Black's Law Dictionary 1124 (10th ed. 2014)). "In other words, the relator must bring something to the table that would add value for the government." *Maur,* 981 F.3d at 527.

The district court determined that Rahimi's allegations failed the materiality requirement because the general fraudulent scheme "was easily inferred from the Connecticut publicity[,] [a]nd Relator's specific examples of Defendant's implementation of the scheme [did] not materially add to the public disclosures." Rahimi now argues that his allegations were material because "[n]othing in the public disclosures spoke to whether the Rx Savings price was the usual and customary price that Rite Aid charged, or whether Rite Aid's billing systems took those prices into account when computing charges to government payers." Thus, the argument goes that "[w]ithout that information, neither the public, nor the government payers, had sufficient information to determine whether Rite Aid was liable for violating U&C billing rules."

We first observe that Rahimi is attempting to rewrite what he disclosed to the government. He contends on appeal that his pre-suit disclosure "reveal[ed] whether the Rx Savings Program price was so prevalent that it had become the usual and customary price under the rules of almost every government health program." But his pre-suit disclosure did nothing of the sort; he reported to the government that he thought the Rx Savings Program price became the U&C price once it was "offered" to plan participants. The only information he relayed about public participation in the Rx Savings Program was that John Doe had reported that ninety percent of cash buyers at his pharmacy were enrolled—he did not disclose any information about broader consumer participation in the Rx Savings Program.

But more to the merits, relator's allegations do not materially add to the public disclosures because the government was already on notice that Rite Aid had not been applying its Rx Savings Programs discount when making its U&C rate calculation by operation of the Connecticut Publicity. Even though Rahimi was able to add additional state-specific information and examples of government beneficiaries paying more than its Rx Savings Program rate, "[o]ffering specific examples [of the alleged fraud] does not provide any significant new information where the underlying conduct already has been publicly disclosed." *Winkelman,* 827 F.3d at 212; *see also ABLE,* 816 F.3d at 432 ("A *qui tam* plaintiff 'is not allowed to proceed independently if it merely adds details to what is already known in outline." (quoting *United States ex rel. Bogina v. Medline Indus., Inc.,* 809 F.3d 365, 370 (7th Cir. 2016) (internal quotations marks and brackets omitted))); *Maur,* 981 F.3d at 528 ("[B]y p.832 merely providing additional instances of the same type of fraud . . ., Maur has failed to offer information of 'such a nature that knowledge' of it 'would affect' the 'government's decision-making.'" (quoting *ABLE,* 816 F.3d at 431-32)). In sum, we agree with the district court that Rahimi proffered no information to change the government's thinking or decision-making with respect to the alleged fraud. He therefore does not qualify as an original source under the 2010 version of the FCA.

D.

For these reasons, the district court properly applied the FCA's public-disclosure bar to Rahimi's FCA claim.

III.

Finally, we consider whether the district court abused its discretion by declining supplemental jurisdiction over four of Rahimi's state-law claims. In declining supplemental jurisdiction, the district court determined that it should, in most cases, avoid deciding novel issues of state law and further observed that the general practice of federal district courts is to dismiss supplemental state-law claims if the federal claims are dismissed before trial.

Rahimi argues that even if the district court properly dismissed his federal claim, it should have exercised supplemental jurisdiction over his equivalent claims brought under state law (and for which, unlike the federal government here, the states waived application of the public-disclosure bars). Generally, he argues that the district court did not adequately balance the interests because it failed to give due weight to judicial economy (the case had been pending in district court for almost nine years) and the avoidance of multiplicity of litigation.

We are unpersuaded. Even though the seal had been lifted for more than three years, the case was still about two years away from its scheduled trial date when the district court granted Rite Aid's motion for judgment on the pleadings. And while the parties had exchanged some discovery while the motion was under advisement, it was largely an exchange of documents—no depositions or expert discovery took place. And finally, the district court was correct to highlight that resolution of the remaining state-law claims would require it to opine on the intricacies of various states' false-claim statutes. *See Landefeld v. Marion Gen. Hosp.*, 994 F.2d 1178, 1182 (6th Cir. 1993) (holding that a district court did not abuse its discretion by declining supplemental jurisdiction when novel state-law questions outweighed judicial-economy interests). For these reasons, the district court permissibly declined to exercise supplemental jurisdiction.

IV.

We affirm the district court's judgment.

[1] The reimbursement aspect of Rahimi's FCA claim stems from the government-sponsored program's insurance coverage for prescription drug costs. For example, Medicare Part D is a federal, voluntary prescription drug benefit program available to persons eligible for Medicare. It is overseen by the Centers for Medicare and Medicaid Services (CMS), which contracts with private companies (called Part D Sponsors) to handle claim submissions and payment processes for Medicare Part D beneficiaries. Under this model, Part D Sponsors work directly with retail pharmacies to provide covered prescriptions at negotiated rates. The Part D Sponsor then tenders payment to the pharmacy and seeks reimbursement from CMS. State-administered Medicaid programs and TRICARE similarly operate on a reimbursement system.

[2] The list of potential "public" disclosures shrank with the 2010 amendments to exclude filings and rulings associated with state-court proceedings. *Compare* 31 U.S.C. § 3730(e)(4)(A) (2010), *with* 31 U.S.C. § 3730(e)(4)(A) (1986). That distinction is not relevant to this case.

[3] There appears to be a reason for this. Upon review of the briefs in those cases, we note the parties failed to bring the conflict between *Rockwell* and *McKenzie* to our attention, and so gave us no reason to reconsider our prior authority.

981 F.3d 516 (2020)

UNITED STATES of America EX REL. Gurpreet MAUR, M.D., Plaintiff-Appellant,
v.
Elie HAGE-KORBAN; Delta Clinics, PLC, dba The Heart and Vascular Center of West Tennessee; Knoxville HMA Holdings, LLC, dba Tennova Healthcare; Jackson Hospital Corporation, dba Regional Hospital of Jackson; Dyersburg Hospital Company, LLC, dba Dyersburg Regional Medical Center, Defendants-Appellees.

No. 20-5301.

United States Court of Appeals, Sixth Circuit.

Argued: October 7, 2020.
Decided and Filed: December 1, 2020.

US ex rel. Maur v. Hage-Korban, 981 F. 3d 516 (6th Cir. 2020)

Appeal from the United States District Court for the Western District of Tennessee at Jackson, No. 1:17-cv-01079—S. Thomas Anderson, District Judge.

ARGUED: Shelby Serig, MORGAN & MORGAN P.A., Jacksonville, Florida, for Appellant. Jeffrey Scott Newton, BAKER DONELSON BEARMAN CALDWELL & BERKOWITZ, PC, Jackson, Mississippi, for Appellees Elie Hage-Korban and Delta Clinics. Brian D. Roark, BASS, BERRY & SIMS PLC, Nashville, Tennessee, for Appellees Knoxville HMA Holdings and Dyersburg Hospital Company. ON BRIEF Shelby Serig, MORGAN & p.520 MORGAN P.A., Jacksonville, Florida, for Appellant. Jeffrey Scott Newton, Micahel Thomas Dawkins, Joseph Lott Warren, BAKER DONELSON BEARMAN CALDWELL & BERKOWITZ, PC, Jackson, Mississippi, for Appellees Elie Hage-Korban and Delta Clinics. Brian D. Roark, BASS, BERRY & SIMS PLC, Nashville, Tennessee, for Appellees Knoxville HMA Holdings and Dyersburg Hospital Company. David J. Chizewer, GOLDBERG KOHN LTD., Chicago, Illinois, for Amicus Curiae.

Before: SILER, SUTTON, and LARSEN, Circuit Judges.

p.519 OPINION

LARSEN, Circuit Judge.

In this *qui tam* action, Dr. Gurpreet Maur accuses Dr. Elie Hage-Korban ("Korban") of submitting false claims to Medicare for unnecessary cardiac testing and procedures, in alleged violation of the False Claims Act (FCA). *See* 31 U.S.C. § 3729(a)(1)(A)-(C), (G). The district court dismissed Maur's complaint pursuant to the FCA's public-disclosure bar, 31 U.S.C. § 3730(e)(4). Because we conclude Maur's allegations are "substantially the same" as those exposed in a prior *qui tam* action and Maur is not an "original source" as defined in the FCA, we AFFIRM the district court's dismissal.

I.

Dr. Korban, along with his medical practice Delta Clinics, is engaged in the private practice of diagnostic and interventional cardiology. This is not the first time he has been accused of this alleged scheme to defraud the government.

A.

In June 2007, Dr. Wood Deming filed a *qui tam* action (the "*Deming* action") under the FCA against two of the defendants in this case—Korban and Regional Hospital of Jackson ("Jackson Regional")—as well as other. Tennessee hospitals where Korban performed cardiac procedures. *See United States ex rel. Deming v. Jackson-Madison Cnty. Gen. Hosp.,* No. 1:07-cv-01116-SHL-egb (W.D. Tenn. June 13, 2007). In essence, Deming charged the defendants with submitting fraudulent claims to federal government insurance programs by "ignor[ing] blatant overutilization of cardiac medical services ... by Korban." The United States intervened in the *Deming* action and ultimately settled the case for cardiac procedures performed between 2004 and 2012.

Two of those settlements are pertinent here. First, as a condition of his settlement, Korban entered into an Integrity Agreement (the "Korban IA") with the Office of Inspector General for the United States Department of Health and Human Services (the "Inspector General"). The Korban IA was in effect from November 13, 2013 through November 13, 2016 and was publicly available on the Inspector General's website during that time. It required Korban to engage an Independent Review Organization to monitor "[c]oding, billing, and claims submission to all Federal health care programs by or on behalf of Korban, and reimbursement records for cardiology items." The Korban IA further called for the Organization to conduct a review of "[c]ardiac procedures including interventional cardiac procedures ... performed by Korban" and to "evaluate and analyze the medical necessity and appropriateness" of those procedures. It was then to generate quarterly reports of these findings for the Inspector General, who retained ultimate supervisory authority over Korban's medical practice. The U.S. Department of Justice issued a press release on December 19, 2013 that detailed p.521 the exposed fraudulent scheme and outlined the terms of Korban's settlement. In the second agreement, entered into in July 2015, defendant Jackson Regional agreed to a $510,000 settlement with the Inspector General. The Justice Department and Jackson Regional both issued press releases concerning that settlement too.

B.

Now to the present allegations. Plaintiff-Relator Dr. Maur is a cardiologist who began working for Korban's medical practice, Delta Clinics, in 2016. At bottom, he alleges that Korban is "simply up to his old tricks." Specifically, his complaint lists five examples of "unnecessary angioplasty and stenting" and four examples of "unnecessary cardiology testing" performed by Korban on patients between March and November 2016. Those allegedly unnecessary procedures were paid for in part by Medicare.

In his complaint, Maur recognizes that "this exact scheme was previously detailed and exposed in" the *Deming* action, though the named defendants differ slightly. In addition to Korban and Jackson Regional, Maur has also sued Jackson Regional's corporate parent (Tennova Healthcare), a second Tennova subsidiary where Maur performed cardiac procedures (Dyersburg Regional Medical Center), and Tennova's corporate parent (Community Health Systems). He alleges these entities knew or should have known that many of Korban's procedures were medically unnecessary.

C.

Maur filed his initial *qui tam* complaint in April 2017. The United States declined to intervene. The defendants then moved to dismiss, arguing that Maur's claims could not proceed because of the FCA's public-disclosure bar, 31 U.S.C. § 3730(e)(4). The district court agreed. It found that "[a]lthough Maur includes several new Defendants, and describes different specific patient examples, there is not only 'substantial identity' between the fraudulent scheme he alleges in his Amended Complaint and the fraudulent scheme that the *Deming qui tam* action publicly exposed—it is the same fraudulent scheme." *United States ex rel. Maur v. Hage-Korban,* No. 1:17-cv-01079-STA-jay, 2020 WL 912753, at *5 (W.D. Tenn. Feb. 25, 2020). The district court further determined that "Maur is not an original source" as defined in the FCA. *Id.* Thus, it dismissed Maur's *qui tam* action in its entirety. *Id.* Maur appealed.

II.

The FCA "prohibits submitting false or fraudulent claims for payment to the United States, [31 U.S.C.] § 3729(a), and authorizes *qui tam* suits, in which private parties bring civil actions in the Government's name, § 3730(b)(1)." *Schindler Elevator Corp. v. United States ex rel. Kirk,* 563 U.S. 401, 404, 131 S.Ct. 1885, 179 L.Ed.2d 825 (2011). The Act encourages relators "to act as private attorneys-general in bringing suits for the common good," *United States ex rel. Poteet v. Medtronic, Inc.,* 552 F.3d 503, 507 (6th Cir. 2009) (internal quotation mark omitted), and provides often-lucrative incentives to do so. If the government proceeds with the action, the *qui tam* plaintiff is entitled to "at least 15 percent but not more than 25 percent of the proceeds of the action or settlement of the claim." 31 U.S.C. § 3730(d)(1). If the government chooses not to intervene, the *qui tam* plaintiff can recover even more—"not less than 25 percent and not more than 30 percent" of the same. *Id.* § 3730(d)(2).

To guard against potential "parasitic lawsuits" and "opportunistic plaintiffs," p.522 Congress included a public-disclosure bar in the FCA. *Poteet,* 552 F.3d at 507 (citation omitted); *see* 31 U.S.C. § 3730(e)(4)(A). That provision "bars *qui tam* actions that merely feed off prior public disclosures of fraud." *United States ex rel. Holloway v. Heartland Hospice, Inc.,* 960 F.3d 836, 843 (6th Cir. 2020). The bar is "wide-reaching," but it "stop[s] short of 'wiping out *qui tam* suits that rest on genuinely new and material information.'" *Id.* at 851 (alteration adopted) (citations omitted). As most recently amended in 2010, the FCA's public-disclosure bar directs that:

The court shall dismiss an action or claim under [the FCA], unless opposed by the Government, if substantially the same allegations or transactions as alleged in the action or claim were publicly disclosed—

(i) in a Federal criminal, civil, or administrative hearing in which the Government or its agent is a party;

(ii) in a congressional, Government Accountability Office, or other Federal report, hearing, audit, or investigation; or

(iii) from the news media, unless the ... person bringing the action is an original source of the information.

31 U.S.C. § 3730(e)(4)(A).

We employ a three-step analysis to decide whether this public-disclosure bar applies. First, we ask whether, before the filing of the *qui tam* complaint, there had been any public disclosures from which fraud might be inferred. *Holloway,* 960 F.3d at 844. Second, we assess whether the allegations in the complaint are "substantially the same" as those contained in the public disclosures. *Id.* at 849. And third, we ask whether the *qui tam* plaintiff is nevertheless an "original source of the information." *See id.* at 843. Maur claims that the district court erred at all three steps.

A.

At the first step, Maur concedes that the *Deming* action and the press releases were all publicly disclosed. However, he contends that the Korban IA was not a public disclosure as defined in the FCA.

As an initial matter, Maur has forfeited this argument by failing to raise it below. *See Armstrong v. City of Melvindale,* 432 F.3d 695, 700 (6th Cir. 2006). The hospital defendants specifically argued in their motion to dismiss that the Korban IA was a public disclosure. Yet Maur failed to contest this argument in his response. But even if the issue were not forfeited, we would still conclude that the contents of the Korban IA qualify as a public disclosure.

The Korban IA was publicly available through the Inspector General's website from November 2013 to November 2016. And it undoubtedly qualifies as a "Federal report" within the meaning of 31 U.S.C. § 3730(e)(4)(A).

The "sources of public disclosure in § 3730(e)(4)(A) ... suggest that the public disclosure bar provides 'a broa[d] sweep.'" *Schindler Elevator,* 563 U.S. at 408, 131 S.Ct. 1885 (second alteration in original) (quoting *Graham Cnty. Soil & Water Conservation Dist. v. United States ex rel. Wilson,* 559 U.S. 280, 290, 130 S.Ct. 1396, 176 L.Ed.2d 225 (2010)). Consistent with this "generally broad scope," the Supreme Court has interpreted "'report'" expansively to include "'something that gives information' or a 'notification.'" *Id.* at 407-08, 131 S.Ct. 1885 (quoting Webster's Third New International Dictionary 1925 (1986)); *see also* Random House Dictionary 1634 (2d ed. 1987) ("an account or statement describing in detail an event, p.523 situation, or the like"). Applying this ordinary meaning here, the Korban IA constitutes a "Federal report." It gave information about the term and scope of the agreement, an extensive list of Korban's obligations following the settlement, and detailed requirements for engaging an Independent Review Organization that would report to the Inspector General. By posting the Korban IA on its publicly available website, the Inspector

General "release[d] the information into the public domain." *United States ex rel. Whipple v. Chattanooga-Hamilton Cnty. Hosp. Auth.*, 782 F.3d 260, 270 (6th Cir. 2015); *accord United States ex rel. Oliver v. Philip Morris USA Inc.*, 826 F.3d 466, 476 (D.C. Cir. 2016). Thus, the district court properly considered the Korban IA as a public disclosure.

B.

We next consider whether the publicly disclosed sources present "substantially the same allegations or transactions" as Maur's complaint. 31 U.S.C. § 3740(e)(4)(A). We hold that they do.

"To decide whether a claim has been publicly disclosed, courts look at the essential elements of alleged fraud to determine if enough information exists in the public domain to expose the fraudulent transaction." *United States ex rel. Ibanez v. Bristol-Myers Squibb Co.*, 874 F.3d 905, 918 (6th Cir. 2017). The key inquiry is whether the disclosures could have "put[] the government on notice of the fraud alleged in the *qui tam* complaint." *Holloway*, 960 F.3d at 851. Yet there need not be a "*complete* identity of allegations, even as to time, place, and manner" to trigger the public-disclosure bar. *Poteet*, 552 F.3d at 514 (citation omitted).[1] There need only a "'substantial identity'" between the public disclosures and the *qui tam* complaint such that "the prior disclosures depict 'essentially the same' scheme." *Holloway*, 960 F.3d at 848 (quoting *Poteet*, 552 F.3d at 514). This is because "once the government knows the essential facts of a fraudulent scheme," it generally "has enough information to discover related frauds." *Poteet*, 552 F.3d at 516 (citation omitted); *accord Holloway*, 960 F.3d at 848, 851; *United States ex rel. Armes v. Garman*, 719 F. App'x 459, 464 (6th Cir. 2017); *United States ex rel. Antoon v. Cleveland Clinic Found.*, 788 F.3d 605, 616 (6th Cir. 2015).

1.

Maur himself states in his complaint that this "exact scheme was previously detailed and exposed in" the *Deming* action. He readily admits that his "complaint make[s] nearly identical claims" about the "same types" of fraudulent conduct. And he does not purport to offer any "unique new details or dramatic twists to the aforementioned scheme, which was previously investigated and seemingly resolved." Indeed, he copies much of the *Deming* complaint verbatim.

Maur nonetheless protests that our decision in *Ibanez* allows his case to proceed. In *Ibanez*, we stated in considered dictum[2] p.524 that "the mere resemblance of ... allegations to a scheme resolved years earlier [was] not by itself enough to trigger the public disclosure bar." *Ibanez*, 874 F.3d at 919. Once the integrity agreements in that case had "putatively ended the scheme," we could not "assume[] that the government [was] aware" that the fraud "continue[d] (or was restarted) simply because [the government] had uncovered, and then resolved, a similar scheme before." *Id.* This was true, we hypothesized, at least "to the extent that the new allegations [were] temporally distant from the previously resolved conduct." *Id.* at 919 n.4. Maur argues that because this case, like *Ibanez*, alleges fraud occurring after the execution of an integrity agreement, the new allegations cannot be "substantially the same" as those publicly disclosed.

For their part, the defendants claim that the rigorous oversight mechanism contained in the Korban IA distinguishes this case from *Ibanez*. Because the Korban IA "requires substantial independent oversight, review, and reports to the government," *Maur*, 2020 WL 912753, at *4, the defendants contend that the government here must have had "notice of the likelihood of related fraudulent activity" by Korban, *United States ex rel. Gilligan v. Medtronic, Inc.*, 403 F.3d 386, 389 (6th Cir. 2005). In defendants' view, then, Maur's new allegations should be treated as "substantially the same" as those previously disclosed. We cannot fully embrace either party's understanding.

Both theories falter because the presence (or lack) of a robust mechanism for reporting future fraud *to the government* has no bearing on whether "substantially the same allegations or transactions" of fraud have been previously "publicly disclosed." 31 U.S.C. § 3730(e)(4)(A); *see also United States ex rel. Booker v. Pfizer, Inc.*, 9 F. Supp. 3d 34, 46 (D. Mass. 2014). Indeed, we have rejected the view that "disclosure to the government in an audit or investigation would be sufficient to trigger the bar," because then "the term 'public' would be superfluous." *Whipple*, 782 F.3d at 268. Instead, the "operative question" for deciding whether allegations are "substantially the same" is whether the *public disclosures* would themselves be "sufficient to set the government on the trail of the alleged fraud without the relator's assistance." *United States ex rel. Reed v. KeyPoint Gov't Sols.*, 923 F.3d 729, 744 (10th Cir. 2019) (alteration adopted) (internal quotation marks omitted); *see Holloway*, 960 F.3d at 848; *United States ex rel. Lager v. CSL Behring, L.L.C.*, 855 F.3d 935, 944 (8th Cir. 2017); *United States ex rel. Winkelman v. CVS Caremark Corp.*, 827 F.3d 201, 210 (1st Cir. 2016); *Oliver*, 826 F.3d at 473. If so, then regardless of what the government knows or how the government behaves, the relator's allegations are "substantially the same" as those contained in the disclosures.

That being said, we agree with defendants, and with the district court, that the character of the government's oversight arrangements can sometimes matter. And we agree with *Ibanez*, and with Maur, that post-settlement allegations of a substantially similar fraudulent scheme can sometimes serve to avoid the public-disclosure bar. *See* 874 F.3d at 919. But we think that both insights are best applied in conducting the "original source" inquiry, rather than when asking whether new allegations are "substantially the same" as those previously "publicly disclosed."

p.525 **2.**

Even if a *qui tam* complaint contains "substantially the same allegations or transactions" as those previously "publicly disclosed," the suit may continue if "the person bringing the action is an original source of the information." 31 U.S.C. § 3730(e)(4)(A). One way a relator may qualify as an "original source" is to show that he "has knowledge that is independent of and materially adds to the publicly disclosed allegations or transactions" and that he "voluntarily provided the information to the Government before filing" suit. *Id.* § 3730(e)(4)(B)([ii]).

Post-settlement allegations that a substantially similar scheme has continued or restarted could provide the government with "knowledge that is independent of and materially adds" to the public disclosures. *See Booker,* 9 F. Supp. 3d at 48. At the same time, the presence of ongoing government monitoring might detract from the conclusion that these allegations have anything material to add. But analyzing these considerations under the "original source" exception is, in our view, more consistent with the public-disclosure bar's text than the approach either party proposes. *Cf. Reed,* 923 F.3d at 757; *Winkelman,* 827 F.3d at 211. For only the original source exception—which focuses on the "material[ity]" of the new allegations—asks us to consider how a relator's allegations might actually "affect[] the government's decision-making." *United States ex rel. Advocates for Basic Legal Equal., Inc. v. U.S. Bank, N.A.,* 816 F.3d 428, 432 (6th Cir. 2016) [hereinafter *ABLE*].

The structure of the public-disclosure bar further supports this interpretation. The question whether a relator's information "materially adds" to disclosures will "often overlap[]" with "whether the relator's allegations are substantially the same as those prior revelations." *Winkelman,* 827 F.3d at 211. But "the 'materially adds' inquiry must remain conceptually distinct; otherwise, the original source exception would be rendered nugatory." *Id.* at 211-12. If, as the defendants argue, both inquiries were to focus on what "the government may have expected" and how the integrity agreements would influence the government's actions, *Ibanez,* 874 F.3d at 919 & n.4, that would have "the effect of collapsing the materially-adds inquiry into the substantially-the-same inquiry," *Reed,* 923 F.3d at 757. We decline to accept that construction "[a]bsent clear evidence that Congress intended this surplusage." *Nat'l Ass'n of Mfrs. v. Dep't of Def.,* ___ U.S. ___, 138 S. Ct. 617, 632, 199 L.Ed.2d 501 (2018); *see Davis v. Helbling,* 960 F.3d 346, 355 (6th Cir. 2020). The defendants' interpretation would leave an exception that excepts nothing.

Hence, we are left with two distinct inquiries to apply. First, Maur's allegations are "substantially the same" if there exists a "'substantial identity'" between the public disclosures and his complaint such that "the prior disclosures depict 'essentially the same' scheme." *Holloway,* 960 F.3d at 848, 851 (quoting *Poteet,* 552 F.3d at 514). For purposes of this inquiry, "[i]t is not enough" for Maur "to allege new, slightly different, or more detailed factual allegations." *Id.* at 848; *accord ABLE,* 816 F.3d at 432-33; *Armes,* 719 F. App'x at 464. Second, even if Maur has depicted essentially the same scheme, he may still clear the public-disclosure bar under the "original source" exception if he has proffered independently obtained information that "materially adds" to the public disclosures. 31 U.S.C. § 3730(e)(4)(B)([ii]); *see Holloway,* 960 F.3d at 843-44; *Reed,* 923 F.3d at 757.

p.526 **3.**

Turning to the first inquiry, we conclude that Maur's allegations are "substantially the same" as the public disclosures. Indeed, our caselaw demands such a result. In *Holloway,* a relator brought a *qui tam* action alleging the defendant had "orchestrat[ed] a corporate-wide scheme to submit false claims." 960 F.3d at 839. She claimed that the scheme persisted from 2004 through 2018. *See id.* at 842. However, because her "allegations [were] substantially the same as those made" in three *qui tam* actions that had been voluntarily dismissed in 2008, we held that the public-disclosure bar applied. *Id.* at 845, 851. We did so even though those previous actions from a decade earlier "were focused on a single hospice facility," as opposed to "the corporate-wide conduct alleged in [*Holloway*]." *Id.* at 849. What drove our decision was that, as in this case, the prior complaints publicly revealed that the "same... actor" had engaged in "the same type of fraud" alleged. *Id.* at 847, 851. Because those "prior disclosure[s] put[] the government on notice of the fraud alleged," adding "new details to describe essentially the same scheme" was insufficient even to "survive the more lenient post-amendment public-disclosure bar." *Id.* at 850-51.

So too here. "If anything, [Maur]'s allegations add some new details to describe essentially the same scheme by [Dr. Korban]." *Id.*; *see also Bellevue v. Universal Health Servs. of Hartgrove, Inc.*, 867 F.3d 712, 720 (7th Cir. 2017) (finding allegations were "substantially similar" to public disclosures where the defendant's "conduct in subsequent years" was simply part of a "continuing practice" by the "same entity" (citation omitted)); *Oliver*, 826 F.3d at 473 (similar). Both the public disclosures and Maur's complaint were levied against the same actor for the same type of fraud. Both accuse Dr. Korban of performing unnecessary cardiac and stent procedures. Both charge him of doing so at western Tennessee hospitals owned by Tennova Healthcare. And both allege that the wrongful procedures were paid for by Medicare.

It also does not matter that Maur has added another Tennova subsidiary, its parent, and Korban's personally owned business as additional defendants. *See Holloway*, 960 F.3d at 849 (concluding that earlier allegations "focused on a single hospice facility" were sufficient to put the government "on notice of the corporate-wide conduct alleged"); *Poteet*, 552 F.3d at 511, 514 (barring claims where the "defendants involved [were] slightly different," because public disclosures "revealed the same kind of fraudulent activity"). What matters instead is that Maur has presented "substantially the same allegations" concerning a scheme perpetuated by Korban. As Maur admits, that "exact scheme" has already been publicly disclosed. The "wide-reaching public disclosure bar" therefore forecloses Maur's *qui tam* suit unless he qualifies as an "original source." *Schindler Elevator*, 563 U.S. at 408, 131 S.Ct. 1885; *see* 31 U.S.C. § 3730(e)(4)(A). We now turn to that final inquiry.

C.

The amended public-disclosure bar defines "original source" in two ways. First, it covers an individual who "prior to a public disclosure under subsection (e)(4)([A]) has voluntarily disclosed to the Government the information on which allegations or transactions in a claim are based." 31 U.S.C. § 3730(e)(4)(B)(i). Second, it includes one "who has knowledge that is independent of and materially adds to the publicly disclosed allegations or transactions, and who has voluntarily provided the information to the Government before filing p.527 an action." *Id.* § 3730(e)(4)(B)([ii]). Maur claims to meet both definitions. We disagree.

1.

Maur does not fall within the first definition of an "original source" for a simple reason. He does not allege that he relayed anything to the government "prior to a public disclosure under subsection (e)(4)([A])." *Id.* § 3730(e)(4)(B)(i). As already explained, those disclosures include the *Deming* action, the Korban IA, and the press releases, all of which preceded Maur's complaint.

In response, Maur urges that his allegations are not "based" upon those prior public disclosures because they describe conduct occurring after that covered by the *Deming* action. Yet this is just an attempt to repackage the argument that his allegations are not "substantially the same" as the disclosures. *Cf. Armes,* 719 F. App'x at 463 ("A later *qui tam* complaint is based upon a publicly disclosed fraud when a substantial identity exists between the publicly disclosed allegations or transactions and the *qui tam* complaint." (internal quotation marks omitted)). Because Maur did not communicate anything to the government prior to those public disclosures, he does not fit within the first definition of an "original source."[3]

2.

Nor does Maur fall within the second definition of an "original source." He did not provide any additional, "material[ ]" information to the government before filing the present complaint. 31 U.S.C. § 3730(e)(4)(B). "Materiality in this setting requires the claimant to show [he] had information '[o]f such a nature that knowledge of the item would affect a person's decision-making,' is 'significant,' or is 'essential.'" *ABLE,* 816 F.3d at 431 (second alteration in original) (quoting Black's Law Dictionary 1124 (10th ed. 2014)); *accord Reed,* 923 F.3d at 756; *Winkelman,* 827 F.3d at 211. In other words, the relator must bring something to the table that would add value for the government. *See Reed,* 923 F.3d at 759; *United States ex rel. Hastings v. Wells Fargo Bank, NA, Inc.,* 656 F. App'x 328, 332 (9th Cir. 2016).

Here, Maur cites nine additional patient examples, but there "is nothing significant or new" about them. *ABLE,* 816 F.3d at 431. Maur even concedes in his complaint that his allegations are "not new" and provide "no unique new details."

Yet that alone is not necessarily fatal to Maur's claim. We noted in *Ibanez* that "the mere resemblance of [the current] allegations to a scheme resolved years earlier is not by itself enough to trigger the public disclosure bar." 874 F.3d at 919. But here, p.528 Maur's allegations are neither novel nor so removed from the "resolved" conduct that we can say that he has added anything "material" to the "prior problematic [procedures] already disclosed" by the *Deming* action. *ABLE,* 816 F.3d at 431; *see Armes,* 719 F. App'x at 464.

To see why, compare this case to one like *Ibanez.* There, the defendants' scheme persisted seven years after they entered the integrity agreements, and two years after both had expired. In those circumstances, we could not "assume[] that the government [was] aware [the] fraudulent scheme continue[d] (or was restarted) simply because it had uncovered, and then resolved, a similar scheme before." *Ibanez,* 874 F.3d at 919. Bringing to light that the scheme had in fact continued well after the execution of the agreements—after they had expired even—might well have "affected the government's decision-making." *ABLE,* 816 F.3d at 432; *see Ibanez,* 874 F.3d at 919 n.4.

By contrast, Maur alleges the perpetuation of—in his words—the "exact scheme" exposed in the *Deming* action, only months after the 2015 settlement and *while* the Korban IA was still in effect. This temporal proximity to the prior settlement, combined with the ongoing effect of the Korban IA, dooms Maur's claim that he is an original source. The Korban IA required Korban to engage an Independent Review Organization for the submission of quarterly reviews to the federal government throughout the period of Maur's allegations. The point of this oversight arrangement was to subject Korban to heightened scrutiny—to monitor whether the fraudulent scheme was continuing. With this arrangement in place, "simply asserting a longer duration for the same allegedly fraudulent practice does not materially add to the information already publicly disclosed." *Winkelman*, 827 F.3d at 212. The government was still dealing with the *Deming* allegations and scrutinizing the precise set of transactions Maur believes were fraudulent, with the benefit of an independent reviewer's assistance. And that robust review system suggests "the government may have expected" the fraud to continue even "after the agreement[was] entered." *Ibanez*, 874 F.3d at 919 n.4.

Thus, by merely providing additional instances of the same type of fraud during the oversight period, Maur has failed to offer information of "such a nature that knowledge" of it "would affect" the "government's decision-making." *ABLE,* 816 F.3d at 431-32. After all, in these circumstances, where there is no allegation of falsification in the reports,[4] it *can* "be assumed that the government [would be] aware" if the same "fraudulent scheme continue[d] (or was restarted)." *Ibanez*, 874 F.3d at 919.

p.529 One final point bears mentioning. We agree with Maur and Amicus that "[e]ngaging in a scheme to defraud cannot immunize a fraudulent action from *qui tam* suits regarding related forms of fraud in perpetuity; what was once a hot trail of fraud must cool at some point." *Booker,* 9 F. Supp. 3d at 45; *see Ibanez*, 874 F.3d at 919. But not only did the public disclosures here "set the government on the trail of the alleged fraud without [Maur's] assistance," *Reed,* 923 F.3d at 744 (citation omitted), the government was still *in fact* on that trail. Maur does not allege that Korban did anything to throw the government off that scent. Accordingly, Maur has proffered no new information that materially adds to what is already contained in public disclosures. He does not qualify as an original source. And he cannot overcome the public-disclosure bar.

* * *

For the foregoing reasons, we hold that Maur's action is foreclosed by the FCA's public-disclosure bar. We therefore AFFIRM the district court's dismissal.

[1] Though *Poteet* interpreted the pre-2010 public-disclosure bar, "we have adopted principles from our pre-amendment cases that are compatible with the amended statutory text." *Holloway,* 960 F.3d at 851. The amended version of the statute expressly incorporates the "substantial identity" standard that this circuit and most other circuits had applied before 2010. *Id.* at 850.

[2] *Ibanez* went on to dismiss the claims because the relators "failed to plead a violation of the FCA with adequate particularity." 874 F.3d at 922. Thus, the discussion as to why the amended public-disclosure bar was *not* implicated in that

case was neither necessary nor sufficient to support the judgment. *Wright v. Spaulding,* 939 F.3d 695, 701 (6th Cir. 2019).

[3] Maur points us to language from *Rockwell International Corporation v. United States,* 549 U.S. 457, 127 S.Ct. 1397, 167 L.Ed.2d 190 (2007), for support. But that case interpreted the pre-2010 version of the FCA's original source definition. *See id.* at 470-71, 127 S.Ct. 1397. This case concerns the post-2010 enactment. And those two provisions differ in important respects. The old version did not have any pre-public disclosure notification requirement. *Compare* 31 U.S.C. § 3730(e)(4)(B) (1986) (defining "original source" as "an individual who has direct and independent knowledge of the information on which the allegations are based and has voluntarily provided the information to the Government before filing an action under this section which is based on the information"), *with* 31 U.S.C. § 3730(e)(4)(B) (2010) (defining "original source" to include "an individual who ... prior to a public disclosure under subsection (e)(4)([A]), has voluntarily disclosed to the Government the information on which allegations or transactions in a claim are based"). *See also United States ex rel. Davis v. District of Columbia,* 679 F.3d 832, 839 n.4 (D.C. Cir. 2012) (explaining the import of the amendment).

[4] We do not speculate whether this case might have come out differently if Maur had alleged that Korban was submitting fraudulent reports or masking some transactions from review during the oversight period. Perhaps such allegations would "change [government] decisions made regarding the allegations of wrongdoing" and thereby materially add to the public disclosures. *United States ex rel. Vitale v. MiMedx Grp., Inc.,* 381 F. Supp. 3d 647, 658 (D.S.C. 2019) (citing *ABLE,* 816 F.3d at 431). But there are no such allegations here. At oral argument, Maur claimed that Korban violated his integrity agreement by failing to train Maur properly. But this "alleged breach of the[] agreement[] did not, by itself, constitute an obligation to pay the government," as such a breach only "'may' have led to obligations to pay stipulated penalties." *Ibanez,* 874 F.3d at 922; *see* R. 51-2, PageID 325-27 (providing that the Inspector General "may" "exercise its contractual right to demand payment" for certain failures by Korban "after determining that Stipulated Penalties are appropriate").

960 F.3d 836 (2020)

UNITED STATES of America EX REL. Kathi HOLLOWAY, Relator-Appellant,
v.
HEARTLAND HOSPICE, INC., Defendant,
Heartland Hospice Services, LLC; HCR Manorcare, Inc.; HCR Home Health Care
& Hospice, LLC; Manorcare Health Services, LLC, Defendants-Appellees.

No. 19-3646.

United States Court of Appeals, Sixth Circuit.

Decided and Filed: June 3, 2020.

United States v. Heartland Hospice, Inc., 960 F. 3d 836 (6th Cir. 2020)

Appeal from the United States District Court for the Northern District of Ohio at Toledo, No. 3:10-cv-01875—James G. Carr, District Judge.

ON BRIEF: Brad J. Pigott, PIGOTT LAW FIRM, P.A., Jackson, Mississippi, for Appellant. Eric A. Dubelier, Katherine J. Seikaly, REED SMITH LLP, Washington, D.C., James C. Martin, Colin E. Wrabley, Devin M. Misour, REED SMITH LLP, Pittsburgh, Pennsylvania, for Appellees.

Before: MERRITT, MOORE, and MURPHY, Circuit Judges.

p.839 OPINION

KAREN NELSON MOORE, Circuit Judge.

The *qui tam* provisions of the False Claims Act ("FCA") encourage whistleblowers to act as private attorneys general and sue companies making false claims for federal money. *See* 31 U.S.C. §§ 3729-3733. Kathi Holloway, the *qui tam* relator in this action, sued Heartland Hospice and related entities ("Heartland") under the FCA for orchestrating a corporate-wide scheme to submit false claims for payments from Medicare and Medicaid to cover hospice care. Heartland allegedly enrolled patients in hospice when they were not terminally ill and kept them there, even when employees like Holloway urged their release.

Heartland, however, shoots back that Holloway is not a genuine whistleblower, that her claims are drawn from prior allegations against Heartland, and accordingly p.840 that her *qui tam* action is prohibited by the FCA's public-disclosure bar. In the alternative, Heartland argues that Holloway has not satisfied the FCA's heightened pleading standard for allegations of fraud and, in particular, that she has not satisfied the limited exception to that standard that we announced in *U.S. ex rel. Prather v. Brookdale Senior Living Cmtys., Inc.,* 838 F.3d 750 (6th Cir. 2016). We hold that Holloway's action is barred in light of prior public disclosures. We accordingly AFFIRM the district court's judgment of dismissal.

I. BACKGROUND[1]

Holloway alleges that Heartland fraudulently claimed Medicare and Medicaid payments to cover hospice care by "recruiting" and keeping patients in hospice despite the fact that many of them were not terminally ill. R. 69 (1st Am. Compl. at 11-12, ¶ 24) (Page ID #485-86).[2] Because these patients were placed into hospice, they were not provided curative treatment for their non-terminal illnesses. *Id.* at 17, ¶ 34 (Page ID #491). Meanwhile, Heartland leeched millions of dollars from the federal government in payments for unnecessary hospice care. *Id.* at 43, ¶ 88 (Page ID #517).

A. Heartland's Scheme

Heartland orchestrated its alleged scheme through incentives, punishments, and training. To incentivize recruitment of hospice patients, Heartland paid out bonuses to regional directors of operations, administrators in charge of the hospice agencies, and its "sales team"—equal to 30% of their salaries—if they met "targets" for admitting and retaining hospice patients. *Id.* at 15-16, ¶¶ 31-32 (Page ID #489-90). Heartland set the targets based on its revenue goals. *Id.* at 15-16, ¶ 31 (Page ID #489-90). It authorized the sales team to ask prospective patients to consent to hospice treatment, rather than curative care, before physician "Medical Directors" received any information regarding patients' medical history and prognosis. *See id.* It even incentivized registered nurses employed as "Patient Care Coordinators" to distort clinical records of patients' medical conditions and progress in a way that would enable the Medical Directors to certify patients as hospice-eligible. *Id.* at 16-17, ¶¶ 33-34 (Page ID #490-91). They, too, would receive a 30%-of-salary bonus if Heartland met its targets. *Id.* Heartland also handed out paid vacation hours to the clinical and non-clinical staffs of the facilities that increased their "census," or patient enrollment, the most within each corporate region. *Id.* at 17-18, ¶ 35 (Page ID #491-92). On the flipside, Heartland threatened to terminate sales team members and clinical staff if they fell short of their required census count. *Id.* at 18, ¶ 36 (Page ID #492).

To cover its tracks, Heartland "trained its hospice agency nurses and other clinical personnel ... to focus their documentation [of patients' clinical status], not on truthful clinical evidence of a patient's stability or need for curative treatment, but instead on purported clinical indicia of medical decline." *Id.* at 22-23, ¶ 43 (Page ID #496-97). Clinical personnel were trained to avoid "Ship Sinkers" like "improving," "stable," or "no change" because they p.841 could render patients hospice-ineligible. *Id.* Guided by the "Heartland Best Practice" manual, executives, regional officers, and local administrators enforced Heartland's corporate-wide practice of "negative charting" designed to paint patients as in decline. *Id.* at 22-23, ¶¶ 43-44 (Page ID #496-97). At the same time, clinicians were encouraged to use phrases that suggest hospice eligibility like "new skin tears," "unable to carry on a conversation without shortness of breath," "new episodes of chest pain," and "eating only sweets, snacks — refusing meals." *Id.* at 23, ¶ 45 (Page ID #497).

Effectively useless physician oversight paved the way for claims with no sound clinical basis to go forward. Heartland did not require its physician Medical Directors to personally examine patients, or to review the underlying clinical records, "before accepting non-physician employees' conclusions that patients were terminally ill." *Id.* at 25, ¶ 52 (Page ID #499). And where Medical Directors or other physicians did determine that patients should be discharged, they were vetoed. Local hospice facility "Directors of Clinical Services" —who were registered nurses, not physicians—were authorized to override physicians' recommendations of discharge. *Id.* at 27-28, ¶ 56 (Page ID #501-02). "Heartland likewise ... authoriz[ed] *regional* and ... *corporate-wide* administrators to veto, override, or ignore recommendations [of discharge] by physician Medical Directors...." *Id.* at 28, ¶ 57 (Page ID #502). On the occasions when Heartland did discharge patients, it was company policy not to review the patients' records to determine when they became hospice-ineligible and how much money should be refunded to the government. *Id.* at 35, ¶ 76 (Page ID #509).

Holloway also learned that Heartland was misleading the Medicare auditors. She witnessed a Heartland senior officer direct a physician to change a patient's general "cancer" diagnosis to "Stage IV cancer" in response to an audit request, without evidence supporting the change. *Id.* at 38, ¶ 80 (Page ID #512). When requests came in from Medicare auditors to review patients' files to verify hospice-eligibility, "Heartland's practice ... was to refuse to respond to such requests as to patients Heartland knew (or realized upon inquiry) were not eligible for hospice services." *Id.* at 37-38, ¶ 79 (Page ID #511-12). Failing to respond came with a minor penalty worth one month's payment, whereas answering honestly would make Heartland liable for refunds stretching back months or years. *Id.* Answering honestly could also prompt the auditors to search for evidence of fraud. *Id.* By accepting the minor penalty, Heartland strategically averted a substantial loss of profits and the discovery of its scheme. *Id.*

Corporate executives were at the helm of Heartland's scheme. *Id.* at 18-19, ¶ 37 (Page ID #492-93). Heartland Vice President Mike Reed, for example, encouraged employees to err on the side of certifying hospice-eligibility. *Id.* He reassured them that they would not be penalized if an auditor later rebuked their determination. *Id.* Executives would also use monthly conference calls to "badger and discipline" local and regional managers who failed to meet census requirements. *Id.* at 19, ¶ 38 (Page ID #493). And, of course, executives doled out incentives and trained employees. *See supra* p. 841. "[T]hrough its corporate headquarters and its most senior corporate leadership[, Heartland] acted with reckless disregard (a) for the truth of patients' actual medical conditions and needs, (b) for the clinical accuracy of the resulting clinical records as to each such patient[], and (c) for the medical necessity of resulting claims to Medicare and Medicaid p.842 for resulting hospice services." *Id.* at 19-20, ¶ 39 (Page ID #493-94).

Thus, Heartland employees certified patients as hospice-eligible under Medicare regulations, even though many of them were not. *Id.*; *see also* 42 C.F.R. § 418.20. The clinical documents that purportedly supported the certification of hospice-eligibility were distorted. R. 69 (1st Am. Compl. at 20, ¶ 40) (Page ID #494). "Heartland did not and could not reasonably rely on or affirm the accuracy of physician certifications made in reliance on its non-physician staff's clinical records, since Heartland knew that its marketing, training and clinical practices had substantially corrupted the reliability of such records as a credible and neutral basis for making such physician certifications." *Id.* at 25, ¶ 51 (Page ID #499). Accordingly, Holloway alleges that the claims based on false certifications that Heartland submitted to Medicare and Medicaid for payment are "factually and legally false." *Id.* at 21-22, ¶ 42 (Page ID #495-96).

B. Procedural History

Holloway brings this action under three provisions of the FCA: presenting false claims under 31 U.S.C. § 3729(a)(1)(A) (2009), use of false records or statements under § 3729(a)(1)(B), and wrongfully retaining government funds under § 3729(a)(1)(G). *Id.* at 45-49, ¶¶ 92-108 (Page ID #519-23). She filed her initial *qui tam* complaint against Heartland Hospice, Inc., HCR ManorCare, Inc. ("HCR"), and The Carlyle Group on August 24, 2010. R. 1 (Compl. at 1, ¶ 1) (Page ID #1). After the government declined to intervene, R. 55 (Election to Decline Intervention) (Page ID #184), Holloway amended her complaint on August 27, 2018 to delete claims against Heartland Hospice, Inc. and the Carlyle Group, and to add claims against HCR Home Health Care and Hospice, LLC, Heartland Hospice Services, LLC, and ManorCare Health Services, R. 69 (1st Am. Compl. at 1-2, ¶ 1) (Page ID #475-76). The conduct implicated in this case began "no later than 2004 and continu[ed] to the time of the filing of [the] First Amended Complaint." *Id.* at 11-12, ¶ 24 (Page ID #485-86).

Heartland initially moved to dismiss this action on August 6, 2018, R. 68-1 (Motion to Dismiss) (Page ID #230), and then moved to dismiss the First Amended Complaint on December 3, 2018, R. 82 (Motion to Dismiss) (Page ID #650). The district court entered judgment dismissing this action with prejudice on June 26, 2019. R. 86 (Judgment) (Page ID #1141). Although the district court held that Holloway's complaint was not barred by a prior public disclosure, the court dismissed her suit for insufficient pleading. *U.S. ex rel. Holloway v. Heartland Hospice, Inc.,* 386 F. Supp. 3d 884, 899, 902 (N.D. Ohio 2019). We have jurisdiction over Holloway's timely appeal. *See* 28 U.S.C. § 1291.

II. DISCUSSION

To be eligible for hospice care under Medicare or Medicaid, a patient must be certified by a physician as "terminally ill"—meaning that the patient's prognosis "is for a life expectancy of 6 months or less if the terminal illness runs its normal course." 42 C.F.R. § 418.20(b); 418.22(b)(1). Without that certification, the hospice provider is not entitled to payment. *See* § 418.20; 42 U.S.C. § 1395f(a)(7). For the certification to be valid, the hospice medical director "must consider at least the following information: (1) Diagnosis of the terminal condition of the patient; (2) Other health conditions, whether related or unrelated to the terminal condition; [and] (3) Current clinically relevant information supporting all diagnoses." 42 C.F.R. § 418.25(b). Submitting a fraudulent certified p.843 claim for payment for care provided to a hospice-ineligible patient constitutes a false claim. *See* 31 U.S.C. § 3729(a); *Prather,* 838 F.3d at 761. Holloway alleges that Heartland submitted false claims by knowingly or recklessly certifying patients' eligibility for hospice care and billing for those claims.

For Holloway to survive a motion to dismiss, she must surmount the public-disclosure bar and the heightened standard for pleading FCA claims. We begin and end with the public-disclosure bar.

The FCA bars *qui tam* actions that merely feed off prior public disclosures of fraud. *See* 31 U.S.C. § 3730(e)(4)(A) (2010); *Walburn v. Lockheed Martin Corp.*, 431 F.3d 966, 970 (6th Cir. 2005). Congress amended aspects of the public-disclosure bar on March 23, 2010, and we have decided that the amendments are not retroactive. *U.S. ex rel. Antoon v. Cleveland Clinic Found.*, 788 F.3d 605, 614-15 (6th Cir. 2015); Patient Protection and Affordable Care Act, § 10104(j)(2) Pub. L. 111-148, 124 Stat. 119, 901-02 (Mar. 23, 2010); *compare* 31 U.S.C. § 3730(e)(4)(A) (2010) ("The court shall dismiss [a *qui tam*] action or claim ... if substantially the same allegations or transactions as alleged in the action or claim were publicly disclosed—(i) in a Federal criminal, civil, or administrative hearing in which the Government or its agent is a party; (ii) in a congressional, Government Accountability Office or other Federal report, hearing, audit, or investigation; or (iii) from the news media, unless... the person bringing the action is an original source of the information.") *with* 31 U.S.C. § 3730(e)(4)(A) (1986) ("No court shall have jurisdiction over an [FCA action brought by a *qui tam* relator that is] based upon the public disclosure of allegations or transactions in a criminal, civil, or administrative hearing, in a congressional, administrative, or Government Accounting Office report, hearing, audit, or investigation, or from the news media unless ... the person bringing the action is an original source of the information.").

Holloway's complaint alleges FCA violations spanning from 2004 to the date of filing, so both the pre- and post-amendment versions of the public-disclosure bar apply.[3] Under either version of the public-disclosure bar, Holloway must demonstrate "(1) that the factual premise of [her] claim was not publicly disclosed before [she] filed the lawsuit, or (2) even if it was, that [she] was the original source of the information." *U.S. ex rel. Advocates for Basic Legal Equal., Inc. v. U.S. Bank, N.A.*, 816 F.3d 428, 430 (6th Cir. 2016). Under the post-amendment public-disclosure bar, a relator qualifies as an "original source" if she either (1) "voluntarily disclosed to the Government the information on which allegations or transactions in a claim are based" "prior to a public disclosure" or (2) "has knowledge that is independent of and materially adds to the publicly disclosed allegations or transactions, and [she] has voluntarily provided the information to the Government before filing an action under [the FCA]." 31 U.S.C. § 3730(e)(4)(B) (2010). Critically, Holloway has not argued that she is an original source. She waived this argument in the district court by stating that it was "irrelevant," *see* R. 83 (Resp. to Mot. to Dismiss at 8-9 n.20) (Page ID #958-59), and she has made no argument on appeal that the p.844 original source exception applies. This might have been the type of case in which the new allegations materially add to what has been publicly disclosed. We cannot say one way or the other in light of Holloway's decision to waive this line of argument.

A. Overview of Potential Public Disclosures

Because Holloway does not argue that she was an original source, she either must show that the purported prior disclosures were not "public," or that their contents did not "disclose" her allegations.[4]

First, Heartland points to a Department of Justice ("DOJ") settlement of FCA claims with SouthernCare Inc., an entity that fraudulently billed Medicare for hospice-ineligible patients but that is in no way connected with Heartland. *See* R. 82-14 (SouthernCare Settlement) (Page ID #874). The accompanying DOJ press release describes only misconduct by SouthernCare Inc., not an industry-wide scheme. *Id.* Similarly (and second), Heartland points to a *qui tam* complaint filed by Holloway against her former employer and its affiliates, which are also in no way connected with Heartland. *See* R. 82-2 (CLP Compl.) (Page ID #702). The complaint portrays a similar scheme to that alleged here. *See id.* Critically, all that these actions have in common is the same type of fraud in the same industry—without a shared corporate parent. We have never inferred an industry-wide disclosure from a set of allegations against a particular company. That can only work the other way around, when the prior disclosures describe "industry-wide abuses and investigations." *See U.S. ex rel. Gear v. Emergency Med. Assocs. of Ill., Inc.,* 436 F.3d 726, 729 (7th Cir. 2006). Accordingly, neither of these sources disclosed the fraud alleged in Holloway's complaint.

Third, Heartland points to a report issued by the Health and Human Services Office of Inspector General ("OIG report") that found that four percent of claims "did not meet certification of terminal illness requirements." R. 82-16 (OIG Report at ii, 16) (Page ID #897, 916). The OIG report does not itself constitute a public disclosure. Although a report need not use the word "fraud" to qualify as a disclosure, it still must carry an inference of wrongdoing. *U.S. ex rel. Burns v. A.D. Roe Co.,* 186 F.3d 717, 724 (6th Cir. 1999) (quoting *U.S. ex rel. Jones v. Horizon Healthcare Corp.,* 160 F.3d 326, 332 (6th Cir. 1998)). The OIG report even falls short of that. It calls out what it perceives to be a compliance problem stemming from the technical nature of the claims process. *See* R. 82-16 (OIG Report at iii, 17) (Page ID #898, 917). Its recommended action is not an investigation, but instead better education, training, and monitoring. *See id.* There is no insinuation of fraud, but at most noncompliance.

That said, a disclosure can arise from multiple documents taken together, rather than from a single document. *See U.S. ex rel. Poteet v. Medtronic, Inc.,* 552 F.3d 503, 512 (6th Cir. 2009). Courts use the following formula to explain that concept: "[I]f X + Y = Z, Z represents the *allegation* of fraud and X and Y represent its essential elements. In order to disclose the fraudulent *transaction* publicly, the combination of X and Y must be revealed, from which readers or listeners may infer Z, *i.e.,* the conclusion that fraud has been committed." *Jones,* 160 F.3d at 331 (quoting p.845 *U.S. ex rel. Springfield Terminal Ry. Co. v. Quinn,* 14 F.3d 645, 654 (D.C. Cir. 1994)). In the district court's view, the OIG report "further marks, however slightly, the trail of fraud in this case" by "set[ting] out the then-current state of affairs." *Heartland Hospice,* 386 F. Supp. 3d at 896. But we do not see how a disclosure of the "current state of affairs" matters because the South Carolina complaints expressly allege fraud in the first place (*i.e.,* the South Carolina complaints are the "Z" and there is no need for an "X" or "Y"). At best, the OIG report lends some support to Heartland's industry-wide disclosure theory, which we have already rejected.

Finally, Heartland points to three *qui tam* complaints filed in the United States District Court for the District of South Carolina against HCR ManorCare—Heartland's parent company—and other Heartland entities ("South Carolina complaints"). *See* R. 82-6 (Litwin Compl.) (Page ID #794); R. 82-7 (Olson Compl.)

(Page ID #803); R. 82-8 (Williams Compl.) (Page ID #813). The government declined to intervene, and the initial complaints were unsealed on July 9, 2007. R. 82-9 (Unsealing Order at 1-2) (Page ID #824-25). Each of the relators jointly stipulated to dismissal on November 12, 2008. R. 82-13 (Joint Stipulation of Dismissal at 2-9) (Page ID #865-72).

Holloway's first line of defense against the South Carolina complaints is that they are not "public" under the amended public-disclosure bar. The amended statutory text bars claims that were publicly disclosed in a federal proceeding "in which the Government or its agent is a party." 31 U.S.C. § 3730(e)(4)(A)(i) (2010). Holloway argues that a *qui tam* relator is not the government's agent and, therefore, that the case is not "public" unless the government intervenes. District courts are split over this question, and we have yet to weigh in. *See, e.g., U.S. ex rel. Forney v. Medtronic, Inc.,* 327 F. Supp. 3d 831 (E.D. Pa. 2018); *U.S. ex rel. Gilbert v. Virginia College, LLC,* 305 F. Supp. 3d 1315 (N.D. Ala. 2018). Courts that have adopted Holloway's position reason that a *qui tam* relator is not the government's agent because the relator is not authorized by statute to act in the government's place, is not labeled an "agent" under the statutory scheme, and is not subject to the government's control. *See Forney,* 327 F. Supp. 3d at 842-44. A majority of courts have rejected that reasoning and instead have held that a *qui tam* relator is the government's agent because the government "is the real party in interest," "the relator is the assignee of the Government's damages claim," and the government "exerts a fair amount of control over *qui tam* litigation." *Gilbert,* 305 F. Supp. 3d at 1324. Even when the government declines to intervene, it "still receives copies of all pleadings and deposition transcripts, can move to stay discovery if it interferes with an ongoing criminal or civil investigation, and has the right to approve or reject a stipulated dismissal." *Id.* (citing § 3730(b)(1), (c)(2)(D)(3), (c)(4)). It "may even intervene at a later date upon a showing of a good cause and subsequently dismiss a case over the relators' objections." *Id.* (citing § 3730(c)(2)(D)(3); § 3730(c)(2)(A)). The district court in this case added that Holloway's position "would render the phrase 'or its agent' ... meaningless." *Holloway,* 386 F. Supp. 3d at 895. "Who, if not the private relator, is the government's agent?" *Id.* We are persuaded by the majority of district courts' and our own district court's reasoning and hold that the *qui tam* relator is, in all cases, the government's agent under § 3730(e)(4)(A)(i). Accordingly, the South Carolina cases are public under both versions of the public-disclosure p.846 bar, despite the fact that the government did not intervene.

Now we turn to the substance of the South Carolina complaints. The relators in the South Carolina cases were registered nurses who worked at a single South Carolina Heartland hospice facility until they were fired for calling out its practice of making false claims for Medicare payments for patients who were not terminally ill. *See* R. 82-10 (Litwin Am. Compl. at 7, ¶ 26) (Page ID #838); R. 82-11 (Olson Am. Compl. at 9, ¶ 37) (Page ID #850); R. 82-12 (Williams Am. Compl. at 7, ¶ 26 (Page ID #860)). They initially alleged FCA violations alongside wrongful termination and tort claims. R. 82-6 (Litwin Compl. at 5-8, ¶¶ 29-53) (Page ID #798-801); R. 82-7 (Olson Compl. at 6-8, ¶¶ 29-53) (Page ID #808-10); R. 82-8 (Williams Compl. at 6-8, ¶¶ 29-53) (Page ID #818-20). Specifically, the relators alleged that Heartland "engaged in a practice and pattern of altering medical records or omitting crucial information from the charts," and in doing so, "systematically misrepresented ...

information concerning the patients' diagnosis and need for hospice care." R. 82-6 (Litwin Compl. at 5, ¶¶ 21, 26) (Page ID #798); R. 82-7 (Olson Compl. at 5, ¶¶ 21, 26) (Page ID #807); R. 82-8 (Williams Compl. at 5, ¶¶ 21, 26) (Page ID #817). According to all three relators, there were "several occasions" when they were told not to verify a patient's hospice-eligibility and "to let the office handle it so they could continue to identify the patient as being eligible." R. 82-6 (Litwin Compl. at 5, ¶ 25) (Page ID #798); R. 82-7 (Olson Compl. at 5, ¶ 25) (Page ID #807); R. 82-8 (Williams Compl. at 5, ¶ 25) (Page ID #817). When the relators instead insisted that their patients' diagnoses were not "supported in their medical charts," they were fired. R. 82-6 (Litwin Compl. at 5, ¶ 25) (Page ID #798); R. 82-7 (Olson Compl. at 5, ¶ 25) (Page ID #807); R. 82-8 (Williams Compl. at 5, ¶ 25) (Page ID #817).

Two of the three South Carolina relators ultimately abandoned their FCA claims in their amended complaint, but all three added examples of particular patients they thought were hospice-ineligible. R. 82-10 (Litwin Am. Compl. at 4, ¶¶ 17-23) (Page ID #835-38); *id.* at 8-9, ¶¶ 37-45 (Page ID #839-40); R. 82-11 (Olson Am. Compl. at 5-8, ¶¶ 21-27) (Page ID #846-49); *id.* at 9-11, ¶¶ 41-54 (Page ID #850-52); R. 82-12 (Williams Am. Compl. at 4-7, ¶¶ 17-23 (Page ID #857-60)); *id.* at 8-9, ¶¶ 37-45 (Page ID #861-62).[5] In each example, they stated that they "were told they would be fired if they didn't continue to work with patients whether they met the criteria or not." R. 82-10 (Litwin Am. Compl. at 4, ¶¶ 17-23) (Page ID #835-38); R. 82-11 (Olson Am. Compl. at 5-8, ¶¶ 21-27) (Page ID #846-49); R. 82-12 (Williams Am. Compl. at 4-7, ¶¶ 17-23 (Page ID #857-60)). They also alleged for the first time that Heartland was "attempting to develop a 'census' of patients under continuous care." R. 82-10 (Litwin Am. Compl. at 7, ¶ 26) (Page ID #838); R. 82-11 (Olson Am. Compl. at 9, ¶ 37) (Page ID #850); R. 82-12 (Williams Am. Compl. at 7, ¶ 26 (Page ID #860)). All in all, "twenty-two (22) of the approximately forty-three (43) patients [at the South Carolina facility] failed to meet the criteria and should [have] be[en] discharged." R. 82-10 (Litwin Am. Compl. at 7, ¶ 26) (Page ID #838); R. 82-11 (Olson Am. Compl. at 9, ¶ 37) (Page ID #850); R. 82-12 (Williams Am. Compl. at 7, ¶ 26 (Page ID #860)). Because the South Carolina p.847 complaints concerned the same corporate parent and the same type of fraud implicated in this case, we will analyze more fully below whether they bar Holloway's *qui tam* action.

B. The South Carolina Complaints

Having discarded three of the four potential public disclosures, we assess whether Holloway's action is barred by the South Carolina complaints. Our decision could, in theory, turn on which version of the public-disclosure bar applies because the amendments are not retroactive. *See Antoon,* 788 F.3d at 614-15. Previously, the 1986 version of the statute barred claims that were "based upon" allegations or transactions that had already been publicly disclosed. 31 U.S.C. § 3730(e)(4)(A) (1986). Now, the statute bars claims "if *substantially the same* allegations or transactions" have been publicly disclosed. 31 U.S.C. § 3730(e)(4)(A) (2010) (emphasis added). We must decide whether the South Carolina complaints disclosed the fraud alleged in Holloway's complaint under either version of the public-disclosure bar.[6]

Heartland argues that Holloway's claims must be dismissed under either version of the public-disclosure bar because Holloway's allegations depict essentially the same scheme as that described in the South Carolina complaints. Appellee Br. at 37-38. We agree and hold that Holloway's claims must be dismissed under either version of the public-disclosure bar.

1. The Pre-Amendment Public-Disclosure Bar

We begin with the pre-amendment public-disclosure bar. Prior to the 2010 amendments, we held that a claim is "based upon" a prior public disclosure when it is "'supported by' the previously disclosed information," *Poteet*, 552 F.3d at 514 (quoting *U.S. ex rel. McKenzie v. BellSouth Telecomm., Inc.,* 123 F.3d 935, 940 (6th Cir. 1997))—meaning that a "substantial identity exists between the publicly disclosed allegations or transactions and the *qui tam* complaint," *id.* (quoting *Jones,* 160 F.3d at 332).[7] In applying the substantial-identity test, we held that the relator's claims are based on prior public disclosures where "essentially the same ... scheme" was "the primary focus" of each. *Id. Qui tam* actions are barred if they are "based *even partly* upon public disclosures." *McKenzie,* 123 F.3d at 940 (emphasis added).

Heartland asserts, based on *McKenzie,* that Holloway's claims are barred because they are at least partly based on the South Carolina complaints. *McKenzie* was our first opportunity to decide how to interpret the "based upon" language in the public-disclosure bar. In doing so, we declined to adopt the Fourth Circuit's interpretation of "based upon," which would have required a relator to personally know about the prior disclosures, and instead adopted the Tenth Circuit's approach. *Id.* We stated that, under a plain text analysis, the Tenth Circuit interpreted "based upon" to "include[] any action based *even partly* upon public disclosures." *Id.* (citing *United States ex rel. Precision Co. v. Koch Indus.,* 971 F.2d 548, 552 (10th Cir. 1992)) (emphasis added). The Tenth Circuit reasoned that "Congress chose not to insert the adverb 'solely,' and we cannot, because to p.848 do so would dramatically alter the statute's plain meaning." *Id.* (quoting *Precision,* 971 F.2d at 552). After explaining the Tenth Circuit's textual analysis, we noted that "[t]he Tenth Circuit later clarified its interpretation by explaining that a court 'must determine whether 'substantial identity' exists between the publicly disclosed allegations or transactions and the qui tam complaint." *Id.* (quoting *U.S. ex rel. Fine v. Advanced Sciences, Inc.,* 99 F.3d 1000, 1006 (10th Cir. 1996)).

We have described the test for "substantial identity" as whether the relator's complaint and the prior disclosures depict "essentially the same" scheme. *Poteet,* 552 F.3d at 514. That, in turn, is informed by the principle that *qui tam* actions will be barred only when "enough information exists in the public domain" to put the government on notice of the fraud alleged. *Walburn,* 431 F.3d at 975; *Poteet,* 552 F.3d at 512. The simple reason is that the entire point of *qui tam* actions is "to prosecute fraud of which the government is unaware." *U.S. ex rel. Dingle v. Bioport Corp.,* 388 F.3d 209, 215 (6th Cir. 2004).

To decide whether the government is already on notice of the fraud alleged, we ask whether the relator "merely 'adds details' to what is already known in outline." *U.S. Bank,* 816 F.3d at 432 (quoting *U.S. ex rel. Bogina v. Medline Indus., Inc.,* 809 F.3d 365, 370 (7th Cir. 2016)). We can presume that the government is on notice of particular frauds once a general disclosure of fraud has been made. *See id.* at 431-32;

Dingle, 388 F.3d at 215; *U.S. ex rel. Gilligan v. Medtronic, Inc.,* 403 F.3d 386, 391 (6th Cir. 2005). Thus, relators cannot avoid the public-disclosure bar "by focusing [their] allegations... on sub-classes of potential claims covered by the initial [disclosure]." *U.S. Bank,* 816 F.3d at 432. It is not enough to allege new, slightly different, or more detailed factual allegations. *Dingle,* 388 F.3d at 215; *Poteet,* 552 F.3d at 514.

For instance, in *Dingle,* we barred a relator's *qui tam* action alleging a scheme in which a company supplied the U.S. government with FDA-noncompliant vaccines. 388 F.3d at 215. Prior public disclosures revealed that the FDA had cited the company for unspecified "deviations" from FDA requirements and that there were allegations that the company's vaccine was not FDA-approved. *Id.* at 214. Because the prior disclosures were "more general and could have referred to several types of fraud," the government was on notice of the particular scheme that the relator alleged. *Gilligan,* 403 F.3d at 391 (citing *Dingle,* 388 F.3d at 213). The same was true in *Gilligan,* where the relators alleged that a company caused doctors and hospitals to submit false claims to Medicare for use of its FDA-noncompliant pacemakers with malfunctioning leads. *See id.* Prior allegations disclosed that the leads were not safe, that there was manufacturing fraud, and that there were design deviations. *Id.* Even though the new allegations concerned a "slightly different type of fraud," the prior allegations "were sufficiently general, and like the allegations in *Dingle,* could have encompassed the claim of manufacturing fraud and design deviations surrounding the ... leads." *Id.* "So long as the government is put on notice to the potential presence of fraud, even if the fraud is slightly different than the one alleged in the complaint, the *qui tam* action" must be dismissed. *Dingle,* 388 F.3d at 214-15.

Heartland contends that that is exactly what we have in this case—Holloway is simply adding new, slightly different, or more detailed allegations to what has already been disclosed in the South Carolina complaints. We agree. Both sets of allegations were levied against the same p.849 corporate parent for the same type of fraud. Both accuse Heartland of making false claims for payment from Medicare for hospice patients. Both allege a systemic and patterned practice of altering or omitting information from clinical documents to make these patients appear to be terminally ill. Both allege that staff were fired if they challenged this practice, and that Heartland set a "census," or required number of patients, for enrollment. We acknowledge, as the district court observed, that Holloway's complaint "alleges a complex, sophisticated scheme" that targets corporate-wide conduct. *Heartland Hospice,* 386 F. Supp. 3d at 898 (quotation omitted). But we disagree with the district court's conclusion that the scheme that Holloway alleges "differ[s] in both degree and in kind from" the South Carolina complaints. *Id.* at 899. Even if the South Carolina complaints were focused on a single hospice facility, the allegations against Heartland as a whole were sufficiently general and alike to those alleged here such that the government was put on notice of the corporate-wide conduct alleged in this case. We therefore hold that Holloway's claims are barred by the pre-amendment public-disclosure bar.

2. The Post-Amendment Public-Disclosure Bar

Having held that Holloway's claims do not survive the pre-amendment public-disclosure bar, we must decide whether they surmount the "more lenient" post-amendment public-disclosure bar. *See U.S. Bank,* 816 F.3d at 430. The 2010 amendments to the public-disclosure bar replaced "based upon" with "substantially the same." *See* 31 U.S.C. § 3730(e)(4)(A) (2010). Accordingly, the text now reads, "The court shall dismiss an [FCA] action or claim ... if substantially the same allegations or transactions as alleged in the action or claim were publicly disclosed...." *Id.* How we interpret the post-amendment public-disclosure bar is informed by the statutory text and the competing purposes of the *qui tam* provisions.

Prior to the amendments, a majority of circuits adopted interpretations of "based upon" analogous to our "substantial-identity" test, using the same or slightly different language. *See U.S. ex rel. Ondis v. City of Woonsocket,* 587 F.3d 49, 57 (1st Cir. 2009) (collecting cases). Many circuits described their test as whether "the relator's allegations are *substantially similar* to information disclosed publicly," *see id.* (emphasis added),[8] while others described their test as whether "the allegations in the complaint were *substantially the same* as allegations in the public disclosures," *U.S. ex rel. Fine v. Sandia Corp.,* 70 F.3d 568, 572 (10th Cir. 1995) (emphasis added).[9] Still others asked whether "material p.850 elements" of the allegations were publicly disclosed, *U.S. ex rel. Kirk v. Schindler Elevator Corp.,* 601 F.3d 94, 103 (2d Cir. 2010), *rev'd on other grounds by Schindler Elevator Corp. v. U.S. ex rel. Kirk,* 563 U.S. 401, 131 S.Ct. 1885, 179 L.Ed.2d 825 (2011), or whether the relator made "essentially the same" allegations, *U.S. ex rel. Reagan v. E. Tex. Med. Ctr. Reg'l Healthcare Sys.,* 384 F.3d 168, 176 (5th Cir. 2004).[10] By the time the public-disclosure bar was amended in 2010, all but one circuit had adopted some version of this interpretation. *See Ondis,* 587 F.3d at 57. The Fourth Circuit was the lonely outlier, interpreting "based upon" as barring suits only if the relator *actually* knew about the public information—a reading the majority of circuits rejected. *See U.S. ex rel. Siller v. Becton Dickinson & Co.,* 21 F.3d 1339, 1348 (4th Cir. 1994) (barring suits "only where the relator has *actually* derived from that disclosure the allegations upon which his *qui tam* action is based" (emphasis added)); *Ondis,* 587 F.3d at 57.

Unsurprisingly, then, the circuits that were in the majority have held that their pre-amendment precedent continues to control, to varying degrees.[11] *See Bellevue v. Universal Health Servs. of Hartgrove, Inc.,* 867 F.3d 712, 718 (7th Cir. 2017) ("The current version of the statute expressly incorporates the 'substantially similar' standard in accordance with the interpretation of this circuit and most other circuits."); *U.S. ex rel. Reed v. KeyPoint Gov't Sols.,* 923 F.3d 729, 743-45 (10th Cir. 2019) ("holding that its pre-amendment precedent should "primarily guide" its post-amendment inquiry"); *U.S. ex rel. Osheroff v. Humana Inc.,* 776 F.3d 805, 812, 814 (11th Cir. 2015) (slotting the new "substantially the same" test into its existing analytical framework); *U.S. ex rel. Winkelman v. CVS Caremark Corp.,* 827 F.3d 201, 208 n.4 (1st Cir. 2016) (stating that "[t]he revised statutory language— 'substantially the same'—merely confirms [its] earlier understanding," but also that the amended language "has no substantive effect *in this case*" (emphasis added)).

For our part, we indicated in an unpublished case, *United States ex rel. Armes v. Garman,* that we would continue to be guided by our "based upon" precedent as we embark on interpreting the amended public-disclosure bar. 719 F. App'x 459, 463 n.2 (6th Cir. 2017) ("Because this court had already interpreted the "based upon" language to mean a "substantial identity," *Poteet,* 552 F.3d at 514, the 2010 amendment does not affect our public-disclosure analysis at this second step."). But we have not expressly adopted our pre-amendment precedent in a published case. In one post-amendment case, both versions technically applied, but we used the "more lenient" amended version for the sake of simplicity because the relator would lose either way. *U.S. Bank,* 816 F.3d at 430. We implicitly adopted two principles from our pre-amendment precedent: (1) an action is barred if a prior p.851 disclosure puts the government on notice of the fraud alleged in the *qui tam* complaint, *id.* at 431, and (2) a broader prior disclosure bars a *qui tam* action based on a narrower set of allegations stemming from the same fraud, *id.* at 432. In another case, we decided that the outcome would be the same under either version of the bar because, even after the amendments, "a common principle remains[:] public disclosure occurs 'when enough information exists in the public domain to expose the fraudulent transaction.'" *United States ex rel. Ibanez v. Bristol-Myers Squibb Company,* 874 F.3d at 918 (quoting *Antoon,* 788 F.3d at 614-15). We stated that courts must "look at the essential elements of alleged fraud to determine if enough information exists in the public domain to expose the fraudulent transaction." *Id.* "Thus, the public disclosure bar is not implicated—even if one or more of a claim's essential elements are in the public domain—unless the exposed elements, taken together, provide adequate notice that there has been a fraudulent transaction." *Id.* at 918-19. So far, then, we have adopted principles from our pre-amendment cases that are compatible with the amended statutory text.[12]

From a textual standpoint, "substantially the same" facially demands a greater degree of similarity between the *qui tam* complaint and the prior disclosures than "based upon" does. And "substantially the same" undoubtedly is more rigorous than "even partly based upon," as we interpreted "based upon" to mean. Without the "based upon" language in the statute, there is no textual hook for *McKenzie*'s "even-partly-based-upon" rule. *See McKenzie,* 123 F.3d at 940 (citing *Precision,* 971 F.2d at 552).[13] We can think of no reason why that plain text interpretation of "based upon" should influence our reading of the amended text.

At the same time, we continue to be guided by the statute's general purpose of encouraging genuine whistleblower actions while snuffing out parasitic suits. *See Walburn,* 431 F.3d at 970. The public-disclosure bar was intended to be "wide-reaching," *Schindler,* 563 U.S. at 408, 131 S.Ct. 1885, but to stop short of "wip[ing] out *qui tam* suits that rest on genuinely new and material information," *Goldberg,* 680 F.3d at 935-36. In light of this purpose and the statute's plain text, we read "substantially the same" as more sensitive to differences between the *qui tam* complaint and prior disclosures than the prior "based upon" language.

Holloway's claims, nevertheless, cannot survive the more lenient post-amendment public-disclosure bar. As we have already described, Holloway's allegations are substantially the same as those made in the South Carolina complaints. If anything, Holloway's allegations add some new details to describe essentially the same scheme by the same corporate actor. We accordingly hold that Holloway's claims must be dismissed under the amended public-disclosure bar as well. Because both versions of the public-disclosure bar apply, we need not address whether Holloway's allegations were sufficient under p.852 Federal Rule of Civil Procedure 9(b) or the limited exception to that standard that we announced in *Prather,* 838 F.3d 750. The district court rightly dismissed Holloway's claims.

III. CONCLUSION

We AFFIRM the district court's judgment of dismissal because Holloway's action is barred in light of prior public disclosures.

[1] The facts are taken from Holloway's First Amended Complaint, as we take all factual allegations to be true at the motion-to-dismiss stage. *See Guertin v. Michigan,* 912 F.3d 907, 916 (6th Cir. 2019).

[2] We will refer to the Defendants-Appellees collectively as "Heartland" because HCR, the parent company, "uses that brand name in its hospice operations." R. 69 (1st Am. Compl. at 4, ¶ 6) (Page ID #478).

[3] After the 2010 amendments, the public-disclosure bar is no longer jurisdictional. *U.S. ex rel. Advocates for Basic Legal Equal., Inc. v. U.S. Bank, N.A.,* 816 F.3d 428, 433 (6th Cir. 2016). Because Heartland argued its motion to dismiss under Rule 12(b)(6), and Holloway has not taken issue with that, we will presume that a Rule 12(b)(6) motion to dismiss is appropriate for both the pre- and post-amendment claims.

[4] The list of potential "public" disclosures shrank with the 2010 amendments to exclude filings and rulings associated with state court proceedings. *U.S. Bank,* 816 F.3d at 430; *compare* 31 U.S.C. § 3730(e)(4)(A) (2010) *with* 31 U.S.C. § 3730(e)(4)(A) (1986). That change does not affect our analysis of the purported disclosures in this case.

[5] It does not matter that the relators dropped the FCA claims because "the disclosure is not required to use the word 'fraud' or provide a specific allegation of fraud," let alone a specific allegation of an FCA violation. *See Poteet,* 552 F.3d at 512.

[6] Both parties believe that they should prevail under either version of the public-disclosure bar. Heartland states in a conclusory fashion that the amendments do not affect our analysis. Appellee Br. at 37 n.12. Holloway neither disputes nor concedes that, and she cites both pre- and post-amendment precedent. *See* Reply Br. at 16.

[7] We have also used the term "substantial likeness." *See Poteet,* 552 F.3d at 514.

[8] *See U.S. ex rel. Atkinson v. Pa. Shipbuilding Co.,* 473 F.3d 506, 519-21 (3d Cir. 2007) (substantially similar); *Glaser v. Wound Care Consultants, Inc.,* 570 F.3d 907, 910 (7th Cir. 2009) (substantially similar); *U.S. ex rel. Newell v. City of St. Paul,* 728 F.3d 791, 797 (8th Cir. 2013) (substantially similar); *U.S. ex rel. Meyer v. Horizon Health Corp.,* 565 F.3d 1195, 1199 (9th Cir. 2009) (using "substantial identity" and "substantially similar" interchangeably), *overruled on other grounds by U.S. ex rel. Hartpence v. Kinetic Concepts, Inc.,* 792 F.3d 1121, 1128 n.6 (9th Cir. 2015); *U.S. ex rel. Osheroff v. Humana, Inc.,* 776 F.3d 805, 814 (11th Cir. 2015) (using "substantially similar" and "substantially the same" interchangeably); *U.S. ex rel. Findley v. FPC-Boron Employees' Club,* 105 F.3d 675, 690 (D.C. Cir. 1997) (substantially similar), *overruled on other grounds by U.S. ex rel. Davis v. District of Columbia,* 679 F.3d 832, 838-39 (D.C. Cir. 2012).

[9] The Tenth Circuit has occasionally used the "substantial identity" language that our circuit has used. *See, e.g., U.S. ex rel. Grynberg v. Praxair, Inc.,* 389 F.3d 1038,

1051 (10th Cir. 2004); *U.S. ex rel. Precision Co. v. Koch Industries, Inc.,* 971 F.2d 548, 553-54 (10th Cir. 1992).

[10] The Fifth Circuit also used "substantively identical" in this case. *See id.*

[11] "Similar" obviously has a different meaning than "same." "Same" means identical; "similar" means analogous, comparable, or resembling the other. The Merriam-Webster dictionary would have us believe otherwise, as it dubiously defines "same" as (among other things) "something identical with *or similar to* another." *Same,* MERRIAM-WEBSTER ONLINE DICTIONARY (last visited Feb. 14, 2020). We instead are guided by the wisdom of Judge Learned Hand, that "it is one of the surest indexes of a mature and developed jurisprudence not to make a fortress out of the dictionary." *See Cabell v. Markham,* 148 F.2d 737, 739 (2d Cir. 1945).

[12] We have not cited *McKenzie* in any of our binding post-amendment precedent. *See U.S. Bank,* 816 F.3d 428; *Ibanez,* 874 F.3d 905.

[13] The Tenth Circuit, which created the "even-partly-based upon" rule in *Precision,* conspicuously has avoided citing to that case for that rule in its post-amendment precedent. *See Reed,* 923 F.3d at 743-45. It has instead emphasized its substantial-identity test from *Fine,* 99 F.3d at 1006. *See Reed,* 923 F.3d at 743-45. Moreover, it has said only that prior precedent should "*primarily* guide [its] substantially-the-same inquiry." *Reed,* 923 F.3d at 745 (emphasis added).

892 F.3d 822 (2018)

UNITED STATES of America ex rel. Marjorie Prather, Relator-Appellant,
v.
BROOKDALE SENIOR LIVING COMMUNITIES, INC. et al., Defendants-Appellees.

No. 17-5826.

United States Court of Appeals, Sixth Circuit.

Argued: April 25, 2018.
Decided and Filed: June 11, 2018.

US v. Brookdale Sr. Living Communities, Inc., 892 F. 3d 822 (6th Cir. 2018)

Appeal from the United States District Court for the Middle District of Tennessee at Nashville. No. 3:12-cv-00764—Aleta Arthur Trauger, District Judge.

ARGUED: Patrick Barrett, Barrett Law Office, PLLC, Nashville, Tennessee, for Appellant. Brian D. Roark, Bass, Berry & Sims PLC, Nashville, Tennessee, for Appellees. Megan Barbero, United States Department of Justice, Washington, D.C., for Amicus Curiae. ON BRIEF: Patrick Barrett, Barrett Law Office, PLLC, Nashville, Tennessee, Michael Hamilton, Provost Umphrey Law Firm, LLP, Nashville, Tennessee, for Appellant. Brian D. Roark, J. Taylor Chenery, Angela L. Bergman, Bass, Berry & Sims PLC, Nashville, Tennessee, for Appellees. Megan Barbero, Charles W. Scarborough, United States Department of Justice, Washington, D.C., for Amicus Curiae.

Before: MOORE, McKEAGUE, and DONALD, Circuit Judges.

MOORE, J., delivered the opinion of the court in which DONALD, J., joined. McKEAGUE, J. (pp. 838-53), delivered a separate dissenting opinion.

p.825 OPINION

KAREN NELSON MOORE, Circuit Judge.

Brookdale Senior Living Communities employed Marjorie Prather to review Medicare claims prior to their submission for payment. Many of these claims were missing the required certifications from physicians attesting to the need for the medical services that the defendants had provided. These certifications need to "be obtained at the time the plan of care is established or as soon thereafter as possible." 42 C.F.R. § 424.22(a)(2). But the defendants were allegedly obtaining certifications months after patients' plans of care were established.

In July 2012, Prather filed a complaint pleading violations of the False Claims Act under an implied false certification theory. The district court dismissed her complaint, holding that Prather did not allege fraud with particularity or that the claims were false. This panel reversed the district court in part, holding that Prather had pleaded two of her claims with the required particularity and that the claims submitted were false. *United States ex rel. Prather v.* p.826 *Brookdale Senior Living Cmties.,*

Inc. (Prather I), 838 F.3d 750, 775 (6th Cir. 2016). In doing so, we interpreted the phrase "as soon thereafter as possible" in 42 C.F.R. § 424.22(a)(2) to mean that a delay in certification is "acceptable only if the length of the delay is justified by the reasons the home-health agency provides for it" and held that the reason alleged for the defendants' delay was not justifiable. *Id.* at 765.

On remand, the district court granted Prather leave to file her Third Amended Complaint ("complaint") in light of the Supreme Court's clarification of the materiality element of a False Claims Act claim in *Universal Health Services., Inc. v. United States ex rel. Escobar,* ___ U.S. ___, 136 S.Ct. 1989, 195 L.Ed.2d 348 (2016). The defendants moved to dismiss again on the grounds that Prather did not plead sufficiently the materiality and scienter elements of her two alleged False Claims Act violations. The district court granted that motion, and Prather now appeals. For the reasons set forth below, we REVERSE the district court's dismissal of Prather's complaint and REMAND for proceedings consistent with this opinion.

I. BACKGROUND

A. Legal Background

The False Claims Act, 31 U.S.C. § 3729 *et seq.,* imposes civil liability that is "essentially punitive in nature" on those who defraud the U.S. government. *Escobar,* 136 S.Ct. at 1996 (quoting *Vt. Agency of Nat. Res. v. United States ex rel. Stevens,* 529 U.S. 765, 784, 120 S.Ct. 1858, 146 L.Ed.2d 836 (2000)). Here, Prather is asserting a theory of liability under the False Claims Act known as "implied false certification." Under this theory, "liability can attach when the defendant submits a claim for payment that makes specific representations about the goods or services provided, but knowingly fails to disclose the defendant's non-compliance with a statutory, regulatory, or contractual requirement." *Id.* at 1995. This misrepresentation through omission "renders the claim 'false or fraudulent' under § 3729(a)(1)(A)." *Id.* "A misrepresentation about compliance with a statutory, regulatory, or contractual requirement must be material to the Government's payment decision in order to be actionable under the False Claims Act." *Id.* at 1996.

The claims and alleged misrepresentations at issue in this case arise in the context of Medicare and home-health services. Medicare Parts A and B provide coverage for certain home-health services. *Prather I,* 838 F.3d at 755 (citing 42 U.S.C. §§ 1395c and 1395k(a)(2)(A)). These services include: "skilled nursing services, home health aide services, physical therapy, speech-language pathology services, occupational therapy services, and medical social services." *Id.* (internal quotation marks and brackets denoting alterations omitted). "'Medicare Part A or Part B pays for home health services only if a physician certifies and recertifies' the patient's eligibility for and entitlement to those services." *Id.* (quoting 42 C.F.R. § 424.22).

These certifications are projections about the patient's medical need and plan of care, and Medicare payments for the care provided are made on a prospective system of 60-day periods, known as an "episode of care." *Id.* at 756. Payments for each episode are made in two parts. The initial payment—the "request for anticipated payment" or "RAP"—is a percentage of the total expected reimbursement. *Id.* (citing

42 C.F.R. § 484.205(b)). The second payment—the "residual final payment"—is disbursed at the end of the episode. *Id.* (citing 42 C.F.R. § 484.205(b)).

p.827 "The certification of need for home health services must be obtained at the time the plan of care is established or as soon thereafter as possible and must be signed and dated by the physician who establishes the plan." 42 C.F.R. § 424.22(a)(2). This regulation "permits a home-health agency to complete a physician certification of need after the plan of care is established, but ... such a delay [is] acceptable only if the length of the delay is justified by the reasons the home-health agency provides for it." *Prather I,* 838 F.3d at 765.[1] If the required certification was not obtained in compliance with the timing requirement in 42 C.F.R. § 424.22(a)(2), the RAP and final payment claims are "impliedly false." *Id.* at 766-67.

B. Factual Background

Prather, the relator in this case, "was employed by Brookdale Senior Living, Inc. as a Utilization Review Nurse from September of 2011 until November 23, 2012."[2] R. 98 (Third. Am. Compl. ¶ 10) (Page ID #1462). Defendant Brookdale Senior Living, Inc., along with defendants Brookdale Senior Living Communities, Inc., Brookdale Living Communities, Inc., Innovative Senior Care Home Health of Nashville, LLC, and ARC Therapy Services, LLC, "are interconnected corporate siblings who operate senior communities, assisted living facilities, and home health care providers." *Id.* ¶ 3 (Page ID #1460).

Prather alleges that it was the defendants' policy to "enroll[] as many of their assisted living facility residents as possible in home health care services that were billed to Medicare," *id.,* even when these treatments "were not always medically necessary or did not need to be performed by nurses who billed to Medicare." *Prather I,* 383 F.3d at 765; R. 98 (Third. Am. Compl. ¶¶ 70, 105, 110) (Page ID #1477, p.828 1486, 1488). This "aggressive solicitation of their senior community and assisted living facility residents ultimately generated thousands of Medicare claims that were 'held' because they did not meet basic Medicare requirements ...." R. 98 (Third Am. Compl. ¶ 3) (Page ID #1460). "In September of 2011, there was a large backlog of about 7,000 unbilled Medicare claims worth approximately $35 million." *Id.* ¶ 77 (Page ID #1478). To facilitate the processing of these claims, the defendants initiated the "Held Claims Project," and Prather was hired to work on this specific assignment. *Id.* ¶ 77-80 (Page ID #1478-49).

Prather's job responsibilities included:

> (1) pre-billing chart reviews in order to ensure compliance with the requirements and established policies of Defendants, as well as state, federal, and insurance guidelines; (2) working directly with the Regional Directors, Directors of Professional Services, and clinical associates to resolve documentation, coverage, and compliance issues; (3) acting as resource person to the agencies for coverage and compliance issues, (4) reviewing visits utilization for appropriateness pursuant to care guidelines and patient condition; and (5) keeping Directors of Professional Services apprised of problem areas requiring intervention.

Id. ¶ 80 (Page ID #1479).

The Held Claims Project team "used a 'billing release checklist' to identify items that needed to be completed before [a] claim could be released for final billing to Medicare." *Id.* ¶ 82 (Page ID #1480). The checklist and corresponding documents for each claim were then given to the billing office. *Id.* Once the billing office had all the documentation required, it submitted the bill to Medicare. *Id.*

One of the required documents frequently missing was the physician certification. Initially, Prather and the other project members "sent attestation forms to doctors for them to sign to correct the problem of missing signatures," but they "only received a few signed and completed forms back from the doctors." *Id.* ¶ 86 (Page ID #1481). Beginning in May 2012, to facilitate the process of gathering the required certifications, "Defendants paid physicians to review outstanding held claims and sign orders for previously provided care." *Id.* ¶ 98 (Page ID #1483). Additionally, team members visited physicians in order to obtain certifications. *Id.* ¶ 104 (Page ID #1818-19). Prather also alleges that the defendants repeatedly "billed RAPs without having physician certifications, and then re-billed them immediately after the RAPs were canceled in order to keep the funds received through the RAPs, while still lacking the required physician certifications." *Id.* ¶ 99 (Page ID #1484).

Prather alleges that she, and the other employees in the Held Claims Project, "raised concerns" about "compliance problems" with supervisors. *Id.* ¶ 91-92 (Page ID #24). But the defendants told the utilization review nurses to ignore problems they found and only cursorily to review the documentation. *Id.* ¶ 23, 91, 94-95 (Page ID #1481-83). In response to Prather's repeated comments to her supervisors that she was discovering compliance issues, she was told that the defendants could "just argue in our favor if we get audited." *Id.* ¶ 114 (Page ID #1489).

To support her allegations that the defendants failed to comply with the timing requirement in 42 C.F.R. § 424.22(a)(2), Prather included five examples in her complaint and incorporated by reference two exhibits containing spreadsheets listing information about hundreds of other untimely certifications. In the examples in her complaint, Prather describes physician certifications obtained from a few months p.829 to nearly a year after an episode of care began. *Id.* ¶ 104-13 (Page ID #1485-89). In her attached Exhibit A, Prather identifies 489 claims submitted to Medicare for which she alleges "Defendants did not obtain the required physician certification of need until after the episode was complete and/or the patient was discharged." *Id.* ¶ 115-17 (Page ID #1489-90); R. 98-1 (Third Am. Compl. Ex. A) (Page ID #1497-1520). Similarly, in Exhibit B, Prather identifies 771 claims that were allegedly submitted to Medicare with physician certifications of the required face-to-face encounter that were not obtained "until after the patient had been discharged and/or the episode was complete." R. 98 (Third Am. Compl. ¶ 118-20) (Page ID #1491); R. 98-2 (Third Am. Compl. Ex. B) (Page ID #1521-54).

C. Procedural History

Prather filed her complaint in this lawsuit under seal in July 2012 asserting multiple False Claim Act violations and state-law claims. R. 1 (Sealed Compl. at 28-45) (Page ID #28-45). In April 2014, the United States declined to intervene, and Prather's complaint was unsealed and served on the defendants. R. 23 (Notice of Election to Decline Intervention) (Page ID #103-04); R. 24 (Apr. 10, 2014 Dist. Ct.

Order) (Page ID #107-08). Before the defendants had responded to the initial complaint, Prather filed her First Amended Complaint. R. 52 (First Am. Compl.) (Page ID #178-211). The defendants subsequently moved to dismiss for failure to comply with Federal Rule of Civil Procedure 9(b), R. 56 (First Mot. to Dismiss at 1) (Page ID #217), and the district court granted the motion without prejudice, R. 71 (Mar. 31, 2015 Dist. Ct. Op.) (Page ID #889-922).

In June 2015, Prather filed her Second Amended Complaint. R. 73 (Second Am. Compl.) (Page ID #924-57). She alleged three claims: (1) the presentation of false claims to the United States government in violation of 31 U.S.C. § 3729(a)(1)(A); (2) the making or use of material false records or statements in the submission of claims to the government in violation of 31 U.S.C. § 3729(a)(1)(B); and (3) the wrongful retention of overpayments in violation of 31 U.S.C. § 3729(a)(1)(G). *Id.* at 29-32 (Page ID #952-55). The defendants again moved to dismiss for failure to comply with Federal Rule of Civil Procedure 9(b). R. 78 (Second Mot. to Dismiss at 1) (Page ID #1028). The district court granted the motion with respect to all three counts. R. 89 (Nov. 5, 2015 Dist. Ct. Op.) (Page ID #1358-1402).

Prather appealed, and this panel reversed the district court's "dismissal of Prather's claims regarding the submission of false or fraudulent claims for payment and the fraudulent retention of payments," but affirmed the "dismissal of Prather's claim regarding the use of false records." *Prather I,* 838 F.3d at 775. The briefs in *Prather I* were filed prior to the Supreme Court's decision in *Escobar,* so we did not address any potential impact that decision may have had on Prather's complaint. *Id.* at 761 n.2. On remand to the district court:

> the defendants stated their intent to file a motion to dismiss the Second Amended Complaint for failure to meet the standards set forth in *Escobar.* Because the Second Amended Complaint was filed before *Escobar* was issued, the court afforded the relator an opportunity to amend her complaint again, specifically to attempt to satisfy the pleading obligations identified in that case.

United States ex rel. Prather v. Brookdale Senior Living Cmties., Inc., *265 F.Supp.3d 782, 787 (M.D. Tenn. 2017).*

Prather filed her Third Amended Complaint in March 2017. R. 98 (Third. Am. Compl.) (Page ID #1459-96). She asserted p.830 two claims: (1) the presentation of false claims to the United States government in violation of 31 U.S.C. § 3729(a)(1)(A); and (2) the wrongful retention of overpayments in violation of 31 U.S.C. § 3729(a)(1)(G). *Id.* ¶ 121-31 (Page ID #1492-94). The defendants moved again to dismiss the complaint. R. 102 (Third Mot. to Dismiss) (Page ID #1571-73). The defendants argued that Prather had failed to plead adequately the required elements of materiality and scienter under *Escobar. Id.* at 1 (Page ID #1571). The district court granted the defendants' motion to dismiss with prejudice, holding that Prather had not sufficiently pleaded materiality. *Prather,* 265 F.Supp.3d at 801; R. 113 (June 22, 2017 Dist. Ct. Order) (Page ID #2142); R. 114 (Dist. Ct. J.) (Page ID #2143). It did not reach the issue of scienter. *Prather,* 265 F.Supp.3d at 801.

Prather's timely appeal from the district court's judgment is now before the same panel that heard her original appeal in *Prather I.*

II. STANDARD OF REVIEW

Federal Rule of Civil Procedure 9(b)'s requirement that fraud be pleaded with particularity applies to complaints alleging violations of the False Claims Act, because "defendants accused of defrauding the federal government have the same protections as defendants sued for fraud in other contexts." *Prather I,* 838 F.3d at 760 (quoting *Chesbrough v. VPA, P.C.,* 655 F.3d 461, 466 (6th Cir. 2011)). "To satisfy Rule 9(b), a complaint of fraud, 'at a minimum, must allege the time, place, and content of the alleged misrepresentation on which [the plaintiff] relied; the fraudulent scheme; the fraudulent intent of the defendants; and the injury resulting from fraud.'" *United States ex rel. Marlar v. BWXT Y-12, L.L.C.,* 525 F.3d 439, 444 (6th Cir. 2008) (quoting *United States ex rel. Bledsoe v. Cmty. Health Sys., Inc. (Bledsoe I),* 342 F.3d 634, 643 (6th Cir. 2003)). If the complaint "alleges 'a complex and far-reaching fraudulent scheme,' then that scheme must be pleaded with particularity and the complaint must also 'provide[] examples of specific' fraudulent conduct that are 'representative samples' of the scheme." *Id.* at 444-45 (alteration in original) (quoting *United States ex rel. Bledsoe v. Cmty. Health Sys. (Bledsoe II),* 501 F.3d 493, 510 (6th Cir. 2007)).

"This Court reviews *de novo* a district court's dismissal of a complaint for failure to state a claim, including dismissal for failure to plead with particularity under [Rule] 9(b)." *United States ex rel. Ibanez v. Bristol-Myers Squibb Co.,* 874 F.3d 905, 914 (6th Cir. 2017) (alteration in original) (quoting *United States ex rel. Eberhard v. Physicians Choice Lab. Servs., LLC,* 642 Fed.Appx. 547, 550 (6th Cir. 2016)), *cert. denied,* No. 17-1399, ___ U.S. ___, 138 S.Ct. 2582, ___ L.Ed.2d ___, 2018 WL 1697046 (U.S. May 29, 2018). We "must construe the complaint in the light most favorable to the plaintiff, accept all factual allegations as true, and determine whether the complaint contains 'enough facts to state a claim to relief that is plausible on its face.'" *Bledsoe II,* 501 F.3d at 502 (quoting *Bell Atl. Corp. v. Twombly,* 550 U.S. 544, 570, 127 S.Ct. 1955, 167 L.Ed.2d 929 (2007)).

III. ANALYSIS

To plead a claim under the False Claims Act, the plaintiff must sufficiently allege that: (1) the defendant made a false statement or created a false record; (2) with scienter; (3) that was "material to the Government's decision to make the payment sought in the defendant's claim"; and (4) that the defendant submitted to the U.S. government causing it to pay the claim. *United States ex rel. Sheldon v.* p.831 *Kettering Health Network,* 816 F.3d 399, 408 (6th Cir. 2016) (quoting *United States ex rel. SNAPP, Inc. v. Ford Motor Co.,* 618 F.3d 505, 509 (6th Cir. 2010)); *see also United States ex rel. Campie v. Gilead Scis., Inc.,* 862 F.3d 890, 902 (9th Cir. 2017), *petition for cert. filed,* 86 U.S.L.W. 3361 (U.S. Dec. 26, 2017) (No. 17-936). In *Prather I,* we resolved in Prather's favor the issue of whether Prather had sufficiently pleaded facts supporting the first element. 838 F.3d at 762. The parties are now contesting whether Prather sufficiently pleaded the second and third elements: scienter and materiality. Appellant Br. at 12; Appellees Br. at 14-15. These two elements are integral to both of Prather's alleged claims and therefore Count One and Count Two of Prather's complaint rise or fall together. *Prather,* 265 F.Supp.3d at 801. Because the district court addressed only materiality and not scienter, we will discuss the two elements in that order.

A. Materiality

"[A] misrepresentation about compliance with a statutory, regulatory, or contractual requirement must be material to the Government's payment decision in order to be actionable under the False Claims Act." *Escobar,* 136 S.Ct. at 2002. The Act defines "material" as "having a natural tendency to influence, or be capable of influencing, the payment or receipt of money or property." 31 U.S.C. § 3729(b)(4). In *Escobar,* the Supreme Court clarified this materiality requirement and emphasized that the "standard is demanding." 136 S.Ct. at 2003.

"[M]ateriality 'look[s] to the effect on the likely or actual behavior of the recipient of the alleged misrepresentation.'" *Escobar,* 136 S.Ct. at 2002 (second alteration in original) (quoting 26 SAMUEL WILLISTON & RICHARD A. LORD, A TREATISE ON THE LAW OF CONTRACTS § 69:12 (4th ed. 2003)). Something is material if a reasonable person "would attach importance to [it] in determining his choice of action in the transaction" or "if the defendant knew or had reason to know that the recipient of the representation attaches importance to the specific matter 'in determining his choice of action,' even though a reasonable person would not." *Id.* at 2002-03 (alteration in original) (quoting RESTATEMENT (SECOND) OF TORTS § 538 (AM. LAW INST. 1977)).

The analysis of materiality is "holistic." *United States ex rel. Escobar v. Universal Health Servs., Inc.,* 842 F.3d 103, 109 (1st Cir. 2016). Relevant factors include: (1) "the Government's decision to expressly identify a provision as a condition of payment"; (2) whether "the Government consistently refuses to pay claims in the mine run of cases based on noncompliance with the particular statutory, regulatory, or contractual requirement" or if, with actual knowledge of the non-compliance, it consistently pays such claims and there is no indication that its practice will change; and (3) whether the "noncompliance is minor or insubstantial" or if it goes "to the very essence of the bargain." *Escobar,* 136 S.Ct. at 2003 & n.5. None of these considerations is dispositive alone, nor is the list exclusive. *Id.* at 2001-04.

1. Express Condition of Payment

"A misrepresentation cannot be deemed material merely because the Government designates compliance with a particular statutory, regulatory, or contractual requirement as a condition of payment." *Escobar,* 136 S.Ct. at 2003. But such a designation is a relevant factor in determining materiality. *Id.*

The parties vigorously dispute whether the timing requirement in 42 C.F.R. § 424.22(a)(2) is an express condition of payment for RAPs and residual final payments.[3] p.832 Appellant Br. at 25-27; Appellees Br. at 28-35; Appellant Reply Br. at 4-6. The district court concluded that the timing requirement was an express condition of payment for both, *Prather,* 265 F.Supp.3d at 796, and we agree.

Medicare Parts A and B condition payment for services on a physician's certification regarding the necessity of such services. 42 U.S.C. §§ 1395f(a)(2) & 1395n(a)(2); 42 C.F.R. § 424.10. Thus, "[i]n order for home health services to qualify for payment under the Medicare program," 42 C.F.R. § 409.41 mandates that "[t]he physician certification and recertification requirements for home health services described in [42 C.F.R.] § 424.22" be met. 42 C.F.R. § 409.41(b). The timing requirement at issue in this case is located in 42 C.F.R. § 424.22.

Prather argues that this analysis answers the question. Section 409.41(b) expressly conditions payment on meeting the certification requirements in § 424.22. Section 424.22(a)(2) contains the timing requirement for the certification Prather alleges the defendants violated. Thus, Prather argues, § 424.22(a)(2) must be an express condition of payment. Appellant Br. at 26.

Not so fast argue the defendants. Section 409.41(b) directs the reader to the requirements "described in § 424.22." So the reader must then look to the language in § 424.22 itself. Appellees Br. at 30. Section 424.22 states: "Medicare Part A or Part B pays for home health services only if a physician certifies and recertifies the content specified in paragraphs (a)(1) and (b)(2) of this section, as appropriate." The defendants argue that this language limits the broader language of 42 C.F.R. § 409.41 by making only the requirements in 42 C.F.R. § 424.22(a)(1) and (b)(2) express conditions of payment. Appellees Br. at 29.

The defendants are correct that § 409.41(b) incorporates the requirements in § 424.22, and thus it is necessary to examine the latter section to understand the scope of the former. For example, if § 424.22 contained a provision that stated "certifications may be submitted via U.S. mail" then § 409.41(b) could not be read as to make it an express condition of payment that the certification must be submitted via U.S. mail merely by reference to § 424.22 as a whole. But the defendants' reading of the introductory clause in § 424.22 is overly crabbed.

The prefatory language states that payment requires the physician to certify (or recertify) the contents specified in § 424.22(a)(1) and (b)(2). Section 424.22(a), entitled "[c]ertification," then explains in further detail what a certification requires. Thus, § 424.22(a) gives meaning to the word "certifies" in the introductory clause. The required certification is not a certification unless it complies with all provisions of § 424.22(a), both (a)(1) and (a)(2). And § 424.22(a)(2) states that the certification "*must* be obtained at the time the plan of care is established or as soon thereafter as possible and *must* be signed and dated by the physician who establishes the plan."[4] p.833 *Cf. Ebeid ex rel. United States v. Lungwitz,* 616 F.3d 993, 1000-01 (9th Cir. 2010) (holding that 42. C.F.R. § 424.22(d), which limits which physicians may certify or recertify the need for home-health services, is an express condition of payment), *cert. denied,* 562 U.S. 1102, 131 S.Ct. 801, 178 L.Ed.2d 546 (2010).

Consequently, we agree with the district court that the timing requirement in 42 C.F.R. § 424.22(a)(2) is an express condition of payment. Thus, this factor weighs in favor of the conclusion that a misrepresentation with respect to this requirement is material.[5] *Escobar,* 136 S.Ct. at 2003.

2. Past Government Action[6]

Another relevant factor in determining materiality is the government's past response to claims violating the same requirement. As the Supreme Court explained:

[P]roof of materiality can include, but is not necessarily limited to, evidence that the defendant knows that the Government consistently refuses to pay claims in the mine run of cases based on non-compliance with the particular statutory, regulatory, or contractual requirement. Conversely, if the Government pays a particular claim in full despite its actual knowledge that certain requirements were violated, that is very strong evidence that those requirements are not material. Or if the Government regularly pays a particular type of claim in full despite actual knowledge that certain requirements were violated, and has signaled no change in position, that is strong evidence that the requirements are not material.

Escobar, 136 S.Ct. at 2003-04.

Prather made no allegations regarding the government's past practice with respect to claims that the government knew did not comply with 42 C.F.R. § 424.22(a)(2). Rather, she only alleged facts regarding the government's reactions to claims submitted by the defendants: "The United States, unaware of the falsity of the claims that Defendants submitted, and in reliance on the accuracy thereof, paid Defendants and other health care providers for claims that would otherwise not have been allowed." R. 98 (Third. Am. Compl. ¶ 125) (Page ID #1493). Without allegations regarding past government action p.834 taken in response to known noncompliance with 42 C.F.R. § 424.22(a)(2), this factor provides no support for the conclusion that the timing requirement is material.

In its analysis, the district court went one step further and drew a negative inference from the absence of any allegations about past government action. It held that Prather's "inability to point to a single instance where Medicare denied payment based on violation of § 424.22(a)(2), or to a single other case considering this precise issue, weighs strongly in favor of a conclusion that the timing requirement is not material." *Prather,* 265 F.Supp.3d at 797. This is one step too far.

Although a relator in a *qui tam* action faces a demanding standard at the motion-to-dismiss stage with respect to pleading materiality, she is not required to make allegations regarding past government action. The Supreme Court was explicit that none of the factors it enumerated were dispositive. *Escobar,* 136 S.Ct. at 2003. Thus, it would be illogical to require a relator (or the United States) to plead allegations about past government action in order to survive a motion to dismiss when such allegations are relevant, but not dispositive. *Escobar,* 842 F.3d at 112 ("We see no reason to require Relators at the Motion to Dismiss phase to learn, and then to allege, the government's payment practices for claims unrelated to services rendered to the deceased family member in order to establish the government's views on the materiality of the violation. Indeed, given applicable federal and state privacy regulations in the healthcare industry, it is highly questionable whether Relators could have even accessed such information."); *see also Campie,* 862 F.3d at 907 (holding that although discovery may reveal "that the government regularly pays this particular type of claim in full despite actual knowledge that certain requirements were violated, such evidence is not before us" and the relator had sufficiently alleged facts supporting that the requirement at issue was material).

Furthermore, we "must construe the complaint in the light most favorable to the plaintiff." *Bledsoe II,* 501 F.3d at 502. Inferring from the absence of allegations regarding past government action, as the district court did, that this means the timing requirement is not material is an inference adverse to the relator and in favor of the defendant. This improperly inverses the pleading standard.

Prather alleges that the government did not know that the claims the defendants submitted were false. R. 98 (Third. Am. Compl. ¶ 125) (Page ID #1493). Without actual knowledge of the alleged non-compliance, the government's response to the claims submitted by the defendants—or claims of the same type also in violation of 42 C.F.R. § 424.22(a)(2)—has no bearing on the materiality analysis.

3. Essence of the Bargain

Another factor relevant to materiality is whether the "non-compliance is minor or insubstantial" or if it goes "to the very essence of the bargain." *Escobar,* 136 S.Ct. at 2003 & n.5. The defendants concede that the physician certification does go to the essence of the bargain between themselves and the government—and therefore is material —but argue that the timing of the certification does not. Appellees Br. at 35. In response, Prather makes two arguments for why the timing requirement goes to the essence of the bargain. She first argues that the timing requirement is necessary to prevent fraud. Appellant Br. at 32-34; Appellant Reply Br. at 6-10. Prather next contends that the federal government's guidance as to the importance of the certification's timeliness demonstrates p.835 materiality. Appellant Br. at 35-37; Appellant Reply Br. at 10-14.

In *Prather I,* we discussed the timing requirement's connection to fraud prevention when interpreting the phrase "as soon thereafter as possible" in 42 C.F.R. § 424.22(a)(2). 838 F.3d at 764. We noted that the timing requirement

> makes it more difficult to defraud Medicare. Absent a deadline, a home-health agency might be able to provide unnecessary treatment absent a doctor's supervision and take the time to find doctors who are willing to validate that care retroactively. A deadline allowing only a short—and justified—delay between the beginning of care and the completion of the physician certification could make such a scheme difficult to pull off.

Id. at 764.[7] Whether the party on the other side of a transaction complied with the regulations aimed at preventing unnecessary or fraudulent certifications is a fact that a reasonable person would want to know before entering into that transaction.[8] *Escobar,* 136 S.Ct. at 2002-03; *cf. United States v. Luce,* 873 F.3d 999, 1007-08 (7th Cir. 2017) (holding material a misrepresentation that none of the officers of a loan-originating company were currently subject to criminal proceedings on a certification that "addressed a foundational part of the Government's mortgage insurance regime, which was designed to avoid the systemic risk posed by unscrupulous loan originators").

In her complaint, Prather referred to numerous guidance documents issued by the Department of Health and Human Services that she argues shows that the timing requirement goes to the essence of the bargain between the defendants and the government. R. 98 (Third Am. Compl. ¶ 47-52) (Page ID #1471-73); Appellant Br. at 35-36. Although this guidance was over ten years old at the time of the alleged false claims, it does provide some support for Prather's assertion that the timing requirement is material. Prather references three publications issued by the Office of

Inspector General for the Department of Health and Human Services which emphasize the timing requirement for physician certifications and highlight "untimely and/or forged physician certifications on plans of care" as an "area[] of special concern." OIG Compliance Program Guidance for Home Health Agencies, 63 Fed. Reg. 42,410, 42,414 (Aug. 7, 1998); OIG p.836 Special Fraud Alert on Physician Liability for Certifications in the Provision of Medical Equipment and Supplies and Home Health Services, 64 Fed. Reg. 1813, 1814 (Jan. 12, 1999); OFFICE OF INSPECTOR GEN., U.S. DEP'T OF HEALTH & HUMAN SERVS., OEI-02-00-00620, THE PHYSICIAN'S ROLE IN MEDICARE HOME HEALTH 2-4 (2001). Prather also cites 2015 guidance from the Centers for Medicare and Medicaid Services, which states: "It is not acceptable for HHAs to wait until the end of a 60-day episode of care to obtain a completed certification/recertification." R. 86-2 (Medicare Benefit Policy Manual (2015) § 30.5.1— Physician Certification at 32) (Page ID #1270). This specific manual was not in effect at the time of the defendants' alleged conduct, but it provides some support for Prather's allegation that the government has consistently emphasized the importance of the timing requirement and its longstanding policy has been to mandate that home-healthcare providers complete the physician certification prior to the end of the episode of care.[9] R. 98 (Third Am. Compl. ¶ 51) (Page ID #1473).

The defendants argue that the government's decision not to intervene in this case indicates that the timing requirement is not material. Appellees Br. at 37-38. This argument is unpersuasive. In *Escobar* itself, the government chose not to intervene, and the Supreme Court did not mention this as a relevant factor in its materiality analysis. 136 S.Ct. at 1998. On remand, the First Circuit held that the relators had sufficiently pleaded materiality, without reference to the government's declination of intervention. *Escobar*, 842 F.3d at 112. Furthermore, the False Claims Act is designed to allow relators to proceed with a *qui tam* action even after the United States has declined to intervene. 31 U.S.C. § 3730(d)(2). If relators' ability to plead sufficiently the element of materiality were stymied by the government's choice not to intervene, this would undermine the purposes of the Act. *See* Trevor W. Morrison, *Private Attorneys General and the First Amendment*, 103 MICH. L. REV. 589, 600-01 (2005) (describing how the False Claims Act is structured such that it encourages private citizens to pursue enforcement actions on behalf of the government).

* * *

After considering the factors implicated in this case that *Escobar* identified as indicative of materiality, we conclude that Prather has sufficiently alleged the required materiality element. The timing requirement in 42 C.F.R. § 424.22(a)(2) is an express condition of payment. Furthermore, Prather alleges that the government paid the claims submitted by the defendants without knowledge of the non-compliance, thus making the government's payment of the claims irrelevant to the question of materiality. Lastly, § 424.22(a)(2) is a mechanism of fraud prevention, which the government has consistently p.837 emphasized in its guidance regarding physician certifications.

B. Scienter

The defendants also argue that Prather failed to plead sufficiently the element of scienter. Appellees Br. at 41. The district court did not reach this issue in its decision. *Prather,* 265 F.Supp.3d at 801.

"False Claims Act liability for failing to disclose violations of legal requirements" will not attach unless "the defendant knowingly violated a requirement that the defendant knows is material to the Government's payment decision." *Escobar,* 136 S.Ct. at 1996. The Act "defines 'knowing' and 'knowingly' to mean that a person has 'actual knowledge of the information,' 'acts in deliberate ignorance of the truth or falsity of the information,' or 'acts in reckless disregard of the truth or falsity of the information.'" *Id.* (quoting 31 U.S.C. § 3729(b)(1)(A)). "Knowing" and "knowingly" does not require "proof of specific intent to defraud." 31 U.S.C. § 3729(b)(1)(B). And, at the motion-to-dismiss stage, a plaintiff need only allege the scienter element generally. FED. R. CIV. P. 9(b).

"[A]n aggravated form of gross negligence (i.e. reckless disregard) will satisfy the scienter requirement for an FCA violation." *United States ex rel. Wall v. Circle C Constr., L.L.C.,* 697 F.3d 345, 356 (6th Cir. 2012) (alteration in original) (quoting *United States ex rel. Burlbaw v. Orenduff,* 548 F.3d 931, 945 n.12 (10th Cir. 2008)). Congress added the "reckless disregard" prong to the definition of knowledge in the False Claims Act "to target that defendant who has 'buried his head in the sand' and failed to make some inquiry into the claim's validity." *United States ex rel. Williams v. Renal Care Grp., Inc.,* 696 F.3d 518, 530 (6th Cir. 2012) (quoting S. Rep. 99-345, at 21 (1986), *reprinted in* 1986 U.S.C.C.A.N. 5266, 5286). This inquiry must be "reasonable and prudent under the circumstances." *Id.* (quoting S. Rep. 99-345, at 21 (1986), *reprinted in* 1986 U.S.C.C.A.N. at 5286).

In her complaint, Prather alleges sufficient facts that support the reasonable inference that the defendants acted with "reckless disregard" with respect to their compliance with 42 C.F.R. § 424.22(a)(2). First, Prather alleges that she and the other nurses employed to review claims were instructed to review the claims only cursorily. R. 98 (Third Am. Compl. ¶ 87) (Page ID #1481). Those working for the Held Claims Project were told that they needed to release claims more quickly. *Id.* ¶ 88 (Page ID #1481-82). To that end, Prather and her co-workers were instructed not to review the content of much of the documentation. *Id.* ¶ 94-95 (Page ID #1483).

Second, Prather alleges that both she and the other nurses raised concerns about the defendants' compliance with Medicare regulations, but were told to ignore any problems. *Id.* at ¶ 91-92 (Page ID #1482). Prather states that her concerns were repeatedly dismissed and she was told that "there is such a push to get the claims through." *Id.* ¶ 92, 96 (Page ID #1482, 1483). Additionally, Prather was told on multiple occasions that "[w]e can just argue in our favor if we get audited" as a solution to any compliance issues. *Id.* ¶ 114 (Page ID #1489).

Lastly, Prather alleges facts demonstrating that the defendants knew that their practices with respect to claims were potentially in violation of governing regulations. The defendants sent an email acknowledging that not all physicians would be "comfortable" with signing untimely certifications and that the defendants could not "force" them to sign. *Id.* ¶ 98 (Page ID #1484). Drawing all inferences in favor of Prather, as we must, this email suggests p.838 that the defendants knew that their conduct was, at least, perilously close to noncompliance such that doctors might refuse to be complicit in the defendants' billing practices.[10] Furthermore, Prather alleges that a supervisor in the billing office alerted the employees that the defendants' practice of cancelling and re-submitting RAPs because of a lack of physician certifications might prompt an audit from Medicare. *Id.* ¶ 100 (Page ID #1484-85).

All these factual allegations support the inference that the defendants were on notice that their claim-submission process was resulting in potential compliance problems. Once the defendants had been informed by the employees explicitly hired to review these claims that there may be compliance issues, they had an obligation to inquire into whether they were actually in compliance with all appropriate regulations, including 42 C.F.R. § 424.22(a)(2). According to Prather, however, the defendants did not conduct such an inquiry and instead repeatedly pushed their employees to ignore problems, which they knew might trigger an audit, in a rush to get the claims submitted. In doing so, the defendants acted with "reckless disregard" as to the truth of their certification of compliance and to whether these requirements were material to the government's decision to pay.[11]

These factual allegations suffice, at the motion-to-dismiss stage, to demonstrate scienter. Discovery may reveal that the defendants did conduct an inquiry into their compliance with 42 C.F.R. § 424.22(a)(2) that was "reasonable and prudent under the circumstances." *Williams,* 696 F.3d at 530 (quoting S. Rep. 99-345, at 21 (1986), *reprinted in* 1986 U.S.C.C.A.N. at 5286). But, at this stage in the litigation, Prather has alleged sufficient facts supporting the inference that the defendants deliberately ignored multiple employees' concerns about their compliance with relevant regulations, and instead pressured their employees only cursorily to review claims for compliance problems so that they could be quickly submitted for reimbursement.

IV. CONCLUSION

Prather has sufficiently pleaded that the defendants misrepresented their compliance with the material timing requirement in 42 C.F.R. § 424.22(a)(2), and that they acted with "reckless disregard" as to whether they had complied with this requirement and whether this requirement was material. For the foregoing reasons, we REVERSE the district court's judgment and REMAND for proceedings consistent with this opinion.

DAVID W. McKEAGUE, Circuit Judge, dissenting.

DISSENT

For the second time, this panel has reversed a well-reasoned decision by the district p.839 court to dismiss Prather's complaint. *See United States ex rel. Prather v. Brookdale Senior Living Cmtys., Inc.,* 838 F.3d 750, 775 (6th Cir. 2016) (*Prather I*) (McKeague, J., concurring and dissenting). Two years ago, the majority invented a more stringent timing-and-explanation requirement out of whole cloth and grafted it onto the Medicare regulations. Today, the majority decides both that this requirement (created by the court in 2016) was somehow material to the government's decision to pay claims in 2011 and 2012, and that the defendants knew, seven years ago, that it was material—even though Prather identifies no authority in support of that position. Since Prather's complaint does not satisfy Rule 8 or Rule 9(b), I respectfully dissent from the majority's opinion.

I

This case involves home-health services billed to Medicare by the defendants (collectively, "Brookdale"). *Id.* at 755. Brookdale is a Home-Health Agency ("HHA") that coordinates the provision of care and the billing of those services to Medicare.

A

Medicare covers the cost of certain home-health services for patients who are confined to the home and need in-house medical care. 42 U.S.C. § 1395f(a)(2)(C); 42 C.F.R. § 424.22. Before Medicare will pay for these services, a physician must (among other things) certify that the patient is eligible for the home-health benefit, must establish a plan of care, and must complete a face-to-face encounter with the patient. 42 C.F.R. § 424.22(a). The signatures on these certifications "must be obtained at the time the plan of care is established or as soon thereafter as possible." *Id.* § 424(a)(2); *Prather I,* 838 F.3d at 762-63.

Billing for home-health services occurs in sixty-day cycles. In other words, Medicare pays the HHA a fixed amount, designed to reimburse it for all costs associated with sixty days of covered services. *Prather I,* 838 F.3d at 756. The sixty-day period is known as the "episode of care." Reimbursement under this prospective payment system is done in two steps. First, the HHA submits a Request for Anticipated Payment ("RAP"), which prompts Medicare to transmit a percentage of the total payment to the HHA. *Id.* Once care is completed, the provider submits a final bill to Medicare. Medicare then settles the account and submits the balance of the payment. *Id.* Medicare itself is not directly involved in these transactions —the agency contracts with Medicare Administrative Coordinators ("MACs"), companies who handle the process on Medicare's behalf. For the purposes of this case, a false statement to a MAC is a false statement to Medicare.

A HHA can submit a RAP even if the certifications have not been signed. *See* Medicare Claims Processing Manual, Ch. 10, § 10.1.10.3 (stating that a RAP may be billed once "the OASIS assessment is complete," "verbal orders for home care have been received and documented," "[a] plan of care has been established and sent to the physician," and "[t]he first service visit under that plan has been delivered"). Thus, while the provider must have the plan of care in place to bill a RAP, it need not have all the signatures squared away before billing the RAP. *See id.* However, the same guidance prohibits HHAs from submitting a final bill "until after all services are provided for the episode and the physician has signed the plan of care and any subsequent verbal order." *Id.* § 10.1.10.4. The signed certifications must be kept on file with the provider and must be produced if the MAC or Medicare requests them. 42 C.F.R. § 424.22(c).

p.840 In *Prather I,* the court held that late signatures, if unexplained, could be "impliedly false" under the False Claims Act ("FCA"). 31 U.S.C. § 3729(a)(1)(A); *Prather I,* 838 F.3d at 765-66. Specifically, the court held that "delay [is] acceptable only if the length of the delay is justified by the reasons the home-health agency provides for it." *Prather I,* 838 F.3d at 765. If those reasons are inadequate, then the claim is false, and a relator or the United States can recover damages under the FCA. *Id.* at 765-66. Between the briefing and the decision in *Prather I,* however, the Supreme Court held that implied-false-certification claims that rely on a misleading omission are only actionable if the omission is material. *Universal Health Servs., Inc. v. United States ex rel. Escobar,* ___ U.S. ___, 136 S.Ct. 1989, 1999-2001, 195 L.Ed.2d 348 (2016). We declined to address materiality in *Prather I,* opting to leave that issue for the parties on remand. *Prather I,* 838 F.3d at 761 n.2.

B

After Prather amended her complaint on remand to better comply with *Escobar,* Brookdale moved to dismiss. The district judge granted the motion, reasoning that Prather failed to plead materiality. Prather appeals that order.

I will not belabor the facts, which are addressed in detail elsewhere. However, it is important to understand what Prather has *not* claimed. Her complaint does not allege that Brookdale backdated the certifications so that they only appeared to be signed in a timely manner (which would be fraud). She does not allege that the certifications were not signed before final bills were submitted to Brookdale's MAC (which would also be fraud). Neither does she allege that Brookdale withheld information from the MAC or from Medicare, nor does it appear any request was ever issued (if that were true, this would be a fraudulent-concealment case, rather than a fraud-by-omission case). *Compare* Restatement (Second) of Torts § 550 (Liability for Fraudulent Concealment) *with* § 551 (Liability for Nondisclosure). Finally, it does not appear that the certification forms were part of the billing package sent to the MAC. Stated differently, the mechanics of the billing process would not inherently disclose to the MAC that the certification signatures were late.[1]

Instead, Prather alleges that the defendants submitted over 1,000 claims where the certifications or other crucial documents were not signed until long after the episode of care had ended. She offers up four patients as exemplars:

p.841 [Table]

Prather alleges that these delays would be material to the MAC's payment decisions, and therefore that Brookdale committed fraud by failing to disclose them and explain the delay.

To state a claim for fraud, Prather must make two related showings in her complaint. First, she must plead, with particularity, that these omissions were material to the government. Second, she must allege facts plausibly suggesting that Brookdale acted with fraudulent intent. In my opinion, her complaint accomplishes neither of these things.

II

I address the materiality issue first. To survive a motion to dismiss, the plaintiff must show that the *Prather I* requirement was material to the government's decision to pay Brookdale's claims. In other words, even if the length of the delay was unacceptable or if the explanation for such delay was insufficient, Prather must show that these errors were significant enough to influence the government's actual payment decisions, not merely its abstract legal rights.

A

Fraud is typically premised on affirmative misrepresentations. This is because a party to a business transaction ordinarily has no duty to disclose facts to his adversary. *See* Restatement (Second) of Torts § 551(1). However, in *Escobar* the Court clarified that the False Claims Act imposes, at least, a duty to avoid certain misleading omissions in claims for monetary reimbursement from the government. *Escobar,* 136 S.Ct. at 1999-2000. Because this kind of "silent fraud" is an exception to the rule, the Court limited its application to cases where a person "state[s] the truth so far as it goes" but knows the statement to be "materially misleading because of his failure to state additional or qualifying matter." *Escobar,* 136 S.Ct. at 1999-2000 (quoting Restatement, § 529). Under this rule, a "half-truth may be as misleading as a statement wholly false" and is equally tortious. Restatement, § 529; *Escobar,* 136 S.Ct. at 2000.

The Court was also painfully clear that not all regulatory violations are material. The government frequently requires contractors to "aver their compliance" with all relevant regulations, and the Court was unwilling to embrace the "extraordinarily expansive" liability that would exist if "failing to mention noncompliance with any of those requirements" would be fraudulent. *Escobar,* 136 S.Ct. at 2004. This statement was not mere dicta—it was in direct response to the United States' argument that every undisclosed regulatory violation would trigger FCA liability. *See id.*

Instead, the fundamental question here is whether the government agents on the ground would have acted differently if they p.842 knew of the omitted fact. Stated differently, Prather must show that the government justifiably relied on the nondisclosure, assuming that if something had been out of place, Brookdale would have said so. *See* Restatement (Second) of Torts §§ 537-38 (observing that materiality is inextricably rooted in the concept of justifiable reliance); 31 U.S.C. § 3729(b)(4) (stating that a fact is material if it has "a natural tendency to influence, or be capable of influencing, the payment or receipt of money or property"). Although this broad standard is clear, applying it to the particulars of this case has proven difficult for everyone involved. When pressed at oral argument, Prather was unable to provide an answer to this question, and the United States was unwilling to do so. In my mind, the majority opinion is equally unenlightening on this issue. Before explaining why Prather has failed to plead materiality, then, I attempt to put more flesh on the skeleton provided by *Escobar*.

B

All agree that Prather bears the burden of showing that these omissions were material. *Escobar,* 136 S.Ct. at 2004. But exactly how is she supposed to accomplish that, in this context? It's a fair question, and it has not been answered by us or any of the other Circuits. Since I would affirm the dismissal of her complaint, it is only fair that I explain, in detail, why she has fallen short of the goal.

1

Whenever a plaintiff alleges fraud, he or she must "state with particularity the circumstances constituting fraud." Fed. R. Civ. P. 9(b). The Sixth Circuit has never asked whether the materiality of an omission is one of those circumstances and, if so, what it means to plead the material nature of an omission with particularity. I would hold that the particularity requirement applies here, and that it requires Prather to explain how and why these omissions deceived the government.

Rule 9(b) imposes the particularity requirement for several reasons. Requiring the plaintiff to plead the "circumstances constituting fraud" provides notice, alerting the defendants "as to the particulars of their alleged misconduct" so that they can respond. *United States ex rel. Bledsoe v. Cmty. Health Sys., Inc.,* 501 F.3d 493, 503 (6th Cir. 2007). It also "protect[s] defendants against spurious charges of immoral and fraudulent behavior," *Prather I,* 838 F.3d at 771 (internal citations and quotation marks omitted), and discourages "fishing expeditions," *Bledsoe,* 501 F.3d at 503 n.11. We have stated that the particulars of fraud include, "at a minimum ... the time, place, and content of the alleged misrepresentation on which [the plaintiff] relied; the fraudulent scheme; the fraudulent intent of the defendants; and the injury resulting from the fraud." *United States ex rel. Marlar v. BWXT Y-12, LLC,* 525 F.3d 439, 444 (6th Cir. 2008) (internal citations and quotation marks omitted).

The Court has strongly suggested that materiality should be added to this list. In *Escobar,* the Court recognized that "the common law could not have conceived of fraud without proof of materiality." *Escobar,* 136 S.Ct. at 2002 (quoting *Neder v. United States,* 527 U.S. 1, 22, 119 S.Ct. 1827, 144 L.Ed.2d 35 (1999)). Indeed, the purpose of the *Escobar* opinion was to emphasize that materiality is essential to a successful silent-fraud claim; it is the lodestar by which the courts separate the careless from the nefarious. Add to this the Court's decision to characterize the materiality standard as "demanding," a label that fits more comfortably with the "special pleading" framework of Rule 9 than the p.843 notice-pleading regime established by Rule 8.

Furthermore, every Circuit to address this question agrees that Rule 9(b) governs materiality allegations. *See Minzer v. Keegan,* 218 F.3d 144, 151 (2d Cir. 2000); *Grabcheski v. Am. Int'l Grp., Inc.,* 687 Fed.Appx. 84, 87 (2d Cir. 2017) ("Materiality must be pleaded with particularity under Rule 9(b).") (interpreting the False Claims Act); *In re Donald J. Trump Casino Securities Litig.,* 7 F.3d 357, 374-75 (3d Cir. 1993); *Shandong Yinguang Chem. Indus. Joint Stock Co. v. Potter,* 607 F.3d 1029, 1033 (5th Cir. 2010); *United States ex rel. Vigil v. Nelnet, Inc.,* 639 F.3d 791, 798-800 (8th Cir. 2011); *Hemmer Grp. v. SouthWest Water Co.,* 527 Fed.Appx. 623, 626 (9th Cir. 2013); *Hopper v. Solvay Pharms., Inc.,* 588 F.3d 1318, 1329-30 (11th Cir. 2009); *Sampson v. Wash. Mut. Bank,* 453 Fed.Appx. 863, 866 (11th Cir. 2011).

In *Prather I*, we relaxed the Rule 9(b) standard slightly. We did so because Prather was close enough to the billing department to say with near certainty that the claims were submitted to the government. *Prather I*, 838 F.3d at 769-73. But Prather has no similar proximity to the government's payment decisions, and so she cannot avail herself of the relaxed standard in this context. Thus, she must overcome the full force of the particularity requirement if her complaint is to survive.

2

What does it mean to plead a material omission with particularity? Although our precedent is sparse on the issue, other Circuits have offered a near-uniform test for answering this question. Put simply, a plaintiff must explain *why* the omissions were material to the government and *how* the government was misled by those omissions. *See Vigil*, 639 F.3d at 798-800 ("[T]he Complaint fails to allege with particularity... why these alleged regulatory violations were material to the government's decision to pay...."); *Hopper*, 588 F.3d at 1330 (holding a complaint deficient when it "d[id] not link the alleged false statements to the government's decision to pay false claims."); *Hemmer Grp.*, 527 Fed.Appx. at 626 ("A plaintiff must 'show with particularity how the [accounting irregularities] affected the company's financial statements and whether they were material in light of the company's overall financial position.'" (quoting *In re Daou Sys., Inc.*, 411 F.3d 1006, 1018 (9th Cir. 2005)); *Sampson*, 453 Fed.Appx. at 866 ("[A] plaintiff must state with particularity... the content and manner in which the[] statements misled the Plaintiffs.") (internal quotation marks omitted).)

The Eighth Circuit provides a particularly enlightening analysis of this issue. In *Vigil*, the court addressed a False Claims Act complaint alleging that a student-loan contractor was using false certifications to defraud the U.S. Department of Education of interest subsidies. Although the plaintiff set out, in detail, how the certifications were false, the panel held that this was not enough to plead materiality. *Vigil*, 639 F.3d at 798-800. "Merely alleging *why* the Certifications were false is insufficient" to satisfy Rule 9(b); instead, the court required the complaint to allege "why these alleged regulatory violations were material to the government" and to connect "the alleged false statements to the government's decision to pay false claims." *Id.* at 799-800; *see also Grabcheski*, 687 Fed. Appx. at 87 (holding that the plaintiff "failed to allege with particularity facts that demonstrate how th[e] difference in value ... was likely to have had any effect on the Agreements" with the government).

A product-safety case from California also provides excellent guidance into what p.844 the particularity rule requires in this context. *Arroyo v. Chattem, Inc.*, 926 F.Supp.2d 1070, 1078-80 (N.D. Cal. 2012). In *Arroyo*, the plaintiff alleged that a pharmaceutical company committed fraud by promoting a weight-loss supplement as "safe," while failing to disclose the existence of a chemical (hexavalent chromium) in the product. *Id.* at 1073. The court noted that the labels did not affirmatively state that the product was hexavalent-chromium free, and therefore that "Plaintiff must specifically allege that hexavalent chromium at the level present in [the product] makes statements about the product's safety false or misleading." *Id.* at 1079. The plaintiff relied on general statements that "hexavalent chromium is unsafe" to plead materiality. *Id.*

The district court dismissed the claim, holding that the materiality allegations in the complaint did not satisfy Rule 9(b). *Id.* at 1078-79. In doing so, the district court reasoned:

> Many foods and drugs on the market are not one hundred percent safe, and general allegations that a product's safety is less than one hundred percent do not give rise to a lawsuit for fraud ... Under this theory of materiality ... Plaintiff's FAC is insufficient because it does not allege a level of hexavalent chromium [in the product] that materially changes its safety profile from safe to unsafe.

Id. at 1079. This theory provides a helpful framework for evaluating materiality. In a silent-fraud case where violations occur by degree, the plaintiff must allege, with particularity, the point at which the defendants crossed from innocuous mistakes to fraudulent omissions. In a product-safety case like *Arroyo,* that means the plaintiff must plead the scientific threshold for safe levels of the offending chemical. Here, Prather has a similar task.

3

In *Prather I,* we held that a late certification is false if "the length of the delay is [not] justified by the reasons the home-health agency provides for it." *Prather I,* 838 F.3d at 765. This general standard leaves crucial issues unresolved. At what point does a late signature require an explanation? It depends. When an explanation is required, how detailed must the explanation be? It depends. What kind of justifications suffice? Again, it depends: In *Prather I,* the majority refused to answer these questions, suggesting instead that each case must rise and fall on its own facts, and even noting that "the rare excuse... could justify a delay" beyond the 60-day episode of care, despite the fact that the government has said such delays are "not acceptable." *Id.* at 765 n.6.

It follows that Prather (or any other relator) must plead facts connecting the defendant's insufficient justifications to Medicare's decision to pay. She must explain to us (and to Brookdale) why and how the government would have been deceived by the failure to include the explanations omitted here. Put another way, she must pinpoint the limits of the government's patience, as applied to her allegations. Even assuming that the delay was "due only to the fact that Brookdale had accumulated a large backlog of Medicare claims," *id.* at 765, Prather must allege facts showing that this excuse is either unacceptable to the government in all cases, or that the government would not have accepted it under the circumstances of this case. Otherwise, we have no basis for finding (a) that the government wanted Brookdale to disclose this delay and explain it at the billing stage, and (b) that if had Brookdale done so, then the government probably would have denied reimbursement.

p.845 This might seem like an unduly harsh requirement. But it is essential if Rule 9 is to serve the notice-providing function Congress ascribed to it. Particularly when the regulation offers a vague threshold ("as soon thereafter as possible") and where we have made it even more vague by interpretation, a silent-fraud plaintiff *must* be able to explain, with particularity, if and how the specific violation would have influenced the government's payment decision. Otherwise, Brookdale is left to guess about how it has allegedly defrauded the government.

C

How can Prather—or any other relator —meet this threshold? *Escobar* made it clear that the world is Prather's oyster: No "single fact or occurrence [i]s always determinative" in deciding whether something is material. *Escobar,* 136 S.Ct. at 2001. Instead, the Court subscribes to an approach that treats everything as relevant, so long as it sheds light on the government's behavior, rather than its abstract legal rights. *Id.* at 2001-03 (observing that the relevant barometer of influence is "the effect on the likely or actual behavior of the recipient," not merely whether "the Government would have the option to decline to pay"). Relevant facts include the government's payment history, the way the government characterizes the requirement, and whether the omission goes to the essence of the bargain. *Id.* at 2001-04. Prather may use any combination of these facts (and others) to demonstrate that Brookdale's excuses are unacceptable to the government in all cases, or that the government would not have accepted the excuses due to the larger delays present in this case. She has not accomplished this.

1

The government's payment habits are, by far, the best evidence of materiality. If the government "refuses to pay claims in the mine run of cases based on noncompliance" with a particular rule, then the requirement is almost certainly material. *Id.* at 2003. In contrast, if the government "regularly pays a particular type of claim in full despite actual knowledge" of the violations, then Prather would be hard-pressed to demonstrate materiality. *Id.* at 2003-04.

Unfortunately, neither Prather nor Brookdale offer this information. Instead, each argues that the other's silence on the subject is evidence that the government cares (or doesn't care) about the information. This does not hurt Brookdale, who bears no legal burden in this context. Neither does it (technically) hurt Prather, except to say that it moves her no closer to the goal. *See id.* at 2000-02 (suggesting that a plaintiff need not present payment statistics to survive a motion to dismiss). Although we granted the United States' motion to appear as an amicus at oral argument, counsel refused to say whether or not she knew of the government's payment habits. Perhaps discovery will dredge up helpful information about the payment policies of Brookdale's MAC; perhaps it won't. The answer to that question will weigh heavily on Prather's case at the summary-judgment stage. The Court has, however, indicated that we cannot deny a motion to dismiss simply because discovery might help flesh out a plaintiff's claim. *Ashcroft v. Iqbal,* 556 U.S. 662, 684-86, 129 S.Ct. 1937, 173 L.Ed.2d 868 (2009).

So we are no closer to answering the materiality question than we were before. An inquiry into the government's payment habits has placed no facts on the scale. Again, this does not technically hurt Prather; it has just removed one of her weapons.

In other words, Prather need not present us with this information now, but p.846 she still needs to present *something* to satisfy Rule 9(b).

2

I agree that we have made the timing-and-explanation requirement a condition of payment. However, this only means that the government would have the option to decline payment if it knew that the requirement had been violated. *Escobar* requires that we look beyond this bare fact and ask about the importance of the requirement under the circumstances of this case. *Escobar*, 136 S.Ct. at 2003. To do so, we must naturally examine what the government has said about it, and the way a provider might disclose a violation to the government. Prather can draw little solace from this information—indeed, a thorough examination shows that it hurts her case.

Medicare prescribes the method by which providers submit claims for reimbursement. *See* 42 U.S.C. §§ 1302, 1395hh; 42 C.F.R. § 424.32. Providers must use the forms indicated by the regulations. 42 C.F.R. § 424.32(a)-(b). Home health service providers primarily use Form CMS-1450 (Uniform Institutional Provider Bill) and sometimes use CMS-1500 (Health Insurance Claim Form). *Id.* § 424.32(b); Medicare Claims Processing Manual, Ch. 10, §§ 10.A, 40. This data usually must be submitted electronically, but both the paper and electronic claims forms contain substantially the same information. *See id.;* 42 C.F.R. § 424.32(d)(2).

The CMS-1450 has 81 fields. Most are for boilerplate information about the patient, the provider, and the services provided. *See* Medicare Claims Processing Manual, Ch. 25, § 75. The form also contains fields for the date of admission, start of care, and statement period. *See id.,* Ch. 10, § 40.1; *id.,* Ch. 25, § 75.1; CMS-1450, FL 6, 12-15. For HHA claims, the "statement period" field is the sixty-day episode of care mandated by the Prospective Payment System. Medicare Claims Processing Manual, Ch. 10, §§ 40.1-40.2.

The form also contains a blank, lined field titled "Remarks." *See* CMS-1450, FL 80. The general instructions for completing the form indicate that this field should be used to enter "any remarks needed to provide information that is not shown elsewhere on the bill but which is necessary for proper payment." Medicare Claims Processing Manual, Ch. 25, § 75.6, FL 80. The specific guidance for HHA claims state that this field is "[c]onditional," *id.,* Ch. 10, § 40.1-40.2, meaning that it is a field "that must be completed if other conditions exist," *id.,* Ch. 1, § 70.2.3.1. For a final bill, remarks are "required only in cases where the claim is cancelled or adjusted." *Id.,* Ch. 10, § 40.2.

The rear of the form lists multiple typewritten warranties, all of which are adopted (if applicable) by the provider when it submits the form. The general warranty affirms that "the billing information as shown on the face hereof is true, accurate and complete," and that "the submitter did not knowingly or recklessly disregard or conceal material facts." *See* CMS-1450, Gen. Warranty. Among the specific warranties is a verification that "[p]hysician's certifications and re-certifications, if required by contract or Federal regulations, are on file" with the provider. *See id.,* Spec. Warranty No. 3. Two observations can be drawn from this data.

First, nothing in the forms, regulations, or guidance suggests that the government cares to review the certifications during the billing process. The general warranty only refers to the accuracy and completeness of the data "shown on the face hereof." *See id.,* Gen. Warranty. It does not require a provider to aver that it has fastidious recordkeeping policies. At most, the p.847 regulations require HHAs to keep the forms "on file" and provide the certifications and other medical records "upon request." *Id.,* Spec. Warranty No. 3; 42 C.F.R. § 424.22(c). It appears that production is only necessary if the MAC initiates a medical review because it suspects improper payment. *See* Medicare Program Integrity Manual, Ch. 3, §§ 3.2.1, 3.2.3.A, 3.3.1.1; *id.,* Ch. 6, §§ 6.1-6.3. Indeed, the physicians need not actually use the CMS-485 (certification template) to certify patient need, "as long as a physician certifies that the five certification requirements" are satisfied. *Id.,* Ch. 6, § 6.2.1.

Second, the form does not contemplate that a provider would disclose a late certification at the billing stage. Neither does it request the date of the physician certification so that billing officials can compare it to the episode of care and evaluate lateness issues. The only place where they might do so on the face of the form would be in the remarks section. But the form instructions identify only two limited circumstances where a provider should complete this field before submitting a bill: "only in cases where the claim is cancelled or adjusted." Medicare Claims Processing Manual, Ch. 10, § 40.2. Thus, by Medicare's own definitions, a bill submitted without a late-signature disclosure would still be "complete," because it would not omit any required information. *Id.,* Ch. 1, § 70.2.3.1. Although this is not dispositive, it fails to provide any support for Prather's assertion that the omissions are material.

Prather's theory fares no better in light of the Medicare Guidance. Medicare's *Program Integrity Manual* devotes nearly 100 pages to instructing Medicare Administrative Coordinators ("MACs") on how to identify "potential errors" and take "corrective actions." *See generally* Medicare Program Integrity Manual, Ch. 3. The mine run of claims submitted to Medicare only include the bill, not the underlying medical records. *See id.,* § 3.3.1.1. Thus, records are only submitted to the MAC if it initiates a medical review to ensure that the services provided were medically necessary. *See id.,* §§ 3.2.1, 3.3.1.1; *id.,* Ch. 7, § 7.2. Although a MAC has the authority to demand records and "review any claim at any time," the sheer size of Medicare "doesn't allow for review of every claim." *See id.,* Ch. 3, §§ 3.2.1, 3.2.3.A; *see also* 42 C.F.R. § 424.22(c).

Consequently, this guidance commands the MACs to prioritize their review efforts. In doing so, they must focus on "areas with the greatest potential for improper payment," or "where the services billed have significant potential to be non-covered or incorrectly coded." Medicare Program Integrity Manual, Ch. 3, § 3.2.1. The guidance lists five red flags that the MACs may use to set priorities.[2] *Id.* Nowhere in this guidance or any of the regulations does the government even hint that any late signatures are so important to a MAC's auditing or payment decisions that a provider would be expected to disclose them every time.

Prather directs us to two pieces of information suggesting that *some* late signatures might be material. Reports from the HHS Inspector General addressing home-health service compliance indicate that a special area of concern to the agency was "[u]ntimely and/or forged physician certifications on plans of care." *Compliance Program Guidance for Home Health Agencies,* HHS Office of Inspector General, 63 p.848

Fed. Reg. No. 152, 42410, 42414 (Aug. 7, 1998). Such statements count as one of the red flags that a MAC may use to set its auditing priorities. Medicare Program Integrity Manual, Ch. 3, § 3.2.1. Related guidance, addressed to the HHAs (rather than the MACs) states that "[i]t is not acceptable for HHAs to wait until the end of a 60-day episode of care to obtain a completed certification/recertification." Medicare Benefit Policy Manual, Ch. 7, § 30.5.1 (2015).[3]

Taken as a whole, the guidance and the forms undercut Prather's case. In the first place, they provide no support for Prather's (conclusory) allegation that the government would not have paid Brookdale's claims had they known about the late certifications. In other words, Prather has not pointed us to *any* governmental statements disapproving of Brookdale's alleged excuses, either as a per se matter or in the context of these particular delays. Neither has she used any of this information to explain how and why the government was misled by Brookdale's alleged omissions. Indeed, the forms and the guidance are completely silent about what excuses suffice to justify delays of this magnitude.

Second, the regulatory framework suggests that the government is not interested in the timing-and-explanation issue during the billing stage. The sheer size of the Medicare program requires a streamlined approach to billing review. To serve this purpose, CMS created a uniform billing form that applies to most claims—a single page containing all the information necessary to process and pay the claim. 42 C.F.R. § 424.32(b); Medicare Claims Processing Manual, Ch. 10, §§ 10.A, 40. The form is not designed to accommodate the explanations contemplated by *Prather I*. The "remarks" field—the only conceivable place to offer such a justification—is tiny and ill-suited to accommodate the complete explanations necessary to avoid more accusations of silent fraud.

Instead, the timing-and-explanation requirement is probably enforced by auditing. No one disputes that the government might initiate an audit of Brookdale's files and decide that it had not satisfied the certification requirements. In this context, Brookdale could offer the kind of detailed, patient-specific explanations for lateness that we required in *Prather I*. Under *Prather I*, a MAC might well be dissatisfied with those reasons and demand reimbursement. At the billing stage, however, it seems that the billing agents only look at the face of the form to ask whether "the services billed have significant potential to be non-covered or incorrectly coded." Medicare Program Integrity Manual, Ch. 3, § 3.2.1. At a higher level, the MACs also use sophisticated algorithms and pattern-matching p.849 (e.g., unnatural spikes in volume, high-cost services) to identify potential areas for audits. *See id.* Although this is not dispositive, it does give us some insight into what the government is looking for at the billing stage—and if the government is not looking for the information that Brookdale omitted, then such information is probably not material.

Ultimately, this is another dead end for Prather. If the timing of the signatures was truly a fulcrum of the government's payment decisions, one would expect to find some reference to it in the instructions that CMS gives to the companies who make those judgments. Again, this is not fatal to Prather's case—it simply removes another arrow from her quiver. Without concrete evidence of the government's payment history or any helpful regulatory guidance, Prather must present some other particular information showing how and why these omissions deceived the government. *See Escobar,* 136 S.Ct. at 2001-03.

3

The government need not specify every single detail of a transaction in order to protect itself from silent fraud. *Id.* at 2001-02. Some things go without saying. The government is entitled to presume that the guns it orders "must actually shoot," even if it does not expressly require that function. *Id.* Such omissions go to the very essence of the bargain and are usually material. *Id.* at 2001-03 & n.5. Prather and the majority conclude that Brookdale's failure to disclose an adequate justification goes to the very essence of the bargain; therefore, Prather can proceed even though she has not otherwise satisfied the particularity requirement.

The case law refutes this position. Start with *Escobar*. The defendants in *Escobar* provided mental health services to children and billed Medicaid for those services. *Id.* at 2000. However, they failed to disclose that their social workers did not have the training or credentials expressly required by the regulations. *Id.* This omission went to the essence of the bargain—the defendants did not (and could not) perform the mental-health services for which they were paid. Another leading case cited by the majority involved similar facts—a mortgage lending executive who certified that he was eligible for a FHA-sponsored loan problem without revealing that he had been indicted for wire fraud and obstruction of justice. *United States v. Luce,* 873 F.3d 999, 1001-03 (7th Cir. 2017). One might compare these cases to a person who bills the government for public-defender services without mentioning that he has never been licensed to practice law (*Escobar*) or that he is in imminent danger of disbarment (*Luce*).

History also provides colorful examples. The FCA was enacted during the Civil War to combat fraud (including silent fraud) in defense contracts. *See United States ex rel. Spay v. CVS Caremark Corp.,* 875 F.3d 746, 753 (3d Cir. 2017). Among the culprits in those cases were contractors who sold "artillery shells filled with sawdust instead of explosives," and uniforms "made of shredded, often decaying rags, pressed ... into a semblance of cloth that would fall apart in the first rain." *Id.* (internal citations and quotation marks).

Prather's claims, as currently pled, are not in the same universe. Medicare was established to "provide[] basic protection against the costs of ... home health services" for the elderly. 42 U.S.C. §§ 1395c, 1395j. The enforcing regulations for home-health services require physician certifications to ensure that Medicare does not pay for those services when they are not necessary, in order to preserve the financial integrity of the program for those who p.850 truly need it. *See* 42 C.F.R. § 424.22. The regulations accordingly require the certifications to be done by a person with one of five specific levels of training. *See id.* § 424.22(a)(1)(v)(A). Had Prather alleged that the forms were signed by individuals not covered by the regulation, her case would be squarely covered by *Escobar,* and Brookdale would have deprived the government of the essence of its bargain. That is not the case here—Prather's only theory of relief is that the forms were signed too late and that the lateness was unjustified, not that the caretakers were inherently unqualified or that the care was fundamentally defective.

The majority claims that these omissions are crucial because the timing-and-explanation requirement is an antifraud measure. This argument is a non-starter. Of course the regulations are designed to prevent fraud. Most (if not all) Medicare regulations exist to make sure the government gets what it paid for. But *Escobar* made it clear that only *significant* regulatory violations can be the basis for silent-fraud liability. *Escobar,* 136 S.Ct. at 2003-04. Thus, antifraud rhetoric set aside, all Prather can derive from this theory is the bare assertion that Brookdale violated § 424.22. This does not satisfy *Escobar.* Prather still has not offered an explanation for how and why Brookdale's omissions actually deceived the government.

Perhaps the closest she comes to this goal is by pointing to the sixty-day period mentioned in the 2015 guidance revisions. That guidance states that "[i]t is not acceptable for HHAs to wait until the end of a 60-day episode of care to obtain a completed certification/recertification." Medicare Benefit Policy Manual, Ch. 7, § 30.5.1 (2015). Although this language was added after the conduct at issue here, Prather claims that this is longstanding policy that goes to the essence of the government's bargain. *See Prather I,* 838 F.3d at 765 n.6. This argument fails on two fronts. First, *Prather I* expressly refused to say that such lateness was categorically inexcusable, even while concluding that it was unjustified here. *Id.* at 765 n.6. If this is true, then it is hard to see how this kind of a violation is so egregious that it always goes to the very essence of the bargain.

Second, and in a related vein, the argument does nothing to explain why *this* delay is material. If a lengthy delay can be justified in some circumstances, Prather must show us why this is not one of those cases. The only excuse she identifies is a massive paperwork backlog. But she makes no compelling argument that disclosure of this excuse would have caused some adverse reaction from the government. Of all the problems faced by Medicare's antifraud contractors, "Paperwork backlog" is not Public Enemy No. 1, or anywhere close to it. Perhaps there is no excuse for Brookdale's conduct here. But my point is that Prather has utterly failed to explain *why* this is the case. Rule 9(b) expects more from someone making accusations of fraud under a statute that is inherently punitive. *See Vigil,* 639 F.3d at 798-80 ("The Complaint fails to allege with particularity ... why these alleged regulatory violations were material to the government's decision to pay...."); *Hopper,* 588 F.3d at 1330 (holding a complaint deficient when it "d[id] not link the alleged false statements to the government's decision to pay false claims.").

4

At the end of the day, Prather is left with an empty quiver. Though none of the factors discussed above are dispositive, Prather can only claim victory in half of one analysis (she correctly identifies the requirement as a condition of payment). This is not enough to demonstrate materiality. p.851 Accordingly, I would affirm the district court.

To some extent, the deficiency in Prather's complaint is not her fault. To show materiality, the plaintiff must make some showing that the omission would influence the government. Since past behavior and administrative guidance is the best predictor of future conduct, a plaintiff can typically mine the agency's publications and industry experience for guidance on what is material. But the timing-and-explanation requirement does not appear in any regulation. It does not come from any agency guidance, adjudication, or notice-and-comment process. It has no history in the Medicare billing system. It sprung, fully formed, from the minds of two federal judges. Consequently, Prather has no history, commentary, or guidance she can use to demonstrate materiality.

Judicial legislation always has pernicious consequences, and this case is no different. By inventing a rule out of whole cloth to preserve this case at the falsity stage, the *Prather I* majority failed to realize it was also crippling the plaintiff's case on materiality grounds. Today, rather than confessing its first error, the majority compounds it by twisting the law of materiality to cover up the mistakes it made two years ago. It would not surprise me if this case returns to us in a few years, presenting us again with a third opportunity to correct ourselves or warp the law even further. The lesson, then, is clear: Leave rulemaking to the legislators and administrators, even when the present outcome appears unjust. The orderly development of the law is not without rough patches, but it is better than living under the law of unintended consequences.

III

The majority also addresses the scienter requirement of the statute, although the district judge did not. And again, the majority gets it wrong.

Like with all fraud claims, the FCA imposes a "rigorous" scienter requirement. *Escobar,* 136 S.Ct. at 2002. Even if a defendant's claim suffers from a material omission, fraud liability does not attach unless the defendant *knows* that the requirement is material to the government's payment decision. *Id.* at 1996. The majority admits as much. Maj. Op. at 837. A defendant acts knowingly if it "has actual knowledge of the information," "acts in deliberate indifference of the truth or falsity of the information," or "acts in reckless disregard of the truth or falsity of the information." 31 U.S.C. § 3729(b)(1)(A). Finally, although Rule 9 does not apply to alleging a person's state of mind, this "does not give [the plaintiff] license to evade the less rigid—though still operative—strictures of Rule 8." *Ashcroft v. Iqbal,* 556 U.S. 662, 686-87, 129 S.Ct. 1937, 173 L.Ed.2d 868 (2009).

Thus, Prather still faces a tough standard. She must allege facts plausibly showing that Brookdale knew omitting the explanations would influence the government's payment decisions or that it recklessly disregarded that possibility. The majority claims she has pled recklessness. She has not.

The first problem with the majority's argument is that the allegedly wrongful conduct occurred between 2011 and 2012. The timing-and-explanation requirement did not exist until we decided *Prather I* in 2016. True, the regulation states that the certifications must be obtained "at the time the plan of care is established or as soon thereafter as possible." 42 C.F.R. § 424.22(a)(2). But before *Prather I,* no one had any reason to think that this regulation required HHAs to submit explanations for all late signatures, or that a p.852 delay is "acceptable only if the length of the delay is justified by the reasons the home-health agency provides for it." *Prather I,* 838 F.3d at 765. I struggle to see how Brookdale can be held responsible for recklessly disregarding such a specific requirement when nothing—absolutely nothing—in the existing law required it to provide affirmative justifications for late signatures during the billing process.

The second problem is that most of Prather's scienter allegations have no relationship to the signatures. Though the nurses were instructed to review claims "only cursorily," Maj. Op. at 837-38, Prather concedes that they *were* told to "make sure the orders are signed, the face to face documentation is complete, and the therapy reassessments are present in the charts," R. 98, Third Amended Compl., ¶¶ 87, 91, PID 1481-82. So even while they were allegedly instructed to ignore other compliance issues, they were expressly told not to ignore the signature requirements. *Id.* I fail to see how this is evidence of reckless disregard as to the timing-and-explanation theory on which Prather relies.

The same symptoms infect Prather's other scienter allegations. Prather alleges that management ignored her complaints about noncompliance in the forms. Maj. Op. at 837-38 (citing R. 98, Third Amended Compl., ¶¶ 91-92, PID 1482). But these paragraphs reveal that Brookdale only ignored her complaints about general flaws in the underlying medical records, not missing signatures—indeed, she was told specifically, and on several occasions, to scour the documents for missing signatures so the errors could be corrected. R. 98, Third Amended Compl., ¶¶ 91-93, PID 1482-83. The majority also cites an email where management said "not all physicians would be 'comfortable' with signing" the late certifications. Maj. Op. at 837. But again, this is not the whole picture: In the same breath, the emails acknowledge that "we can not force this process," suggesting that Brookdale was trying to speed up the process as much as they could without resorting to the kind of unsavory methods indicative of fraud. R. 98, Third Amended Compl., ¶¶ 98, PID 1483-84.

The closest Prather comes to alleging scienter is in paragraphs 99 and 100. There, she alleges that Medicare would frequently cancel Brookdale's RAPs because the final bill was not submitted in time, but then Brookdale would immediately re-bill the RAP without having the physician signatures on file. *Id.,* ¶¶ 99-100, PID 1484-85. Prather's supervisors admitted in an email that this practice might "trigger a probe or review by Medicare." *Id.,* ¶ 100, PID 1485. Thus, at least superficially, this suggests that Brookdale knew some of its billing practices might draw the ire of Medicare auditors.

But again, these allegations fail because they are not connected to Prather's theory of relief: That Brookdale acted with reckless disregard for the materiality of the late signatures and omitted explanations. As explained earlier, a provider may bill a RAP—but not a final claim—without the physician signatures on file. *See supra,* at 23, 119 S.Ct. 1827. Although this could be done with a nefarious or reckless motive, it is equally plausible that Brookdale was simply keeping the window open while it collected the signatures and explanations that the regulation requires. Nothing in this behavior inherently suggests that Brookdale was rebilling these claims with the intent to submit final bills that omitted material information. Since Prather has alleged facts that are, at best, only consistent with recklessness, she has not satisfied the requirements of Rule 8. *Iqbal,* 556 U.S. at 678, 129 S.Ct. 1937.

p.853 IV

My dissent today should not be understood as endorsing Brookdale's conduct. Medicare providers can and should be much more careful and meticulous with their recordkeeping. But accusing someone of fraud is a serious thing, and I simply am not convinced that Prather has alleged anything more than sloppy management and negligence. Medicare has a myriad of tools to prevent and remedy the problems associated with these lesser forms of culpability, but no one contends that this power has also been delegated to relators. If Congress wants to permit relators to pursue negligence claims on behalf of the government, so be it. But we lack the authority to make that policy judgment by equating negligence with fraud.

For the reasons stated above, I respectfully dissent from the opinion of the court.

[1] The dissent attempts to re-litigate the issues decided in *Prather I,* including efforts to muddy the holding of that decision. Dissent Op. at 838-39, 844-45, 850-51. Both 42 C.F.R. § 424.22(a)(2) and our corresponding interpretation are not hard to understand. Certifications are timely in two situations. First, they are timely if they were "obtained at the time the plan of care is established." 42 C.F.R. § 424.22(a)(2). This is a binary rule: either the certification was obtained at the time the plan of care was established or it was not. Second, certifications are timely if they were signed as soon as possible after the plan of care is established. *Id.* This is a standard. Although the dissent is unhappy that it is a standard and not a rule, Dissent Op. at 844, this was how the regulation was written and neither we, the parties, nor the U.S. government can pretend this away. *Prather I,* 838 F.3d at 765 n.6. The strength, and weakness, of standards is that they are fact-specific in their application. Thus, whether a certification complies with the standard that it be signed "as soon thereafter as possible," 42 C.F.R. § 424.22(a)(2), depends on the reason it was not completed at the time the plan of care was established. Imagine if the certification is signed one day after the plan of care is established. The reason? The certifying physician had to leave work early the day before because of a family emergency, and therefore delayed signing the certification. In this hypothetical, the length of the delay—one day—is plausibly justified by the reason for the delay —a personal emergency. Now imagine another certification that is signed months after the plan of care was established. In this case, the reason is because the home-healthcare provider is incompetent with its paperwork. This appears to be a situation in which the delay of several months is not justified by the excuse. This is a commonsense approach to which we continue to adhere.

[2] These facts are drawn from Prather's complaint and attached exhibits. R. 98 (Third. Am. Compl.) (Page ID #1459-96). Because of the case's procedural posture—it is before us on an appeal from the district court's grant of a motion to dismiss—we presume all factual allegations in the complaint to be true. Furthermore, as this court and the parties are familiar with the basic factual allegations in this case, we recite only those alleged facts that are relevant to the issues currently being litigated before us.

[3] The relevant "provision[s] ... do[] not distinguish between requests for final payment and requests for anticipated payment" in stating the conditions of payment, *Prather I,* 838 F.3d at 766 (citing 42 C.F.R. § 424.10(a)), and thus we will not do so here either.

[4] The opposite conclusion would produce results that are antithetical to common sense. Under the defendants' approach, it is not an express condition of payment that the certification be signed and dated by the physician who establishes the plan of care. But an unsigned and undated document stating that the patient is eligible for a home-health benefit is not a certification. *See Certification,* BLACK'S LAW DICTIONARY (10th ed. 2014) ("1. The act of attesting; esp., the process of giving someone or something an official document stating that a specified standard has been satisfied."); *Attest,* BLACK'S LAW DICTIONARY (10th ed. 2014) ("1. To bear witness; testify .... 2. To affirm to be true or genuine; to authenticate by signing as a witness.").

[5] The dissent seeks to reduce the weight of this factor by discussing the mechanisms by which a home healthcare provider would disclose violations of 42 C.F.R. § 424.22(a)(2). Dissent Op. at 845-49. In doing so, it loses sight of the woods for the trees. The implied false certification theory of liability is premised on the notion that parties submitting claims to the government must not "fail[] to disclose noncompliance with material statutory, regulatory, or contractual requirements." *Escobar,* 136 S.Ct. at 2001. Thus, a provider who has committed a material violation cannot submit a claim in silence—regardless of whether its claim form has a box for reporting violations. An inquiry, therefore, into how mechanically providers could report violations is not helpful in determining materiality.

[6] The United States filed an amicus brief and appeared at oral argument taking a position only on this "past-government-action prong" of the materiality analysis. Amicus Br. at 4. It argued that the district court erred in its evaluation of this factor. *Id.* The United States appeared, as it is authorized to do so, to speak only on this issue. 28 U.S.C. § 517; FED. R. APP. P. 29. The dissent's implied criticism of the United States' counsel taking only a limited position in this case is not well-founded. Dissent Op. at 841-42, 845-46. The legislative branch has created the scheme that gives the executive branch the ability to "attend to the interests of the United States," 28 U.S.C. § 517, as it—not we—may choose.

[7] Prather does not allege that the dates on the certifications were fraudulently backdated. Thus, a government agent reviewing each claim could determine that the physician certifications were not obtained in accordance with 42 C.F.R. § 424.22(a)(2) by looking at the underlying documentation and comparing the dates of the episode of care with the date on the physician certification. But merely because the government had an alternate way to assess the timeliness of the certifications does not negate the materiality of the defendants' alleged misrepresentation about their compliance with § 424.22(a)(2). *See* 31 U.S.C. § 3729(b)(4) (defining material as "having a natural tendency to influence, or be capable of influencing, the payment or receipt of money or property"); *United States ex rel. Miller v. Weston Educational, Inc.,* 840 F.3d 494, 505 (8th Cir. 2016) ("To the extent Heritage asserts that its statements, even if false, did not cause any actual harm, this is not an element of materiality.").

[8] The dissent suggests that concern about fraud is illusory in this context. Dissent Op. at 849-50. But in her complaint, Prather points to evidence that "untimely and/or forged physician certifications on plans of care" are a key focus for the Inspector General for the Department of Health and Human Services. R. 98 (Third. Am. Comp. ¶ 47) (citing OIG Compliance Program Guidance for Home Health Agencies, 63 Fed. Reg. 42,410, 42,414 (Aug. 7, 1998)); *see also infra.* Reasonable

people want to know if a party has complied with regulations addressing an area of historical concern. *Escobar,* 136 S.Ct. at 2002-03.

[9] The dissent claims that this manual's relevance is undercut by our decision in *Prather I.* Dissent Op. at 849-51. But the dissent is conflating this case with *Prather I* and the two ways Prather has utilized this evidence. In *Prather I,* Prather pointed to the manual to support her argument that certifications could never be timely if signed after the end of the episode of care. We rejected this argument as contrary to the plain language of the regulation. *Prather I,* 838 F.3d at 765 n.6. In the case currently before us, Prather points to this manual as evidence that the government has consistently emphasized the importance of the timing requirement, thus making it more likely that the requirement is material to the government's decision to pay these kinds of claims. This second inference is the one that is relevant to this case, and it supports the conclusion that Prather has pleaded sufficiently the materiality element.

[10] Contrary to the dissent's suggestion, Dissent Op. at 851-53, awareness that coercing physicians to sign certifications would be a separate unlawful act does not negate this scienter.

[11] The dissent constructs a strawman and complains that we are saying that Prather alleges that the defendants violated a requirement that did not exist at the time of the conduct at issue. Dissent Op. at 851-53. This misreads our opinion. As the defendants themselves note, Appellee Br. at 24, the timing requirement in 42 C.F.R. § 424.22(a)(2) is longstanding and was in effect during the alleged wrongdoing. Thus, when the defendants were put on notice that they may be violating regulations, including 42 C.F.R. § 424.22(a)(2), they had an obligation to investigate. It is this alleged failure to make a reasonable inquiry that supports Prather's allegations of scienter, *Wall,* 697 F.3d at 356, and not—as the dissent states—the defendants' ability to anticipate the development of the law in this area.

[1] This is an important concern raised by the United States as an *amicus* in this case. If the MAC reviewed the physician certifications alongside the bills, then it would be nearly impossible for Prather to show materiality. If the government was able to compare the date of the signature on the certification to the episode of care on the bill itself, then it had all the information it needed to deny the claim as not properly payable due to a late signature. *See Escobar,* 136 S.Ct. at 2003-04. If the government paid those hypothetical claims anyway, Prather would struggle to show materiality. *See id.* However, since the government had no reason to know about the potential defect in the signatures, I agree with the United States that Medicare's decision to pay in this context cannot be held against them (in a FCA prosecution) or against a relator (in a declined FCA case).

[2] These flags include (1) a high volume of services, (2) high cost of services, (3) a dramatic change in frequency, (4) high risk and problem-prone areas, and (5) data from OIG and other agencies indicating vulnerability. MEDICARE PROGRAM INTEGRITY MANUAL, Ch. 3, § 3.2.1.

[3] Prather identifies two other pieces of guidance that are only minimally persuasive. First, she points to a policy factsheet from another MAC, which states that no payment will be made if the certification is not obtained prior to the care being given. R. 98, Third Amended Compl., ¶ 50, PID 1472. Although this somewhat relevant, it has little bearing on what *Brookdale*'s MAC requires, which is the real

question here. Prather does not provide similar information from Palmetto GBA, which processes claims for Brookdale. *Id.,* ¶ 57, PID 1474. Second, Prather identifies a CMS outreach pamphlet, stating that a HHA "may not add late signatures to medical records (beyond the short delay that occurs during the transcription process)." *Id.,* ¶ 52, PID 1473. However, she neglects to mention that the same guidance, in the very next sentence, states: "If the practitioner's signature is missing from the medical record, submit an attestation statement from the author of the medical record." *Complying with Medicare Signature Requirements,* CENTERS FOR MEDICARE AND MEDICAID SERVS., at 2 (March 2016). Elsewhere in her complaint, Prather appears to acknowledge that this "attestation method" was exactly how Brookdale obtained the late signatures. *See* R. 98, Third Amended Compl., ¶ 86, PID 1481.

846 F.3d 879 (2017)

UNITED STATES of America ex rel. Andrew Hirt, Relator-Appellant,
v.
WALGREEN COMPANY, Defendant-Appellee.

No. 16-6232.

United States Court of Appeals, Sixth Circuit.

Decided and Filed: January 25, 2017.

US v. Walgreen Co., 846 F. 3d 879 (6th Cir. 2017)

p.880 Appeal from the United States District Court for the Middle District of Tennessee at Nashville. No. 3:13-cv-00870—William J. Haynes Jr., District Judge.

ON BRIEF: G. Kline Preston IV, KLINE PRESTON LAW GROUP, P.C., Nashville, Tennessee, for Appellant. Frederick Robinson, NORTON ROSE FULBRIGHT US LLP, Washington, D.C., for Appellee.

Before: SUHRHEINRICH, SUTTON, and MCKEAGUE, Circuit Judges.

OPINION

SUTTON, Circuit Judge.

Andrew Hirt, owner of Andy's Pharmacies, alleges that Walgreen Company distributed kickbacks to Medicare and Medicaid recipients when they transferred their prescriptions to Walgreens. By sending these fraudulent insurance claims to the government, Hirt maintains that Walgreens violated the False Claims Act, and he filed this *qui tam* claim as a result. The district court rejected Hirt's claim as a matter of law. Because Hirt failed to state his claim with particularity, as Civil Rule 9(b) requires, we affirm.

Hirt owns two pharmacies, one of which is located in Cookeville, Tennessee. His Cookeville pharmacy competes with a Walgreens in the area. Between November 19, 2012 and August 25, 2014, Hirt alleges that the Willow Walgreens offered $25 gift cards to lure his customers to Walgreens in violation of the Anti-Kickback Statute, 42 U.S.C. § 1320a-7b(b), and that Walgreens submitted the resulting prescription-drug claims by Medicare and Medicaid recipients to the government in violation of the False Claims Act, 31 U.S.C. § 3729.

Hirt filed this *qui tam* action under the whistleblower provision of the False Claims Act on behalf of himself and the United States. The government declined to intervene in the action, and Walgreens moved to dismiss it. The district court granted the motion, holding (among other things) that Hirt failed to state his claims with sufficient particularity under Civil Rule 9(b).

The False Claims Act imposes civil liability for "knowingly present[ing]... a false or fraudulent claim" to the government "for payment or approval." 31 U.S.C. § 3729(a)-(b). The statute provides for public enforcement and private (*qui tam*) lawsuits. *Id.* § 3730(b). At the same time that the statute encourages whistleblowers, it discourages "opportunistic" plaintiffs who "merely feed off a previous disclosure of fraud." *U.S. ex rel. Poteet v. Medtronic, Inc.,* 552 F.3d 503, 507 (6th Cir. 2009). For that reason, individual plaintiffs cannot bring *qui tam* complaints based upon information already in the public domain. *See* 31 U.S.C. § 3730(e)(4). But if they can show that they are an original source of the information — someone "who has knowledge that is independent of and materially adds" to the prior public disclosure — the public-disclosure bar does not apply. *Id.; see U.S. ex rel. Advocates for Basic Legal Equal., Inc. v. U.S. Bank, N.A.,* 816 F.3d 428, 430 (6th Cir. 2016).

In addition to satisfying the False Claims Act's requirements, *qui tam* plaintiffs must meet the heightened pleading standards of Civil Rule 9(b). *U.S. ex rel. Bledsoe v. Cmty. Health Sys., Inc.,* 501 F.3d 493, 503 (6th Cir. 2007). In all averments of "fraud or mistake," the plaintiff must state with "particularity the circumstances p.881 constituting fraud or mistake." Fed. R. Civ. P. 9(b). The identification of at least one false claim with specificity is "an indispensable element of a complaint that alleges a [False Claims Act] violation in compliance with Rule 9(b)." *Bledsoe,* 501 F.3d at 504. Adherence to this requirement not only respects Civil Rule 9(b), but it also helps in determining whether the public-disclosure bar applies.

Hirt has not met this standard. His complaint does not identify a single false claim. He describes the unlawful distribution of gift cards in general but not the submission of any claims obtained with those gift cards. All that Hirt says is that "his [Medicaid and Medicare] customers accepted the $25.00 gift cards to move their business to (Willow) Walgreens in Cookeville during the period November 19, 2012 through August 25, 2014," and that Walgreens "induce[d] ... false or fraudulent claims to the United States Government for the payment of pharmaceuticals." R. 29 at 5, 9. But he does not identify any false claim arising from any of those (allegedly) induced customers. He does not tell us the names of any such customers or their initials. He does not tell us the dates on which they filled prescriptions at Walgreens. He does not tell us the dates on which Walgreens filed the reimbursement claims with the government. He does not, indeed, even say that these unnamed customers filled any prescriptions at Walgreens at all, let alone that Walgreens processed them and filed reimbursement claims with the government. We are left to infer these essential elements from the fact that Hirt's customers moved their business from his pharmacies. But inferences and implications are not what Civil Rule 9(b) requires. It demands specifics — at least if the claimant wishes to raise allegations of fraud against someone.

Relying on an unpublished decision from the Eleventh Circuit, we raised the possibility in 2007 of "relaxing" the requirement that a plaintiff identify at least one false claim with particularity if that plaintiff, through no fault of his own, "cannot allege the specifics of actual false claims that in all likelihood exist." *Bledsoe,* 501 F.3d at 504 n.12. But we did not resolve the point, ultimately "express[ing] no opinion as to the contours or existence of any such exception." *Id.* In two later decisions, we repeated the "relax" language. *Chesbrough v. VPA, P.C.,* 655 F.3d 461, 471 (6th Cir. 2011); *U.S. ex rel. Prather v. Brookdale Senior Living Comtys., Inc.,* 838 F.3d 750, 769 (6th Cir. 2016). The Eleventh Circuit's use of the word "relax," and our repetition of it in later cases, runs the risk of misleading lawyers and their clients. We have no more authority to "relax" the pleading standard established by Civil Rule 9(b) than we do to increase it. Only by following the highly reticulated procedures laid out in the

Rules Enabling Act can anyone modify the Civil Rules, whether in the direction of relaxing them or tightening them. *See* 28 U.S.C. §§ 2071-2077. To the extent the words of Civil Rule 9(b) need elaboration, and it's not obvious that they do, the most that can be said is that "particular" allegations of fraud may demand different things in different contexts.

In practice, we have applied the "relax[ed]" standard just once, and that application has no purchasing power here. *See Prather,* 838 F.3d at 769. Prather's allegations satisfied the particularity requirement because she had sufficient personal knowledge of the defendant's claims submission and billing processes. Her job required her to review the company's Medicare claims documentation to ensure compliance with state and federal insurance guidelines. *Id.* at 770. This review took place, according to Prather, for the sole purpose of submitting the claims to p.882 Medicare. Compl. at 18, *id.* (No. 15-6377). After her review, Prather would deliver the claims documents to the billing department, whose job it was to submit the claims for payment. *Id.* at 19. In context, that set of pleading statements sufficed to establish with particularity that the defendant "submitted a claim for payment," — as it described when, where, and how the defendant submitted the claim. *See U.S. ex rel. Marlar v. BWXT Y-12, LLC,* 525 F.3d 439, 445 (6th Cir. 2008); *Chesbrough,* 655 F.3d at 470.

Hirt offers no equivalent basis for satisfying the particularity requirement here. The reason is straightforward. Unlike Prather, Hirt failed to provide the factual predicates necessary to convince us that "actual false claims" "in all likelihood exist." *Bledsoe,* 501 F.3d at 504 n.12. He does not allege personal knowledge of Walgreen's claim submission procedures. *Prather,* 838 F.3d at 770. And he does not otherwise allege facts "from which it is highly likely that a claim was submitted to the government." *Chesbrough,* 655 F.3d at 472. At the least, Hirt could have described a prescription filled by one of his previous customers at the Willow Walgreens. In the same way that Hirt discovered that his former customers had accepted the gift cards, he could have determined whether they used those gift cards when filling a prescription at Walgreens. And if that is somehow not the case, how could he know that Walgreens violated the False Claims Act — the first requirement for filing an action?

Hirt's general allegations that Walgreens offered gift cards and some Medicare and Medicaid recipients accepted them do not meet the particularity requirement. "To conclude that a claim was presented" in this setting "requires a series of assumptions," leaving only a "possibility" of fraudulent submissions rather than an establishment of them. *Id.* Hirt failed to describe even one unlawful prescription purchase — that customer X of his pharmacy filled prescription Y with Willow Walgreens on date Z after receiving a gift card from Walgreens. If Hirt lacked the information to do even this, he was not the right plaintiff to bring this *qui tam* claim — and almost certainly not the right one to do so in a way that would allow a court to decide whether the public-disclosure bar applies to the allegation. We have no basis for excluding a lack of personal knowledge when it comes to the essential — the primary — illegal conduct at issue. *Id.* The point of Civil Rule 9(b) is to prevent, not facilitate, casual allegations of fraud.

The privacy concerns reflected in the Health Insurance Portability and Accountability Act (HIPAA) do not permit us to overlook this problem. Hirt could have used customer initials, dates, or other non-identifying descriptions. Exposing a false claim with particularity does not require risking the personal privacy of the claimant.

For these reasons, we affirm.

874 F.3d 905 (2017)

UNITED STATES of America ex rel. Joseph Ibanez and Jennifer Edwards, Relators-Appellants,

v.

BRISTOL-MYERS SQUIBB COMPANY; Otsuka America Pharmaceutical, Inc., Defendants-Appellees.

No. 16-3154.

United States Court of Appeals, Sixth Circuit.

Argued: December 6, 2016.
Decided and Filed: October 27, 2017.
Rehearing En Banc Denied January 3, 2018.[*]

US v. Bristol-Myers Squibb Co., 874 F. 3d 905 (6th Cir. 2017)

Appeal from the United States District Court for the Southern District of Ohio at Cincinnati, No. 1:11-cv-00029—William O. Bertelsman, District Judge.

ARGUED: William C. Meyers, Goldberg Kohn LTD., Chicago, Illinois, for Relators. Jessica L. Ellsworth, Hogan Lovells US LLP, Washington, D.C., for Appellee Bristol-Myers Squibb. Jennifer L. Spaziano, Skadden, Arps, Slate, Meagher & Flom LLP, Washington, D.C., for Appellee Otsuka. ON BRIEF: William C. Meyers, David J. Chizewer, Emily D. Gilman, Goldberg Kohn LTD., Chicago, Illinois, Jennifer M. Verkamp, Frederick M. Morgan, Jr., Chandra Napora, Morgan Verkamp LLC, Cincinnati, Ohio, for Relators. Jessica L. Ellsworth, Mitchell J. Lazris, Eugene A. Sokoloff, Hogan Lovells US LLP, Washington, D.C., for Appellee Bristol-Myers Squibb. Jennifer L. Spaziano, Mitchell S. Ettinger, Caroline Van Zile, Skadden, Arps, Slate, Meagher & Flom LLP, Washington, D.C., Daniel E. Izenson, Thomas F. Hankinson, Keating Muething & Klekamp, PLL, Cincinnati, Ohio, for Appellee Otsuka.

Before: McKEAGUE, KETHLEDGE, and STRANCH, Circuit Judges.

McKEAGUE, J., delivered the opinion of the court in which KETHLEDGE, J., joined, and STRANCH, J., joined in part. STRANCH, J. (pp. 922-26), delivered a separate opinion concurring in part and dissenting in part.

p.911 **OPINION**

McKEAGUE, Circuit Judge.

Relators Joseph Ibanez and Jennifer Edwards, former employees of Bristol-Myers Squibb Co. (BMS), bring this *qui tam* action alleging that BMS, together with Otsuka America Pharmaceutical, Inc. (Otsuka), engaged in a complex, nationwide scheme to improperly promote the antipsychotic drug Abilify. Relators assert that this scheme caused claims for reimbursement for the drug to be submitted to the government, in violation of the False p.912 Claims Act (FCA), 31 U.S.C. § 3729 *et seq.*, and several state-law analogues. The district court dismissed the complaint in part and subsequently denied relators' motion to amend. Because neither the second amended complaint nor the proposed third amended complaint satisfies Rule 9(b)'s pleading requirements, we affirm the district court's orders.

I

A. Factual Background

Since 1999, BMS and Otsuka have sold and marketed the drug Abilify. Both relators Joseph Ibanez and Jennifer Edwards worked as BMS sales representatives marketing Abilify from 2005 to 2010.

Abilify is an antipsychotic drug approved for various prescriptive uses by the FDA. It has three approved adult uses. It was approved to treat schizophrenia in 2002; to treat symptoms related to Bipolar I Disorder in 2004; and as a supplemental treatment for major depressive disorder in 2007. Abilify also has three approved uses for pediatrics. It was approved to treat schizophrenia in 13 to 17 year-olds in 2007; to treat symptoms associated with Bipolar I Disorder in patients 10 to 17 years old in 2008; and to treat irritability associated with autistic disorder for patients 6 to 17 years old in 2009. There are no expressly disapproved treatments for elderly patients, but the FDA has included a warning since 2007 that Abilify is associated with increased mortality rate in elderly patients with dementia-related psychosis.

Relators' FCA complaint boils down to two separate theories. First, relators allege that defendant pharmaceutical companies engaged in a scheme to encourage providers to prescribe Abilify for unapproved ("off-label") uses and that some of those off-label prescriptions were paid for by government programs. Second, relators assert that defendants improperly induced providers to prescribe Abilify through remunerations and benefits in violation of the Anti-Kickback Statute. Relators assert that requests for government reimbursement for off-label prescriptions and prescriptions induced by kickbacks constitute false claims under the FCA.

These allegations come on the heels of a set of nearly identical allegations leveled against BMS and Otsuka some nine years earlier. In 2007, BMS entered into a five-year Corporate Integrity Agreement as part of a settlement of a *qui tam* action which also involved improper promotion of Abilify. In 2008, Otsuka entered into its own five-year Corporate Integrity Agreement as a result of yet another *qui tam* action alleging the same misconduct. The two agreements used similar language to require Otsuka and BMS to adopt procedures and programs designed to ensure compliance with the FCA, the Anti-Kickback Statute, and cease off-label promotion of Abilify. The relators allege that, despite those agreements, the two companies continued to promote Abilify off-label and offer kickbacks to physicians who prescribed it.

B. Procedural Background

Relators brought this action under the False Claims Act, 31 U.S.C. § 3729 *et seq.*, and twenty-eight state-law analogues after disclosure to the government, which declined to intervene. Specifically, the complaint alleges that defendants' illegal promotion of Abilify caused the government to pay off-label prescriptions in violation of 31 U.S.C. § 3729(a)(1)(A). The complaint further alleges that, as part of these fraudulent schemes, defendants violated the Anti-Kickback Statute, 42 U.S.C. § 1320-7b(b); caused the use or creation of false records material to false claims, 31 U.S.C. § 4729(a)(1)(B); failed to reimburse the p.913 United States for overpayments, *id.* § 3729(a)(1)(G); conspired to violate the FCA, *id.* § 3729(a)(1)(C); and that BMS retaliated against Ibanez and Edwards for internally reporting the company's alleged failure to comply with federal and state laws and the Corporate Integrity Agreements, *id.* § 3730(h).

In response to relators' second amended complaint, defendants filed motions to dismiss pursuant to Fed. R. Civ. P. 12(b)(6). The district court granted Otsuka's motion to dismiss, and granted in part and denied in part BMS's motion, dismissing all of the *qui tam* claims. As a result, the only claims that survived were the retaliation claims brought against BMS and Edwards' Arizona-employment claim analogue. The court declined to exercise supplemental jurisdiction over the remaining state law claims. Proceedings continued in the district court on the retaliation claims.

However, relators moved to file a third amended complaint under Fed. R. Civ. P. 15(a)(2), and attached the proposed complaint. The district court directed the parties to address changes made in the complaint that it saw as potentially implicating the FCA's public-disclosure bar. Following responsive filings, the court found the public-disclosure bar precluded many of the amendments and that the amended complaint otherwise failed to plead presentment with adequate particularity to survive a Rule 12(b)(6) motion. Accordingly, the court denied relators' motion to file a third amended complaint on the basis of futility. The court subsequently granted a Rule 54(b) motion staying litigation on the retaliation claims and granting final judgment certification on both the order resolving the partial motion to dismiss and the order denying the motion to amend. Relators now timely appeal those certified orders.

II

A. Jurisdiction

The district court had jurisdiction over claims arising under the False Claims Act claims pursuant to 28 U.S.C. § 3732(a). The district court certified its order partially granting defendants' Rule 12(b)(6) motion and its order denying relators' Rule 15(a)(2) motion under Fed. R. Civ. P. 54(b). "Although Rule 54(b) relaxes the traditional finality requirement for appellate review, it does not tolerate immediate appeal of every action taken by a district court." *Gen. Acquisition, Inc. v. GenCorp, Inc.,* 23 F.3d 1022, 1026 (6th Cir. 1994). Neither party challenges this court's jurisdiction to hear the certified orders on appeal. Nonetheless, we must still satisfy ourselves that the certification was proper. Otherwise, appellate jurisdiction is lacking. *Lowery v. Fed. Express Corp.,* 426 F.3d 817, 820 (6th Cir. 2005).

The district court's determination that certification was proper has two components. First, entry of final judgment as to one or more but fewer than all of the claims or parties; and second, that there is no just reason for delay. The first component is reviewed de novo and the second for abuse of discretion. *Id.* at 821.

The district court's orders collectively ended the litigation of relators' *qui tam* claims against Otsuka and BMS, leaving only relators' personal, employment-based retaliation claims against BMS. *See* R. 73, Dist. Ct. Op. I, PID 1228; R. 97, Dist. Ct. Op. II, PID 2168. There was no error in deeming these orders final. That is, no matter how the record might develop in further proceedings on the unresolved retaliation claims against BMS, there are no grounds on which the dismissed claims would be subject to reopening. Second, the district court did not abuse its discretion in finding there was "no reason to delay" p.914 appeal of the orders. As noted by the district court in its certification order, "the *qui tam* and employment-based retaliation claims are sufficiently distinct, such that permitting immediate appeal will not cause piecemeal appeals" and so allowing this appeal to go forward would "create judicial and economic efficiencies." *See* R. 102, Order, PID 2195-96. Thus, the court weighed relevant considerations and did not abuse its discretion in determining that there was no reason for delay. *See Lowery*, 426 F.3d at 821-22. We now consider the orders certified for appeal.

B. Standard of Review

"This Court reviews *de novo* a district court's dismissal of a complaint for failure to state a claim, including dismissal for failure to plead with particularity under [Rule] 9(b)." *United States ex rel. Eberhard v. Physicians Choice Lab. Servs., LLC*, 642 Fed.Appx. 547, 550 (6th Cir. 2016) (quoting *United States ex rel. Bledsoe v. Cmty. Health Sys., Inc.* ("*Bledsoe II*"), 501 F.3d 493, 502 (6th Cir. 2007)). "Complaints alleging FCA violations must comply with Rule 9(b)'s requirement that fraud be pled with particularity because 'defendants accused of defrauding the federal government have the same protections as defendants sued for fraud in other contexts.'" *Chesbrough v. VPA, P.C.*, 655 F.3d 461, 466 (6th Cir. 2011) (quoting *Yuhasz v. Brush Wellman, Inc.*, 341 F.3d 559, 563 (6th Cir. 2003)). Thus, "[w]here a relator pleads a complex and far-reaching fraudulent scheme," she also must provide "examples of specific false claims submitted to the government pursuant to that scheme" in order to proceed to discovery on the scheme. *United States ex rel. Prather v. Brookdale Senior Living Cmtys., Inc.*, 838 F.3d 750, 768 (6th Cir. 2016) (quoting *Bledsoe II*, 501 F.3d at 510). "In the *qui tam* context, 'the Court must construe the complaint in the light most favorable to the plaintiff, accept all factual allegations as true, and determine whether the complaint contains enough facts to state a claim to relief that is plausible on its face.'" *United States ex rel. SNAPP, Inc. v. Ford Motor Co.*, 532 F.3d 496, 502 (6th Cir. 2008) (quoting *Bledsoe II*, 501 F.3d at 502).

C. Second Amended Complaint

1. Section 3729(a)(1)(A) Claims

Section 3729(a)(1)(A) of the FCA prohibits "knowingly present[ing], or caus[ing] to be presented, a false or fraudulent claim for payment or approval." 31 U.S.C. § 3729(a)(1)(A). A claim under § 3729(a)(1)(A) "requires proof that the alleged false or fraudulent claim was 'presented' to the government." *United States ex rel. Marlar v. BWXT Y-12, LLC*, 525 F.3d 439, 445 (6th Cir. 2008). At the pleading stage, this requirement is stringent: "where a relator alleges a 'complex and far-reaching fraudulent scheme,' in violation of § 3729(a)(1), it is insufficient to simply plead the scheme; [s]he must also identify a representative false claim that was actually submitted to the government." *Chesbrough*, 655 F.3d at 470 (quoting *Bledose II*, 501 F.3d at 510). Alternatively, a claim may survive a Rule 12(b)(6) motion if it includes allegations showing "specific personal knowledge" supporting a "strong inference that a [false] claim was submitted." *Prather*, 838 F.3d at 769.

Relators allege defendants participated in a complex, nationwide scheme to improperly promote Abilify which caused false claims to be submitted to the government. These allegations include a long chain of causal links from defendants' conduct to the eventual submission of claims. Rule 9(b) requires relators to adequately allege the entire chain — from start to finish — to fairly show defendants caused false claims to be filed.

p.915 To cover the ground from one end of this scheme — defendants' improper promotion — to the other — claims for reimbursement — the complaint must allege specific intervening conduct. First, a physician to whom BMS and Otsuka improperly promoted Abilify must have prescribed the medication for an off-label use or because of an improper inducement. Next, that patient must fill the prescription. Finally, the filling pharmacy must submit a claim to the government for reimbursement on the prescription. While this chain reveals just what an awkward vehicle the FCA is for punishing off-label promotion schemes,[1] a single adequately pled claim of this nature would allow relators to satisfy Rule 9(b)'s pleading requirement and proceed to discovery on the entire scheme.

In order to survive defendants' motion, relators must provide a representative claim that describes each step with particularity: a prescription reimbursement submitted to the government for a tainted prescription of Abilify. *See Prather*, 838 F.3d at 768. Relators do not adequately identify a representative false claim. Relators allege knowledge of a complex scheme related to the promotion of Abilify, but they do not provide any representative claim that was actually submitted to the government for payment. Lacking a specific claim, relators encourage the court to apply a "relaxed" Rule 9(b) pleading standard that, despite having been suggested by prior opinions, had not been applied by this court until very recently. *See id.* The *Prather* standard is an exception to our usual rule, and applies only if "a relator alleges specific personal knowledge that relates directly to billing practices," supporting a "strong inference that a [false] claim was submitted." *Id.* (citing *Chesbrough*, 655 F.3d at 471).

Prather's personal knowledge exception applies in limited circumstances. *See United States ex rel. Hirt v. Walgreen Co.*, 846 F.3d 879, 881 (6th Cir. 2017). In *Chesbrough*, an independent radiology consultant — alleging the radiology billings he reviewed were fraudulent — had insufficient personal knowledge to support the necessary inference that false claims were submitted because he had no involvement with billing procedures. *Chesbrough*, 655 F.3d at 471. Likewise, in *Eberhard*, relators failed to adequately plead knowledge because they could not show they had "personal knowledge of billing practices or contracts with the government." *Eberhard*, 642 Fed.Appx. at 552 (6th Cir. 2016) (citing *Chesbrough*, 655 F.3d at 471-72). In fact, the only time this court has ever applied a personal knowledge exception to FCA pleading requirements was in *Prather* itself. *See Prather*, 838 F.3d at 770. There, the exception applied under circumstances where the relator was specifically employed to review medical treatment documentation allegedly submitted to Medicare — i.e., she reviewed allegedly false claims themselves. *Id.* at 768. It was only this "detailed knowledge of the billing and treatment documentation related to the p.916 submission of requests for final payment, combined with her specific allegations regarding requests for anticipated payments" that satisfied a relaxed 9(b) standard. *Id.* at 770.

Here, relators do not allege this type of personal knowledge. Relators were sales representatives of BMS and, unlike the relator in *Prather,* did not directly engage with claims whatsoever. In order for the *Prather* exception to apply, it is not enough to allege personal knowledge of an allegedly fraudulent scheme; a relator must allege adequate personal knowledge of billing practices themselves. *Id.* at 768. Relators fail to do so. Thus, absent a representative false claim derived from the alleged promotional scheme, the second amended complaint fails to adequately plead a violation of 31 U.S.C. § 3729(a)(1)(A).

Accordingly, relators have failed to adequately allege a violation of 31 U.S.C. § 3729(a)(1)(A) in their second amended complaint.

2. Section 3729(a)(1)(B), (C) and (G) Claims

In addition to their claims under 31 U.S.C. § 3729(a)(1)(A), relators allege violations of three other sections of the FCA. Section 3729(a)(1)(B) imposes liability on one who "knowingly makes, uses, or causes to be made or used, a false record or statement material to a false or fraudulent claim." Section 3729(a)(1)(G) imposes liability on one who accepts overpayment from the government and fails to refund that overpayment — a so-called "reverse false claim." Section 3729(a)(1)(C) imposes liability on anyone who "conspires to commit a violation" of the FCA's other prohibitions. The district court dismissed relators' claims relating to all three.

Section 3719(a)(1)(B) requires a relator to "plead a connection between the alleged fraud and an actual claim made to the government." *Chesbrough,* 655 F.3d at 473. The alleged connection must be evident. *See Allison Engine Co. v. U.S. ex rel. Sanders,* 553 U.S. 662, 671-72, 128 S.Ct. 2123, 170 L.Ed.2d 1030 (2008). Otherwise, "a cause of action under the FCA for fraud directed at private entities would threaten to transform the FCA into an all-purpose antifraud statute." *Id.* at 672, 128 S.Ct. 2123. Thus, although relators allege defendants made false or fraudulent statements in order to increase the number of Abilify prescriptions, there are no allegations connecting these statements to any claim made to the government. Such statements, even if false, rely on a "link between the false statement and the Government's decision to pay or approve a false claim [that] is too attenuated to establish liability." *Id.* Thus, relators fail to adequately plead a 31 U.S.C. § 3729(a)(1)(B) claim because they rely on a too-attenuated chain connecting alleged false statements to the submission of claims. *See Chesbrough,* 655 F.3d at 473.

Section 3719(a)(1)(G) requires a relator to allege facts that show defendants received overpayments from the government and failed to refund those payments. *See* 31 U.S.C. § 3729(a)(1)(G); *Prather,* 838 F.3d at 774. Alternatively, a section 3729(a)(1)(G) violation is made out if the relator pleads adequate "'proof that the defendant made a false record or statement at a time that the defendant owed to the government an obligation' — a duty to pay money or property." *Chesbrough,* 655 F.3d at 473 (quoting *Am. Textile Mfrs. Inst., Inc. v. The Ltd., Inc.,* 190 F.3d 729, 736 (6th Cir.

1999)); 31 U.S.C. § 3729(a)(3). The district court held relators failed to adequately plead a reverse false claim.

p.917 We agree. Relators do not plead facts that show defendants received overpayment, much less that they retained it. Moreover, relators provide no facts showing defendants were under an affirmative obligation to the government at the time the alleged false statements were made. 31 U.S.C. § 3729(a)(3); *see Am. Textile Mfrs. Inst.,* 190 F.3d at 741. Thus, these allegations amount to nothing more than an impermissible "formulaic recitation of the elements of a cause of action" and were properly dismissed. *Bell Atlantic Corp., et al. v. Twombly,* 550 U.S. 544, 555, 127 S.Ct. 1955, 167 L.Ed.2d 929 (2007).

Section 3719(a)(1)(C), prohibiting FCA conspiracies, requires a relator to plead facts showing that there was a plan or agreement "to commit a violation of" one or more of the FCA subsections. *See* 31 U.S.C. § 3729(a)(1)(C). The district court determined relators failed to adequately plead an FCA conspiracy. In the court's words,

> [e]ven accepting all factual allegations as true and drawing all reasonable inferences in their favor, Relators have alleged, at most, a single plan to get doctors to prescribe [Abilify] for off-label uses.... [T]he Court must make several assumptions in Relators' favor in order to construe the alleged fraudulent schemes as one *designed to* induce the government to pay false claims.

R. 73, Dist. Ct. Op. I, PID 1218 (emphasis added).

We agree. There are insufficient allegations to show there was a plan to get false claims paid. The alleged plan was to increase Abilify prescriptions through improper promotion. While this may be condemnable, it does not amount to a conspiracy to violate the FCA. Even if it was foreseeable that somewhere down the line off-label prescriptions of Abilify would be submitted to the government for payment, that foreseeable consequence does not subsume the aim of the agreement. In other words, to adequately allege an FCA conspiracy, it is not enough for relators to show there was an agreement that made it *likely* there would be a violation of the FCA; they must show an agreement was made *in order to* violate the FCA. *See United States ex rel. Ladas v. Exelis, Inc.,* 824 F.3d 16, 27 (2d Cir. 2016) (affirming the holding that a "claim of conspiracy to violate the FCA was deficient because the [complaint] 'fails to identify a specific statement where [defendants] agreed to defraud the government'").

The chain that connects defendants' alleged misconduct to the eventual submission of false claims to the government is an unusually attenuated one and relators provide no specific statement showing the plan was made in order to defraud the government. *Id.* at 27. The absence of such a conspiratorial statement, in conjunction with relators' failure to adequately plead a violation of any other section of the FCA, renders insufficient the otherwise bare allegation that there was an FCA conspiracy. *Twombly,* 550 U.S. at 556, 127 S.Ct. 1955. Accordingly, we uphold the dismissal of the conspiracy claim.

We therefore affirm the district court's order dismissing in part relators' second amended complaint.

D. Third Amended Complaint

Relators also appeal the district court's denial of their motion to file a third amended complaint. Although a court should freely give leave to amend a complaint when justice so requires, it does not need to give leave if doing so would be futile, such as when the amended complaint cannot survive a motion to dismiss. *SFS Check, LLC v. First Bank of Del.,* 774 F.3d 351, 355 (6th Cir. 2014). After partially p.918 dismissing the second amended complaint, the district court granted relators leave to file a Rule 15 motion to amend and provided a deadline by which to do so.[2] Relators timely filed the motion, attaching the third amended complaint. The district court denied relators' motion for futility because it could not survive a Rule 12(b)(6) motion to dismiss. A district court's order denying a Rule 15(a) motion to amend is typically reviewed for abuse of discretion. *Rose v. Hartford Underwriters Ins. Co.,* 203 F.3d 417, 420 (6th Cir. 2000). However, where the district court denies leave to amend because the complaint, as amended, would not withstand a motion to dismiss, that denial is reviewed de novo. *Seaton v. TripAdvisor LLC,* 728 F.3d 592, 596 (6th Cir. 2013). Thus, we review the district court's order de novo.

1. Public-Disclosure Bar

Generally, unless the relator was an "original source" within the meaning of the statute, the FCA bars a claim based on publicly disclosed information. *U.S. ex rel. Antoon v. Cleveland Clinic Found.,* 788 F.3d 605, 614 (6th Cir. 2015); 31 U.S.C. § 3730(e)(4)(A)-(B) (2012). The district court determined that several of the new facts and allegations included in the third amended complaint ran afoul of the public-disclosure bar, undermining the viability of the claims. Relators challenge that conclusion on appeal.

On March 23, 2010, the public-disclosure bar was amended by the Patient Protection and Affordable Care Act. Pub. L. 111-148, 124 Stat. 119 (2010). What constitutes "public disclosure" and an "original source" changed with the FCA amendment, but a common principle remains; public disclosure occurs "when enough information exists in the public domain to expose the fraudulent transaction." *See Antoon,* 788 F.3d at 614-15. Because relators' complaint alleges fraud spanning from 2005 to 2015, the amended complaint is subject to both versions of the public-disclosure bar. *See id.* at 614-15 (holding that the FCA public disclosure bar in effect at the time of the alleged fraud, not the time of filing, applies). But, as conceded by both parties, any difference in statutory language is irrelevant if the outcome would be the same under either version. *See U.S. ex rel. Lockey v. City of Dallas,* 576 Fed.Appx. 431, 437-38 (5th Cir. 2014) ("While the language in the current version of the [FCA] differs from [that] in the prior version of the statute... on the facts of this case, the outcome is the same."). Here, the outcome is the same under both versions of the statute.

To decide whether a claim has been publicly disclosed, courts look at the essential elements of alleged fraud to determine if enough information exists in the public domain to expose the fraudulent transaction. *See Dingle v. Bioport Corp.,* 388 F.3d 209, 212 (6th Cir. 2004); *Antoon,* 788 F.3d at 614-15. Thus, the public disclosure bar is not implicated — even if one or more of a claim's essential elements are in p.919 the public domain — unless the exposed elements, taken together, provide adequate notice that there has been a fraudulent transaction. *See Dingle,* 388 F.3d at 212; *U.S. ex rel. Poteet v. Medtronic, Inc.,* 552 F.3d 503, 512-13 (6th Cir. 2009) (holding public disclosure barred a federal claim that alleged substantially the same conduct as a previously filed state civil action).

Exposing a fraudulent transaction under an off-label promotion scheme requires a relator to string together several necessary elements. Here, relators must connect defendants' promotion of Abilify to the eventual submission of a related claim to the government. But it is this first link in the chain — the improper promotion of the drug — that is crucial. This is because, even if the scheme's other elements were publicly disclosed — e.g., it was publicly disclosed that the government had paid claims for off-label prescriptions of Abilify — the FCA is implicated only if that conduct is somehow tied back to improper promotion.[3] Thus, no fraud was publicly disclosed without disclosure of this key element.

Here, defendants assert that the government's previous FCA actions and resultant Corporate Integrity Agreements constitute disclosure of defendants' improper promotion of Abilify. The district court agreed, finding that relators' alleged scheme "closely track[s]" the pre-agreement promotion scheme. R. 97, Dist. Ct. Order, PID 2160. However, it was error for the court to hold that this resemblance alone called for dismissal under the public disclosure bar.

If a fraudulent off-label promotion scheme was publicly disclosed and then resolved, allegations of improper promotion that took place before the agreements putatively ended the scheme would necessarily implicate the public disclosure bar. But allegations that the scheme either continued despite the agreements or was restarted after the agreements are different. It cannot be assumed that the government is aware a fraudulent scheme continues (or was restarted) simply because it had uncovered, and then resolved, a similar scheme before.[4] Indeed, the most logical inference to draw from defendants' agreements to cease improper promotion of Abilify is that they had done so. Thus, to the extent that relators are able to describe with particularity post-agreement, improper promotion of Abilify, the mere resemblance of those allegations to a scheme resolved years earlier is not by itself enough to trigger the public disclosure bar.[5]

Here, other than the fact that the alleged scheme resembled that described in the prior enforcement action, defendants p.920 do not otherwise show the alleged improper promotion was publicly disclosed. Thus, there was not enough information in the public domain to expose the alleged fraudulent transactions, meaning the public disclosure bar does not implicate fraud connected to post-agreement improper promotion of Abilify.

2. Representative False Claims Under Section 3729(a)(1)(A)

As previously discussed, outside the narrow circumstances described in *Prather,* Rule 9(b) requires relators to provide facts identifying a representative claim that was presented to the government, i.e., "[t]he actual *submission* of a *specific* request for anticipated payment to the government." *Prather,* 838 F.3d at 768-69. Because relators do not allege personal knowledge supporting the strong inference that claims were submitted such that the *Prather* exception could apply, they must provide the court with a specific representative claim submitted to the government pursuant to the alleged scheme. *See id.* at 768.

In this context, a representative claim consists of a request for a prescription reimbursement submitted to the government for either an off-label prescription of Abilify or one induced and written by a specific provider to whom either or both defendants improperly promoted the drug. To that end, relators must identify a representative claim with *specificity* as to each necessary component of the alleged scheme; identifying a claim that merely infers one or more of these elements is inadequate. *See Yuhasz,* 341 F.3d at 564 ("[A] plaintiff should not be able to avoid the specificity requirements of Rule 9(b) by relying upon the complexity of the edifice which he created") (internal quotation marks); *SNAPP, Inc.,* 532 F.3d at 506 ("Rule 9(b) 'does not permit an [FCA] plaintiff merely to describe a private scheme in detail but then to allege simply... that claims requesting illegal payments must have been submitted, were likely submitted or should have been submitted to the Government.'") (quoting *Sanderson v. HCA-The Healthcare Co.,* 447 F.3d 873, 877 (6th Cir. 2006)). The third amended complaint identifies many inference-based claims. All are inadequate under our FCA pleading standard.

Relators' failure to identify a representative claim with adequate specificity warrants a few examples. For one, relators attach an exhibit identifying reimbursement for prescriptions of Abilify paid to various pharmacies by Massachusetts Medicaid for prescriptions of Abilify filled for pediatric patients before the drug had any pediatric indication. However, nothing connects any of the prescribing physicians, not identified by name or care facility, to defendants' improper promotion. Similarly, relators attach an exhibit identifying Abilify prescriptions paid by California Medi-Cal as prescribed by two physicians with whom the defendants allegedly had a relationship. All the same, the patient diagnoses by these doctors are not identified; meaning it is not a necessary inference that any one of the Abilify prescriptions they wrote was for an off-label use. Moreover, there is nothing about the alleged relationship between these physicians and the defendants that can be characterized as a violation of the Anti-Kickback Statute or that any particular Abilify prescription they wrote was improperly induced. The same failures undercut Abilify prescriptions paid by Kentucky Medicaid.

Relators also attempt to identify a representative claim by describing a patient identified as "D.M." and two Abilify prescriptions written for him. First, relators attach a receipt for an Abilify prescription written to treat D.M. and filled by a Kroger Pharmacy in 2015. Second, p.921 relators attach a 2013 diagnostic assessment of D.M., reporting that he was taking Abilify as prescribed by another doctor in July of that year. Both prescriptions were for off-label uses, but neither is an adequately pled representative claim.

First, the complaint fails to adequately allege that the 2013 prescription was presented to the government for payment. The complaint does not identify a pharmacy or any other entity that may have submitted a claim for reimbursement to a government program for the 2013 prescription. However, relators allege that, because D.M. had been a Medicaid beneficiary "for nearly all of his life," the prescription was reimbursed by Ohio Medicaid. R. 82-1, Third Amd. Complt., ¶ 341. But absent any factual support for this allegation and lacking any identifying information on who may have submitted a claim to the government for the 2013 prescription, we are not to simply assume a claim was presented to the government because relators say so. *See Ashcroft v. Iqbal,* 556 U.S. 662, 678-79, 129 S.Ct. 1937, 173 L.Ed.2d 868 (2009); *Prather,* 838 F.3d at 768. In this regard, the 2013 prescription lacks the specificity of the 2015 prescription — which at least identifies the relevant pharmacy and notes that D.M. paid nothing to fill that prescription — though even that additional detail neither confirms nor denies that Ohio Medicaid (or any other government program) was presented with a prescription for reimbursement. In sum, absent any support for the allegation that the 2013 prescription was submitted to a government program or any more specificity as to that claim, it is not representative of the alleged scheme.

Second, the 2015 prescription fails at an earlier link in the scheme's chain because it is not adequately connected to defendants' improper promotion. Relators allege that the prescription was written by a physician who was working as a provider at a facility to which defendants allegedly promoted Abilify from 2005 to 2007. Thus, the complaint relies on inference to bridge a gap of approximately eight years between the alleged promotion in 2007 and D.M.'s 2015 prescription. This hardly satisfies the *Twombly* standard. *See Twombly,* 550 U.S. at 556, 127 S.Ct. 1955. In short, the D.M. prescriptions are not adequately pled representative claims.

There are many other claims identified in the complaint which are similarly inadequate to provide the single, specific claim for reimbursement required to survive a motion to dismiss. We will not belabor the point by individually discussing the inadequacies of each claim (there are many), but suffice it to say that relators have not identified a single request for prescription reimbursement submitted to the government for a prescription of Abilify written by a provider to whom either or both defendants improperly promoted the drug. Relators have therefore failed to adequately plead a violation of 31 U.S.C. § 3729(a)(1)(A). Accordingly, the district court correctly held that those claims would not survive a motion to dismiss.

3. Claims Under Section 3729(a)(1)(B), (C), and (G)

Relators' three related claims, under 31 U.S.C. § 3729(a)(1)(B), (C), and (G), would likewise not survive a motion to dismiss.

Relators nowhere cure the inadequacy of their pleadings as to the section 3729(a)(1)(C) conspiracy claim. As in the second amendment complaint, there is no alleged plan to get a false claim paid and the allegations remain no more than threadbare recitations of the elements of the cause of action. *See Twombly,* 550 U.S. at 555, 127 S.Ct. 1955. Accordingly, as amended, that claim would not survive a Rule 12(b)(6) motion to dismiss.

p.922 Relators do beef up allegations relating to their section 3729(a)(1)(B) claim, but the claim continues to fall short. Despite amending the complaint to include a plethora of data showing Abilify claims submitted to government reimbursement programs, those claims, as before, are not adequately tied to any allegedly false statements made by defendants. Thus, the connection between false statements and claims submitted to the government remains "too attenuated to establish liability." *See Allison Engine Co.,* 553 U.S. at 671-72, 128 S.Ct. 2123.

The amended reverse false claims allegations rely on the Corporate Integrity Agreements, attached to the third amended complaint. Relators assert these documents created an obligation to pay the government under the FCA. However, section 3729(a)(1)(G)'s "obligation" does not include "those contingent obligations that arise only because the government has prohibited an act, or arising after the exercise of government discretion." *Am. Textile Mfrs. Inst.,* 190 F.3d at 741. The district court found the Corporate Integrity Agreements to be "contingent obligations" and failed to trigger a reverse false claim.

We agree. Both defendants were subject to nearly identical Corporate Integrity Agreements, the breach of which "may" have led to obligations to pay stipulated penalties. R. 82-2, BMS CIA, PID 1758; R. 82-3, Otsuka CIA, PID 1825. Yet even an alleged breach of these agreements did not, by itself, constitute an obligation to pay the government. This is because the penalties for a breach of the agreements were subject to discretionary enforcement by the Office of the Inspector General, who was to determine whether the penalties were "appropriate" before triggering an administrative review process to collect those penalties. R. 82-2, BMS CIA, PID 1760-61; R. 82-3, Otsuka CIA, PID 1827. This is the type of non-obligation that fails to satisfy 31 U.S.C. § 3729(a)(1)(G). *See Am. Textile Mfrs. Inst.,* 190 F.3d at 738 ("[e]xamples of contingent obligations include those arising from civil and criminal penalties that impose monetary fines after a finding of wrongdoing ... [and] attach only after the exercise of administrative or prosecutorial discretion"). Accordingly, relators fail to adequately plead a reverse false claim in their third amended complaint.

In sum, even considering the newly pled facts, amending the complaint would be futile as it would not survive a motion to dismiss. Accordingly, we affirm the district court's denial of relators' motion to amend.

III.

Because relators have failed to plead a violation of the FCA with adequate particularity, we AFFIRM the orders certified for appeal by the district court and REMAND for further proceedings consistent with this opinion.

JANE B. STRANCH, Circuit Judge, concurring in part and dissenting in part.

CONCURRING IN PART AND DISSENTING IN PART

The American health care system, the context for this case, is not only a life and death industry, but also the source of one in every eight jobs in the United States and one dollar of every six in our gross domestic product. *See* Employment by Major Industry Sector, Bureau of Labor Statistics (Dec. 8, 2015), https://www.bls.gov/emp/ep_table_201.htm; National Health Expenditure Projections 2016-2025, Ctrs. for Medicare & Medicaid Servs. at 1, https://www.cms.gov/Research-Statistics-Data-and-Systems/Statistics-Trends-and-Reports/NationalHealthExpendData/Downloads/proj2016.pdf p.923 (last visited Oct. 20, 2017). The scale of health care fraud is comparably huge. As I have previously discussed, rampant health care fraud in the United States likely costs

Medicare and Medicaid between \$30 and \$98 billion each year. *United States ex rel. Doghramji v. Cmty. Health Sys., Inc.,* 666 Fed.Appx. 410, 419 (6th Cir. 2016) (Stranch, J., concurring). That cost is transferred to us all in the forms of higher health care bills, premiums, co-pays, and taxes. The False Claims Act (FCA), the legal vehicle that relators use to bring claims identifying and combatting that fraud, operates on the same massive scale, having allowed the United States to recover over \$31 billion between 2009 and 2016. *See* Justice Department Recovers Over \$4.7 Billion From False Claims Act Cases in Fiscal Year 2016, U.S. Dep't of Justice (Dec. 14, 2016), https://www.justice.gov/opa/pr/justice-department-recovers-over-47-billion-false-claims-act-cases-fiscal-year-2016.

Qui tam relators are critical to the FCA's operation. Their suits are responsible for over sixty-three percent of FCA recoveries between 1986 and 2008. *Doghramji,* 666 Fed.Appx. at 419 (Stranch, J., concurring). When drafting the FCA, "Congress wrote expansively, meaning 'to reach all types of fraud, without qualification, that might result in financial loss to the Government.'" *Cook County v. United States ex rel. Chandler,* 538 U.S. 119, 129, 123 S.Ct. 1239, 155 L.Ed.2d 247 (2003) (quoting *United States v. Neifert-White Co.,* 390 U.S. 228, 232, 88 S.Ct. 959, 19 L.Ed.2d 1061 (1968)). Congress has not backed down from this expansive position. To the contrary, Congress amended the Act in 1986 "to strengthen the Government's hand in fighting false claims, and to encourage more private enforcement suits," *Graham Cty. Soil & Water Conservation Dist. v. United States ex rel. Wilson,* 559 U.S. 280, 298, 130 S.Ct. 1396, 176 L.Ed.2d 225 (2010) (citations and internal quotation marks omitted), and then expanded its scope again in 2009, *Boegh v. EnergySolutions, Inc.,* 772 F.3d 1056, 1062 (6th Cir. 2014). In the 2009 amendments, Congress recognized the important role of *qui tam* relators, explained that the "effectiveness of the False Claims Act ha[d] recently been undermined by court decisions which limit the scope of the law," and expanded FCA protections for relators. S. Rep. No. 111-10, at 4 (2009). This case arises in the context of that Congressional concern and is reviewed under the post-2009 provisions of the FCA.

I respectfully dissent from the majority opinion except for its public-disclosure bar analysis in Part II(D)(1). I concur in the holding that the public-disclosure bar does not apply to fraudulent schemes that continue or are restarted following a defendant's entry into an agreement with the government. Maj. Op. at 917-20. A contrary rule would allow a company to use publicly disclosed agreements to avoid liability for future bad acts that mirror previous misdeeds. The rule announced today, on the other hand, ensures that the public-disclosure bar does not prohibit a challenge to improper post-agreement behavior. I turn to the reasons for my dissent.

The relators allege that the defendants violated the FCA by once again submitting hundreds of millions of dollars of claims for prescriptions of an illegally promoted drug. The complaint alleges facts based on the relators' personal knowledge, collaboration with others, and extensive research. At this stage in the proceedings, "the Court must construe the complaint in the light most favorable to the plaintiff, accept all factual allegations as true, and determine whether the complaint contains enough facts to state a claim to relief that is plausible on its face." *United States ex* p.924 *rel. Prather v. Brookdale Senior Living Cmtys., Inc.,* 838 F.3d 750, 761 (6th Cir. 2016) (quoting *United States ex rel. SNAPP, Inc. v. Ford Motor Co.,* 532 F.3d 496, 502 (6th Cir. 2008)).

When sounding in fraud, claims brought under the FCA must satisfy Rule 9(b)'s requirement that the relevant fraudulent circumstances be stated "with particularity." Fed. R. Civ. P. 9(b); *see also United States ex rel. Bledsoe v. Cmty. Health Sys., Inc.*, 501 F.3d 493, 504 (6th Cir. 2007). Particularized pleading in this context typically requires a showing of a false claim that was actually submitted to the government. *Bledsoe,* 501 F.3d at 505 ("A relator cannot meet this [pleading] standard without alleging which specific false claims constitute a violation of the FCA."). But, as our sister circuits have concluded, particularity is not necessarily synonymous with representative samples. Particularity may also be satisfied where a relator "alleg[es] particular details of a scheme to submit false claims paired with reliable indicia that lead to a strong inference that claims were actually submitted." *United States ex rel. Grubbs v. Kanneganti,* 565 F.3d 180, 190 (5th Cir. 2009); *see also United States ex rel. Chorches v. Am. Med. Response, Inc.,* 865 F.3d 71, 86 (2d Cir. 2017); *United States ex rel. Heath v. AT&T, Inc.,* 791 F.3d 112, 126 (D.C. Cir. 2015); *United States ex rel. Thayer v. Planned Parenthood of the Heartland,* 765 F.3d 914, 917-18 (8th Cir. 2014); *Foglia v. Renal Ventures Mgmt., LLC,* 754 F.3d 153, 156-57 (3d Cir. 2014); *Ebeid v. Lungwitz,* 616 F.3d 993, 998-99 (9th Cir. 2010); *United States ex rel. Lemmon v. Envirocare of Utah, Inc.,* 614 F.3d 1163, 1172 (10th Cir. 2010); *United States ex rel. Duxbury v. Ortho Biotech Prods., L.P.,* 579 F.3d 13, 30 (1st Cir. 2009); *United States ex rel. Lusby v. Rolls-Royce Corp.,* 570 F.3d 849, 854 (7th Cir. 2009).

When applying a strict pleading standard in cases prior to *Prather,* we left open the possibility that a relator can survive a motion to dismiss when the relator "has pled facts which support a strong inference that a claim was submitted." *Prather,* 838 F.3d at 769 (quoting *Chesbrough v. VPA, P.C.,* 655 F.3d 461, 471 (6th Cir. 2011)); *see also United States ex rel. Sheldon v. Kettering Health Network,* 816 F.3d 399, 414 (6th Cir. 2016). In *Prather,* we noted that every circuit that has applied a heightened pleading standard "has retreated from such a requirement in cases in which other detailed factual allegations support a strong inference that claims were submitted." *Prather,* 838 F.3d at 772 (citing *Thayer,* 765 F.3d at 917-18; *Lemmon,* 614 F.3d at 1172; *United States ex rel. Walker v. R&F Props. of Lake Cty., Inc.,* 433 F.3d 1349, 1360 (11th Cir. 2005)). We then "confirm[ed] our adoption of that exception," holding that a plaintiff can "survive a motion to dismiss by pleading specific facts based on her personal billing-related knowledge that support a strong inference that specific false claims were submitted for payment." 838 F.3d at 773.

As was the case in *Prather,* we are confronted in this case with "detailed factual allegations [that] support a strong inference that claims were submitted." *Id.* at 772. In light of our governing precedent, I think that the majority erred by failing to read the third amended complaint in the light most favorable to the plaintiff and to accept all factual allegations as true. That complaint points to off-label prescriptions that were written by physicians targeted in the alleged scheme and paid for by state Medicaid programs — and so, ultimately, submitted to the United States government. For example, "Dr. 3" was targeted by defendants in their marketing scheme to increase off-label sales of Abilify starting in May 2007. Dr. 3 wrote a prescription for a twelve-year-old patient that was filled p.925 on January 29, 2008 at a specific CVS pharmacy; the $370.59 bill was paid by Massachusetts Medicaid. The use was off-label because, at the time, Abilify had not been medically indicated for patients under the age of thirteen. As another example, in April 2010, relator Ibanez personally sat in on a meeting discussing how to promote off-label use of Abilify to a specific child and adolescent psychiatrist in Cincinnati. That doctor had just written 124 prescriptions for Abilify that had been filled between November 2009 and January 2010 and paid for by Kentucky Medicaid. As discussed in the majority opinion, prescriptions for off-label use of Abilify were written for juvenile D.M. and paid for by Ohio Medicaid. Maj. Op. at 920-21. The majority is concerned with the lack of information about D.M.'s receipt of Medicaid reimbursements and the gap between promotion and filling the prescription. *Id.* But the complaint explains that relator Ibanez himself targeted the facility where D.M. was first prescribed Abilify during the year when he was first prescribed it. The complaint alleges that D.M. "routinely filled his Abilify prescriptions at Kroger pharmacies" and was reimbursed by Ohio Medicaid; the 2015 prescription the majority finds insufficiently linked to the initial promotion is offered as "but one example" of that continuous trend from the initial prescription in 2010. These examples, and the many others with which the complaint abounds, provide adequate and fair notice to defendants of the claims brought against them.

The First Circuit correctly recognized that a relator alleging that the defendant induced third parties to file false claims can "satisfy Rule 9(b) by providing 'factual or statistical evidence to strengthen the inference of fraud beyond possibility' without necessarily providing details as to each false claim." *Duxbury,* 579 F.3d at 29 (quoting *United States ex rel. Rost v. Pfizer, Inc.,* 507 F.3d 720, 733 (1st Cir. 2007)). These relators employed this method to support the examples of false claims described above. First and foremost, the relators have personal knowledge of the corporate strategies employed to promote off-label uses of Abilify. They also provide extensive statistical evidence that creates the strong inference both that this scheme occurred and that it resulted in substantial claims paid by the government.

The majority opinion points out that the facts in this complaint are not identical to those in *Prather,* where the relator alleged "specific personal knowledge that relates directly to billing practices." Maj. Op. at 915 (quoting *Prather,* 838 F.3d at 769). I agree that the relators in this case were not personally involved in billing. However, the relators here have nonetheless "pled facts which support a strong inference that a claim was submitted." *Prather,* 838 F.3d at 769 (quoting *Chesbrough,* 655 F.3d at 471). Relators, unlike the government, do not have many legal tools available to discern details of claims during the pleading stage. Making those legal tools available is precisely the purpose of discovery. The facts in the third amended complaint — detailed examples of the alleged scheme backed by personal knowledge and statistical evidence — are sufficient to satisfy Rule 9(b)'s requirement that the "circumstances constituting fraud" are stated with particularity. Fed. R. Civ. P. 9(b).

In summary, I concur in the majority opinion's holding that the public-disclosure bar does not apply here. I cannot agree with the remainder of the majority opinion because the relators have pled facts sufficient to satisfy Rule 9(b) by identifying specific claims and supplementing those identifications with personal knowledge and statistical evidence. Thus, under our precedent and in accordance with the purposes of the FCA specified by Congress, p.926 this case should not be dismissed. I therefore respectfully dissent.

[*] Judge White recused herself from participation in this ruling.

[1] A recent opinion from the Second Circuit described the FCA's awkward application to off-label promotion schemes well:

[I]t is unclear just whom Pfizer could have caused to submit a "false or fraudulent" claim: The physician is permitted to issue off-label prescriptions; the patient follows the physician's advice, and likely does not know whether the use is off-label; and the script does not inform the pharmacy at which the prescription will be filled whether the use is on-label or off. We do not decide the case on this ground, but we are dubious of [relator]'s assumption that any one of these participants in the relevant transactions would have knowingly, impliedly certified that any prescription for Lipitor was for an on-label use.

United States ex rel. Polansky v. Pfizer, Inc., *822 F.3d 613, 619-20 (2d Cir. 2016)*.

[2] The parties do not challenge this particular order, but we note that, in these circumstances, the district court was under no obligation to grant relators leave to file a Rule 15 motion to amend. Where parties have fully argued the merits of a 12(b)(6) motion to dismiss and the district court has duly considered those arguments and issued an opinion resolving the motion, it is a stretch to say justice requires granting leave to cure the complaint's deficiencies as identified in adversarial pleadings and the district court's order — even where the initial order turned on a failure to meet Rule 9(b)'s particularity requirements. *See SNAPP, Inc.,* 532 F.3d at 510-11 (noting that "*Bledsoe II* should not be taken to imply that the district court must grant Relator leave to file an amended complaint") (Suhrheinrich, J., concurring).

[3] Highlighting, once again, just how awkward it is to use the FCA to punish pharmaceutical companies for improper promotion of prescription medication. *See Polansky,* 822 F.3d at 615.

[4] This may be true only to the extent that the new allegations are temporally distant from the previously resolved conduct. *See U.S. ex rel. Kester v. Novartis Pharm. Corp.,* 43 F.Supp.3d 332, 353 (S.D.N.Y. 2014) ("Allegations that an extensive fraudulent scheme occurred [and was resolved] on February 14 strongly indicate that the scheme is still taking place on February 15 and February 16"). Here, instantaneous compliance with the Corporate Integrity Agreements was unlikely, but relators' allegations that the fraud continued intentionally for years after the agreements were entered into goes well beyond any reasonable period the government may have expected it to.

[5] We note that Rule 9(b)'s particularity requirements prevent a relator from proceeding to discovery on bare allegations that generally describe the same or similar conduct as a prior FCA action. The particularity requirement is stringent. *See Chesbrough,* 655 F.3d at 470.

SEVENTH CIRCUIT DECISIONS
Qui Tam Actions

41 F.4th 854 (2022)

Noreen LANAHAN, Plaintiff-Appellant,
v.
COUNTY OF COOK, Defendant-Appellee.

No. 21-1852.

United States Court of Appeals, Seventh Circuit.

Argued February 17, 2022.
Decided July 20, 2022.

Lanahan v. County of Cook, 41 F. 4th 854 (7th Cir. 2022)

Appeal from the United States District Court for the Northern District of Illinois, Eastern Division, No. 17-cv-5829 — Harry D. Leinenweber, *Judge.*

John Lanahan, I, Law Office of John Lanahan, Chicago, IL, for Plaintiff-Appellant.

Jennifer C. King, Office of the Cook County State's Attorney, Labor & Employment Division, Chicago, IL, Robert Thomas Shannon, Gretchen Harris Sperry, Attorneys, Hinshaw & Culbertson LLP, Chicago, IL, for Defendant-Appellee.

Before Rovner, Hamilton, and St. Eve, Circuit Judges.

p.858 St. Eve, Circuit Judge.

Relator Noreen Lanahan was a longtime employee of Cook County's Department of Public Health responsible for managing federal grants. After her retirement, Relator filed a *qui tam* suit against Cook County, alleging various violations of the False Claims Act arising out of the use of federal grants. The district court dismissed Relator's Second Amended Complaint with prejudice, and Relator now appeals. We affirm.

I. Background

Appellant Noreen Lanahan ("Relator") worked as a director of financial control in Cook County's Department of Public Health ("CCDPH"), a certified public health department, from 1994 until her retirement in 2017. In this capacity, Relator oversaw Cook County's claim and reimbursement policies for hundreds of federal grants and crafted budgets submitted to the federal government in order to qualify for grant funding. During this period, Cook County received approximately $20 million annually from the federal government for services related to federal public health priorities. Between 2008 and 2017, Relator repeatedly warned Cook County it was seeking federal reimbursement for unincurred expenses. Relator identifies four examples of Cook County's purportedly fraudulent practices.

A. 2009-11 H1N1 Influenza Grant

In September 2009, the Centers for Disease Control and Prevention ("CDC") awarded Cook County $2.5 million in federal grant funds to distribute the H1N1 vaccine. Prior to performing under the grant, Cook County prepared an anticipated budget. By regulation, Cook County could only be reimbursed for costs associated with work actually performed under the grant. Instead, Relator asserts Cook County estimated the time dedicated to federal service after the fact and pinned the salary allocations submitted for reimbursement to the CDC to pre-performance budget estimates. Relator herself "never tracked [] federal service dedication," never asked other managers how they apportioned employee time and was never solicited for an estimate of how individual employees apportioned their time p.859 among federal and local service. Indeed, Relator never tracked her own dedication to federal service.

On September 1, 2011, Cook County submitted two Certified Grant Allocation Cost Reports, one associated with the IDPH Pandemic Flu program and one with the IDPH Mass Vaccination program. Although the line-item shared expenses for each individual employee are identical, the IDPH Pandemic Flu expense report requested $1,065,506.05 in federal reimbursement while the IDPH Mass Vaccination expense report requested $1,210,802.33 in federal reimbursement. On September 26, 2011, the CDC transmitted reimbursement vouchers to the Cook County Comptroller.

Cook County was also required by regulation to segregate federal reimbursement funds from unaffiliated Cook County revenue. Upon receiving federal funds, Cook County submitted credit vouchers to apply the reimbursements to accounts in the CCDPH's general ledger. On November 30, 2011, the Cook County Comptroller moved the H1N1 funds into a discretionary account for the benefit of Cook County Health and Hospital Systems ("CCHHS"). Relator asserts this transfer "frustrated the allocations" in the September 1, 2011, report and "undermined any truth to the budget and compliance certifications" represented to qualify for and close out the grants.

B. 2012-14 WIC Grant

The Supplemental Nutrition Assistance Program ("SNAP") for Women, Infants and Children ("WIC") provides supplemental nutrition, education, and healthcare to low-income citizens. Individual WIC grant business units occasionally retain positive balances at the end of the fiscal year as a product of deferred personnel costs. By July 2014, Cook County had accumulated approximately $6.8 million in deferred WIC credits. In an email to Cook County's Director of Grants Management, Relator explained the $6.8 million "provides funding for Salaries and Fringe Benefits of grant employees should current grants not be renewed" and the "deferred revenue rolls forward from the previous grant year and is adjusted at grant closing." To avoid "distort[ing] current period grant expenses," Relator opined the "funds need[ed] to be segregated by the use of a unique Cost Center." Instead, Cook County opted to move the $6.8 million in deferred revenue into the general health fund of the CCHHS as, according to Cook County's Chief Budget Officer, "[p]resumably these are expenses that were absorbed by the general/health fund when they occurred."

Relator asserts CCHHS did not itself incur any expense in connection with the WIC grants.

C. Alleged Hektoen Kickback Scheme

The Hektoen Institute of Medicine ("Hektoen") is a nonprofit fiscal agent that processes claims and collects reimbursement revenue on behalf of Cook County for personal service costs incurred by Cook County physicians for federal grants. Hektoen did not have a formal agreement with Cook County but instead unofficially contracted with Cook County physicians in an "Exhibit A" package. Hektoen retained the only executed copies of these agreements, which Relator alleges violated recordkeeping regulations. Hektoen submits claims upon and collects revenue from federal research grants on behalf of Cook County physicians in exchange for 10-15% of the awarded grant amount. Hektoen reallocated this collected revenue into a "Dean's Fund" and gave physicians "near autonomy" over the money.

In 2015, Hektoen collected and retained $5 million in restricted federal funds. Relator points to a 2018 Chicago Tribune article p.860 detailing allegations against Dr. Bala Hota, a former Cook County hospital physician, as an example of the problems with Hektoen's practices. Dr. Hota allegedly embezzled almost $280,000 from Hektoen's salary reallocation account, which he spent on personal expenses such as iTunes, luxury travel, and couture cupcakes.

D. 2009-12 PHIMC Grant Management

The Public Health Institute of Metropolitan Chicago ("PHIMC") is a nonprofit fiscal agent. PHIMC is not a certified health department. In 2010, the CDC awarded CCDPH $15.9 million as an up-front payment for services to be rendered during a two-year period of performance. In the funding notice, the CDC limited funding to certified public health departments. The CCHHS Board approved PHIMC to serve as the fiscal agent for these funds. In June 2011, the CCHHS Board passed a resolution authorizing the transfer of grant funds to PHIMC, even though Relator alleges it had transferred the funds previously. PHIMC lacked the resources and financial controls to qualify for the award independently and the CCDPH would have to account for the funds in an annual audit.

E. Procedural History

Relator filed an initial *qui tam* complaint alleging various violations of the False Claims Act ("FCA"), 31 U.S.C. § 3729 *et seq.* After investigating Relator's allegations, the United States declined to intervene. Cook County moved to dismiss Relator's complaint for failure to state a claim under Rule 12(b)(6) and Rule 9(b). Instead of responding, Relator filed a First Amended Complaint which differed very little from the initial complaint. Cook County moved to dismiss the First Amended Complaint under Rule 12(b)(6) and Rule 9(b) as well.

The district court dismissed Relator's First Amended Complaint without prejudice in a thorough and detailed opinion. The chief deficiencies of Relator's FCA claims were twofold. First, Relator failed to plead the submission of a false statement to the government, and certainly not with the particularity required under Rule 9(b). Indeed, most of the activities Relator described occurred after federal payments had been disbursed to Cook County. Second, Relator failed to allege any false claim for payment submitted by Cook County to the government. The district court observed accounting failures, procedural irregularities, and regulatory violations could not themselves give rise to an FCA claim.

In response, Relator filed the operative Second Amended Complaint, alleging four causes of action under the FCA: a claim for presenting false claims for payment, in violation of 31 U.S.C. § 3729(a)(1)(A) (Count I); a claim for use of false statements, in violation of 31 U.S.C. § 3729(a)(1)(B) (Count II); a claim for conversion, in violation of 31 U.S.C. § 3729(a)(1)(D) (Count III); and a claim for reverse false claims, in violation of 31 U.S.C. § 3729(a)(1)(G) (Count IV). Again, Cook County moved to dismiss the Second Amended Complaint based on Rule 12(b)(6) and Rule 9(b).

The district court dismissed the Second Amended Complaint with prejudice against Relator.[1] The district court noted p.861 that, despite painstakingly explaining the Rule 9(b) pleading standard in its previous opinion, Relator failed to cure the deficiencies that warranted dismissal of the First Amended Complaint. The defects that doomed the Second Amended Complaint mirror those that doomed the First Amended Complaint. Specifically, with respect to Count I and Count II, Relator failed to adequately plead any false statements or claims, let alone any false statements connected with any government payments. While Relator's allegations surrounding the administration of the H1N1 grant reimbursement were more detailed, they nonetheless did not identify any specific falsities in the reports Cook County submitted. Even had Relator adequately pled a false statement, she did not link it to a government payment. The district court deemed Relator's improper retention claims in Count III and Count IV inadequate because the Second Amended Complaint did not contain sufficient facts indicating Cook County had retained any funds that properly belonged to the government. Because Relator enjoyed two opportunities to amend her complaint, one with the benefit of the district court's detailed assessment of the claims' flaws, the district court dismissed the Second Amended Complaint with prejudice. The district court observed the Second Amended Complaint contained "the same mistakes" as Relator's previous iteration, and these deficiencies were "not small and provide th[e] Court with no indication that Relator may be able to adequately plead an FCA claim in the future." Relator now appeals the district court's order dismissing the Second Amended Complaint with prejudice.

II. Discussion

Relator presents two arguments on appeal.[2] First, that the district court improperly dismissed her suit for failure to state a claim. Second, that the district court improperly did so with prejudice. Both arguments fail.

The FCA imposes civil liability on a series of actions related to fraudulent treatment of government funds. 31 U.S.C. § 3729(a)(1). The Attorney General may bring suit under the FCA directly in the name of the United States. *Id.* at § 3730(a). Alternatively, a private citizen referred to as a "relator" may bring a *qui tam* action "in the name of the Government." *Id.* at § 3730(b)(1). If the *qui tam* action results in damages, the relator shares in the award. *See id.* at § 3730(d).

We review a district court's dismissal of a complaint de novo, construing "all allegations and any reasonable inferences in the light most favorable to the plaintiff." *Jauquet v. Green Bay Area Catholic Educ., Inc.,* 996 F.3d 802, 807 (7th Cir. 2021) (internal quotations omitted). Rule 12(b)(6) requires a complaint contain sufficient facts "to state a claim to relief that is plausible on its face." *Bell Atl. Corp. v. Twombly,* 550 U.S. 544, 570, 127 S.Ct. 1955, 167 L.Ed.2d 929 (2007).

Claims arising under the FCA, an antifraud statute, are subject to Rule 9(b)'s heightened pleading standard. *United* p.862 *States ex rel. Mamalakis v. Anesthetix Mgmt. LLC,* 20 F.4th 295, 301 (7th Cir. 2021). To state such a claim, Relator "must state with particularity the circumstances constituting fraud or mistake." Fed. R. Civ. P. 9(b). To satisfy Rule 9(b)'s strictures, Relator must plead "the first paragraph of any newspaper story," i.e., the "who, what, when, where, and how of the fraud." *United States ex rel. Berkowitz v. Automation Aids, Inc.,* 896 F.3d 834, 839 (7th Cir. 2018) (internal quotations omitted). None of Relator's causes of action meet this rigorous pleading standard.

A. Counts I-II: False Claims and False Statements

Relator's first two causes of action both involve allegations of false submissions to the government. Section 3729(a)(1)(A) imposes civil liability where a person "knowingly presents, or causes to be presented, a false or fraudulent claim for payment or approval" to the government. 31 U.S.C. § 3729(a)(1)(A). To maintain a cause of action under § 3729(a)(1)(A), Relator must plead with particularity (1) the existence of a false or fraudulent claim that (2) Cook County presented to the government for payment (3) with knowledge the claim was false. *United States v. Sanford-Brown, Ltd.,* 788 F.3d 696, 709 (7th Cir. 2015), *reinstated in part, superseded in part on other grounds by United States v. Sanford-Brown, Ltd.,* 840 F.3d 445 (7th Cir. 2016). Section 3729(a)(1)(B) prohibits "knowingly mak[ing], us[ing], or caus[ing] to be made or used, a false record or statement material to a false or fraudulent claim." To survive a motion to dismiss under this section, Relator must plead Cook County (1) made a statement in order to receive money from the government, (2) the statement was false, (3) Cook County knew the statement was false at the time it made the statement, and (4) the statement was material to the government's decision to give Cook County money. *Berkowitz,* 896 F.3d at 840.

Relator's claims under § 3729(a)(1)(A) and § 3729(a)(1)(B) falter at the first element. Relator has not alleged any false claim or statement for payment with the degree of granularity Rule 9(b) requires. Rule 9(b) demands Relator "allege... specific facts demonstrating what occurred at the individualized transactional level" to maintain a claim. *Id.* at 841. This "includes 'the identity of the person making the misrepresentation, the time, place, and content of the misrepresentation, and the method by which the misrepresentation was communicated to the [defendant].'" *United States ex rel. Hanna v. City of Chi.,* 834 F.3d 775, 779 (7th Cir. 2016) (quoting *United States ex rel. Grenadyor v. Ukrainian Vill. Pharmacy, Inc.,* 772 F.3d 1102, 1106 (7th Cir. 2014)).

We dismiss outright Relator's conclusory assertions that Cook County profited from "reimbursement of WIC false claims" and that Hektoen was reimbursed "[d]espite the falsity of the underlying claims." We are not obligated to accept "sheer speculation, bald assertions, and unsupported conclusory statements" on a motion to dismiss. *Taha v. Int'l Bhd. of Teamsters, Local 781*, 947 F.3d 464, 469 (7th Cir. 2020). With respect to Relator's allegations regarding the WIC grant funds, Hektoen, and PHIMC's treatment of federal grant money, she does not identify any statement or claim, false or otherwise, Cook County made to the government. For each of these sources of federal grant money, Relator objects only to Cook County's treatment of the funds after they were disbursed. The Second Amended Complaint is utterly silent as to the events leading up to Cook County's receipt of these funds. Relator's assertions of regulatory p.863 or contractual violations are similarly incapable of establishing an FCA claim absent some connection between the breaches and a false statement or claim for payment, which Relator has not pleaded. *See Berkowitz*, 896 F.3d at 839; *Hanna*, 834 F.3d at 779.

Relator's assertions about the expense reports Cook County submitted to the CDC for reimbursement under the H1N1 vaccination grant provide some additional details, but these, too, fail. Relator asserts generally that the expense reports are false because the allocations were estimated after the fact instead of recorded contemporaneously. Relator, however, does not support this claim with particularized information about how the allocations were calculated or the expense reports prepared. Indeed, Relator states she "never discussed ... how individual employees apportioned their time among various federal and local services."

Nor does Relator assert any particular line item in the expense reports is false. Tellingly, while Relator pleads she "never tracked her own dedication to federal services," Relator does not claim her allocation is false. Relator's presentation of the differing claimed total reimbursements between the two expense reports despite "indistinguishable" individual line items is superficially tempting but does not bear up under closer scrutiny. Both the IDPH Pandemic Flu and the IDPH Mass Vaccination expense reports calculate a total shared expense of $1,862,772.82, a product of each recorded employee's salary and the amount of time they dedicated to federal service. The ultimate claimed reimbursement, however, is the sum of the government share amount and the fringe benefits amount. The government share amount is calculated by taking a specified percentage of the total shared expenses. For the IDPH Mass Vaccination expense report, this percentage is 50%, yielding a government share amount of $931,386.41. The fringe benefits amount is calculated by taking a specified percentage of the government share amount. For both the IDPH Mass Vaccination expense report and the IDPH Pandemic Flu expense report, the fringe benefits rate is 30%. For the IDPH Mass Vaccination expense report, the fringe benefits amount comes to $279,415.92. In total, the ultimate reimbursement claimed under the IDPH Mass Vaccination expense report—the sum of the $931,386.41 government share amount and the $279,415.92 fringe benefits amount—is $1,210,802.33.

The government share amount and the fringe benefits amount in the IDPH Pandemic Flu expense report differ from their counterparts in the IDPH Mass Vaccination expense report. The IDPH Pandemic Flu expense report does not indicate the government share rate, and this appears to be the source of the discrepancy. The total government share amount reported in the IDPH Pandemic Flu expense report is $819,620.04, which amounts to 44% of the total calculated shared expenses of $1,862,772.82. The fringe benefits rate for the IDPH Pandemic Flu expense report, like that of the IDPH Mass Vaccination expense report, is 30%. When applied to the reported government share amount this yields a fringe benefits amount of $245,886.01. All told, Cook County claimed $1,065,506.05 in reimbursements from the government under the IDPH Pandemic Flu expense report. Based on the actual submissions, it appears the differential in claimed reimbursements between the two expense reports is a product of the structure of the grants themselves, not to the value of federal services claimed as Relator suggests. And yet, Relator does not allege the government share rates applied in either the IDPH Pandemic Flu expense p.864 report or the IDPH Mass Vaccination expense report are false.

Even if Relator had adequately pleaded the falsity of the expense reports, she did not sufficiently link them to any government payments. Relator pleads Cook County submitted the two expense reports to the CDC on September 1, 2011. Next, Relator alleges the CDC transmitted reimbursement vouchers to Cook County on September 26, 2011. Relator asks us to infer the former caused the latter but offers no specific factual pleadings to support this logical leap. The Second Amended Complaint is entirely silent as to the purpose of the expense report, how the CDC uses such reports, or whether they are a prerequisite to government reimbursement. Relator's claim fails.

Further, while Relator alleges Cook County improperly reallocated restricted H1N1 grant funds to an unrestricted CCDPH account thereby "undermin[ing] the truth to the budget and compliance certifications represented by program managers to qualify and closeout the grants," she does not allege the certifications were false at the time they were made, as the FCA requires. *See Grenadyor,* 772 F.3d at 1105-06. Instead, Relator relies upon conduct which, according to the Second Amended Complaint, took place on November 30, 2011—well after the September 1, 2011, certification—to infer the certification itself was false at inception. Finally, although intent may be alleged generally in an FCA claim, Relator neglects to plead any facts from which we may infer Cook County intended to defraud the government. *See United States ex rel. Presser v. Acacia Mental Health Clinic, LLC,* 836 F.3d 770, 781 n.29 (7th Cir. 2016).

The district court properly dismissed Relator's claims under §§ 3729(a)(1)(A)-(B) of the FCA.

B. Counts III-IV: Improper Retention of Government Funds

In Count III and Count IV, Relator suggests Cook County improperly retained government funds. Section 3729(a)(1)(D) prohibits conversion of government funds and assigns civil liability where someone "has possession, custody, or control of property or money used, or to be used, by the Government and knowingly delivers, or causes to be delivered, less than all of that money or property." 31 U.S.C. § 3729(a)(1)(D). Similarly, a reverse false claim under § 3729(a)(1)(G) proscribes "knowingly mak[ing], us[ing], or caus[ing] to be made or used, a false record or statement material to an obligation to pay or transmit money or property to the

Government, or knowingly conceal[ing] or knowingly and improperly avoid[ing] or decreas[ing] an obligation to pay or transmit money or property to the Government." *Id.* at § 3729(a)(1)(G). Claims under both § 3729(a)(1)(D) and § 3729(a)(1)(G) require Relator to plead Cook County possessed funds that rightfully belonged to the government.[3] *See United States ex rel. Yannacopoulos v. Gen. Dynamics,* 652 F.3d 818, 835 (7th Cir. 2011); *see also United States ex rel. Foreman v. AECOM,* 19 F.4th 85, 122 (2d Cir. 2021) (analyzing § 3729(a)(1)(D)). Relator failed to do so in the Second Amended Complaint.

At most, Relator pleads Cook County placed federal funds from the H1N1 grant and the WIC grant in improper accounts. Relator does not plead the funds were due back to the government. p.865 Relator alleges Cook County transferred H1N1 grant funds into a CCHHS discretionary account, in violation of regulations which mandated segregation of restricted government funds. Nowhere does Relator claim Cook County was not entitled to the H1N1 funds.

Similarly, Relator objects only to Cook County's decision to place the $6.8 million of deferred restricted federal WIC funds into the CCHHS Enterprise Fund. In the email exchange attached to, and cited liberally throughout, the Second Amended Complaint, Relator emphasizes the $6.8 million in deferred WIC funds are intended to "provide[] funding for Salaries and Fringe Benefits of grant employees should current grants not be renewed" and "roll[] forward from the previous grant year and [are] adjusted at grant closing." This characterization strongly suggests Cook County was permitted to retain those WIC funds even after the federal grant expired. Relator's recommendation to place the $6.8 million in WIC funds in a segregated "unique Cost Center" reinforces this conclusion. If Cook County was not entitled to the $6.8 million in deferred federal revenue, it would certainly be odd to recommend Cook County keep the money. Cook County ultimately rejected Relator's suggestion and, instead, placed the WIC funds into a CCHHS account. Relator claims this was an error, not because Cook County decided to keep the funds instead of remitting them back to the government, but because the WIC funds were deposited into the account of an agency that did not incur costs related to the grant. At root, Relator objects to the location of the WIC funds, not Cook County's custody of the WIC funds. Moreover, the Second Amended Complaint is entirely bare of allegations regarding when, how, and under what circumstances Cook County had an obligation to return these funds to the government. Once again, Relator's allegations amount to nothing more than a putative regulatory violation.

Finally, Relator fails to plead any facts suggesting Cook County knew it was in possession of government funds to which it was not entitled. *Grenadyor,* 772 F.3d at 1105-06. With respect to the reclassified H1N1 funds, the Second Amended Complaint is wholly silent as to Cook County's knowledge or lack thereof. As to the WIC funds, while Relator alleges the assignment to the CCHHS account amounted to a "windfall" and that she disagreed with this decision, there is no indication whatsoever Cook County knew it was not entitled to those funds. *See* 31 U.S.C. § 3729(a)(1)(G) (requiring knowledge); *see also, e.g., United States ex rel. Harper v. Muskingum Watershed Conservancy Dist.,* 842 F.3d 430, 438-39 (6th Cir. 2016) (interpreting § 3729(a)(1)(D) to require knowledge that the property belongs to the government); *Foreman,* 19 F.4th at 122 (same). Indeed, Cook County's Chief Budget Officer justified placing the funds in the CCHHS account because, "[p]resumably these are expenses that were absorbed by the general/health fund when they occurred." This suggests Cook County was under the impression that the WIC deferred revenue mirrored already-incurred expenditures.

The district court properly dismissed Relator's causes of action for conversion under § 3729(a)(1)(D) and for reverse false claims under § 3729(a)(1)(G).

C. Dismissal with Prejudice

Relator nominally presents the district court's decision to dismiss the Second Amended Complaint with prejudice and without leave to amend as a basis for appeal. Beyond listing the issue as a question presented, however, Relator entirely fails to expound on the position. Indeed, p.866 even when Cook County suggested Relator forfeited this argument such that plain error applied, Relator did not respond to Cook County's position or even contest forfeiture on reply. Relator's challenge to the dismissal with prejudice is waived as perfunctory, underdeveloped, and cursory. *Shipley v. Chi. Bd. of Election Comm'rs*, 947 F.3d 1056, 1063 (7th Cir. 2020). Furthermore, Relator failed to adequately present her claims even after the district court dismissed her First Amended Complaint with a detailed discussion of its deficiencies. The dismissal with prejudice was proper.

III. Conclusion

For the foregoing reasons, the judgment of the district court is AFFIRMED.

[1] Initially, the district court dismissed the Second Amended Complaint with prejudice without specifying whether it pertained only to Relator or to the United States as well. The district court granted the government's resultant motion to clarify the dismissal and specified the action was dismissed with prejudice as to Relator but without prejudice as to the United States.

[2] Although the district court did not enter a separate final judgment in this case per Federal Rule of Civil Procedure 58, we are nonetheless confident in our appellate jurisdiction. The district court clearly "indicated its intent to finally dispose of all claims," *Law Offices of David Freydin, P.C. v. Chamara*, 24 F.4th 1122, 1128 (7th Cir. 2022), in dismissing the Second Amended Complaint with prejudice, expressly noting the "deficiencies in the [Second Amended Complaint] ... provide this Court with no indication that Relator may be able to adequately plead an FCA claim in the future." The district court's judgment is therefore final within the meaning of 28 U.S.C. § 1291. *See id.*

[3] Section 3729(a)(1)(G) also requires Relator to adequately plead a false statement. *See Yannacopoulos*, 652 F.3d at 835-36. For all the reasons articulated in Section II.A, Relator's reverse false claims cause of action fails on this basis as well.

17 F.4th 732 (2021)

UNITED STATES of America and the State of Illinois ex rel. Thomas Prose, Plaintiffs-Appellants, v. MOLINA HEALTHCARE OF ILLINOIS, INC., and Molina Healthcare, Inc., Defendants-Appellees.

No. 20-2243.

United States Court of Appeals, Seventh Circuit.

Argued January 15, 2021.

Amended November 15, 2021.

United States v. Molina Healthcare of Illinois, 17 F. 4th 732 (7th Cir. 2021)

Appeal from the United States District Court for the Northern District of Illinois, Eastern Division, No. 17 C 6638, Virginia M. Kendall, *Judge.*

Neil M. Rosenbaum, Damon E. Dunn, Attorneys, Funkhouser Vegosen Liebman & Dunn, Bruce C. Howard, Attorney, Howard Law LLC, Paul M. King, Attorney, Pedersen & Houpt, P.C., Chicago, IL, Tejinder Singh, Attorney, Goldstein & Russell, P.C., Bethesda, MD, for Plaintiff-Appellant Thomas Prose.

Albert Giang, Kelly Perigoe, Attorneys, King & Spalding LLP, Los Angeles, CA, Quyen Ta, Attorney, King & Spalding, San Francisco, CA, for Defendants-Appellees.

Before SYKES, Chief Judge, and WOOD and HAMILTON, Circuit Judges.

p.736 WOOD, Circuit Judge.

Sophisticated players in the healthcare market know that services come at a cost; providers charge fees commensurate with the services rendered; and payors expect to receive value for their money. There are many options from which to choose when designing a payment scheme, including fee-for-service, prepaid services using the health-maintenance organization model (HMO), and capitation payments, to name just a few. Each of these models attempts to balance expected services against expected costs.

The present case involves a capitation system, which is similar to the traditional HMO approach in which parties agree to a fixed per-patient fee that covers all services within the scope of a governing plan. Molina Healthcare of Illinois (Molina) contracted with the state's Medicaid program (which in turn is largely funded by the federal government, see Illinois Medicaid, https://www.benefits.gov/benefit/1628) to provide multiple tiers of medical-service plans with scaled capitation rates. Among those, the Nursing Facility (NF) plan required Molina to provide Skilled Nursing Facility (SNF) services. Molina itself, however, did not deliver those services; instead, it subcontracted with GenMed to cover this obligation. Molina received a general capitation payment from the state, out of which it was to pay GenMed for the SNF component. But little time passed before Molina breached its contract with GenMed and GenMed terminated the contract. After GenMed quit, Molina continued to collect money from the state for the SNF services, but it was neither providing those services itself nor making them available through any third party. Molina never told the government about this breakdown, nor did it seek out a replacement service provider.

p.737 Thomas Prose, the founder of GenMed, brought this *qui tam* action under both the federal and the state False Claims Acts. See 31 U.S.C. § 3729 *et seq.*; 740 ILCS 175/1 *et seq.* (Because the state law does not differ in any meaningful way from the federal law, we refer in this opinion only to the federal law for the sake of simplicity.) Prose alleged that Molina submitted fraudulent claims for payments to the Department (which was for the most part just a conduit for federal funds—a point we will not repeat) for skilled nursing facility services. Although the district court agreed with Prose that the SNF services were material to the contract, it dismissed the case at the pleading stage because it found that the complaint insufficiently alleged that Molina knew that this condition was material. But on our independent reading of the complaint, we conclude that it plausibly alleges that as a sophisticated player in the medical-services industry, Molina was aware that these kinds of services play a material role in the delivery of Medicaid benefits. We therefore reverse and remand for further proceedings.

I

We present the facts in the light most favorable to Prose, the party opposing dismissal for failure to state a claim. Molina, a subsidiary of Molina Healthcare, Inc. (Molina Healthcare), is a Managed Care Organization (MCO). It has contracted with the Illinois Department of Healthcare and Family Services to provide healthcare services for Illinois Medicaid beneficiaries. Molina's contract with the state was a "risk contract," in which the parties agree to an expected cost for services for a patient and Molina assumed the risk that the cost of those services might exceed the contracted payment amount. 42 C.F.R. § 438.2.

As part of this risk contract, Molina and the Department agreed to capitation payments—periodic contractual fees, calculated per enrollee. These fees must be "actuarily sound." *Id.* Each enrollment category had its own schedule of payments. A given category's capitation rate reflected the anticipated costs per person on an amortized basis. There was nothing unusual about this arrangement. In the late 1980s and 1990s, the capitation-payment model became common in the healthcare industry. It is similar to the more traditional health maintenance organization (HMO), in which a health insurance provider covers all care over a fixed annual fee, but it differs in some important ways. Capitation rates, in a word, are more flexible. They allow providers to establish distinct rate tiers, and the providers agree to delineate at the outset exactly what services they will furnish within each tier. Membership in each tier is correlated with factors such as age, health, and needed services. See, *e.g.,* Nina Novak, *Health Care Risk Contracting: The Capitation Alternative,* 3 HEALTH LAW. 4, 4-5 (1987). A Managed Care Organization plays an active role in the creation of the plan, as it needs to understand the risk it is assuming through its guarantee of services. See Andrew Ruskin, *Capitation: The Legal Implication of Using Capitation to Affect Physician Decision-Making Processes,* 13 J. CONTEMP. HEALTH L. & POL'Y 391, 397, 409, 411 (1997).

Molina's contract created "rate cells" that were "stratified by age ..., geographic services area (Greater Chicago and Central Illinois), and setting-of-care." It defined five care settings: Nursing Facility, Waiver, Waiver Plus, Community, and Community Plus. The lowest cost and most populous of these cells was the Community group. For the Greater Chicago Community category during the contract period for February to December 2014, for example, the projected enrollee count was 261,108, p.738 and the monthly capitation rate the state paid to Molina was $53.51 for each person 65 years and older. By contrast, the highest-cost category—Nursing Facility—had 70,836 enrollees covered at a monthly rate of $3,180.30 per person 65 and older. Our case concerns this latter category.

Molina contracted to provide Skilled Nursing Facility (universally abbreviated as SNF) services for Nursing Facility enrollees. Under Illinois state law, SNF providers, known as "SNFists," are "medical professional[s] specializing in the care of individuals residing in nursing homes employed by or under contract with a MCO." 305 ILCS 5/5F-15. Molina's contract further specified that a SNFist's "entire professional focus is the general medical care of individuals residing in a Nursing Facility and whose activities include Enrollee care oversight, communication with families, significant others, PCPs, and Nursing Facility administration." SNFists perform valuable long-term care for sick, disabled, or elderly patients who need long-term medical and nursing care without hospitalization. Molina's contract with the Department emphasized that SNFist services were integral to improving the enrollee's quality of life and potentially to enabling her to be discharged from the nursing home.[1]

In order to deliver these expensive services, in April 2014 Molina entered into an agreement with GenMed, because Molina did not have the necessary qualified personnel. This contract provided that GenMed would provide SNF services for Molina's Nursing Facility enrollees. The Department was not a party to the contract, and so it continued to pay Molina the full capitation payments for the SNF recipients. Molina then used those funds to pay GenMed the agreed amount. This arrangement, however, lasted only about nine months. In January 2015, Molina stopped reimbursing GenMed and sought to renegotiate the price terms of the service agreement. GenMed continued to provide SNF services through March 2015, but it terminated the contract on April 2, 2015, after Molina continued to refuse to pay it.

From April 2, 2015, until at least April 5, 2017, Molina was not delivering SNF services to anyone, either with its own personnel or through a subcontractor. Indeed, it was not even looking for a replacement for GenMed. It did not inform the Department or the federal authorities of this change, and so the Department continued to pay it the full capitation amount for SNF services—in essence, payments for nothing. Aware of the situation because of his association with GenMed, Thomas Prose filed this *qui tam* action on September 14, 2017, alleging that Molina violated the False Claims Act by seeking and obtaining compensation despite failing to provide material services under its contract with the Department.

II

Since we are evaluating the district court's decision to grant a motion to dismiss under Rule 12(b)(6), we accept all p.739 well-pleaded facts as true and draw all reasonable inferences in favor of the non-moving party. *O'Brien v. Village of Lincolnshire,* 955 F.3d 616, 621 (7th Cir. 2020). Critically, however, this is not a case that is governed by the usual notice-pleading standards of Federal Rule of Civil Procedure 8. See, *e.g., Ashcroft v. Iqbal,* 556 U.S. 662, 678, 129 S.Ct. 1937, 173 L.Ed.2d 868 (2009). A party bringing a case alleging fraud must satisfy the heightened pleading standards set forth in Rule 9(b), which says that "[i]n alleging fraud or mistake, a party must state with particularity the circumstances constituting fraud or mistake." FED. R. CIV. P. 9(b). At the same time, Rule 9(b) carves out several matters that may be alleged generally, including "[m]alice, intent, knowledge, and other conditions of a person's mind." *Id.*

Rule 9(b)'s more demanding pleading requirements apply to suits brought under the False Claims Act. The complaint must describe the "who, what, when, where, and how" of the fraud to survive a motion to dismiss. *United States ex rel. Presser v. Acacia Mental Health Clinic, LLC,* 836 F.3d 770, 776 (7th Cir. 2016) (quoting *United States ex rel. Lusby v. Rolls-Royce Corp.,* 570 F.3d 849, 853 (7th Cir. 2009)). Nonetheless, courts and litigants should not "take an overly rigid view of the formulation"; the allegation must be "precis[e]" and "substantiat[ed]," but the specific details that are needed to support a plausible claim of fraud will depend on the facts of the case. *Presser,* 836 F.3d at 776 (quoting *Pirelli Armstrong Tire Corp. Retiree Med. Benefits Tr. v. Walgreen Co.,* 631 F.3d 436, 442 (7th Cir. 2011)). As we noted earlier, the Illinois False Claims Act applies the same standards as the federal statute. *Bellevue v. Universal Health Servs. of Hartgrove, Inc.,* 867 F.3d 712, 716 n. 2 (7th Cir. 2017).

A

Before assessing Prose's complaint, it is helpful to take a more detailed look at the False Claims Act. This statute creates a right of action under which private parties may, on behalf of the federal government, bring lawsuits alleging fraud. 31 U.S.C. § 3730(b). The actions go by the hoary Latin term "*qui tam*" (short for *qui tam pro domino rege quam pro se ipso in hac parte sequitur,* meaning "who as well for the king as for himself sues in this matter," see Bryan A. Garner, ed., BLACK'S LAW DICTIONARY at 1444 (10th ed. 2014)). The party seeking to represent the government's interest is called a "relator." Successful relators are motivated by the prospect of recovering sizable shares of the money paid to the government after bringing a successful claim. *Glaser v. Wound Care Consultants, Inc.,* 570 F.3d 907, 912 (7th Cir. 2009). The government has the right, but is not obligated, to proceed on a claim brought by a relator; it may elect to dismiss the action notwithstanding the party's objection. 31 U.S.C. § 3730(c)(2)(B). When the government chooses not to proceed with the action but does not dismiss the action either, the initiating party retains the right to proceed against the defendant. 31 U.S.C. § 3730(c)(3).

The Act makes it unlawful knowingly (1) to present or cause to be presented a false or fraudulent claim for payment to the United States, (2) to make or use a false record or statement material to a false or fraudulent claim, or (3) to use a false record or statement to conceal or decrease an obligation to pay money to the United States. *United States ex rel. Yannacopoulos v. Gen. Dynamics,* 652 F.3d 818, 822 (7th Cir. 2011). A successful claim requires proof both that the defendant made a statement to receive money from the government and that he made that p.740 statement knowing it was false. *Id.* But there is more. Not all false statements are actionable under the Act. The plaintiff also must prove that the violation proximately caused the alleged injury. *United States v. Luce,* 873 F.3d 999, 1011-14 (7th Cir. 2017). In other words, the pecuniary losses must be "within the foreseeable risk of harm" that the false statement created. *Id.* at 1012. In addition, the defendant's conduct must meet a strict materiality requirement. *Universal Health Servs., Inc. v. United States ex rel. Escobar,* 579 U.S. 176, 136 S. Ct. 1989, 1996, 195 L.Ed.2d 348 (2016). It is not enough simply to say that the government required compliance with a certain condition for payment. The facts must indicate that the government actually attaches weight to that requirement and relies on compliance with it. In sum, as the Third Circuit has put it, the relator must establish (1) falsity, (2) causation, (3) knowledge, and (4) materiality. *United States ex rel. Petratos v. Genentech Inc.,* 855 F.3d 481, 487 (3d Cir. 2017).

The Act is not limited to claims that are facially false. It covers a defendant's more general decision fraudulently to procure payment from the government. Consequently, while the archetypical claim is one in which a "claim for payment is itself literally false and fraudulent," *United States ex rel. Hendow v. Univ. of Phoenix,* 461 F.3d 1166, 1170 (9th Cir. 2006), courts have identified particular theories that support FCA claims, including (1) false certification to the government that the party has complied with a statute, regulation, or condition of payment; (2) promissory fraud, or fraud in the inducement, *id.* at 1172-73; and (3) implied false certification, see *Escobar,* 136 S. Ct. at 2001. The implied false certification claim involves the omission of key facts rather than affirmative misrepresentations. This type of liability arises if the "defendant makes representations in submitting a claim but omits its violations of statutory, regulatory, or contractual requirements[;] those omissions can be a basis for liability if they render the defendant's representations misleading with respect to the goods or services provided." *Id.* at 1999.

B

Prose's complaint raises allegations under all three of these approaches: factual falsity, fraud in the inducement, and implied false certification. At the same time, he contends that these labels should be jettisoned. Taking our guidance from *Escobar,* we decline to distill one unified approach for all cases. The Court's focus on the implied false certification theory in *Escobar* signals that it continues to find that there are distinct ways in which the statute may be violated. We will follow suit.

As we now explain, we conclude that Prose has adequately stated a claim under the Act. His detailed allegations support a strong inference that Molina was making false claims. At this stage, that is enough; as the litigation proceeds, it is possible that one or more of these theories will lack support. But there is time enough for that assessment at trial or upon a motion for summary judgment.

Fraud is a serious matter. Rule 9 represents a policy decision to protect potential fraud defendants from litigation based on nothing but rumor or speculation. Instead, the relator must set forth the basis for her conclusion that fraud is afoot. *United States ex rel. Grenadyor v. Ukrainian Vill. Pharmacy, Inc.,* 772 F.3d 1102, 1108 (7th Cir. 2014). But as we have been saying, that does not require the impossible. Relators with a legitimate basis for bringing False Claims Act cases will not generally have propriety information of the company they are trying to sue, and p.741 so courts do not demand voluminous *documentation* substantiating fraud at the pleading stage. All that is necessary are sufficiently detailed *allegations*.

We begin with the allegations that would support a claim for direct factual falsity—the canonical FCA claim. The question is whether Prose's allegations alert Molina in sufficient detail for Rule 9(b) purposes of how it allegedly made a "claim for payment [that] is itself literally false and fraudulent." *Hendow,* 461 F.3d at 1170. Prose contends that after April 2, 2015, Molina submitted to the government materially fraudulent enrollment forms for each *new* enrollee in the Nursing Facility category of patients. As of that date, its contract with GenMed had ended, and it could not, and did not, provide SNF services.

Rule 9(b) requires specificity, but it does not insist that a plaintiff literally prove his case in the complaint. Prose provided numerous details indicating when, where, how, and to whom allegedly false representations were made. He hardly can be blamed for not having information that exists only in Molina's files. He did provide information that plausibly supports the inference that Molina included false information about the pertinent services for new enrollees. How else could it have asked for its capitation payments based on these additional beneficiaries? A direct assertion that Molina had new enrollees who were in the skilled nursing facility tier, coupled with an assertion that Molina was seeking reimbursement for their SNF services, is not an omission. It is a statement, and in this case a statement that Prose asserts was false. He did not need any more to defeat the challenge to the adequacy of his complaint.

Prose also alleged circumstantial evidence of promissory fraud, or fraud in the inducement. Here, he needed to alert Molina with the necessary specificity of how it allegedly misrepresented its compliance with a condition of payment in order to induce the government to enter into a contract. *Hendow,* 461 F.3d at 1172-73 (citing *United States ex rel. Marcus v. Hess,* 317 U.S. 537, 542, 63 S.Ct. 379, 87 L.Ed. 443 (1943)); *cf. United States v. Sanford-Brown, Ltd.,* 788 F.3d 696, 709 (7th Cir. 2015), *abrogated by Escobar,* 579 U.S. 176, 136 S. Ct. 1989 ("[F]raud entails making a false representation, such as a statement that the speaker will do something *it plans not to do.*"). Prose charges that Molina fraudulently induced the Department to enter into contract renewals with Molina in 2016 and 2017 by affirmatively misrepresenting that it would continue to provide SNF services in its package for NF-category enrollees while not intending to do so.

The district court concluded that the complaint in this respect fell short because it did not include any details about the contract-renewal negotiations between Molina and the Department. But how would Prose have had access to those documents or conversations? The obligation to set out the "who, what, when, where, and how" of the fraud does not require such granular detail. Prose set forth precise allegations about the beneficiaries, the time period, the mechanism for the fraud, and the financial consequences. Once again, at trial or upon a motion for summary judgment he will face a different burden, but for now, this was enough.

Claims of fraudulent inducement also require the plaintiff to show that the defendant never intended to perform the promised act that induced the government to enter the contract. *United States ex rel. Main v. Oakland City Univ.,* 426 F.3d 914, 917 (7th Cir. 2005) ("[F]ailure to honor one's promise is (just) breach of contract, but making a promise that one intends not p.742 to keep is fraud."). Prose put Molina on notice of this aspect of his case, too. He included details about statements made by Molina's chief operating officer (COO), Benjamin Schoen, who stated in his deposition that Molina's "staff did not have the ability or licensure to render [SNF] services." Taken together with Molina's defunct contract with GenMed and its failure to seek out a replacement SNF provider, the complaint alleges that any promise by Molina to provide SNF services during the contract-renewal process was fraudulent on its face.

This may even have been more detail than was necessary, taking into account the fact that Rule 9(b) permits intent to be alleged generally. Construing the allegations liberally, the complaint asserts that Molina made some representations about actual SNF services that would be offered. Schoen acknowledged that Molina did not have the personnel available to perform those services. The complaint thus concludes that Molina did not and never intended to seek out another SNF service provider. This sufficed to allege intent.

Finally, even if the complaint fell short of the required specificity under Rule 9 for the first two approaches, it was sufficient to state a claim for implied false certification. The Supreme Court described that version of fraud as follows in *Escobar*:

> ... [T]he implied false certification theory can be a basis for liability. Specifically, liability can attach when the defendant submits a claim for payment that makes specific representations about the goods or services provided, but knowingly fails to disclose the defendant's noncompliance with a statutory, regulatory, or contractual requirement. In these circumstances, liability may attach if the omission renders those representations misleading.
>
> We further hold that False Claims Act liability for failing to disclose violations of legal requirements does not turn upon whether those requirements were expressly designated as conditions of payment. Defendants can be liable for violating requirements even if they were not expressly designated as conditions of payment. Conversely, even when a requirement is expressly designated a condition of payment, not every violation of such a requirement gives rise to liability. What matters is not the label the Government attaches to a requirement, but whether the defendant knowingly violated a requirement that the defendant knows is material to the Government's payment decision.

136 S. Ct. at 1995-96.

Even before *Escobar*, courts recognized express false certification—that is, an affirmative misstatement of compliance with a statute, regulation, or other contractual obligation to obtain payment from the government—as a basis of liability. *United States ex rel. Absher v. Momence Meadows Nursing Ctr., Inc.,* 764 F.3d 699, 710-11 (7th Cir. 2014). Implied and express statements raise distinct issues, however.

Implied false certification is just another genre of fraud, and so plaintiffs must as usual satisfy Rule 9(b)'s requirements to plead falsity, materiality, and causation with particularity. (Knowledge is also an element, but it falls within the Rule's carve-out.) As the Supreme Court did in *Escobar*, we focus first on the "rigorous materiality requirement" that the plaintiff must meet. 136 S. Ct. at 1996. A misrepresentation is not material "merely because the Government designates compliance with a particular statutory, regulatory, or contractual requirement as a condition of payment." *Id.* at 2003. Such a stipulation is "relevant, but not automatically p.743 dispositive." *Id.* But materiality requires more: typically, proof either that (1) a reasonable person would view the condition as important to a "choice of action in the transaction" or (2) the defendant knew or had reason to know that the recipient of the representation attaches importance to that condition. *Id.* at 2002-03. Should the government decide to pay despite knowing of the party's noncompliance, that would be "very strong evidence" (though not dispositive) that the condition is not material. *Id.* In short, facts matter. The complaint must include specific allegations that show that the omission in context significantly affected the government's actions.

Prose's complaint points to many factual representations that Molina made that, he charges, amounted to implied false certification. For instance, he alleges that Molina's contract with the Department carefully created different rate cells for enrollees based on the level of care they would need; the level of care in turn yields a reasonable estimate of cost for each tier. Both are essential if the capitation payments are to be actuarially sound. The difference between the Community group and the Nursing Facility group is a whopping $3,127 per head. The middle-tier group costs roughly $600 less apiece than the Nursing Facility group. The size of the price differential alone offers strong support for a finding of materiality: it is hard to see why the government would be indifferent about paying $3,180 for services that should have been at the $54 level. The district court concluded that each enrollment form, which constituted a specific request for payment connected to the NF enrollees, was "impliedly false because it requested payment of the SNF capitation rate" when those services were not being rendered.[2]

Molina responds that the enrollment forms did not contain misleading omissions because Molina did not fraudulently manipulate the beneficiary pool to increase the number of people in the more expensive category. But that is just one way in which liability could be shown; it is not the only one.

The complaint, read in Prose's favor, contains specific allegations showing that Molina was far from a passive recipient of a favorable capitation rate. Prose was not relying on Molina's receipt of capitation payments for existing enrollees. Rather, the complaint alleges that by submitting enrollment forms for *new* enrollees after Molina canceled its contract with GenMed, Molina implicitly falsely certified that Nursing Facility enrollees had access to SNF services. But they did not. Construed in Prose's favor, the complaint describes Molina's noncompliance with a contractual requirement to provide SNF services to Nursing Facility enrollees. This is akin to the defendant's actions in *Escobar,* in which the Court found that the defendant "misleadingly omit[ted] [the] critical facts" that its care providers were not qualified to render services for which it nevertheless requested payments. 136 S. Ct. at 2001.

Molina's strongest argument against materiality relies on its contention that the government continued to contract with Molina after learning that Molina could no p.744 longer provide SNF services. Molina emphasized that the government not only continued paying it after Prose brought this case, but it also renewed its contract with Molina twice during that time. It is true that the government's continued payment of a claim despite "actual knowledge" that certain requirements are not met "is very strong evidence that those requirements are not material." *Escobar,* 136 S. Ct. at 2003.

But this argument is better saved for a later stage, once both sides have conducted discovery. At this juncture, it appears that Molina is offering only part of the story. Later exploration will be needed before anyone can say what the government did and did not know about Molina's provision of SNF services.

For pleading purposes, Molina's barebones assertion that the government was aware of all material facts is not enough to sweep away the elaborate facts that Prose furnished. The contract itself, which fixes the cost of the NF category well above the other tiers, is powerful evidence of the materiality of the SNF services. See *Ruckh v. Salus Rehab., LLC,* 963 F.3d 1089, 1105 (11th Cir. 2020) (finding materiality when the issue "went to the heart" of the bargain). Many things could explain the government's continued contracting with Molina. It may have expected to purge the underserved NF enrollees from the books; it may have needed time to work out a way not to prejudice Medicaid recipients who had nothing to do with this problem. Medicaid (along with the Children's Health Insurance Program, or CHIP) serves more than 71 million people nationally and accounts for $600 billion in federal spending. See Center for Medicare and Medicaid Services, Medicaid Facts and Figures, at https://www.cms.gov/newsroom/fact-sheets/medicaid-facts-and-figure.   An organization like that does not turn on a dime.

For all these reasons, we conclude that Prose's complaint adequately alleged materiality for purposes of his *qui tam* action. The district court was also willing to go that far. Where Prose foundered, it thought, was on the final element of the claim: knowledge. The court found that the complaint failed adequately to allege that Molina knew that the government viewed SNF services as material. In *Escobar,* the Supreme Court identified a two-layered knowledge requirement: the defendant must (1) knowingly violate a requirement while (2) knowing that the government viewed the requirement as material to payment. 136 S. Ct. at 1996. Even though Molina necessarily knew that it had violated the contractual requirement to provide SNF services, the district court thought that Prose's allegations that Molina knew that these services were material were conclusory and need not be accepted as true. The allegations, it said, at most supported a conclusion that Molina's actuarial consultants coordinated the payment scheme with the government. Missing, it thought, was a contention that Molina was involved in calculating the capitation rates.

This was error. First, the court failed to give proper weight to the complaint's description of Molina as a highly sophisticated member of the medical-services industry. Molina was quite familiar with capitation rates, and it knew that they are designed to allow the provider to be reimbursed for services rendered. And recall that this was a risk contract: Molina had a strong incentive to ensure that the capitation rate was high enough to cover its costs plus a reasonable profit, because it would be left holding the bag if the rate were too low. Ruskin, *supra,* at 397, 409; Novak, *supra,* at 5.

In addition, knowledge may be alleged generally, even in a case under Rule 9(b), and so the district court was wrong to p.745 insist that Prose identify concrete evidence of actual knowledge. A party seeking to establish liability under the FCA may satisfy the Act's knowledge requirement through proof of actual knowledge, deliberate ignorance of truth or falsity, or reckless disregard for truth or falsity. 31 U.S.C. 3729(b)(1)(A)(i)-(iii). Construing the allegations in Prose's favor, there is ample detail to support a finding that Molina either had actual knowledge that the government would view skilled nursing services as a critical part of the Nursing Facility rate cell (*i.e.,* as material), or that it was deliberately ignorant on this point. Once again, these high-cost services, essential to the nursing-home population, were the very reason why the government paid a capitation rate more than fifty times as much to support them.

Molina subcontracted for SNF services because it could not provide those services. Its contract with GenMed recognized that these SNF services "fill the primary care gap" for Nursing Facility patients. The deal fell apart when Molina attempted to renegotiate its contract with GenMed to reduce the cost of those services and thus to increase its own profit margin. Molina therefore knew these services' cost and their importance, and it knew that it was unable to provide these services without a partner such as GenMed. Prose's complaint plausibly alleges this knowledge, insofar as it notes that before the actuarial consultant's resolution of the cost breakdown, Molina and the government discussed these services at the proposal stage. Requiring more concrete proof of knowledge would run afoul of Rule 9(b).

In light of this, we need not rely on Prose's other arguments. He alleges a scheme to cover up Molina's noncompliance by having its own personnel perform non-skilled work for the nursing, such as face-to-face comprehensive assessments and annual comprehensive exams. That practice does not shed much light on the problem: Molina always admitted that its personnel were not qualified to provide SNF services, and it appears that these exams were merely non-SNF functions that Molina had delegated to GenMed.

Last, we say a word about causation. This too is an element of an FCA claim: the plaintiff must establish that the defendant's fraud "was a material element and a substantial factor in bringing about the injury." *Luce,* 873 F.3d at 1012 (internal quotation omitted). Causation here is evident. By submitting enrollment forms requesting payment for services Molina could not provide to Illinois Medicaid, Molina caused the government to pay significant sums that it would not have paid with full knowledge. That is enough to satisfy the pleading burden on causation.

Prose's complaint sufficiently alleges that Molina knew that SNF services played a major role in the significantly higher capitation rate for the NF category. It thus suffices for purposes of his False Claims Act theories. We of course express no opinion on the ultimate fate of this litigation; we hold only that Prose may proceed.

III

The final loose end we must address is Molina Healthcare's request that it be dismissed from the case. Molina Healthcare (as we briefly noted at the outset) is Molina's parent company. It contends that corporate affiliation is not enough to support its liability. Given the decision on the merits, the district court did not reach the question of parent-company liability. Neither do we; it is far too underdeveloped at this point. But it is an issue that, if properly p.746 raised again, the district court should address on remand.

The judgment of the district court is REVERSED and the case REMANDED for further proceedings consistent with this opinion.

SYKES, Chief Judge, dissenting.

"The False Claims Act is not 'an all-purpose antifraud statute[ ]' or a vehicle for punishing garden-variety breaches of contract or regulatory violations." *Universal Health Servs., Inc. v. United States ex rel. Escobar,* 579 U.S. 176, 136 S. Ct. 1989, 2003, 195 L.Ed.2d 348 (2016) (quoting *Allison Engine Co. v. United States ex rel. Sanders,* 553 U.S. 662, 672, 128 S.Ct. 2123, 170 L.Ed.2d 1030 (2008)). Our own precedent aligns with this understanding of the FCA's reach. *See United States v. Sanford-Brown, Ltd.* ("*Sanford-Brown II*"), 840 F.3d 445, 447 (7th Cir. 2016). The majority moves our circuit law in a different direction, establishing a new rule that a mere request for payment from the government, coupled with material noncompliance with a contractual condition, is a cognizable FCA violation subject to the full panoply of remedies authorized by the Act, including qui tam suits and treble damages. Because that rule conflicts with *Escobar* and circuit precedent, I respectfully dissent.

* * *

The government and Molina Healthcare of Illinois have a risk contract. Each month the government pays Molina a fixed sum to provide health coverage for a Medicaid beneficiary, and no matter how expensive that beneficiary's medical costs are, Molina is responsible. Molina profits when the fixed sum—the "capitation rate"—exceeds actual expenses; it swallows a loss when expenses are in excess.

The contract creates five risk pools called "rate cells" that correspond to health status, and it fixes capitation payments by rate cell—higher capitation rates are paid for rate cells that are likely to require more intensive care. The most expensive of these rate cells is for an enrollee living in a nursing facility. To enroll a beneficiary, Molina submits a form to the government categorizing the enrollee by rate cell, and in response the government pays Molina the corresponding amount.

Molina's contract with the government specifies the "covered services" that it must provide to enrollees depending on their rate cells. As relevant here, an enrollee who resides in a skilled nursing facility is entitled to "SNFist" services, generally described as "intensive clinical management of Enrollees in Nursing Facilities." Plaintiff-relator Thomas Prose alleges that for approximately two years, Molina submitted enrollment forms to the government but knowingly did not deliver SNFist services to its nursing-facility enrollees.

To place this allegation in proper context, some background on the nature of these services is needed. The term "SNFist" is defined in the contract as a medical professional "whose entire professional focus is the general medical care of individuals residing in a Nursing Facility and whose activities include Enrollee care oversight, communication with families, significant others, [primary-care providers], and Nursing Facility administration." Or as the contract puts it more succinctly, a SNFist is a medical professional who "provide[s] Care Management and care coordination activities" for enrollees residing in nursing facilities. Importantly, "care management" is not the direct provision of medical care, personal care, or social services to nursing-home residents; rather, as the contract defines the term, "care management" comprises "[s]ervices that assist p.747 Enrollees *in gaining access to needed services,* including medical, social, education, and other services."[1] (Emphasis added.)

The contract gives Molina the option to provide SNFist services "either through direct employment or a subcontractual relationship," and its "SNFist Program" may use either a "facility-based Provider (Physician or nurse practitioner)" or "telephonic or field-based Registered Nurses or licensed clinical social workers," depending on the circumstances.

Because SNFist services are provided only to enrollees in nursing facilities, it's reasonable to assume that the inclusion of these services plays at least *some* role in the difference between the capitation rate for the nursing-facility rate cell and the rate cell below it. How large a role is unclear; a key question is whether Prose has alleged sufficient facts to show that the delivery of SNFist services was material to the government's decision to pay Molina for nursing-facility enrollees during the relevant time period. I will return to the materiality point later. For now, it's enough to note that SNFist services are one component of nursing-home care among many, and as explained, are contractually defined as care coordination and management. Moreover, a nursing-home enrollee is inherently a riskier beneficiary for Molina to cover than a lower-tier enrollee, which also partly explains the difference in capitation rates.

In the majority's view, because Prose has alleged that Molina billed the government for the full nursing-facility capitation rate while failing to provide SNFist services, he has adequately pleaded an FCA claim for making materially false statements to the government. That reasoning might have surface appeal, but once we understand that SNFist services are just one component of nursing-home care among many, the error in the majority's reasoning becomes clear. Prose's complaint states a claim for breach of contract, but it relies on too many factually unsupported inferences to state a claim for an FCA violation.

* * *

My colleagues begin the analysis by identifying the three recognized theories of FCA liability: fraud in the inducement (or promissory fraud), express factual falsity, and implied false certification. Majority op. at 740. They also explain that Rule 9(b) of the Federal Rules of Civil Procedure requires an FCA plaintiff to plead fraud allegations with particularity rather than simply satisfy the usual plausibility standard. *Id.* at 740-41. I have no disagreement with these basic doctrinal points. The majority concludes, however, that even under Rule 9(b)'s demanding standards, Prose has stated an FCA claim under all three theories. In my view the complaint does not satisfy the heightened pleading standard under *any* of these theories.

A. Fraud in the Inducement

Prose alleges that Molina fraudulently induced the government to renew its contract in 2016 and 2017 by representing that it would provide SNFist services for nursing-facility enrollees while never intending to do so. I agree with the district judge that Prose's allegations are too generalized and conclusory to state a claim under this theory.

p.748 To satisfy Rule 9(b), "[t]he complaint must state the identity of the person making the misrepresentation, the time, place, and content of the misrepresentation, and the method by which the misrepresentation was communicated." *United States ex rel. Grenadyor v. Ukrainian Vill. Pharmacy, Inc.,* 772 F.3d 1102, 1106 (7th Cir. 2014) (quotation marks omitted). Prose's complaint falls far short of checking these boxes. It includes no details of the contract renewals in 2016 and 2017 and does not point to any specific misleading statement made by an identified Molina representative, let alone specify the "time, place, and content" of the statement. The allegations of promissory fraud are not only vague and highly generalized, but they are made "[o]n information and belief," which is insufficient under Rule 9(b). *United States ex rel. Bogina v. Medline Indus., Inc.,* 809 F.3d 365, 370 (7th Cir. 2016) ("'[O]n information and belief' can mean as little as 'rumor has it that ....'"). In essence, Prose simply invites us to assume that because the contract was renewed at a time when Molina was not providing SNFist services, Molina necessarily made false statements to the government.

Surprisingly, the majority accepts this invitation to deviate from Rule 9(b) and forgives Prose for not describing the "who, what, when, where, and how" of the fraud, as required by the rule. *United States ex rel. Presser v. Acacia Mental Health Clinic, LLC,* 836 F.3d 770, 776 (7th Cir. 2016) (quotation marks omitted). My colleagues say that Prose cannot be expected to provide these factual particulars at the pleading stage because he lacks access to information about the contract-renewal discussions until discovery opens that door. Majority op. at 740-41. But we are not at liberty to loosen pleading standards under circumstances where a specific false statement is hard to identify. Rule 9(b) raises the pleading burden "because of the stigmatic injury that potentially results from allegations of fraud." *Presser,* 836 F.3d at 776. Pleading a fraud claim is challenging, but that's the point: the rule "deters the filing of suits solely for discovery purposes" and "guards against the institution of a fraud-based action in order to discover whether unknown wrongs actually have occurred." 5A ARTHUR R. MILLER ET AL., FEDERAL PRACTICE & PROCEDURE § 1296 (4th ed. 2021). By permitting Prose to proceed on generic allegations of promissory fraud pleaded "on information and belief," this case will become the very "fishing expedition" that Rule 9(b) is meant to avoid. *Vicom, Inc. v. Harbridge Merch. Servs., Inc.,* 20 F.3d 771, 777 (7th Cir. 1994).

B. Express Factual Falsity

As my colleagues explain, the archetypal FCA violation is an express factual falsehood—a "claim for payment [that] is itself literally false or fraudulent." *United States ex rel. Hendow v. Univ. of Phoenix,* 461 F.3d 1166, 1170 (9th Cir. 2006). The majority reasons that Molina's enrollment forms were factually false on their face because they amounted to "[a] direct assertion that Molina had new enrollees who were in the skilled nursing facility tier, coupled with an assertion that [it] was seeking reimbursement for their SNF services." Majority op. at 741. This reasoning extends the factual-falsity theory too far.

A direct falsehood is an affirmative misrepresentation, not an omission. For example, in *Presser* the plaintiff alleged that a medical clinic submitted claims to the government for payment using billing codes corresponding to specific psychiatric services but in fact had performed only nonpsychiatric evaluations. 836 F.3d at 778-79. Thus, the clinic made an affirmative factual misrepresentation: it billed the government specifically for service X when it p.749 actually provided service Y. *Id.* at 779 ("Acacia ... allegedly billed Medicaid for a completely different treatment. The claim therefore does not involve a misrepresentation by omission; it involves an express false statement.").

Here, by contrast, Prose alleges a falsehood by omission: Molina requested capitation payments at the nursing-facility rate without disclosing that it did not deliver one of the many services required by the contract. This allegation does not describe an affirmative misrepresentation. At most, it alleges a fraudulent omission, which situates this case within the theory of implied false certification. We should analyze Prose's complaint under that framework, not expand the theory of facial factual falsity to include misleading omissions.

That was the approach taken by the Supreme Court in *Escobar*. There, the plaintiffs alleged that a medical-services contractor submitted claims for payment to the government for counseling services it had provided and listed billing codes and identification numbers corresponding to the specific services its counselors had provided, along with their job titles, respectively. The problem was that the counselors "lacked licenses to provide mental health services, yet—despite regulatory requirements to the contrary—they counseled patients and prescribed drugs without supervision." 136 S. Ct. at 1997.

The complaint thus alleged a falsehood by omission. The Court held that allegations of fraudulent omissions might suffice to state an FCA claim based on a theory of implied false certification. *Id.* at 1999. In so holding, the Court described the paradigm case of implied false certification as follows: "When, as here, a defendant makes representations in submitting a claim but omits its violations of statutory, regulatory, or contractual requirements, those omissions can be a basis for liability if they render the defendant's representations misleading with respect to the goods or services provided." *Id.*

Prose's allegations are best conceptualized as a possible claim under a theory of implied falsehood. Following *Escobar*'s lead, we should not stretch the facial-falsehood concept but instead analyze the allegations under the rubric of implied false certification.

C. Implied False Certification

Turning now to the theory that is the closest fit with Prose's allegations, I note for starters that my colleagues skip the threshold requirements announced in *Escobar* and instead move straight to the second-tier question of materiality. That approach cannot be squared with *Escobar*'s requirements for this type of FCA claim.

Escobar held that a claim for payment might be an actionable violation of the FCA under a theory of an implied false certification *if* two conditions are present: "first, the claim does not merely request payment[ ] but also makes specific representations about the goods or services provided; and second, the defendant's failure to disclose noncompliance with material statutory, regulatory, or contractual requirements makes those representations misleading half-truths." 136 S. Ct. at 2001.

Prose's allegations do not satisfy the first of these threshold conditions. Molina's enrollment forms did not make any specific representation about the goods or services provided. They simply enrolled Medicaid beneficiaries by rate cell, which designated the appropriate capitation rate for a given enrollee. This rate-cell information was nothing more than a request for a specific amount of payment for a very broad swath of services. In *Escobar,* by contrast, the medical contractor "submit[ed] claims for p.750 payment using payment codes *that corresponded to specific counseling services.*" 136 S. Ct. at 2000 (emphasis added). In other words, the claims for payment at issue in *Escobar* were specific claims that misled the government into believing something false. Here, Molina's enrollment forms made broad payment requests covering a host of services, only one of which was not delivered. That does not satisfy *Escobar*'s first condition for a cognizable claim of implied false certification.

Indeed, our own precedent confirms that a general request for payment coupled with some degree of contractual or regulatory noncompliance is not enough to support a claim of implied false certification. In *United States v. Sanford-Brown, Ltd.* ("*Sanford-Brown I*"), 788 F.3d 696 (7th Cir. 2015), *vacated United States ex rel. Nelson v. Sanford-Brown, Ltd.,* ___ U.S. ___, 136 S. Ct. 2506, 195 L.Ed.2d 836 (2016), *reinstated in part by Sanford-Brown II,* 840 F.3d at 447, we considered an FCA action brought against a for-profit college. The school signed a Program Participation Agreement with the Department of Education in which the college agreed to comply with all regulations under Title IV in exchange for federal subsidies. *Id.* at 707-08. The college did not comply with all regulations, yet it submitted requests for funds anyway. *Id.* at 708. On remand from the Supreme Court, we held that the plaintiff had not satisfied *Escobar*'s first condition because he "offered no evidence that defendant Sanford-Brown College ... made any representations at all in connection with its claims for payment, much less false or misleading representations." *Sanford-Brown II,* 840 F.3d at 447. In other words, a generic payment request—without specific representations about the goods or services provided—does not satisfy *Escobar*'s first condition and thus cannot suffice as an implied false certification.

Escobar's second condition requires the plaintiff to adequately allege (and later prove) that the defendant's failure to disclose its noncompliance with a statutory or regulatory requirement made the specific representation a misleading half-truth. A half-truth is a "representation[ ] that state[s] the truth only so far as it goes, while omitting critical qualifying information." *Escobar,* 136 S. Ct. at 2000. Imagine that the Green Bay Packers have a bye week and someone makes the statement, "the Packers didn't win today." That's a classic half-truth. The statement is true as far as it goes, but it directly implies a specific falsehood to an unaware fan: that the Packers lost that day.

Escobar identified some helpful examples of half-truths. "A classic example of an actionable half-truth in contract law is the seller who reveals that there may be two new roads near a property he is selling[ ] but fails to disclose that a third potential road might bisect the property." *Id.* "Likewise, an applicant for an adjunct position at a local college makes an actionable misrepresentation when his resume lists prior jobs and then retirement[ ] but fails to disclose that his 'retirement' was a prison stint for perpetrating a $12 million bank fraud." *Id.* Or consider the half-truth at issue in *Escobar* itself: the medical contractor's submission of claims with payment codes and identification numbers corresponding to specific job titles and counseling services while not disclosing that the counselors providing the services were unlicensed. What we can distill from these examples is that a misleading half-truth arises when a defendant makes a specific statement (the Packers didn't win today) that inevitably leads the recipient to assume by implication a particular falsehood (that the Packers lost).

Prose's allegations operate at a much higher level of generality than the allegations p.751 in *Escobar*. In that case there was a tight link between the specific representations (payment codes for counseling services and ID numbers for job titles) and the falsehood inevitably implied by omission (the counselors corresponding to the identified job titles were in fact licensed for those positions). Here, there is at most only a loose association between Molina's nonspecific representation (enrolling a Medicaid beneficiary in the nursing-facility rate cell) and the alleged false implication (that SNFist services—one among many nursing-facility services—were actually provided). Where, as here, the defendant's claim for payment wouldn't necessarily lead the recipient to assume the specific falsehood alleged in the complaint, there is no half-true statement and thus no falsehood by implication.

Indeed, Molina's enrollment forms made no specific representations about the services provided beyond enrolling a beneficiary in a given rate cell, which after all, is just a request for a certain payment amount. Considering the multitude of services provided to nursing-home enrollees, the enrollment forms wouldn't inevitably lead the government to assume any specific falsehood by implication. The enrollment forms, though perhaps misleading in a general sense, did not contain a specific half-true statement as required by *Escobar*.

* * *

The majority concentrates its implied-falsehood analysis on the question of materiality, an additional requirement for a viable FCA claim and one that *Escobar* also addressed at some length. A representation is material if "a reasonable man would attach importance to [it] in determining his choice of action in the transaction" or if "the defendant knew or had reason to know that the recipient of the representation attaches importance to the specific matter." *Id.* at 2002-03 (quotation marks omitted).

My colleagues rely almost entirely on the difference in capitation rates among rate cells: \$3,127 per month for a nursing-facility enrollee; about \$2,500 per month for a middle-tier enrollee; and \$54 for a low-tier enrollee. They conclude that "[t]he size of the price differential alone offers strong support for a finding of materiality." Majority op. at 743; *see also id.* at 744 ("The contract itself, which fixes the cost of the NF category well above the other tiers, is powerful evidence of the materiality of the SNF services."). But by omitting SNFist services, Molina didn't provide middle-tier service at high-tier rates. Instead, it provided something close to high-tier service at high-tier rates. By itself, the difference in capitation rates sheds little light on the materiality question because nothing in the complaint connects that difference to SNFist services.

In some cases a large pay differential between two billing rates might alone be enough to support an inference of materiality. Not so here. The problem turns again on the nature of SNFist services. To repeat, SNFist services are care-coordination services—one of many services provided to nursing-home enrollees that in the aggregate contribute to the higher capitation rate. The complaint offers nothing to explain the effect of these particular services on the government's willingness to pay the nursing-facility capitation rate for these enrollees. Without some factual contextualization, we cannot draw an inference that Molina's nondisclosure was material to the government's decision to pay its claims during the relevant time period.

Think of it this way: If rate cell 1 corresponds to 10 services provided at a rate of $2,000 and rate cell 2 corresponds to those same 10 services plus SNFist services at a rate of $3,000, then billing at the level 2 p.752 rate while not providing SNFist services would support an inference of materiality at the pleading stage. If SNFist services are not delivered, then the contractor is providing only level 1 services, and a reasonable person would not pay much higher level 2 rates for receiving only level 1 services.

But now consider a scenario in which rate cell 2 corresponds to *30* services—the 10 in rate cell 1 plus 20 others, one of which is SNFist services. In that scenario it doesn't make sense to rely on the $1,000 price differential in considering whether the omission of SNFist services is material because the differential may be largely explained by the 19 other services separating rate cell 1 and rate cell 2. That's the situation here—the difference in capitation rates between the nursing-home rate and the middle-tier rate is only partially explained by SNFist services, and nothing in the complaint illuminates the extent to which those services account for the differential. Without at least some contextualizing factual allegations, the capitation-rate differentials are not a useful metric for assessing materiality.

Of course, materiality might be established in other ways, but Prose's remaining arguments are unpersuasive; even the majority doesn't make use of them. For example, he points to the fact that the government specifically discussed SNFist services during 2013 contract negotiations and asks us to infer that they were material to the government's decision to pay Molina in 2015, 2016, and 2017. But the mere discussion of a contract term earlier in negotiations doesn't mean that its fulfillment is material to a later decision to pay, especially when the negotiations occurred years before. Prose also asks us to infer materiality because SNFist services were supposed to be available 24/7 and were coupled with reporting obligations. But the contract requires *every* covered service to be provided 24/7 and is replete with reporting obligations, which undermines any suggestion that SNFist services had special status.

Finally, Prose argues that SNFist services are necessarily material because payment rates are derived from actuarially precise calculations that included them. This reasoning suggests that *every* service under a contract with actuarial pricing is material. That's an unsound approach to the materiality question in this context. Although the contract may have calibrated the capitation rates to the services the government expected to be delivered, it doesn't follow that the government would withhold payment if a *single one* of those services wasn't provided.

Escobar characterized the materiality standard as "demanding," 136 S. Ct. at 2003, and Prose has failed to meet it. Perhaps he could have done so with factual allegations showing that SNFist services account to a significant degree for the difference in capitation rates. Or perhaps he could have alleged that Molina was aware that the government "consistently refuses to pay claims in the mine run of cases" if SNFist services are omitted. *Id.* But we know the opposite is true, as my colleagues acknowledge. Majority op. at 744 (explaining that "the government not only continued paying [Molina] after Prose brought this case, but it also renewed its contract with Molina twice during that time"). *Escobar* explained that "if the [g]overnment regularly pays a particular type of claim in full despite actual knowledge that certain requirements were violated, and has signaled no change in position, that is strong evidence that the requirements are not material." *Id.* at 2003-04. As it is, we're left with only generic statements about the importance of SNFist services and a rate differential p.753 without any contextualizing factual allegations connecting the differential to the omitted services. That doesn't clear the bar.

Even if my analysis of materiality is wrong, the majority's conclusion that Prose has stated a claim for implied false certification essentially establishes a new rule that *any* claim for payment while in material noncompliance with a contract or governing law is an actionable violation of the FCA. As already explained, that conclusion conflicts with *Escobar* and circuit caselaw.

* * *

For these reasons, I would affirm the judgment dismissing the complaint for failure to state a claim. Prose's allegations fall short of satisfying Rule 9(b)'s heightened pleading standard for an actionable FCA claim under any of the three recognized theories of liability.

[1] The dissent suggests that the SNFist services provided by Molina were contractually limited to "care coordination and management." That was true in some circumstances, but not all. Providers employed through the SNFist program were also expected to "deliver care" "when appropriate or necessary." And in its general definition of SNF facility services, the contract included all of "Skilled Nursing care, continuous Skilled Nursing observations, restorative nursing, and other services under professional direction with frequent medical supervision." Construing the allegations in the light most favorable to Prose, as we must, this shows that SNFist services are comprehensive, not just one of a bundle of 20 or 30 different items, as the dissent contends.

[2] The dissent takes issue with the numbers here, asserting that Molina provided "something close to high-tier service at high-tier rates." But that claim appears to spring from the redefinition of SNFist services as nothing more than care coordination—a definition that neither the contract nor the pleadings reflect. Just how close to "high-tier services" Molina got is best decided on summary judgment or at trial, not here. For present purposes, Prose's complaint adequately alleges that SNFist services explain much of the cost difference between the Nursing Facility tier and the less expensive tiers.

[1] The majority uses the term "SNF services," which loosely suggests that what's at stake here is a broader spectrum of nursing-facility services. Not so. Prose's complaint alleges that from April 2, 2015, to April 5, 2017, Molina failed to deliver

"SNFist services," a contractually defined term that is limited to care coordination performed by a SNFist—not a broader set of services provided by skilled nursing facilities.

20 F.4th 295 (2021)

UNITED STATES of America EX REL. John MAMALAKIS, Plaintiff-Appellant,

v.

ANESTHETIX MANAGEMENT LLC d/b/a Anesthetix of TeamHealth, et al.,[*]
Defendants-Appellees.

No. 19-3117.

United States Court of Appeals, Seventh Circuit.

Argued April 13, 2020.
Decided December 8, 2021.

US ex rel. Mamalakis v. Anesthetix Management LLC, 20 F. 4th 295 (7th Cir. 2021)

Appeal from the United States District Court for the Eastern District of Wisconsin, No. 14-CV-349, David E. Jones, Magistrate Judge.

Daniel N. Rosen, Attorney, Kluger Kaplan Silverman Katzen & Levine, P.L., Minneapolis, MN, David Smart Stone, Attorney, Stone & Magnanini, Berkeley Heights, NJ, for Plaintiff-Appellant.

Daniel Barnowski, Eric Thomas Werlinger, Mary Fleming, Attorneys, Katten Muchin Rosenman LLP, Washington, DC, for Defendants-Appellees.

Before SYKES, Chief Judge, and HAMILTON and ST. EVE, Circuit Judges.

p.297 SYKES, Chief Judge.

Dr. John Mamalakis, a Wisconsin anesthesiologist, filed this *qui tam* lawsuit under the False Claims Act, 31 U.S.C. §§ 3729 *et seq.,* alleging that Anesthetix Management LLC, his former employer, fraudulently billed Medicare and Medicaid for services performed by its anesthesiologists. His central allegation is that the anesthesiologists regularly billed the government using the code for "medically directed" services when their services qualified for payment only at the lower rate for services that are "medically supervised." A magistrate judge dismissed the case, ruling that the complaint did not provide enough factual particularity to satisfy Rule 9(b)'s heightened pleading standard for fraud claims. FED. R. CIV. P. 9(b). The judge gave Mamalakis a chance to amend, directing him to provide representative examples of the alleged fraudulent billing.

Mamalakis obliged, filing an amended complaint that included ten specific examples of inflated billing. Each example identified a particular procedure and anesthesiologist and provided details about how the services did not qualify for payment at the medical-direction billing rate. Six of the ten examples included a specific allegation that the anesthesiologist billed the services using that code; the other four relied on general allegations regarding the group's uniform policy of billing at the medical-direction rate.

The judge held that the amended complaint still fell short under Rule 9(b) and dismissed the case with prejudice. That was error. Although Rule 9(b) imposes a high pleading bar to protect defendants from baseless accusations of fraud, Mamalakis cleared it. The ten examples, read in context with the other allegations in the amended complaint, provide sufficient particularity about the alleged fraudulent billing to survive dismissal. We reverse and remand for further proceedings.

I. Background

We begin with the government's billing rules for anesthesiologists. Under Medicare and Medicaid regulations, anesthesiologists may submit claims for payment to the government under one of three billing codes corresponding to the level of services provided. 42 C.F.R. § 414.46(b). The p.298 highest billing rate is reserved for cases in which the anesthesiologist "personally performed" the procedure. This rate applies if the anesthesiologist (1) performed the anesthesia services alone; (2) was the teaching physician directing a resident or intern physician during the procedure; or (3) continuously participated in a single procedure involving a certified registered nurse anesthetist, an anesthesiologist assistant, or a student nurse anesthetist. *Id.* § 414.46(c).

The "medical direction" rate is half the personal-performance rate. *Id.* § 414.46(d)(3)(v). An anesthesiologist may bill at the medical-direction rate if he directed a resident or intern, certified registered nurse anesthetist, anesthesiologist assistant, or student nurse anesthetist in two, three, or four concurrent procedures *and* he personally performed or participated in each of the following steps in each procedure: (1) conducted the preanesthetic examination and evaluation; (2) prescribed the anesthesia plan; (3) participated in the most demanding parts of the plan, including induction and emergence, if applicable; (4) ensured that any procedure he did not personally perform was performed by a qualified individual; (5) monitored the anesthesia administration at frequent intervals; (6) remained physically present and available for immediate diagnosis and treatment of an emergency; and (7) provided postanesthetic care as indicated. *Id.* §§ 414.46(d), 415.110(a)(1). To qualify for payment at the medical-direction rate, the anesthesiologist must personally document that the seven conditions were satisfied and specifically confirm that he performed requirements 1, 3, and 7. *Id.* § 415.110(b).

The lowest billing rate applies when the physician "medically supervises anesthesia services" performed by other anesthesia professionals. *Id.* § 414.46(f). Special billing rules apply when the anesthesiologist medically supervises more than four concurrent procedures. *Id.*

With the regulatory framework in place, we recount the facts as alleged in the operative amended complaint. In 2008 Dr. Mamalakis began working as an anesthesiologist at All Saints Hospital in Racine, Wisconsin. He was employed by Southeastern Anesthesia Consultants, which contracted with All Saints to provide anesthesia services for the hospital's patients. Southeastern did not employ nurse anesthetists, so its anesthesiologists personally performed the anesthesia services and Southeastern billed Medicare and Medicaid at the personal-performance rate.

In early January 2010, All Saints dropped Southeastern as its provider of anesthesia services and awarded the contract to Anesthetix Management LLC. Mamalakis accepted an offer of employment from the new provider. At around the same time, Anesthetix Management was acquired by TeamHealth Holdings, Inc., a nationwide holding company of providers of clinical services to hospital systems around the country. Both Anesthetix Management, doing business as Anesthetix of TeamHealth, and the holding company TeamHealth are named as defendants. We refer to them collectively as "TeamHealth."

Unlike Southeastern, TeamHealth employs nurse anesthetists and planned to have its anesthesiologists medically direct procedures rather than personally perform them. At an orientation session on January 10, 2010, Dr. Sonya Pease, the new medical director, told the anesthesiologists that they should "document each procedure with the goal of fitting it within the Medicare guidelines for medical direction." She explained that the anesthesiologists should sign the anesthesia record every 15 minutes indicating that they had checked in on the patient. Mamalakis alleges that he and p.299 other anesthesiologists interpreted her statement as an instruction that they should sign the patient record as if they were present at every 15-minute interval during the procedure even if they were not.

TeamHealth thereafter converted the anesthesia practice at All Saints to "100% medical direction across the board." The new system "was designed to allow TeamHealth anesthesiologist[s] to perform more procedures concurrently[] and bill for the procedures in accordance with the regulatory framework" for medically directed anesthesia services.

Mamalakis alleges that after this transition, his fellow anesthesiologists frequently failed to satisfy the conditions required for billing at the medical-direction rate yet routinely billed at that rate in accordance with the new business model. More specifically, he alleges that anesthesiologists regularly failed to perform preanesthetic exams and evaluations, did not personally prescribe anesthesia plans, did not monitor the patient at frequent intervals during procedures, did not participate in the most demanding parts of the procedure, and sometimes were not physically present to handle emergencies. He alleges that TeamHealth was aware that its anesthesiologists did not comply with these conditions for payment at the medical-direction rate but billed at that rate anyway and therefore knowingly submitted false bills to the government for payment.

Mamalakis further alleges that he brought his concerns about fraudulent billing to Dr. Pease, but she instructed him not to inform All Saints because it might jeopardize TeamHealth's contract. Dr. Pease also directed him to let the nurse anesthetists prescribe the anesthesia plans for his procedures—even though an anesthesiologist must do so in order to bill at the medical-direction rate. Mamalakis claims that Dr. Pease stated on numerous occasions that all TeamHealth anesthesia services were to be billed as medically directed regardless of whether the procedure qualified for that rate.

In May 2011 TeamHealth CEO Dr. Steve Gottlieb visited the hospital and met with doctors and administrators. During this visit, Mamalakis tried to tell him about the fraudulent billing practices, but Dr. Gottlieb "abruptly stood up and ran out of the room in an attempt to avoid hearing any more." Dr. Pease thereafter placed Mamalakis under "strict scrutiny" and was "look[ing] for any excuse to terminate his employment." She fired Mamalakis two months later, at the end of July 2011.

In March 2014 Mamalakis filed this *qui tam* suit against TeamHealth alleging violations of several sections of the False Claims Act and similar laws in several states.

The case remained sealed for more than a year while the government considered whether to step in and assume control of the litigation. *See* 31 U.S.C. § 3730(b)(4)(B). In June 2015 the government declined to do so, leaving Mamalakis in charge of the action as the relator. *Id.* § 3730(c)(3). The case was then unsealed, and nearly a year later, Mamalakis filed an amended complaint on behalf of the United States, the District of Columbia, and 16 states seeking treble damages for multiple violations of the Act and similar false-claims laws in six states and the District of Columbia.

TeamHealth moved to dismiss. The case then stalled for about 18 months due to the retirement of the assigned judge and the administrative process of reassigning it to a magistrate judge presiding by consent. Once the case got back on track, the magistrate judge granted TeamHealth's dismissal motion, ruling that the allegations of fraud were too generalized to satisfy the particularity requirement of Rule 9(b). The p.300 judge gave Mamalakis a final opportunity to amend, setting a 60-day deadline and instructing him to provide representative examples of fraudulent billing.

Mamalakis timely filed another amended complaint adding ten specific examples of procedures at All Saints in which TeamHealth anesthesiologists failed to comply with the requirements for the medical-direction billing code. Each example identified the procedure in question, the anesthesiologist involved, and the specific ways in which he or she did not perform the services required to bill at the medicaldirection rate. For six of the ten examples, the amended complaint affirmatively alleges that the anesthesiologist billed for his or her services at the medical-direction rate. The other four examples rely on the complaint's more general allegations that TeamHealth anesthesiologists uniformly used the medical-direction billing code whether their services qualified for it or not.

TeamHealth again moved to dismiss, and the magistrate judge again granted the motion. He began by noting that Mamalakis's response to the motion was limited to the alleged violation of § 3729(a)(1)(A) of the Act. That section provides a cause of action on behalf of the United States against any person who "knowingly presents, or causes to be presented, a false or fraudulent claim for payment or approval." Because Mamalakis offered no argument regarding the other counts in the complaint, the judge summarily dismissed all other claims. Mamalakis does not challenge that ruling, so we limit our discussion accordingly.

Regarding the alleged § 3729(a)(1)(A) violation, the judge held that the ten examples in the latest amended complaint did not cure the deficiencies in the earlier version. He determined that nine of the ten examples failed to provide adequately particularized factual support for the allegation that the anesthesiologists fraudulently billed at the medical-direction rate. The single remaining example, the judge ruled, was not enough by itself to satisfy the heightened pleading burden under Rule 9(b). The judge also rejected Mamalakis's background allegations regarding TeamHealth's billing policies as insufficient to plead fraud with the specificity required by the rule. Focusing on the allegations about Dr. Pease's instructions to anesthesiologists at the January 2010 orientation, the judge explained that her remarks suggested only that the anesthesiologists should provide medically directed care and bill accordingly— not that the doctors should fraudulently bill at the medical-direction rate. On this reasoning the judge dismissed the case in its entirety, and Mamalakis appealed.

II. Discussion

This once-sprawling case has been narrowed to Mamalakis's claim that TeamHealth violated § 3729(a)(1)(A) of the False Claims Act. That section provides that any person who "knowingly presents, or causes to be presented, a false or fraudulent claim for payment or approval" by the government is liable to the government for civil penalties and treble damages. To prevail on a claim under this provision, the plaintiff "generally must prove (1) that the defendant made a statement in order to receive money from the government; (2) that the statement was false; and (3) that the defendant knew the statement was false." *United States ex rel. Presser v. Acacia Mental Health Clinic, LLC,* 836 F.3d 770, 777 (7th Cir. 2016) (quotation marks omitted). In addition, the defendant's misrepresentation must have been material to the government's payment decision; the Supreme Court has characterized the materiality requirement as "rigorous." *Universal Health Servs., Inc. v.* p.301 *United States ex rel. Escobar,* 579 U.S. 176, 181, 136 S.Ct. 1989, 195 L.Ed.2d 348 (2016).[1]

The Act rewards private relators with a generous share of the proceeds of a successful claim: 15-25% if the government takes over the case; 25-30% if the government declines to do so and the private relator handles it solo. 31 U.S.C. § 3730(d)(1)-(2).

Because the False Claims Act is an antifraud statute, Rule 9(b)'s heightened pleading standard applies, so the complaint must allege the circumstances of the fraud with factual particularity. We have described this burden as requiring the plaintiff to "describe the 'who, what, when, where, and how' of the fraud." *Presser,* 836 F.3d at 776 (quoting *United States ex rel. Lusby v. Rolls-Royce Corp.,* 570 F.3d 849, 853 (7th Cir. 2009)). This more rigorous pleading standard guards against "the stigmatic injury that potentially results from allegations of fraud." *Id.* However, the knowledge element of the claim may be alleged generally. FED. R. CIV. P. 9(b). What is essential is that the complaint allege with sufficient particularity the facts showing that the defendant made a false statement to obtain money from the government, "injecting precision and some measure of substantiation" into the allegations of fraud. *Presser,* 836 F.3d at 776 (quotation marks omitted).

It follows that alleging fraud "on information and belief" is normally insufficient to satisfy Rule 9(b)'s heightened pleading standard. *United States ex rel. Bogina v. Medline Indus., Inc.,* 809 F.3d 365, 370 (7th Cir. 2016). While the relator need not "produce the invoices (and accompanying representations) at the outset of the suit," it is nevertheless "essential to show a false statement," though this can be accomplished by including particularized factual allegations that give rise to a plausible inference of fraud. *Lusby,* 570 F.3d at 854.

Mamalakis lacked access to TeamHealth's billing records and thus has not identified specific false invoices. As we've just noted, however, that omission is not fatal to the claim. He has alleged that he has direct knowledge that anesthesiologists regularly falsely coded their procedures for billing purposes after TeamHealth took over the practice group. He provided some factual background about the change in approach to the delivery of anesthesia services under TeamHealth's ownership and the billing policies implemented by the new upper management. Among other things, he described: (1) statements Dr. Pease made at the 2010 orientation about the shift to the medical-direction billing rate; (2) her instruction to him that he should not micromanage the nurse anesthetists and instead let them create anesthesia plans; (3) her insistence that he not inform All Saints of his suspicions of fraudulent billing activity; and (4) her repeated direction that it was the policy of TeamHealth to bill all procedures as medically directed, whether or not a procedure met the requirements for that rate. He also described his attempt to bring his allegations of fraudulent billing to Dr. Gottlieb's attention, alleging that Dr. Gottlieb ran out of the room to avoid hearing more.

These generalized allegations that anesthesiologists engaged in fraudulent billing after the transition to TeamHealth's p.302 ownership are insufficient under Rule 9(b), even when read against the backdrop of the complaint's more particularized allegations about Dr. Pease and Dr. Gottlieb. We therefore cannot fault the magistrate judge for insisting that Mamalakis provide specific representative examples of fraudulent billing. But we disagree with the judge's conclusion that the examples in the latest version of the complaint fall short of the mark. Mamalakis provided ten specific examples in which an anesthesiologist failed to comply— sometimes egregiously— with the requirements to submit a bill at the medical-direction rate. He alleged that each procedure involved a patient insured by Medicare or Medicaid and that he knew that each procedure was billed to the government. For six procedures Mamalakis affirmatively alleged that the anesthesiologist billed at the medical-direction rate despite failing to comply with the requirements for that rate. These allegations are as follows:

- In June 2011 Dr. Lee billed three procedures as medically directed (one general-surgery procedure, one urology procedure, and one hysterectomy), but he left the hospital before noon and spent the afternoon waiting for a piano to be delivered. Mamalakis learned of this situation when Dr. Disque called him to say that he was already directing two procedures and could not direct all three of Dr. Lee's rooms without exceeding the four-procedure maximum required to qualify for the medical-direction rate.

- In spring 2010 Dr. Peters billed a hip replacement as medically directed, but she left the hospital after inducing anesthesia. Dr. Peters called Mamalakis from out of state and asked him to treat the patient's low blood pressure during the procedure.

- In fall 2010 Dr. Peters billed two procedures as medically directed while she was absent from All Saints. When Dr. Pease made a surprise visit, Mamalakis called Dr. Peters and told her to return immediately.

- In spring 2011 Dr. Stroupe billed a knee arthroscopy as medically directed. But when the patient experienced distress, the nurse anesthetist administering the procedure asked Mamalakis to come to the room. When he asked her why Dr. Stroupe wasn't there, she said that he was never present for a knee arthroscopy.

- In winter 2011 Dr. Stroupe billed a gynecological procedure as medically directed, but he was never present in the operating room, didn't prescribe the anesthesia plan, and didn't provide postoperative care. When the patient suffered distress after emerging from anesthesia, Dr. Stroupe was called. When he arrived at All Saints over 30 minutes later, he was wearing street clothes and then left without examining the patient, ordering studies, or prescribing any treatment. When the patient required further care, Mamalakis was called to assist. Nurse Anesthetist Fitzpatrick told Mamalakis that Dr. Stroupe had billed the procedure as medically directed despite several failures to comply with the requirements for medical direction.

• In fall 2010 Dr. Dean billed a cataract extraction as medically directed, but Nurse Anesthetist Fisher told Mamalakis that Dr. Dean never entered the operating room (even after complications), did not create the anesthesia plan, and did not perform the preanesthetic examination required for medical direction.

p.303 These examples are detailed, identifying specific doctors and procedures and describing why each procedure should not have been billed as medically directed. And Mamalakis alleged that he became personally involved in some of these procedures after a care provider asked him for assistance—in several cases entering the operating room itself.

The remaining four examples are similarly detailed, although Mamalakis did not include a specific allegation that the anesthesiologist in question billed for the services using the medical-direction code. For these four examples, he relied on his more generalized allegations about Team-Health's uniform policy of billing at the medical-direction rate.

Together, these representative examples provide a particularized basis from which to plausibly infer that at least on these occasions, TeamHealth presented false claims to the government. Mamalakis has injected enough precision and substantiation into his allegations of fraud to entitle him to move forward with his case.

Indeed, the allegations here are roughly analogous to the allegations of fraudulent Medicaid billing at issue in *Presser*. There the plaintiff alleged that a medical clinic submitted claims for payment to the government using billing codes corresponding to specific psychiatric services but in fact had performed only nonpsychiatric services. 836 F.3d at 778-79. As we summarized the allegations, the provider "billed Medicaid *for a completely different treatment*" and thus made an express false statement by "misus[ing] a billing code and falsely represent[ing] to the state and federal governments that a certain treatment was given by certain medical staff when in fact it was not." *Id.* at 779. We held that the plaintiff's allegations regarding up-coded billing were sufficient to satisfy the particularity requirement of Rule 9(b). *Id.* at 781.

The ten specific examples of TeamHealth anesthesiologists falsely billing at the medical-direction rate are likewise sufficient to lift the latest version of Mamalakis's complaint over Rule 9(b)'s pleading benchmark. The case may proceed, but it calls for carefully managed discovery to test whether it in fact has evidentiary support. If early managed discovery reveals that TeamHealth did not submit false claims on these occasions, then it can respond as appropriate. But Mamalakis has pleaded fraud with enough particularity to entitle him to move forward on his claim.

REVERSED AND REMANDED.

[*] The parties misspelled the defendant's name as "Anesthestix Management LLC" in the case caption. We use the correct spelling.

[1] Mamalakis alleges that TeamHealth's bills contained express false-hoods; he does not rely on a theory of implied false certification. *See Universal Health Servs., Inc. v. United States ex rel. Escobar,* 579 U.S. 176, 187, 136 S.Ct. 1989, 195 L.Ed.2d 348 (2016); *United States ex rel. Prose v. Molina Healthcare of Ill., Inc.,* 17 F.4th 732, 742 (7th Cir. 2021).

970 F.3d 835 (2020)

UNITED STATES of America ex rel. CIMZNHCA, LLC, Plaintiff-Appellee,
v.
UCB, INC., et al., Defendants,
Appeal of: United States of America, Appellant.

No. 19-2273.

United States Court of Appeals, Seventh Circuit.

Argued January 23, 2020.
Decided August 17, 2020.

US v. UCB, Inc., 970 F. 3d 835 (7th Cir. 2020)

Appeal from the United States District Court for the Southern District of Illinois, No. 3:17-cv-00765-SMY-MAB, Staci M. Yandle, *Judge*.

Melissa N. Patterson, Charles W. Scarborough, Attorneys, DEPARTMENT OF JUSTICE, Civil Division, Appellate Staff, Washington, DC, Nathan D. Stump, Attorney, OFFICE OF THE UNITED STATES ATTORNEY, Civil Division, Fairview Heights, IL, for Plaintiff-Appellant.

Julie Fix Meyer, Attorney, ARMSTRONG TEASDALE, St. Louis, MO, W. Jason Rankin, I, Attorney, HEPLER BROOM, LLC, Edwardsville, IL, for Defendants CVS HEALTH CORPORATION and OMNICARE, INCORPORATED.

Scott D. Stein, Attorney, SIDLEY AUSTIN LLP, Chicago, IL, for Defendants RXC ACQUISITION COMPANY and UCB, INC.

C. Lance Gould, Leslie Pescia, Attorneys, BEASLEY ALLEN, Montgomery, AL, for Appellee.

James F. Segroves, Attorney, REED SMITH LLP, Washington, DC, for Amicus Curiae.

Before Rovner, Hamilton, and Scudder, Circuit Judges.

p.838 Hamilton, Circuit Judge.

The False Claims Act allows the United States government to dismiss a relator's qui tam suit over the relator's objection with notice and opportunity for a hearing. 31 U.S.C. § 3730(c)(2)(A). The Act does not indicate how, if at all, the district court is to review the government's decision to dismiss. The D.C. Circuit has said not at all; the Ninth Circuit has said for a rational basis. Compare *Swift v. United States,* 318 F.3d 250 (D.C. Cir. 2003), with *United States ex rel. Sequoia Orange Co. v. Baird-Neece Packing Corp.,* 151 F.3d 1139 (9th Cir. 1998). In this case, the district court said it agreed with the Ninth Circuit but applied something closer to administrative law's "arbitrary and capricious" p.839 standard and denied dismissal. The government has appealed. The relator contends we should either dismiss for want of appellate jurisdiction or affirm.

We find that we have jurisdiction and reverse. First, we interpret the Act to require the government to intervene as a party before exercising its right to dismiss under § 3730(c)(2)(A). We think it best, however, to construe the government motion here as a motion to both intervene and dismiss. This solves the jurisdictional problem without needing to create a new category of collateral-order appeals. On the merits, we view the choice between the competing standards as a false one, based on a misunderstanding of the government's rights and obligations under the False Claims Act. And by treating the government as seeking to intervene, which it should have been allowed to do, we can apply a standard for dismissal informed by Federal Rule of Civil Procedure 41.

I. Factual and Procedural Background

In 1863, "a series of sensational congressional investigations" revealed that war-profiteering military contractors had billed the federal government for "nonexistent or worthless goods, charged exorbitant prices for goods delivered, and generally robbed" the government's procurement efforts. *United States v. McNinch,* 356 U.S. 595, 599, 78 S.Ct. 950, 2 L.Ed.2d 1001 (1958). In response, Congress passed the False Claims Act, now codified at 31 U.S.C. §§ 3729-3733. The Act authorizes a private person, called a relator, to enforce its terms by filing suit "for the person and for the United States Government." § 3730(b)(1). Suits of this type were once so common that "[a]lmost every" penal statute could be enforced by them. *Adams v. Woods,* 6 U.S. (2 Cranch) 336, 341, 2 L.Ed. 297 (1805). Such suits are called "qui tam" suits, from a Latin tag meaning, "who as well for the lord king as for himself sues in this matter." If the relator's qui tam action is successful, she receives a portion of the recovery as a bounty; the lion's share goes to the government. § 3730(d).

The False Claims Act prohibits, among other acts, presenting to the government "a false or fraudulent claim for payment or approval." § 3729(a)(1)(A). One way to present a false claim is to present to a federal healthcare program a claim for payment that violates the Anti-Kickback Statute, 42 U.S.C. § 1320a-7b(b), which prohibits giving or receiving "remuneration" in return for such programs' business. See 42 U.S.C. § 1320a-7b(g) (violations of the Anti-Kickback Statute also violate the False Claims Act). For a limited liability company called Venari Partners, doing business as the "National Health Care Analysis Group," this law presented a business opportunity.

Venari Partners has four members (Sweetbriar Capital, LLC; 101 Partners, LLC; Min-Fam-Holding, LLC; and Uptown Investors, LP), themselves composed of one or two individual investors, six in total. Venari Partners formed eleven daughter companies, each for the single purpose of prosecuting a separate qui tam action. All eleven actions allege essentially identical violations of the False Claims Act via the Anti-Kickback Statute by dozens of defendants in the pharmaceutical and related industries across the country.

The relator in this case is CIMZNHCA, LLC, one of those Venari companies. Its complaint, filed in 2017 in the Southern District of Illinois, alleges that defendants illegally paid physicians for prescribing or recommending Cimzia, a drug manufactured by defendant UCB, Inc. to treat Crohn's disease, to patients who received benefits under federal healthcare programs. p.840 The relator alleges that the illegal kickbacks took the form of free education services provided by nurses to physicians and their patients and free reimbursement support services, that is, assistance with insurance paperwork.

Once the relator filed this action, the government had the right "to intervene and proceed" as the plaintiff with the "primary responsibility" for prosecuting it. 31 U.S.C. §§ 3730(b)(2), 3730(c)(1). The government chose not to exercise that right. The False Claims Act also gives the government the right to dismiss the action over the relator's objection if the relator is provided notice and an opportunity for a hearing. § 3730(c)(2)(A). This right the government has sought to exercise. On December 17, 2018, the government filed a motion to dismiss, representing that it had investigated the Venari companies' claims, including CIMZNHCA's, and found them "to lack sufficient merit to justify the cost of investigation and prosecution and otherwise to be contrary to the public interest." The district court held a hearing on the government's motion and issued an opinion denying it.

The court considered first what standard of review applied to the government's motion under § 3730(c)(2)(A), which itself supplies none. The government urged adoption of the standard announced in *Swift v. United States,* 318 F.3d 250, 253 (D.C. Cir. 2003), which gives the government "unfettered" discretion to dismiss. Relator argued for the more demanding burden-shifting test announced in *United States ex rel. Sequoia Orange Co. v. Baird-Neece Packing Corp.,* 151 F.3d 1139 (9th Cir. 1998). Under that test, the government must first identify a "valid government purpose" and then show "a rational relation between dismissal and accomplishment of the purpose." *Id.* at 1145. If the government does so, the burden shifts to the relator to show that "dismissal is fraudulent, arbitrary and capricious, or illegal." *Id.*

Reasoning that Congress would not command the hollow ritual of convening a hearing on a preordained outcome (no one deliberates about the fall of Troy, as Aristotle said), the district court concluded that *Sequoia Orange* supplied the proper standard. Deeming the government's general evaluation of the Venari companies' claims to be insufficient as to CIMZNHCA in particular, and hearing notes of mere "animus towards the relator" in the government's arguments, the court concluded further that the government's decision to dismiss was "arbitrary and capricious" and "not rationally related to a valid governmental purpose."

After the district court denied its motion to reconsider, the government took this appeal, pending which the district court proceedings have been stayed. Our jurisdiction is contested. On the merits, the government argues that *Swift,* not *Sequoia Orange,* supplies the proper standard and that it satisfied the Ninth Circuit's test in any event. Relator argues that *Swift* should be rejected and that the district court correctly applied *Sequoia Orange.* We conclude first that we have jurisdiction and second that the choice presented to us on the merits is a false one, though the correct answer lies much nearer to *Swift* than *Sequoia Orange.* We reverse and remand with instructions to dismiss this action.

II. Analysis

A. The False Claims Act

We begin with an overview of the False Claims Act's most relevant provisions.[1] A p.841 qui tam action under the Act is brought "for the person and for the United States Government" and must be filed "in the name of the Government." 31 U.S.C. § 3730(b)(1). The relator may voluntarily dismiss the action "only if the court and the Attorney General give written consent to the dismissal and their reasons for consenting." *Id.*

The relator's complaint must be filed under seal and may not be served on the defendants until the court so orders. § 3730(b)(2). Upon filing, the relator must serve the government with a copy of the complaint and a "written disclosure of substantially all material evidence" in the relator's possession. *Id.* The government then has sixty days, *id.,* extendable for "good cause shown," § 3730(b)(3), to decide whether "to intervene and proceed with the action" while the complaint remains under seal. § 3730(b)(2). At the end of the seal period, "the Government shall (A) proceed with the action, in which case the action shall be conducted by the Government; or (B) notify the court that it declines to take over the action, in which case the person bringing the action shall have the right to conduct the action." § 3730(b)(4).

Before 1986, if the government intervened in the action, the relator's participation was at an end. In 1986, however, Congress amended the False Claims Act to allow for the relator's continued participation even after the government intervenes. Allowing two plaintiffs has given rise to a new set of tensions that the provisions at the heart of this case were designed to manage. See *Sequoia Orange,* 151 F.3d at 1143-44, citing *United States ex rel. Kelly v. Boeing Co.,* 9 F.3d 743, 745 (9th Cir. 1993), among others. "If the Government proceeds with the action," it assumes "primary responsibility" for prosecuting it. § 3730(c)(1). The relator retains "the right to continue as a party to the action," but critically for our purposes, that right is "subject to the limitations set forth in paragraph (2)." *Id.*

The most relevant of these limits is the government's right to dismiss the action:

> The Government may dismiss the action notwithstanding the objections of the person initiating the action if the person has been notified by the Government of the filing of the motion and the court has provided the person with an opportunity for a hearing on the motion.

§ 3730(c)(2)(A). The other limits are the government's right to settle the action "notwithstanding the objections of the person initiating the action if the court determines, after a hearing, that the proposed settlement is fair, adequate, and reasonable under all the circumstances," § 3730(c)(2)(B); the government's right to seek a court order restraining the relator's abusive litigation conduct, § 3730(c)(2)(C); and the defendant's right to do the same. § 3730(c)(2)(D).

"If the Government elects not to proceed with the action," the relator "shall have the right to conduct the action." § 3730(c)(3). The relator's sole obligations to the government thereafter are to supply it on request with copies of all pleadings and, at the government's expense, copies of all deposition transcripts. *Id.* The court may "nevertheless permit the Government to intervene at a later date upon a showing of good cause." *Id.* "Whether or not the Government proceeds with the action," the government may seek a stay of discovery if it would interfere with an ongoing investigation into the same facts. § 3730(c)(4). Finally, if the government elects to pursue "any alternate remedy" for the challenged conduct, the relator may not be cut out; she has "the same rights" in the alternate proceeding as in the qui tam action. § 3730(c)(5).

p.842 *B.* Appellate Jurisdiction: Appeal from the Denial of a Motion to Intervene

We must decide our jurisdiction first. *West v. Louisville Gas & Elec. Co.,* 920 F.3d 499, 503 (7th Cir. 2019). Ordinarily we have appellate jurisdiction of the district courts' final judgments under 28 U.S.C. § 1291 and a few categories of interlocutory orders under § 1292. Denials of motions to dismiss rarely fit into those categories, but the government argues here that the denial of its motion to dismiss under 31 U.S.C. § 3730(c)(2)(A) was a "collateral order," not a final judgment but by a "practical construction" of 28 U.S.C. § 1291 still a "final decision" within its terms. See *Ott v. City of Milwaukee,* 682 F.3d 552, 554 (7th Cir. 2012) (internal quotation marks omitted). We see no need to create a new category of appealable collateral orders. In substance, the government appeals a denial of what should be deemed a motion to intervene and then to dismiss. It is well established that denials of motions to intervene are appealable.

Collateral orders are orders that are final with respect to the issue they decide and important enough to be immediately appealable. *Mohawk Industries v. Carpenter,* 558 U.S. 100, 103, 130 S.Ct. 599, 175 L.Ed.2d 458 (2009), citing *Cohen v. Beneficial Indus. Loan Corp.,* 337 U.S. 541, 546, 69 S.Ct. 1221, 93 L.Ed. 1528 (1949). Protecting the default rule of one appeal per case, however, means that the universe of appealable collateral orders "must remain narrow and selective in its membership." *Mohawk Industries,* 558 U.S. at 113, 130 S.Ct. 599, quoted in *Ott,* 682 F.3d at 555. The question is not whether the particular order is collateral but whether "the entire category" of orders to which it belongs is. *JPMorgan Chase Bank, N.A. v. Asia Pulp & Paper Co.,* 707 F.3d 853, 868 (7th Cir. 2013), quoting *Mohawk,* 558 U.S. at 107, 130 S.Ct. 599.

This categorical analysis is difficult here because the type of order appealed here is very rare. In the history of the False Claims Act since 1986, the government tells us, only one other district court has denied its § 3730(c)(2)(A) motion to dismiss, which the Ninth Circuit recently declined to hold a collateral order.[2] The power of a non-party to force dismissal of another's lawsuit is otherwise unheard of in our law. See, e.g., Fed. R. Civ. P. 17(a)(3) (real party in interest must "ratify, join, or be substituted into" action brought on its behalf); *Minneapolis-Honeywell Regulator Co. v. Thermoco, Inc.,* 116 F.2d 845, 847 (2d Cir. 1941) (L. Hand, J.) ("[T]he companies could not make any motion unless they became parties ... although they might ... have combined a motion to intervene with a motion to dismiss.").

1. Eisenstein, Footnote 2

The government argues that the jurisdictional issue has already been resolved in its favor by *United States ex rel. Eisenstein v. City of New York,* 556 U.S. p.843 928, 129

S.Ct. 2230, 173 L.Ed.2d 1255 (2009), the Supreme Court's most recent word on the relationship between the relator and the government in a qui tam case in which the government has declined to intervene. The holding of *Eisenstein* is that, absent intervention, the government is not a "party" for the purpose of determining applicable appeal deadlines. 556 U.S. at 937, 129 S.Ct. 2230; see 28 U.S.C. § 2107(b) (deadline where United States is "party"); Fed. R. App. P. 4(a)(1)(B) (same). Along the way, the Court observed that, the government's non-party status notwithstanding, it need not intervene to appeal "any order" in a qui tam suit. 556 U.S. at 931 n.2, 129 S.Ct. 2230. Rather, its immediate appeal would lie from the relator's voluntary dismissal of the case without the government's written consent. *Id.,* citing 31 U.S.C. § 3730(b)(1). And denials of motions to intervene have long been held immediately appealable. *Id.,* citing § 3730(c)(3).

The government maintains there is "no basis for distinguishing" *Eisenstein*'s examples from an order *denying* a motion to a dismiss under § 3730(c)(2)(A). But the bases are obvious: voluntary dismissal ends the case, and the immediate appealability of a denial of intervention is even older than the collateral-order doctrine announced in *Cohen.* See *Brotherhood of R.R. Trainmen v. Baltimore & Ohio R.R. Co.,* 331 U.S. 519, 524-25, 67 S.Ct. 1387, 91 L.Ed. 1646 (1947). Footnote 2 of *Eisenstein* does not stand for the proposition stated by the government. It nonetheless indicates the correct path to solving the jurisdictional problem: treat the government's motion to dismiss as a motion both to intervene and to dismiss.

2. Intervention in Substance

An intervenor comes between the original parties to ongoing litigation and interposes between them its claim, interest, or right, which may be adverse to either or both of them. See *Eisenstein,* 556 U.S. at 933, 129 S.Ct. 2230; *Rocca v. Thompson,* 223 U.S. 317, 330-31, 32 S.Ct. 207, 56 L.Ed. 453 (1912). That is exactly what the government wants to do here. The government claims a superior right to dispose of this lawsuit between the relator and the defendants by ending it on terms it deems suitable. The relator holds the present statutory right "to conduct the action," 31 U.S.C. § 3730(b)(4)(B), as well as a partial congressional assignment of any resulting damages, *Vermont Agency of Nat. Res. v. United States ex rel. Stevens,* 529 U.S. 765, 773, 120 S.Ct. 1858, 146 L.Ed.2d 836 (2000), both of which the government asserts the right to nullify. The defendants, as their pending motions to dismiss reveal, desire the finality of a dismissal with prejudice. The government asserts the right to deny defendants that finality by having the action dismissed with prejudice as to the relator but without prejudice as to it. In sum, the government wants a say—the final say—in conducting this lawsuit. The district court's order denying that wish is in substance an order denying a motion to intervene.

3. Intervention in Form

There is another reason to construe for jurisdictional purposes the government's motion to dismiss as a motion to intervene and dismiss: it ought to have been filed that way to begin with. Cf. *Swift v. United States,* 318 F.3d 250, 252 (D.C. Cir. 2003) (if government were required to intervene before dismissing, "we could construe the government's motion to dismiss as including a motion to intervene").

As a matter of form, the government did not move to intervene before filing its motion to dismiss under § 3730(c)(2)(A). Several courts of appeals have expressly or p.844 tacitly endorsed its prerogative not to do so. *Chang v. Children's Advocacy Ctr. of Del.,* 938 F.3d 384, 386 (3d Cir. 2019); *Ridenour v. Kaiser-Hill Co.,* 397 F.3d 925, 933-34 (10th Cir. 2005); *Swift,* 318 F.3d at 251-52; *United States ex rel. Kelly v. Boeing Co.,* 9 F.3d 743, 753 n.10 (9th Cir. 1993); see also *United States v. Everglades Coll., Inc.,* 855 F.3d 1279, 1285-86 (11th Cir. 2017) (settlements under § 3730(c)(2)(B)). These decisions did not address appeals of denials of dismissal, but adhering to them in this case of a denial would require in effect creation of a new category of appealable collateral orders. The Supreme Court has firmly discouraged that step. See *Mohawk,* 558 U.S. at 113-14, 130 S.Ct. 599.

There is a better solution. We read the False Claims Act as requiring the government to intervene before exercising any right under § 3730(c)(2). Accord, *United States ex rel. Poteet v. Medtronic, Inc.,* 552 F.3d 503, 519 (6th Cir. 2009) ("Section 3730(c)(2)(A) applies only when the government has decided to 'proceed[ ] with the action' and has assumed 'primary responsibility for prosecuting the action.'").

a. Text and Structure of § 3730(c)

To explain our solution of the jurisdictional problem, we begin with the statute's text. E.g., *Ross v. Blake,* ___ U.S. ___, 136 S. Ct. 1850, 1856, 195 L.Ed.2d 117 (2016). Subsection (c) of § 3730 bears the heading, "Rights of the parties to qui tam actions." One would thus expect subsection (c) to treat the rights of *parties* to qui tam actions, which the government is not unless and until "it intervenes in accordance with the procedures established by federal law." *Eisenstein,* 556 U.S. at 933, 129 S.Ct. 2230. In fact, the structure of subsection (c) guides its proper interpretation as to which rights litigants possess under which procedural circumstances. See *Ortega v. Holder,* 592 F.3d 738, 743 (7th Cir. 2010) ("we must consider not only the words of the statute, but also the statute's structure."). Each paragraph of subsection (c)—except paragraph (2)—announces at its outset the procedural posture to which it applies. Paragraph (1) applies "If the Government proceeds with the action." Paragraph (3) applies "If the Government elects not to proceed with the action." Paragraph (4) applies "Whether or not the Government proceeds with the action." Paragraph (5) applies "Notwithstanding subsection (b)," that is, notwithstanding the relator's qui tam action altogether. Where, then, does paragraph (2) fit into this structure?

Nowhere, the D.C. Circuit answered in *Swift.* According to *Swift,* paragraph (2) is entirely free-floating; it is not "constrained by" and operates "independent[ly] of" the rest of subsection (c), including specifically paragraph (1). 318 F.3d at 252. There are several reasons to question this reading. First, it makes surplusage of paragraph (4)'s introductory phrase, "Whether or not the Government proceeds with the action." But see, e.g., *Reiter v. Sonotone Corp.,* 442 U.S. 330, 339, 99 S.Ct. 2326, 60 L.Ed.2d 931 (1979) (anti-surplusage canon); see also Antonin Scalia & Bryan A. Garner, *Reading Law* 156 (2012) ("Material within an indented subpart relates only to that subpart."). If the background assumption of subsection (c) were that each of its paragraphs applied no matter whether the government had intervened, Congress would not have specified that paragraph (4), and only paragraph (4), applies "Whether or not the Government proceeds with the action."

The *Swift* analysis also makes surplusage of the provision in paragraph (1) that a post-intervention relator has the right to continue as a party "subject to the limitations set forth in paragraph (2)." Again, if p.845 the government enjoyed its rights under paragraph (2) under all circumstances and in any posture, there would have been no reason to specify that the relator's continued participation as a party, and only the relator's continued participation as a party, is "subject to" paragraph (2).

Along these lines, § 3730(b)(4)(B) gives the relator "the right to conduct the action" —without qualification—when the government has declined to intervene. That phrase is picked up by paragraph (c)(3), which provides that, "If the Government elects not to proceed with the action," the relator "shall have the right to conduct the action," while reserving certain rights (to be served with copies of certain papers, to intervene later for good cause) to the government. Thus, when Congress wanted to qualify the relator's "right to conduct the action" absent intervention, it did so in paragraph (c)(3). It would be odd if the unqualified "right to conduct the action" in subparagraph (b)(4)(B) and the nearly unqualified "right to conduct the action" in paragraph (c)(3) were in fact the profoundly qualified right to conduct the action so long as the government does not wish to have it dismissed or settled under subparagraphs (c)(2)(A) or (B)—neither of which even mentions the relator's "right to conduct the action."

So where does paragraph (2) best fit in? The second half of the paragraph plainly operates against the backdrop of government intervention. Specifically, subparagraph (C) provides for "limitations" on the relator's participation where its "unrestricted participation ... would interfere with or unduly delay *the Government's prosecution* of the case." (Emphasis added.) Similarly, subparagraph (D) provides that the relator's "participation" may be "limit[ed]" where its "unrestricted participation" would harass or unduly burden the defendant. Obviously a defendant cannot "restrict the participation" of its sole adversary in a lawsuit. We find subparagraph (D) even more telling than subparagraph (C) for our purposes because subparagraph (C) makes the government's participation explicit while subparagraph (D) tacitly assumes it—suggesting that so too does the rest of paragraph (2).

We conclude that paragraph (2) fits in best right where paragraph (1) puts it: as a limit on the right of the relator to continue as a party after the government has intervened. It can have no other independent operation without disrupting the structure of the statute as a whole. *Swift* reasoned that, to justify this reading, "either § 3730(c)(2) would have to be a subsection of § 3730(c)(1)—which it is not—or § 3730(c)(2) would have to contain language stating that it is applicable only in the context of § 3730(c)(1)—which it does not." 318 F.3d at 252. The first minor premise, that paragraph (c)(2) is not a subsection of paragraph (c)(1), is true as a typographic matter but otherwise fails to capture how the five paragraphs of subsection (c) relate to one another in text and logic. As our premises differ, so too does our conclusion: paragraph (c)(2) is better read to operate only "If the Government proceeds with the action." § 3730(c)(1).

The remaining arguments advanced by *Swift* and cases adopting its reading against a need for intervention to dismiss are not persuasive. First, *Swift* neutered the binary choice put to the government by Congress—intervene, § 3730(b)(4)(A), or decline, § 3730(b)(4)(B)—by finding a third way to dismiss without intervention under § 3730(c)(2)(A). From the provision that the government "may elect to intervene *and proceed* with the action," § 3730(b)(2), the court reasoned that "[e]nding the case by dismissing it is not proceeding with the action; to 'proceed with the action' means ... that the case p.846 will go forward with the government running the litigation." 318 F.3d at 251. Accord, *Everglades Coll., Inc.,* 855 F.3d at 1285 (settlement under § 3730(c)(2)(B)); *Ridenour,* 397 F.3d at 933.

In our view, this awkward reading of the provision is not the better reading. "Proceeding" in the litigation context is chiefly defined as "the regular and orderly progression of a lawsuit." *Proceeding,* Black's Law Dictionary 600 (4th pocket ed. 2011). We find no support in *Swift* or elsewhere for the proposition that the regular and orderly progression of a lawsuit requires litigating to favorable judgment or involuntary dismissal, to the exclusion of voluntary dismissal, particularly upon settlement. If "proceed" were understood that way, how much litigating would the government have to do before it could then dismiss without running afoul of the command to "proceed"? This reading of "proceed" suggests further that "electing not to proceed" would include electing to dismiss voluntarily. That cannot be right because paragraph (c)(3) gives the relator "the right to conduct the action" where "the Government elects not to proceed with the action." One cannot "conduct" a lawsuit that has been dismissed.

b. Serious Constitutional Doubts?

Second, the Tenth Circuit in *Ridenour,* invoking the Take Care Clause of Article II, § 3, and the constitutional-doubt canon of statutory interpretation, see *Zadvydas v. Davis,* 533 U.S. 678, 689, 121 S.Ct. 2491, 150 L.Ed.2d 653 (2001), rejected the reading we adopt here in part because "to condition the Government's right ... to dismiss an action in which it did not initially intervene upon a requirement of ... good cause [under § 3730(c)(3)] would place the FCA on constitutionally unsteady ground" by "unnecessarily bind[ing] the Government." 397 F.3d at 934; see also *Kelly,* 9 F.3d at 753 n.10 (because statute does not "prohibit[ ]" it, interpretation allowing dismissal without intervention is "entirely appropriate" as illustration of "meaningful [executive] control" over relators' FCA suits). Respectfully, we do not find constitutional doubt a sound reason to follow this path.

The canon of constitutional doubt teaches that when two interpretations of a statute are "fairly possible," one of which raises a "serious doubt" as to the statute's constitutionality and the other does not, a court should choose the interpretation "by which the question may be avoided." *Zadvydas,* 533 U.S. at 689, 121 S.Ct. 2491; see *United States ex rel. Att'y General v. Del. & Hudson Co.,* 213 U.S. 366, 407-08, 29 S.Ct. 527, 53 L.Ed. 836 (1909). The canon does *not* hold that any reading of a statute not expressly "prohibited" must be adopted if it will relieve the executive of any burden of undefined weight which the judiciary deems without analysis to be "unnecessary." But that is how the canon was applied in *Ridenour* and *Kelly.* In our view, this analysis is misguided for two reasons. First, it indulges every presumption in favor of the statute's invalidity rather than its validity. Second, it simply does not show that the False Claims Act is in serious danger of unconstitutionality unless dismissal under § 3730(c)(2)(A) applies only after the government has declined to intervene.

First, *Ridenour* and *Kelly* inverted the constitutional-doubt canon, and constitutional avoidance principles generally, by creating constitutional problems in one section of a statute to solve them in a different section of the statute. "Good cause" is a uniquely flexible and capacious concept. See *Good Cause,* s.v. *Cause,* Black's Law Dictionary 101 (4th pocket ed. 2011) ("A legally sufficient reason."). But neither *Ridenour* nor *Kelly* offered p.847 an interpretation of what constitutes "good cause" under § 3730(c)(3). Neither acknowledged the variety of situations calling for that decision.[3] Both assumed without analysis that any "good cause" requirement would tend to fetter the executive unconstitutionally—neglecting, at minimum, the possibility that avoiding offense to the separation of powers in a case that actually risks it would itself weigh heavily in any "good cause" determination.

Both decisions thus defaulted to the most constitutionally offensive reading of § 3730(c)(3) rather than the least. Both thereby created rather than avoided doubtful questions of constitutional law, which then required "solving" by doubtful interpretation of § 3730(c)(2)(A). Our duty, though, is to indulge "[e]very presumption... in favor of the validity of the statute." *Graves v. Minnesota,* 272 U.S. 425, 428, 47 S.Ct. 122, 71 L.Ed. 331 (1926). Our reading of § 3730(c)(2)(A), by contrast, presumes § 3730(c)(3) is valid on its face and simply defers consideration of genuine constitutional concerns until they ripen in a specific context and are thus more properly presented for decision. See *Ashwander v. T.V.A.,* 297 U.S. 288, 347, 56 S.Ct. 466, 80 L.Ed. 688 (1936) (Brandeis, J., concurring).

Second, because neither *Ridenour* nor *Kelly* offered an account of what "good cause" requires nor of what Article II requires in relation to "good cause" dismissals, neither decision raises a serious possibility that the constitutionality under Article II of the False Claims Act depends on a particular construction of § 3730(c)(2)(A). As a general matter, the Supreme Court has reserved decision on the constitutionality under Article II of qui tam actions. *Vermont Agency of Nat. Res. v. United States ex rel. Stevens,* 529 U.S. 765, 778 n.8, 120 S.Ct. 1858, 146 L.Ed.2d 836 (2000). Their ancient pedigree, however, together with their widespread use at the time of the Founding, suggests that the False Claims Act as a whole is not in imminent danger of unconstitutionally usurping the executive power. See *id.* at 774-77, 120 S.Ct. 1858 ("originated around the end of the 13th century"); *Marvin v. Trout,* 199 U.S. 212, 225, 26 S.Ct. 31, 50 L.Ed. 157 (1905) ("in existence for hundreds of years in England, and in this country ever since the foundation of our government"); *Adams v. Woods,* 6 U.S. (2 Cranch) 336, 341, 2 L.Ed. 297 (1805) (Marshall, C.J.) ("Almost every fine or forfeiture under a penal statute, may be recovered by an action of debt [qui tam]."); 3 William Blackstone, Commentaries *160 (Forfeitures created by penal statutes "more usually are given at large, to any common informer; or ... to the people in general .... [I]f any one hath begun a *qui tam,* or *popular,* action, no other person can pursue it; and the verdict passed upon the defendant ... is... conclusive even to the king himself."). Indeed, a common function of qui tam actions, and one of the earliest, has been to regulate the exercise of executive power itself. Randy Beck, *Qui Tam Litigation Against Government Officials,* 93 Notre Dame L. Rev. 1235, 1260-61 (2018) p.848 (discussing Statute of York 1318, 12 Edw. 2); *id.* at 1269-1304 (early American use of such qui tam actions).

While reserving decision on the Article II consequences, as a matter of statutory interpretation, *Stevens* rejected an agency theory of the government-relator relationship under the False Claims Act: "to say that the relator here is simply the statutorily designated agent of the United States, in whose name ... the suit is brought

... is precluded ... by the fact that the statute gives the relator himself an interest *in the lawsuit.*" 529 U.S. at 772, 120 S.Ct. 1858 (some emphasis omitted). That interest is reflected in the rights retained by the relator even after the government has intervened. *Id.*, citing § 3730(c)(1), (c)(2)(A), & (c)(2)(B). It is reflected as well in "the right to conduct the action" that indisputably belongs to the relator once the government declines to intervene and can be wrested from the relator later only on a showing of good cause. § 3730(b)(4)(B) & (c)(3). That right includes, for example, the right to choose which claims to pursue, the right to engage the machinery of discovery, and the right to settle claims without government oversight (excepting the government's veto power under § 3730(b)(1) if the settlement is entered as a voluntary dismissal, though it need not be).

We are not persuaded that a serious marginal risk of unconstitutionality is created by including dismissal in the list of powers reclaimable by the government only for good cause. The power to terminate the action is simply part of the power "to conduct the action." See Fed. R. Civ. P. 41(a); see also *Kelly,* 9 F.3d at 754 & n.14 ("[O]nce prosecution has been initiated, the government has greater authority to ... ultimately *end* the litigation in a qui tam action than it does in an independent counsel's action;" true no matter whether § 3730(c)(2)(A) requires intervention), applying *Morrison v. Olson,* 487 U.S. 654, 108 S.Ct. 2597, 101 L.Ed.2d 569 (1988). The government's automatic intervention rights during the seal period are themselves extendable only for "good cause," § 3730(b)(3), and even in criminal cases, the government must have "leave of court" to dismiss the prosecution. Fed. R. Crim. P. 48(a); *Rinaldi v. United States,* 434 U.S. 22, 29-32, 98 S.Ct. 81, 54 L.Ed.2d 207 (1977). Accordingly, we do not see a serious possibility that the constitutionality of the False Claims Act will stand or fall on a requirement that the government show good cause to intervene and dismiss after its automatic intervention rights have expired.

We have warned before that the constitutional-doubt canon "must be used with care, for it is a closer cousin to invalidation than to interpretation. It is a way to enforce the constitutional penumbra." *United States v. Marshall,* 908 F.2d 1312, 1318 (7th Cir. 1990) (en banc); see also Richard A. Posner, *The Federal Courts* 285 (1985) (The canon "enlarge[s] the ... reach of constitutional prohibition ... to create a... 'penumbra' that has much the same prohibitory effect as the ... Constitution itself.").

The application of the canon in *Ridenour* and *Kelly* illustrates this warning. The canon can produce a hazy penumbra of quasi-constitutional law that is used to limit legislative power when statutes are construed, without constitutional adjudication of a concrete case or controversy, to exclude all "unnecessar[y]" executive restrictions and to require all "entirely appropriate" executive prerogatives. See *Ridenour,* 397 F.3d at 934; *Kelly,* 9 F.3d at 753 n.10.

Our task is not to chip away at the legislation under the guise of interpreting p.849 it until every conceivable constitutional concern is assuaged. See *Salinas v. United States,* 522 U.S. 52, 59-60, 118 S.Ct. 469, 139 L.Ed.2d 352 (1997), citing among others *United States v. Albertini,* 472 U.S. 675, 680, 105 S.Ct. 2897, 86 L.Ed.2d 536 (1985). Our task is to apply the Act until a party with standing convinces us or the Supreme Court that to do so would be unconstitutional. The constitutional-doubt canon can be used to resolve genuine doubts when the language is ambiguous and the constitutional danger clear and present. *Marshall,* 908 F.2d at 1318. It should not be used where, as here, the constitutional questions are more dubious than the statutory text. Statutory clarity should not yield to penumbral obscurity.

In sum, we treat the government's motion to dismiss as a motion both to intervene and then to dismiss under § 3730(c)(3) because intervention was in substance what the government sought and in form what the False Claims Act requires. Cf. *Swift,* 318 F.3d at 252 ("[I]f there were such a requirement, we could construe the government's motion to dismiss as including a motion to intervene."). The Supreme Court in *Eisenstein* could not "disregard" the "congressional assignment of discretion" to the government to intervene under the Act by treating the government as a party "even after it has declined to assume the rights and burdens attendant to full party status." 556 U.S. at 933-34, 129 S.Ct. 2230. Neither will we. The government cannot eat its cake and have it too. If the government wishes to control the action as a party, it must intervene as a party, as provided for by Congress.

Having concluded that the government's case for dismissal was not even rational, the district court here has necessarily expressed its view on the government's lack of "good cause" to intervene under the Act. Accordingly, we have jurisdiction over the appeal of what amounted to an order denying a motion to intervene. E.g., *Planned Parenthood of Wis., Inc. v. Kaul,* 942 F.3d 793, 796-97 (7th Cir. 2019). We may proceed to the merits.

C. Merits: The Government Was Entitled to Dismissal

Treating the government as having sought to intervene solves the jurisdictional problem and offers a standard on the merits of dismissal, in the absence of a specific standard in 31 U.S.C. § 3730(c)(2)(A). The standard is that provided by the Federal Rules of Civil Procedure, as limited by any more specific provision of the False Claims Act and any applicable background constraints on executive conduct in general. In this case, no such substantive limits apply, so the Rules are the beginning and the end of our analysis.

Federal Rule of Civil Procedure 41(a)(1)(A)(i) provides that "the plaintiff may dismiss an action" by serving a notice of dismissal any time "before the opposing party serves either an answer or a motion for summary judgment." Dismissal is without prejudice unless the notice states otherwise. Fed. R. Civ. P. 41(a)(1)(B). This right is "absolute." *Marques v. Federal Reserve Bank of Chi.,* 286 F.3d 1014, 1017 (7th Cir. 2002). "[O]ne doesn't need a good reason, or even a sane or any reason" to serve notice under the Rule, *id.,* and the notice is self-executing and case-terminating. *Id.* at 1018; *Smith v. Potter,* 513 F.3d 781, 782-83 (7th Cir. 2008). In other words, once a valid Rule 41(a) notice has been served, "the case [is] gone; no action remain[s] for the district judge to take," and her further orders are void. *Smith,* 513 F.3d at 782-83. Here, the government filed its "motion to dismiss" before the defendants had answered or p.850 moved for summary judgment, seeking dismissal without prejudice as to it and with prejudice as to the relator. It does not matter that the paper was labeled a "motion" rather than a "notice." *Id.* at 782. That looks like the end of the case, on terms of the government's choosing.

Actually, that was *almost* the end of the case because the provisions of Rule 41(a) are "[s]ubject to ... any applicable federal statute." Fed. R. Civ. P. 41(a)(1)(A). By itself, Rule 41(a) provides that "the plaintiff may dismiss an action," *id.,* which obviously does not authorize an intervenor-plaintiff to effect involuntary dismissal of the original plaintiff's claims. See *Washington Elec. Coop., Inc. v. Mass. Mun. Wholesale Elec. Co.,* 922 F.2d 92, 97 (2d Cir. 1990). But § 3730(c)(2)(A) provides otherwise. Picking up the language of Rule 41, the statute provides: "The Government may dismiss the action" without the relator's consent if the relator receives notice and opportunity to be heard. § 3730(c)(2)(A). This procedural limit is the only authorized statutory deviation from Rule 41. Cf. § 3730(c)(2)(B) (authorizing settlement without relator's consent only "if the court determines, after a hearing, that the proposed settlement is fair, adequate, and reasonable under all the circumstances"). Nor, because § 3730(c)(2)(A) twice refers to the government's "motion," should the statute be construed to eliminate the right to dismiss under the first half of Rule 41(a), whose language it mirrors. See *Adams v. Woods,* 6 U.S. (2 Cranch) 336, 337, 341, 2 L.Ed. 297 (1805) (Marshall, C.J.) (where statute of limitations provided that no person shall be "*prosecuted, tried or punished* ... for *any* fine or forfeiture ..., unless the *indictment or information*" was filed within two years, statute was construed to bar actions of debt qui tam: otherwise "a distinct member of the sentence ... would be rendered almost totally useless"). Here, the relator received notice and took its opportunity to be heard. Once these had been accomplished, that should have been the end of the case.

This conclusion may seem counterintuitive. The law does not require the doing of a useless thing. *Mashi v. I.N.S.,* 585 F.2d 1309, 1314 (5th Cir. 1978). What, then, is the purpose of the statute's additional process if the government's litigation right is absolute and there is no substantive standard to apply? Congress sometimes demands that parties to a nascent legal dispute simply "communicate in some way" to attempt to resolve the dispute without court action, and there the judicial role is confined to ensuring that the communication has in fact taken place on the terms specified by statute. *Mach Mining, LLC v. E.E.O.C.,* 575 U.S. 480, 494, 135 S.Ct. 1645, 191 L.Ed.2d 607 (2015) (Title VII conciliation); cf. Fed. R. Civ. P. 26(c)(1) (parties must confer or attempt to confer before seeking court order on discovery dispute); Fed. R. Civ. P. 37(a)(1) (same). In such cases, however, the court is not called upon to serve as a mere convening authority— "and perhaps," as the district judge put it here, "serve you some donuts and coffee" —while the parties carry on an essentially private conversation in its presence. Like the district court, we find unpersuasive *Swift*'s suggestion that "the function of a hearing when the relator requests one is simply to give the relator a formal opportunity to convince the government not to end the case." 318 F.3d at 253.

Not every case, though, will be like this one. For example, if the conditions of Rule 41(a)(1) do not apply, "an action may be dismissed at the plaintiff's request only by court order, on terms that the court considers proper." Fed. R. Civ. P. 41(a)(2). Thus, if the government's chance to serve notice of dismissal has passed, see Fed. R. p.851 Civ. P. 41(a)(1)(A)(i), and the relator by hypothesis refuses to agree to dismissal, see Fed. R. Civ. P. 41(a)(1)(A)(ii), then a hearing under § 3730(c)(2)(A) could serve to air what terms of dismissal are "proper." Cf. *Swift,* 318 F.3d at 252-53.

Further, there are always background constraints on executive action, even in the quasi-prosecutorial context of qui tam actions and the decisions to dismiss them. *Heckler v. Chaney,* 470 U.S. 821, 105 S.Ct. 1649, 84 L.Ed.2d 714 (1985), cited by the government here, is not to the contrary. *Heckler* held that an administrative agency's decision not to take certain "investigatory and enforcement actions" had been "committed to agency discretion by law" and was thus not subject to judicial review under the Administrative Procedure Act. 470 U.S. at 824, 838, 105 S.Ct. 1649; see 5 U.S.C. § 701(a)(2).

Heckler is an imperfect fit for the False Claims Act because the Court relied in part on the fact that "when an agency refuses to act it generally does not exercise its coercive power over an individual's liberty or property rights." 470 U.S. at 832, 105 S.Ct. 1649 (emphasis omitted). That is not the case when the government dismisses a relator's action under the False Claims Act because "the statute gives the relator himself an interest *in the lawsuit*" as well as a partial assignment of the government's damages. *Vermont Agency of Nat. Res. v. United States ex rel. Stevens,* 529 U.S. 765, 772, 773, 120 S.Ct. 1858, 146 L.Ed.2d 836 (2000); cf. *Logan v. Zimmerman Brush Co.,* 455 U.S. 422, 428-430, 102 S.Ct. 1148, 71 L.Ed.2d 265 (1982) (Due Process Clause protects causes of action); *id.* at 438, 102 S.Ct. 1148 (Blackmun, J., concurring for four Justices) (same for Equal Protection Clause).

More important, *Heckler* reserved decision on what result would follow if there were a "colorable claim ... that the agency's refusal to institute proceedings violated any constitutional rights" of the plaintiffs. 470 U.S. at 838, 105 S.Ct. 1649. Its accompanying citation to *Yick Wo v. Hopkins* suggests the limits of executive nonenforcement decisions:

> [E]nforcing these notices may ... bring ruin to ... those against whom they are directed, while others, from whom they are withheld, may be actually benefited by what is thus done to their neighbors; and, when we remember that this action of non-action may proceed from enmity or prejudice, from partisan zeal or animosity, from favoritism and other improper influences ..., it becomes unnecessary to suggest ... the injustice capable of being wrought.

118 U.S. 356, 373, 6 S.Ct. 1064, 30 L.Ed. 220 (1886); see *Heckler,* 470 U.S. at 839, 105 S.Ct. 1649 (Brennan, J., concurring) ("It is possible to imagine other nonenforcement decisions made for entirely illegitimate reasons, for example, ... in return for a bribe.").

In this light, *Sequoia Orange* may be read to hold no more than that the government's § 3730(c)(2)(A) dismissal may not violate the substantive component of the Due Process Clause. Demanding "no greater justification ... than is mandated by the Constitution itself," *Sequoia Orange* equated its rational-relation test to the test used to determine "whether executive action violates substantive due process." 151 F.3d at 1145, 1146. *Swift* rejected as contrary to *Heckler* the *Sequoia Orange* point that "arbitrary or irrational" decisions not to prosecute could violate due process, 318 F.3d at 253, but *Heckler* does not warrant such a strong statement. See *Yick Wo,* 118 U.S. at 370, 6 S.Ct. 1064 (no room "for the play and action of purely personal and arbitrary power"). In arguing a similar p.852 case before the Ninth Circuit,[4] the government suggested that its § 3730(c)(2)(A) dismissal may not violate the Equal Protection Clause. See *Oyler v. Boles,* 368 U.S. 448, 456, 82 S.Ct. 501, 7 L.Ed.2d 446 (1962). Before this court, the government suggested, and even *Swift* entertained the possibility of, review for fraud on the court. See 318 F.3d at 253. We agree in principle with both suggestions, though we hope that these generous limits would be breached rarely if ever. We say only that in exceptional cases they could supply grist for the hearing under § 3730(c)(2)(A).

Not in this case, though. Wherever the limits of the government's power lie, this case is not close to them. At bottom, the district court faulted the government for having failed to make a particularized dollar-figure estimate of the potential costs and benefits of CIMZNHCA's lawsuit, as opposed to the more general review of the Venari companies' activities undertaken and described by the government. No constitutional or statutory directive imposes such a requirement. None is found in the False Claims Act. The government is not required to justify its litigation decisions in this way, as though it had to show "reasoned decisionmaking" as a matter of administrative law, as in, for example, *Motor Vehicle Mfrs. Ass'n v. State Farm Mut. Auto. Ins. Co.,* 463 U.S. 29, 51-52, 103 S.Ct. 2856, 77 L.Ed.2d 443 (1983).

We must disagree with the suggestion that the government's decision here fell short of the bare rationality standard borrowed by *Sequoia Orange* from substantive due process cases. "[T]he Due Process Clause was intended to prevent government officials from abusing their power, or employing it as an instrument of oppression," and "only the most egregious official conduct can be said to be arbitrary in the constitutional sense." *County of Sacramento v. Lewis,* 523 U.S. 833, 846, 118 S.Ct. 1708, 140 L.Ed.2d 1043 (1998) (internal quotation marks and alterations omitted); see also *Yick Wo,* 118 U.S. at 369-70, 6 S.Ct. 1064 ("[O]ur institutions of government... do not mean to leave room for the play and action of purely personal and arbitrary power."). Executive action is not due process of law when it "shocks the conscience;" when it "offend[s] even hardened sensibilities;" or when it is "too close to the rack and the screw to permit of constitutional differentiation." *Rochin v. California,* 342 U.S. 165, 172, 72 S.Ct. 205, 96 L.Ed. 183 (1952).

The government proposed to terminate this suit in part because, across nine cited agency guidances, advisory opinions, and final rulemakings, it has consistently held that the conduct complained of is probably lawful. Not only lawful, but beneficial to patients and the public. As the government argued in the district court, "These relators" —created as investment vehicles for financial speculators—"should not be permitted to indiscriminately advance claims on behalf of the government against an entire industry that would undermine ... practices the federal government has determined are ... appropriate and beneficial to federal healthcare programs and their beneficiaries." This is not government irrationality. It oppresses no one and shocks no one's conscience.[5]

p.853 Accordingly, where the government's conduct does not bump up against the Rules, the statute, or the Constitution, the notice and hearing under § 3730(c)(2)(A) serve no great purpose. But that will not be true in every case. Our reading of § 3730(c)(2)(A) does not render its process futile as a general matter. Rather, this particular relator simply had no substantive case to make at the hearing to which the statute entitled it. Whenever a party has the right to invoke the court's aid, it has the obligation to do so with at least a non-frivolous expectation of relief under the governing substantive law. Fed. R. Civ. P. 11(b). That is not always possible, but that does not make the right meaningless.

In any event, the danger that the § 3730(c)(2)(A) hearing may often serve little purpose does not justify imposing on the government in each case the burden of satisfying *Sequoia Orange*'s "two-step test" before the burden is put back on the relator to show unlawful executive conduct. 151 F.3d at 1145; cf. *United States v. Armstrong,* 517 U.S. 456, 464, 116 S.Ct. 1480, 134 L.Ed.2d 687 (1996) ("in the absence of clear evidence to the contrary," courts presume regularity of prosecutorial decision-making). Nor does a Senate report on an unenacted version of the 1986 amendments frame a proper standard for § 3730(c)(2)(A) dismissals where Congress itself has supplied none in the enacted statute. See *Swift,* 318 F.3d at 253, discussing S. Rep. No. 99-345, at 26 (1986). If Congress wishes to require some extra-constitutional minimum of fairness, reasonableness, or adequacy of the government's decision under § 3730(c)(2)(A), it will need to say so. See § 3730(c)(2)(B).

Two final matters relating to § 3730(c)(3). First, because we have construed the government's motion to dismiss as a motion to intervene and dismiss for both jurisdictional and merits purposes, it might be thought proper to remand the case for the district court to consider the government's "good cause" to intervene under § 3730(c)(3). We see no need for a further hearing here because the proper outcome is clear. In light of the government's unrestricted substantive right under Rule 41(a) and the absence of countervailing factors, such as fairness to the relator or conservation of judicial resources (likely not factors in any case at an early enough stage for Rule 41(a)(1)(A)(i) to apply), we see no basis for denying intervention here. A denial would be an abuse of discretion, so we need not remand for that purpose. *United States v. Ford,* 627 F.2d 807, 811 (7th Cir. 1980).

Second, because § 3730(c)(3) instructs the district court not to "limit[ ] the status and rights" of the relator when permitting the government to intervene, it might be argued that § 3730(c)(1) and (2) do not apply when the government intervenes under § 3730(c)(3). Presumably in such cases the government would be treated as an ordinary Rule 24(b) intervenor-plaintiff with the same rights as the original plaintiff. See 7C Charles Alan Wright, Arthur R. Miller, et al., *Federal Practice and Procedure* § 1920 (3d ed. 1998 & supp. 2019). But intervention is already given to the government on basically identical terms under Rule 24(b)(2). There is no need to construe § 3730(c)(3) so that it would add nothing. We find it unlikely that Congress meant to introduce a new configuration of the government-relator relationship (that is, as co-equal plaintiffs) in an ancillary p.854 provision without otherwise providing for its terms in § 3730(c). See *Whitman v. American Trucking Ass'ns,* 531 U.S. 457, 468, 121 S.Ct. 903, 149 L.Ed.2d 1 (2001) (Congress does not hide "elephants in mouseholes"). The better reading is that § 3730(c)(3) instructs the district court not to limit the relator's "status and rights" as they are defined by §§ 3730(c)(1) and (2). Thus, the government cannot gain an advantage by intervening after the seal period; the relator cannot gain an advantage by engaging in gamesmanship or delay during the seal period.

The decision of the district court is REVERSED and the case is REMANDED with instructions to enter judgment for the defendants on the relator's claims under the False Claims Act, dismissing those claims with prejudice as to the relator and without prejudice as to the government.

Appendix: 31 U.S.C. § 3730(b)-(c)

(b) Actions by Private Persons.—(1) A person may bring a civil action for a violation of section 3729 for the person and for the United States Government. The action shall be brought in the name of the Government. The action may be dismissed only if the court and the Attorney General give written consent to the dismissal and their reasons for consenting.

(2) A copy of the complaint and written disclosure of substantially all material evidence and information the person possesses shall be served on the Government pursuant to Rule 4(d)(4) of the Federal Rules of Civil Procedure. The complaint shall be filed in camera, shall remain under seal for at least 60 days, and shall not be served on the defendant until the court so orders. The Government may elect to intervene and proceed with the action within 60 days after it receives both the complaint and the material evidence and information.

(3) The Government may, for good cause shown, move the court for extensions of the time during which the complaint remains under seal under paragraph (2). Any such motions may be supported by affidavits or other submissions in camera. The defendant shall not be required to respond to any complaint filed under this section until 20 days after the complaint is unsealed and served upon the defendant pursuant to Rule 4 of the Federal Rules of Civil Procedure.

(4) Before the expiration of the 60-day period or any extensions obtained under paragraph (3), the Government shall—

(A) proceed with the action, in which case the action shall be conducted by the Government; or

(B) notify the court that it declines to take over the action, in which case the person bringing the action shall have the right to conduct the action.

(5) When a person brings an action under this subsection, no person other than the Government may intervene or bring a related action based on the facts underlying the pending action.

(c) Rights of the Parties to Qui Tam Actions.—(1) If the Government proceeds with the action, it shall have the primary responsibility for prosecuting the action, and shall not be bound by an act of the person bringing the action. Such person shall have the right to continue as a party to the action, subject to the limitations set forth in paragraph (2).

(2)(A) The Government may dismiss the action notwithstanding the objections of the person initiating the action if the person has been notified by the Government of the filing of the motion and the court has provided the person with an opportunity for a hearing on the motion.

(B) The Government may settle the action with the defendant notwithstanding p.855 the objections of the person initiating the action if the court determines, after a hearing, that the proposed settlement is fair, adequate, and reasonable under all the circumstances. Upon a showing of good cause, such hearing may be held in camera.

(C) Upon a showing by the Government that unrestricted participation during the course of the litigation by the person initiating the action would interfere with or unduly delay the Government's prosecution of the case, or would be repetitious, irrelevant, or for purposes of harassment, the court may, in its discretion, impose limitations on the person's participation, such as—

(i) limiting the number of witnesses the person may call;

(ii) limiting the length of the testimony of such witnesses;

(iii) limiting the person's cross-examination of witnesses; or

(iv) otherwise limiting the participation by the person in the litigation.

(D) Upon a showing by the defendant that unrestricted participation during the course of the litigation by the person initiating the action would be for purposes of harassment or would cause the defendant undue burden or unnecessary expense, the court may limit the participation by the person in the litigation.

(3) If the Government elects not to proceed with the action, the person who initiated the action shall have the right to conduct the action. If the Government so requests, it shall be served with copies of all pleadings filed in the action and shall be supplied with copies of all deposition transcripts (at the Government's expense). When a person proceeds with the action, the court, without limiting the status and rights of the person initiating the action, may nevertheless permit the Government to intervene at a later date upon a showing of good cause.

(4) Whether or not the Government proceeds with the action, upon a showing by the Government that certain actions of discovery by the person initiating the action would interfere with the Government's investigation or prosecution of a criminal or civil matter arising out of the same facts, the court may stay such discovery for a period of not more than 60 days. Such a showing shall be conducted in camera. The court may extend the 60-day period upon a further showing in camera that the Government has pursued the criminal or civil investigation or proceedings with reasonable diligence and any proposed discovery in the civil action will interfere with the ongoing criminal or civil investigation or proceedings.

(5) Notwithstanding subsection (b), the Government may elect to pursue its claim through any alternate remedy available to the Government, including any administrative proceeding to determine a civil money penalty. If any such alternate remedy is pursued in another proceeding, the person initiating the action shall have the same rights in such proceeding as such person would have had if the action had continued under this section. Any finding of fact or conclusion of law made in such other proceeding that has become final shall be conclusive on all parties to an action under this section. For purposes of the preceding sentence, a finding or conclusion is final if it has been finally determined on appeal to the appropriate court of the United States, if all time for filing such an appeal with respect to the finding or conclusion has expired, or if the finding or conclusion is not subject to judicial review.

Scudder, Circuit Judge, concurring in the judgment.

I agree with the majority's analysis of the jurisdictional question and bottom-line p.856 conclusion. But because I prefer to decide the government's challenge to the district court's denial of its motion to dismiss on narrower grounds, I concur in the judgment.

The majority opinion rightly observes that Section 3730(c)(2)(A) of the False Claim Act is an odd provision. It is strange to grant the government broad dismissal authority but then condition any dismissal on the district court holding a hearing (to allow a relator to voice objections) that leads to no judicial review. The oddity of that outcome contributes to the difficulty of landing on the right answer to the question of statutory construction analyzed in depth in the majority opinion.

What I am more confident saying is that this appeal does not require us to answer the question. We can (and should) resolve this case without deciding whether the D.C. Circuit got it right in holding that Section 3730(c)(2)(A) confers unfettered discretion upon the government to dismiss a *qui tam* action or instead whether the Ninth Circuit has the better end of the reasoning in requiring a dismissal decision to survive rational basis review. Compare *Swift v. United States,* 318 F.3d 250 (D.C. Cir. 2003), with *United States ex rel. Sequoia Orange Co. v. Baird-Neece Packing Corp.,* 151 F.3d 1139 (9th Cir. 1998). Even under the Ninth Circuit's standard, the government's dismissal request easily satisfied rational basis review, and the district court committed error concluding otherwise. See *FCC v. Beach Commc'ns, Inc.,* 508 U.S. 307, 314-15, 113 S.Ct. 2096, 124 L.Ed.2d 211 (1993) (underscoring that the rational basis standard requires "a paradigm of judicial restraint" and indeed ruling out "every conceivable basis" otherwise supporting the challenged measure).

I would stop there. While the majority opinion contains a sophisticated discussion of whether principles of constitutional avoidance should play any role in a question of statutory interpretation under the False Claims Act, I would rather confront that question in a case where the outcome hinged on the answer. In my respectful view, the narrower ground is the best ground to stand on to resolve this appeal.

[1] The text of 31 U.S.C. § 3730(b)-(c) is attached as an appendix to this opinion.

[2] *United States v. Academy Mortgage Corp.,* No. 3:16-cv-02120-EMC, 2018 WL 3208157, at *2-*3 (N.D. Cal. June 29, 2018), appeal dismissed sub nom. *United States ex rel. Thrower v. Academy Mortgage Corp.,* No. 18-16408, 968 F.3d 996 (9th Cir. Aug. 4, 2020). The Ninth Circuit in *Thrower* rejected the government's argument that an order denying a motion to dismiss under 31 U.S.C. § 3730(c)(2)(A) is appealable as a collateral order. The *Thrower* court was not presented with and did not consider the possibility of treating the government's motion to dismiss as a motion both to intervene and to dismiss, as suggested in *Swift v. United States,* 318 F.3d 250, 252 (D.C. Cir. 2003), which is the path we follow in finding that we have jurisdiction over this appeal, as explained below.

[3] For example, the Article II implications of denying good cause to intervene could vary widely. Compare a case where the government seeks to dismiss at an early stage because it has consistently held the challenged conduct to be lawful and desirable, to a case where the government seeks to dismiss on the eve of trial of meritorious claims only to protect a high-ranking executive official's private business interests. See *Yick Wo v. Hopkins,* 118 U.S. 356, 372-74, 6 S.Ct. 1064, 30 L.Ed. 220 (1886), cited by *Heckler v. Chaney,* 470 U.S. 821, 838, 105 S.Ct. 1649, 84 L.Ed.2d 714 (1985); see also Andrew Kent et al., *Faithful Execution and Article II,* 132 Harv. L. Rev. 2111 (2019) (original public meaning of duty to "faithfully execute" was "fiduciary").

[4] See n.2, supra.

[5] At the hearing, the government cited the following: Medicare and State Health Care Programs, HHS Final Rule, 81 Fed. Reg. 88,368 (Dec. 7, 2016); Special Fraud Alert, HHS Notice, 79 Fed. Reg. 40,115 (July 11, 2014); Medicare and State Health Care Programs, HHS Final Rule, 78 Fed. Reg. 79,202 (Dec. 27, 2013); OIG

Advisory Op. No. 12-20, HHS, 2012 WL 7148096 (Dec. 12, 2012); OIG Advisory Op. No. 12-10, HHS, 2012 WL 4753657 (Aug. 23, 2012); OIG Compliance Program Guidance for Pharmaceutical Manufacturers, HHS Notice, 68 Fed. Reg. 23,731 (May 5, 2003); OIG Advisory Op. No. 00-10, HHS, 2000 WL 35747420 (Dec. 15, 2000); Publication of OIG Special Fraud Alerts, HHS Notice, 59 Fed. Reg. 65,372 (Dec. 19, 1994); Medicare and State Health Care Programs, HHS Final Rule, 56 Fed. Reg. 35,952 (July 29, 1991).

957 F.3d 743 (2020)

STOP ILLINOIS HEALTH CARE FRAUD, LLC, Plaintiff-Appellant,

v.

Asif SAYEED, et al., Defendants-Appellees.

No. 19-2635.

United States Court of Appeals, Seventh Circuit.

Argued April 8, 2020.
Decided April 29, 2020.

Stop Illinois Health Care Fraud, LLC v. Sayeed, 957 F. 3d 743 (7th Cir. 2020)

Appeal from the United States District Court for the Northern District of Illinois, Eastern Division, No. 1:12-cv-9306, Sharon Johnson Coleman, Judge.

Christopher D. Willis, Attorney, GRASSE LEGAL, LLC, Schaumburg, IL, for Plaintiff-Appellant STOP ILLINOIS HEALTH CARE FRAUD, LLC.

Barry A. Spevack, Attorney, MONICO & SPEVACK, Chicago, IL, for Defendants-Appellees ASIF SAYEED, MANAGEMENT PRINCIPLES, INC., VITAL HOME & HEALTHCARE, INC., PHYSICIAN CARE SERVICES, S.C., doing business as HOME PHYSICIAN CARE SERVICES.

Linda A. Wawzenski, Attorney, OFFICE OF THE UNITED STATES ATTORNEY, Chicago, IL, for Defendant UNITED STATES DEPARTMENT OF HEALTH & HUMAN SERVICES.

Before RIPPLE, BRENNAN, and SCUDDER, Circuit Judges.

p.744 SCUDDER, Circuit Judge.

Stop Illinois Health Care Fraud, LLC brought a *qui tam* lawsuit against Management Principles, Inc. and some of its associates as well as the Healthcare Consortium of Illinois, alleging that they had an illegal referral practice that violated the Anti-Kickback Statute and, by extension, the federal and state False Claims Acts. The MPI defendants proceeded to a bench trial. At the close of the plaintiff's case, the district court entered judgment for the defendants, concluding that there was no evidence that MPI paid any renumeration with the intent to induce referrals. Stop Illinois Health Care Fraud appeals that judgment.

The trial evidence plainly showed that MPI made monthly payments to HCI in return for access to the non-profit's client records and then used that information to solicit clients. The defendants contend that the arrangement constitutes a kickback offered p.745 in exchange for a referral, and that the district court came to the contrary conclusion because it employed too narrow an understanding of a referral. Review of the district court's reasoning leaves us concerned that the court did not account for the evidence regarding MPI's solicitation of HCI clients, and we are unable to confirm that the court employed the proper definition of a proscribed referral. We therefore reverse and remand for further proceedings.

I

A

The Healthcare Consortium of Illinois, or HCI, was an organization that contracted with the Illinois Department of Aging to coordinate services for low-income seniors in an effort to keep them at home and out of nursing homes. HCI sometimes referred clients who needed in-home healthcare services to Vital Home & Healthcare, Inc. and Physician Care Services, S.C., two companies housed under the same umbrella entity, Management Principles, Inc. Also known by its acronym, MPI is owned and managed by Asif Sayeed. Stop Illinois Health Care Fraud, LLC— an entity whose name leaves few doubts about its mission—sued MPI, its two home healthcare companies, Sayeed, and HCI, alleging that they orchestrated an illegal patient referral scheme.

The plaintiff brought its claims under the federal False Claims Act and its Illinois analogue. In recognition of the limited resources available for the government to police violations on its own, both statutes allow enforcement to be outsourced to private parties, known as relators, who sue alleged wrongdoers on the government's behalf in exchange for a cut of the recovery. See 31 U.S.C. § 3730(b)(1), (d); 740 ILCS 175/4(b)(1), (d). We call this a *qui tam* action, which comes from an abbreviation of a Latin phrase meaning "who [*qui*] sues in this matter for the king as well as [*tam*] for himself." See *U.S. ex rel. Bogina v. Medline Indus., Inc.,* 809 F.3d 365, 368 (7th Cir. 2016). Stop Illinois Health Care Fraud sued in this matter for the United States and the State of Illinois. Though both governments had the ability to intervene and take the matter over for themselves, they declined to do so.

The operative complaint alleged that MPI and HCI had a contract and that MPI paid HCI gift cards in substantial amounts in return for the ability to access the detailed information that HCI employees gathered about clients during in-home assessments. Using that information, MPI called Medicare-eligible seniors and offered them the services of its two home healthcare companies. MPI's payments to HCI, the complaint alleged, ran afoul of the Anti-Kickback Statute, 42 U.S.C. § 1320a-7b(b)(2), which makes it illegal to pay someone to induce them to refer a patient for services that will be paid for by a federal healthcare program. The plaintiff sued under the federal and state False Claims Acts, which prohibit claims for payment on services resulting from violations of the Anti-Kickback Statute.

HCI settled the claims against it, but Sayeed and his companies proceeded to a bench trial. Ella Grays, who used to be a supervisor at HCI, testified about her former employer's usual referral practices. She explained that the organization dispatched caseworkers to seniors' homes to assess whether they could safely remain living on their own and, if so, whether they needed additional services like meal deliveries or aides to assist with daily living. When a client needed in-home healthcare, the HCI caseworker would make a referral from a prepared list of providers. To ensure a fair distribution, HCI caseworkers p.746 rotated the referrals by methodically going down the list. MPI's companies received referrals in this manner, and Grays did not believe that any of the referrals were given in exchange for something of value.

The parties expended little trial time on the topic of gift cards. Grays testified she did not know of caseworkers ever receiving gift cards from anyone at MPI. The plaintiff presented the video testimony of Alice Piwowarski, a former MPI employee who said that she gave HCI caseworkers Dunkin' Donuts gift cards on special occasions like birthdays and charged them to her expense account. Sayeed confirmed that his employee handed out the small gift cards—in $5 or $10 amounts—as friendly birthday gifts but denied that the purpose was to receive referrals.

Most of the trial testimony focused instead on a 2010 Management Services Agreement under which MPI paid HCI $5,000 a month. What HCI was paying MPI to do was the topic of much discussion, since the contract itself was vague. HCI's only stated obligations were to "assist MPI in the management of the case management Program and appoint personnel as Associate Managers." For their part, HCI's associate managers had to "[d]evote sufficient time for the performance of all assigned duties" and "[p]rovide periodic written reports of activities." The plaintiff's theory, as laid out in its opening statement, was that the ambiguous Management Services Agreement was a sham contract meant to disguise a kickback offered for patient referrals.

Sayeed testified that the idea for the agreement came about because HCI was in need of financial help and MPI was looking to become an Accountable Care Organization, which required enrolling 5,000 Medicare recipients as patients. Believing that MPI could not acquire that many patients on its own, Sayeed thought the company could rely on HCI records to find them—a process he referred to as "data mining." Sayeed explained that the executed agreement fulfilled this purpose by requiring HCI to do two things—give MPI access to the comprehensive forms that caseworkers filled out when they assessed clients and teach MPI about how it coordinated care. He also said that HCI's attorney not only had contributed to drafting the agreement but also approved of it.

MPI's acquiring access to HCI's caseworker paperwork was important because those documents included information about the clients' medical diagnoses, healthcare needs, and living situations. Sayeed clarified that before the Management Services Agreement took effect, MPI had access only to the assessment forms of clients who HCI had referred to its providers, but the agreement opened the door to those of all HCI's patients.

The trial testimony also shed light on how MPI acquired access and what its employees then did with the information gleaned from HCI's files. Sayeed testified that MPI employees would go to HCI's office and copy the information from caseworkers' forms to an intake tracking log and a client referral log. He explained that the data was helpful because MPI could extract patterns from it to forecast future events, allowing for earlier intervention that was cheaper and more efficient. The purpose of collecting HCI clients' information, he said, was not to solicit them for home health services but rather to help HCI and to mine data.

But Sayeed's testimony showed that his companies did use the information obtained from HCI's files to solicit and acquire new patients. MPI would call individuals from the logs and, if the person did not have a doctor and was unable to travel to one, it would send a doctor from MPI's sister company Physicians Care Services p.747 to the client's house. Something similar occurred for seniors in need of in-home nursing. MPI used the HCI data to forecast when a client would need help and then call the person's doctor. If the doctor prescribed home assistance, MPI would send a nurse to evaluate the patient.

Rosetta Cutright Woods, a former MPI employee whose job it had been to go to HCI and retrieve their clients' information from the forms, confirmed that the solicitation process worked just this way. She testified that, upon arriving at HCI, she would access the caseworkers' files and then write down the clients' diagnoses and contact information. After returning to MPI, she would speak with the doctor who ran Physicians Care Services, and the doctor would review the list of HCI clients and instruct Woods who to call. Woods would then make the calls and asked the prospective clients if they needed additional medical assistance. If the person responded in the affirmative, Woods recorded the information and later relayed it to Physicians Care Services.

According to Sayeed, the Management Services Agreement also required HCI to teach MPI about the care coordination work that it did, and HCI provided an employee who was available to MPI for questions. But Sayeed could not name the HCI liaison, and he admitted to never having seen a written report of the person's activities as was contemplated by the agreement. Ella Grays—the former HCI supervisor—testified that she could not think of a time any HCI employee ever did work for MPI under the agreement.

Indeed, Grays offered a different understanding of the Management Services Agreement. She testified that its purpose was for MPI to collect and analyze HCI's data in an effort to help HCI better understand their clients' needs and in doing so facilitate the organization's grant-writing process. She recalled that as part of the agreement, MPI would call HCI's clients to see if they needed additional services and, if so, they would make a referral that had to be approved by HCI's director.

The agreement remained in effect for 18 months, and MPI's payments to HCI totaled $90,000. Sayeed testified that MPI then ceased the payments, but HCI nevertheless continued to give the company access to its clients' information, which he attributed to the mutually beneficial nature of the arrangement.

Finally, John Mininno, the head of Stop Illinois Health Care Fraud, offered testimony about his company's relator practices and how the defendants and their practices came to his attention. But, unsurprisingly given his role in the litigation, Mininno had little firsthand information to offer on the topic of the Management Services Agreement's purpose and operation.

B

After the plaintiff's case concluded, the defendants moved for a directed verdict. They argued that the plaintiff had shown no impropriety in the HCI referrals as needed to meet its prima facie burden, both failing to substantiate the complaint's allegations about using gift cards as bribes and presenting no evidence that the parties intended the Management Services Agreement to enable and facilitate referrals from HCI to MPI and its sister companies. The district court held oral argument on the motion, where the plaintiff put forth a different view of the evidence. Pointing to Woods's testimony about collecting client information from HCI's files and then using it to place solicitation calls, the plaintiff explained that the defendants used the agreement "to get referrals for essentially any patients that they wanted by having HCI open their files and allowing p.748 them, rather than getting a referral from an HCI case manager directly, to call those individuals up."

The following day the district court issued a brief written order finding that the plaintiff had fallen short of its burden. Because the trial had been before a judge and not a jury, the court construed the defendants' motion for a directed verdict as one for judgment on partial findings under Federal Rule of Civil Procedure 52(c). The court's factual findings touched lightly on the topic of the Management Services Agreement, noting that it provided for MPI to pay HCI $5,000 per month in exchange for "administrative advice and counsel"; that Sayeed discussed his "data mining" objectives with HCI's lawyer, who gave his blessing; and that, even though John Mininno testified that the payments under the agreement constituted a kickback, he had not specifically explained why.

The district court's legal conclusions were succinct. While acknowledging the undisputed evidence that an MPI employee gave low-value gift cards to a few HCI caseworkers and that the Management Services Agreement existed, the court found no evidence that either was intended to induce patient referrals. The evidence, the court continued, compelled the contrary conclusion. Sayeed testified that the payments his company made under the agreement were unaccompanied by any expectation of referrals, HCI's lawyer had signed off on the contract, and other witnesses denied knowledge that the defendants had given anything of value in return for referrals. On that basis, the district court granted the defendants' motion and entered judgment in their favor on all counts. The plaintiff now appeals.

II

Rule 52(c) provides for judgment based on partial findings, the bench trial equivalent of its more well-known cousin, a motion for judgment as a matter of law (or a directed verdict) under Rule 50(a). Both rules allow the trial court to resolve an issue after a party has been fully heard but before the trial has concluded. See FED. R. CIV. P. 50(a), 52(c). But Rule 50(a) applies to jury trials, and Rule 52(c) applies to bench trials. The other crucial difference between the two is that a district court resolving a Rule 50(a) motion must consider the evidence in the light most favorable to the non-moving party to avoid usurping the jury's role as factfinder, but there is no such concern in a bench trial, so under Rule 52(c) the court can weigh evidence, determine witness credibility, and make factual findings on the way to its legal conclusions. See *Wilborn v. Ealey*, 881 F.3d 998, 1008 (7th Cir. 2018). The court's findings of fact and conclusions of law must comply with Rule 52(a)'s requirement that the court "find the facts specially and state its conclusions of law separately." See FED. R. CIV. P. 52(c).

Recognizing that the district court is in the better position to determine facts, we defer to its factual findings unless there is a clear error. See *Fillmore v. Page*, 358 F.3d 496, 503 (7th Cir. 2004). But the court's legal conclusions are not entitled to that deference and we review them *de novo*. See *id.*; 9A C. WRIGHT & A. MILLER, FEDERAL PRACTICE AND PROCEDURE § 2573.1 (3d ed.) (explaining that a Rule 52(c) judgment "is reversible only if the appellate court finds it to be clearly erroneous, even though the underlying conclusions of law are reviewed de novo").

A

The plaintiff's claims arose under the False Claims Act, but they hinged on whether the defendants violated the Anti-Kickback p.749 Statute. See 42 U.S.C. § 1320a-7b(g) ("[A] claim that includes items or services resulting from a violation of [the Anti-Kickback Statute] constitutes a false or fraudulent claim for purposes of [the False Claims Act]."); see also *New York v. Amgen Inc.,* 652 F.3d 103, 113 (1st Cir. 2011) (concluding the same is true of the Illinois False Claims Act). Section 1320a-7b(b)(2)(A) of the Anti-Kickback Statute makes it unlawful (indeed a felony) to knowingly and willfully offer or pay a renumeration to someone in order to induce that person to "refer" an individual for a service for which payment may be made under a federal healthcare program.

The district court broadly concluded that the plaintiff offered "no evidence" that the gift cards or Management Services Agreement were intended to induce referrals. That is certainly true as to the gift cards. The agreement, however, presents a more difficult issue. No doubt nothing linked the monthly payments to HCI caseworkers telling their clients that they should use MPI's services. But the plaintiff put forward another, less direct theory— that MPI's payments under the agreement were intended to secure access to the client information in the HCI files that it then used to place solicitation calls. The question is whether this arrangement could constitute a prohibited referral under the Anti-Kickback Statute.

We expounded on what it means to "refer" a patient in *United States v. Patel,* 778 F.3d 607 (7th Cir. 2015). Dr. Kamal Patel prescribed home healthcare for some of his patients, and he was convicted of violating the Anti-Kickback Statute for accepting undisclosed payments from Grand Home Health Care. See *id.* at 609, 611. The evidence showed that Dr. Patel did not expressly direct his patients to Grand but instead allowed them to choose from among a stack of brochures for an assortment of home healthcare options. See *id.* at 610-11. To receive Medicare reimbursement for a patient who had selected Grand, the provider had to submit certification and recertification forms signed by a doctor to demonstrate that home care was medically necessary. See *id.* at 610. The government presented evidence that Grand and Dr. Patel had monthly meetings at which he signed certification forms and accepted cash payments. See *id.* at 611.

On appeal Dr. Patel argued that since his patients selected Grand on their own initiative, he could not be said to have referred them at all, let alone in exchange for payment. He urged us to construe Congress's use of "refer" in the Anti-Kickback Statute in a limited way—as meaning "to personally recommend to a patient that he seek care from a particular entity." *Id.* at 612.

We rejected that narrow definition of a referral in favor of a "more expansive" one that includes "a doctor's authorization to receive medical care." *Id.* at 613. Under that definition, Dr. Patel had referred patients to the healthcare provider that paid him, Grand Home Health Care, because he signed the mandatory certification forms necessary for the patients to receive Medicare-reimbursed home care. See *id.* at 614. The central characteristic of the referral, we explained, was that the doctor "facilitate[d] or authorize[d]" the patient's choice of provider. *Id.* A doctor stands between the patient and his chosen provider because his approval is necessary to obtain the services, and "[e]xercising this gatekeeping role is one way that doctors refer their patients to a specific provider." *Id.* In so concluding, we observed that our holding was consistent with Congress's broad objectives in the Anti-Kickback Statute of preventing Medicare and Medicaid fraud p.750 and protecting patient choice. See *id.* at 615.

Patel's holding that a physician "refers" patients to a home healthcare provider when he approves them for services does not directly control this case, which concerns not a gatekeeping doctor but an organization (here, HCI) with no certification authority. The applicable lesson is instead that the definition of a referral under the Anti-Kickback Statute is broad, encapsulating both direct and indirect means of connecting a patient with a provider. It goes beyond explicit recommendations to include more subtle arrangements. And the inquiry is a practical one that focuses on substance, not form.

B

The district court was required to employ this inclusive understanding of a referral when evaluating whether the plaintiff had proven an illegal kickback scheme. The breadth of the definition was particularly vital to the plaintiff's theory that MPI's payments to HCI under the Management Services Agreement constituted kickbacks intended to obtain referrals in the form of receiving access to the HCI files that the defendants then exploited to solicit clients. A factfinder applying an erroneously narrow understanding of a referral might find those facts, devoid of an explicit direction of a patient to a provider, to fall outside its scope. But application of the proper standard—the more inclusive, practical approach illustrated in *Patel*—presents a much closer question.

We cannot tell with any certainty which route the district court took. The opinion contains no express articulation of what constitutes a referral for the purposes of the Anti-Kickback Statute. And the fact that some material evidence makes no appearance in the factual findings causes us to question whether the court applied the broader definition intended by Congress and underscored in our prior opinion in *Patel*. We have observed before that although "the district court cannot be expected to explain the significance of every bit of evidence in the record," the failure to address material and potentially dispositive evidence "violates the command of Rule 52(a) to 'find the facts specially' and precludes effective appellate review." *Mozee v. Jeffboat, Inc.*, 746 F.2d 365, 370 (7th Cir. 1984); see also *Schneiderman v. United States*, 320 U.S. 118, 129-30, 63 S.Ct. 1333, 87 L.Ed. 1796 (1943) ("The pertinent findings of fact on these points ... are but the most general conclusions of ultimate fact. It is impossible to tell from them upon what underlying facts the court relied, and whether proper statutory standards were observed.").

The district court's opinion contains no mention of the evidence showing that MPI used its access to HCI's files to solicit and obtain patients, though the testimony on that point was considerable and unambiguous. Rosetta Cutright Woods explained with specificity how she was employed by MPI to go to HCI, copy down the medical and contact information from client files, and then contact those people to see if they needed medical care. If someone said they did, then Woods relayed the information to Physicians Care Services. Sayeed confirmed that his companies used the information in that manner. A practical analysis of this arrangement would allow, but perhaps not compel, a finding that it qualifies as a referral. Though no evidence suggested that HCI directed its clients to MPI or its home healthcare companies, one could conclude that the effect of the file access was the same. Instead of giving its clients MPI's name, the reasoning would go, HCI simply gave MPI its clients' names and the information needed to contact them.

p.751 But it seems the district court rejected this file-access theory of referral. We come to that view from the court's statement that the plaintiff presented "no evidence" that the Management Services Agreement was intended to induce referrals. The broad statement could mean one of two things with respect to the file access— either the court concluded that the so-called "data mining" did not constitute a referral under the Anti-Kickback Statute or that it was not the intent of the agreement. The court must have meant the former, because the plaintiff did present some evidence that the agreement was intended to give MPI access to HCI's files so that it could place solicitation calls. For example, Sayeed testified that the agreement's purpose was to mine data, and Woods's testimony about her collection of HCI's "data" and what she did with it (solicit clients) allowed a finding that MPI's intent to mine data was synonymous with an intent to use the information to reach HCI's clients.

In the end, we are left with uncertainty. The district court did not acknowledge any of the evidence supporting the file-access theory of referral, and we cannot discern why it was rejected. The court may have applied the correct definition of "refer" but found that the proof fell short of it, or it may have instead committed a legal error by adopting an unduly narrow understanding of the term. In the absence of more explanation of the court's reasoning, we are unable to tell. The proper course in these circumstances—where the district court "made the necessary ultimate finding" that the Management Services Agreement was not intended to induce referrals but "failed to make the subsidiary findings necessary for us to follow its chain of reasoning"—is to remand for additional proceedings. *Mozee,* 746 F.2d at 370.

* * *

We VACATE the judgment and remand the case for further proceedings. We leave it to the district court to decide whether to reach new findings of fact and conclusions of law on the existing record or to reopen the record and receive additional evidence.

896 F.3d 834 (2018)

UNITED STATES EX REL. Jeffrey BERKOWITZ, Plaintiff-Appellant,
v.
AUTOMATION AIDS, INC., et al., Defendants-Appellees.

No. 17-2562.

United States Court of Appeals, Seventh Circuit.

Argued February 14, 2018.
Decided July 25, 2018.

US ex rel. Berkowitz v. Automation Aids, Inc., 896 F. 3d 834 (7th Cir. 2018)

Appeal from the United States District Court for the Northern District of Illinois, Eastern Division, No. 13-cv-08185, Edmond E. Chang, *Judge.*

Daniel R. Hergott, Attorney, Linda Wyetzner, Attorney, Behn & Wyetzner, Chartered, Chicago, IL, H. Vincent McKnight, Jr., Attorney, Cleveland Lawrence, III, Attorney, John Wesley McKnight, Attorney, Sanford Heisler, LLP, Washington, DC, for Plaintiff-Appellant.

Adelicia R. Cliffe, Attorney, Brian Tully McLaughlin, Attorney, Crowell & Moring LLP, Washington, DC, Sabena Auyeung, Attorney, Stephen H. Pugh, Attorney, Pugh, Jones & Johnson P.C., Chicago, IL, Ming Yuan Zhou, Attorney, Crowell & Moring LLP, Los Angeles, CA, for Defendant-Appellee Automation Aids.

Kevin P. Shea, Attorney, Nixon Peabody LLP, Chicago, IL, for Defendant-Appellee A&E Office and Industrial Supply.

Christopher Michael Loveland, Attorney, Sheppard, Mullin, Richter & Hampton, LLP, Washington, DC, David Mitchell Poell, Attorney, Sheppard, Mullin, Richter & Hampton LLP, Chicago, IL, for Defendant-Appellee Support of Microcomputers Associated.

Christopher B. Mead, Attorney, London & Mead, Washington, DC, Steven M. Kowal, Attorney, K&L Gates LLP, Chicago, IL, for Defendant-Appellee Aprisa Technology LLC.

Richard C. Landon, Attorney, Gray Plant Mooty, Minneapolis, MN, for Defendant-Appellee United Office Solutions, Inc.

Brian Tully McLaughlin, Attorney, Crowell & Moring LLP, Washington, DC, Sabena Auyeung, Attorney, Stephen H. Pugh, Attorney, Pugh, Jones & Johnson P.C., Chicago, IL, for Defendant-Appellee Caprice Electronics, Inc.

David J. Chizewer, Attorney, Goldberg Kohn Ltd., Chicago, IL, for Amicus Curiae.

p.838 Before Easterbrook and Rovner, Circuit Judges, and Griesbach, District Judge.[*]

p.837 Griesbach, District Judge.

Relator Jeffrey Berkowitz filed a *qui tam* complaint against nine separate defendants, alleging violations of the False Claims Act (FCA), 31 U.S.C. § 3730. The defendants moved to dismiss Berkowitz' third amended complaint for failure to state a claim. The district court granted the defendants' motions and dismissed the case. We affirm.

I. Background

Berkowitz is the president of Complete Packaging and Shipping Supplies, Inc., a company that holds a General Service Administration (GSA) multiple award schedule contract. Under the GSA schedule contract, Complete Packaging sells office supplies, packaging and shipping supplies, information technology products, and janitorial maintenance supplies to various government agencies and departments. The defendants — Automation Aids, Inc.; A&E Office and Industrial Supply; Support of Microcomputers Associated; Aprisa Technology LLC; Supply Saver Corporation; United Office Solutions, Inc.; Vee Model Management Consulting; Caprice Electronics, Inc.; and Computech Data Systems — also hold separate GSA schedule contracts and compete with Berkowitz' company. Vendors with GSA schedule contracts are responsible for complying with the requirements of the Trade Agreements Act (TAA), 19 U.S.C. § 501 *et seq.* As relevant to this case, GSA requires that a vendor only offer and sell U.S.-made or other designated country end products to governmental agencies in accordance with the TAA. The Federal Acquisition Regulations (FAR) catalogues the designated countries for the purposes of the TAA and defines "designated country end product" as a product made in a designated country. FAR 52.225-5. It also requires that a vendor's GSA agreement contain a "Trade Agreements Certificate," certifying that each end product sold through the GSA services contract is a U.S.-made or designated country end product and explicitly listing the other end products that are not U.S.-made or designated country end products. FAR 52.225-6.

Once a vendor enters into a GSA schedule contract with the government, the vendor uploads its price list to the GSA Advantage online portal, GSA's online shopping and ordering system. From there, government employees may purchase millions of commercial products and services from the vendors.

According to Berkowitz, as early as 2005, he became aware that other vendors offered and sold products from non-designated countries, such as China or Thailand, to the government. He claims he came to this realization by comparing the sales other vendors made on the GSA Advantage online portal with certain product lists he obtained through the normal course of his business that identify the country of origin for various products. Berkowitz contends that while he carefully screens out the non-compliant products he places on the online portal, he realized many other vendors were not doing the same. As a result, he began compiling reports that compared non-TAA compliant products with sales made on GSA Advantage. He determined that the defendants sold end products that were from non-designated countries.

Berkowitz claims the defendants violated the FCA by making material false statements and presenting false claims to the United States. He alleges the defendants p.839 knowingly sold products from non-designated countries to the government even though they filed Trade Agreements Certificates, in accordance with FAR 52.225-6, affirming they would only sell products from designated countries. It therefore follows, Berkowitz contends, that any invoices the defendants submitted to the government for payment for products that did not comply with the TAA constitute material false statements as defined by the FCA. Berkowitz recognizes there are limited exceptions to GSA's restriction on buying non-compliant products from vendors but asserts none of these exceptions apply to the defendants.

Berkowitz filed his complaint on November 14, 2013. On January 13, 2016, the government elected not to intervene in Berkowitz' case. Berkowitz subsequently amended his complaint multiple times and filed a third amended complaint, the subject of the instant appeal, on April 4, 2016. He attached as exhibits to the complaint lists describing the number of alleged non-compliant products the defendants sold as well as GSA notices advising certain defendants to remove non-compliant products from their product catalogs maintained on the GSA Advantage online portal.

All defendants, excluding Aprisa, moved to dismiss the complaint for failure to state a claim under Rules 12(b)(6) and 9(b) of the Federal Rules of Civil Procedure. Aprisa filed a motion to dismiss under Rule 12(b)(1) asserting the district court lacked subject matter jurisdiction over Berkowitz' claims against it. On March 16, 2017, the district court denied Aprisa's 12(b)(1) motion but granted the other defendants' Rule 12(b)(6) motions to dismiss and dismissed Berkowitz' claims against them with prejudice. Aprisa then filed a motion to dismiss under Rule 12(b)(6). The district court granted the motion on July 12, 2017 and dismissed Berkowitz' complaint with prejudice.

II. Analysis

We review the district court's grant of a motion to dismiss pursuant to Rule 12(b)(6) of the Federal Rules of Civil Procedure *de novo. Volling v. Kurtz Paramedic Servs., Inc.,* 840 F.3d 378, 382 (7th Cir. 2016). In construing the complaint, we accept all of the well-pleaded facts as true and "draw all reasonable inferences in favor of the plaintiff." *Kubiak v. City of Chicago,* 810 F.3d 476, 480-81 (7th Cir. 2016). To survive a motion to dismiss, the complaint must contain sufficient factual information to "state a claim to relief that is plausible on its face." *Bell Atl. Corp. v. Twombly,* 550 U.S. 544, 555, 127 S.Ct. 1955, 167 L.Ed.2d 929 (2007). "Threadbare recitals of the elements of a cause of action, supported by mere conclusory statements, do not suffice." *Ashcroft v. Iqbal,* 556 U.S. 662, 678, 129 S.Ct. 1937, 173 L.Ed.2d 868 (2009). In other words, a claim has facial plausibility when "the plaintiff pleads factual content that allows the court to draw the reasonable inference that the defendant is liable for the misconduct alleged." *Id.*

Because Berkowitz' claims arise under the FCA, an anti-fraud statute, they are subject to the heightened pleading requirements of Rule 9(b). *United States ex rel. Gross v. AIDS Research Alliance — Chicago,* 415 F.3d 601, 604 (7th Cir. 2005). Under Rule 9(b), a plaintiff "alleging fraud or mistake ... must state with particularity the circumstances constituting fraud or mistake." Fed. R. Civ. P. 9(b). The plaintiff must describe the "who, what, when, where, and how" of the fraud — "the first paragraph of any newspaper story." *United States ex rel. Lusby v. Rolls-Royce Corp.,* 570 F.3d 849, 853 (7th Cir. 2009) (internal quotation marks omitted). What constitutes "particularity," however, may depend on the facts of a given case. *See Pirelli Armstrong*

Tire Corp. Retiree Med. p.840 *Benefits Trust v. Walgreens Co.,* 631 F.3d 436, 442 (7th Cir. 2011) (citations omitted). Plaintiffs must "use some ... means of injecting precision and some measure of substantiation into their allegations of fraud." *United States ex rel. Presser v. Acacia Mental Health Clinic, LLC,* 836 F.3d 770, 776 (7th Cir. 2016) (quoting 2 James Wm. Moore et al., MOORE'S FEDERAL PRACTICE § 9.03[1][b], at 9-22 (3d ed. 2015)). The heightened pleading requirement in fraud cases "forces the plaintiff to conduct a careful pretrial investigation" to minimize the risk of damage associated with a baseless claim. *Fidelity Nat'l Title Ins. Co. of N.Y. v. Intercounty Nat'l Title Ins. Co.,* 412 F.3d 745, 748-49 (7th Cir. 2005).

The FCA allows private persons, or relators, to prosecute *qui tam* actions "against alleged fraudsters on behalf of the United States government." *United States ex rel. Watson v. King-Vassel,* 728 F.3d 707, 711 (7th Cir. 2013); 31 U.S.C. § 3730. If the government does not intervene in the action, as is the case here, the relator may proceed with the case on his own, though still on behalf of the government. 31 U.S.C. § 3730(c)(3). If the action is successful, the relator is eligible to receive a percentage of the recovery. *Id.* § 3730(d)(1)-(2).

The fraudulent conduct alleged in Berkowitz' complaint appears to be governed by both the current FCA statute, which was amended in 2009 by the Fraud Enforcement Recovery Act, and the pre-amendment statute. Prior to the amendment, the FCA limited liability to an individual who "knowingly presents, or causes to be presented, to an officer or employee of the United States Government or a member of the Armed Forces of the United States a false or fraudulent claim for payment or approval" or "knowingly makes, uses, or causes to be made or used, a false record or statement to get a false or fraudulent claim paid or approved by the government." 31 U.S.C. § 3729(a)(1)-(3) (2006). Under the current version of the statute, which applies only to claims pending on or after June 7, 2008, a person is liable under the FCA if he "knowingly presents, or causes to be presented, a false or fraudulent claim for payment or approval" or "knowingly makes, uses, or causes to be made or used, a false record or statement material to a false or fraudulent claim." 31 U.S.C. § 3729(a)(1)(A)-(B). Both versions of the FCA define "knowledge" or "knowingly" to encompass the conduct of an individual who either has "actual knowledge of the information," "acts in deliberate ignorance of the truth or falsity of the information," or "acts in reckless disregard of the truth or falsity of the information." *Id.* § 3729(b)(1)(A).

Berkowitz asserts four counts under both versions of the statute based on when the defendants' alleged fraudulent activity occurred. To state an FCA claim under either version of the statute, Berkowitz must allege the following essential elements with particularity: "(1) the defendant made a statement in order to receive money from the government; (2) the statement was false; and (3) the defendant knew the statement was false." *Gross,* 415 F.3d at 604 (citing 31 U.S.C. § 3729(a)(2); *United States ex rel. Lamers v. City of Green Bay,* 168 F.3d 1013, 1018 (7th Cir. 1999)).

Berkowitz concedes he cannot allege that the defendants made any express misrepresentations to the government. Instead, his claims are premised on an implied false certification theory. The Supreme Court recently recognized that this theory may be a basis for FCA liability when a defendant not only requests payment on a claim "but also makes specific representations about the goods or services provided" and "the defendant's failure p.841 to disclose noncompliance with material statutory, regulatory, or contractual requirements makes those representations misleading half-truths." *Universal Health Servs., Inc. v. United States ex rel. Escobar*, ___ U.S. ___, 136 S.Ct. 1989, 2001, 195 L.Ed.2d 348 (2016). Though *Universal Health* clarified the circumstances under which a plaintiff may proceed on an implied false certification claim, its analysis does not change the fact that a plaintiff must sufficiently plead the essential elements of an FCA claim.

We must therefore consider whether the third amended complaint states, with sufficient particularity, the facts necessary to demonstrate that the defendants knowingly made false statements to receive payment from the government. Berkowitz alleges that the defendants knowingly or with gross disregard sold products from non-designated countries to the government and presented false claims for the payment for the sale of these items. Because the defendants did not properly or truthfully complete the Trade Agreements Certificate and offered and sold products from non-designated countries in the face of misrepresentations and omissions in their Trade Agreements Certificates, he continues, the defendants knowingly violated the FCA when they submitted a claim to the government for payment and impliedly certified that the products were compliant with TAA regulations. The government then paid for the non-compliant products and sustained damages because of the defendants' actions. If the defendants had properly identified the non-compliant products prior to their sale, the entire offer would have been rejected or subject to a non-availability analysis.

Though Berkowitz alleges the defendants defrauded the government by knowingly submitting false statements for payment, the third amended complaint does not contain the underlying details of the fraud scheme. What the complaint fails to allege are any specific facts demonstrating what occurred at the individualized transactional level for each defendant. Berkowitz contends that the Rule 9(b) standard should be relaxed in this context because, as one of the defendants' competitors, he does not have access to the detailed information that would substantiate his claims. Indeed, this court has recognized that a party may make allegations on information and belief in the fraud context when "(1) the facts constituting the fraud are not accessible to the plaintiff and (2) the plaintiff provides the grounds for his suspicions." *Pirelli*, 631 F.3d at 442 (citing *Uni*Quality, Inc. v. Infotronx, Inc.*, 974 F.2d 918, 924 (7th Cir. 1992)). Even under this standard, however, the relator must still describe the predicate acts with some specificity to inject "precision and some measure of substantiation" into his allegations of fraud. *Presser*, 836 F.3d at 776 (citation omitted); *see also Pirelli*, 631 F.3d at 443 ("The grounds for the plaintiff's suspicions must make the allegations *plausible*, even as courts remain sensitive to information asymmetries that may prevent a plaintiff from offering more detail."). Berkowitz has not done so here.

Berkowitz alleges that he compiled reports showing the defendants sold thousands of non-compliant products over a three-year period. He does not, however, describe the nature of the product lists he used to assist in the compilation of the reports, indicate how these lists relate to the defendants' actual sales, or say what particular information any sales orders submitted by the defendants contained. The fact that the defendants may have sold non-compliant products during a certain time period in violation of the TAA does not equate to the defendants making p.842 a knowingly false statement in order to receive money from the government.

In *Universal Health,* the Court suggested that "concerns about fair notice and open-ended liability [in FCA cases based on an implied false certification theory should] be 'effectively addressed through strict enforcement of the Act's materiality and scienter requirements.'" 136 S.Ct. at 2002 (quoting *United States v. Science Applications Int'l Corp.,* 626 F.3d 1257, 1270 (D.C. Cir. 2010)). That is what the district court did here. At most, Berkowitz' allegations amount to claims that the defendants made mistakes or were negligent. This alone is insufficient to infer fraud under the FCA. *United States ex rel. Fowler v. Caremark RX, L.L.C.,* 496 F.3d 730, 742 (7th Cir. 2007), *overruled on other grounds by Glaser v. Wound Care Consultants, Inc.,* 570 F.3d 907 (7th Cir. 2009) (noting that "'innocent' mistakes or negligence are not actionable" under FCA (citations omitted)). The FCA is not "'an all-purpose antifraud statute' ... or a vehicle for punishing garden-variety breaches of contract or regulatory violations." *Universal Health,* 136 S.Ct. at 2003; *see also United States ex rel. Yannacopoulos v. Gen. Dynamics,* 652 F.3d 818, 832 (7th Cir. 2011) (The FCA "does not penalize all factually inaccurate statements, but only those statements made with knowledge of their falsity."). This court has recognized that a violation of a regulation "is not synonymous with filing a false claim." *United States ex rel. Grenadyor v. Ukrainian Vill. Pharmacy, Inc.,* 772 F.3d 1102, 1107 (7th Cir. 2014). If this were the standard, every allegedly inaccurate claim would transform "into a false claim and consequently replace the Act's knowledge requirement with a strict liability standard." *Fowler,* 496 F.3d at 743; *see also United States ex rel. Main v. Oakland City Univ.,* 426 F.3d 914, 917 (7th Cir. 2005) ("[F]raud requires more than breach of promise: fraud entails making a false representation, such as a statement that the speaker will do something it plans not to do. Tripping up on a regulatory complexity does not entail a knowingly false representation."). Without any specific allegations regarding the particularities of the fraud scheme, Berkowitz cannot satisfy the requirements of Rule 9(b) for these claims.

Even if he did not sufficiently plead that the defendants had actual knowledge of the false information, Berkowitz maintains that he has alleged that the defendants acted with reckless disregard of the truth or falsity of the information. This court has recognized that "a person acts with reckless disregard 'when the actor knows or has reason to know of facts that would lead a reasonable person to realize' that harm is the likely result of the relevant act." *Watson,* 728 F.3d at 713 (quoting BLACK'S LAW DICTIONARY 540-41 (9th ed. 2009)). In other words, Berkowitz is only required to allege that the defendants "had reason to know of facts that would lead a reasonable person to realize that [the defendants were] causing the submission of a false claim ... or that [the defendants] failed to make a reasonable and prudent inquiry into that possibility." *Id.*

To establish that the defendants acted with reckless disregard, Berkowitz relies on GSA notices directing certain defendants to remove non-compliant products from their GSA Advantage online portal product inventories. But these notices were sent to some, not all, of the defendants. In addition, Berkowitz does not allege that, after being instructed to remove non-compliant products from their lists, the defendants who received the notices subsequently submitted claims for payment for these products anyway or that any of the defendants received non-compliant warnings regarding actual product sales. It also seems worth noting that the p.843 fact that the government has allegedly paid millions of dollars for the non-compliant products suggests that Berkowitz cannot satisfy the materiality prong of the implied certification theory. *See Universal Health,* 136 S.Ct. at 2002-03 (It is not enough to demonstrate that "the Government would have the option to decline to pay if it knew of the defendant's noncompliance.... [M]ateriality looks to the effect on the *likely* or *actual* behavior of the recipient of the alleged misrepresentation."). Setting materiality aside, however, Berkowitz has not alleged that the defendants acted with reckless disregard of the truth or falsity of the information they provided to the government. Simply put, Berkowitz has failed to plead the elements of an FCA claim with particularity.

We acknowledge that it is difficult for a relator to allege with accuracy what occurs inside a competitor's operations. But this difficulty does not relieve Berkowitz of his obligation to adequately plead all of the elements of an FCA claim or to fully investigate his claim before filing a complaint. *See Ackerman v. Nw. Mut. Life Ins. Co.,* 172 F.3d 467, 469 (7th Cir. 1999) ("The purpose ... of the heightened pleading requirement in fraud cases is to force the plaintiff to do more than the usual investigation before filing his complaint.").

One final point warrants comment. Berkowitz hints in his reply brief that he offered to cure any perceived pleading deficiencies through the filing of an amended complaint, but the district court denied his request for leave to amend and dismissed the complaint with prejudice. Arguments raised for the first time in an appellate reply brief are waived. *Hess v. Reg-Ellen Mach. Tool Corp.,* 423 F.3d 653, 665 (7th Cir. 2005). Even reaching the merits, Berkowitz has not established that the district court erred in denying him leave to file a fourth amended complaint. "We review a district court's denial of leave to amend for abuse of discretion and reverse only if no reasonable person could agree with that decision." *Huon v. Denton,* 841 F.3d 733, 745 (7th Cir. 2016) (quoting *Schor v. City of Chicago,* 576 F.3d 775, 780 (7th Cir. 2009)). The district court explained in denying his request to amend that Berkowitz did not actually specify what the additional allegations might be and that he had ample opportunity to cure the deficiencies in his complaint through his previous amendments. In short, the district court did not err in denying leave to amend.

For the above reasons, the decision of the district court is AFFIRMED.

[*] Of the Eastern District of Wisconsin, sitting by designation.

EIGHTH CIRCUIT DECISIONS
Qui Tam Actions

963 F.3d 733 (2020)

UNITED STATES of America, EX REL. Rafik BENAISSA, M.D., Relator Plaintiff-Appellant

v.

TRINITY HEALTH; Trinity Hospital; Trinity Kenmare Community Hospital; Trinity Hospital-St. Joseph's Defendants-Appellees.

No. 19-1207.

United States Court of Appeals, Eighth Circuit.

Submitted: February 12, 2020.
Filed: June 25, 2020.

US ex rel. Benaissa v. Trinity Health, 963 F. 3d 733 (8th Cir. 2020)

Appeal from United States District Court for the District of North Dakota — Bismarck

Anthony L. DeWitt, Bartimus & Frickleton, Jefferson City, MO, Daniel M. Twetten, Loevy & Loevy, Boulder, CO, for Plaintiff-Appellant.

Brian D. Roark, Molly K. Ruberg, Bass Berry & Sims PLC, Nashville, TN, for Defendants-Appellees.

Before LOKEN, BENTON, and KELLY, Circuit Judges.

p.737 KELLY, Circuit Judge.

This is a qui tam action brought by Dr. Rafik Benaissa against Trinity Health, Trinity Hospital, Trinity Kenmare Hospital, and Trinity Hospital — St. Joseph's (collectively, Trinity). Dr. Benaissa alleges that Trinity violated the False Claims Act (FCA) by knowingly presenting a false or fraudulent claim to the government in violation of 31 U.S.C. § 3729(a)(1)(A), making a false statement material to a false or fraudulent claim in violation of 31 U.S.C. § 3729(a)(1)(B), and retaliating against him in violation of 31 U.S.C. § 3730(h). The district court[1] granted Trinity's motion to dismiss for failure to state a claim. Finding no error, we affirm.

I. Background

Trinity operates a regional healthcare system based in Minot, North Dakota. Dr. Benaissa was a trauma surgeon at one of Trinity's hospitals from 2003 to 2015. In his Amended Complaint, Dr. Benaissa alleges that Trinity paid physicians for referrals in violation of the federal Stark and Anti-Kickback laws.[2] He asserts that these underlying violations of the Stark and Anti-Kickback laws resulted in the presentment of false or fraudulent claims to the government, in violation of the FCA, because "services provided in violation of the Stark and Anti-Kickback laws are ineligible for government payment," see 42 U.S.C. §§ 1320a-7b(g); 1395nn(a)(1)(B) and (g)(1), and "Trinity submitted bills for these services."

To support his claim that Trinity violated the Stark and Anti-Kickback laws, Dr. Benaissa identifies five physicians whom Trinity paid in excess of the 90th percentile of compensation for their specialties. He contends that these physicians' high salaries were not merited by their skills, credentials, or personal productivity. Instead, he alleges that Trinity paid them in part for illegally referring patients for additional services at Trinity. He asserts that, if these physicians were not making illegal referrals, Trinity would have lost money by paying their high salaries.

Dr. Benaissa further alleges that, as a consequence of Trinity's compensation scheme, these physicians performed unnecessary surgeries to justify their high salaries. He states that two dental surgeons performed reconstructive surgeries that were within "the field of a plastic surgeon or an ENT surgeon" and not usually performed by dental surgeons. He also asserts that a cardiologist performed unnecessary vascular surgeries that were not within the standard of care. And he describes five instances in which an orthopedic surgeon, Dr. Joshi, performed operations p.738 that were not necessary or were medically ill-advised.

Dr. Benaissa alleges that he and others complained about Dr. Joshi's unnecessary surgeries. In 2012, he reported to Trinity's leadership that Dr. Joshi was "not ethical and was doing a large number of unnecessary surgeries," and he requested that leadership review one of Dr. Joshi's surgeries. He was told, "Don't say that in public." A member of Trinity's leadership later informed Dr. Benaissa that there were "problems" with Dr. Joshi's care, but the results of Trinity's review were confidential. In 2015, a neurosurgeon told Dr. Benaissa that Trinity knew Dr. Joshi was performing unnecessary surgeries, but it was difficult to prove. Later that year, an operating-room technician told Dr. Benaissa that Dr. Joshi was "out of control" and was doing an unnecessary surgery to repair ankle fractures. A medical-device representative also told Dr. Benaissa that he believed some of Dr. Joshi's operations were not "kosher." And Dr. Joshi's former nurse sent Dr. Benaissa a letter alleging that Dr. Joshi was performing unnecessary surgeries, some of which had resulted in deaths, and that Trinity "simply covered up all his mistakes and let them go." The nurse later repeated these allegations to Dr. Benaissa in person.

Another physician told Trinity's CEO that Dr. Joshi was writing abnormally long consults so he could bill Medicare at a higher rate. Dr. Benaissa alleges that, after this meeting, the physician told him that Dr. Joshi was "untouchable" because he was "a big money maker." Dr. Benaissa also alleges that, after he was in a dispute with Dr. Joshi, the Chief of Surgery "fabricated" a story about Dr. Benaissa behaving in an unprofessional manner. A few weeks later, Dr. Benaissa was informed that Trinity would not be renewing his contract.

Dr. Benaissa argues that these allegations give rise to a plausible inference that Trinity paid these five physicians for referrals in violation of the Stark and Anti-Kickback laws. See 42 U.S.C. §§ 1395nn(a)(1); 1320a-7b(b)(1). And he contends that, because the government will not pay claims that are tainted by violations of these statutes, see 42 U.S.C. §§ 1320a-7b(g); 1395nn(a)(1)(B) and (g)(1), every claim submitted by these physicians constitutes a false or fraudulent claim in violation of 31 U.S.C. § 3729(a)(1)(A). Further, Dr. Benaissa alleges that Trinity submitted provider agreements and annual cost reports to the government that were necessary to participate in the Medicare program, and that these agreements and reports falsely stated that Trinity had not violated and would not violate the Stark and Anti-Kickback laws. He contends that these were false statements material to false or fraudulent claims in violation of 31 U.S.C. § 3729(a)(1)(B). Finally, Dr. Benaissa argues that he was terminated in retaliation for his complaints about Trinity's unlawful scheme in violation of 31 U.S.C. § 3730(h).

The district court granted Trinity's motion to dismiss for failure to state a claim. As to the § 3729(a)(1)(A) claim, the court concluded that Dr. Benaissa had failed to allege with particularity that Trinity presented a false or fraudulent claim to the government. As to the § 3729(a)(1)(B) claim, the court held that Dr. Benaissa had failed to allege with particularity that Trinity made, used, or caused to be used a false record or statement. And as to the retaliation claim, the district court concluded that Dr. Benaissa had failed to allege that he engaged in "protected activity" or that Trinity had knowledge of his protected activity. This appeal followed.

II. Analysis

"Because the FCA is an anti-fraud statute, complaints alleging violations p.739 of the FCA must comply with Rule 9(b)" of the Federal Rules of Civil Procedure. United States ex rel. Joshi v. St. Luke's Hosp., Inc., 441 F.3d 552, 556 (8th Cir. 2006). Rule 9(b) requires plaintiffs to "state with particularity the circumstances constituting fraud." Fed. R. Civ. P. 9(b). "This particularity requirement demands a higher degree of notice than that required for other claims," and "is intended to enable the defendant to respond specifically and quickly to the potentially damaging allegations." United States ex rel. Costner v. URS Consultants, Inc., 317 F.3d 883, 888 (8th Cir. 2003). To satisfy Rule 9(b)'s particularity requirement, "the complaint must plead such facts as the time, place, and content of the defendant's false representations, as well as the details of the defendant's fraudulent acts, including when the acts occurred, who engaged in them, and what was obtained as a result." Joshi, 441 F.3d at 556.

"This court reviews de novo the district court's dismissal of a claim under Rule 9(b), accepting the allegations contained in the complaint as true and drawing all reasonable inferences in favor of the nonmoving party." United States ex rel. Strubbe v. Crawford Cty. Mem'l Hosp., 915 F.3d 1158, 1162-63 (8th Cir. 2019) (cleaned up).

A. The § 3729(a)(1)(A) Claim

The FCA imposes liability on any person who "knowingly presents, or causes to be presented, a false or fraudulent claim for payment or approval." 31 U.S.C. § 3729(a)(1)(A). "The FCA is not concerned with regulatory noncompliance. Rather, it serves a more specific function, protecting the federal fisc by imposing severe penalties on those whose false or fraudulent claims cause the government to pay money." United States ex rel. Dunn v. N. Mem'l Health Care, 739 F.3d 417, 419 (8th Cir. 2014) (citation omitted). "Accordingly, the FCA generally attaches liability, not to the underlying fraudulent activity, but to the claim for payment." Id. (cleaned up).

The first element of a § 3729(a)(1)(A) claim, often referred to as the "presentment requirement," requires a plaintiff to allege with particularity that the defendant presented, or caused to be presented, a claim for payment or approval. When a plaintiff alleges that a defendant engaged in a systematic practice or scheme of submitting fraudulent claims, the plaintiff is not required to "allege specific details of *every* alleged fraudulent claim forming the basis of [their] complaint." Joshi, 441

F.3d at 557. However, the plaintiff must provide "sufficient details to enable the defendant to respond specifically and quickly" to their allegations that the defendant presented false claims for payment or approval. See Strubbe, 915 F.3d at 1163 (citation omitted). A plaintiff can satisfy this requirement "by pleading (1) representative examples of the false claims, or (2) the particular details of a scheme to submit false claims paired with reliable indicia that lead to a strong inference that claims were actually submitted." See id. (cleaned up).

Dr. Benaissa concedes that he has not alleged representative examples of false claims that Trinity presented for payment or approval. However, he argues that "two facts" show that his allegations satisfy the second method of pleading with particularity that false claims were submitted. First, he alleges that Trinity received a large Medicare reimbursement representing approximately 28-29% of its annual revenue. Second, he asserts that, if Trinity compensated physicians for illegal referrals in violation of the federal Stark and Anti-Kickback statutes, every claim submitted for services provided by those p.740 physicians would be a false or fraudulent claim under the FCA. Thus, he asks, "which is more likely: that Trinity did not submit any claims for the services associated with these physicians or that Trinity submitted at least some claims for such services?"

We have previously rejected allegations of this sort as insufficient. In Joshi, the plaintiff argued that he had alleged presentment with particularity "by his allegations that 'all the nurse anesthetists' work was illegal,' and that 'every invoice for nurse anesthetist work was fraudulent because no nurse anesthetist was medically supervised or directed.'" 441 F.3d at 556. We held that "Rule 9(b) requires more than such conclusory and generalized allegations." Id. To support this conclusion, we cited the Eleventh Circuit's rule that the plaintiff's allegations of presentment must contain "indicia of reliability" to satisfy Rule 9(b)'s particularity requirement. See id. at 557 (citing Corsello v. Lincare, Inc., 428 F.3d 1008, 1013 (11th Cir. 2005)). The Eleventh Circuit had held that, because "[t]he act of submitting a fraudulent claim to the government is the *sine qua non* of a False Claims Act violation," it was insufficient to "describe[ ] in detail a private scheme to defraud" and then speculate that claims "must have been submitted, were likely submitted or should have been submitted to the Government." Corsello, 428 F.3d at 1012-13 (cleaned up). However, it had allowed claims to go forward where the plaintiff had an "underlying basis" for asserting that false claims had been presented, such as "'firsthand information' about the billing practices of the defendant." Id. at 1013-14 (citation omitted).

Applying this rule in Joshi, we concluded that the plaintiff's allegations lacked sufficient "indicia of reliability" because the plaintiff "was an anesthesiologist ..., not a member of the billing department, and his conclusory allegations [we]re unsupported by specific details of [the defendants'] alleged fraudulent behavior." 441 F.3d at 557. In Thayer, by contrast, we concluded that the plaintiff's allegations contained sufficient "indicia of reliability" because the plaintiff oversaw the defendant's billing and claims systems and pleaded personal, firsthand knowledge of the defendant's submission of false claims. See United States ex rel. Thayer v. Planned Parenthood of the Heartland, 765 F.3d 914, 917 (8th Cir. 2014).

As a trauma surgeon, Dr. Benaissa does not have firsthand knowledge of Trinity's billing practices. He also has not pleaded details about Trinity's billing practices indicating a reliable "basis for knowledge" regarding the submission of fraudulent claims. See Joshi, 441 F.3d at 558. For example, he has not provided dates and descriptions of particular services coupled with "a description of the billing system that the records were likely entered into." See Strubbe, 915 F.3d at 1165 (quoting United States ex rel. Grubbs v. Kanneganti, 565 F.3d 180, 190 (5th Cir. 2009)). Instead, he relies solely on two general facts—Trinity's receipt of a large Medicare reimbursement and his allegation that every claim submitted by certain physicians was false or fraudulent—to draw the conclusion that Trinity most likely submitted false claims to the government.

This sort of general inference is "not specific enough to give defendants notice of the particular misconduct which is alleged to constitute the fraud charged so that they can defend against the charge and not just deny that they have done anything wrong." See Joshi, 441 F.3d at 557 (quoting Costner, 317 F.3d at 889). As a result, it is not sufficient to satisfy Rule 9(b)'s particularity requirement. See Thayer, 765 F.3d at 919-20 (affirming the dismissal p.741 of an FCA claim where the plaintiff "failed to provide a factual basis for her knowledge" and was "only able to speculate that false claims were submitted" by certain hospitals); Dunn, 739 F.3d at 420 (stating that a plaintiff may not "rely on the broad allegation that every claim submitted... is false in order to satisfy the particularity requirement"); Joshi, 441 F.3d at 557 (conclusory allegations unsupported by firsthand knowledge or particular details are insufficient).

Dr. Benaissa argues that this means that "only members of the billing department or the financial services department of a hospital could qualify as a relator," which is "wildly contrary to the purposes of the [FCA]." We disagree. We have recognized that "an insider might have an easier time obtaining information about billing practices and meeting the pleading requirements under the FCA." Joshi, 441 F.3d at 560 (cleaned up). But we have not precluded others with reliable allegations from serving as relators. See Strubbe, 915 F.3d at 1164 (noting that claims by paramedics and EMTs were "close to meeting this standard"). Other courts applying this same standard have allowed individuals outside of a hospital's billing department to serve as relators where they were able to plead "particular and reliable indicia that false bills were actually submitted as a result of the scheme—such as dates that services were fraudulently provided or recorded, by whom, and evidence of the department's standard billing procedure." See Grubbs, 565 F.3d at 189 (psychiatrist); see also United States ex rel. Walker v. R&F Props. of Lake Cty, Inc., 433 F.3d 1349, 1360 (11th Cir. 2005) (nurse practitioner); United States ex rel. Dicken v. Nw. Eye Ctr., No. 13-CV-2691, 2017 WL 2345579, at *2-3 (D. Minn. May 30, 2017) (ophthalmologist).

There is no requirement that a relator must be a member of a hospital's billing or financial-services department. However, a relator must allege representative examples of false claims or particular details of a scheme to submit false claims paired with reliable indicia that lead to a strong inference that claims were actually submitted. Strubbe, 915 F.3d at 1163. Dr. Benaissa's general allegations that Trinity's compensation scheme most likely resulted in the presentment of claims for payment or approval are insufficient to meet this requirement.

B. The § 3729(a)(1)(B) Claim

Next, Dr. Benaissa alleges that Trinity falsely certified in its provider agreement and cost reports that it would comply with the Stark and Anti-Kickback laws. The FCA imposes liability on any person who "knowingly makes, uses, or causes to be made or used, a false record or statement material to a false or fraudulent claim." 31 U.S.C. § 3729(a)(1)(B). The elements of a § 3729(a)(1)(B) claim are: "(1) the defendant made a false record or statement; (2) the defendant knew the statement was false; (3) the statement was material; and (4) the statement made a claim for the government to pay money or forfeit money due." United States ex rel. Miller v. Weston Educ., Inc., 840 F.3d 494, 500 (8th Cir. 2016) (cleaned up).

There is no "presentment" requirement for a § 3729(a)(1)(B) claim. However, the plaintiff must "plead a connection between the alleged fraud and an actual claim made payable to the government." See Strubbe, 915 F.3d at 1166 (cleaned up). Because Dr. Benaissa has failed to allege with particularity that Trinity submitted a claim for payment to the government, he cannot establish that Trinity's allegedly false statements were "material" p.742 to any claim that was actually submitted. See id.

C. The Retaliation Claim

Finally, Dr. Benaissa alleges that Trinity retaliated against him in violation of 31 U.S.C. § 3730(h). There are four elements to an FCA retaliation claim: (1) the relator was engaged in protected activity; (2) his employer knew he was engaged in protected activity; (3) his employer retaliated against him; and (4) the retaliation was motivated solely by his protected activity. Id. at 1166-67. To constitute "protected activity," an employee's conduct must have been (1) in furtherance of an FCA action or an effort to stop one or more FCA violations, and (2) aimed at matters which are calculated, or reasonably could lead, to a viable FCA action. Id. at 1167. To show that an employer knew that an employee was engaged in protected activity, the employee "must connect the alleged misconduct to fraudulent or illegal activity under the FCA." Id. at 1168.

Dr. Benaissa alleges that he complained, on two occasions, that Dr. Joshi was performing unnecessary surgeries. However, he does not allege that he connected his complaints to a concern over improper billing or the submission of false claims to the government. Rather, his concern was with the medical propriety and ethical ramifications of Dr. Joshi's procedures. Even assuming that complaining about these issues constitutes "protected activity" under the FCA, Dr. Benaissa has not alleged that he told Trinity the "behavior was fraudulent or potentially subjected it to FCA liability." See id. Therefore, his allegations are insufficient to establish that Trinity knew he was engaged in a protected activity.

III. Conclusion

The district court's judgment is affirmed.

[1] The Honorable Daniel L. Hovland, then Chief Judge, United States District Court for the District of North Dakota.

[2] The Stark law prohibits physicians from making referrals to hospitals or other entities with which they have a financial relationship. See 42 U.S.C. § 1395nn(a)(1). The Anti-Kickback statute prohibits soliciting or receiving anything of value in exchange for a referral of medical services. See 42 U.S.C. § 1320a-7b(b)(1).

915 F.3d 1158 (2019)

UNITED STATES of America, EX REL. Stephanie STRUBBE; Carmen Trader; Richard Christie, Relators, Plaintiffs-Appellants

v.

CRAWFORD COUNTY MEMORIAL HOSPITAL; Bill Bruce, Individually, Defendants-Appellees.

No. 18-1022.

United States Court of Appeals, Eighth Circuit.

Submitted: November 13, 2018.

Filed: February 11, 2019.

Rehearing and Rehearing En Banc Denied March 20, 2019.

US ex rel. Strubbe v. Crawford Cnty. Mem. Hosp., 915 F. 3d 1158 (8th Cir. 2019)

Appeal from United States District Court for the Northern District of Iowa — Sioux City.

Angela L. Campbell, Attorney, DICKEY & CAMPBELL, Des Moines, IA, Michael J. Carroll, COPPOLA & MCCONVILLE, West Des Moines, IA, for Plaintiffs-Appellants.

Randall D. Armentrout, Leslie C. Behaunek, NYEMASTER & GOODE, Edwin N. McIntosh, Brian Andrew Melhus, Kirk W. Schuler, DORSEY & WHITNEY, Des Moines, IA, Alex P. Hontos, DORSEY & WHITNEY, Minneapolis, MN, for Defendants-Appellees.

Before BENTON, BEAM, and ERICKSON, Circuit Judges.

p.1161 BENTON, Circuit Judge.

Stephanie A. Strubbe, Carmen Trader, and Richard Christie sued Crawford County Memorial Hospital (CCMH) as relators in a qui tam action for violations of the False Claims Act. 31 U.S.C. § 3729(a). They also sued CCMH and its Chief Executive Officer, Bill Bruce, for violating the FCA's anti-retaliation provision. § 3730(h). The district court[1] granted CCMH's motion to dismiss all counts of the complaint, except Strubbe's retaliation claim. As for it, the district court granted CCMH's motion for summary judgment. *Strubbe v. Crawford Cty. Mem'l Hosp.,* 2017 WL 8792692 (N.D. Iowa Dec. 6, 2017). Having jurisdiction under 28 U.S.C. § 1291, this court affirms.

I.

Crawford County Memorial Hospital is a county-owned nonprofit hospital in Iowa. In April 2012, Bruce became its Chief Executive Officer.

At CCMH, Strubbe was an Emergency Medical Technician (EMT), and Christie p.1162 and Trader were paramedics. They filed a sealed qui tam complaint as relators in April 2015. The United States declined to intervene. The relators filed an amended complaint. It alleges that CCMH submitted false claims for Medicare reimbursement and made false statements or reports to get fraudulent claims paid. Specifically, Count I alleges that CCMH violated the FCA by submitting (1) claims for breathing treatments administered by paramedics; (2) claims for laboratory services done by paramedics and EMTs; (3) claims with false credentials of service providers; (4) claims for EMT and paramedic services at Eventide, L.L.C. and Denison Care Center; and (5) cost reports with improper reimbursements and payments to vendors for non-CCMH expenses. Count II alleges CCMH knowingly made or used false statements to get false claims paid, including (1) records documenting breathing treatments at 30 minutes; (2) records listing paramedics as "specialized ancillary staff" for breathing treatments; (3) reimbursement requests and invoices for improper payments for non-CCMH expenses; (4) documents with false credentials for emergency medical staff; and (5) cost reports with false costs. Count III alleges that CCMH conspired with Eventide to violate the Anti-Kickback Statute, 42 U.S.C. § 1320a-7b.

Strubbe, Trader, and Christie also sued CCMH and Bruce for violating the FCA's anti-retaliation provision. According to the complaint, Strubbe began reviewing hospital financial documents in July 2014. Soon after, she "spoke to all Board members about the financial situation of CCMH [and] her belief that the finances were not adding up." In November, Strubbe tore her rotator cuff at work. Initially, CCMH put her on "light duty." In July 2015, however, CCMH told Strubbe her light-duty assignments were a financial hardship for the hospital and moved her to part-time status. CCMH removed Strubbe from part-time status in March 2016 (effectively a termination).

Christie and Trader also began investigating CCMH's finances in 2014. They complained to other hospital staff that "there was something wrong with the changes in the breathing treatments." Christie also complained there was "potentially something wrong with the financial statements provided by CCMH to the Board." In January 2015, Christie reported to her supervisor that Jonathan Richard was "not properly licensed" as a paramedic. Both Christie and Trader then reported the license violation to the Iowa Department of Public Health. Four months later, CCMH transitioned Christie from night shifts to day shifts. It terminated Christie later that month for speeding while driving an ambulance. Trader still works at CCMH as a paramedic, but claims that it subjects him to harrassment and other discriminatory treatment.

CCMH moved to dismiss the complaint. The district court dismissed the substantive FCA claims for failure to plead with particularity because the complaint did not set forth facts showing any false claims were submitted, or plead how the relators acquired this information. It also dismissed Christie and Trader's retaliation claims as not stating a plausible claim for relief. However, the court denied CCMH's motion to dismiss Strubbe's retaliation claim. CCMH then moved for summary judgment on it. Concluding that Strubbe could not prove a prima facie case of retaliation, the district court granted summary judgment to CCMH.

II.

This court reviews de novo the district court's dismissal of a claim under Rule 9(b), "accepting the allegations contained in the complaint as true and drawing all reasonable inferences in favor of the p.1163 nonmoving party." *United States ex rel. Joshi v. St. Luke's Hosp., Inc.,* 441 F.3d 552, 555 (8th Cir. 2006). The False Claims Act (FCA) imposes liability on anyone who "knowingly presents, or causes to be presented, a false or fraudulent claim for payment or approval" or who "knowingly makes, uses, or causes to be made or used, a false record or statement material to a false or fraudulent claim." 31 U.S.C. § 3729(a)(1)(A)-(B). "The FCA attaches liability, not to the underlying fraudulent activity, but to the claim for payment." *Olson v. Fairview Health Servs. of Minn.,* 831 F.3d 1063, 1070 (8th Cir. 2016). Qui tam provisions permit private persons, relators, to sue for violations in the name of the United States and to recover part of the proceeds if successful. § 3730(b), (d).

"Because the FCA is an anti-fraud statute, complaints alleging violations of the FCA must comply with Rule 9(b)." *Joshi,* 441 F.3d at 556. Under Rule 9(b), "a party must state with particularity the circumstances constituting fraud or mistake." This gives defendants notice and protects them from baseless claims. *United States ex rel. Thayer v. Planned Parenthood of the Heartland,* 765 F.3d 914, 918 (8th Cir. 2014). While Rule 9(b) is "context specific and flexible," *id.,* a plaintiff cannot meet this burden with conclusory and generalized allegations. *Joshi,* 441 F.3d at 557. Where "the facts constituting the fraud are peculiarly within the opposing party's knowledge," the "allegations may be pleaded on information and belief" if "accompanied by a statement of facts on which the belief is founded." *Drobnak v. Andersen Corp.,* 561 F.3d 778, 783-84 (8th Cir. 2009).

To satisfy the particularity requirement for FCA claims, "the complaint must plead such facts as the time, place, and content of the defendant's false representations, as well as the details of the defendant's fraudulent acts, including when the acts occurred, who engaged in them, and what was obtained as a result." *Joshi,* 441 F.3d at 556. A relator can meet the Rule 9(b) requirements by pleading (1) "representative examples of the false claims," or (2) the "particular details of a scheme to submit false claims paired with reliable indicia that lead to a strong inference that claims were actually submitted." *Thayer,* 765 F.3d at 918. To satisfy the particular details requirement, the complaint must "provide sufficient details to enable the defendant to respond specifically and quickly to the potentially damaging allegations." *Id.* at 918-19.

A.

In Count I, the relators contend that CCMH submitted false claims through a wide-ranging fraudulent scheme. First, the complaint alleges that shortly after Bruce became CEO, CCMH required paramedics to perform breathing treatments previously provided by nursing staff. Hospital management told employees this change was for "billing" and "cost reimbursement purposes" and required them to document each treatment at 30 minutes, regardless of its length. The complaint alleges—upon information and belief—that these changes allowed CCMH to bill these treatments separately to get a higher reimbursement from Medicare. Further, the complaint alleges that CCMH treats paramedics as "specialized staff," making the treatments separately billable. Relators also contend —upon information and belief—that patients are receiving breathing treatments who do not need them.

Second, the complaint alleges that CCMH ordered paramedics and EMTs to perform laboratory services, like blood draws. The relators claim—upon information and belief—that this change, like the breathing treatments, was intended to increase Medicare reimbursement by allowing p.1164 CCMH to bill these services separately. Third, the complaint identifies three employees with misclassified titles. For example, the complaint alleges—upon information and belief—that CCMH billed Medicare for Richard's services as a paramedic, though he was "not properly licensed." Fourth, the relators claim paramedics and EMTs provided services at two other health care facilities—Eventide and Denison. Based on information and belief, CCMH instituted this change to increase Medicare reimbursement. Finally, the complaint alleges that CCMH reported improper expenses to Medicare. Relators contend— upon information and belief— that CCMH submitted cost reports to Medicare with payments to Bruce's relatives above the market value and with duplicate payments to the credit card companies and the sellers.

Relators did not plead representative samples of false claims. In *Joshi,* a hospital anesthesiologist brought a qui tam claim alleging that the hospital sought Medicare reimbursements at higher rates and submitted claims for services and supplies not provided. *Joshi,* 441 F.3d at 554. Joshi did not provide representative samples, but alleged that every claim over a sixteen-year period was fraudulent. *Id.* at 556-57. Though Rule 9(b) does not require alleging the "specific details of *every* alleged fraudulent claim," this court dismissed Joshi's claim because a relator "must provide *some* representative examples of [the] alleged fraudulent conduct, specifying the time, place, and content of [the] acts and the identity of the actors." *Id.* at 557.

The relators here pleaded more than the relator in *Joshi.* However, like *Joshi,* the complaint here alleges a fraudulent scheme without representative examples with the required specificity. For instance, the complaint alleges CCMH submitted false claims for unnecessary breathing treatments. It gives one example of a patient who received an unnecessary breathing treatment, but fails to include the date, the provider performing the treatment, any specific information about the patient, what money was obtained, and most importantly, whether a claim was actually submitted for that particular patient.

Under *Thayer,* a relator can also satisfy Rule 9(b) by pleading the "particular details of a scheme to submit false claims paired with reliable indicia that lead to a strong inference that claims were actually submitted." *Thayer,* 765 F.3d at 918. The allegations in Count I are close to meeting this standard. The complaint includes some details of the fraudulent scheme. It pleads the names of the individuals that instructed them to carry out the breathing treatments and blood draws, the two-year period when these services were provided, and statements by their supervisor that the changes to the breathing treatments were for billing and cost reimbursement purposes. The complaint also pleads how hospital management told them to document each breathing treatment at 30 minutes, regardless of its length. It includes the names of three individuals who relators believed were misclassified, and how Christie and Trader learned of Richard's licensure violation. The relators also give some details about one receipt for gas and moving expenses that was allegedly altered.

However, the complaint lacks the sufficient indicia of reliability leading to a strong inference that claims were actually submitted. In *Thayer,* the relator—a center manager for several Planned Parenthood clinics—alleged a fraudulent scheme. *Id.* at 919. This court emphasized that the relator's position as center manager gave her personal knowledge that false claims were submitted and allowed her to plead specific details about the billing system p.1165 and practices, providing sufficient indicia of reliability for two of Thayer's claims. *Id.* This court dismissed another claim where Thayer did not have "access to the billing systems ... [or] knowledge of their billing practices," leaving her "only able to speculate that false claims were submitted...." *Id.* at 919-20.

The relators here—paramedics and EMTs—did not have access to the billing department. The complaint did not include any details about CCMH's billing practices. *See United States ex rel. Grubbs v. Kanneganti,* 565 F.3d 180, 190-91 (5th Cir. 2009) ("Confronting False Claims Act defendants with both an alleged scheme to submit false claims and details leading to a strong inference that those claims were submitted—such as dates and descriptions of recorded, but unprovided, services and a description of the billing system that the records were likely entered into—gives defendants adequate notice of the claims."). Nor did the complaint allege that the relators had personal knowledge of the billing system or the submission of false claims. *See United States ex rel. Prather v. Brookdale Senior Living Cmtys.,* 838 F.3d 750, 769-70 (6th Cir. 2016) (relator's allegations gave reliable indicia because she had knowledge of billing documentation and pleaded specific details like the treatment of four patients, the dates of care, the dates the false certification occurred, and the amount requested for final payment). Some of the facts pleaded—such as their supervisor's statements that the changes to breathing treatments were for billing and cost reimbursement purposes— shows the *possibility* that CCMH submitted claims. However, the facts pleaded do not "lead to a *strong inference* that claims were actually submitted." *Thayer,* 765 F.3d at 918 (emphasis added). *See Chesbrough v. VPA, P.C.,* 655 F.3d 461, 472 (6th Cir. 2011) ("[T]his is not a situation in which the alleged facts support a strong inference—rather than simply a possibility —that a false claim was presented to the government."); *Corsello v. Lincare, Inc.,* 428 F.3d 1008, 1013 (11th Cir. 2005) (declining to "make inferences about the submission of fraudulent claims because such an assumption would 'strip[ ] all meaning from Rule 9(b)'s requirements of specificity'") (alteration in original).

The relators pleaded many key facts upon information and belief, without providing a "statement of facts on which the belief is founded." *Drobnak,* 561 F.3d at 784. *See, e.g.,* Compl. ¶ 59 ("Upon information and belief, Richard's services were billed, in part, to Medicare. Richard was not, however, licensed in the State of Iowa as a paramedic."). They allege, "Certain vendors paid by the hospital are personally related to Bruce and their services are paid well above market value. For example, thousands of dollars have been paid to Bruce's brother, who, upon information and belief, owns an out-of-state moving company ... [which] is paid from CCMH funds to move doctors ... when it would be more economical to use a local moving company." *Id.* ¶ 74. Relators then claim, upon information and belief, that these expenses were included in cost reports to Medicare. They do not explain how they know Bruce's brother owns a moving company or that CCMH is using it. A generalized allegation that the hospital paid vendors above market value and submitted a false cost report—without a statement of facts on which the belief is founded—does not sufficiently demonstrate that these were improper expenses or were included on cost reports. *See Drobnak,* 561 F.3d at 784 (when pleading on information and belief, allegations must be "accompanied by a statement of facts on which the belief is founded").

Other allegations, which are not pleaded upon information and belief, similarly do not identify the underlying basis for the p.1166 assertions. *See Thayer,* 765 F.3d at 919 ("Thayer's claims thus have sufficient indicia of reliability because she provided the underlying factual bases for her allegations."). For instance, the relators plead, "The paramedics were told by their managers, in writing, that no matter how long the breathing treatments took, to document on the timesheets that the treatments took at least 30 minutes. These timesheets are used in billing to Medicare." Compl. ¶ 30. The relators—who do not allege personal knowledge of the hospital's billing practices—do not explain how they knew the timesheets were used to bill Medicare. They also do not plead a single example where they performed a breathing treatment in less than 30 minutes.

Because the relators failed to plead fraud with particularity, the district court properly dismissed Count I under Rule 9(b).

B.

In Count II, relators sued under 31 U.S.C. § 3729(a)(1)(B), which imposes liability on anyone who "knowingly makes, uses, or causes to be made or used, a false record or statement material to a false or fraudulent claim." The false statements alleged include: records for 30-minute breathing treatments, records for breathing treatments listing paramedics as "specialized ancillary staff," improper payment requests for non-CCMH expenses, documents misclassifying employees like Richard, and cost reports listing false costs. Though claims under § 3729(a)(1)(B) do not require proof that CCMH submitted a false claim, relators must still "plead a connection between the alleged fraud and an actual claim made to the government." *United States ex rel. Ibanez v. Bristol-Myers Squibb Co.,* 874 F.3d 905, 916 (6th Cir. 2017). *See United States ex rel. Grant v. United Airlines, Inc.,* 912 F.3d 190, 200 (4th Cir. 2018) (reasoning that a relator asserting a claim under § 3729(a)(1)(B) "is still required to show that a false claim was submitted to the government"). *Cf. Grubbs,* 565 F.3d at 193 ("[T]he recording of a false record, when it is made with the requisite intent" to get a false claim paid "is enough to satisfy the statute...."). The complaint here, as discussed above, fails to connect the false records or statements to any claim made to the government. Further, like Count I, many of the allegations are founded upon information and belief without a statement of facts on which the belief is founded. *Drobnak,* 561 F.3d at 784. Count II was properly dismissed.

C.

Count III alleges that CCMH conspired with Eventide to violate the Anti-Kickback Statute. To satisfy Rule 9(b)'s particularity requirements, this claim must plead the details of a conspiracy, including an agreement between CCMH and Eventide, and an overt act in furtherance of the conspiracy. *Grubbs,* 565 F.3d at 193. Because the complaint does not include any details about an agreement, the relators fail to plead the conspiracy with particularity. The district court properly dismissed the conspiracy claim.

III.

The FCA protects employees who are "discharged, demoted, ... harassed, or in any other manner discriminated against in the terms and conditions of employment because of lawful acts done by the employee... in furtherance of" a civil action under the FCA "or other efforts to stop 1 or more violations" of the FCA. 31 U.S.C. § 3730(h). To prove retaliation in violation of the FCA, a plaintiff must prove that "(1) the plaintiff was engaged in conduct protected by the FCA; (2) the plaintiff's employer knew that the plaintiff engaged in the protected activity; (3) the employer p.1167 retaliated against the plaintiff; and (4) the retaliation was motivated solely by the plaintiff's protected activity." *Schuhardt v. Washington Univ.*, 390 F.3d 563, 566 (8th Cir. 2004).

The relators allege that Bruce can be held individually liable for his acts in their FCA retaliation claims. CCMH—not Bruce—is the relators' employer. They appear to argue that a 2009 amendment to the FCA—which removed an explicit reference to retaliatory acts by an "employer" —expands liability. Before the 2009 amendment, federal courts—including this court—uniformly held that the FCA did not impose individual liability for retaliation claims. *See United States ex rel. Golden v. Arkansas Game & Fish Comm'n*, 333 F.3d 867, 870-71 (8th Cir. 2003). After the 2009 amendment, numerous courts still hold that the FCA does not create individual liability because Congress deleted the word "employer" so contractors and agents could bring FCA retaliation claims. *E.g., Howell v. Town of Ball*, 827 F.3d 515, 529-30 (5th Cir. 2016). "Congress acts with knowledge of existing law, and [ ] absent a clear manifestation of contrary intent, a ... revised statute is presumed to be harmonious with existing law and its judicial construction." *Estate of Wood v. C.I.R.*, 909 F.2d 1155, 1160 (8th Cir. 1990). Because Congress did not amend the FCA to impose individual liability, the FCA does not impose individual liability for retaliation claims. The district court correctly dismissed the claims against Bruce.

A.

To survive a motion to dismiss, the complaint must "state a claim to relief that is plausible on its face," meaning that the "plaintiff pleads factual content that allows the court to draw the reasonable inference that the defendant is liable for the misconduct alleged." *Ashcroft v. Iqbal*, 556 U.S. 662, 678, 129 S.Ct. 1937, 173 L.Ed.2d 868 (2009), *quoting Bell Atlantic Corp. v. Twombly*, 550 U.S. 544, 570, 127 S.Ct. 1955, 167 L.Ed.2d 929 (2007). This court reviews de novo the dismissal for failure to state a claim. *Drobnak*, 561 F.3d at 783.

The district court found that Christie and Trader did not engage in protected activity and dismissed their claims. Christie and Trader claim they engaged in two different types of protected activity: (1) complaining to hospital staff about the breathing treatments, and (2) reporting Richard's license violation to the State. Additionally, Christie claims his investigations into CCMH's financial matters are protected activity. An employee's conduct must satisfy two conditions to constitute protected activity. *Schuhardt,* 390 F.3d at 567. First, it "must have been in furtherance of an FCA action" or an effort to stop one or more FCA violations. § 3730(h); *Schuhardt,* 390 F.3d at 567. Second, the conduct "must be aimed at matters which are calculated, or reasonably could lead, to a viable FCA action," meaning the employee "in good faith believes, and ... a reasonable employee in the same or similar circumstances might believe, that the employer is possibly committing fraud against the government." *Schuhardt,* 390 F.3d at 567.

Even assuming Christie and Trader engaged in protected activity, their retaliation claims fail to state a plausible claim because they did not adequately plead that CCMH knew they were engaging in protected activity. They must show CCMH knew they were "either taking action in furtherance of a private *qui tam* action ... [,] assisting in an FCA action brought by the government," or taking some other action to stop an FCA violation. *Id.* at 568; § 3730(h). Christie and Trader both complained to hospital staff p.1168 about the breathing treatments and the financial situation at CCMH. Christie also emailed the compliance manager to inform CCMH he made a report about Richard's license "as required by Iowa law." However, to provide actual or constructive knowledge, employees must connect the alleged misconduct to fraudulent or illegal activity or the FCA. *See Schuhardt,* 390 F.3d at 568-69 (plaintiff gave her employer notice of protected activity after she advised her supervisor that the organization's conduct could be "fraudulent and illegal" and that "if the OIG would come in they would frown upon us and they'd pretty much wipe us out"). The complaint here does not allege that Christie and Trader told CCMH or the State that CCMH's behavior was fraudulent or potentially subjected it to FCA liability. Reporting a license violation to the State does not tell CCMH that these employees believe it is acting fraudulently, especially where Christie pleaded he was "required to tell" state officials about Richard's license because "otherwise he himself could lose his licensure" under state law. Likewise, complaining to hospital staff about CCMH's financial situation and the changes to breathing treatments does not give CCMH notice that Christie and Trader were taking action in furtherance of a qui tam action or to stop an FCA violation. *Id.* at 568.

Because the relators did not sufficiently plead that CCMH knew they were engaging in protected activity, the district court properly dismissed their retaliation claims.

B.

This court reviews de novo the grant of summary judgment, viewing all evidence most favorably to the nonmoving party. *Id.* at 566. Summary judgment is appropriate if there is no genuine issue of material fact and the moving party is entitled to judgment as a matter of law. Fed. R. Civ. P. 56(a). CCMH is entitled to summary judgment if Strubbe "has failed to make a sufficient showing on an essential element of her case with respect to which she has the burden of proof." *See Celotex Corp. v. Catrett,* 477 U.S. 317, 323, 106 S.Ct. 2548, 91 L.Ed.2d 265 (1986).

In the absence of direct evidence of retaliation, courts apply the *McDonnell Douglas* framework to retaliation claims. *McDonnell Douglas Corp. v. Green,* 411 U.S. 792, 93 S.Ct. 1817, 36 L.Ed.2d 668 (1973). While this court has not explicitly adopted this framework for FCA retaliation claims, it applies it to other whistleblower statutes. *See, e.g., Elkharwily v. Mayo Holding Co.*, 823 F.3d 462, 470 (8th Cir. 2016) (assuming without deciding that the framework applies to the Emergency Medical Treatment Active Labor Act). Most of the other circuits use the framework for FCA retaliation claims. *See Diaz v. Kaplan Higher Educ., L.L.C.*, 820 F.3d 172, 175 & n.3 (5th Cir. 2016) (collecting cases and adopting the framework for FCA retaliation claims). This court will apply the *McDonnell Douglas* framework to FCA retaliation claims.

Under *McDonnell Douglas*, Strubbe bears the initial burden of establishing a prima facie case of FCA retaliation. *Elkharwily*, 823 F.3d at 470. To establish a prima facie case, Strubbe must show that (1) she engaged in protected conduct, (2) CCMH knew she engaged in protected conduct, (3) CCMH retaliated against her, and (4) "the retaliation was motivated solely by [Strubbe's] protected activity." *Schuhardt*, 390 F.3d at 566. If Strubbe establishes a prima facie case, the burden shifts to CCMH to "articulate a legitimate reason for the adverse action." *Elkharwily*, 823 F.3d at 470. The burden then shifts back to Strubbe to demonstrate that "the proffered reason is merely a pretext and that retaliatory animus motivated the adverse action." *Id.*

p.1169 Like Christie and Trader, Strubbe's complaints to the CCMH Board and sheriff about "financial wrongdoing" and her investigations into CCMH's finances are not protected activity. There is no indication they were made in furtherance of an FCA action or were an effort to stop an FCA violation. She did not connect her concerns about CCMH's finances to fraud, the FCA, or any unlawful activity. *See Green v. City of St. Louis*, 507 F.3d 662, 667-68 (8th Cir. 2007) (reasoning the plaintiff did not engage in protected activity because he admitted he did not know whether the city submitted any document with false information when he complained about the city's policy). *See also Robertson v. Bell Helicopter Textron, Inc.*, 32 F.3d 948, 951 (5th Cir. 1994) (recognizing that to engage in protected activity, an employee should "express concerns about possible fraud to their employers"). However, Strubbe's filing of an FCA claim is protected conduct. § 3730(h).

The complaint was unsealed in November 2015, alerting CCMH that Strubbe engaged in protected activity. Strubbe claims that CCMH had notice before this because the federal government sent informal interrogatories to CCMH in August 2015 that mimicked the open records request her attorney sent in March. Strubbe presented no evidence, however, that CCMH knew her attorney sent that records request. Strubbe has shown only that CCMH had knowledge of her protected activity beginning in November 2015.

Retaliatory acts under the FCA include discharging, demoting, suspending, threatening, harrassing, or otherwise discriminating against an employee. § 3730(h)(1). Strubbe's removal from part-time status— effectively a termination—in March 2016 is a retaliatory act.

Strubbe cannot prove that her termination was solely motivated by protected activity. She contends causation can be inferred because CCMH assigned her light-duty work after she was injured, but stopped once it learned of her FCA claim. Meanwhile, Stacey Kruse, another employee with a shoulder injury, continued to get light-duty work. Strubbe claims that an email from CCMH to Kruse, describing Kruse as a "low key injured employee," provides further proof CCMH removed her from part-time status because of her protected conduct. However, these events all occurred before CCMH knew Strubbe brought the FCA claim. They do not demonstrate CCMH terminated Strubbe solely because of her protected conduct.

CCMH did not terminate Strubbe until four months after learning of her involvement in the FCA claim. By then, she had not performed work at CCMH for six months. A temporal connection between the protected conduct and adverse action may be sufficient to establish a prima facie case where the proximity is "very close." *Clark Cty. Sch. Dist. v. Breeden,* 532 U.S. 268, 273, 121 S.Ct. 1508, 149 L.Ed.2d 509 (2001) (per curiam); *Smith v. Allen Health Sys., Inc.,* 302 F.3d 827, 833 (8th Cir. 2002) (two weeks between protected conduct and adverse action sufficient to establish prima facie case). Generally, however, "more than a temporal connection between the protected conduct and the adverse employment action is required to present a genuine factual issue on retaliation." *Kiel v. Select Artificials, Inc.,* 169 F.3d 1131, 1136 (8th Cir. 1999) (en banc). Here, the four months between the unsealing of the complaint and her removal from part-time status is too attenuated to establish a prima facie case. *See Kipp v. Missouri Highway & Transp. Comm'n,* 280 F.3d 893, 897 (8th Cir. 2002) (two months between complaint and termination "dilutes any inference of causation").

Even if the facts suggested Strubbe's removal was solely motivated by her protected p.1170 conduct, CCMH has provided a legitimate, non-discriminatory reason. CCMH claims it removed Strubbe from part-time status under its policy requiring employees to have worked in the previous six months. Strubbe can prove this reason is pretextual by showing CCMH "(1) failed to follow its own policies, (2) treated similarly-situated employees in a disparate manner, or (3) shifted its explanation of the employment decision." *Schaffhauser v. United Parcel Serv., Inc.,* 794 F.3d 899, 904 (8th Cir. 2015). CCMH's policy states, "The minimum requirement to remain a per diem employee is to have worked in the past six months...." CCMH followed this policy when it terminated Strubbe. By the time it removed her from part-time status, Strubbe had not worked as an EMT for over a year and had not performed any work for CCMH for six months. CCMH has not changed its explanation for Strubbe's termination.

Strubbe claims that CCMH treated Kruse, a similarly situated employee, differently by giving her light-duty work. Strubbe has not demonstrated that Kruse is similarly situated. She did not provide sufficient information detailing the significance of Kruse's injury, her physical limitations, her position at CCMH, or whether she had worked in the last six months. Further, CCMH sent Kruse the email describing her as a "low key injured employee" before CCMH learned of Strubbe's FCA claim. Strubbe cannot show that CCMH's reason for her termination was pretextual.

The district court properly granted summary judgment for CCMH.

* * * * * * *

The judgment is affirmed.

BEAM, Circuit Judge, dissenting in part and concurring in part.

I acknowledge that fraud cases receive more scrutiny at the pleadings stage than the average civil case. In a fraud case, rather than simply providing notice in the pleadings under Federal Rule of Civil Procedure 8, a plaintiff must "state with particularity the circumstances constituting fraud." Fed. R. Civ. P. 9(b). Originally, Rule 8 required something akin to, "I'm hurt, you did it, pay me." See Conley v. Gibson, 355 U.S. 41, 45-46, 78 S.Ct. 99, 2 L.Ed.2d 80 (1957) (holding that "a complaint should not be dismissed for failure to state a claim unless it appears beyond doubt that the plaintiff can prove no set of facts in support of his claim which would entitle him to relief"). But see Bell Atl. Corp. v. Twombly, 550 U.S. 544, 127 S.Ct. 1955, 167 L.Ed.2d 929 (2007) & Ashcroft v. Iqbal, 556 U.S. 662, 129 S.Ct. 1937, 173 L.Ed.2d 868 (2009) (effecting a landslide erosion of Conley's liberal construction of Rule 8's pleading standard). Because the FCA is an anti-fraud statute, the complaint's false-claim allegations must comply with Rule 9(b). However because Rule 9 does not eliminate Rule 8's notice pleading standard, Zayed v. Associated Bank, N.A., 779 F.3d 727, 733 (8th Cir. 2015), and the relators' pleadings in Counts I and II of their complaint more than adequately give notice, with particularity, of the fraud they are alleging, I dissent in part.

"To satisfy the particularity requirement of Rule 9(b), the complaint must plead such facts as the time, place, and content of the defendant's false representations, as well as the details of the defendant's fraudulent acts, including when the acts occurred, who engaged in them, and what was obtained as a result." United States ex rel. Joshi v. St. Luke's Hosp., Inc., 441 F.3d 552, 556 (8th Cir. 2006). As the majority opinion acknowledges, "[t]he relators here pleaded more than the relator in Joshi" and that "[t]he allegations in Count I are *close* to meeting this standard." Ante at 1164-65 (emphasis added). And yet, the court still requires more of a relator than p.1171 is necessary at this stage of the proceedings.

I would find that the relators have met Rule 8 and 9 (and Joshi's) requirement for pleading fraud with particularity. 441 F.3d at 556. Indeed, the majority opinion and the district court essentially require that the relators here witness the Medicare forms being submitted in order to get past the pleading stage in this case. If that were the case, only someone with access to the hospital's internal accounting records could successfully bring a qui tam action in this situation. Indeed, as relators point out, the accounting records became unaccessible to employees and the public once Bill Bruce became CEO (and incidentally, the HR manager) of the hospital. Bruce and the hospital can thus effectively eliminate any civil liability for false claims by eliminating access to financial information.

The complaint contained 198 paragraphs, including 55 paragraphs in the "Specific and Detailed Allegations" section, and spelled out the impropriety of EMTs and paramedics being asked to perform work differently, and to perform work— (i.e., breathing treatments on *inpatients*) —that EMTs and paramedics were not the most qualified and certainly not the most conveniently situated to perform. The complaint alleges the relators were told the reason for this abrupt change in procedure and policy was for "billing" purposes. Comp. ¶¶ 26-28. The complaint detailed the exponential increase in separately billed "breathing" treatments even while the number of hospital patients declined. ¶¶ 33-35. The complaint detailed how relators were required to make false entries into the computer system that was used for Medicare billing—averring that the treatments lasted at least thirty minutes regardless of how long the treatment lasted. ¶¶ 30, 98. Requiring the relators to plead an exact day in which any one of them performed a breathing treatment in less than 30 minutes, see ante at 1165-66, is more than is necessary. United States ex. rel Thayer v. Planned Parenthood of the Heartland, 765 F.3d 914, 917-18 (8th Cir. 2014) (holding that a relator does not have to plead specific examples in every case, and instead a "relator can satisfy Rule 9(b) by 'alleging particular details of a scheme to submit false claims paired with reliable indicia that lead to a strong inference that claims were actually submitted'") (quoting United States ex rel. Grubbs v. Kanneganti, 565 F.3d 180, 190 (5th Cir. 2009)).

Further, the relators did provide a concrete example of a terminal patient who clearly did *not* need a breathing treatment but was required to get one. ¶ 37. Relators pleaded with particularity that "Patient A, known to Relator Trader, was ordered to receive breathing treatments despite having been in a traumatic, clearly terminal, accident." Id. Two of the relators questioned the hospital's nurses about giving breathing treatments to other patients who clearly did "not need the treatments, but they were told to give the treatments anyway." ¶ 38. The complaint goes on to explain that breathing treatments given by paramedics, as opposed to nurses, are billed differently and generate more revenue for the hospital. ¶¶ 39-53. There are links to governmental and industry documents explaining this process.[2] The complaint details specific accounts of staff who were held out to be, and required to perform, acts of paramedics and phlebotomists despite their lack of certification. ¶¶ 59-63.

Although relators were not in a position to see the bills generated after such computer entries, the pleadings gave adequate notice of the natural inference that the p.1172 breathing treatments were fraudulently and inflatedly billed the way they were entered. Further, evidence of fraud— Bruce's purported misuse of a hospital credit card—is documented with particularity in the complaint including: the day of payment to "Money Gram," the amount of payment, and the outcome of an open records request which resulted in the production of an altered receipt. ¶ 70.

In short, the district court, and a majority of this court, essentially hold that short of the relators committing criminal activity by illegally accessing the hospital's billing records, they cannot successfully plead a false claims act case of Medicare billing fraud. This should not be the state of the law, especially as here "when the opposing party is the only practical source for discovering the specific facts supporting a pleader's conclusion." Bos. & Maine Corp. v. Town of Hampton, 987 F.2d 855, 866 (1st Cir. 1993), overruled on other grounds by Educadores Puertorriquenos en Accion v. Hernandez, 367 F.3d 61, 66-67 (1st Cir. 2004). In such cases, "less specificity of pleading may be required pending discovery." 987 F.2d at 866. See also United States ex rel. Nargol v. DePuy Orthopaedics, Inc., 865 F.3d 29, 37-41 (1st Cir. 2017) (noting that inferences can be used at the pleading stage of a fraud case, especially where the relators have little access to documentation, but clear knowledge of the scheme), cert. denied, ___ U.S. ___, 138 S.Ct. 1551, 200 L.Ed.2d 770 (2018). Accordingly, I dissent from Part IIA and IIB of the opinion affirming the dismissal of Counts I and II of the complaint. I concur in the remainder of the court's opinion.

[1] The Honorable Leonard T. Strand, Chief Judge, United States District Court for the Northern District of Iowa.

[2] Some of the government website links no longer work or have been moved, but many of the links do indeed provide the documentation described in the complaint.

NINTH CIRCUIT DECISIONS
Qui Tam Actions

945 F.3d 1237 (2020)

UNITED STATES EX REL. ALEXANDER VOLKHOFF, LLC, Plaintiff-Appellant,[*]

v.

JANSSEN PHARMACEUTICA N.V.; Janssen Pharmaceuticals, Inc.; Janssen Research And Development, LLC; Johnson & Johnson; Ortho-McNeil, Defendants-Appellees.

No. 18-55643.

United States Court of Appeals, Ninth Circuit.

Argued and Submitted November 14, 2019 Pasadena, California.

Filed January 2, 2020.

US ex rel. Alexander Volkhoff v. Janssen Pharma., 945 F. 3d 1237 (9th Cir. 2020)

Appeal from the United States District Court for the Central District of California; R. Gary Klausner, District Judge, Presiding, D.C. No. 2:16-cv-06997-v. RGK-RAO AND.

C. Brooks Cutter (argued) and John R. Parker, Jr., Cutter Law P.C., Sacramento, California; Audra Ibarra, Law Office of Audra Ibarra, Palo Alto, California; Mychal Wilson, Law Offices of Mychal Wilson, Santa Monica, California; for Plaintiff-Appellant.

Michael A. Schwartz (argued) and Erin Colleran, Pepper Hamilton LLP, Philadelphia, Pennsylvania; Jeffrey M. Goldman, Pepper Hamilton LLP, Los Angeles, California; for Defendants-Appellees.

Before: FERDINAND F. FERNANDEZ, MILAN D. SMITH, JR., and ERIC D. MILLER, Circuit Judges.

p.1239 OPINION

M. SMITH, Circuit Judge:

Alexander Volkhoff, LLC (Volkhoff) appeals the district court's dismissal of the qui tam complaint filed by relator Jane Doe pursuant to the False Claims Act (FCA), 31 U.S.C. §§ 3729-3733, and analogous state false claims laws.[1] However, Volkhoff was not a party to Jane Doe's complaint. Moreover, it is not clear from Volkhoff's notice of appeal (Notice), as required by Federal Rule of Appellate Procedure 3(c), that Jane Doe also sought to take an appeal. Because Volkhoff is a non-party that cannot appeal, and Jane Doe was not properly named as an appellant, we dismiss this appeal for lack of appellate jurisdiction.

FACTUAL AND PROCEDURAL BACKGROUND

On September 16, 2016, shortly after its incorporation as a Delaware limited liability company, Volkhoff filed a qui tam complaint (the Original Complaint) in federal p.1240 district court. The Original Complaint named Volkhoff as the relator and alleged violations of the FCA and various states' false claims laws by Defendants Janssen Pharmaceutica N.V., Janssen Pharmaceuticals, Inc., Janssen Research & Development, LLC, Johnson & Johnson, and Ortho-McNeil (Defendants). In particular, the Original Complaint alleged that Defendants fraudulently and unlawfully marketed their medications. Neither the United States nor any state elected to intervene, allowing Volkhoff to proceed with the Original Complaint.[2]

Following Defendants' motion to dismiss the Original Complaint, Volkhoff did not oppose the motion. Instead, Volkhoff's counsel filed a First Amended Complaint (FAC). The FAC alleged the same claims as those Volkhoff alleged in the Original Complaint. The FAC, however, removed Volkhoff as the relator and named Jane Doe, an anonymous natural person, as the only relator.

The FAC did not mention Volkhoff or its relationship to Jane Doe. In filings before the district court and our court, Jane Doe and Volkhoff acknowledge that the replacement of Volkhoff by Jane Doe was a tactical decision aimed at avoiding the dismissal of the Original Complaint's FCA employment retaliation claim. The change responded to Defendants' first motion to dismiss, which argued that Volkhoff, as a limited liability company, lacked standing to assert an FCA retaliation claim.

Defendants moved to dismiss Jane Doe's FAC. The district court dismissed the FAC on April 19, 2018. In relevant part, the district court dismissed Jane Doe's FCA claims for lack of subject matter jurisdiction based on the so-called "first-to-file bar," which prevents private third parties from intervening in or filing similar FCA qui tam lawsuits after an initial relator has filed one. *See* 31 U.S.C. 3730(b)(5); *United States ex rel. Lujan v. Hughes Aircraft Co.,* 243 F.3d 1181, 1187 (9th Cir. 2001). In concluding that the first-to-file bar applied, the district court found that Jane Doe was not a party to the Original Complaint that Volkhoff had filed, and that she and Volkhoff were distinct legal persons. The district court dismissed Jane Doe's FCA employment retaliation claim because she failed to demonstrate a need for proceeding anonymously. Finally, the court declined to exercise supplemental jurisdiction over Jane Doe's remaining state law claims and dismissed those claims without prejudice.

Within thirty days of the dismissal, Volkhoff filed the Notice challenging the district court's order. Fed. R. App. P. 4. The Notice names Volkhoff as the sole relator and plaintiff. It does not mention Jane Doe, nor refer to any other relator, plaintiff, or appellant. The "Representation Statement" filed concurrently with the Notice, and subsequent papers filed with this court, designate Volkhoff variously as the only relator, plaintiff, or appellant. On appeal, Volkhoff contends that Jane Doe is Volkhoff's sole owner.

JURISDICTION AND STANDARD OF REVIEW

Generally, we have jurisdiction over appeals "from all final decisions of the district p.1241 courts of the United States," 28 U.S.C. § 1291, such as the district court's final decision dismissing Jane Doe's FAC.

However, whether a nonparty has the ability to appeal is a jurisdictional question, *see Cal. Dep't of Toxic Substances Control v. Com. Realty Projects, Inc.,* 309 F.3d 1113, 1121 (9th Cir. 2002), and a failure to comply with the filing and content requirements of the Federal Rules of Appellate Procedure may "present a jurisdictional bar to appeal." *Le v. Astrue,* 558 F.3d 1019, 1021, 1024 (9th Cir. 2009). As a result, our inquiry into whether this appeal is proper is jurisdictional. "We have jurisdiction to determine our own jurisdiction." *Havensight Capital LLC v. Nike, Inc.,* 891 F.3d 1167, 1171 (9th Cir. 2018) (quoting *Agonafer v. Sessions,* 859 F.3d 1198, 1202 (9th Cir. 2017)). We review whether we have appellate jurisdiction de novo. *Le,* 558 F.3d at 1021 (citing *Perez-Martin v. Ashcroft,* 394 F.3d 752, 756 (9th Cir. 2005)).

ANALYSIS

Volkhoff argues both that it and Jane Doe appealed the district court's dismissal, and that, under either circumstance, the appeal is proper. However, Volkhoff and Jane Doe each face distinct jurisdictional problems that foreclose this appeal. First, Volkhoff's appeal violates the general rule that only parties to a lawsuit may appeal it. Second, because Volkhoff's Notice does not name Jane Doe or otherwise refer to her, Jane Doe's purported appeal does not conform to Federal Rule of Appellate Procedure 3(c). We discuss each jurisdictional defect in turn.

I. Volkhoff's Nonparty Appeal

Volkhoff claims that it may appeal the dismissal of Jane Doe's FAC even though it was not a party to her lawsuit. "The rule that only parties to a lawsuit, or those that properly become parties, may appeal an adverse judgment, is well settled." *Marino v. Ortiz,* 484 U.S. 301, 304, 108 S.Ct. 586, 98 L.Ed.2d 629 (1988) (per curiam) (citing *United States ex rel. Louisiana v. Jack,* 244 U.S. 397, 402, 37 S.Ct. 605, 61 L.Ed. 1222 (1917); Fed. R. App. P. 3(c)). This rule echoes the requirements of standing. *See Raley v. Hyundai Motor Co., Ltd.,* 642 F.3d 1271, 1274 (10th Cir. 2011) ("After all, it is usually only *parties* who are sufficiently aggrieved by a district court's decision that they possess Article III and prudential standing to be able to pursue an appeal of it." (emphasis added) (citations omitted)). But while the rule is sometimes described as "standing to appeal," it is distinct from the requirements of constitutional standing. *See United States v. Kovall,* 857 F.3d 1060, 1068-69 (9th Cir. 2017); *In re Proceedings Before Fed. Grand Jury,* 643 F.2d 641, 642-643, 642 n.1 (9th Cir. 1981).

As required by this rule, we hear nonparties' appeals only in "exceptional circumstances." *S. Cal. Edison Co. v. Lynch,* 307 F.3d 794, 804 (9th Cir. 2002) (quoting *Citibank Int'l v. Collier-Traino, Inc.,* 809 F.2d 1438, 1441 (9th Cir. 1987)). "We have allowed such an appeal only when (1) the appellant, though not a party, participated in the district court proceedings, and (2) the equities of the case weigh in favor of hearing the appeal." *Hilao v. Estate of Marcos,* 393 F.3d 987, 992 (9th Cir. 2004) (citation and internal quotation marks omitted); *see also United States v. Badger,* 930 F.2d 754, 756 (9th Cir. 1991).

The cases in which we have applied this test illustrate the level and nature of participation in the district court proceedings that is required for a nonparty to be permitted to appeal. We have allowed nonparties to appeal when they were significantly involved in the district p.1242 court proceedings—often because they were compelled to participate by one of the parties or the court. *Commodity Futures Trading Comm'n v. Topworth Int'l, Ltd.,* 205 F.3d 1107, 1113-14 (9th Cir. 1999), *as amended* (9th Cir. 2000) (non-party "participated in the proceedings below to the full extent possible" and "participated for several years, rather than coming in at the end of the proceedings" (citation omitted)); *Keith v. Volpe,* 118 F.3d 1386, 1389-91 (9th Cir. 1997) (after objecting, nonparty responded to order to show cause filed by party, filed memorandum of points and authorities at court's request, and participated in oral argument); *S.E.C. v. Wencke,* 783 F.2d 829, 834-35 (9th Cir. 1986) (nonparty appeared in the district court to contest the same issues it was asserting on appeal, the district court accepted nonparty's briefs, and it allowed him to cross-examine witnesses). This requirement is in accordance with the Supreme Court's admonition in *Marino* that "the better practice is for... a nonparty to seek intervention for purposes of appeal." 484 U.S. at 304, 108 S.Ct. 586; *see also* Fed. R. Civ. P. 24.

In contrast, we have denied nonparties the right to appeal when they choose not to meaningfully involve themselves in the district court proceedings. In *Citibank,* we dismissed a nonparty's appeal from a judgment when the nonparty "was well-apprised of the proceedings" but "chose not to intervene, join or make an appearance to contest jurisdiction [in district court], even though it had actual knowledge of the proceedings and their substance." 809 F.2d at 1441; *see also Washoe Tribe v. Greenley,* 674 F.2d 816, 818-19 (9th Cir. 1982) (concluding that nonparty state could not appeal where, by deciding not to intervene in the district court, it avoided waiving its immunity).

We conclude that Volkhoff's participation in the district court proceedings cannot serve as the basis for a right to appeal. Its activity in the case all but ceased with the filing of the FAC. The substitution of Jane Doe in place of Volkhoff was a strategic choice. *See Citibank,* 809 F.2d at 1441. Although Volkhoff, in what appears to be a scrivener's error, was listed as the only relator in the opposition to Defendants' motion to dismiss the FAC, the district court's order dismissing the FAC explicitly noted that Volkhoff had been substituted out of the lawsuit by Jane Doe. Moreover, the district court's application of the first-to-file bar to dismiss the FAC was premised upon on its finding that Volkhoff, the initial sole relator, had been completely replaced by Jane Doe, the second sole relator. Like the nonparty in *Citibank,* Volkhoff "chose not to participate" in the district court proceedings and instead substituted itself out when Jane Doe filed the FAC. *Id.*

We also find that Volkhoff fails to show that the equities favor hearing its appeal. The equities will support a nonparty's appeal "when a party has haled the non-party into the proceeding against his will, and then has attempted to thwart the nonparty's right to appeal by arguing that he lacks standing or when judgment has been entered against the nonparty." *Hilao,* 393 F.3d at 992 (citations and internal quotation marks omitted); *see also Commodity Futures Trading Comm'n,* 205 F.3d at 1114 n.1 (nonparty was "brought into the proceedings by the Receiver's notice indicating that [nonparty] would forfeit his right to recover anything ... unless he filed a claim, and by the later schedule requiring him to file a written objection or waive it"); *Keith,* 118 F.3d at 1391; *Badger,* 930 F.2d at 756.

Here, Volkhoff was not haled into court by one of the parties or the court. Instead, p.1243 its participation ceased after it made the tactical decision to substitute Jane Doe for itself. *See Washoe,* 674 F.2d at 818-819 (concluding that equities did not favor appeal of party that avoided appearing in district court). Moreover, the district court's judgment is against Jane Doe, not Volkhoff. At most, Volkhoff concludes, with little support, that its appeal is not *inequitable* to Defendants, which does not meet its burden as a nonparty appellant to demonstrate that the equities are in its favor. *See S. Cal. Edison Co.,* 307 F.3d at 804.[3] Thus, we conclude that we lack jurisdiction to hear nonparty Volkhoff's appeal of the district court's dismissal of Jane Doe's FAC.

II. Jane Doe's Purported Appeal

Alternatively, Volkhoff argues that we should infer from the Notice that Jane Doe, a party in the district court proceedings, intended to appeal. Federal Rule of Appellate Procedure 3(c) governs the required contents of a notice of appeal. *Smith v. Barry,* 502 U.S. 244, 247-48, 112 S.Ct. 678, 116 L.Ed.2d 678 (1992). Rule 3(c) requires that the notice "specify the party or parties taking the appeal by naming each one in the caption or body of the notice, but an attorney representing more than one party may describe those parties with such terms as 'all plaintiffs,' 'the defendants,' 'the plaintiffs A, B, et al.,' or 'all defendants except X.'" Fed. R. App. P. 3(c)(1)(A).

Rule 3(c), however, instructs us not to dismiss an appeal "for failure to name a party whose intent to appeal is otherwise clear from the notice [of appeal]." Fed. R. App. P. 3(c)(4). The Advisory Committee Note to the 1993 amendment to Rule 3(c) makes clear that its current version aims "to prevent the loss of a right to appeal through inadvertent omission[s]" of party names on the notice of appeal, but also that it still requires that it be "objectively clear that a party intended to appeal."

In interpreting Rule 3(c), the Supreme Court has instructed that "[a]lthough courts should construe Rule 3 liberally when determining whether it has been complied with, noncompliance is fatal to an appeal." *Le,* 558 F.3d at 1022 (quoting *Smith,* 502 U.S. at 248, 112 S.Ct. 678) (brackets in original). In particular, we interpret Rule 3(c)(1)(A)'s appellant-naming requirements strictly, following the Supreme Court's decision in *Torres v. Oakland Scavenger Co.,* 487 U.S. 312, 108 S.Ct. 2405, 101 L.Ed.2d 285 (1988), *superseded by statute as recognized in Retail Flooring Dealers of America, Inc. v. Beaulieu of America, LLC,* 339 F.3d 1146, 1148 (9th Cir. 2003).

In *Torres,* the Court dismissed an appeal pursuant to Rule 3(c) because the appellant was not named in the notice of appeal. *Torres,* 487 U.S. at 314-18, 108 S.Ct. 2405. Although the 1993 amendments to Rule 3(c) responded to *Torres* by allowing appellants more flexibility in meeting its requirements, *Retail Flooring,* 339 F.3d at 1148, *Torres* nevertheless continues to guide our interpretation of Rule 3(c). *Le,* 558 F.3d at 1022 ("[T]he 'failure to name a party in a notice of appeal is more p.1244 than excusable informality,' but rather 'it constitutes a failure of that party to appeal.'" (quoting *Torres,* 487 U.S. at 314, 108 S.Ct. 2405)); *Argabright v. United States,* 35 F.3d 472, 474 (9th Cir. 1994) (applying *Torres* to dismiss appeals of appellants not named or implicitly indicated through the use of "et al." or "plaintiffs" in the notice of appeal), *superseded by statute on other grounds as recognized in Hinck v. United States,* 550 U.S. 501, 504, 127 S.Ct. 2011, 167 L.Ed.2d 888 (2007); *see also West v. United States,* 853 F.3d 520, 522-24 (9th Cir. 2017) (contrasting our court's liberal interpretation of Rule 3(c)(1)(B) with the Supreme Court's "narrow application of Rule 3(c)(1)(A)" in *Torres* (citing *Le,* 558 F.3d at 1022)).

We are not alone in relying on *Torres* to find that the failure to name an appellant in a notice of appeal can result in dismissal. The Tenth Circuit relied on *Torres* in dismissing an appeal in a case that we find to be on point. In *Raley,* the initial plaintiff, Misty Raley, asked the district court to substitute her for the entity BancFirst as the sole plaintiff in the case. 642 F.3d at 1273-74. The court granted the requested substitution. *Id.* Defendant Hyundai prevailed at trial, but the district court's judgment erroneously identified Raley as the losing plaintiff. *Id.* at 1274. After Raley appealed the judgment in her name, the district court entered an amended judgment identifying only BancFirst as the losing party. *Id.* Raley filed another notice of appeal, again in her name, to appeal the amended judgment. *Id.*

The Tenth Circuit, quoting *Torres* for the proposition that Rule 3(c) was part of a "jurisdictional threshold" to appellate review, dismissed the appeal. 642 F.3d at 1274, 1276 (quoting 487 U.S. at 315, 108 S.Ct. 2405). The Tenth Circuit refused to look beyond the notice of appeal to determine whether BancFirst intended to appeal. *Id.* at 1277. Because the notice specified only Raley as the appellant and did not "use terms that objectively and clearly encompass[ed]" BancFirst, the court would not infer that BancFirst intended to appeal. *Id.* Although the court noted the apparent harshness of the result, it emphasized that "[t]hroughout most of the briefing of [the] appeal it was unclear whether BancFirst wanted to pursue an appeal," creating an unfair situation for Hyundai, which "ha[d] to write its briefs and prepare its arguments without any way of being sure who [was], and who [was] not, seeking to undo its district court victory." *Id.* at 1278.

The defects in Volkhoff's Notice are akin to those in Raley's notice of appeal. It is not clear from the Notice that Jane Doe intended to appeal the district court's dismissal. As already discussed, the Notice does not mention Jane Doe or her alleged ownership of Volkhoff, and instead designates Volkhoff as the only relator, plaintiff, and appellant.

Perhaps in light of this notable absence, Volkhoff urges us to view "Alexander Volkhoff, LLC" and "Jane Doe" as interchangeable. We do not accept the proposition that an LLC is interchangeable with a natural person. *See, e.g.,* 6 Del. Code tit. 6, §§ 18-201(b), 18-303(a); *In re Carlisle Etcetera LLC,* 114 A.3d 592, 605 (Del. Ch. 2015) (observing that the "core attributes of the LLC" include "its separate legal existence ... and limited liability for its members" (citation omitted)). Moreover, the alleged unity of identity between Volkhoff and Jane Doe is not clear from the Notice.

Volkhoff also argues that Rule 3(c), as amended in 1993, precludes dismissal because the Notice *mistakenly* named Volkhoff as the relator. The record undermines this argument. Before the district court, Jane Doe indicated that she changed the
p.1245 relator's name from "Alexander Volkhoff LLC" to "Jane Doe" to maintain the FAC's FCA employment retaliation claim, which could only be brought by an individual. In its appeal, Volkhoff acknowledges that the decision to switch relators in the FAC was tactical. In the shadow of this tactical choice, Volkhoff filed the Notice, which failed to designate Jane Doe as an appellant. That omission has been repeated in subsequent filings since the Notice. We cannot accept that Volkhoff's failure to name Jane Doe as an appellant was an "inadvertent omission" that Rule 3(c) requires us to overlook. Fed. R. App. P. 3(c) advisory committee's note to 1993 amendment.

Finally, Volkhoff relies on Rule 3(c)(4), which instructs us not to dismiss an appeal "for failure to name a party whose intent to appeal is otherwise clear from the notice." But Jane Doe's intent to appeal is not clear from the Notice, nor would it be any clearer even if we were permitted to look beyond the Notice. The lack of identity between Doe and Volkhoff was the central merits problem before the district court. The fact that Volkhoff is not Doe, and vice versa, is precisely why the district court dismissed Doe's FCA claim in the first place—and even before that, why Volkhoff voluntarily substituted itself out of the case so that Doe could pursue her retaliation claim. Under these circumstances, we cannot find that Jane Doe's intent to appeal was clear when Volkhoff, and only Volkhoff, filed a Notice.

The cases on which Volkhoff relies that invoke Rule 3(c)(4) involve attorneys who mistakenly appealed sanctions orders in the names of their parties, when the attorneys signed and were otherwise named in the filings. *See Detabali v. St. Luke's Hosp.*, 482 F.3d 1199, 1204 (9th Cir. 2007) (attorney "prepared, signed, and filed Detabali's notice of appeal" challenging sanctions order); *Retail Flooring*, 339 F.3d at 1149 (notice directly challenged sanctions against counsel, counsel's name appeared on the notice as the attorney, and counsel signed and filed the notice of appeal); *Aetna Life Ins. Co. v. Alla Med. Servs., Inc.*, 855 F.2d 1470, 1473 (9th Cir. 1988) (attorney listed on notice of appeal, where only appealable order was that imposing sanctions against attorney). None of the considerations that underlie these cases' applications of Rule 3(c)(4) applies here. Jane Doe is not serving as Volkhoff's attorney, is not otherwise mentioned on the Notice, and Volkhoff is not appealing a sanctions order against Jane Doe entered by the district court.

We are mindful of Rule 3(c)'s goal of avoiding dismissals of appeals solely due to matters of form. However, Volkhoff has failed to establish that Rule 3(c) forecloses dismissal of this appeal for lack of jurisdiction. Because Volkhoff, a nonparty, and Jane Doe, a purported appellant not named in the Notice, both fail to meet the requirements of appellate jurisdiction, we DISMISS this appeal.

APPEAL DISMISSED.

[*] The caption's reference to Alexander Volkhoff, LLC as "Plaintiff-Appellant" reflects the appeal-initiating documents. As we explain herein, Alexander Volkhoff, LLC is neither a plaintiff in this action nor a proper appellant of the district court order at issue on appeal.

[1] In a qui tam action brought pursuant to the FCA, a private plaintiff, referred to as a "relator," initiates a suit on behalf of the government for alleged fraud. *See* 31 U.S.C. § 3730; *United States ex rel. Eisenstein v. City of New York*, 556 U.S. 928, 932, 129 S.Ct. 2230, 173 L.Ed.2d 1255 (2009). Herein, we use "relator," except where necessary to indicate that the parties used (or did not use) the term "plaintiff."

[2] FCA suits are subject to certain procedural requirements, including the government's sole right to intervene, generally within 60 days of the suit's filing. *See* 31 U.S.C. § 3730; *Eisenstein*, 556 U.S. at 932, 129 S.Ct. 2230. Like the FCA, the state false claims laws invoked by the Original Complaint provide their respective state governments with an opportunity to intervene. *See, e.g.,* Cal. Gov't Code §§ 12650-12656; Colo. Rev. Stat. §§ 25.5-4-303.5-25.5-4-310. Because we dismiss this appeal for lack of appellate jurisdiction, we do not reach any other procedural issues relating to qui tam suits that are raised on appeal.

[3] Volkhoff briefly raises the possibility that Defendants might later argue, in a subsequent lawsuit, that the district court's dismissal of Jane Doe's FAC has a preclusive effect against Volkhoff. The cases that Volkhoff relies on to argue that this consideration should affect our analysis are inapposite. *American Games, Inc. v. Trade Products, Inc.* concerned an intervenor. 142 F.3d 1164, 1166 (9th Cir. 1998). *Wencke,* described above, involved a nonparty that was extensively involved at the district court. 783 F.2d 829, 834-835. Furthermore, we do not see how the possibility of future legal arguments regarding issue or claim preclusion tips the balance of equities in Volkhoff's favor.

968 F.3d 996 (2020)

UNITED STATES of America, Appellant,

v.

United States ex rel. Gwen Thrower, Plaintiff-Appellee,

v.

ACADEMY MORTGAGE CORPORATION, Defendant.

No. 18-16408.

United States Court of Appeals, Ninth Circuit.

Argued and Submitted November 14, 2019 San Francisco, California.
Filed August 4, 2020.

US v. Academy Mortg. Corp., 968 F. 3d 996 (9th Cir. 2020)

Appeal from the United States District Court for the Northern District of California; Edward M. Chen, District Judge, Presiding, D.C. No. 3:16-cv-02120-EMC.

Melissa N. Patterson (argued), Michael S. Raab, and Charles W. Scarborough, Appellate Staff; David L. Anderson, United States Attorney; Joseph H. Hunt, Assistant Attorney General; Civil Division, United States Department of Justice, Washington, D.C.; for Plaintiff-Appellant.

J. Nelson Thomas (argued), Thomas & Solomon LLP, Rochester, New York; Sanford J. Rosen and Van Swearingen, Rosen Bien Galvan & Grunfeld LLP, San Francisco, California; for Plaintiff-Appellee.

Jeffrey S. Bucholtz, Anne M. Voigts, and Bethany L. Rupert, King & Spalding LLP, Washington, D.C.; Steven P. Lehotsky and p.1000 Michael B. Schon, United States Chamber Litigation Center, Washington, D.C.; for Amicus Curiae Chamber of Commerce of the United States of America.

Claire M. Sylvia, Phillips & Cohen LLP, San Francisco, California; Jacklyn N. DeMar, Taxpayers Against Fraud Education Fund, Washington, D.C.; Jennifer M. Verkamp, Morgan Verkamp LLP, Cincinnati, Ohio; for Amicus Curiae Taxpayers Against Fraud Education Fund.

Before: Kim McLane Wardlaw, William A. Fletcher, and Richard Linn,[*] Circuit Judges.

p.999 OPINION

WARDLAW, Circuit Judge.

The False Claims Act (FCA) allows any person with knowledge that false or fraudulent claims for payment have been submitted to the federal government to bring a *qui tam* suit[1] on behalf of the United States against the perpetrator. If successful, the individual initiating the suit, known as the "relator," keeps a percentage of any recovery, with the remainder going to the Government. Each year, suits initiated by private relators return billions of dollars to the public fisc.[2]

When a *qui tam* suit is filed, the Government may choose to intervene and prosecute the case itself. 31 U.S.C. § 3730(b)(4)(A). If it declines to intervene, the relator has "the right to conduct the action." *Id.* § 3730(b)(4)(B). Here, the Government notified the district court that it declined to intervene in a *qui tam* suit filed by relator Gwen Thrower. It then filed a motion seeking dismissal of the action under § 3730(c)(2)(A) of the FCA. The district court denied the motion both because the Government failed to meet its burden of demonstrating a valid governmental purpose related to the dismissal and because it failed to fully investigate the allegations of the amended complaint.

The Government filed an immediate appeal, asserting appellate jurisdiction under the collateral order doctrine. We are thus presented with a question of first impression in the federal courts: is a district court order denying a Government motion to dismiss an FCA case under § 3730(c)(2)(A) an immediately appealable collateral order? We conclude that such orders fall outside the collateral order doctrine's narrow scope and dismiss the appeal for lack of jurisdiction.

I.

Academy Mortgage Corporation (Academy) is a mortgage lender that participates in residential mortgage insurance programs run by the Federal Housing Administration (FHA). These government programs insure lenders against losses incurred on certain qualifying mortgages. While the insurance programs are designed to encourage the extension of credit to low income borrowers, they are also a boon to lenders, who earn income from the mortgages without bearing the risk of loss in the event of default. Because the Government is financially responsible if p.1001 borrowers default on their loans, both borrowers and loans must meet certain eligibility criteria to qualify for FHA insurance. Participating lenders must certify that the mortgages they originate comply with these requirements.

Gwen Thrower works for Academy as an underwriter. She filed this FCA suit, detailing a scheme through which Academy certified loans for FHA insurance even though they failed to meet the Government's requirements. Some of the insured loans were subsequently defaulted upon, resulting in financial losses that the Government was required to cover. Thrower alleged that the Government would not have insured the loans had it known about Academy's lending practices, so Academy's false certifications of compliance with government requirements amounted to false claims within the meaning of the FCA.

The Government declined to exercise its statutory right to intervene and prosecute the case itself and so notified the court. Under the FCA, Thrower then had the right to conduct the action herself. *Id.* § 3730(b)(4)(B). But instead of permitting her to do so, the Government moved to dismiss under 31 U.S.C. § 3730(c)(2)(A), which allows the United States to move to dismiss an FCA action "notwithstanding the objections of the person initiating the action if the person has been notified by the Government of the filing of the motion and the court has provided the person with an opportunity for a hearing on the motion." The Government argued that if the case proceeded, it would be "burdened by discovery requests" that would "tax many of the same resources being used in other litigation and investigations." It asserted a "right to undertake a cost-benefit analysis and to conclude it is not in the public interest to spend further time and resources on [Thrower's] litigation of this matter."

Whether a motion to dismiss under § 3730(c)(2)(A) should be granted is governed by a two-step test. *United States ex rel. Sequoia Orange Co. v. Baird-Neece Packing Corp.*, 151 F.3d 1139, 1145 (9th Cir. 1998). The Government bears the initial burden of identifying a "valid governmental purpose" and showing a "rational relation between dismissal and accomplishment of the purpose." *Id.* If the Government makes this showing, the burden shifts to the relator "to demonstrate that dismissal is fraudulent, arbitrary and capricious, or illegal." *Id.*

Applying the *Sequoia Orange* test, the district court concluded that the Government's asserted cost-benefit justification fell short at both steps of the analysis. Specifically, the court determined that the Government could not have meaningfully assessed the potential recovery from the suit—i.e., the benefit side of the cost-benefit analysis—because it had not sufficiently investigated Thrower's claims, including by failing to investigate the detailed allegations of wrongdoing Thrower had added when she amended her original complaint. The district court therefore denied the Government's motion to dismiss.

The Government immediately appealed, invoking appellate jurisdiction under the collateral order doctrine.[3]

II.

We have jurisdiction to determine our jurisdiction, which includes authority to decide whether the district court's denial of the motion to dismiss under § 3730(c)(2)(A) is immediately appealable under the collateral order doctrine. *Metabolic* p.1002 *Research, Inc. v. Ferrell,* 693 F.3d 795, 798 (9th Cir. 2012).

III.

A.

Under 28 U.S.C. § 1291, the courts of appeals have jurisdiction over "appeals from all final decisions of the district courts." This statute is most often invoked as the basis for appellate jurisdiction over quintessential "final decisions," such as final judgments. But it also encompasses "a small set of prejudgment orders that are 'collateral to' the merits of an action and 'too important' to be denied immediate review." *Mohawk Indus., Inc. v. Carpenter,* 558 U.S. 100, 103, 130 S.Ct. 599, 175 L.Ed.2d 458 (2009) (quoting *Cohen v. Beneficial Indus. Loan Corp.,* 337 U.S. 541, 546, 69 S.Ct. 1221, 93 L.Ed. 1528 (1949)). This has become known as the "collateral order doctrine."

To fall within the limited scope of the collateral order doctrine, a district court order must satisfy three requirements first described by the Supreme Court in *Cohen*: it must (1) be "conclusive" on the issue at hand, (2) "resolve important questions separate from the merits," and (3) be "effectively unreviewable" after final judgment. *Id.* at 106, 130 S.Ct. 599; *see Cohen,* 337 U.S. at 545-46, 69 S.Ct. 1221. These conditions are "stringent," *Digital Equip. Corp. v. Desktop Direct, Inc.,* 511 U.S. 863, 868, 114 S.Ct.

1992, 128 L.Ed.2d 842 (1994), and efforts to expand the scope of the collateral order doctrine have been repeatedly rebuffed, *Will v. Hallock,* 546 U.S. 345, 350, 126 S.Ct. 952, 163 L.Ed.2d 836 (2006).

Stringent application of the final judgment rule avoids encroachment on the "special role" that district judges play as initial arbiters of "the many questions of law and fact that occur in the course of a trial." *Firestone Tire & Rubber Co. v. Risjord,* 449 U.S. 368, 374, 101 S.Ct. 669, 66 L.Ed.2d 571 (1981). As the Supreme Court has explained, "[i]mplicit in § 1291 is Congress' judgment that the *district judge* has primary responsibility to police the prejudgment tactics of litigants, and that the district judge can better exercise that responsibility if the appellate courts do not repeatedly intervene to second-guess prejudgment rulings." *Richardson-Merrell, Inc. v. Koller,* 472 U.S. 424, 436, 105 S.Ct. 2757, 86 L.Ed.2d 340 (1985). The final judgment rule also furthers the strong interest in judicial efficiency and the avoidance of piecemeal appellate proceedings. *Mohawk Indus.,* 558 U.S. at 106, 130 S.Ct. 599. Under a more relaxed standard, "cases could be interrupted and trials postponed indefinitely as enterprising appellants bounced matters between the district and appellate courts." *SolarCity Corp. v. Salt River Project Agric. Improvement & Power Dist.,* 859 F.3d 720, 723 (9th Cir. 2017) (citing *Bank of Columbia v. Sweeny,* 26 U.S. (1 Pet.) 567, 569, 7 L.Ed. 265 (1828)).

B.

The Government first contends that the Supreme Court has already held that the denial of a government motion to dismiss a *qui tam* suit over the relator's objection is an appealable collateral order. *See United States ex rel. Eisenstein v. City of New York,* 556 U.S. 928, 129 S.Ct. 2230, 173 L.Ed.2d 1255 (2009). But that question was not before the Court in *Eisenstein;* nor was it even addressed. The question in *Eisenstein* was whether the Government is a "party" to a *qui tam* action under the FCA when it has declined to intervene. *See id.* at 930-31, 129 S.Ct. 2230. The Supreme Court unanimously answered: "No."

In *Eisenstein,* the Government declined to intervene in a *qui tam* action filed by Eisenstein, and the defendants successfully moved to dismiss. *Id.* at 930, 129 S.Ct. p.1003 2230. Eisenstein filed his notice of appeal within the 60-day period of Federal Rule of Appellate Procedure 4(a)(1)(B), which is the time limit applicable when the United States or its officer or agency is a party, rather than within the 30-day period that applies to everyone else. *Id.* The Court stated that the question presented was "whether the 30-day time limit to file a notice of appeal in Federal Rule of Appellate Procedure 4(a)(1)(A) or the 60-day time limit in Rule 4(a)(1)(B) applies when the United States declines to formally intervene in a *qui tam* action brought under the False Claims Act." *Id.* at 929, 129 S.Ct. 2230. After considering the plain meaning of the word "party" and its prior precedent, which instructed that a litigant becomes a party only through intervention, the Court held that "[a]lthough the United States is aware of and minimally involved in every FCA action ... it is not a 'party'... for purposes of the appellate filing deadline unless it has exercised its right to intervene in the case." *Id.* at 932-34, 129 S.Ct. 2230.

In Footnote 2 of the *Eisenstein* opinion, the Court noted that its holding "d[id] not mean that the United States must intervene before it can appeal *any order* of the court in an FCA action." *Id.* at 931 n.2, 129 S.Ct. 2230 (emphasis added). And it gave some examples of situations in which "the Government is a party for purposes of appealing the specific order at issue even though it is not a party for purposes of the final judgment and Federal Rule of Appellate Procedure 4(a)(1)(B)." *Id.*

The Court explained that the Government may appeal "the dismissal of an FCA action over its objection," citing to FCA § 3730(b)(1), which prohibits the dismissal of an FCA case without the Attorney General's written consent. *Id.* It also pointed out that a denial of a Government motion to intervene under FCA § 3730(c)(3) would be immediately appealable, *id.,* as denials of motions to intervene of right generally are, *see, e.g., Citizens for Balanced Use v. Mont. Wilderness Ass'n,* 647 F.3d 893, 896 (9th Cir. 2011). These examples of when non-parties may appeal from a specific order meet the *Cohen* requirements for appealability of a collateral order, thus giving the appellate court jurisdiction to entertain them. *See Robert Ito Farm, Inc. v. County of Maui,* 842 F.3d 681, 687-88 (9th Cir. 2016) (explaining that the collateral order doctrine is the source of the right to immediately appeal the denial of a motion to intervene).

In no place in Footnote 2 or elsewhere in *Eisenstein* did the Court indicate that the denial of a Government motion to dismiss an FCA action that the relator has a statutory right to prosecute, where the Government declined to intervene as a party, is an appealable order under *Cohen.* And, unlike in *Eisenstein,* whether or not the United States is a party is not the focus of our analysis here. Rather, the question is whether the district court's order satisfies the collateral order doctrine requirements and is thus a "final decision" within the meaning of 28 U.S.C. § 1291. We disagree with the Government's assertion that there is "no basis for distinguishing the appealability of an order rejecting the United States' objection to dismissal under Section 3730(b)(1) and an order rejecting the United States' request for such dismissal under Section 3730(c)(2)(A)." The former order ends the action and is therefore prototypically "final,"[4] while the latter p.1004 order allows the case to continue, and the motion can be renewed as circumstances change.[5]

In sum, Footnote 2 of *Eisenstein* stands for the narrow proposition that even when the Government is not a party to an FCA action because it has not intervened, there are some orders that determine important rights with sufficient finality that the Government may appeal them under the collateral order doctrine. It says nothing about whether orders denying a Government motion to dismiss under § 3730(c)(2)(A) satisfy the collateral order doctrine requirements. We now turn to that question.

C.

The small class of district court decisions immediately appealable under the collateral order doctrine includes only orders that are conclusive, that resolve important questions separate from the merits, and that are effectively unreviewable after final judgment. *Mohawk Indus.,* 558 U.S. at 106, 130 S.Ct. 599. Here, whether the order resolved important questions separate from the merits is dispositive.

1.

Explicit in the second requirement of the collateral order test, the question of importance is also implicated by the third *Cohen* condition—effective unreviewability —because whether an order is effectively unreviewable "cannot be answered without a judgment about the value of the interests that would be lost through rigorous application of a final judgment requirement." *Digital Equip.,* 511 U.S. at 878-79, 114 S.Ct. 1992. Whether a particular category of district court orders is "important" enough to merit immediate appellate consideration turns on "whether delaying review... 'would imperil a substantial public interest' or 'some particular value of a high order.'" *Mohawk Indus.,* 558 U.S. at 107, 130 S.Ct. 599 (quoting *Will,* 546 U.S. at 352-53, 126 S.Ct. 952). Even orders implicating rights that are generally considered "important" in the abstract have been found to fall outside the collateral order doctrine's scope. *See, e.g., id.* at 114, 130 S.Ct. 599 (order finding a waiver of attorney-client privilege); *Flanagan v. United States,* 465 U.S. 259, 262-63, 104 S.Ct. 1051, 79 L.Ed.2d 288 (1984) (order disqualifying a criminal defendant's chosen counsel); *see also Mohawk Indus.,* 558 U.S. at 117, 130 S.Ct. 599 (Thomas, J., concurring) (explaining that the Supreme Court has narrowed the scope of the collateral order doctrine "principally by raising the bar on what types of interests are 'important enough' to justify collateral order appeals").

In determining whether a district court order is immediately appealable, we do not focus on the exigencies presented by any individual case. *Mohawk Indus.,* 558 U.S. at 107, 130 S.Ct. 599. Instead, "the issue of appealability under § 1291 is to be determined for the entire category to which a claim belongs, without regard to the chance that the litigation at hand might be speeded, or a particular injustice averted by a prompt appellate court decision." *Digital Equip.,* 511 U.S. at 868, 114 S.Ct. 1992 (internal citation, quotation p.1005 marks, and alteration omitted). The mere fact that a class of orders may never be subject to appellate review after final judgment is not, on its own, sufficient to justify an immediate appeal. *Cf. id.* at 878, 114 S.Ct. 1992 (emphasizing that a collateral order appeal is available only if the right implicated is important).

2.

The interests implicated by orders denying a Government motion to dismiss under § 3730(c)(2)(A) of the FCA are not sufficiently important to justify expanding the collateral order doctrine's narrow scope, at least in cases where the Government has not exercised its right to intervene.

In support of its motion to dismiss, the Government cited the likelihood that it would face burdensome discovery requests if the litigation proceeded. We have previously acknowledged that the Government may legitimately consider the avoidance of litigation costs as a basis for moving to dismiss an FCA case. *Sequoia Orange,* 151 F.3d at 1146. But the mere fact that an erroneous denial of a § 3730(c)(2)(A) motion could lead to unnecessary government expenditures does not render the denial order immediately appealable. The Supreme Court has made clear that an interest in "abbreviating litigation troublesome to Government employees" is not important enough to justify a collateral order appeal. *Will,* 546 U.S. at 353, 126

S.Ct. 952. Otherwise, the valuable interests served by the final judgment rule "would fade out whenever the Government or an official lost an early round that could have stopped the fight." *Id.* at 354, 126 S.Ct. 952.

The Government argues that motions to dismiss under § 3730(c)(2)(A) "further[ ] interests similar to the doctrine of qualified immunity" in that they exist to protect the Government from "the burdens associated with the litigation itself." Without an immediate appeal, the Government contends, its interest in avoiding litigation burdens would be lost forever.

This is not the first time a litigant has sought to analogize its interests to those served by the doctrine of qualified immunity to support an immediate appeal.[6] *See Will,* 546 U.S. at 350-51, 126 S.Ct. 952; *Digital Equip.,* 511 U.S. at 871, 114 S.Ct. 1992; *SolarCity,* 859 F.3d at 725. But we are mindful of the Supreme Court's instruction that "claims of a 'right not to be tried'" must be viewed "with skepticism, if not a jaundiced eye." *Digital Equip.,* 511 U.S. at 873, 114 S.Ct. 1992. After all, with a "lawyer's temptation to generalize," *Will,* 546 U.S. at 350, 126 S.Ct. 952, almost any right that could be vindicated through a motion to dismiss could be characterized as providing immunity from further proceedings. *Digital Equip.,* 511 U.S. at 873, 114 S.Ct. 1992.

Even accepting that one purpose of § 3730(c)(2)(A) is to provide the Government with a mechanism for dismissing financially burdensome cases, that is not enough to treat the provision as tantamount to a grant of immunity. The Government's interest in cost avoidance is simply not a "value of a high order" on par with those the collateral order doctrine has been held to protect. *Will,* 546 U.S. at 352-54, 126 S.Ct. 952; *see, e.g., P.R. Aqueduct & Sewer Auth. v. Metcalf & Eddy, Inc.,* 506 U.S. 139, 146, 113 S.Ct. 684, 121 L.Ed.2d 605 (1993) (allowing immediate appeal of the denial of Eleventh Amendment immunity to protect the "dignitary interests" of states); *Nixon v. Fitzgerald,* p.1006 457 U.S. 731, 743, 102 S.Ct. 2690, 73 L.Ed.2d 349 (1982) (allowing immediate appeal of the denial of absolute presidential immunity to protect "essential Presidential prerogatives under the separation of powers"); *Abney v. United States,* 431 U.S. 651, 661, 97 S.Ct. 2034, 52 L.Ed.2d 651 (1977) (allowing an immediate appeal to protect the Double Jeopardy Clause's guarantee that an individual "will not be forced ... to endure the personal strain, public embarrassment, and expense of a criminal trial more than once for the same offense").

The Government argues that cases like *Will* are inapposite because they addressed a *defendant's* ability to appeal the denial of a motion to dismiss, whereas in FCA cases, the United States should be viewed as akin to a plaintiff seeking to voluntarily dismiss its own case.[7] But *Eisenstein* makes clear that the United States is not a party, and therefore not a plaintiff, when it has declined to exercise its right to intervene. 556 U.S. at 933, 129 S.Ct. 2230 ("[I]ntervention is the requisite method for a nonparty to become a party to a lawsuit."). Instead, the Government is more akin to a third-party assignor, albeit one that retains some statutory rights to participate in the proceedings. *Vt. Agency of Nat. Res. v. United States ex rel. Stevens,* 529 U.S. 765, 773, 120 S.Ct. 1858, 146 L.Ed.2d 836 (2000) ("The FCA can reasonably be regarded as effecting a partial assignment of the Government's damages claim."); *see also* 31 U.S.C. § 3730(c)(3)-(4) (detailing rights retained by the Government when it declines to intervene).[8]

As a third party, the Government and its agencies are subject to the same discovery obligations as other non-parties under Federal Rule of Civil Procedure 45, including the obligation to respond to subpoenas for documents and testimony. *Exxon Shipping Co. v. U.S. Dep't of Interior,* 34 F.3d 774, 779 (9th Cir. 1994); *see also Yousuf v. Samantar,* 451 F.3d 248, 256-57 (D.C. Cir. 2006); John T. Boese, *Civil False Claims and Qui Tam Actions* § 5.07 (4th ed. 2011) (explaining the use of Rule 45 subpoenas to obtain discovery from government agencies in FCA cases). When third-party discovery obligations become onerous, Rule 45 allows the subject of a subpoena to file a motion to quash on grounds of undue burden. Fed. R. Civ. P. 45(d)(3)(A)(iv). We have previously identified this procedural mechanism as a means by which the Government can vindicate its "serious and legitimate" interest in ensuring "that its employee resources [are] not... commandeered into service by private litigants to the detriment of the smooth functioning of government operations." *Exxon Shipping,* 34 F.3d at 779.

Yet notwithstanding the important interest in ensuring that non-parties are not subjected to burdensome discovery requests, orders denying a motion to quash a Rule 45 subpoena generally cannot be immediately appealed under the collateral order doctrine. *Perry v. Schwarzenegger,* 602 F.3d 976, 979 (9th Cir. 2010) (per curiam) (citing *In re Subpoena Served on Cal. Pub. Utils. Comm'n,* 813 F.2d 1473, 1476 (9th Cir. 1987)). Instead, a non-party can obtain p.1007 appellate review only by ignoring the subpoena, accepting the consequences of being held in contempt, and appealing the ensuing contempt citation.[9] *Cal. Pub. Utils. Comm'n,* 813 F.2d at 1476; *see also Mohawk Indus.,* 558 U.S. at 111-12, 130 S.Ct. 599 (explaining that noncompliance and contempt is a means by which an individual subject to a discovery order can obtain appellate review). It would be incongruous to hold, as we are asked to here, that the Government's interest in dismissing the case to avoid the *possibility* of future onerous discovery requests is important enough to merit an immediate appeal, when third parties *actually faced* with burdensome subpoenas have no such right.

Inherent in the final judgment rule is the possibility that some cases will proceed further than they should have, resulting in increased costs for parties and non-parties alike. But a mere interest in avoiding these costs has never been enough to justify an immediate appeal, even when they will be borne by the Government, and consequently, the taxpayers. *Will,* 546 U.S. at 353-54, 126 S.Ct. 952. While we have recognized that the Government may move to dismiss under § 3730(c)(2)(A) when an FCA case will impose an undue burden on the taxpayers or impose "enormous internal staff costs," *Sequoia Orange,* 151 F.3d at 1146, this interest in government efficiency is not a "value of a high order" that may be vindicated through collateral order review, *Will,* 546 U.S. at 352-53, 126 S.Ct. 952.

3.

In its reply brief, the Government recharacterizes its interest as one of protecting "fundamental Executive Branch prerogatives"—namely its "wide latitude to determine which enforcement actions will proceed in the United States' name to remedy the United States' injuries." We do not question the validity of this interest, but it is hardly at its apex here. Through the *qui tam* provisions of the FCA, Congress has assigned some enforcement responsibility to private relators, *Stevens,* 529 U.S. at

773, 120 S.Ct. 1858, and that partial assignment has "to some degree diminish[ed] Executive Branch control over the initiation and prosecution of [FCA cases]," *United States ex rel. Kelly v. Boeing Co.,* 9 F.3d 743, 754-55 (9th Cir. 1993).

Our decisions addressing the motion to dismiss procedures of § 3730(c)(2)(A) make clear that the Government's interests in this area are qualified. In *Kelly,* we held that the FCA does not offend the principle of separation of powers even though it requires the Government to obtain judicial approval before dismissing an FCA suit. *Id.* at 754 n.12, 756. We expanded on this holding in *Sequoia Orange,* where we explicitly recognized that § 3730(c)(2)(A) creates a "check," albeit a limited one, on the Government's prosecutorial discretion. 151 F.3d at 1144-45. By requiring the Government to make an adequate showing to justify dismissal, *Sequoia Orange* implicitly contemplated that in some circumstances, an FCA case may proceed even over the Government's objection. *Id.* at 1145.

p.1008 Because the FCA's broad intervention rights are a primary means by which the Executive Branch can exercise control over a given case, *id.* at 1144, the Government's interests are particularly attenuated where, as here, it has declined to intervene. In FCA cases initiated by a private relator, the Government has an unfettered right to intervene within 60 days after service of the complaint and all material evidence the relator possesses, with extensions of the period for intervention available for good cause. 31 U.S.C. § 3730(b)(2)-(3). And, even if the Government initially declines to intervene, it may intervene later upon a showing of good cause, *id.* § 3730(c)(3), at which point it enjoys the same rights as if it had intervened from the outset, *Sequoia Orange,* 151 F.3d at 1145.

When the Government intervenes, "it shall have the primary responsibility for prosecuting the action, and shall not be bound by an act of the [relator]." 31 U.S.C. § 3730(c)(1). While the relator may remain a party to the case, *id.,* the Government, with the district court's approval, may impose significant limitations on the relator's participation, *id.* § 3730(c)(2)(C). In short, intervention by the Government "reduce[s] substantially the relator's role." *United States v. Northrop Corp.,* 59 F.3d 953, 964 (9th Cir. 1995).

By contrast, when the Government declines to intervene, the relator "shall have the right to conduct the action." 31 U.S.C. § 3730(b)(4)(B); *see United States ex rel. Killingsworth v. Northrop Corp.,* 25 F.3d 715, 722 (9th Cir. 1994) (noting Congress' intent "to place full responsibility for False Claims Act litigation on private parties, absent early intervention by the government or later intervention for good cause"); *see also* H.R. Rep. 99-660, at 22 (1986) (reflecting that Congress intended the 1986 amendments to the FCA to restore incentives for *qui tam* suits). As a practical matter, the Government need not do anything beyond respond to discovery requests like any other third party, Fed. R. Civ. P. 45, provide its views if the relator seeks to dismiss the case, 31 U.S.C. § 3730(b)(1), and wait to see if the suit succeeds, in which case the Government receives the bulk of any recovery, *id.* § 3730(d)(2). Thus, by denying the motion to dismiss here, the district court in no way forced the Government to actively prosecute an action against its will.[10]

For all the separation-of-powers discussion, we cannot escape the conclusion that the Government's true interest in dismissing this case is what it has repeatedly maintained throughout this litigation: avoiding burdensome discovery expenses in a case the Government does not think will ultimately be worth the cost. While this may be a legitimate reason for moving to dismiss, *Sequoia Orange,* 151 F.3d at 1146, it is not an interest important enough to merit expanding the narrow scope of the collateral order doctrine, *Will,* 546 U.S. at 350, 126 S.Ct. 952.

D.

We are not swayed by the Government's argument that refusing to allow an immediate appeal will render orders denying a motion to dismiss under § 3730(c)(2)(A) effectively unreviewable.

First, any concerns in this area are substantially diminished by the extraordinarily low likelihood of an erroneous denial of a motion to dismiss under § 3730(c)(2)(A). *Cf. Mohawk Indus.,* 558 U.S. at 110 n.2, 130 S.Ct. 599. The test set out in *Sequoia Orange* is not especially demanding, as evidenced by the fact that this is the first p.1009 time a district court in our circuit has *ever* found the Government's argument for dismissal lacking.[11] There is therefore no reason to think that a new exception to the final judgment rule is necessary to accommodate this rare situation.

Moreover, in many cases, there will be other mechanisms available to mitigate any harms that could flow from the erroneous denial of a motion to dismiss. For example, in moving to dismiss here, the Government claimed that it would be subjected to burdensome discovery requests if the litigation proceeded. But to the extent these requests materialize, the Government can seek to quash or modify them, including on grounds of undue burden. *See* Fed. R. Civ. P. 45(d); *Exxon Shipping,* 34 F.3d at 779. The Government also argues that it has an interest in dismissing cases to prevent the creation of unfavorable precedent. But if the Government is concerned about the direction in which a case is moving, it can move to intervene upon a showing of good cause and take over the prosecution itself. 31 U.S.C. § 3730(c)(3).

We recognize that in some cases, the Government may seek dismissal to protect more unique interests. For example, in *Sequoia Orange,* we affirmed the district court's decision to dismiss a case at the Government's behest in order "to end the divisiveness in the citrus industry caused by over ten years of litigation." 151 F.3d at 1142, 1146. The Government has also sought dismissal when it contended that continued prosecution of a *qui tam* action would risk the disclosure of classified information. *See, e.g., United States ex rel. Mateski v. Mateski,* 634 F. App'x 192, 193-94 (9th Cir. 2015). But it would not be appropriate for us to expand the collateral order doctrine to accommodate these atypical cases. The issue of appealability must be determined "for the entire category to which a claim belongs," *Digital Equip.,* 511 U.S. at 868, 114 S.Ct. 1992, and we cannot allow immediate appeal of *all* orders denying § 3730(c)(2)(A) motions simply because a subset of them may implicate interests more important than simple cost avoidance, *Mohawk Indus.,* 558 U.S. at 112, 130 S.Ct. 599. We also see no need to do so because, at least to this point, district courts have invariably granted motions to dismiss when concerns of a higher order have been raised. *Cf. id.* at 110 n.2, 130 S.Ct. 599.

We emphasize that our decision does not leave the Government without options for seeking appellate review. *See id.* at 110-11, 130 S.Ct. 599. Most obviously, the Government could ask the district court to certify, and our court to accept, an interlocutory appeal under 28 U.S.C. § 1292(b), which allows for appeal of orders that "involve[ ] a controlling question of law as to which there is substantial ground for difference of opinion," when an immediate appeal "may materially advance the ultimate termination of the litigation." And, in extraordinary circumstances, such as where the unjustified disclosure of classified information is at risk, *see Mateski,* 634 F. App'x at 193-94, the Government may seek a writ of mandamus. *Mohawk Indus.,* 558 U.S. at 111, 130 S.Ct. 599. These "safety valves" are more than adequate to address denials of motions to dismiss that implicate interests more important than run-of-the-mill litigation burdens. *Id.* (alterations omitted).

p.1010 IV.

As the Supreme Court has emphasized time and again, the "small class" of immediately appealable collateral orders must remain "narrow and selective in its membership." *Will,* 546 U.S. at 350, 126 S.Ct. 952. Because the interests implicated by an erroneous denial of a Government motion to dismiss a False Claims Act case in which it has not intervened are insufficiently important to justify an immediate appeal, we conclude that they fall outside of the collateral order doctrine's scope. We therefore dismiss this appeal for lack of jurisdiction.[12]

DISMISSED.

[*] The Honorable Richard Linn, United States Circuit Judge for the U.S. Court of Appeals for the Federal Circuit, sitting by designation.

[1] "[T]he phrase *qui tam* means an action under a statute that allows a private person to sue for a penalty, part of which the government or some specified public institution will receive." *United States ex rel. Kelly v. Serco, Inc.,* 846 F.3d 325, 330 n.4 (9th Cir. 2017) (internal alterations and quotation marks omitted).

[2] In Fiscal Year 2019, FCA suits initiated by private relators recovered more than $2.2 billion, including almost $300 million in cases in which the Government declined to intervene. U.S. Dep't of Justice, *Fraud Statistics — Overview: October 1, 1986 — September 30, 2019* (2020), https://tinyurl.com/vvbvx5h.

[3] A motions panel of our court stayed further district court proceedings pending the resolution of this appeal.

[4] The Government hypothesizes that in cases where FCA claims are joined in a single action with other claims, an order dismissing the FCA claims over the Government's objection would not necessarily end the case. In those circumstances, it contends, Footnote 2 of *Eisenstein* allows the Government to take an immediate appeal even before the remaining claims are resolved in a final judgment. But we do not believe Footnote 2 was directed toward this unusual scenario. Footnote 2 of *Eisenstein* says that under the collateral order doctrine, "the United States may appeal... the dismissal of an FCA *action* over its objection." 556 U.S. at 931 n.2, 129 S.Ct. 2230 (emphasis added). We assume that by using the word "action" instead of "claim," the Court meant to refer to an order that ended the entire case.

[5] This is particularly true in this case because the district court rejected the Government's motion to dismiss for lack of a meaningful cost-benefit analysis, in which the Government might still engage.

[6] Denials of qualified immunity may be immediately appealed under the collateral order doctrine to the extent they turn on questions of law. *Mitchell v. Forsyth,* 472 U.S. 511, 530, 105 S.Ct. 2806, 86 L.Ed.2d 411 (1985).

[7] Federal Rule of Civil Procedure 41(a)(1)(A)(i) provides that a plaintiff may voluntarily dismiss a case without a court order if it files a notice of dismissal before the opposing party serves an answer or a motion for summary judgment.

[8] These include the right to be served with pleadings and receive copies of deposition transcripts, the right to seek a stay of discovery if it "would interfere with the Government's investigation or prosecution of a criminal or civil matter arising out of the same facts," and the right to intervene at a later date upon a showing of good cause. 31 U.S.C. § 3730(c)(3)-(4).

[9] We have recognized limited exceptions to this rule "when a subpoena is issued by a district court in favor of a nonparty in connection with a case pending in a district court of another circuit," *Cal. Pub. Utils. Comm'n,* 813 F.2d at 1476, or when the subject of the subpoena is a "disinterested third-party custodian of privileged documents" who "would most likely produce the documents rather than submit to a contempt citation," *United States v. Krane,* 625 F.3d 568, 572 (9th Cir. 2010) (quoting *United States v. Griffin,* 440 F.3d 1138, 1143 (9th Cir. 2006)); *see Perlman v. United States,* 247 U.S. 7, 38 S.Ct. 417, 62 L.Ed. 950 (1918).

[10] We do not decide whether the Government may immediately appeal the denial of a motion to dismiss in a case in which it *has* intervened.

[11] We are aware of only one other instance of a district court denying a Government motion to dismiss under § 3730(c)(2)(A). *See United States ex rel. CIMZNHCA, LLC v. UCB, Inc.,* No. 17-CV-765-SMY-MAB, 2019 WL 1598109, at *2-4 (S.D. Ill. Apr. 15, 2019), *appeal docketed* No. 19-2273 (7th Cir. July 8, 2019). An appeal of that decision is currently pending before the Seventh Circuit.

[12] Thrower's motion to strike documents from the Government's Excerpts of Record is DENIED as moot.

953 F.3d 1108 (2020)

Jane WINTER, EX REL. UNITED STATES of America, Plaintiff-Appellant,

v.

GARDENS REGIONAL HOSPITAL AND MEDICAL CENTER, INC., dba Tri-City Regional Medical Center, a California corporation; RollinsNelson LTC Corp., a California corporation; p.1109 Vicki Rollins; Bill Nelson; S&W Health Management Services, Inc., a California corporation; Beryl Weiner; Prode Pascual, M.D.; Rafaelito Victoria, M.D.; Arnold Ling, M.D.; Cynthia Miller-Dobalian, M.D.; Edgardo Binoya, M.D.; Namiko Nerio, M.D.; Manuel Sacapano, M.D., Defendants-Appellees.

No. 18-55020.

United States Court of Appeals, Ninth Circuit.

Argued and Submitted September 13, 2019, Pasadena, California.
Filed March 23, 2020.

Appeal from the United States District Court for the Central District of California; D.C. No. 2:14-cv-08850-JFW-E, John F. Walter, District Judge, Presiding.

Michael J. Khouri (argued), Andrew G. Goodman, and Jennifer W. Gatewood, Khouri Law Firm APC, Irvine, California, for Plaintiff-Appellant.

Thad A. Davis (argued), Gibson Dunn & Crutcher LLP, San Francisco, California; James L. Zelenay Jr., Gibson Dunn & Crutcher LLP, Los Angeles, California; for Defendants-Appellees Beryl Weiner and S&W Health Management Services, Inc.

Matthew Umhofer (argued) and Elizabeth J. Lee, Spertus Landes & Umhofer LLP, Los Angeles, California, for Defendants-Appellees RollinsNelson LTC Corp., Vicki Rollins, and Bill Nelson.

Raymond J. McMahon, Doyle Schafer McMahon, Irvine, California, for Defendants-Appellees Arnold Ling, M.D.; Cynthia Miller-Dobalian, M.D.; and Edgardo Binoya, M.D.

Michael D. Gonzalez and Andrea D. Vazquez, Law Offices of Michael D. Gonzalez, Glendale, California; Kenneth R. Pedroza and Matthew S. Levinson, Cole Pedroza LLP, for Defendant-Appellee Prode Pascual, M.D.

Craig B. Garner, Garner Health Law Corporation, Marina Del Rey, California, for Defendant-Appellee Rafaelito Victoria, M.D.

No appearance by Defendants-Appellees Gardens Regional Hospital and Medical Center, Inc.; Namiko Nerio, M.D.; and Manuel Sacapano, M.D.

Benjamin M. Shultz (argued), Michael S. Raab, and Charles W. Scarborough, Appellate Staff; Nicola T. Hanna, United States Attorney; Civil Division, United States Department of Justice, Washington, D.C.; for Amicus Curiae United States of America.

James F. Segroves, Kelly H. Hibbert, and Nancy B. Halstead, Reed Smith LLP, Washington, D.C.; Mark E. Reagan, Hooper Lundy & Bookman PC, San Francisco,

California; for Amici Curiae American Health Care Association, National Center for Assisted Living, and California Association of Health Facilities.

Before: JOHNNIE B. RAWLINSON, JOHN B. OWENS, and MARK J. BENNETT, Circuit Judges.

p.1112 **OPINION**

BENNETT, Circuit Judge:

Appellant-Relator Jane Winter ("Winter"), the former Director of Care Management at Gardens Regional Hospital ("Gardens Regional"), brought this *qui tam* action under the False Claims Act ("FCA"), 31 U.S.C. §§ 3729-33. Winter alleges Defendants[1] submitted, or caused to be submitted, Medicare claims falsely certifying that patients' inpatient hospitalizations were medically necessary. Winter alleges that the admissions were not medically p.1113 necessary and were contraindicated by the patients' medical records and the hospital's own admissions criteria. The district court dismissed Winter's second amended complaint ("the complaint") for failure to state a claim. The district court held that "to prevail on an FCA claim, a plaintiff must show that a defendant knowingly made an objectively false representation," so a statement that implicates a doctor's clinical judgment can never state a claim under the FCA because "subjective medical opinions ... cannot be proven to be objectively false."

We have jurisdiction under 28 U.S.C. § 1291. We hold that a plaintiff need not allege falsity beyond the requirements adopted by Congress in the FCA, which primarily punishes those who submit, conspire to submit, or aid in the submission of false or fraudulent claims. Congress imposed no requirement of proving "objective falsity," and we have no authority to rewrite the statute to add such a requirement. A doctor's clinical opinion must be judged under the same standard as any other representation. A doctor, like anyone else, can express an opinion that he knows to be false, or that he makes in reckless disregard of its truth or falsity. *See* 31 U.S.C. § 3729(b)(1). We therefore hold that a false certification of medical necessity can give rise to FCA liability.[2] We also hold that a false certification of medical necessity can be material because medical necessity is a statutory prerequisite to Medicare reimbursement. Accordingly, we reverse and remand.

BACKGROUND

A. The "Medical Necessity" Requirement

The Medicare program provides basic health insurance for individuals who are 65 or older, disabled, or have end-stage renal disease. 42 U.S.C. § 1395c. "[N]o payment may be made ... for any expenses incurred for items or services ... [that] are not reasonable and necessary for the diagnosis or treatment of illness or injury or to improve the functioning of a malformed body member[.]" 42 U.S.C. § 1395y(a)(1)(A). Medicare reimburses providers for inpatient hospitalization only if "a physician certifies that such services are required to be given on an inpatient basis for such individual's medical treatment, or that inpatient diagnostic study is medically required and such services are necessary for such purpose[.]" 42 U.S.C. § 1395f(a)(3).

The Department of Health and Human Services, Centers for Medicare & Medicaid Services ("CMS"), administers the Medicare program and issues guidance governing reimbursement. CMS defines a "reasonable and necessary" service as one that "meets, but does not exceed, the patient's medical need," and is furnished "in accordance with accepted standards of medical practice for the diagnosis or treatment of the patient's condition ... in a setting appropriate to the patient's medical needs and condition[.]" CMS, Medicare Program Integrity Manual § 13.5.4 (2019). The Medicare program tells patients that "medically necessary" means health care services that are "needed to diagnose or treat an illness, injury, condition, disease, or its symptoms and that meet accepted standards of medicine." CMS, Medicare & You 2020: The Official U.S. Government Medicare Handbook 114 (2019).

Admitting a patient to the hospital for inpatient—as opposed to outpatient— treatment requires a formal admission order from a doctor "who is knowledgeable p.1114 about the patient's hospital course, medical plan of care, and current condition." 42 C.F.R. § 412.3(b). Inpatient admission "is generally appropriate for payment under Medicare Part A when the admitting physician expects the patient to require hospital care that crosses two midnights," but inpatient admission can also be appropriate under other circumstances if "supported by the medical record." *Id.* § 412.3(d)(1), (3).

The Medicare program trusts doctors to use their clinical judgment based on "complex medical factors," but does not give them unfettered discretion to decide whether inpatient admission is medically necessary: "The factors that lead to a particular clinical expectation *must be documented in the medical record* in order to be granted consideration." *Id.* § 412.3(d)(1)(i) (emphasis added). And the regulations consider medical necessity a question of fact: "No presumptive weight shall be assigned to the physician's order under § 412.3 or the physician's certification... in determining the medical necessity of inpatient hospital services .... A physician's order or certification will be evaluated in the context of the evidence in the medical record." *Id.* § 412.46(b).

B. The False Claims Act

The FCA imposes significant civil liability on any person who, *inter alia,* (A) "knowingly presents, or causes to be presented, a false or fraudulent claim for payment or approval," (B) "knowingly makes, uses, or causes to be made or used, a false record or statement material to a false or fraudulent claim," or (C) "conspires to commit a violation of subparagraph (A), [or] (B)[.]" 31 U.S.C. § 3729(a)(1). The Act allows private plaintiffs to enforce its provisions by bringing a *qui tam* suit on behalf of the United States. *Id.* § 3730(b).

A plaintiff must allege: "(1) a false statement or fraudulent course of conduct, (2) made with the scienter, (3) that was material, causing, (4) the government to pay out money or forfeit moneys due." *United States ex rel. Campie v. Gilead Scis., Inc.,* 862 F.3d 890, 899 (9th Cir. 2017). Winter's allegations fall under a "false certification" theory of FCA liability.[3] *See Universal Health Servs., Inc. v. United States ex rel. Escobar,* ___ U.S. ___, 136 S. Ct. 1989, 2001, 195 L.Ed.2d 348 (2016). Because medical necessity is a condition of payment, every Medicare claim includes an express or implied certification that treatment was medically necessary. Claims for unnecessary treatment are false claims. Defendants act with the required scienter if they know the treatment was not medically necessary, or act in deliberate ignorance or reckless disregard of whether the treatment was medically necessary. *See* 31 U.S.C. § 3729(b)(1).

C. The Allegations in Winter's Complaint[4]

Winter, a registered nurse, became the Director of Care Management and Emergency Room at Gardens Regional in August 2014, and came to the job with thirteen years of experience as a director of case management at hospitals in Southern California and Utah.

Winter reviewed hospital admissions using the admissions criteria adopted by Gardens Regional—the InterQual Level of Care Criteria 2014 ("the InterQual criteria"). The InterQual criteria, promulgated p.1115 by McKesson Health Solutions LLC and updated annually, "are reviewed and validated by a national panel of clinicians and medical experts," and represent "a synthesis of evidence-based standards of care, current practices, and consensus from licensed specialists and/or primary care physicians." Medicare uses the criteria to evaluate claims for payment. And, as the criteria require a secondary review of all care decisions, Winter's job included reviewing Garden Regional patients' medical records and applying the criteria to evaluate the medical necessity of hospital admissions.

In mid-July 2014, Defendant RollinsNelson—which owned and operated nursing facilities in the Los Angeles area—acquired a 50% ownership interest in Defendant S&W, the management company that oversaw operations at Gardens Regional. RollinsNelson then began jointly managing the hospital with S&W. When Winter started work, she noticed that the emergency room saw an unusually high number of patients transported from RollinsNelson nursing homes, including from a facility sixty miles away. The RollinsNelson patients were not just treated on an outpatient basis or held overnight for observation—most were admitted for inpatient hospitalization. In August 2014, 83.5% of the patients transported from RollinsNelson nursing homes were admitted to Gardens Regional for inpatient treatment—an unusually high admissions rate based on Winter's experience and judgment.

Winter was concerned about this pattern and scrutinized Gardens Regional's admissions statistics, comparing July and August 2014 to prior months. She realized that the spike in admissions from Rollins-Nelson nursing homes corresponded with RollinsNelson's acquisition of S&W. Not only did the number of admissions increase, the number of Medicare beneficiaries admitted rose as well. The number of Medicare beneficiaries admitted in August 2014, for example, surpassed that of any month before RollinsNelson began managing the hospital. Winter alleges that RollinsNelson and S&W—including the individual owners of both entities— "exerted direct pressure on physicians to admit patients to [Gardens Regional] and cause false claims to be submitted based on false certifications of medical necessity."

Winter's complaint details sixty-five separate patient admissions—identified by the admitting physician, patient's initials, chief complaint, diagnosis, length of admission, the Medicare billing code, and the amount billed to Medicare—that Winter alleges did not meet Gardens Regional's admissions criteria and were unsupported by the patients' medical records. She alleges that none of the admissions were medically necessary. Winter observed several trends: i) admitting patients for urinary tract infections ("UTIs") ordinarily treated on an outpatient basis with oral antibiotics; ii) admitting patients for septicemia with no evidence of sepsis in their records; and iii) admitting patients for pneumonia or bronchitis with no evidence of such diseases in their medical records. Winter estimates that in less than two months—between July 14 and September 9, 2014—Gardens Regional submitted $1,287,701.62 in false claims to the Medicare program.

Winter repeatedly tried to bring her concerns to the attention of hospital management, with no success. In her first week, she reported the high number of unnecessary admissions to the hospital's Chief Operating Officer. After receiving no response, she reached out to the hospital's Chief Executive Officer. When she still received no response, she tried confronting Dr. Sacapano directly. He told her: "You know who I'm getting pressure from." Winter understood Dr. Sacapano to mean the hospital management.

p.1116 At the beginning of September 2014, Defendants Rollins, Nelson and Weiner— the owners of S&W and RollinsNelson— "called an urgent impromptu meeting," and "instructed case management not to question the admissions to [Gardens Regional.]" When Winter tried to speak up, Rollins cut her off, using profanity. Shortly after the meeting, Rollins instructed one of the hospital's case managers to "coach" physicians, explaining in an email that "[t]hese Mds will most likely increase their admits because their documentation will be 'assisted.'"

In November 2014, Gardens Regional fired Winter and replaced her with an employee who had never questioned any inpatient admissions. Winter filed her complaint a week later.

D. Procedural History

In November 2017, after the Government had declined to intervene and Winter had filed the second amended complaint, Defendants RollinsNelson, Rollins, Nelson, S&W, Weiner and Dr. Pascual filed motions to dismiss the complaint for failure to state a claim.[5] The district court granted the motions, dismissing Winter's three FCA claims against all Defendants for the same reasons: (1) because a determination of "medical necessity" is a "subjective medical opinion[ ] that cannot be proven to be objectively false," and (2) because the alleged false statements, which the district court characterized as the "failure to meet InterQual criteria," were not material.[6]

STANDARD OF REVIEW

We review the grant of a motion to dismiss de novo. *Manzarek v. St. Paul Fire & Marine Ins. Co.,* 519 F.3d 1025, 1030 (9th Cir. 2008). "In reviewing the dismissal of a complaint, we inquire whether the complaint's factual allegations, together with all reasonable inferences, state a plausible claim for relief." *Cafasso, United States ex rel. v. Gen. Dynamics C4 Sys., Inc.,* 637 F.3d 1047, 1054 (9th Cir. 2011). As with all fraud allegations, a plaintiff must plead FCA claims "with particularity" under Federal Rule of Civil Procedure 9(b). *Id.*

DISCUSSION

A. Winter properly alleges false or fraudulent statements

We interpret the FCA broadly, in keeping with the Congress's intention "to reach all types of fraud, without qualification, that might result in financial loss to the Government." *United States v. Neifert-White Co.,* 390 U.S. 228, 232, 88 S.Ct. 959, 19 L.Ed.2d 1061 (1968). For that reason, the Supreme Court "has consistently refused to accept a rigid, restrictive reading" of the FCA, *id.,* and has cautioned courts against "adopting a circumscribed view of what it means for a claim to be false or fraudulent," *Escobar,* 136 S. Ct. at 2002 (quoting *United States v. Sci. Applications Int'l Corp.,* 626 F.3d 1257, 1270 (D.C. Cir. 2010)).

"[W]e start, as always, with the language of the statute." *Id.* at 1999 (quoting *Allison Engine Co. v. United* p.1117 *States ex rel. Sanders,* 553 U.S. 662, 668, 128 S.Ct. 2123, 170 L.Ed.2d 1030 (2008)). The plain language of the FCA imposes liability for presenting, or causing to be presented, a "false or fraudulent claim for payment or approval," making "a false record or statement material to a false or fraudulent claim," or conspiring to do either. 31 U.S.C. § 3729(1)(A)-(C). Because Congress did not define "false or fraudulent," we presume it incorporated the common-law definitions, including the rule that a statement need not contain an "express falsehood" to be actionable. *Escobar,* 136 S. Ct. at 1999 ("[I]t is a settled principle of interpretation that, absent other indication, Congress intends to incorporate the well-settled meaning of the common-law terms it uses." (quoting *Sekhar v. United States,* 570 U.S. 729, 732, 133 S.Ct. 2720, 186 L.Ed.2d 794 (2013))). And, in at least one respect, Congress intended for the FCA to be broader than the common law: Under the FCA, "'knowingly' ... require[s] no proof of specific intent to defraud." 31 U.S.C. § 3729(b)(1)(B).

"[O]pinions are not, and have never been, completely insulated from scrutiny." *United States v. Paulus,* 894 F.3d 267, 275-76 (6th Cir. 2018) (upholding conviction for Medicare fraud where physician justified unnecessary procedures by exaggerating his interpretation of medical tests); *see also Hooper v. Lockheed Martin Corp.,* 688 F.3d 1037, 1049 (9th Cir. 2012) (holding that false estimates "can be a source of liability under the FCA"). Under the common law, a subjective opinion is fraudulent if it implies the existence of facts that do not exist, or if it is not honestly held. Restatement (Second) of Torts § 525; *id.* § 539. As the Supreme Court recognized, "the expression of an opinion may carry with it an implied assertion, not only that the speaker knows no facts which would preclude such an opinion, but that he does know facts which justify it." *Omnicare, Inc. v. Laborers Dist. Council Const. Indus. Pension Fund,* 575 U.S. 175, 191, 135 S.Ct. 1318, 191 L.Ed.2d 253 (2015) (quoting W. Page Keeton et al., Prosser and Keeton on the Law of Torts § 109, at 760 (5th ed. 1984)).

Defendants and amici curiae American Health Care Association, National Center for Assisted Living, and California Association of Health Facilities urge this court to hold the FCA requires a plaintiff to plead an "objective falsehood." But "[n]othing in the text of the False Claims Act supports [Defendants'] proposed restriction." *Escobar,* 136 S. Ct. at 2001. Under the plain language of the statute, the FCA imposes liability for all "false or fraudulent claims"—it does not distinguish between "objective" and "subjective" falsity or carve out an exception for clinical judgments and opinions.

Defendants are correct that if clinical judgments can be fraudulent under the FCA, doctors will be exposed to liability they would not face under Defendants' view of the law. "But policy arguments cannot supersede the clear statutory text." *Id.* at 2002. Our role is "to apply, not amend, the work of the People's representatives." *Henson v. Santander Consumer USA Inc.,* ___ U.S. ___, 137 S. Ct. 1718, 1726, 198 L.Ed.2d 177 (2017). And the Supreme Court has already addressed Defendants' concern: "Instead of adopting a circumscribed view of what it means for a claim to be false or fraudulent, concerns about fair notice and open-ended liability can be effectively addressed through strict enforcement of the Act's materiality and scienter requirements." *Escobar,* 136 S. Ct. at 2002 (quotation marks, alterations, and citation omitted).

We have similarly explained that the FCA requires "the 'knowing presentation of what is known to be false'" and that "[t]he phrase 'known to be false'... does not mean 'scientifically untrue'; it p.1118 means 'a lie.' The Act is concerned with ferreting out 'wrongdoing,' not scientific errors." *Wang v. FMC Corp.,* 975 F.2d 1412, 1421 (9th Cir. 1992) (citations omitted), *overruled on other grounds by United States ex rel. Hartpence v. Kinetic Concepts, Inc.,* 792 F.3d 1121 (9th Cir. 2015) (en banc). This does not mean, as the district court understood it, that only "objectively false" statements can give rise to FCA liability. It means that falsity is a necessary, but not sufficient, requirement for FCA liability—after alleging a false statement, a plaintiff must still establish scienter. *Id.* ("What is false as a matter of science is not, by that very fact, wrong as a matter of morals."). To be clear, a "scientifically untrue" statement is "false"—even if it may not be actionable because it was not made with the requisite intent. And an opinion with no basis in fact can be fraudulent if expressed with scienter.

We are not alone in concluding that a false certification of medical necessity can give rise to FCA liability. In *United States ex rel. Riley v. St. Luke's Episcopal Hospital,* the Fifth Circuit recognized that "claims for medically unnecessary treatment are actionable under the FCA." 355 F.3d 370, 376 (5th Cir. 2004). The plaintiff alleged the defendants filed false claims "for services that were ... medically unnecessary," *id.* at 373, and the Fifth Circuit reversed the district court's dismissal for failure to state a claim, explaining that because the complaint alleged that the defendants ordered medical services "knowing they were unnecessary," the statements were lies, not simply errors. *Id.* at 376.

Likewise, in *United States ex rel. Polukoff v. St. Mark's Hospital,* the Tenth Circuit recognized "[i]t is possible for a medical judgment to be 'false or fraudulent' as proscribed by the FCA[.]" 895 F.3d 730, 742 (10th Cir. 2018). The court looked to CMS's definition of "medically necessary," and held, "a doctor's certification to the government that a procedure is 'reasonable and necessary' is 'false' under the FCA if the procedure was not reasonable and necessary under the government's definition of the phrase." *Id.* at 743. The Third Circuit reached a similar conclusion in *United States ex rel. Druding v. Care Alternatives,* 952 F.3d 89 (3d Cir. 2020), rejecting the "bright-line rule that a doctor's clinical judgment cannot be 'false.'" *Id.* at 98 (holding that, in the context of certifying terminal illness, "for purposes of FCA falsity, a claim may be 'false' under a theory of legal falsity, where it fails to comply with statutory and regulatory requirements," and that "a physician's judgment may be scrutinized and considered 'false,'" *id.* at 100-01).

The Eleventh Circuit's recent decision in *United States v. AseraCare, Inc.,* 938 F.3d 1278 (11th Cir. 2019), is not directly to the contrary. In *AseraCare,* the Eleventh Circuit held that "a clinical judgment of terminal illness warranting hospice benefits under Medicare cannot be deemed false, for purposes of the False Claims Act, when there is *only* a reasonable disagreement between medical experts as to the accuracy of that conclusion, *with no other evidence* to prove the falsity of the assessment." *Id.* at 1281 (emphases added). We recognize that the court also said "a claim that certifies that a patient is terminally ill... cannot be 'false'—and thus cannot trigger FCA liability—if the underlying clinical judgment does not reflect an objective falsehood." *Id.* at 1296-97. But we conclude that our decision today does not conflict with *AseraCare* for two reasons.

First, the Eleventh Circuit was not asked whether a medical opinion could ever be false or fraudulent, but whether a reasonable disagreement between physicians, *without more,* was sufficient to prove falsity at summary judgment. *Id.* at p.1119 1297-98. Notwithstanding the Eleventh Circuit's language about "objective falsehoods," the court clearly did not consider all subjective statements—including medical opinions—to be incapable of falsity, and identified circumstances in which a medical opinion would be false.[7]

Second, the Eleventh Circuit recognized that its "objective falsehood" requirement did not necessarily apply to a physician's certification of medical necessity—explicitly distinguishing *Polukoff. Id.* at 1300 n.15. Rather, the court explained that the "hospice-benefit provision at issue" purposefully defers to "whether a physician has based a recommendation for hospice treatment on a genuinely-held clinical opinion" whether a patient was terminally ill.[8] *Id.; see also id.* at 1295. In fact, after holding that physicians' hospice-eligibility determinations are entitled to deference, the Eleventh Circuit explained that the less-deferential medical necessity requirement remained an important safeguard: "The Government's argument that our reading of the eligibility framework would 'tie CMS's hands' and 'require improper reimbursements' is contrary to the plain design of the law" because "CMS is statutorily prohibited from reimbursing providers for services 'which are not reasonable and necessary[.]'" *Id.* at 1295 (alteration and citation omitted). Thus, for the same reason the Eleventh Circuit recognized *AseraCare* did not conflict with *Polukoff,* we believe our decision does not conflict with *AseraCare.* And to the extent that *AseraCare* can be read to graft any type of "objective falsity" requirement onto the FCA, we reject that proposition. *See Druding,* 952 F.3d at 99-100.

In sum, we hold that the FCA does not require a plaintiff to plead an "objective falsehood." A physician's certification that inpatient hospitalization was "medically necessary" can be false or fraudulent for the same reasons any opinion can be false or fraudulent. These reasons include if the opinion is not honestly held, or if it implies the existence of facts—namely, that inpatient hospitalization is needed to diagnose or treat a medical condition, in accordance with accepted standards of medical practice—that do not exist. *See Polukoff,* 895 F.3d at 742-43.

We now turn to Winter's complaint. We accept all facts alleged as true and draw all inferences in Winter's favor, and conclude that her complaint plausibly alleges false certifications of medical necessity.

First, the complaint "alleges a 'scheme' connoting knowing misconduct." *Riley,* 355 F.3d at 376. RollinsNelson and S&W—and their individual owners Rollins, Nelson and Weiner—had a motive to falsify Medicare claims and pressure doctors to increase admissions. Gardens Regional relied on Medicare for a "significant portion" of its revenue, and the spike in admissions corresponded with an increased number of Medicare beneficiaries in its care. Moreover, p.1120 the increased admissions of RollinsNelson patients began when RollinsNelson started managing Gardens Regional.

Second, not only does Winter identify suspect trends in inpatient admissions—for example, hospitalizing patients for UTIs—she also alleges statistics showing an overall increase in hospitalizations once RollinsNelson started managing the hospital. For example, the daily occupancy rate jumped by almost 10%, the number of Medicare beneficiaries became the highest it had ever been by a significant margin, and the admissions rate from RollinsNelson nursing homes was over 80%. Plus, the large number of admissions that did not meet the criteria, and the fact that the vast majority of admissions came from a single doctor—Dr. Pascual, who had contractually agreed to use the InterQual criteria— decreases the likelihood that any given admission was an outlier.

Third, Winter's detailed allegations as to each Medicare claim support an inference of falsity. This is not a complaint that "identifies a general sort of fraudulent conduct but specifies no particular circumstances of any discrete fraudulent statement[.]" *Cafasso,* 637 F.3d at 1057. The complaint identifies sixty-five allegedly false claims in great detail, listing the date of admission, the admitting physician, the patient's chief complaint and diagnosis, and the amount billed to Medicare. The complaint alleges that each admission failed to satisfy the hospital's own admissions criteria—the InterQual criteria that Gardens Regional and Dr. Pascual had contractually agreed to use and that Winter's job as Director of Care Management required her to apply. And, as the district court recognized, the InterQual criteria represent the "consensus of medical professionals' opinions," so a failure to satisfy the criteria also means that the admission went against the medical consensus.

Finally, we note that many of the allegations supporting an inference of scienter also support an inference of falsity. *Cf. AseraCare,* 938 F.3d at 1304-05 (remanding for district court to consider evidence related to scienter in determining falsity on summary judgment). For example, when confronted, Dr. Sacapano corroborated Winter's suspicions, telling her that hospital management pressured him into recommending patients for medically unnecessary inpatient admission. And following Winter's numerous attempts to bring her concerns to the attention of hospital management, Defendants Rollins, Nelson, and Weiner held a meeting where they instructed Winter and other staff not to question the admissions.

Defendants argue that "Winter has alleged nothing more than her competing opinion with the treating physicians who actually saw the patients at issue." The district court similarly dismissed the complaint because Winter's "contention that the medical provider's certifications were false is based on her own after-the-fact review of [Gardens Regional's] admission records." To begin with, an opinion can establish falsity. *See Paulus,* 894 F.3d at 270, 277 (affirming doctor's conviction for healthcare fraud by performing medically unnecessary procedures and holding that experts' "opinions, having been accepted into evidence, are sufficient to carry the government's burden of proof"); *cf. AseraCare,* 938 F.3d at 1300 (distinguishing *Paulus* because in *AseraCare* "the Government's expert witness declined to conclude that [the clinical judgments of] AseraCare's physicians ... were unreasonable or wrong"). Winter alleges more than just a reasonable difference of opinion. In addition to the allegations discussed above, she alleges that a number of the hospital admissions were for diagnoses that had been disproven by laboratory tests, and that several admissions were for psychiatric p.1121 treatment, even though Gardens Regional was not a psychiatric hospital—and one of those patients never even saw a psychiatrist. Even if we were to discount Winter's evaluation of the medical records, as the district court did, the other facts she alleges would be sufficient to make her allegations of fraud plausible.

But more importantly, assessing medical necessity based on an "after-the-fact review" of patients' medical records *was Winter's job.* At the motion to dismiss stage, her assessment is "entitled to the presumption of truth[.]" *Starr v. Baca,* 652 F.3d 1202, 1216 (9th Cir. 2011). "The standard at this stage of the litigation is not that plaintiff's explanation must be true or even probable. The factual allegations of the complaint need only 'plausibly suggest an entitlement to relief.'" *Id.* at 1216-17 (quoting *Ashcroft v. Iqbal,* 556 U.S. 662, 681, 129 S.Ct. 1937, 173 L.Ed.2d 868 (2009)). Winter's complaint satisfies that standard.[9]

B. Winter properly alleges material false or fraudulent statements

The district court also held that Winter failed to allege any material false statements. We disagree.

"[T]he term 'material' means having a natural tendency to influence, or be capable of influencing, the payment or receipt of money or property." 31 U.S.C. § 3729(b)(4). "Under any understanding of the concept, materiality 'looks to the effect on the likely or actual behavior of the recipient of the alleged misrepresentation.'" *Escobar,* 136 S. Ct. at 2002 (quoting 26 Samuel Williston & Richard A. Lord, Williston on Contracts § 69:12 (4th ed. 2003)) (alteration omitted). No "single fact or occurrence" determines materiality— "the Government's decision to expressly identify a provision as a condition of payment is relevant, but not automatically dispositive." *Id.* at 2001, 2003 (citation omitted). For a false statement to be material, a plaintiff must plausibly allege that the statutory violations are "so central" to the claims that the government "would not have paid these claims had it known of these violations." *Id.* at 2004; *see also id.* at 2003 ("[P]roof of materiality can include... evidence that the defendant knows that the Government consistently refuses to pay claims in the mine run of cases based on noncompliance with the particular statutory, regulatory, or contractual requirement.").

The district court analyzed whether failure to meet the InterQual criteria was material and concluded that it was not because "[t]here is no mention of the InterQual criteria in any of the relevant statutes or regulations." This misreads the complaint. Winter does not allege that failure to satisfy the InterQual criteria made Defendants' Medicare claims per se false— although, as discussed above, she claims that the InterQual criteria support her allegations because they reflect a medical consensus. Rather, she alleges that "[Defendants'] claims for payment ... were false in that the services claimed for (inpatient hospital admissions) were not medically p.1122 necessary and economical," and that Defendants submitted "false certifications of ... medical necessity."

We conclude that a false certification of medical necessity can be material. The medical necessity requirement is not an "insignificant regulatory or contractual violation[.]" *Escobar,* 136 S. Ct. at 2004. Congress *prohibited* payment for treatment "not reasonable and necessary for the diagnosis or treatment of illness or injury or to improve the functioning of a malformed body member[.]" 42 U.S.C. § 1395y(a)(1)(A). And Medicare pays for inpatient hospitalization "*only if* ... such services are required to be given on an inpatient basis for such individual's medical treatment[.]" *Id.* § 1395f(a)(3) (emphasis added). In fact, Medicare regulations require all doctors to sign an acknowledgment that states,

> Medicare payment to hospitals is based in part on each patient's principal and secondary diagnoses and the major procedures performed on the patient, as attested to by the patient's attending physician by virtue of his or her signature in the medical record. Anyone who misrepresents, falsifies, or conceals essential information required for payment of Federal funds, may be subject to fine, imprisonment, or civil penalty under applicable Federal laws.

42 C.F.R. § 412.46(a)(2). In addition to highlighting the above Medicare statutes and regulations, Winter's complaint alleges that the government "would not" have "paid" Defendants' false claims "if the true facts were known." In sum, Winter alleges that Defendants' false certification of the medical necessity requirement is "so central" to the Medicare program that the government "would not have paid these claims had it known" that the inpatient hospitalizations were, in fact, unnecessary. *Escobar,* 136 S. Ct. at 2004. Thus, Winter has "sufficiently ple[d] materiality at this stage of the case." *Campie,* 862 F.3d at 907.

C. Scienter

Defendants urge us to determine whether Winter adequately alleged scienter. The district court did not reach this issue but expressed doubt that Winter had. Although we may consider alternate grounds for upholding the district court's decision, *see Islamic Republic of Iran v. Boeing Co.,* 771 F.2d 1279, 1288 (9th Cir. 1985), we decline to do so here.

We remind the district court, however, that under Rule 9(b), scienter need not be pleaded with particularity, but may be alleged generally. Fed. R. Civ. P. 9(b). A complaint needs only to allege facts supporting a plausible inference of scienter. *United States ex rel. Lee v. Corinthian Colls.,* 655 F.3d 984, 997 (9th Cir. 2011). And unlike in common law fraud claims, a plaintiff need not prove a "specific intent to defraud" under the FCA—the Act imposes liability on any person acting "knowingly," which includes acting with "actual knowledge," as well as acting "in deliberate ignorance," or "in reckless disregard of the truth or falsity of the information[.]" 31 U.S.C. § 3729(b)(1). As the Supreme Court noted in another Medicare case, "[p]rotection of the public fisc requires that those who seek public funds act with scrupulous regard for the requirements of law[.]" *Heckler v. Cmty. Health Servs. of Crawford Cty., Inc.,* 467 U.S. 51, 63, 104 S.Ct. 2218, 81 L.Ed.2d 42 (1984).

CONCLUSION

We hold that a plaintiff need not plead an "objective falsehood" to state a claim under the FCA, and that a false certification of medical necessity can be material. Accordingly, we reverse the district court's dismissal of Winter's complaint and remand p.1123 for further proceedings consistent with this opinion.

[1] The Defendants include Gardens Regional Hospital, the hospital management company (S&W Health Management Services) and its owners (RollinsNelson, Rollins, Nelson, and Weiner), and individual physicians who diagnosed and admitted patients.

[2] The FCA covers claims that are "false or fraudulent." 31 U.S.C. § 3729(a)(1). For convenience, we will generally use "false" to mean "false or fraudulent."

[3] The complaint alleges both express and implied false certification.

[4] All facts are taken from Winter's second amended complaint. "We accept all factual allegations in the complaint as true and construe the pleadings in the light most favorable to the nonmoving party." *Outdoor Media Grp., Inc. v. City of Beaumont,* 506 F.3d 895, 900 (9th Cir. 2007).

[5] At oral argument, Winter's counsel acknowledged that Dr. Sacapano and Dr. Nerio had not yet been served with the second amended complaint when the district court, in granting the moving Defendants' motions to dismiss, sua sponte dismissed the complaint against them as well. Oral Argument at 10:58, *Winter v. Gardens Regional Hosp., et al.,* No. 18-55020 (9th Cir. Sept. 13, 2019), https://www.ca9.uscourts.gov/media/view_video.php?pk_vid=XXXXXXXXXX.

[6] The district court did not dismiss Winter's retaliation claim against Gardens Regional. Winter voluntarily dismissed that claim without prejudice to allow for an appeal.

[7] For example, "if the [doctor] does not actually hold that opinion" or simply "rubber-stamp[s] whatever file was put in front of him," if the opinion is "based on information that the physician knew, or had reason to know, was incorrect," or if "no reasonable physician" would agree with the doctor's opinion, "based on the evidence[.]" *AseraCare,* 938 F.3d at 1302.

[8] A patient must have less than six months to live to be eligible for hospice care. *AseraCare,* 938 F.3d at 1282. But, as the Eleventh Circuit explained, CMS "repeatedly emphasized that '[p]redicting life expectancy is not an exact science,' [and that] 'certifying physicians have the best clinical experience, competence and judgment to make the determination that an individual is terminally ill.'" *Id.* at 1295 (quoting 75 Fed. Reg. 70372, 70448 (Nov. 17, 2010) and 78 Fed. Reg. 48234, 48247 (Aug. 7, 2013)). By contrast, a certification of medical necessity is not entitled to deference. 42 C.F.R. § 412.46(b).

[9] FCA claims must also be pleaded with particularity under Federal Rule of Civil Procedure 9(b). *Cafasso,* 637 F.3d at 1054. While a plaintiff need not "allege 'all facts supporting each and every instance' of billing submitted," she must "provide enough detail 'to give [defendants] notice of the particular misconduct which is alleged to constitute the fraud charged so that [they] can defend against the charge

and not just deny that [they have] done anything wrong.'" *Ebeid ex rel. United States v. Lungwitz*, 616 F.3d 993, 999 (9th Cir. 2010) (quoting *United States ex rel. Lee v. SmithKline Beecham, Inc.,* 245 F.3d 1048, 1051-52 (9th Cir. 2001)). Winter's detailed allegations clearly suffice to put Defendants on notice of their alleged false statements.

937 F.3d 1201 (2019)

Geraldine GODECKE, Relator; ex rel. United States of America, Plaintiff-Appellant,
v.
KINETIC CONCEPTS, INC.; KCI-USA, Inc., Defendants-Appellees.

No. 18-55246.

United States Court of Appeals, Ninth Circuit.

Argued and Submitted April 12, 2019 Pasadena, California.
Filed September 6, 2019.

Godecke v. Kinetic Concepts, Inc., 937 F. 3d 1201 (9th Cir. 2019)

Appeal from the United States District Court for the Central District of California; Christina A. Snyder, District Judge, Presiding, D.C. No. CV 08-6403 CAS.

p.1205 Kurt Kuhn (argued), Kuhn Hobbes PLLC, Austin, Texas; Patrick J. O'Connell, Law Offices of Patrick J. O'Connell PLLC, Austin, Texas; Mark I. Labaton, Glancy Prongay & Murray LLP, Los Angeles, California; Michael A. Hirst, Hirst Law Group P.C., Davis, California; for Plaintiff-Appellant.

Gregory M. Luce (argued), Skadden Arps Slate Meagher & Flom LLP, Washington, D.C.; Matthew E. Sloan and Kevin J. Minnick, Skadden Arps Slate Meagher & Flom LLP, Los Angeles, California; for Defendants-Appellees.

Before: A. WALLACE TASHIMA and JAY S. BYBEE, Circuit Judges, and M. DOUGLAS HARPOOL,[*] District Judge.

p.1204 **OPINION**

TASHIMA, Circuit Judge:

Relator Geraldine Godecke appeals the district court's dismissal of her qui tam case against Defendants Kinetic Concepts, Inc. and KCI USA, Inc. (collectively, "KCI"), brought under the federal False Claims Act ("FCA"). Godecke alleges that KCI submitted false claims to Medicare. Specifically, Godecke alleges that KCI delivered durable medical equipment to Medicare patients before obtaining a detailed written order from a physician, which was a requirement for Medicare reimbursement. She alleges that if Medicare knew that this delivery requirement had not been satisfied prior to delivery, Medicare's policy would have been to refuse payment on KCI's claims. She alleges that KCI knew that it should not have been able to receive payment, but sought reimbursement regardless of this fact and chose not to alert Medicare to the issue. On this appeal, we must determine whether Godecke sufficiently alleges that (1) KCI submitted false claims, (2) KCI acted with scienter, and (3) the false claims were material to the government. We hold that she does so. Therefore, we reverse and remand for further proceedings.

BACKGROUND

The facts as presented here are taken from the allegations in the Fourth Amended Complaint ("FAC"). For the purposes of a motion to dismiss, we must take all of the factual allegations in the complaint as true, although we are not bound to accept as true a legal conclusion couched as a factual allegation. *Ashcroft v. Iqbal,* 556 U.S. 662, 678-79, 129 S.Ct. 1937, 173 L.Ed.2d 868 (2009); *Bell Atlantic Corp v. Twombly,* 550 U.S. 544, 555, 127 S.Ct. 1955, 167 L.Ed.2d 929 (2007).[1]

In 2001, Godecke became an employee of MedClaim, Inc., a specialized billing company that was under contract with KCI to submit KCI's claims to Medicare and to provide evidentiary and other support for appeals of claims denied by Medicare. In 2003, KCI purchased MedClaim, and Godecke became an employee of KCI. She was the Director of Medicare Cash and Collections at MedClaim and then KCI from June 1, 2001 to October 1, 2007. Her position required her to work with KCI's information systems related to billing, and also required her to review communications regarding claim payments that were made or denied by Medicare. She was also responsible for the creation of a new department within KCI, informally known as the "back end" of the billing department, that dealt specifically with the p.1206 appeal process for KCI's claims that had been denied by the Medicare billing and payment system. She and her staff evaluated whether KCI should appeal those denials and provided supporting information for challenging those denials in administrative hearings.

KCI manufactures a piece of durable medical equipment known as a Vacuum Assisted Closure device ("VAC"), which is used to perform negative pressure wound therapy ("NPWT"). The VAC was added to the list of Medicare covered devices starting on October 1, 2000, and, at that time, no other NPWT pump was approved for Medicare reimbursement. Pursuant to Medicare Part B, the VAC device is rented on a monthly basis, and the supplies needed for VAC treatment, such as dressings and a canister, are purchased. In 2006, the total monthly cost for a VAC for a Medicare patient was about $2,224 for the first 3 months and $ 1,794 for each subsequent month; Medicare pays 80% of this cost and the patient is liable for the remaining 20%. Between 2001 and 2011, KCI's Medicare Part B revenue totalled $ 1.325 billion.

Medicare administers the rules for use of the VAC and similar NPWT devices through private claims processing contractors known as Durable Medical Equipment Medicare Administrative Contractors ("DME MACs"). These DME MACs have issued Local Coverage Determinations ("LCDs") that govern reimbursement rules for VACs. DME MACs are also authorized to make payments on behalf of the government to Medicare claimants. Because Medicare is required to pay claims submitted within just a few weeks of receipt of the claim, the Medicare program has historically paid claims quickly without verifying the accuracy of the claims before payment. Medicare accepts claims as submitted by providers as being a true representation that the claim either qualifies for reimbursement or does not qualify and automatically pays those claims represented as qualifying. Medicare must then seek reimbursement or recoupment if it later determines that the claim should not have been paid. This payment system has become known as "pay and chase," and relies on the honesty of providers and the accuracy of the claims they submit.

Under the LCD, KCI must receive, prior to delivery of the VAC to a patient, a detailed written order from a physician, also known as a written order prior to delivery ("WOPD"), referred to as a "prior written order" by KCI. If KCI does not receive a WOPD prior to delivery of the VAC, then KCI is not entitled to payment from Medicare. This requirement to obtain a WOPD before delivering the VAC has been in the Medicare Program Integrity Manual since KCI first started billing Medicare in 2000. Importantly, if KCI does not receive a detailed written order prior to delivery, payment will not be made for the device *even if* KCI was able subsequently to obtain a written order after delivery.

When KCI submitted claims to Medicare, it used certain billing code modifiers on the claims to indicate whether all of the reimbursement requirements had been met. The KX billing code modifier specifically represents to Medicare that all requirements for payment have been satisfied. By adding the KX modifier to a claim, KCI attested that the specific required documentation is on file before submitting the claim to the DME MAC. As early as 1999, the Office of Inspector General of the U.S. Department of Health and Human Services warned that misuse of the KX modifier could result in false claims.[2] In p.1207 contrast, there is a separate billing code modifier that must be used in order to represent to Medicare that not all requirements for payment have been satisfied. In 2003, the billing code modifier "EY" was adopted for use when a NPWT item was delivered before a signed written order had been received by the supplier. KCI is allowed to submit claims for costs that are presumptively non-reimbursable, but must do so openly by using the proper Medicare billing code modifier, describing the claims accurately while challenging the presumption and seeking reimbursement.

Godecke alleges that KCI delivered many VACs without the required WOPD. Due to time constraints and business pressures, KCI management would authorize "exceptions" to KCI's standard operating procedures, which were based on Medicare's requirements. These exceptions would allow KCI employees to release the VAC and supplies for delivery to the patient before receiving the written order. The exception granted by management would make the claim appear to be billable under KCI's internal procedures, even though Medicare's WOPD requirements had not been satisfied. KCI was not required to disclose the actual date on which it received the written order, and there was a 30-day window after a patient's treatment started before KCI had to bill Medicare. During this 30-day window, KCI could get a detailed written order from a physician for the VAC. In such cases, of course, the order was not technically a WOPD because it was not written *prior to delivery*. Based on reviews of reports and conversations with customer service representatives and KCI management, Godecke learned that KCI management granted these exceptions and allowed customer service representatives to deliver VACs to patients before all the WOPD requirements had been satisfied. She also knew that KCI management understood the Medicare requirements and the rules for reimbursement, and she also helped KCI management set up tracking systems specifically for following up on orders for VACs that had been delivered but did not satisfy the WOPD requirements.

Godecke next alleges that KCI knowingly used the wrong billing code modifiers to conceal from Medicare that these VACs were delivered before receiving a WOPD. KCI would routinely submit claims for payment when KCI either did not have any

WOPD in its possession or had some form of a WOPD, but the order was defective. KCI would bill Medicare using the KX modifier as long as it was able to obtain a detailed written order before the 30-day window to submit bills had closed. KCI would submit these claims without including the EY modifier, even though it was required to do so. Because of the 30-day window and the fact that KCI was not required to submit the actual date the WOPD was received, KCI's alleged scheme avoided detection by Medicare, unless Medicare chose to audit a claim and knew exactly what to look for and where to look.

Godecke provides fifteen representative examples of false claims that were submitted for reimbursement without the EY code. These claims are identified by Rental Order Entry ("ROE") numbers, a unique identifying number assigned to each VAC delivery request. Godecke used an internal KCI report to identify ROEs for a group of VACs delivered without a WOPD (or with an incomplete WOPD). By cross-referencing this group with another internal report, Godecke was able to identify the ROEs in this group for which KCI management granted an exception in order to approve the delivery and billing of these VACs without a WOPD. Then, Godecke generated a report through KCI's billing and appeals databases to confirm that these ROEs had been either paid or appealed. p.1208 Therefore, because claims with the EY modifier would not be paid and could not be appealed, these ROEs not only were delivered despite noncompliance, but also were billed by KCI without the required EY modifier.

After gathering evidence and customized reports, Godecke brought her concerns about the billing noncompliance issues to the attention of KCI's management. Godecke presented her findings at a meeting with her boss Rich Brinkley, KCI Senior Vice President Steve Hartpence, and with Godecke's former supervisor Deb Smith on the phone. Smith disputed Godecke's interpretation of the Medicare rules, but Hartpence requested that Godecke continue her research on the issue. Within hours of the meeting, Hartpence was fired and escorted out of KCI's building. About a month later, Brinkley was also fired, and he called Godecke to say that she was going to be fired "because senior management told him she was going to be a whistleblower." Godecke was fired a few weeks later on October 1, 2007.[3]

JURISDICTION AND STANDARD OF REVIEW

We have jurisdiction pursuant to 28 U.S.C. § 1291. We review the dismissal of claims under the FCA de novo. *U.S. ex rel. Hendow v. Univ. of Phx.,* 461 F.3d 1166, 1170 (9th Cir. 2006). We assume that the facts as alleged are true and examine only whether the relator's allegations support a cause of action under the FCA, under the theories presented. *Id.* A Rule 12(b)(6) dismissal "can be based on the lack of a cognizable legal theory or the absence of sufficient facts alleged under a cognizable legal theory." *Balistreri v. Pacifica Police Dep't,* 901 F.2d 696, 699 (9th Cir. 1990). A complaint must plead "sufficient factual matter, accepted as true, to 'state a claim to relief that is plausible on its face.'" *Iqbal,* 556 U.S. at 678, 129 S.Ct. 1937 (quoting *Twombly,* 550 U.S. at 570, 127 S.Ct. 1955). A claim under the FCA must not only be plausible, Fed. R. Civ. P. 8(a), but pled with particularity under Rule 9(b), *U.S. ex rel. Cafasso v. Gen. Dynamics C4 Sys., Inc.,* 637 F.3d 1047, 1054-55 (9th Cir. 2011). Rule 9(b) requires that the circumstances alleged to constitute fraud be specific enough to give the defendant notice of the particular misconduct so that it can defend against the charge. *Kearns v. Ford Motor Co.,* 567 F.3d 1120, 1124 (9th Cir. 2009). The party must allege the "who, what, when, where, and how" of the misconduct. *Id.*

DISCUSSION

I. Godecke sufficiently alleged that KCI violated the FCA.

The FCA makes liable anyone who "knowingly presents, or causes to be presented, a false or fraudulent claim for payment or approval," or "knowingly makes, uses, or causes to be made or used, a false record or statement material to a false or fraudulent claim." 31 U.S.C. § 3729(a)(1)(A), (B). A claim under the FCA requires a showing of: "(1) a false statement or fraudulent course of conduct, (2) made with scienter, (3) that was material, causing (4) the government to pay out money or forfeit moneys due." *U.S. ex rel. Campie v. Gilead Sci., Inc.,* 862 F.3d 890, 899 (9th Cir. 2017), *cert. denied,* ___ U.S. ___, 139 S. Ct. 783, 202 L.Ed.2d 566 (2019).

The district court dismissed the FAC on the ground that it failed to plead a violation of the FCA. Godecke challenges the district court's determination that she failed sufficiently to allege that, either (1) p.1209 KCI actually submitted any claim without the EY modifier when it was required, or (2) there were "reliable indicia" leading to "a strong inference" that KCI actually submitted claims without an EY modifier. Godecke also challenges the district court's determination that her claims failed to meet the FCA's scienter requirements. KCI, on the other hand, argues that Godecke failed to allege sufficient facts to meet the FCA's materiality requirement. The district court denied KCI's motion to dismiss on materiality grounds in an earlier ruling on the Second Amended Complaint.

A. Godecke adequately alleges a fraudulent scheme to submit false claims and reliable indicia that lead to a strong inference that false claims were actually submitted.

To state an FCA claim, a relator is not required to identify actual examples of submitted false claims; instead, "it is sufficient to allege 'particular details of a scheme to submit false claims paired with reliable indicia that lead to a strong inference that claims were actually submitted.'" *Ebeid ex rel. U.S. v. Lungwitz,* 616 F.3d 993, 998-99 (9th Cir. 2010) (quoting *U.S. ex rel. Grubbs v. Kanneganti,* 565 F.3d 180, 190 (5th Cir. 2009)). A relator is not required to identify representative examples of false claims to support every allegation, although the use of representative examples is one means of meeting the pleading obligation. *Id.* at 998.

Godecke sufficiently alleged particular details of a scheme to submit false claims paired with reliable indicia that lead to a strong inference that the claims were actually submitted. Godecke alleges that she learned about KCI's scheme to submit false claims through her role as KCI's Director of Medicare Cash and Collections. Even though Godecke never personally was directed not to include an EY modifier or directly observed other employees omitting the EY modifier, her complaint alleges particular details of a KCI management scheme to submit claims omitting the EY modifier when it should have been included. Based on knowledge gained from talking with sales representatives, Godecke learned that KCI often delivered VAC devices without receiving a prior written order at the urging of sales executives. She alleges that she "knew from management explanations" that KCI management knew that Medicare would not pay for the VAC devices delivered under these "exceptions" to the rules, and KCI management "set up tracking systems to expedite [the] effort... to mask the fact that VACs were delivered without all of the required elements in hand." Godecke has alleged personal knowledge that KCI management was actively and knowingly looking for ways to conceal the fact that certain VAC devices would not be reimbursable.

Godecke's ROEs analysis shows reliable indicia that raise a strong inference that KCI actually submitted false claims. The district court found that Godecke's analysis did not sufficiently support the theory that KCI actually submitted false claims because Godecke's analysis of ROEs in KCI's appeals database was entirely consistent with an equally plausible interpretation that the ROEs instead represented claims that were submitted with an EY modifier and were consequently denied. But Godecke shows that her system of cross-referencing ROEs in different databases allowed her to rule out that interpretation. In paragraphs 157 through 160 of the FAC, Godecke specifically alleges that she could pinpoint those ROEs for claims without a WOPD where the claim was either paid or appealed, which would have been impossible had the claim included the EY modifier as it should have had.

p.1210 Furthermore, the FAC includes detailed allegations from Theresa Duffy, a former colleague of Godecke, who personally reviewed KCI's claims denied by Medicare to determine whether KCI should appeal the denials. Starting in 2002, "Duffy complained to Godecke about the inadequate documentary support for submitted claims," and Duffy and Godecke "discussed that numerous claims lacked required documentation." Less than two weeks before Godecke filed the FAC (in 2017), Duffy confirmed to Godecke "that KCI's claims submitted to Medicare that Duffy had personally reviewed lacked appropriate documentation, including claims which required an EY modifier because KCI did not have a valid WOPD before delivery of a VAC." In 2017, Duffy also confirmed to Godecke that she "personally saw that claims for first cycle treatment had routinely been billed to Medicare, and paid by Medicare, even though the VAC had been delivered before KCI had obtained a valid WOPD."[4] Duffy also stated that she "did not recall ever seeing an EY modifier placed on any first cycle claims, even when Medicare required that an EY modifier be included." Duffy also confirmed that when she "reported to KCI management, including Deb Smith, that she had not found any WOPD for claims submitted, Smith directed Duffy not to appeal the claim ... because Smith was worried that Medicare would notice the lack of a WOPD."

Duffy's allegations provided the necessary reliable indicia that give a strong inference that KCI actually submitted false claims to Medicare, and the district court incorrectly disregarded the information provided by Duffy. The district court recognized that, "[w]hile it is certainly suspect that Plaintiff is on her Fourth Amended Complaint, and Plaintiff now, for the first time, alleges facts pertaining to conversations that occurred starting in 2002, the Court must accept Plaintiff's allegations as true when deciding a motion to dismiss." In spite of that acknowledgement, however, the district court did not accept the allegations as true, stating that the "allegations regarding [Godecke's] conversations with Duffy are not particularly reliable, given that Duffy was allegedly recounting what she recalled from fifteen years prior." The district court ultimately held that "Plaintiff's allegations regarding her 2002 conversations with Duffy and Duffy's recollections that Plaintiff 'confirmed' in 2017 do not provide the necessary "reliable indicia" that KCI actually submitted false claims to Medicare."

The district court imposed too high of a hurdle to test the sufficiency of these allegations. The only unreliable aspect of Duffy's allegations is the fact that Duffy's recollection is based on events that happened fifteen years prior. Although it is true that a fifteen year old memory is less reliable than a more recent one, Duffy's memories clearly allege a false claim: she "personally saw that claims for first cycle treatment had routinely been billed to Medicare, and paid by Medicare, even though the VAC had been delivered before KCI had obtained a valid WOPD." Duffy's recollections can be more closely examined in a deposition, and it is possible that they would not hold up under cross-examination. But a motion to dismiss is too early a stage to render a judgment on the reliability of Duffy's recollections when the only indication that they might be less than reliable is the length of time that has elapsed since she witnessed the events at issue.

Godecke alleges details of a scheme to submit claims that were fraudulent because they lacked the EY modifier when it should have been included. And Duffy's recollections and Godecke's cross-referencing p.1211 of ROEs are enough reliable indicia to lead to a strong inference that KCI actually submitted false claims to Medicare.

B. Godecke sufficiently alleges that KCI acted with the requisite scienter under the FCA.

Liability under the FCA is established only when the defendant "knowingly" presents a false or fraudulent claim for payment. 31 U.S.C. § 3729(a)(1)(A). "Knowingly" is defined as having: (1) actual knowledge of the information; (2) deliberate ignorance of the truth or falsity of the information; or (3) reckless disregard of the truth or falsity of the information. 31 U.S.C. § 3729(b)(1)(A). The FCA's "knowingly" requirement "require[s] no proof of specific intent to defraud." 31 U.S.C. § 3729(b)(1)(B). Instead of pleading specific intent to defraud, it is sufficient to plead that the defendant knowingly filed false claims, or that the defendant submitted false claims with reckless disregard or deliberate ignorance as to the truth or falsity of its representations. *United States v. Bourseau*, 531 F.3d 1159, 1167 (9th Cir. 2008). The deliberate ignorance standard can cover "the ostrich type situation where an individual has buried his head in the sand and failed to make simple inquiries which would alert him that false claims are being submitted." *United States v. United Healthcare Ins. Co.*, 848 F.3d 1161, 1174 (9th Cir. 2016) (internal quotation marks omitted). "Congress adopted the concept that individuals and contractors receiving public funds have some duty to make a limited inquiry so as to be reasonably certain they are entitled to the money they seek." *Id.* (internal quotation marks omitted).

The district court erred in holding that Godecke failed to plead the requisite scienter under the FCA.[5] The district court indicated that Godecke and Duffy's knowledge of the appeals process would only support an inference that KCI found out during the appeals process that it was submitting false claims to the government, not that it knew they were false at the time of submission.

But Godecke sufficiently alleges that KCI knowingly submitted claims without the requisite EY modifier when KCI had not gotten a written order prior to delivery. First, Godecke alleges that KCI knowingly delivered VAC devices without receiving a prior written order, as evidenced by the "exceptions" authorized by managers. Although this allegation by itself would not be sufficient to allege that KCI knowingly *submitted* false claims, it is an important building block in the overall allegations sufficiently to plead FCA violations. Building on the allegations that KCI knowingly delivered VAC devices without a WOPD, Godecke sufficiently alleges that KCI knowingly submitted these claims without a WOPD to Medicare without the p.1212 requisite EY modifier. Godecke alleges that KCI management explained they knew that Medicare would not pay for the VAC devices delivered under the "exceptions" to the rules, and KCI management "set up tracking systems to expedite [the] effort ... to mask the fact that VACs were delivered without all of the required elements in hand."

Godecke's scienter allegations are bolstered by information from her former co-worker Theresa Duffy. Godecke alleges that Duffy recently confirmed to her "that KCI's claims submitted to Medicare that Duffy had personally reviewed lacked appropriate documentation, including claims which required an EY modifier because KCI did not have a valid WOPD before delivery of a VAC." Duffy also confirmed to Godecke that KCI's billing and management head Deb Smith told her not to appeal denials of certain claims "because Smith was worried that Medicare would notice the lack of a WOPD." Partially through Duffy's recollection, the FAC alleged that false claims were submitted without the proper WOPD documentation and KCI management deliberately avoided appealing denials of claims that lacked a WOPD. Combined, this is sufficient to allege scienter. The district court explained away Godecke's conversations with Duffy as not alleging the requisite scienter, saying "at most, Duffy 'confirmed' that KCI realized after the fact, during the appeals process, that it had submitted claims to Medicare without a WOPD or the required EY modifier." But at the very least, Duffy's recollections are sufficient to show the "ostrich type situation" of deliberate ignorance on the part of KCI, where KCI "has buried his head in the sand and failed to make simple inquiries which would alert [it] that false claims are being submitted." *See United Healthcare Ins. Co.,* 848 F.3d at 1174.

Furthermore, when Godecke raised concerns about whether KCI was following proper rules for billing Medicare, KCI quickly fired not only Godecke, but also her supervisor, and the senior vice president to whom they both reported. Godecke's supervisor told her that KCI management was afraid she was gathering information on false claims and was going to be a whistleblower. While the circumstances of the firings does not establish on its own that KCI knowingly submitted false claims, KCI's extraordinarily aggressive reaction to these concerns suggest that KCI was at least trying to remain willfully ignorant of the falsity of its VAC claims. When combined with Duffy's recollection and the tracking systems, the firings are added support of the allegation that KCI knowingly submitted false claims.

In sum, the allegations of scienter were sufficient, at least under the "deliberate ignorance" standard, based on the FAC's discussion of the tracking systems set up by KCI management, Godecke's colleague's assertions that she personally reviewed claims that lacked appropriate documentation, KCI management's instructions not to appeal denials for fear that Medicare would notice the lack of a written order prior to delivery, and the quick termination of Godecke, her supervisor, and the senior vice president after they raised concerns about false claims being submitted.

C. Godecke sufficiently alleges that KCI's false claims were material to the government's payment decision.

KCI argues that the FAC fails the FCA's materiality requirement because it does not allege with particularity that the allegedly false submissions would have affected Medicare's ultimate payment p.1213 decision. In an earlier order, the district court denied KCI's motion to dismiss the Second Amended Complaint on the issue of materiality. "In reviewing decisions of the district court, we may affirm on any ground finding support in the record. If the decision below is correct, it must be affirmed, even if the district court relied on the wrong grounds or wrong reasoning." *Cigna Prop. & Cas. Ins. Co. v. Polaris Pictures Corp.,* 159 F.3d 412, 418 (9th Cir. 1998).

The FCA defines the term "material" as "having a natural tendency to influence, or be capable of influencing, the payment or receipt of money or property." 31 U.S.C. § 3729(b)(4). Although the requirement is "demanding," the Supreme Court has held that there is not a bright-line test for determining whether the FCA's materiality requirement has been met. *See Universal Health Servs., Inc. v. U S. ex rel. Escobar,* ___ U.S. ___, 136 S. Ct. 1989, 2003, 195 L.Ed.2d 348 (2016). Instead, the Supreme Court has given a list of relevant, but not necessarily dispositive, factors in determining whether the false claims were material, such as whether the government decided "to expressly identify a provision as a condition of payment." *Id.* "Likewise, proof of materiality can include, but is not necessarily limited to, evidence that the defendant knows that the Government consistently refuses to pay claims in the mine run of cases based on noncompliance with the particular statutory, regulatory, or contractual requirement." *Id.* "Conversely, if the Government pays a particular claim in full despite its actual knowledge that certain requirements were violated, that is very strong evidence that those requirements are not material." *Id.* "Or, if the Government regularly pays a particular type of claim in full despite actual knowledge that certain requirements were violated, and has signaled no change in position, that is strong evidence that the requirements are not material." *Id.* at 2003-04. "Materiality, in addition, cannot be found where noncompliance is minor or insubstantial." *Id.* at 2003.

Filing for Medicare payment for a VAC and related supplies without disclosing that no written order was received prior to delivery is a material false claim. Godecke's allegations, taken together, sufficiently allege materiality to survive a motion to dismiss. According to the FAC, the LCDs explicitly provide that payment would not be made if a VAC was delivered before the written order was received. Although this express identification of a condition of payment "may not be sufficient, without more, to prove materiality, ... it is certainly probative evidence of materiality." *See U.S. ex rel. Rose v. Stephens Inst.,* 909 F.3d 1012, 1020 (9th Cir. 2018). Godecke further alleges that the prior written order requirement was not just some "paperwork issue" but the result of extensive negotiations KCI had with Medicare representatives in order to prevent fraud and abuse. Although this is not an allegation based on how Medicare "has treated similar violations," the fact that the requirement was "extensively negotiated" is also probative. *See id.* KCI simply suggests that because the government "*may* reimburse a particular claim in full despite its not meeting the LCD guidelines (including the EY modifier requirement), those guidelines cannot be said to be material to the government's payment determination." (Emphasis added.) But KCI has not shown that Medicare has paid a particular claim in full despite its actual knowledge that there was no prior written order. Nowhere in the record is there evidence that the government actually *has* reimbursed a particular claim in full despite knowing that it did not meet the LCD guidelines related to the EY modifier requirement. Godecke's allegations also do not indicate that non-compliance would be minor or insubstantial. Godecke alleges that Medicare would not pay for the VAC at all if it knew that p.1214 there was no prior written order. Godecke therefore has sufficiently alleged materiality.

CONCLUSION

For the foregoing reasons, we reverse the district court's dismissal of the FAC.[6] REVERSED and REMANDED.

[*] The Honorable M. Douglas Harpool, United States District Judge for the Western District of Missouri, sitting by designation.

[1] Godecke began this action in 2008 when she filed the original complaint under seal. This case has been up to the Ninth Circuit before on the issue of subject matter jurisdiction. *See U.S. ex rel. Hartpence v. Kinetic Concepts,* Inc., 792 F.3d 1121 (9th Cir. 2015).

[2] The KX billing code replaced the ZX billing code in 2002. The only difference between the codes is that ZX was a temporary designation and KX is a permanent designation. For the sake of simplicity, we use "KX" throughout this opinion.

[3] The district court stayed Godecke's retaliation claim and KCI's breach of contract and conversion counterclaims pending the out-come of this appeal.

[4] First cycle treatment refers to the first month of VAC therapy.

[5] The district court misstated the standard for scienter at the conclusion of its scienter analysis, stating that Godecke had not sufficiently alleged that KCI "knowingly submitted false claims with *an intent to deceive the government.*" (Emphasis added.) But this incorrect legal standard was only mentioned once, and it is clear from the rest of the district court's analysis that the district court understood that the proper standard only required KCI knowingly to submit false claims. As the district court stated, "[t]he more appropriate inquiry is whether Plaintiff has pleaded facts indicating that KCI knowingly submitted claims without a completed WOPD to Medicare without the requisite EY modifier." Therefore, reversal would not be warranted solely on the ground that the district court misstated once the proper legal standard for scienter. *See Hooper v. Lockheed Martin Corp.,* 688 F.3d 1037, 1049-50 (9th Cir. 2012) (holding that when the district court applies the wrong legal standard by

requiring the relator to prove that the defendant acted "with the intent to deceive," reversal may be warranted).

[6] Because we hold that the FAC's allegations are sufficient under the FCA, we do not reach Godecke's alternate argument that the district court erred in denying her leave to further amend her complaint.

895 F.3d 619 (2018)

UNITED STATES EX REL. Anita SILINGO, Plaintiff-Appellant,

v.

WELLPOINT, INC., an Indiana corporation; Anthem Blue Cross, business entity, form unknown; Health Net, Inc.; Health Net of California, Inc., a California corporation; Health Net Life Insurance Company, a California corporation; Visiting Nurse Service Choice; Molina Healthcare, Inc., a Delaware corporation; Molina Healthcare of California, a California corporation; Molina Healthcare of California Partner Plan, Inc., a California corporation; Alameda Alliance for Health, a business organization, form unknown; Anthem Blue Cross Life and Health Insurance Company, a California corporation; Blue Cross of California, a California corporation, Defendants-Appellees.

No. 16-56400.

United States Court of Appeals, Ninth Circuit.

Argued and Submitted March 8, 2018 Pasadena, California.
Filed July 9, 2018.

US ex rel. Silingo v. WellPoint, Inc., 895 F. 3d 619 (9th Cir. 2018)

Appeal from the United States District Court for the Central District of California; Fernando M. Olguin, District Judge, Presiding, D.C. No. 8:13-cv-01348-FMO-JC.

Abram Jay Zinberg (argued), The Zinberg Law Firm A.P.C., Huntington Beach, California; William K. Hanagami, The p.623 Hanagami Law Firm A.P.C., Woodland Hills, California; for Plaintiff-Appellant.

David Jeffrey Leviss (argued) and Amanda M. Santella, O'Melveny & Myers LLP, Washington, D.C.; Elizabeth M. Bock, Sabrina Strong, and David Deaton, O'Melveny & Myers LLP, Los Angeles, California; Poopak Nourafchan and Michael M. Maddigan, Hogan Lovells LLP, Los Angeles, California; David J. Schindler, Latham & Watkins LLP, Los Angeles, California; Anne W. Robinson, Latham & Watkins LLP, Washington, D.C.; Paul C. Burkholder and David Jacobs, Epstein Becker & Green PC, Los Angeles, California; Pamela A. Stone and Michael J. Daponde, Daponde Szabo Rowe PC, Sacramento, California; for Defendants-Appellees.

Before: Ronald M. Gould and Mary H. Murguia, Circuit Judges, and Jack Zouhary,[*] District Judge.

p.622 OPINION

GOULD, Circuit Judge:

Qui tam relator Anita Silingo appeals the dismissal of her False Claims Act suit against several Medicare Advantage organizations. We reverse in part, affirm in part, and remand.

I

Medicare Advantage is a modern adaptation of the momentous 1960s-era program. Traditional Medicare uses a fee-for-service payment model, whereby the more services physicians perform, the more money they earn. After Medicare was enacted, however, experts came to realize that this payment structure encourages healthcare providers to order more tests and procedures than medically necessary. *See* Thomas L. Greaney, *Medicare Advantage, Accountable Care Organizations, and Traditional Medicare: Synchronization or Collision?,* 15 Yale J. Health Pol'y, L. & Ethics 37, 38, 41 (2015).

Medicare Advantage seeks to improve the quality of care while safeguarding the public fisc by employing a "capitation" payment system. Capitation means an amount is paid per person. *Capitation,* Black's Law Dictionary (10th ed. 2014). Under Medicare Advantage's capitation system, private health insurance organizations provide Medicare benefits in exchange for a fixed monthly fee per person enrolled in the program — regardless of actual healthcare usage. These organizations pocket for themselves or pay out to their enrollees' providers the difference between their capitation revenue and their enrollees' medical expenses, creating an incentive for the organizations to rein in costs. *See* Patricia A. Davis et al., Cong. Research Serv., R40425, *Medicare Primer* 20 (2017), https://fas.org/sgp/crs/misc/R40425.pdf.

Unfortunately, human nature being what it is, Medicare Advantage organizations also have some incentive to improperly inflate their enrollees' capitation rates, if these organizations fall prey to greed. By design, Medicare Advantage is supposed to compensate these organizations for expected healthcare costs, paying "less for healthier enrollees and more for less healthy enrollees." Establishment of the Medicare Advantage Program, 70 Fed. Reg. 4588, 4657 (Jan. 28, 2005). So capitation rates are based largely on an individual's "risk adjustment data," which reflect several factors that can affect healthcare costs. *See* 42 U.S.C. § 1395w-23(a)(1)(C)(i); p.624 42 C.F.R. § 422.308(c). Chief among these data are individuals' medical diagnoses. *See* Policy and Technical Changes to the Medicare Advantage and the Medicare Prescription Drug Benefit Programs, 74 Fed. Reg. 54,634, 54,673 (Oct. 22, 2009). Medicare Advantage organizations obtain diagnosis codes from healthcare providers after these providers have had medical visits with plan enrollees. *See* CMS, Pub. No. 100-16, *Medicare Managed Care Manual,* ch. 7, § 40 (2014), https://www.cms.gov/Regulations-and-Guidance/Guidance/Manuals/downloads/mc86c07.pdf. In turn, Medicare Advantage organizations report the diagnosis codes that they receive to the Centers for Medicare and Medicaid Services ("CMS") for use in the risk adjustment model that is the key to calculation of capitation rates. *Id.* The risk adjustment model deems a Medicare Advantage enrollee to be as healthy as the average Medicare beneficiary unless CMS receives updated diagnosis codes for the enrollee every year. *See id.* §§ 20, 70, 70.2.5, 120.2.4.

With data for millions of people being submitted each year, CMS is unable to confirm diagnoses before calculating capitation rates. Instead, the agency accepts the diagnoses as submitted, and then audits some of the self-reported data a few years later to ensure that they are adequately supported by medical documentation. *See* 42 C.F.R. §§ 422.310(e), 422.311; Contract Year 2015 Policy and Technical Changes to the Medicare Advantage and the Medicare Prescription Drug Benefit Programs, 79 Fed. Reg. 1918, 2001 (Jan. 10, 2014). These audits have revealed excess payments for unsupported diagnoses steadily increasing over the last decade, reaching an estimated $16.2 *billion* — nearly ten cents of every dollar paid to Medicare Advantage organizations — in 2016 alone. *See* James Cosgrove, U.S. Gov't Accountability Office, GAO-17-761T, *Medicare Advantage Program Integrity: CMS's Efforts to Ensure Proper Payments and Identify and Recover Improper Payments* 1 (2017), https://www.gao.gov/assets/690/685934.pdf; James Cosgrove, U.S. Gov't Accountability Office, GAO-13-206, *Medicare Advantage: Substantial Excess Payments Underscore Need for CMS to Improve Accuracy of Risk Score Adjustments* 9-10 (2013), https://www.gao.gov/assets/660/651712.pdf.

To combat the "incentive for [Medicare Advantage] organizations to potentially over-report diagnoses," Medicare regulations require risk adjustment data to be produced according to certain best practices. Contract Year 2015 Policy and Technical Changes to the Medicare Advantage and the Medicare Prescription Drug Benefit Programs, 79 Fed. Reg. 1918, 2001 (Jan. 10, 2014). Every diagnosis code submitted to CMS must be based on a "face-to-face" visit that is documented in the medical record. *Medicare Managed Care Manual,* ch. 7, §§ 40, 120.1.1. Medical records must be validated by qualifying "physician/practitioner signatures and credentials." Policy and Technical Changes to the Medicare Advantage and the Medicare Prescription Drug Benefit Programs, 75 Fed. Reg. 19,678, 19,743 (Apr. 15, 2010). Further, electronic medical records must meet special signature requirements and use software that is "protected against modification." CMS, Pub. No. 100-08, *Medicare Program Integrity Manual,* ch. 3, § 3.3.2.4 (2018), https://www.cms.gov/Regulations-and-Guidance/Guidance/Manuals/downloads/PIM83c03.pdf.[1]

p.625 Medicare regulations also establish several data certification requirements. Most important here, it is an express condition of payment that a Medicare Advantage organization "certify (based on best knowledge, information, and belief) that the [risk adjustment] data it submits ... are accurate, complete, and truthful." 42 C.F.R. § 422.504(*l*)(2). We have explained that a certification is thus false "when the Medicare Advantage organization has actual knowledge of the falsity of the risk adjustment data *or* demonstrates either 'reckless disregard' or 'deliberate ignorance' of the truth or falsity of the data." *United States ex rel. Swoben v. United Healthcare Ins. Co.,* 848 F.3d 1161, 1169 (9th Cir. 2016) (citing Medicare+Choice Program, 65 Fed. Reg. 40,170, 40,268 (June 29, 2000)). The organization also is required to "[a]dopt and implement an effective compliance program, which must include measures that prevent, detect, and correct non-compliance with CMS' program requirements," such as written standards of conduct, the designation of a compliance officer, and other listed minimum requirements. 42 C.F.R. § 422.503(b)(4)(vi). The importance of accurate data certifications and effective compliance programs is obvious: if enrollee diagnoses are overstated, then the capitation payments to Medicare Advantage organizations will be improperly inflated.

The Medicare Advantage capitation payment system is subject to the False Claims Act. Originally enacted during the Civil War, the False Claims Act was intended to "forfend[] widespread fraud by government contractors." *United States ex rel. Hopper v. Anton,* 91 F.3d 1261, 1265 (9th Cir. 1996). The Act's *qui tam* provisions allow a person — called a "relator" — to bring suit on the federal government's behalf, and then share the recovered damages and civil penalties with the government. *See United States ex rel. Kelly v. Boeing Co.,* 9 F.3d 743, 745-47 (9th Cir. 1993). Liability attaches upon proof that a false claim for payment was made, regardless of whether the government suffered actual damage. *United States ex rel. Aflatooni v. Kitsap Physicians Serv.,* 314 F.3d 995, 1002 (9th Cir. 2002).

II

Anita Silingo is a former Compliance Officer and Director of Provider Relations for Mobile Medical Examination Services, Inc. ("MedXM"). MedXM employs physicians, nurse practitioners, and physician assistants to conduct in-home health assessments of Medicare beneficiaries. Silingo alleges that from 2010 to 2014, MedXM contracted with the defendant Medicare Advantage organizations to provide up-to-date diagnosis codes and medical documentation for enrollees who otherwise may not have had an eligible medical encounter during a calendar year.

In August 2013, Silingo filed an initial complaint against MedXM and the defendant Medicare Advantage organizations under the False Claims Act. In May 2014, Silingo filed her first amended complaint. The United States then declined to intervene, and in January 2015 Silingo filed a second amended complaint.

The crux of the complaint is that the defendant Medicare Advantage organizations retained MedXM to fraudulently increase, or at least maintain, their capitation payments for enrollees whose risk scores were set to expire and revert to the unadjusted Medicare beneficiary average.

First, Silingo claims that MedXM used inappropriate software so that it could edit p.626 health records to exaggerate medical diagnoses. Silingo alleges that MedXM's in-home health assessment reports were prepared in Microsoft Word templates that are not "protected against modification," and were signed by merely typing in the medical examiner's name, which is not an acceptable electronic signature. *Medicare Program Integrity Manual,* ch. 3, § 3.3.2.4. Once in the hands of MedXM's coders, these reports were allegedly modified to delete information showing little risk and insert new information to support diagnoses with higher risk scores. According to Silingo, MedXM then saved these reports as PDF files and submitted them to Medicare Advantage organizations as support for inflated risk adjustment data. Silingo asserts that all of MedXM's health assessment reports violated CMS's requirements for electronic medical records, and that more than half of them had been tampered with in this manner.

Next, Silingo claims that MedXM's fleet of mostly nurse practitioners and physician assistants were not legally authorized to make conclusive medical diagnoses, so their examinations could not support the risk adjustment data that was submitted. Before 2012, MedXM allegedly contracted directly with these healthcare providers without ensuring that they practiced under the supervision of licensed physicians. From 2012 to 2014, MedXM allegedly had contract physicians fraudulently sign standard care agreements with these non-physician providers without properly supervising their work.

Silingo also claims MedXM systematically fabricated complex diagnoses that its medical examiners could not have possibly confirmed during an in-home assessment.

The complaint identifies a variety of ailments — such as chronic obstructive pulmonary disease, hepatitis, and inflammatory bowel disease — that allegedly cannot be diagnosed without a spirometry test, biopsy, follow-up blood test, or other invasive procedure that MedXM's examiners were unequipped and unauthorized to perform in a person's home. Instead, Silingo alleges, MedXM's medical examiners and coders simply recycled prior diagnoses and medical histories in the updated health assessment reports.

Further, Silingo claims that MedXM regularly produced diagnostic information that was not the result of face-to-face medical encounters. By her estimation, in-home health assessments took about 45 minutes plus travel time and could be performed only within an 11-hour window, so MedXM's medical examiners realistically could not perform more than 13 in-home health assessments per day. But Silingo alleges that many examiners consistently reported more than 15 assessments per day, with some reporting as many as 25. Silingo contends that these examiners boosted their assessment numbers by sometimes submitting identical vital statistics (age, weight, sex, and so on) for hundreds of enrollees, and only "correcting" these suspicious data entries when requested by Medicare Advantage organizations, by collecting information over the phone or having MedXM's coders forge new data.

A company offering in-home health assessment services has no intrinsic reason to overstate its findings. Rather, as Silingo alleges, MedXM went to the trouble of editing and forging medical records to provide its clients with more lucrative diagnosis codes — earning the Medicare Advantage organizations higher than warranted capitation payments.

Silingo contends that the defendant Medicare Advantage organizations made false claims for payment by submitting MedXM's risk adjustment data to CMS for several years, either with actual knowledge p.627 that the data were invalid or with reckless disregard or deliberate ignorance as to their validity. In doing so, the organizations allegedly violated the certification requirements of 42 C.F.R. § 422.504(*l*)(2), which is an express condition of payment. And Silingo contends that the failure to catch MedXM's widespread fraud is evidence that these organizations did not have the effective compliance programs required by 42 C.F.R. § 422.503(b)(4)(vi), which is not an express condition of payment.

Silingo advanced six theories of liability under the False Claims Act. She first charged that defendants violated 31 U.S.C. § 3729(a)(1)(A) by making, or causing to be made, a claim for payment that is "factually false." *Mikes v. Straus*, 274 F.3d 687, 697 (2d Cir. 2001), *abrogated on other grounds by Universal Health Servs., Inc. v. United States ex rel. Escobar*, ___ U.S. ___, 136 S.Ct. 1989, 195 L.Ed.2d 348 (2016). A factually false claim is one in which "the claim for payment is itself literally false or fraudulent," *United States ex rel. Hendow v. Univ. of Phoenix*, 461 F.3d 1166, 1170 (9th Cir. 2006), such as when the claim "involves an incorrect description of goods or services provided or a request for reimbursement for goods or services never provided," *Mikes*, 274 F.3d at 697.

In addition, Silingo contended that defendants violated § 3729(a)(1)(A) by making claims that were "legally false." *Id.* There are two cognizable theories of liability for legally false claims: express false certification and implied false certification. Express false certification involves an entity's representation of compliance with the law as part of the process for submitting a claim when it is actually not compliant. *United States ex rel. Ebeid v. Lungwitz,* 616 F.3d 993, 998 (9th Cir. 2010). By contrast, "[i]mplied false certification occurs when an entity has previously undertaken to expressly comply with a law, rule, or regulation, and that obligation is implicated by submitting a claim for payment even though a certification of compliance is not required in the process of submitting the claim." *Id.; see also Escobar,* ___ U.S. ___, 136 S.Ct. 1989, 195 L.Ed.2d 348 (validating the implied false certification theory).

Silingo next raised a false records claim under the following subparagraph, § 3729(a)(1)(B). Such a claim imposes liability where a party "knowingly makes, uses, or causes to be made or used, a false record or statement material to a false or fraudulent claim." 31 U.S.C. § 3729(a)(1)(B).

Silingo also alleged a violation of the False Claims Act's "reverse false claim" provision, § 3729(a)(1)(G). That provision "is designed to cover Government money or property that is knowingly retained by a person even though they have no right to it." S. Rep. No. 111-10, at 13-14 (2009), *reprinted in* 2009 U.S.C.C.A.N. 430, 441.

Finally, Silingo accused defendants of conspiring to violate the False Claims Act. *See* 31 U.S.C. § 3729(a)(1)(C).

In February 2015, defendants separately moved to dismiss Silingo's claims. Silingo opposed defendants' motions, but did not defend her count for reverse false claims. The district court held that the factually false claim cause of action against MedXM was well-pleaded under Federal Rules of Civil Procedure 8 and 9(b) because Silingo sufficiently alleged that MedXM caused false claims to be submitted to CMS. But the court dismissed Silingo's abandoned reverse false claim count and conspiracy claim with prejudice, and dismissed her four remaining claims against the defendant Medicare Advantage organizations without prejudice. In the district court's p.628 view, the latter claims were defective for using an impermissible "group-pleading."

Silingo filed a third amended complaint in October 2015. This time, Silingo separately pleaded her allegations against the Medicare Advantage organizations seriatim. Defendants promptly moved to dismiss the new complaint, and while these motions were pending, MedXM settled out of the case. The district court then dismissed Silingo's claims against the Medicare Advantage organizations with prejudice on the ground that the allegations "remain undifferentiated." Silingo timely appealed the dismissal of her causes of action for factually false claims, express false certifications, false records, and reverse false claims.

III

We review *de novo* a district court's dismissal of a complaint under Federal Rule of Civil Procedure 12(b)(6), "accepting as true all well-pleaded allegations of fact in the complaint and construing them in the light most favorable to the Relator[]." *United States v. Corinthian Colleges,* 655 F.3d 984, 991 (9th Cir. 2011) (citation and alterations omitted). We review for abuse of discretion a district court's denial of leave to amend a complaint. *Id.* at 995.

In the usual case involving dismissal of a complaint, we must evaluate whether the factual allegations, together with all reasonable inferences, state a plausible claim to relief. *Ashcroft v. Iqbal,* 556 U.S. 662, 678, 129 S.Ct. 1937, 173 L.Ed.2d 868 (2009).

Rule 9(b), however, requires that "[i]n alleging fraud or mistake, a party must state with particularity the circumstances constituting fraud or mistake." Fed. R. Civ. P. 9(b). To satisfy this requirement, a pleading must identify "the who, what, when, where, and how of the misconduct charged," as well as "what is false or misleading about [the purportedly fraudulent] statement, and why it is false." *United States ex rel. Cafasso v. Gen. Dynamics C4 Sys., Inc.,* 637 F.3d 1047, 1055 (9th Cir. 2011) (quoting *Ebeid,* 616 F.3d at 998). This heightened pleading standard serves two main purposes. First, allegations of fraud "must be specific enough to give defendants notice of the particular misconduct which is alleged to constitute the fraud charged so that they can defend against the charge and not just deny that they have done anything wrong." *Bly-Magee v. California,* 236 F.3d 1014, 1019 (9th Cir. 2001) (quotation marks and citation omitted). Second, the rule serves "to deter the filing of complaints as a pretext for the discovery of unknown wrongs, to protect [defendants] from the harm that comes from being subject to fraud charges, and to prohibit plaintiffs from unilaterally imposing upon the court, the parties and society enormous social and economic costs absent some factual basis." *Id.* at 1018 (quotation marks and citation omitted).

IV

To satisfy Rule 9(b), a fraud suit against differently situated defendants must "identify the role of each defendant in the alleged fraudulent scheme." *Swartz v. KPMG LLP,* 476 F.3d 756, 765 (9th Cir. 2007) (citation and alterations omitted). In other words, when defendants engage in different wrongful conduct, plaintiffs must likewise "differentiate their allegations." *Id.* at 764 (citation omitted).

This rule is illustrated by *Destfino v. Reiswig,* 630 F.3d 952 (9th Cir. 2011). There, plaintiffs alleged that 29 individuals, 10 businesses, and a church formed an intricate tax avoidance scheme, but the complaint did not "set out which of the defendants made which of the fraudulent p.629 statements/conduct." *Id.* at 954, 958. We explained that in a situation like that in *Destfino,* with different actors playing different parts, it is not enough to "lump" together the dissimilar defendants and assert that "everyone did everything." *Id.* at 958 (quoting *Swartz,* 476 F.3d at 764-65). More is required to plead the circumstances of a fraud with particularity.

On the other hand, a complaint need not distinguish between defendants that had the exact same role in a fraud. We recently addressed this issue in *United States ex rel. Swoben v. United Healthcare Ins. Co.,* 848 F.3d 1161 (9th Cir. 2016), which we decided a few months after the district court dismissed Silingo's complaint. *Swoben* involved allegations of Medicare Advantage organizations — including several of the defendant organizations here — submitting false certifications of the accuracy, completeness, and truthfulness of the risk adjustment data they provided to CMS. *Id.* at 1166-67. In a bit of *deja vu,* these Medicare Advantage organizations faulted the complaint there for using "collective allegations to refer to the defendants rather than differentiating among them." *Id.* at 1184. We dispensed with this argument, holding: "There is no flaw in a pleading... where collective allegations are used to describe the actions of multiple defendants who are alleged to have engaged in precisely the same conduct." *Id.* A good claim against one defendant did not become inadequate simply because a co-defendant was alleged to have committed the same wrongful acts.

To better understand *Swoben*'s ruling, consider an analogy. In the taxonomy of conspiracy theories, a "chain conspiracy" is one in which "each person is responsible for a distinct act within the overall plan," while a "wheel conspiracy" involves "a single member or group (the 'hub') separately agree[ing] with two or more other members or groups (the 'spokes')." *Conspiracy,* Black's Law Dictionary (10th ed. 2014). Broadly speaking, if a fraudulent scheme resembles a chain conspiracy, then a complaint must separately identify which defendant was responsible for what distinct part of the plan. By contrast, if a fraudulent scheme resembles a wheel conspiracy, then any parallel actions of the "spokes" can be addressed by collective allegations.

Applying Swoben here in light of these related principles, we observe that Silingo has pleaded a wheel conspiracy-like fraud in which MedXM was the "hub" and the defendant Medicare Advantage organizations were the "spokes." Each of the defendant organizations allegedly had separate contracts with MedXM, and each of them allegedly passed on MedXM's inflated diagnosis information in the same way. These organizations thus miss the mark when they implore us to consider that they are "unrelated, dissimilar defendants with no relevant business connections to one another and that [they] differ in size, geography, and member populations." Because the Medicare Advantage organizations are largely "alleged to have engaged in precisely the same conduct," there was no reason (and no way) for Silingo to differentiate among those allegations that are common to the group. *Swoben,* 848 F.3d at 1184. Silingo's charges of factually false claims, express false certifications, and false records should not have been dismissed due to her use of group allegations.

V

The defendant Medicare Advantage organizations contend that we should nevertheless affirm the dismissal of the third amended complaint based on arguments that the district court did not reach. We may affirm the dismissal on any ground supported by the record, even if p.630 the district court did not rely on that ground. *Corinthian Colleges,* 655 F.3d at 992. The defendant organizations offer two such grounds: (1) that the complaint did not allege a sufficient factual basis to link MedXM's misconduct to their actual submission of claims or certifications to CMS; and (2) that Silingo's allegations about their knowledge of the fraud did not satisfy Rule 8.[2] We address these points in turn.

A

The defendant Medicare Advantage organizations first contend that the complaint provides inadequate detail of their submission of false claims. When alleging a scheme to submit false claims, a plaintiff must provide "reliable indicia that lead to a strong inference that claims were actually submitted." *Ebeid,* 616 F.3d at 998-99 (quoting *United States ex rel. Grubbs v. Ravikumar Kanneganti,* 565 F.3d 180, 190 (5th Cir. 2009)). We do not require the complaint to identify representative examples of actual false claims, though that is one way to satisfy the heightened pleading requirement. *Id.*

We agree with the district court, in its analysis of the claims against MedXM, that Silingo has carried her burden here. The complaint asserts that the defendant

Medicare Advantage organizations contracted with MedXM to provide health assessment reports and diagnosis codes for at least four years. Silingo details "first-hand experience of the scheme unfolding," describing MedXM's in-home assessments targeting Medicare Advantage enrollees who would otherwise lack risk adjustment data for a given year. *Grubbs,* 565 F.3d at 192. For this population, the Medicare Advantage organizations would face lower capitation payments if they did not procure and submit updated data. *See Medicare Managed Care Manual,* ch. 7, §§ 20, 70, 70.2.5. Conversely, if they submitted data that overstated health problems in the diagnosis codes given, that would result in higher capitated payments to them. And as part of their requests for payment, Medicare Advantage organizations must certify that the data they submit are "accurate, complete, and truthful." 42 C.F.R. § 422.504(*l*)(2). Taking Silingo's allegations as true, as we must, we see ample circumstantial evidence from which to infer that the defendant organizations submitted MedXM's risk adjustment data and certified the data's validity to CMS.

Indeed, "[i]t would stretch the imagination to infer the inverse." *Grubbs,* 565 F.3d at 192. Perhaps it would be possible that some Medicare Advantage organization, after paying for MedXM's services, might have discovered the fraud and then cut ties with the company and thrown out its data. But the organizations here are alleged to have had multi-year relationships with MedXM, apparently encompassing thousands of examinations. There is no reason to believe that these companies consistently paid MedXM for data that they desperately needed but, time after time, did not actually use.

The defendant Medicare Advantage organizations counter that Silingo did not sufficiently plead the "who, what, when, where, why" of their false claims, omitting allegations about their "claims filtering, p.631 verification, or submission processes or outcomes." But these omissions do not justify dismissing the complaint for inadequate pleading. Rule 9(b) does not require a plaintiff to explain *why* a defendant committed fraud; the complaint simply must allege "the who, what, when, where, and *how* of the misconduct charged." *Cafasso,* 637 F.3d at 1055 (quoting *Ebeid,* 616 F.3d at 998) (emphasis added). Whatever their internal processes, Silingo alleges, the defendant organizations ultimately did submit false claims and certifications.

B

The next argument of the defendant Medicare Advantage organizations is that Silingo's allegations about their knowledge of the alleged fraud are not plausible under Rule 8.

To plead the element of knowledge under the False Claims Act, a relator must allege that a defendant knew a claim for payment was false, or that it acted with reckless disregard or deliberate indifference as to the truth or falsity of the claim. *Corinthian Colleges,* 655 F.3d at 996; *see also* 31 U.S.C. § 3729(b)(1) (defining the terms "knowing" and "knowingly"). Although the circumstances of a fraud must be pleaded with particularity, knowledge may be pleaded generally. Fed. R. Civ. P. 9(b); *see also Corinthian Colleges,* 655 F.3d at 996. A complaint therefore must set out sufficient factual matter from which a defendant's knowledge of a fraud might reasonably be inferred. *See Iqbal,* 556 U.S. at 678, 129 S.Ct. 1937.

Here, Silingo plausibly pleads that the defendant Medicare Advantage organizations submitted false claims and certifications and used false records with actual knowledge, reckless disregard, or deliberate ignorance of their falsity. The complaint details a variety of ways in which the defendant organizations knew, or reasonably should have known, that MedXM's risk adjustment data were invalid.

For one thing, Silingo claims that every health assessment report contained a typewritten signature only, violating the requirements for medical records underlying risk adjustment data. *See Medicare Program Integrity Manual,* ch. 3, § 3.3.2.4 (describing requirements for handwritten and electronic signatures); *see also* Policy and Technical Changes, 75 Fed. Reg. at 19,742 ("Medical records with missing signatures or credentials are scored as errors under [risk adjustment data validation] audit procedures."). Similarly, Silingo contends that these errant signatures should have tipped off the defendant organizations that MedXM was editing its examiners' unsecured reports.

For another, Silingo alleges that other parts of MedXM's health assessment reports provided additional reasons for suspicion. According to the complaint, MedXM's frequent use of nurse practitioners and physician assistants as examiners was a "serious red flag" because these practitioners are commonly known to be limited by law in their ability to make diagnoses. MedXM's diagnosis codes themselves could have revealed the fraud because, as Silingo alleges, many complex diagnoses cannot be confirmed during brief and non-invasive in-home assessments. And Silingo claims that duplicative patient data were sometimes sent to the defendant organizations before being "corrected," which would suggest that something was amiss.

Taking all reasonable inferences in Silingo's favor, *see Iqbal,* 556 U.S. at 678, 129 S.Ct. 1937, there are still further grounds for concluding that the allegations of the defendant organizations' knowledge, reckless disregard, or deliberate ignorance of p.632 the fraud is plausible. Even without the concrete signs detailed above, one would expect that a sophisticated company would notice when its contractor's work is too good to be true. MedXM was allegedly obtaining worse-than-average diagnostic information from enrollees who did not otherwise visit a healthcare provider during a calendar year, and thus would not seem to be in such dire health. The defendant organizations' materials show that the use of in-home assessments is controversial, with CMS repeatedly expressing interest in forbidding their use on the ground that they "contribute[] to increased risk scores and differences in coding patterns" between Medicare Advantage and traditional Medicare.[3] And all of these organizations had an incentive to pass along fraudulent data because, by overstating diagnoses, they could yield more revenue and profit under the capitated payment system — and it was not certain that they would get caught. That may not have been what was going on here, but the third amended complaint certainly states a plausible claim for knowingly participating in fraud, even as to the well-respected companies who are defending here.

It is no defense that Silingo's core allegations against the defendant Medicare Advantage organizations are all alike. If a group pleading against similarly situated defendants can satisfy Rule 9(b), then it can also satisfy the lesser notice pleading standard of Rule 8. *See Swoben,* 848 F.3d at 1184. Silingo simply claims that all of the defendant organizations were equally put on notice by the warning signs that allegedly infected MedXM's health assessment reports. These allegations, if true, give rise to the reasonable inference that the defendant organizations knowingly submitted false claims and used false records, or else acted with reckless disregard or deliberate indifference of the falsity of these claims and records. *See Corinthian Colleges,* 655 F.3d at 996. Because each Medicare Advantage organization must certify the validity of its data "based on best knowledge, information, and belief," these same allegations also support Silingo's express false certification claim. 42 C.F.R. § 422.504(*l*)(2); *Swoben,* 848 F.3d at 1169.

VI

Silingo also appeals the dismissal of her second amended complaint's count for a reverse false claim. But she did not defend this claim in response to the motions to dismiss, so she may not revive it on appeal. *See Carvalho v. Equifax Info. Servs., LLC,* 629 F.3d 876, 888 (9th Cir. 2010). And the district court did not abuse its discretion in denying leave to amend here because amendment could not have revived this abandoned claim. *See Corinthian Colleges,* 655 F.3d at 995.

VII

For the reasons set forth above, we conclude that this case was mistakenly dismissed p.633 on the pleadings. Our decision rests on Silingo's group pleadings, the primary focus of the district court decision and the parties' appellate briefing and oral arguments. Although the defendant organizations also challenge Silingo's additional allegations that are specific to each defendant, we see nothing to undermine our conclusion that the group pleadings alone are adequate.[4]

Some discovery appears to have already taken place, but Silingo is entitled to continue taking discovery before her claims are resolved on summary judgment or at trial. We assuredly do not hold now that Silingo showed enough to get to trial, but rather only that her complaint is adequate to proceed to discovery. Accordingly, we REVERSE in part, AFFIRM in part, and REMAND for further proceedings on Silingo's causes of action for factually false claims, express false certifications, and false records.

[*] The Honorable Jack Zouhary, United States District Judge for the Northern District of Ohio, sitting by designation.

[1] Though this chapter was recently updated, the relevant section has existed in the same form for several years. *See, e.g.,* CMS, Pub. No. 100-08, *Medicare Program Integrity Manual,* ch. 3, § 3.3.2.4 (2012), https://web.archive.org/web/XXXXXXXXXXXXXXX/https://www.cms.gov/Re gulations-and-Guidance/Guidance/Manuals/downloads/PIM83c03.pdf.

[2] The defendant Medicare Advantage organizations also argue that as to the implied false certification claim, Silingo did not plead facts with the requisite particularity to show that the organizations lacked the compliance programs required by 42 C.F.R. § 422.503(b)(4)(vi). We need not address this argument, however,

because Silingo has abandoned this claim on appeal by not challenging its dismissal "clearly and distinctly in the opening brief." *McKay v. Ingleson,* 558 F.3d 888, 891 n.5 (9th Cir. 2009).

[3] CMS, Advance Notice of Methodological Changes for Calendar Year (CY) 2015 for Medicare Advantage (MA) Capitation Rates, Part C and Part D Payment Policies and 2015 Call Letter 20 (Feb. 21, 2014), https://www.cms.gov/Medicare/Health-Plans/MedicareAdvtgSpecRateStats/downloads/Advance2015.pdf; see also CMS, Advance Notice of Methodological Changes for Calendar Year (CY) 2014 for Medicare Advantage (MA) Capitation Rates, Part C and Part D Payment Policies and 2014 Call Letter 22-23 (Feb. 15, 2013), https://www.cms.gov/Medicare/Health-Plans/MedicareAdvtgSpecRateStats/Downloads/Advance2014.pdf; CMS, Announcement of Calendar Year (CY) 2016 Medicare Advantage Capitation Rates and Medicare Advantage and Part D Payment Policies and Final Call Letter 144-45 (Apr. 6, 2015), https://www.cms.gov/Medicare/Health-Plans/MedicareAdvtgSpecRateStats/Downloads/Announcement2016.pdf.

[4] At most, the defendant organizations contend that the allegations specific to Molina Healthcare, Inc. "*contradicted* [Silingo's] more general allegations elsewhere ... for lack of oversight." But the alleged contradiction concerns Silingo's implied false certification claim, which is not at issue on appeal. *See supra,* note 2.

909 F.3d 1012 (2018)

UNITED STATES EX REL. Scott ROSE; Mary Aquino; Mitchell Nelson; Lucy Stearns, Plaintiffs-Appellees,

v.

STEPHENS INSTITUTE, dba Academy of Art University, Defendant-Appellant.

No. 17-15111.

United States Court of Appeals, Ninth Circuit.

Argued and Submitted December 6, 2017 San Francisco, California.

Filed August 24, 2018.

Amended November 26, 2018.

US ex rel. **Rose v. Stephens Institute,** 909 F. 3d 1012 (9th Cir. 2018)

Appeal from the United States District Court for the Northern District of California; Phyllis J. Hamilton, Chief Judge, Presiding, D.C. No. 4:09-cv-05966-PJH.

Steven M. Gombos (argued) Gerald M. Ritzert, Jacob C. Shorter, and David A. Obuchowicz, Gombos Leyton PC, Fairfax, Virginia; Leland B. Altschuler, Law Offices of Leland B. Altschuler, Woodside, California; for Defendant-Appellant.

Michael von Loewenfeldt (argued) and James M. Wagstaffe, Kerr & Wagstaffe LLP, San Francisco, California; Stephen R. Jaffe, The Jaffe Law Firm, San Francisco, California; for Plaintiffs-Appellees.

Charles W. Scarborough (argued) and Michael S. Raab, Appellate Staff; Chad A. Readler, Acting Assistant Attorney General; Civil Division, United States Department of Justice, Washington, D.C.; for Amicus Curiae United States of America.

p.1015 John P. Elwood and Ralph C. Mayrell, Vinson & Elkins LLP, Washington, D.C.; Warren Postman and Steven P. Lehotsky, U.S. Chamber Litigation Center, Washington, D.C.; for Amicus Curiae Chamber of Commerce of the United States of America.

Justin S. Brooks, Reuben A. Guttman, and Elizabeth H. Shofner, Philadelphia, Pennsylvania; Asher S. Alavi and David A. Bocian, Kessler Topaz Meltzer and Check LLP, Radnor, Pennsylvania; Daniel Miller, Berger & Montague P.C., Philadelphia, Pennsylvania; David S. Stone, Stone & Magnanini LLP, Berkeley Heights, New Jersey; for Amicus Curiae National Nurses United—California Nurses Association, et al.

Claire M. Sylvia, Phillips & Cohen LLP, San Francisco, California; Jacklyn N. DeMar, Taxpayers Against Fraud Education Fund, Washington, D.C.; Jennifer M. Verkamp, Morgan Verkamp LLC, Cincinnati, Ohio; for Amicus Curiae Taxpayers Against Fraud Education Fund.

Brandon J. Mark, Parsons Behle & Latimer, Salt Lake City, Utah, for Amicus Curiae Veterans Education Success.

Before: Susan P. GRABER and N. Randy SMITH, Circuit Judges, and Jennifer G. ZIPPS,[*] District Judge.

p.1014 **ORDER**

The opinion filed on August 24, 2018, and published at 901 F.3d 1124, is amended by the opinion filed concurrently with this order, as follows:

On slip opinion page 10, begin the first full paragraph with: "As relevant here, the falsity requirement can be satisfied in one of two ways."

With this amendment, Judges Graber and Zipps have voted to deny Appellant's petition for panel rehearing, and Judge Smith has voted to grant it. Judge Graber has voted to deny Appellant's petition for rehearing en banc, and Judge Zipps has so recommended. Judge Smith has recommended granting the petition for rehearing en banc.

The full court has been advised of the petition for rehearing en banc, and no judge of the court has requested a vote on it.

Appellant's petition for panel rehearing and rehearing en banc is DENIED. No further petitions for panel rehearing or rehearing en banc may be filed.

OPINION

GRABER, Circuit Judge:

This qui tam action, brought under the False Claims Act, comes to us on interlocutory appeal from the district court's denial of summary judgment so that we can settle questions of law posed in the wake of *Universal Health Services, Inc. v. United States ex rel. Escobar,* ___ U.S. ___, 136 S.Ct. 1989, 195 L.Ed.2d 348 (2016). We affirm.

FACTUAL AND PROCEDURAL HISTORY[1]

Defendant Stephens Institute, doing business as Academy of Art University, p.1016 is an art school in San Francisco that offers undergraduate and graduate degrees. Defendant receives federal funding —in the form of federal financial aid to its students—through various funding programs available under Title IV of the Higher Education Act. To qualify for that funding, Defendant entered into a program participation agreement with the Department of Education ("Department"), in which it pledged to follow various requirements, including the incentive compensation ban. The incentive compensation ban prohibits schools from rewarding admissions officers for enrolling higher numbers of students. 20 U.S.C. § 1094(a)(20); 34 C.F.R. § 668.14(b)(22).

In 2006, Defendant's admissions department instituted a new policy to encourage admissions representatives to enroll more students. The policy established an enrollment goal for each admissions representative. If a representative succeeded in enrolling that number of students, he or she would receive a salary increase of up to $30,000. Conversely, a representative could have his or her salary decreased by as much as $30,000 for failing to reach the assigned enrollment goal. Defendant characterized those adjustments as dependent on both quantitative success, meaning a representative's enrollment numbers, and qualitative success, meaning the representative's non-enrollment performance. But, in practice, the employees understood that their salary adjustments rested entirely on their enrollment numbers. Defendant rewarded one team of representatives with an expense-paid trip to Hawaii. The team received that reward solely because of their enrollment numbers.

That enrollment incentive policy remained in place until 2009, when Defendant instituted new enrollment goals and a "scorecard" system for calculating salary adjustments. The scorecard system involved separate salary adjustment calculations for qualitative and quantitative performance. An admissions representative could receive an adjustment of as much as $23,000 for quantitative performance alone; adjustments related to qualitative performance topped out at $6,000. Managers were told not to share those scorecards with admissions representatives because of concerns about compliance with the participation agreement. The scorecard policy remained in effect until 2010.

Relators Scott Rose, Mary Aquino, Mitchell Nelson, and Lucy Stearns, who are former admissions representatives for Defendant, brought this False Claims Act action in 2010, claiming that Defendant violated the incentive compensation ban from 2006 through 2010. Defendant filed a motion for summary judgment, which the district court denied on May 4, 2016. But on June 16, 2016, the Supreme Court decided *Escobar,* in which the Court clarified the law surrounding falsity and materiality in False Claims Act claims. 136 S.Ct. at 1999, 2001. Defendant filed a motion for reconsideration in light of *Escobar,* which the district court likewise denied. But the district court granted in part Defendant's motion for an interlocutory appeal, certifying to this court several questions relating to *Escobar*'s effect on our precedent.[2]

p.1017 DISCUSSION

A. Legal Background

The Department of Education oversees the grant of Title IV funds to colleges and universities. To qualify for such funds, schools must comply with a number of statutory, regulatory, and contractual requirements. One such requirement is the incentive compensation ban, which is mandated by statute, regulation, and contractual program participation agreements. The incentive compensation ban prohibits schools from providing "any commission, bonus, or other incentive payment based directly or indirectly on success in securing enrollments or financial aid to any persons or entities engaged in any student recruiting or admission activities." 20 U.S.C. § 1094(a)(20); 34 C.F.R. § 668.14(b)(22). If individuals become aware of a school's violation of the incentive compensation ban, they can bring a qui tam action on behalf of the United States under the False Claims Act. When the Department becomes aware of such violations, it also can take direct action against noncompliant schools by, among other things, mandating corrective action; reaching a settlement agreement; imposing fines; or limiting, suspending, or terminating a school's participation in federal student aid programs.

The False Claims Act imposes liability on anyone who "knowingly presents, or causes to be presented, a false or fraudulent claim for payment or approval." 31

U.S.C. § 3729(a)(1)(A). We articulated the four elements of a False Claims Act claim in *United States ex rel. Hendow v. University of Phoenix,* 461 F.3d 1166 (9th Cir. 2006), another case that involved alleged violations of the incentive compensation ban. Under *Hendow,* a successful False Claims Act claim requires: "(1) a false statement or fraudulent course of conduct, (2) made with scienter, (3) that was material, causing (4) the government to pay out money or forfeit moneys due." *Id.* at 1174. But *Escobar* has unsettled the state of this circuit's law with regard to two of those elements: falsity and materiality.

B. Implied False Certification

As relevant here, the falsity requirement can be satisfied in one of two ways. The first is by express false certification, which "means that the entity seeking payment [falsely] certifies compliance with a law, rule or regulation as part of the process through which the claim for payment is submitted." *Ebeid ex rel. United States v. Lungwitz,* 616 F.3d 993, 998 (9th Cir. 2010). The other is by implied false certification, which "occurs when an entity has *previously* undertaken to expressly comply with a law, rule, or regulation [but does not], and that obligation is implicated by submitting a claim for payment even though a certification of compliance is not required in the process of submitting the claim." *Id.* (emphasis added).

In *Ebeid,* we clarified that, to establish a claim under the implied false certification theory, a relator must show that "(1) the defendant explicitly undertook to comply with a law, rule or regulation that is implicated in submitting a claim for payment and that (2) claims were submitted (3) even though the defendant was not in compliance with that law, rule or regulation." *Id.* Thus, under *Ebeid,* a relator bringing an implied certification claim could show falsity by pointing to p.1018 noncompliance with a law, rule, or regulation that is necessarily implicated in a defendant's claim for payment.

The Supreme Court subsequently addressed implied false certification in *Escobar.* There, the Supreme Court held that

> [t]he implied certification theory can be a basis for liability, *at least* where two conditions are satisfied: first, the claim does not merely request payment, but also makes *specific representations* about the goods or services provided; and second, the defendant's failure to disclose noncompliance with material statutory, regulatory, or contractual requirements makes those representations misleading half-truths.

Escobar, 136 S.Ct. at 2001 (emphases added).

We have addressed *Escobar* in two cases that create uncertainty about the ongoing validity of *Ebeid*'s test for falsity in implied false certification cases. First, in *United States ex rel. Kelly v. Serco, Inc.,* 846 F.3d 325, 332 (9th Cir. 2017), we considered only *Escobar*'s two-part test in determining that the plaintiff's implied false certification claim failed; we did not consider whether the claim met the lower standard for falsity enunciated in *Ebeid.* Then, in *United States ex rel. Campie v. Gilead Sciences, Inc.,* we noted that *Escobar* "'clarif[ied] *some* of the circumstances in which the False Claims Act imposes liability' under [an implied false certification] theory." 862 F.3d 890, 901 (9th Cir. 2017) (emphasis added) (quoting *Escobar,* 136 S.Ct. at 1995), *petition for cert. filed,* 86 U.S.L.W. 3519 (U.S. Dec. 26, 2017) (No. 17-936). But we then stated that the "Supreme Court held that although the implied certification theory can be a basis for liability, two conditions *must* be satisfied." *Id.* (emphasis added) (citing *Escobar,* 136 S.Ct. at 2000).

Were we analyzing *Escobar* anew, we doubt that the Supreme Court's decision would require us to overrule *Ebeid.* The Court did not state that its two conditions were the *only* way to establish liability under an implied false certification theory. But our post-*Escobar* cases—without discussing whether *Ebeid* has been fatally undermined—appear to *require Escobar*'s two conditions nonetheless. We are bound by three-judge panel opinions of this court. *Miller v. Gammie,* 335 F.3d 889, 899 (9th Cir. 2003) (en banc). We conclude, therefore, that Relators must satisfy *Escobar*'s two conditions to prove falsity, unless and until our court, en banc, interprets *Escobar* differently.

On this record, a reasonable trier of fact could conclude that Defendant's actions meet the *Escobar* requirements for falsity. In the Federal Stafford Loan School Certification form, Defendant specifically represented that the student applying for federal financial aid is an "eligible borrower" and is "accepted for enrollment in an eligible program." Because Defendant failed to disclose its noncompliance with the incentive compensation ban, those representations could be considered "misleading half-truths." That is sufficient evidence to create a genuine issue of material fact and, therefore, to defeat summary judgment.

C. Materiality

Under the False Claims Act, "the term 'material' means having a natural tendency to influence, or be capable of influencing, the payment or receipt of money or property." 31 U.S.C. § 3729(b)(4). In *Hendow,* we held that the relators had alleged adequately that the University of Phoenix "engaged in statements or courses of conduct that were *material* to the government's decision with p.1019 regard to funding." 461 F.3d at 1177. In concluding that the alleged violations of the incentive compensation ban were material, we relied on the fact that the statute, regulation, and program participation agreement all explicitly conditioned payment on compliance with the incentive compensation ban. *Id.* We did not explicitly consider any other factors in determining that the relators properly pleaded the materiality of the university's violations. *Id.* We noted, with regard to materiality, that "the question is merely whether the false certification ... was relevant to the government's decision to confer a benefit." *Id.* at 1173.

In *Escobar,* the Supreme Court elaborated on what can and cannot establish materiality in the context of the False Claims Act. The Court clarified that "[w]hether a provision is labeled a condition of payment is *relevant* to but not *dispositive* of the materiality inquiry." *Escobar,* 136 S.Ct. at 2001 (emphases added). Therefore, "even when a requirement is expressly designated a condition of payment, not every violation of such a requirement gives rise to liability." *Id.* at 1996. Instead, the Court explained, "materiality looks to the effect on the likely or actual behavior of the recipient of the alleged misrepresentation," meaning the government. *Id.* at 2002 (internal quotation marks and brackets omitted).[3]

The Supreme Court then laid out three scenarios that may help courts determine the likely or actual behavior of the government with regard to a given requirement. First, "proof of materiality can include, but is not necessarily limited to, evidence that the defendant knows that the Government consistently refuses to pay claims in the mine run of cases based on noncompliance with the particular statutory, regulatory, or contractual requirement." *Id.* at 2003. Second, the Court explained that, "if the Government pays a particular claim in full despite its *actual knowledge* that certain requirements were violated, that is very strong evidence that those requirements are not material." *Id.* (emphasis added). Third, "if the Government regularly pays a particular type of claim in full despite *actual knowledge* that certain requirements were violated, and has signaled no change in position, that is strong evidence that the requirements are not material." *Id.* at 2003-04 (emphasis added). The Court further noted that materiality "cannot be found where noncompliance is minor or insubstantial." *Id.* at 2003.

In our view, *Hendow* is not "clearly irreconcilable with the reasoning or theory of" *Escobar* and, therefore, has not been overruled. *Miller,* 335 F.3d at 893. It is true that *Hendow* explicitly considered only the facts that the defendant had violated a statute, regulation, and contract— by not complying with the incentive compensation ban—and that payment was conditioned on compliance with the ban. 461 F.3d at 1175. But *Hendow* did not state that noncompliance is material in *all* cases. For instance, *Hendow* itself may have been decided differently had there been countervailing evidence of immateriality.[4] p.1020 After *Escobar,* it is clear that noncompliance with the incentive compensation ban is not material per se. Nor does noncompliance automatically revoke institutional eligibility. Rather, we must examine the particular facts of each case. In other words, we view *Escobar* as creating a "gloss" on the analysis of materiality. But the four basic elements of a False Claims Act claim, set out in *Hendow,* remain valid. *See supra* p. 1017.

Applying the *Escobar* standard of materiality to the facts here, we conclude that Defendant has not established as a matter of law that its violations of the incentive compensation ban were immaterial. A reasonable trier of fact could find materiality here because the Department's payment was conditioned on compliance with the incentive compensation ban, because of the Department's past enforcement activities, and because of the substantial size of the forbidden incentive payments.[5]

1. Funds Conditioned on Compliance

We consider first the same factor that *Hendow* did: the government conditioned the payment of Title IV funds on compliance with the incentive compensation ban through statute, regulation, and contract. Had Defendant not certified in its program participation agreement that it complied with the incentive compensation ban, it could not have been paid, because Congress required as much.[6] After *Escobar,* that triple-conditioning of Title IV funds on compliance with the incentive compensation ban may not be sufficient, without more, to prove materiality, but it is certainly probative evidence of materiality.

2. Past Department Actions

We next consider how the Department has treated similar violations. We look to the three scenarios bearing on materiality that the Supreme Court enunciated in *Escobar,* though none of them is necessarily p.1021 required or dispositive. *See Escobar,* 136 S.Ct. at 2003-04 (laying out scenarios that can constitute proof of materiality or immateriality, but noting that such proof "is not necessarily limited to" those scenarios).

First, we ask whether there is "evidence that the defendant knows that the Government consistently refuses to pay claims in the mine run of cases based on noncompliance" with the incentive compensation ban, because such a showing can help establish that the requirement was material. *Escobar,* 136 S.Ct. at 2003. There is no such evidence in this case and, therefore, that inquiry does not factor into our analysis.

Second, we ask whether the Department has paid "a particular claim in full despite its *actual knowledge* that" the incentive compensation ban was violated, because "that is very strong evidence that [the incentive compensation ban is] not material." *Id.* (emphasis added). The record does not establish that, during the relevant time period, the Department had actual knowledge that Defendant was violating the incentive compensation ban. We cannot, therefore, analyze the Department's behavior here to determine whether compliance with the incentive compensation ban was material.[7]

Third, we examine whether the Department "regularly pays a particular type of claim in full despite *actual knowledge* that certain requirements were violated, and has signaled no change in position, [because] that is strong evidence that the requirements are not material." *Id.* at 2003-04 (emphasis added). To show that the Department does regularly pay claims in full despite knowing about violations of the incentive compensation ban, Defendant points to two 2010 Government Accountability Office ("GAO") reports. The first report identifies 32 instances in which schools violated the incentive compensation ban between 1998 and 2009, and the second documents the Department's responses to those 32 violations. Because the Department "did not limit, suspend, or terminate any [of those] school[s'] access to federal student aid," Defendant argues, the Department regularly paid claims in full despite actual knowledge of violations of the incentive compensation ban.

Defendant's argument does not tell the whole story. Of the 32 schools with substantiated violations, the Department ordered 25 of them to take corrective action, which included terminating bonus payments to recruiters and ending referral fees to students. And 2 of those 25 schools were required to pay fines as a penalty, which together totaled $64,000. The Department also identified a liability of more than $187 million in misspent student aid funds at 1 of the 32 schools, meaning that the Department required the school to repay improperly awarded federal funds. The Department recouped more than $16 million of the total liability. The GAO reports also show that the Department took p.1022 no further enforcement action at six schools with violations. But, of those six schools, three of them closed, two were terminated for other reasons, and one school's violations fell within a "safe harbor provision." The GAO reports further reveal that the Department reached settlement agreements with 22 additional schools, which allowed it to recoup funds totaling more than $59 million in payments.

There is evidence, then, that the Department *did* care about violations of the incentive compensation ban and did not allow schools simply to continue violating the ban while receiving Title IV funds. And in many cases, through one means or another, the Department recouped many millions of dollars from the violating schools, showing that it was not prepared to pay claims "in full" despite knowing of violations of the incentive compensation ban. The Department can demonstrate that requirements, such as the incentive compensation ban, are material without directly limiting, suspending, or terminating schools' access to federal student aid. A full examination of the Department's past enforcement habits in similar cases, therefore, reveals that a reasonable trier of fact could find that Defendant's violations of the incentive compensation ban were material.

3. Magnitude of Violation

As mentioned, the Supreme Court also noted in *Escobar* that materiality does not exist "where noncompliance is minor or insubstantial." 136 S.Ct. at 2003. For instance, were a school to offer admissions representatives cups of coffee or $10 gift cards for recruiting higher numbers of students, there would be no viable claim under the False Claims Act. That is not the case here. Under Defendant's 2006-2008 compensation scheme, admissions representatives stood to gain as much as $30,000 and a trip to Hawaii simply by hitting their enrollment goals. And under Defendant's 2009-2010 scorecard compensation scheme, representatives' salaries could be adjusted by as much as $23,000 for meeting their enrollment goals.

Those large monetary awards are quite unlike a small, occasional perk. Rather, those awards are precisely the kind of substantial incentive that Congress sought to prevent in enacting the ban on incentive compensation. Therefore, the tremendous bonuses that Defendant's admissions representatives could receive by achieving their enrollment goals (and the similar decreases that could result from falling short of the targets set by Defendant) also counsel against a finding that Defendant's noncompliance was immaterial.

Overall, then, when we construe the evidence in the light most favorable to Relators, we conclude that a reasonable trier of fact could find that Defendant's noncompliance with the incentive compensation ban was material.

D. Safe Harbor

Finally, Defendant argues that, even if there is a question of fact as to one or more of *Hendow*'s four requirements for claims under the False Claims Act, it should win on summary judgment because any violations of the incentive compensation ban fell within the Department's safe harbor provision. The now-repealed safe harbor provision was in effect from 2003 through 2010. *Compare* Federal Student Aid Programs, 67 Fed. Reg. 67,048-01, 67,072 (Nov. 1, 2002), *with* 34 C.F.R. § 668.14(b)(22)(i)(B). That provision required, among other things, that "any adjustment [in compensation] is not based solely on the number of students recruited, admitted, enrolled, or awarded financial p.1023 aid." Federal Student Aid Programs, 67 Fed. Reg. at 67,072.

Defendant's argument fails, at least on summary judgment. Viewed in the light most favorable to Relators, the record contains evidence that Defendant *did* make compensation adjustments based solely on admissions representatives' enrollment numbers.

AFFIRMED.

N.R. SMITH, Circuit Judge, dissenting in part:

I agree with the Majority's opinion through Section B of the Discussion Section, however we part ways regarding: (1) the validity of *United States ex rel. Hendow v. University of Phoenix,* 461 F.3d 1166 (9th Cir. 2006), in light of the Supreme Court's decision in *Universal Health Services, Inc. v. United States ex rel. Escobar,* ___ U.S. ___, 136 S.Ct. 1989, 195 L.Ed.2d 348 (2016); and (2) whether, under *Escobar*'s "demanding" and "rigorous" materiality standard, there was sufficient evidence of a "material" violation of the Incentive Compensation Ban (ICB) to defeat summary judgment, *id* at 1996, 2003. Instead, I would reverse the district court's materiality finding, vacate the judgment, and remand for additional discovery and further briefing. Why?

The Majority makes three errors in its analysis. First, it fails to recognize that *Hendow*'s materiality holding is no longer good law after *Escobar*. Second, it fails to fully articulate the Supreme Court's materiality standard as outlined in *Escobar*. Finally, the Majority applies its erroneous legal standard to the facts at hand, reaching an erroneous conclusion. Let me explain.

I. *Escobar* overruled the logic of *Hendow*'s materiality holding.

The Majority erroneously concludes that it can still rely—at least in some regard— on *Hendow*'s materiality holding, because it "may have been decided differently had there been countervailing evidence of immateriality." Maj. Op. at 1019. *Escobar,* the Majority concludes, merely "creat[ed] a 'gloss' on the analysis of materiality." Maj. Op. at 1020. I disagree. Instead, *Escobar* explicitly overruled *Hendow*'s materiality standard and imposed a new materiality analysis that we must follow and apply.

The Majority's theory that *Hendow* could have reached a different conclusion in light of "countervailing evidence" does not acknowledge *Hendow*'s own reasoning. *Hendow* explicitly rejected the "countervailing evidence" before it: "questions of enforcement power are *largely academic,* because the eligibility of the University under Title IV and the Higher Education Act of 1965 ... is *explicitly* conditioned, in three different ways, on compliance with the [ICB]." *Hendow,* 461 F.3d at 1175 (last emphasis original). Put another way: the government's enforcement *power*—much less what it actually did with that power— did not matter. Rather, *Hendow* clearly held that "expressly condition[ing] [payment] in three different ways" on compliance with the ICB was sufficient to make compliance with the ICB material. *Id.* at 1177.

However, *Escobar* rejected this *Hendow* materiality standard. In *Escobar,* the First Circuit followed *Hendow* and concluded that the "express and absolute language of the regulation in question, in conjunction with the repeated references to supervision throughout the regulatory scheme, constitute[d] dispositive evidence of materiality." *United States ex rel. Escobar v. Universal Health Servs., Inc.,* 780 F.3d 504, 514 (1st Cir. 2015) (citations and quotation marks omitted), *vacated and remanded* p.1024 *by Escobar,* 136 S.Ct. at 1996. Rejecting that reasoning, the Supreme Court instead held that "the label the Government attaches to a requirement" is not dispositive. *Escobar,* 136 S.Ct. at 1996. Accordingly, the Supreme Court outlined that the proper inquiry is "whether the defendant knowingly violated a requirement that the defendant knows is *material* to the Government's payment decision." *Id.* at 1996 (emphasis added); *see also id.* at 2001 ("[S]tatutory, regulatory, and contractual requirements are not automatically material, even if they are labeled conditions of payment."); *id.* at 2003 ("In sum, when evaluating materiality under the False Claims Act, the Government's decision to expressly identify a provision as a condition of payment is relevant, but not automatically dispositive.").

Thus, under *Escobar,* the analysis focuses not on *whether* payment is conditioned on compliance, but *whether* the Government would truly find such noncompliance material to a payment decision. Because *Hendow* does not follow that analysis, the Majority opinion should conclude that *Hendow*'s materiality holding is "clearly irreconcilable with the reasoning and theory of" *Escobar* and explicitly overrule *Hendow* to that extent. *Miller v. Gammie,* 335 F.3d 889, 893 (9th Cir. 2003).

II. The Majority fails to articulate the "demanding" and "rigorous" nature of the materiality standard imposed by *Escobar.*

There is no question that the Majority outlines part of the *Escobar* materiality standard. However, it leaves out two very significant aspects, both of which are required to determine whether a misrepresentation is actually material.

First, the Supreme Court stated four times that the materiality test was "rigorous" or "demanding." *Escobar,* 136 S.Ct. at 1996 ("We clarify below how that *rigorous materiality requirement* should be enforced." (emphasis added)); *id.* at 2002 ("[The materiality and scienter] requirements are *rigorous.*" (emphasis added)); *id.* at 2003 ("The materiality standard is *demanding.*" (emphasis added)); *id.* at 2004 n.6 ("The standard for materiality that we have outlined is a familiar *and rigorous one.*" (emphasis added)). The Majority states that these descriptors of the analysis merely "give flavor to the Court's discussion," but otherwise ascribes no use to them. Maj. Op. at 1019, n.3. Descriptions of *how* the test is to be applied are not just "flavor[ing]," they are the key in conducting the analysis the Supreme Court has instructed us to do. Anything less is insufficient and the Majority's application of *Escobar* reveals its lack of rigor.

Second, the Supreme Court provided a very clear standard for evaluating whether the misrepresentation was "material to the Government's payment decision." *Id.* at 1996; *see also id.* at 2002-03. The Supreme Court stated that the primary inquiry "looks to the effect on the *likely or actual behavior* of the recipient of the alleged misrepresentation." *Id.* at 2002 (emphasis added and quotation marks omitted). To illustrate *what* the inquiry looks like, the Supreme Court then explicitly referenced both tort and contract law materiality standards. These standards require an analysis of what, for example, "a reasonable man would attach importance to ... in determining his choice of action in the transaction" or whether "the defendant knew or had reason to know that the recipient of the representation attaches importance to the specific matter in determining his choice of action, even though a reasonable person would not." *Id.* at 2002-03 (quotation marks omitted) (citing Restatement (Second) of Torts § 538 at 80); *see* p.1025 *also id.* at 2003 n.5.[1] Again, similar to the "demanding" and "rigorous" nature of the inquiry, the Majority does not even mention the contract or tort guideposts provided by the Supreme Court. *Id.* at 1996, 2003.

In sum, though expressly suggesting that payment can be *relevant, Escobar* requires that the primary inquiry of whether a misrepresentation is material mandates a "rigorous" and "demanding" inquiry into the "likely or actual behavior" of the Government to determine whether it "would attach importance [to the misrepresentation] in determining [its] choice of action in the transaction." *Id.* at 2002-03 (quotation marks omitted). Stated differently, the evidence (regarding the government's response to a misrepresentation) must be specific or directly analogous to the current alleged misrepresentation. Anything else would not be sufficiently "demanding" or "rigorous" to determine the Government's "likely or actual behavior." *Id.*

III. The Majority erroneously concludes that, on this record, there are sufficient questions of material fact to defeat summary judgment.

The Majority, like the district court, fails to properly apply the "demanding" and "rigorous" *Escobar* standard to the evidence in this case. *Id.* at 2002-03.

First, there is simply no evidence before us regarding *how* the Government would respond to the specific ICB violations alleged against Stephens Institute. At most, the Majority relies on aggregate data regarding the Government's *general* enforcement of the ICB.[2] The Majority concludes that this is sufficient: "There is evidence, then, that the Department *did* care about violations of the incentive compensation ban and did not allow schools simply to continue violating the ban while receiving Title IV funds." Maj. Op. at 1022. Certainly, the Majority is correct that this evidence demonstrates that the Government *cares* in a broad sense. But, caring is not enough to make it material under the *Escobar* standard. Whether aggregate data demonstrates that the Government cares is not evidence that, *in this case,* the Government would find these alleged misrepresentations *material.* Significant materiality questions remain, for example: Does a fine for noncompliance represent a "material" aspect? Or, are fines only imposed for minor regulatory violations, which *Escobar* explicitly stated were not material? *Escobar,* 136 S.Ct. at 2003 ("The False Claims Act is not ... a vehicle for punishing garden-variety breaches of contract or regulatory p.1026 violations."). If the fines are material, were they imposed for more or less egregious behavior than the alleged Stephens Institute behavior? The aggregate data answers none of these questions and yet their answers are required before liability under the "demanding" and "rigorous" *Escobar* standard may be imposed. *Id.* at 2002-03.[3]

Second, with no specific evidence regarding how the Government would respond to the instant allegations, the only "relevant" evidence that remains is the fact that compliance with the ICB is a condition for payment. Indeed, to reach its conclusion, the Majority appears to invoke the all or nothing *Hendow* analysis, which the Supreme Court squarely rejected. And, the Majority steps beyond such evidence being "relevant" and concludes that the Government's triple-conditioning of ICB compliance is "probative evidence of materiality." Maj. Op. at 1020.

However, the sole fact that compliance is a condition of payment is not enough. *Escobar,* 136 S.Ct. at 2003 ("In sum, when evaluating materiality under the False Claims Act, the Government's decision to expressly identify a provision as a condition of payment is relevant, but *not automatically dispositive.*" (emphasis added)). Yes, certification of compliance with the ICB is required for payment, but so is certification of compliance with a *host* of additional statutes, regulations, and contractual requirements. There is no indication that the Government holds the ICB out as an exceptionally important requirement and, under *Escobar,* misrepresentations regarding compliance "must be material to the Government's payment decision." *Id.* at 1996. Therefore, absent additional evidence demonstrating that in *this* situation, the Government treated a violation as material, and in *that* situation, it did not, conditioning compliance with the ICB is simply not enough to prove materiality. *Id.* at 2003 & n.5 (holding the misrepresentation must go "to the very essence of the bargain" (quoting *Junius Constr. Co. v. Cohen,* 257 N.Y. 393, 178 N.E. 672, 674 (1931))).

As such, all we have before us is (1) general, aggregate evidence that the Government cares about ICB violations (not that what Stephens Institute is specifically accused of doing is, indeed, material such that it would influence a payment decision by the Government), and (2) the fact that payment is triple-conditioned on compliance with the ICB. This is not enough to meet the "rigorous" and "demanding" inquiry into the "likely or actual behavior" of the Government to determine whether it "would attach importance to [the misrepresentation] in determining [its] choice of p.1027 action in the transaction." *Id.* at 2002-03 (quotation marks omitted).

IV. Conclusion.

It is apparent from both the district court's order and the parties' briefing that there was confusion regarding the materiality question, particularly the role of *Hendow* in light of *Escobar.* And, there is insufficient evidence to establish that the allegations against Stephens Institute would be considered material. However, the clarification of the interaction between *Hendow* and *Escobar* could change what the parties seek in discovery and the district court's ultimate conclusion. Therefore, in light of the clarified reasoning, I would reverse the district court's denial of Stephens Institute's motion for summary judgment, vacate the judgment, and remand for (1) additional discovery to develop the summary judgment record; (2) additional briefing; and, after that, (3) a re-examination by the district court.

[*] The Honorable Jennifer G. Zipps, United States District Judge for the District of Arizona, sitting by designation.

[1] "We review *de novo* the district court's denial of summary judgment. When doing so, we 'must determine whether the evidence, viewed in a light most favorable to the non-moving party, presents any genuine issues of material fact and whether the district court correctly applied the law.'" *Lenz v. Universal Music Corp.,* 815 F.3d 1145, 1150 (9th Cir. 2016) (quoting *Warren v. City of Carlsbad,* 58 F.3d 439, 441 (9th Cir. 1995)). Here, therefore, we view the evidence in the light most favorable to Relators.

[2] The three questions certified for interlocutory appeal are:

(1) Must the "two conditions" identified by the Supreme Court in Escobar always be satisfied for implied false certification liability under the [False Claims Act], or does *Ebeid*'s test for implied false certification remain good law?

(2) Does an educational institution automatically lose its institutional eligibility if it fails to comply [with] the [incentive compensation ban]?

(3) Does *Hendow*'s holding that the [incentive compensation ban] is material under the [False Claims Act] remain good law after *Escobar?*

Although we structure our discussion differently, we have endeavored to answer those questions.

[3] The dissent maintains that we have ignored the Supreme Court's assertion that the materiality standard is "rigorous" or "demanding." Dissent at 1024. Those adjectives, while they give flavor to the Court's discussion, do not establish the *test* that the Court requires us to use. The actual test to be applied is the one that we quote and apply in text: what is the effect of a misrepresentation on the likely or actual behavior of the government. We have, in our view, applied that test rigorously.

[4] The dissent claims that *Hendow* explicitly rejected "the 'countervailing evidence' [of immateriality] before it" when determining that the incentive compensation ban is material. Dissent at 1023. *Hendow* did not do so. The opinion contains no suggestion whatsoever that any countervailing *evidence* existed. Rather, the dissent quotes from a passage in which the opinion considers the parties' *legal* arguments concerning the extent of the enforcement powers of the Department of Education; did "its authority to take 'emergency action'... mean[] that the statutory requirements are causally related to its decision to pay out moneys due"? *Hendow,* 461 F.3d at 1175. *Hendow* simply does not discuss the relevance of evidence that, for example, the Department refused to impose sanctions on schools that violated the incentive compensation ban. *Hendow* and *Escobar,* therefore, are not clearly irreconcilable. *Miller,* 335 F.3d at 893.

[5] In concluding that the existing record is insufficient to create an issue of fact as to materiality, the dissent demands more certainty than *Escobar* and general principles governing summary judgment require. For example, the dissent argues that the government's responses to other schools' similar misrepresentations is insufficient to demonstrate that the government "*would* find" the misrepresentations material in this case. Dissent at 1025 (emphasis added). But *Escobar* speaks in terms of "likely," as well as "actual," behavior. 136 S.Ct. at 2002. As another example, the dissent states that "[s]ignificant materiality questions remain," the answers to which "are required before liability" can attach. Dissent at 1026. But the only question that we are called on to answer in this summary judgment appeal is whether there is a

genuine issue of material fact; we need not and do not decide whether Relators do or should prevail.

[6] Defendant argues that the incentive compensation ban is expressly identified as a condition of *participation* in the government's Title IV programs, not as a condition of *payment*. We addressed that argument in *Hendow* and concluded that it is "a distinction without a difference." 461 F.3d at 1176. Because no subsequent Supreme Court or Ninth Circuit en banc case has undermined our holding, we cannot, and do not, revisit that determination now.

[7] Defendant points to the Department's 2011 program review of Defendant, which took place after Relators filed this action. Defendant argues that the program review, which made no findings regarding the incentive compensation ban and resulted in no action against Defendant for noncompliance, is proof that the incentive compensation ban was not material to the Department. But the letter closing the review cautioned that the review's determination "does not relieve [Defendant] of its obligation to comply with *all* of the statutory or regulatory provisions governing the Title IV, [Higher Education Act] programs," and specifically noted that "compensation *must not* be based in any way on the number of students enrolled." (Emphases added.) Further, at the summary judgment stage, the presence of some contrary evidence does not negate the existence of an issue of fact on materiality.

[1] Indeed, the Supreme Court's illustrations of the inquiry outline the required specificity. It held that "proof of materiality can include" evidence that: (1) "the defendant *knows* that the Government consistently refuses to pay claims *in the mine run of cases* based on noncompliance with the *particular* statutory, regulatory, or contractual requirement"; or (2) "the Government pays a particular claim in full despite its *actual knowledge* that certain requirements were violated ...." *Escobar*, 136 S.Ct. at 2003-04 (emphasis added). Actual knowledge of regular, repeated nonpayment or actual knowledge of violations are both particular and demanding standards.

[2] Plaintiffs establish no more. A plaintiff bears the burden to present sufficient evidence from which a jury could conclude the misrepresentations were material to the government's payment decision. Here, Plaintiffs alleged Stephens Institute knowingly paid significant compensation to recruiters for meeting certain enrollment goals. Yet, the record also indicates that the ICB is only one of many (if not hundreds) of the regulations with which the Department of Education (DOE) requires schools to comply and that the DOE has generally doled out only minor penalties for ICB violations—particularly for several seemingly significant violations. In this light, I think a jury would be left to speculate *how* important the alleged misrepresentations actually are.

[3] The Majority faults my dissent for stating that answers to these questions are required before "liability ... may be imposed." Maj. Op. at 1020, n.5. Particularly, it argues that on summary judgment, we must only determine whether there are questions of material fact, not whether "liability ... may be imposed." The Majority's argument misreads my dissent and confuses the standard. Like we must on summary judgment, I am "view[ing] the evidence in the light *most favorable to the non-moving party*." *Vos. v. City of Newport Beach*, 892 F.3d 1024, 1030 (9th Cir. 2018) (emphasis added) (quoting *Lal v. California*, 746 F.3d 1112, 1115-16 (9th Cir. 2014)). In this case, there

is no real dispute about *what* the evidence is, but whether the evidence proffered is— viewed in the light most favorable to the non-moving party—sufficient to even go to trial, i.e., impute liability in the best case Plaintiffs have. Here, the evidence proffered is simply not enough under *Escobar* —there is *no* evidence about *what* the Government would actually do in this case (or even in a similar case). "The court shall grant summary judgment if the movant shows that there is no genuine dispute as to any material fact and the movant is entitled to judgment as a matter of law." Fed. R. Civ. P. 56(a).

901 F.3d 1124 (2018)

UNITED STATES ex rel. Scott Rose; Mary Aquino; Mitchell Nelson; Lucy Stearns, Plaintiffs-Appellees,

v.

STEPHENS INSTITUTE, dba Academy of Art University, Defendant-Appellant.

No. 17-15111.

United States Court of Appeals, Ninth Circuit.

Argued and Submitted December 6, 2017 — San Francisco, California. Filed August 24, 2018.

US v. Stephens Institute, 901 F. 3d 1124 (9th Cir. 2018)

Appeal from the United States District Court for the Northern District of California; D.C. No. 4:09-cv-05966-PJH, Phyllis J. Hamilton, Chief Judge, Presiding.

Steven M. Gombos (argued), Jacob C. Shorter, and Gerald M. Ritzert, Gombos Leyton PC, Fairfax, Virginia; Leland B. Altschuler, Law Offices of Leland B. Altschuler, Woodside, California; for Defendant-Appellant.

Michael von Lowenfeldt (argued), Kenneth Nabity, Brady R. Dewar, and James M. Wagstaffe, Kerr & Wagstaffe LLP, San Francisco, California; Stephen R. Jaffe, The Jaffe Law Firm, San Francisco, California; for Plaintiffs-Appellees.

Charles W. Scarborough (argued) and Michael S. Raab, Appellate Staff; Chad A. Readler, Acting Assistant Attorney General; Civil Division, United States Department of Justice, Washington, D.C.; for Amicus Curiae United States of America.

John P. Elwood and Ralph C. Mayrell, Vinson & Elkins LLP, Washington, D.C.; Warren Postman and Steven P. Lehotsky, U.S. Chamber Litigation Center, Washington, D.C.; for Amicus Curiae Chamber of Commerce of the United States of America.

Justin S. Brooks, Reuben A. Guttman, and Elizabeth H. Shofner, Philadelphia, Pennsylvania; Asher S. Alavi and David A. Bocian, Kessler Topaz Meltzer and Check LLP, Radnor, Pennsylvania; Daniel Miller, Berger & Montague P.C., Philadelphia, Pennsylvania; David S. Stone, Stone & Magnanini LLP, Berkeley Heights, New Jersey; for Amicus Curiae National Nurses United — California Nurses Association, et al.

Claire M. Sylvia, Phillips & Cohen LLP, San Francisco, California; Jacklyn N. DeMar, Taxpayers Against Fraud Education Fund, Washington, D.C.; Jennifer M. Verkamp, Morgan Verkamp LLC, Cincinnati, Ohio; for Amicus Curiae Taxpayers Against Fraud Education Fund.

Brandon J. Mark, Parsons Behle & Latimer, Salt Lake City, Utah, for Amicus Curiae Veterans Education Success.

Before: Susan P. Graber and N. Randy Smith, Circuit Judges, and Jennifer G. Zipps,[*] District Judge.

p.1127 OPINION

GRABER, Circuit Judge:

This qui tam action, brought under the False Claims Act, comes to us on interlocutory appeal from the district court's denial of summary judgment so that we can settle questions of law posed in the wake of *Universal Health Services, Inc. v. United States ex rel. Escobar*, ___ U.S. ___, 136 S.Ct. 1989, 195 L.Ed.2d 348 (2016). We affirm.

FACTUAL AND PROCEDURAL HISTORY[1]

Defendant Stephens Institute, doing business as Academy of Art University, is an art school in San Francisco that offers undergraduate and graduate degrees. Defendant receives federal funding p.1128 — in the form of federal financial aid to its students — through various funding programs available under Title IV of the Higher Education Act. To qualify for that funding, Defendant entered into a program participation agreement with the Department of Education ("Department"), in which it pledged to follow various requirements, including the incentive compensation ban. The incentive compensation ban prohibits schools from rewarding admissions officers for enrolling higher numbers of students. 20 U.S.C. § 1094(a)(20); 34 C.F.R. § 668.14(b)(22).

In 2006, Defendant's admissions department instituted a new policy to encourage admissions representatives to enroll more students. The policy established an enrollment goal for each admissions representative. If a representative succeeded in enrolling that number of students, he or she would receive a salary increase of up to $30,000. Conversely, a representative could have his or her salary decreased by as much as $30,000 for failing to reach the assigned enrollment goal. Defendant characterized those adjustments as dependent on both quantitative success, meaning a representative's enrollment numbers, and qualitative success, meaning the representative's non-enrollment performance. But, in practice, the employees understood that their salary adjustments rested entirely on their enrollment numbers. Defendant rewarded one team of representatives with an expense-paid trip to Hawaii. The team received that reward solely because of their enrollment numbers.

That enrollment incentive policy remained in place until 2009, when Defendant instituted new enrollment goals and a "scorecard" system for calculating salary adjustments. The scorecard system involved separate salary adjustment calculations for qualitative and quantitative performance. An admissions representative could receive an adjustment of as much as $23,000 for quantitative performance alone; adjustments related to qualitative performance topped out at $6,000. Managers were told not to share those scorecards with admissions representatives because of concerns about compliance with the participation agreement. The scorecard policy remained in effect until 2010.

Relators Scott Rose, Mary Aquino, Mitchell Nelson, and Lucy Stearns, who are former admissions representatives for Defendant, brought this False Claims Act action in 2010, claiming that Defendant violated the incentive compensation ban from 2006 through 2010. Defendant filed a motion for summary judgment, which the district court denied on May 4, 2016. But on June 16, 2016, the Supreme Court decided *Escobar*, in which the Court clarified the law surrounding falsity and materiality in False Claims Act claims. 136 S.Ct. at 1999, 2001. Defendant filed a motion for reconsideration in light of *Escobar,* which the district court likewise denied. But the district court granted in part Defendant's motion for an interlocutory appeal, certifying to this court several questions relating to *Escobar*'s effect on our precedent.[2]

p.1129 DISCUSSION

A. Legal Background

The Department of Education oversees the grant of Title IV funds to colleges and universities. To qualify for such funds, schools must comply with a number of statutory, regulatory, and contractual requirements. One such requirement is the incentive compensation ban, which is mandated by statute, regulation, and contractual program participation agreements. The incentive compensation ban prohibits schools from providing "any commission, bonus, or other incentive payment based directly or indirectly on success in securing enrollments or financial aid to any persons or entities engaged in any student recruiting or admission activities." 20 U.S.C. § 1094(a)(20); 34 C.F.R. § 668.14(b)(22). If individuals become aware of a school's violation of the incentive compensation ban, they can bring a qui tam action on behalf of the United States under the False Claims Act. When the Department becomes aware of such violations, it also can take direct action against noncompliant schools by, among other things, mandating corrective action; reaching a settlement agreement; imposing fines; or limiting, suspending, or terminating a school's participation in federal student aid programs.

The False Claims Act imposes liability on anyone who "knowingly presents, or causes to be presented, a false or fraudulent claim for payment or approval." 31 U.S.C. § 3729(a)(1)(A). We articulated the four elements of a False Claims Act claim in *United States ex rel. Hendow v. University of Phoenix,* 461 F.3d 1166 (9th Cir. 2006), another case that involved alleged violations of the incentive compensation ban. Under *Hendow,* a successful False Claims Act claim requires: "(1) a false statement or fraudulent course of conduct, (2) made with scienter, (3) that was material, causing (4) the government to pay out money or forfeit moneys due." *Id.* at 1174. But *Escobar* has unsettled the state of this circuit's law with regard to two of those elements: falsity and materiality.

B. Implied False Certification

The falsity requirement can be satisfied in one of two ways. The first is by express false certification, which "means that the entity seeking payment [falsely] certifies compliance with a law, rule or regulation as part of the process through which the claim for payment is submitted." *Ebeid ex rel. United States v. Lungwitz,* 616 F.3d 993, 998 (9th Cir. 2010). The other is by implied false certification, which "occurs when an entity has *previously* undertaken to expressly comply with a law, rule, or regulation [but does not], and that obligation is implicated by submitting a claim for payment even though a certification of compliance is not required in the process of submitting the claim." *Id.* (emphasis added).

In *Ebeid,* we clarified that, to establish a claim under the implied false certification theory, a relator must show that "(1) the defendant explicitly undertook to comply with a law, rule or regulation that is implicated in submitting a claim for payment and that (2) claims were submitted (3) even though the defendant was not in compliance with that law, rule or regulation." *Id.* Thus, under *Ebeid,* a relator bringing an implied certification claim could show falsity by pointing to noncompliance with a law, rule, or regulation that is necessarily implicated in a defendant's claim for payment.

The Supreme Court subsequently addressed implied false certification in *Escobar.* There, the Supreme Court held that

> [t]he implied certification theory can be a basis for liability, *at least* where two conditions are satisfied: first, the claim does not merely request payment, but p.1130 also makes *specific representations* about the goods or services provided; and second, the defendant's failure to disclose noncompliance with material statutory, regulatory, or contractual requirements makes those representations misleading half-truths.

Escobar, 136 S.Ct. at 2001 (emphases added).

We have addressed *Escobar* in two cases that create uncertainty about the ongoing validity of *Ebeid*'s test for falsity in implied false certification cases. First, in *United States ex rel. Kelly v. Serco, Inc.,* 846 F.3d 325, 332 (9th Cir. 2017), we considered only *Escobar*'s two-part test in determining that the plaintiff's implied false certification claim failed; we did not consider whether the claim met the lower standard for falsity enunciated in *Ebeid.* Then, in *United States ex rel. Campie v. Gilead Sciences, Inc.,* we noted that *Escobar* "'clarif[ied] *some* of the circumstances in which the False Claims Act imposes liability' under [an implied false certification] theory." 862 F.3d 890, 901 (9th Cir. 2017) (emphasis added) (quoting *Escobar,* 136 S.Ct. at 1995), *petition for cert. filed,* 86 U.S.L.W. 3519 (U.S. Dec. 26, 2017) (No. 17-936). But we then stated that the "Supreme Court held that although the implied certification theory can be a basis for liability, two conditions *must* be satisfied." *Id.* (emphasis added) (citing *Escobar,* 136 S.Ct. at 2000).

Were we analyzing *Escobar* anew, we doubt that the Supreme Court's decision would require us to overrule *Ebeid.* The Court did not state that its two conditions were the *only* way to establish liability under an implied false certification theory. But our post-*Escobar* cases — without discussing whether *Ebeid* has been fatally undermined — appear to *require Escobar*'s two conditions nonetheless. We are bound by three-judge panel opinions of this court. *Miller v. Gammie,* 335 F.3d 889, 899 (9th Cir. 2003) (en banc). We conclude, therefore, that Relators must satisfy *Escobar*'s two conditions to prove falsity, unless and until our court, en banc, interprets *Escobar* differently.

On this record, a reasonable trier of fact could conclude that Defendant's actions meet the *Escobar* requirements for falsity. In the Federal Stafford Loan School Certification form, Defendant specifically represented that the student applying for federal financial aid is an "eligible borrower" and is "accepted for enrollment in an eligible program." Because Defendant failed to disclose its noncompliance with the incentive compensation ban, those representations could be considered "misleading half-truths." That is sufficient evidence to create a genuine issue of material fact and, therefore, to defeat summary judgment.

C. Materiality

Under the False Claims Act, "the term 'material' means having a natural tendency to influence, or be capable of influencing, the payment or receipt of money or property." 31 U.S.C. § 3729(b)(4). In *Hendow,* we held that the relators had alleged adequately that the University of Phoenix "engaged in statements or courses of conduct that were *material* to the government's decision with regard to funding." 461 F.3d at 1177. In concluding that the alleged violations of the incentive compensation ban were material, we relied on the fact that the statute, regulation, and program participation agreement all explicitly conditioned payment on compliance with the incentive compensation ban. *Id.* We did not explicitly consider any other factors in determining that the relators properly pleaded the materiality of the university's violations. *Id.* We noted, with regard to materiality, that p.1131 "the question is merely whether the false certification ... was relevant to the government's decision to confer a benefit." *Id.* at 1173.

In *Escobar,* the Supreme Court elaborated on what can and cannot establish materiality in the context of the False Claims Act. The Court clarified that "[w]hether a provision is labeled a condition of payment is *relevant* to but not *dispositive* of the materiality inquiry." *Escobar,* 136 S.Ct. at 2001 (emphases added). Therefore, "even when a requirement is expressly designated a condition of payment, not every violation of such a requirement gives rise to liability." *Id.* at 1996. Instead, the Court explained, "materiality looks to the effect on the likely or actual behavior of the recipient of the alleged misrepresentation," meaning the government. *Id.* at 2002 (internal quotation marks and brackets omitted).[3]

The Supreme Court then laid out three scenarios that may help courts determine the likely or actual behavior of the government with regard to a given requirement. First, "proof of materiality can include, but is not necessarily limited to, evidence that the defendant knows that the Government consistently refuses to pay claims in the mine run of cases based on noncompliance with the particular statutory, regulatory, or contractual requirement." *Id.* at 2003. Second, the Court explained that, "if the Government pays a particular claim in full despite its *actual knowledge* that certain requirements were violated, that is very strong evidence that those requirements are not material." *Id.* (emphasis added). Third, "if the Government regularly pays a particular type of claim in full despite *actual knowledge* that certain requirements were violated, and has signaled no change in position, that is strong evidence that the requirements are not material." *Id.* at 2003-04 (emphasis added). The Court further noted that materiality "cannot be found where noncompliance is minor or insubstantial." *Id.* at 2003.

In our view, *Hendow* is not "clearly irreconcilable with the reasoning or theory of" *Escobar* and, therefore, has not been overruled. *Miller,* 335 F.3d at 893. It is true that *Hendow* explicitly considered only the facts that the defendant had violated a statute, regulation, and contract — by not complying with the incentive compensation ban — and that payment was conditioned on compliance with the ban. 461 F.3d at 1175. But *Hendow* did not state that noncompliance is material in *all* cases. For instance, *Hendow* itself may have been decided differently had there been countervailing evidence of immateriality.[4] p.1132 After *Escobar,* it is clear that noncompliance with the incentive compensation ban is not material per se. Nor does noncompliance automatically revoke institutional eligibility. Rather, we must examine the particular facts of each case. In other words, we view *Escobar* as creating a "gloss" on the analysis of materiality. But the four basic elements of a False Claims Act claim, set out in *Hendow,* remain valid. *See supra* p. 1129.

Applying the *Escobar* standard of materiality to the facts here, we conclude that Defendant has not established as a matter of law that its violations of the incentive compensation ban were immaterial. A reasonable trier of fact could find materiality here because the Department's payment was conditioned on compliance with the incentive compensation ban, because of the Department's past enforcement activities, and because of the substantial size of the forbidden incentive payments.[5]

1. Funds Conditioned on Compliance

We consider first the same factor that *Hendow* did: the government conditioned the payment of Title IV funds on compliance with the incentive compensation ban through statute, regulation, and contract. Had Defendant not certified in its program participation agreement that it complied with the incentive compensation ban, it could not have been paid, because Congress required as much.[6] After *Escobar,* that triple-conditioning of Title IV funds on compliance with the incentive compensation ban may not be sufficient, without more, to prove materiality, but it is certainly probative evidence of materiality.

2. Past Department Actions

We next consider how the Department has treated similar violations. We look to the three scenarios bearing on materiality that the Supreme Court enunciated in *Escobar,* though none of them is necessarily required or dispositive. *See Escobar,* 136 S.Ct. at 2003-04 (laying out scenarios that can constitute proof of materiality or immateriality, but noting that such proof "is not necessarily limited to" those scenarios).

First, we ask whether there is "evidence that the defendant knows that the Government consistently refuses to pay claims in the mine run of cases based on noncompliance" with the incentive compensation ban, because such a showing can help establish that the requirement was material. *Escobar,* 136 S.Ct. at 2003. There is no such evidence in this case and, therefore, that inquiry does not factor into our analysis.

p.1133 Second, we ask whether the Department has paid "a particular claim in full despite its *actual knowledge* that" the incentive compensation ban was violated, because "that is very strong evidence that [the incentive compensation ban is] not material." *Id.* (emphasis added). The record does not establish that, during the relevant time period, the Department had actual knowledge that Defendant was violating the incentive compensation ban. We cannot, therefore, analyze the Department's behavior here to determine whether compliance with the incentive compensation ban was material.[7]

Third, we examine whether the Department "regularly pays a particular type of claim in full despite *actual knowledge* that certain requirements were violated, and has signaled no change in position, [because] that is strong evidence that the requirements are not material." *Id.* at 2003-04 (emphasis added). To show that the Department does regularly pay claims in full despite knowing about violations of the incentive compensation ban, Defendant points to two 2010 Government Accountability Office ("GAO") reports. The first report identifies 32 instances in which schools violated the incentive compensation ban between 1998 and 2009, and the second documents the Department's responses to those 32 violations. Because the Department "did not limit, suspend, or terminate any [of those] school[s'] access to federal student aid," Defendant argues, the Department regularly paid claims in full despite actual knowledge of violations of the incentive compensation ban.

Defendant's argument does not tell the whole story. Of the 32 schools with substantiated violations, the Department ordered 25 of them to take corrective action, which included terminating bonus payments to recruiters and ending referral fees to students. And 2 of those 25 schools were required to pay fines as a penalty, which together totaled $64,000. The Department also identified a liability of more than $187 million in misspent student aid funds at 1 of the 32 schools, meaning that the Department required the school to repay improperly awarded federal funds. The Department recouped more than $16 million of the total liability. The GAO reports also show that the Department took no further enforcement action at six schools with violations. But, of those six schools, three of them closed, two were terminated for other reasons, and one school's violations fell within a "safe harbor provision." The GAO reports further reveal that the Department reached settlement agreements with 22 additional schools, which allowed it to recoup funds totaling more than $59 million in payments.

There is evidence, then, that the Department *did* care about violations of the incentive compensation ban and did not allow schools simply to continue violating the ban while receiving Title IV funds. And in many cases, through one means or another, the Department recouped many millions p.1134 of dollars from the violating schools, showing that it was not prepared to pay claims "in full" despite knowing of violations of the incentive compensation ban. The Department can demonstrate that requirements, such as the incentive compensation ban, are material without directly limiting, suspending, or terminating schools' access to federal student aid. A full examination of the Department's past enforcement habits in similar cases, therefore, reveals that a reasonable trier of fact could find that Defendant's violations of the incentive compensation ban were material.

3. Magnitude of Violation

As mentioned, the Supreme Court also noted in *Escobar* that materiality does not exist "where noncompliance is minor or insubstantial." 136 S.Ct. at 2003. For instance, were a school to offer admissions representatives cups of coffee or $10 gift cards for recruiting higher numbers of students, there would be no viable claim under the False Claims Act. That is not the case here. Under Defendant's 2006-2008 compensation scheme, admissions representatives stood to gain as much as $30,000 and a trip to Hawaii simply by hitting their enrollment goals. And under Defendant's

2009-2010 scorecard compensation scheme, representatives' salaries could be adjusted by as much as $23,000 for meeting their enrollment goals.

Those large monetary awards are quite unlike a small, occasional perk. Rather, those awards are precisely the kind of substantial incentive that Congress sought to prevent in enacting the ban on incentive compensation. Therefore, the tremendous bonuses that Defendant's admissions representatives could receive by achieving their enrollment goals (and the similar decreases that could result from falling short of the targets set by Defendant) also counsel against a finding that Defendant's noncompliance was immaterial.

Overall, then, when we construe the evidence in the light most favorable to Relators, we conclude that a reasonable trier of fact could find that Defendant's noncompliance with the incentive compensation ban was material.

D. Safe Harbor

Finally, Defendant argues that, even if there is a question of fact as to one or more of *Hendow*'s four requirements for claims under the False Claims Act, it should win on summary judgment because any violations of the incentive compensation ban fell within the Department's safe harbor provision. The now-repealed safe harbor provision was in effect from 2003 through 2010. *Compare* Federal Student Aid Programs, 67 Fed. Reg. 67,048-01, 67,072 (Nov. 1, 2002), *with* 34 C.F.R. § 668.14(b)(22)(i)(B). That provision required, among other things, that "any adjustment [in compensation] is not based solely on the number of students recruited, admitted, enrolled, or awarded financial aid." Federal Student Aid Programs, 67 Fed. Reg. at 67,072.

Defendant's argument fails, at least on summary judgment. Viewed in the light most favorable to Relators, the record contains evidence that Defendant *did* make compensation adjustments based solely on admissions representatives' enrollment numbers.

AFFIRMED.

Opinion by Judge Graber; Dissent by Judge N.R. Smith

N.R. SMITH, Circuit Judge, dissenting in part:

I agree with the Majority's opinion through Section B of the Discussion Section, however we part ways regarding: (1) the validity of *United States ex rel. Hendow v. University of Phoenix*, 461 F.3d 1166 (9th Cir. 2006), in light of the Supreme Court's decision in *Universal* p.1135 *Health Services, Inc. v. United States ex rel. Escobar*, ___ U.S. ___, 136 S.Ct. 1989, 195 L.Ed.2d 348 (2016); and (2) whether, under *Escobar*'s "demanding" and "rigorous" materiality standard, there was sufficient evidence of a "material" violation of the Incentive Compensation Ban (ICB) to defeat summary judgment, *id* at 1996, 2003. Instead, I would reverse the district court's materiality finding, vacate the judgment, and remand for additional discovery and further briefing. Why?

The Majority makes three errors in its analysis. First, it fails to recognize that *Hendow*'s materiality holding is no longer good law after *Escobar*. Second, it fails to fully articulate the Supreme Court's materiality standard as outlined in *Escobar*. Finally, the Majority applies its erroneous legal standard to the facts at hand, reaching an erroneous conclusion. Let me explain.

I. *Escobar* overruled the logic of *Hendow*'s materiality holding.

The Majority erroneously concludes that it can still rely — at least in some regard — on *Hendow*'s materiality holding, because it "may have been decided differently had there been countervailing evidence of immateriality." Maj. Op. at 1131-32. *Escobar*, the Majority concludes, merely "creat[ed] a 'gloss' on the analysis of materiality." Maj. Op. at 1132. I disagree. Instead, *Escobar* explicitly overruled *Hendow*'s materiality standard and imposed a new materiality analysis that we must follow and apply.

The Majority's theory that *Hendow* could have reached a different conclusion in light of "countervailing evidence" does not acknowledge *Hendow*'s own reasoning. *Hendow* explicitly rejected the "countervailing evidence" before it: "questions of enforcement power are *largely academic,* because the eligibility of the University under Title IV and the Higher Education Act of 1965 ... is *explicitly* conditioned, in three different ways, on compliance with the [ICB]." *Hendow,* 461 F.3d at 1175 (last emphasis original). Put another way: the government's enforcement *power* — much less what it actually did with that power — did not matter. Rather, *Hendow* clearly held that "expressly condition[ing] [payment] in three different ways" on compliance with the ICB was sufficient to make compliance with the ICB material. *Id.* at 1177.

However, *Escobar* rejected this *Hendow* materiality standard. In *Escobar,* the First Circuit followed *Hendow* and concluded that the "express and absolute language of the regulation in question, in conjunction with the repeated references to supervision throughout the regulatory scheme, constitute[d] dispositive evidence of materiality." *United States ex rel. Escobar v. Universal Health Servs., Inc.,* 780 F.3d 504, 514 (1st Cir. 2015) (citations and quotation marks omitted), *vacated and remanded by Escobar,* 136 S.Ct. at 1996. Rejecting that reasoning, the Supreme Court instead held that "the label the Government attaches to a requirement" is not dispositive. *Escobar,* 136 S.Ct. at 1996. Accordingly, the Supreme Court outlined that the proper inquiry is "whether the defendant knowingly violated a requirement that the defendant knows is *material* to the Government's payment decision." *Id.* at 1996 (emphasis added); *see also id.* at 2001 ("[S]tatutory, regulatory, and contractual requirements are not automatically material, even if they are labeled conditions of payment."); *id.* at 2003 ("In sum, when evaluating materiality under the False Claims Act, the Government's decision to expressly identify a provision as a condition of payment is relevant, but not automatically dispositive.").

Thus, under *Escobar,* the analysis focuses not on *whether* payment is conditioned on compliance, but *whether* the Government p.1136 would truly find such noncompliance material to a payment decision. Because *Hendow* does not follow that analysis, the Majority opinion should conclude that *Hendow*'s materiality holding is "clearly irreconcilable with the reasoning and theory of" *Escobar* and explicitly overrule *Hendow* to that extent. *Miller v. Gammie,* 335 F.3d 889, 893 (9th Cir. 2003).

II. The Majority fails to articulate the "demanding" and "rigorous" nature of the materiality standard imposed by *Escobar.*

There is no question that the Majority outlines part of the *Escobar* materiality standard. However, it leaves out two very significant aspects, both of which are required to determine whether a misrepresentation is actually material.

First, the Supreme Court stated four times that the materiality test was "rigorous" or "demanding." *Escobar,* 136 S.Ct. at 1996 ("We clarify below how that *rigorous materiality requirement* should be enforced." (emphasis added)); *id.* at 2002 ("[The materiality and scienter] requirements are *rigorous.*" (emphasis added)); *id.* at 2003 ("The materiality standard is *demanding.*" (emphasis added)); *id.* at 2004 n.6 ("The standard for materiality that we have outlined is a familiar *and rigorous one.*" (emphasis added)). The Majority states that these descriptors of the analysis merely "give flavor to the Court's discussion," but otherwise ascribes no use to them. Maj. Op. at 1131, n.3. Descriptions of *how* the test is to be applied are not just "flavor[ing]," they are the key in conducting the analysis the Supreme Court has instructed us to do. Anything less is insufficient and the Majority's application of *Escobar* reveals its lack of rigor.

Second, the Supreme Court provided a very clear standard for evaluating whether the misrepresentation was "material to the Government's payment decision." *Id.* at 1996; *see also id.* at 2002-03. The Supreme Court stated that the primary inquiry "looks to the effect on the *likely or actual behavior* of the recipient of the alleged misrepresentation." *Id.* at 2002 (emphasis added and quotation marks omitted). To illustrate *what* the inquiry looks like, the Supreme Court then explicitly referenced both tort and contract law materiality standards. These standards require an analysis of what, for example, "a reasonable man would attach importance to ... in determining his choice of action in the transaction" or whether "the defendant knew or had reason to know that the recipient of the representation attaches importance to the specific matter in determining his choice of action, even though a reasonable person would not." *Id.* at 2002-03 (quotation marks omitted) (citing Restatement (Second) of Torts § 538 at 80); *see also id.* at 2003 n.5.[1] Again, similar to the "demanding" and "rigorous" nature of the inquiry, the Majority does not even mention the contract or tort guideposts provided by the Supreme Court. *Id.* at 1996, 2003.

In sum, though expressly suggesting that payment can be *relevant, Escobar* requires that the primary inquiry of whether a misrepresentation is material mandates a "rigorous" and "demanding" inquiry into the "likely or actual behavior" of the Government p.1137 to determine whether it "would attach importance [to the misrepresentation] in determining [its] choice of action in the transaction." *Id.* at 2002-03 (quotation marks omitted). Stated differently, the evidence (regarding the government's response to a misrepresentation) must be specific or directly analogous to the current alleged misrepresentation. Anything else would not be sufficiently "demanding" or "rigorous" to determine the Government's "likely or actual behavior." *Id.*

III. The Majority erroneously concludes that, on this record, there are sufficient questions of material fact to defeat summary judgment.

The Majority, like the district court, fails to properly apply the "demanding" and "rigorous" *Escobar* standard to the evidence in this case. *Id.* at 2002-03.

First, there is simply no evidence before us regarding *how* the Government would respond to the specific ICB violations alleged against Stephens Institute. At most, the Majority relies on aggregate data regarding the Government's *general* enforcement of the ICB.[2] The Majority concludes that this is sufficient: "There is evidence, then, that the Department *did* care about violations of the incentive compensation ban and did not allow schools simply to continue violating the ban while receiving Title IV funds." Maj. Op. at 1133. Certainly, the Majority is correct that this evidence demonstrates that the Government *cares* in a broad sense. But, caring is not enough to make it material under the *Escobar* standard. Whether aggregate data demonstrates that the Government cares is not evidence that, *in this case,* the Government would find these alleged misrepresentations *material*. Significant materiality questions remain, for example: Does a fine for noncompliance represent a "material" aspect? Or, are fines only imposed for minor regulatory violations, which *Escobar* explicitly stated were not material? *Escobar,* 136 S.Ct. at 2003 ("The False Claims Act is not ... a vehicle for punishing garden-variety breaches of contract or regulatory violations."). If the fines are material, were they imposed for more or less egregious behavior than the alleged Stephens Institute behavior? The aggregate data answers none of these questions and yet their answers are required before liability under the "demanding" and "rigorous" *Escobar* standard may be imposed. *Id.* at 2002-03.[3]

Second, with no specific evidence regarding how the Government would respond p.1138 to the instant allegations, the only "relevant" evidence that remains is the fact that compliance with the ICB is a condition for payment. Indeed, to reach its conclusion, the Majority appears to invoke the all or nothing *Hendow* analysis, which the Supreme Court squarely rejected. And, the Majority steps beyond such evidence being "relevant" and concludes that the Government's triple-conditioning of ICB compliance is "probative evidence of materiality." Maj. Op. at 1132-33.

However, the sole fact that compliance is a condition of payment is not enough. *Escobar,* 136 S.Ct. at 2003 ("In sum, when evaluating materiality under the False Claims Act, the Government's decision to expressly identify a provision as a condition of payment is relevant, but *not automatically dispositive*." (emphasis added)). Yes, certification of compliance with the ICB is required for payment, but so is certification of compliance with a *host* of additional statutes, regulations, and contractual requirements. There is no indication that the Government holds the ICB out as an exceptionally important requirement and, under *Escobar,* misrepresentations regarding compliance "must be material to the Government's payment decision." *Id.* at 1996. Therefore, absent additional evidence demonstrating that in *this* situation, the Government treated a violation as material, and in *that* situation, it did not, conditioning compliance with the ICB is simply not enough to prove materiality. *Id.* at 2003 & n.5 (holding the misrepresentation must go "to the very essence of the bargain" (quoting *Junius Constr. Co. v. Cohen,* 257 N.Y. 393, 178 N.E. 672, 674 (1931))).

As such, all we have before us is (1) general, aggregate evidence that the Government cares about ICB violations (not that what Stephens Institute is specifically accused of doing is, indeed, material such that it would influence a payment decision by the Government), and (2) the fact that payment is triple-conditioned on compliance with the ICB. This is not enough to meet the "rigorous" and "demanding" inquiry into the "likely or actual behavior" of the Government to determine whether it "would attach importance to [the misrepresentation] in determining [its] choice of action in the transaction." *Id.* at 2002-03 (quotation marks omitted).

IV. Conclusion.

It is apparent from both the district court's order and the parties' briefing that there was confusion regarding the materiality question, particularly the role of *Hendow* in light of *Escobar.* And, there is insufficient evidence to establish that the allegations against Stephens Institute would be considered material. However, the clarification of the interaction between *Hendow* and *Escobar* could change what the parties seek in discovery and the district court's ultimate conclusion. Therefore, in light of the clarified reasoning, I would reverse the district court's denial of Stephens Institute's motion for summary judgment, vacate the judgment, and remand for (1) additional discovery to develop the summary judgment record; (2) additional briefing; and, after that, (3) a re-examination by the district court.

[*] The Honorable Jennifer G. Zipps, United States District Judge for the District of Arizona, sitting by designation.

[1] "We review *de novo* the district court's denial of summary judgment. When doing so, we 'must determine whether the evidence, viewed in a light most favorable to the non-moving party, presents any genuine issues of material fact and whether the district court correctly applied the law.'" *Lenz v. Universal Music Corp.,* 815 F.3d 1145, 1150 (9th Cir. 2016) (quoting *Warren v. City of Carlsbad,* 58 F.3d 439, 441 (9th Cir. 1995)). Here, therefore, we view the evidence in the light most favorable to Relators.

[2] The three questions certified for interlocutory appeal are:

(1) Must the "two conditions" identified by the Supreme Court in Escobar always be satisfied for implied false certification liability under the [False Claims Act], or does *Ebeid*'s test for implied false certification remain good law?

(2) Does an educational institution automatically lose its institutional eligibility if it fails to comply [with] the [incentive compensation ban]?

(3) Does *Hendow*'s holding that the [incentive compensation ban] is material under the [False Claims Act] remain good law after *Escobar?*

Although we structure our discussion differently, we have endeavored to answer those questions.

[3] The dissent maintains that we have ignored the Supreme Court's assertion that the materiality standard is "rigorous" or "demanding." Dissent at 1135-36. Those adjectives, while they give flavor to the Court's discussion, do not establish the *test*

that the Court requires us to use. The actual test to be applied is the one that we quote and apply in text: what is the effect of a misrepresentation on the likely or actual behavior of the government. We have, in our view, applied that test rigorously.

[4] The dissent claims that *Hendow* explicitly rejected "the 'countervailing evidence' [of immateriality] before it" when determining that the incentive compensation ban is material. Dissent at 1135. *Hendow* did not do so. The opinion contains no suggestion whatsoever that any countervailing *evidence* existed. Rather, the dissent quotes from a passage in which the opinion considers the parties' *legal* arguments concerning the extent of the enforcement powers of the Department of Education; did "its authority to take 'emergency action'... mean[] that the statutory requirements are causally related to its decision to pay out moneys due"? *Hendow,* 461 F.3d at 1175. *Hendow* simply does not discuss the relevance of evidence that, for example, the Department refused to impose sanctions on schools that violated the incentive compensation ban. *Hendow* and *Escobar,* therefore, are not clearly irreconcilable. *Miller,* 335 F.3d at 893.

[5] In concluding that the existing record is insufficient to create an issue of fact as to materiality, the dissent demands more certainty than *Escobar* and general principles governing summary judgment require. For example, the dissent argues that the government's responses to other schools' similar misrepresentations is insufficient to demonstrate that the government "*would* find" the misrepresentations material in this case. Dissent at 1137 (emphasis added). But *Escobar* speaks in terms of "likely," as well as "actual," behavior. 136 S.Ct. at 2002. As another example, the dissent states that "[s]ignificant materiality questions remain," the answers to which "are required before liability" can attach. Dissent at 1137-38. But the only question that we are called on to answer in this summary judgment appeal is whether there is a genuine issue of material fact; we need not and do not decide whether Relators do or should prevail.

[6] Defendant argues that the incentive compensation ban is expressly identified as a condition of *participation* in the government's Title IV programs, not as a condition of *payment.* We addressed that argument in *Hendow* and concluded that it is "a distinction without a difference." 461 F.3d at 1176. Because no subsequent Supreme Court or Ninth Circuit en banc case has undermined our holding, we cannot, and do not, revisit that determination now.

[7] Defendant points to the Department's 2011 program review of Defendant, which took place after Relators filed this action. Defendant argues that the program review, which made no findings regarding the incentive compensation ban and resulted in no action against Defendant for noncompliance, is proof that the incentive compensation ban was not material to the Department. But the letter closing the review cautioned that the review's determination "does not relieve [Defendant] of its obligation to comply with *all* of the statutory or regulatory provisions governing the Title IV, [Higher Education Act] programs," and specifically noted that "compensation *must not* be based in any way on the number of students enrolled." (Emphases added.) Further, at the summary judgment stage, the presence of some contrary evidence does not negate the existence of an issue of fact on materiality.

[1] Indeed, the Supreme Court's illustrations of the inquiry outline the required specificity. It held that "proof of materiality can include" evidence that: (1) "the

defendant *knows* that the Government consistently refuses to pay claims *in the mine run of cases* based on noncompliance with the *particular* statutory, regulatory, or contractual requirement"; or (2) "the Government pays a particular claim in full despite its *actual knowledge* that certain requirements were violated ...." *Escobar,* 136 S.Ct. at 2003-04 (emphasis added). Actual knowledge of regular, repeated nonpayment or actual knowledge of violations are both particular and demanding standards.

[2] Plaintiffs establish no more. A plaintiff bears the burden to present sufficient evidence from which a jury could conclude the misrepresentations were material to the government's payment decision. Here, Plaintiffs alleged Stephens Institute knowingly paid significant compensation to recruiters for meeting certain enrollment goals. Yet, the record also indicates that the ICB is only one of many (if not hundreds) of the regulations with which the Department of Education (DOE) requires schools to comply and that the DOE has generally doled out only minor penalties for ICB violations — particularly for several seemingly significant violations. In this light, I think a jury would be left to speculate *how* important the alleged misrepresentations actually are.

[3] The Majority faults my dissent for stating that answers to these questions are required before "liability ... may be imposed." Maj. Op. at 1132, n.5. Particularly, it argues that on summary judgment, we must only determine whether there are questions of material fact, not whether "liability ... may be imposed." The Majority's argument misreads my dissent and confuses the standard. Like we must on summary judgment, I am "view[ing] the evidence in the light *most favorable to the non-moving party.*" *Vos v. City of Newport Beach,* 892 F.3d 1024, 1030 (9th Cir. 2018) (emphasis added) (quoting *Lal v. California,* 746 F.3d 1112, 1115-16 (9th Cir. 2014)). In this case, there is no real dispute about *what* the evidence is, but whether the evidence proffered is — viewed in the light most favorable to the non-moving party — sufficient to even go to trial, i.e., impute liability in the best case Plaintiffs have. Here, the evidence proffered is simply not enough under *Escobar* — there is *no* evidence about *what* the Government would actually do in this case (or even in a similar case). "The court shall grant summary judgment if the movant shows that there is no genuine dispute as to any material fact and the movant is entitled to judgment as a matter of law." Fed. R. Civ. P. 56(a).

Tenth Circuit Decisions
Qui Tam Actions

923 F.3d 729 (2019)

UNITED STATES of America EX REL., Julie REED, Plaintiff - Appellant,
v.
KEYPOINT GOVERNMENT SOLUTIONS, Defendant - Appellee.

No. 17-1379.

United States Court of Appeals, Tenth Circuit.

April 30, 2019.

US ex rel. Reed v. KeyPoint Government Solutions, 923 F. 3d 729 (10th Cir. 2019)

Appeal from the United States District Court for the District of Colorado; (D.C. No. 1:14-CV-00004-CMA-MJW).

Richard E. Condit, Mehri & Skalet PLLC, Washington, District of Columbia (Steven A. Skalet and Brett D. Watson, Mehri & Skalet PLLC, Washington, District of Columbia, and John T. Harrington and Robert S. Oswald, The Employment Law Group, Washington, District of Columbia, with him on the briefs), for Plaintiff-Appellant.

Robert C. Blume, Gibson, Dunn & Crutcher LLP, Denver, Colorado (Ryan T. Bergsieker and Allison Chapin, Gibson, Dunn & Crutcher LLP, Denver, Colorado, with him on the brief), for Defendant-Appellee.

Before BRISCOE, SEYMOUR, and HOLMES, Circuit Judges.

p.735 HOLMES, Circuit Judge.

The False Claims Act (or the "Act") allows for the recovery of civil penalties p.736 and treble damages from anyone who defrauds the government by submitting fraudulent claims for payment. 31 U.S.C. §§ 3729-3733. To enforce its provisions, the Act empowers individuals to file suits on behalf of the government alleging that a third party made a fraudulent claim for payment to the government. *Id.* § 3730(b)(1). These suits are known as *"qui tam"* suits, and the individual plaintiffs are called "relators." Recognizing the risks relators face as prospective whistleblowers, the Act prohibits employers from retaliating against employees who try to stop violations of the Act. *Id.* § 3730(h).

Julie Reed sued her former employer, KeyPoint Government Solutions, LLC ("KeyPoint"), for violating the False Claims Act. Her *qui tam* claims alleged that KeyPoint violated the Act by knowingly and fraudulently billing the government for work that was inadequately or improperly completed. Ms. Reed also claimed that KeyPoint fired her in retaliation for her efforts to stop KeyPoint's fraud.

This case presents two overarching questions. First, did the district court err in granting summary judgment in KeyPoint's favor on Ms. Reed's *qui tam* claims? Second, did the district court err in dismissing Ms. Reed's retaliation claim under Federal Rule of Civil Procedure ("Rule") 12(b)(6)?

Exercising jurisdiction under 28 U.S.C. § 1291, we hold that the district court erred in the first respect but not in the second. We therefore vacate the district court's order insofar as it granted summary judgment on Ms. Reed's *qui tam* claims and remand for further proceedings. We affirm the district court's order insofar as it dismissed Ms. Reed's retaliation claim.

I

This is a whistleblower case. The relevant background has three parts: (1) the statutory background, (2) the underlying (alleged) bad acts, and (3) the whistleblowing and ensuing procedural history. We recount each part below.

A

The False Claims Act "covers all fraudulent attempts to cause the government to pay out sums of money." *United States ex rel. Conner v. Salina Reg'l Health Ctr., Inc.,* 543 F.3d 1211, 1217 (10th Cir. 2008) (quoting *United States ex rel. Boothe v. Sun Healthcare Grp., Inc.,* 496 F.3d 1169, 1172 (10th Cir. 2007)). It does so by permitting the recovery of civil penalties and treble damages from anyone who "knowingly presents ... a false or fraudulent claim for payment or approval." 31 U.S.C. § 3729(a)(1)(A). Liability also attaches to anyone who "knowingly makes, uses, or causes to be made or used, a false record or statement material to a false or fraudulent claim." *Id.* § 3729(a)(1)(B).

The Act's proscriptions may be effectuated in two ways. "First, the Government itself may" sue "the alleged false claimant" to remedy the fraud. *Vt. Agency of Nat. Res. v. United States ex rel. Stevens,* 529 U.S. 765, 769, 120 S.Ct. 1858, 146 L.Ed.2d 836 (2000). Second, "a private person (the relator) may bring a *qui tam*" suit on behalf of the government and also for herself alleging that a third party made fraudulent claims for payment to the government. *Id.* "As a bounty for identifying and prosecuting fraud," relators get to keep a portion "of any recovery they obtain." *Boothe,* 496 F.3d at 1172 (citing 31 U.S.C. § 3730(d)).

But there are limits to a relator's right to bring a *qui tam* suit. One such limit is "known as the public disclosure p.737 bar." *Id.; see State Farm Fire & Cas. Co. v. United States ex rel. Rigsby,* 580 U.S. ___, 137 S.Ct. 436, 440, 196 L.Ed.2d 340 (2016) (describing the public disclosure bar as a threshold relators must pass for their *qui tam* suits to proceed). That bar compels courts to dismiss *qui tam* claims "if substantially the same allegations ... as alleged in the action or claim were publicly disclosed," unless the relator "is an original source of the information."[1] 31 U.S.C. p.738 § 3730(e)(4)(A). The public disclosure bar aims to strike "the golden mean between" encouraging "whistle-blowing insiders with genuinely valuable information" to come forward while discouraging "opportunistic plaintiffs who have no significant information to contribute of their own." *United States ex rel. Fine v. Sandia Corp.,* 70 F.3d 568, 571 (10th Cir. 1995) (quoting *United States ex rel. Springfield Terminal Ry. Co. v. Quinn,* 14 F.3d 645, 649 (D.C. Cir. 1994)).

And because insiders might be reluctant to use these *qui tam* provisions due to fear of employer backlash, the False Claims Act protects whistleblowers from employer retaliation. *See Potts v. Ctr. for Excellence in Higher Educ., Inc.,* 908 F.3d 610, 613-14 (10th Cir. 2018) (discussing 31 U.S.C. § 3730(h)). To qualify for whistleblower protection, an employee must engage in "protected activity." *Armstrong v. Arcanum Grp., Inc.,* 897 F.3d 1283, 1286 (10th Cir. 2018). Until 2009, protected activity included only "lawful acts done by the employee ... in furtherance of an action under this section [i.e., a *qui tam* suit]." 31 U.S.C. § 3730(h) (2008). But Congress amended the anti-retaliation provision in 2009 and 2010, and it now protects employees who take steps "in furtherance of" either a *qui tam* claim *or* "other efforts to stop 1 or more violations" of the Act. 31 U.S.C. § 3730(h)(1). A whistleblower who prevails on her retaliation claim is entitled to reinstatement, double back pay, litigation costs, and attorneys' fees. *Id.* § 3730(h)(2). The events giving rise to this litigation took place against this statutory backdrop.

B

1

KeyPoint is a private company that conducts background investigations for the federal government—specifically, the Office of Personnel Management ("OPM"). OPM uses KeyPoint to investigate prospective federal employees. The depth of KeyPoint's investigations varies according to the level of security clearance involved. Most investigations, though, entail running background checks, interviewing the subject of the investigation, gathering testimony from the subject's neighbors and coworkers, and then compiling the information in a report. Government agencies rely on these reports in making employment decisions and deciding whether to issue (or reject) security clearances.

OPM's contract with KeyPoint rewards timeliness. If KeyPoint finishes its investigations on time, OPM pays KeyPoint a premium. But KeyPoint's pay decreases for each day an investigation runs past the deadline.

The contract also includes safeguards to ensure that KeyPoint's investigations are complete and accurate. For example, KeyPoint must do thorough case reviews of each investigation and reinterview a percentage of all sources. Another safeguard is the Telephone Testimony Program ("TTP"); KeyPoint developed such a program at OPM's request, and OPM endorsed KeyPoint's program. Ordinarily, investigators must conduct in-person interviews. But they may do telephone interviews under some circumstances, so long as they keep their total number of p.739 telephone interviews below a certain percentage threshold. Under the TTP, each month OPM sends KeyPoint a list of investigators who exceeded their allotted number of telephone interviews during the last month. KeyPoint then must send OPM "corrective action report[s]" explaining each infraction and what it is doing to remedy the problem. Aplt.'s App. at 31, ¶ 54 (Second Am. Compl., filed Dec. 5, 2016). The contract and OPM's Investigator's Handbook, which the contract incorporates, spell out these and other quality-control measures.

2

Along with KeyPoint, the background-investigation industry has two other main players—U.S. Investigations Services ("USIS") and CACI International, Inc. ("CACI"). This insular industry has had its share of troubles. From 2008 to 2010, the government prosecuted several individual investigators, including a former KeyPoint employee, for rushing investigations and falsifying information in reports to OPM.

And a 2010 report summarizing an OPM audit concluded that KeyPoint's and its competitors' "quality assurance process" needed improvement. *Id.* at 273 (Final Audit Report, dated June 22, 2010).

The year 2013 was a particularly turbulent one for the industry. That year two federal government contractors—Edward Snowden and Aaron Alexis—committed high-profile crimes after having received security clearances. These embarrassing episodes put the industry under intense scrutiny.

With scrutiny came unflattering news reports. A June 2013 article reporting on allegations against USIS noted that the "concerns about background checks [were] not limited to USIS" and later named KeyPoint and CACI as USIS's "two main competitors." *Id.* at 159, 160 (Wash. Post Article, dated June 27, 2013). Another article that month reported that "a select group of private contractors conducting background checks for high-security jobs were not doing enough to ensure the quality of their investigations." *Id.* at 302 (Reuters Article, dated June 26, 2013). The article noted "problems with procedures and safeguards used by all three private contractors—USIS, KeyPoint ... and CACI." *Id.* at 303. A slew of other news reports covered such allegations roiling the background-investigation industry.

The allegations in the press worried Congress and OPM. Those worries led to several congressional hearings to probe the industry's alleged practice of using "false, incomplete, or rushed information gathering" in its background investigations. *Id.* at 411 & n.3 (Order, entered Sept. 28, 2017). And the bad press of its contractors prompted OPM to commission an audit of KeyPoint's and its competitors' practices. The audit concluded that "OPM need[ed] to strengthen its controls over its Contractors and the background investigation review process." *Id.* at 164 (Audit Report, dated June 4, 2014).[2]

Exacerbating the industry's woes, a federal court unsealed a complaint against USIS in October 2013. *See United States ex rel. Percival v. U.S. Investigations Servs., LLC,* No. 2:11-cv-00527-WKW-WC, 2011 WL 13060142 (M.D. Ala. July 1, 2011) p.740 (complaint reproduced in Aplt.'s Reply Br., Addendum A). That complaint leveled three accusations against USIS: first, that USIS "failed to provide accurate and complete investigations prior to Cases being submitted to the government," Aplt.'s Reply Br., Addendum A, at 10; second, that USIS "knowingly submitted Cases to OPM for payment that [it] knew had not been reviewed," *id.* at 6; and third, that USIS exploited "the Blue Zone software .... to submit Cases to OPM under the false pretense that the Cases had been complete[d] and accurately and properly reviewed," *id.* at 12. This USIS suit and the government's intervention into it incited more press accounts of the industry's shoddy investigations.

3

Ms. Reed worked for KeyPoint during this turbulent period. As a Senior Quality Control Analyst, she reviewed investigators' work and documented incomplete investigations in monthly reports. Ms. Reed also ran KeyPoint's TTP by performing a "regular monthly audit of KeyPoint investigators who violated" the program. Aplt.'s App. at 34, ¶ 81. Along with her "regular duties," Ms. Reed "was occasionally tasked with extra audits of investigators," *id.* at 61, ¶ 165, or assigned "to determine the nature of ... chronic infractions," *id.* at 84, ¶ 228. The precise scope of Ms. Reed's responsibilities as a Senior Quality Control Analyst and where she fell in the KeyPoint hierarchy, however, are not specified in the operative complaint.

Nevertheless, that complaint does clearly aver that, in discharging her duties, Ms. Reed observed what she described as "KeyPoint's systemic violations" of its contract with OPM and persistent submission of fraudulent claims for payment to the government based on incomplete or improperly completed investigations. *Id.* at 29, ¶ 34. Ms. Reed's position allowed her to see investigators falsely reporting applicants' backgrounds as "clean" and omitting information showing otherwise, completing fewer than the required number of interviews, and generally cutting corners. Ms. Reed also believed that she witnessed rampant violations of the TTP and a scheme by KeyPoint management to hide the violations by submitting knowingly false corrective action reports to OPM.

According to Ms. Reed, KeyPoint's management not only knew of the foregoing systemic violations but also encouraged them by pressuring investigators to rush investigations to maximize revenue. Alarmed by the abuses, Ms. Reed voiced her concerns within the company. Periodically, Ms. Reed and her staff uncovered and reported violations. Ms. Reed also "regularly reported [certain] infractions to her supervisor ... by submitting and discussing a monthly spreadsheet." *Id.* at 62, ¶ 171. Along with these monthly reports, Ms. Reed repeatedly shared her concerns with her supervisor. She also discussed the problems with other individuals at KeyPoint, such as the Director of Training, the OPM Contract Director, Regional Managers, and certain Field Managers. But Ms. Reed's efforts to curb the violations failed. In fact, she alleges that the problems multiplied over time.

Eventually, KeyPoint fired Ms. Reed in October 2013. About a month later, Ms. Reed and her counsel contacted the Department of Justice ("DOJ"). She told DOJ about the abuses she claimed to have witnessed while at KeyPoint. To back up her allegations, Ms. Reed provided a pre-disclosure statement and a presentation detailing KeyPoint's alleged violations.

C

At the government's urging, Ms. Reed sued KeyPoint in January 2014. Her operative p.741 complaint raised three *qui tam* claims and a retaliation claim.[3] The *qui tam* claims alleged that KeyPoint violated the False Claims Act by: (1) falsely certifying that it performed complete and accurate investigations, (2) falsely certifying that it did proper case reviews and quality-control checks, and (3) falsifying corrective action reports. Ms. Reed's retaliation claim alleged that KeyPoint fired her for trying to stop it from violating the False Claims Act.

After the government declined to intervene in the case, KeyPoint moved to dismiss the suit. The district court then informed the parties that it intended to convert the portion of KeyPoint's motion concerning the *qui tam* claims into a summary-judgment motion; the court did not perform a similar conversion on KeyPoint's motion to dismiss the retaliation claim. At the court's invitation, Ms. Reed filed additional evidence to defend her *qui tam* claims from summary judgment.

In September 2017, the district court entered judgment for KeyPoint on all counts. Regarding the *qui tam* claims, the court declined to consider some of the supplemental materials that Ms. Reed had proffered to oppose KeyPoint's summary-judgment motion. And, on the merits, the court determined that the allegations in Ms. Reed's *qui tam* claims were "substantially the same" as those that had been publicly disclosed in (1) the criminal investigations of individual investigators, (2) the unflattering news reports about the background-investigation industry, (3) the congressional hearings and OPM audits, and (4) the USIS suit. *Id.* at 411. And, because the court also concluded that Ms. Reed did not qualify as "an 'original source,'" it dismissed her *qui tam* claims under the public disclosure bar. *Id.* at 414. As for Ms. Reed's retaliation claim, the district court granted KeyPoint's Rule 12(b)(6) motion to dismiss after determining that she had inadequately pleaded that KeyPoint was on notice that she was engaging in protected activity.

Ms. Reed now appeals from the district court's order entering judgment for KeyPoint. Her appeal presents two questions. First, did the district court err in granting KeyPoint summary judgment on the *qui tam* claims under the public disclosure bar? And second, did the district court err in granting KeyPoint's Rule 12(b)(6) motion to dismiss the retaliation claim? For the reasons explicated below, we answer the first question in the affirmative and the second in the negative.

II

We start with the first question. The public disclosure bar compels courts to dismiss *qui tam* claims if (1) "substantially the same allegations ... were publicly disclosed," *unless* (2) the relator is "an original source of the information." 31 U.S.C. § 3730(e)(4)(A). The district court thought the allegations in Ms. Reed's *qui tam* claims were substantially the same as those that had been publicly disclosed. And it further reasoned that Ms. Reed was not an original source of that information. Thus, the district court granted KeyPoint summary judgment on Ms. Reed's *qui tam* claims.

We review that conclusion de novo and apply the same legal standard that the district court used. *See United States ex rel. Smith v. Boeing Co.,* 825 F.3d 1138, 1145 (10th Cir. 2016). "Summary judgment is appropriate 'if the movant p.742 shows that there is no genuine dispute as to any material fact and the movant is entitled to judgment as a matter of law.'" *Id.* (quoting FED. R. CIV. P. 56(a)). When, as here, the district court granted the defendant's motion for summary judgment, "we accept as true the relator['s] evidence and draw all reasonable inferences in [her] favor." *Id.*

Ms. Reed argues that the district court erred twice en route to dismissing her *qui tam* claims under the public disclosure bar.[4] Its first error, she says, was concluding that the allegations in her complaint were substantially the same as those aired in earlier public disclosures. Compounding that error, in her view, the district court then wrongly determined that she did not fall under the "original source" exception to the public disclosure bar.

Put differently, the fate of Ms. Reed's *qui tam* claims hangs on two questions. First, are the allegations in those claims substantially the same as those in earlier public disclosures? And second, if so, is Ms. Reed an "original source" of the information in her claims? Our answer to the first question does not favor Ms. Reed, but our answer to the second one does.[5] p.743 Specifically, we hold that Ms. Reed's complaint averments are substantially the same as the allegations in the available public disclosures, but the district court erred in finding that Ms. Reed's averments do not materially add to those disclosures' allegations, such that she does not qualify as an original source. But this holding does not fully resolve the original-source question. Consequently, we vacate the district court's summary-judgment order and remand for further proceedings regarding whether Ms. Reed qualifies as an original source.

A

We agree with the district court that Ms. Reed's allegations undergirding her *qui tam* claims are "substantially the same" as the allegations in the public disclosures. We explain this conclusion in three steps. First, we discuss the applicable legal standard that guides our substantially-the-same inquiry. Second, we compare the allegations in Ms. Reed's *qui tam* claims with those in the public disclosures. And third, we close by concluding that the allegations in the *qui tam* claims are "substantially the same" as the publicly disclosed allegations.

1

Congress amended the False Claims Act in 2010. *See* Pub. L. No. 111-148, § 10104(j)(2), 124 Stat. 119, 901-02 ("2010 amendment"). Before that year, the provision setting out the public disclosure bar read: "No court shall have jurisdiction over an action under this section *based upon* the public disclosure of allegations or transactions ...." 31 U.S.C. § 3730(e)(4)(A) (2008) (emphasis added). The amended provision reads: "The court shall dismiss an action ... if *substantially the same* allegations ... as alleged in the action or claim were publicly disclosed." 31 U.S.C. § 3730(e)(4)(A) (2010) (emphasis added).

Our court has yet to opine on the degree of similarity necessary to satisfy this new substantially-the-same standard. That said, even before 2010, our circuit read the unamended provision's "based upon" language to mean that the public disclosure bar applied when "the allegations in the complaint were substantially the same as allegations in the public disclosures." *Fine,* 70 F.3d at 572; *see also Glaser v. Wound Care Consultants, Inc.,* 570 F.3d 907, 910 (7th Cir. 2009) (noting that "eight other circuits have read the phrase 'based upon'" to encompass allegations that are "substantially similar" to those publicly disclosed). That the substantially-the-same standard adopted in the 2010 amendment resembles the standard we already used is no accident; the amendment "expressly incorporates the 'substantially similar' standard in accordance with the interpretation of this circuit and most other circuits." *Bellevue v. Universal Health Servs. of Hartgrove, Inc.,* 867 F.3d 712, 718 (7th Cir. 2017), *cert. denied,* ___ U.S. ___, 138 S.Ct. 1284, 200 L.Ed.2d 470 (2018). Thus, the 2010 amendment confirms the vitality p.744 of our pre-2010 standard.[6]

In her reply brief, Ms. Reed argues for the first time that the 2010 amendment nullifies our earlier cases. *See* Aplt.'s Reply Br. at 8. In her view, the amendment "made clear" Congress's "desire to narrow the impact of the public disclosure bar." *Id.* Indeed, Ms. Reed believes that Congress acted specifically to jettison the reasoning used in our pre-2010 cases. And so she warns us not to rely on those earlier cases in our substantially-the-same inquiry.

Ms. Reed's argument is too little too late. For starters, by waiting until her reply brief to argue that the 2010 amendment narrowed the public disclosure bar's sweep and undermined our earlier cases, Ms. Reed waived that argument. *See, e.g., White v. Chafin,* 862 F.3d 1065, 1067 (10th Cir. 2017) ("Mr. White waived this contention by waiting to present it for the first time in his reply brief."). Furthermore, were we to overlook this waiver, we nevertheless would decline Ms. Reed's invitation to discard our earlier precedent because of Congress's supposed "desire to narrow the impact of the public disclosure bar." Aplt.'s Reply Br. at 8.

We ordinarily derive Congress's intent "from the text, not from extrinsic sources." Antonin Scalia & Bryan A. Garner, READING LAW: THE INTERPRETATION OF LEGAL TEXTS 56 (2012). The amended text says that the public disclosure bar applies when substantially the same allegations had been publicly disclosed; that is how our circuit (and most others) applied the public disclosure bar pre-amendment, *see Fine,* 70 F.3d at 572, and that is how we will continue to apply it until Congress or the Supreme Court tells us otherwise. In any event, Congress's supposed desire to narrow the public disclosure bar presumably would relate to only those circuits that had used a standard other than the substantially-the-same standard adopted in the 2010 amendment. *See, e.g., United States ex rel. May v. Purdue Pharma L.P.,* 737 F.3d 908, 917 (4th Cir. 2013) (explaining that because the Fourth Circuit had not used the substantially-the-same standard, the 2010 amendment "changed the required connection between the plaintiff's claims and the qualifying public disclosure" in that circuit). But in this circuit—where we already used the substantially-the-same standard—the 2010 amendment "merely confirms our earlier understanding." *United States ex rel. Winkelman v. CVS Caremark Corp.,* 827 F.3d 201, 208 n.4 (1st Cir. 2016). Thus, our pre-2010-amendment cases guide our substantially-the-same inquiry.

Those cases teach that the operative question is whether the public disclosures were sufficient to set the government "on the trail of the alleged fraud without [the relator's] assistance."[7] *Fine,* 70 F.3d at 571. And we must recognize p.745 that the government's nose for fraud may be sensitive enough to pick up the scent even if the public disclosures did not "identify any specific compan[y]."[8] *See In re Nat. Gas Royalties,* 562 F.3d 1032, 1039, 1042 (10th Cir. 2009). The need to identify the defendant by name is particularly weak when "the government has already identified the problem and has an easily identifiable group of probable offenders."[9] *Fine,* 70 F.3d at 572. Similarly, "[a] relator need not have learned of the basis for the *qui tam* action from the public disclosure" to trigger the public disclosure bar. *Kennard v. Comstock Res., Inc.,* 363 F.3d 1039, 1044 (10th Cir. 2004). Nor is "a *complete* identity of allegations, even as to time, place, and manner ... required to implicate the public disclosure bar." *Boothe,* 496 F.3d at 1174. Rather, it is enough if "the essence of" the relator's allegations was "'derived from' a prior public disclosure." *Id.* In fact, the public disclosures need not allege any False Claims Act violations or even "any wrongdoing"; they need only disclose "the material elements of the fraudulent transaction."[10] *Fine,* 70 F.3d at 572.

In summary, the public disclosure bar applies to *qui tam* claims "if substantially the same allegations ... were publicly disclosed." 31 U.S.C. § 3730(e)(4)(A). Our pre-2010-amendment cases primarily guide our substantially-the-same inquiry. And those cases teach that the operative question is whether the public disclosures were sufficient to set the government "on the trail of the alleged fraud without [the relator's] assistance." *Fine,* 70 F.3d at 571.

2

Having settled on the proper standard governing the substantially-the-same inquiry, p.746 we now must compare Ms. Reed's allegations with those in the public disclosures.

Ms. Reed's Allegations. At a high level of generality, Ms. Reed's *qui tam* claims allege that KeyPoint "was engaging in systemic fraud." Aplt.'s Opening Br. at 1. This fraud grew from KeyPoint's "focus[ ] on meeting ... deadlines" and winning bonuses "at the expense of the quality, completeness, and accuracy" of its investigations, Ms. Reed says. Aplt.'s App. at 29, ¶ 38. For instance, Ms. Reed accuses KeyPoint of pressuring investigators to rush investigations to maximize revenue. This pressure led, generally, to rampant violations of KeyPoint's contract with OPM and, in particular, of the TTP. Notably, as to the TTP, the pressure led to the submission of knowingly false corrective action reports designed to hide the violations. At bottom, Ms. Reed alleges that KeyPoint knowingly defrauded the government to "enrich itself and its executives at the expense of national security." Aplt.'s Opening Br. at 6.

Zooming in on the details, Ms. Reed claims that KeyPoint's fraud manifested itself in three main ways. First, she says that KeyPoint falsely certified to OPM that it had performed complete and accurate investigations. To support this charge, Ms. Reed points to specific instances in which investigators failed to do mandatory interviews of sources. She also details how individual investigators uncovered derogatory information about subjects but failed to report that information in their reports to OPM. Piling on, Ms. Reed lists over 100 instances in which investigators cut interviews short and then lied about it to OPM. She adds to this by exposing scores of violations of the TTP.

Ms. Reed contends that the second manifestation of KeyPoint's fraud entailed falsely representing to OPM that it had done proper case reviews and quality-control checks. For instance, she documents at least five times that, "despite ... readily apparent violations," KeyPoint reviewers violated OPM requirements by failing to reopen cases. Aplt.'s App. at 88, ¶ 248. And to circumvent the TTP, "quality control staff failed to perform the proper number of re-interviews." *Id.* at 89, ¶ 252.

The third (related) strain of fraud Ms. Reed identifies is KeyPoint's submission of falsified corrective action reports. Recall that these reports "are supposed to detail the specific actions taken by KeyPoint management to address" violations of OPM rules and programs—most notably, the TTP. *Id.* at 89, ¶ 255. To hide its rampant violations and institutional acquiescence to those violations, Ms. Reed alleges that "KeyPoint falsified corrective action reports to OPM" to give the appearance that it "was actively addressing [violations], when it was not." *Id.* at 89, ¶ 256. To Ms. Reed's knowledge, KeyPoint falsified dozens of reports to hide malfeasance by at least four individual investigators.

Publicly Disclosed Allegations. There are four categories of relevant public disclosures: (1) criminal investigations of individual investigators, (2) the news reports, (3) congressional hearings and OPM audits, and (4) the previously mentioned USIS suit.

Criminal Investigations. Between 2007 and 2013, the government prosecuted individual investigators for allegedly falsifying information in their reports. At least one of these "criminal cases involve[d] ... a former Key[P]oint employee who 'raced through investigations to get more work' and lied about conducting thorough background checks when they were incomplete and rushed." *Id.* at 410.

News Reports. In 2013, a slew of news reports chronicled the suspected fraud and p.747 widespread sloppiness in the background-investigation industry. One article in September 2013 reported that the government was "'pursuing suspected fraud in the granting of security clearances,' including '19 private and government investigators for submitting fabricated reports.'" *Id.* (quoting *id.* at 307-09 (NBC Article, dated Sept. 18, 2013)). Another article in June 2013 relayed that OPM had found problems "with procedures and safeguards used by all three private contractors— USIS, KeyPoint ... and CACI." *Id.* at 303. This article added that "[a]ll three companies have had investigators who were found to have done substandard work in background checks." *Id.* Another June 2013 article reporting on allegations against USIS noted that "concerns about background checks [were] not limited to USIS." *Id.* at 159.

Congressional Hearings & OPM Audits. In 2013, Congress twice held hearings to investigate the background-investigation industry's practice of using "false, incomplete, or rushed information gathering" in its background investigations. *Id.* at 411 & n.3. OPM reacted by commissioning an audit of KeyPoint's and its competitors' practices. This audit determined that OPM "need[ed] to strengthen its controls over its Contractors and the background investigation review process." *Id.* at 164. Back in 2010, OPM had completed a report on another audit of the background-investigation industry. This earlier report concluded that KeyPoint's and its competitors' "quality assurance process" needed improvement. *Id.* at 273. The 2010 report also revealed that KeyPoint sometimes "did not conduct the required amount of re-contacts" in its investigations, *id.* at 289, and that there were "falsification and[ ] integrity issues" with investigations done by USIS, KeyPoint, and CACI, *id.* at 261.

The USIS Suit. In October 2013—a month before Ms. Reed conveyed her allegations to DOJ and two months before she filed her *qui tam* suit—a federal court unsealed a complaint against USIS. The complaint included three *qui tam* claims against USIS. First, it alleged that USIS had a practice of "dumping" cases. That is, USIS allegedly sent cases "to OPM that were represented as Field Finished" when, in truth, they were unreviewed or "had not been investigated at all." Aplt.'s Reply Br., Addendum A, at 5. Second, the complaint claimed that USIS "failed to provide accurate and complete investigations." *Id.* at 10. Third, USIS supposedly falsely represented to OPM the extent to which it used a software program known as the "Blue Zone." *Id.* at 12. But the suit neither mentioned KeyPoint nor implied that USIS's fraud extended to its competitors or the industry as a whole.

3

The question now is: Are the allegations in Ms. Reed's *qui tam* claims substantially the same as those in the publicly disclosed sources? We agree with the district court that the answer to that question is "yes." That is, we conclude that the public disclosures were sufficient to set the government on the trail of KeyPoint's alleged fraud without Ms. Reed's assistance.[11]

p.748 At their most general, Ms. Reed's *qui tam* claims allege systemic sloppiness and fraud in the background-investigation *industry*.[12] But the government and the public knew that much already from the news reports. Those news articles painted a picture of widespread problems with the thoroughness and accuracy of the private contractors' background investigations. And that Congress held hearings to probe the background-investigation industry's alleged practice of using "false, incomplete, or rushed information gathering" underscored the pre-existing public awareness of a strong probability of fraud in the industry. Aplt.'s App. at 411 & n.3. What is more, the criminal prosecutions of individual investigators confirmed that the government knew that investigators in the industry were falsifying information in their reports.

Moving down a rung on the generality ladder to more specific footing, Ms. Reed's claims allege fraud not only in the background-investigation industry generally, but also in KeyPoint's specific background-investigative practices. That information, too, was old news to the government. After all, the government prosecuted a former KeyPoint employee for "rac[ing] through investigations" and lying "about conducting thorough background checks when they were incomplete and rushed." *Id.* at 410. News reports from 2013 added to this knowledge by reporting that OPM had found problems "with procedures and safeguards used by all three private contractors— USIS, KeyPoint ... and CACI." *Id.* at 303. To be sure, the news reports avoided explicitly accusing KeyPoint of defrauding the government. But direct allegations of fraud were unnecessary to put the government on the trail of KeyPoint's fraud. *Cf. Winkelman,* 827 F.3d at 208 (explaining that it is enough that the disclosures "lead to a plausible inference of fraud" (quoting *United States ex rel. Ondis v. City of Woonsocket,* 587 F.3d 49, 54 (1st p.749 Cir. 2009))); *United States ex rel. Osheroff v. Humana Inc.,* 776 F.3d 805, 814 (11th Cir. 2015) (same); *Boothe,* 496 F.3d at 1174 ("[A] *complete* identity of allegations, even as to time, place, and manner [is unnecessary]."); *Fine,* 70 F.3d at 572 (noting that public disclosures need not allege "any wrongdoing"). Moreover, a 2010 OPM audit report revealed both that KeyPoint sometimes "did not conduct the required amount of re-contacts" in its investigations, Aplt.'s App. at 289, and that there were "falsification and[ ] integrity issues" with investigations done by USIS, KeyPoint, and CACI, *id.* at 261. The government, then, did not need Ms. Reed's allegations to pick up the scent of fraud at KeyPoint.

At their most specific, Ms. Reed's claims allege that KeyPoint knowingly defrauded the government by submitting fraudulent reports about the completeness and accuracy of its investigations. The government could have inferred as much from the public disclosures. Consider the USIS lawsuit. That suit alleged that USIS failed to review investigations, failed to do adequate investigations, and sent false reports to OPM. Those are the same basic failings Ms. Reed accuses KeyPoint of. Furthermore, the USIS suit alleged that investigators sent cases "to OPM that were represented as Field Finished" when, in truth, they were unreviewed or "had not been investigated at all." Aplt.'s Reply Br., Addendum A, at 5. Ms. Reed's suit similarly asserts that KeyPoint sent OPM false claims "certifying that [its] investigators conducted complete, accurate, and proper investigations." Aplt.'s App. at 104, ¶ 359.

Considering this information from the USIS lawsuit and the other publicly disclosed matters discussed above, we conclude that the public disclosures were sufficient to set the government on the trail of KeyPoint's alleged fraud without Ms. Reed's assistance. Our cases reinforce this conclusion. Take *Fine,* for example. The relator there accused Sandia Corporation of misappropriating nuclear waste funds. 70 F.3d at 569. At the time, Sandia was one of only nine laboratories receiving federal funds from the Department of Energy. Before the relator's suit, a government report documented how three such laboratories, including Sandia, funded their discretionary research. The report concluded that the two other laboratories—but, notably, not Sandia—were fraudulently "taxing" nuclear waste funds in order to bolster their research programs, possibly in violation of federal law. *Id.* Again without implicating Sandia, a later congressional hearing further probed the Department of Energy's acquiescence to such behavior from its laboratories. As we saw it, that neither the report nor the congressional hearing named Sandia as a wrongdoer was not determinative. *Id.* at 572. We reasoned that because the public disclosures had "identified the problem and [there was] an easily identifiable group of probable offenders," the disclosures "were sufficient to put the government on notice as to Sandia's potential for misappropriating nuclear waste funds." *Id.* Thus, we held that the relator's allegations were substantially the same to those in the report and the congressional hearing. *Id.*

The same reasoning applies here. As in *Fine,* the public disclosures here identified the problem—fraud in background investigations—and traced that problem to an easily identifiable group of probable offenders (USIS, KeyPoint, and CACI). As in *Fine,* Congress held hearings to probe the suspected fraud in this limited industry. Moreover, akin to *Fine,* a government report (here, the 2010 OPM audit report) laid bare the heart of the matter—i.e., the falsification and integrity issues that plagued the background-investigation industry.

p.750 But unlike in *Fine,* some of the public disclosures explicitly linked KeyPoint to the suspected fraud. The OPM audit said that "Contractors" had falsification issues; that defined term meant USIS, KeyPoint, and CACI. And the news reports publicized that OPM had "found problems with procedures and safeguards used by all three private contractors—USIS, KeyPoint... and CACI." Aplt.'s App. at 303. Thus, although the public disclosures did not say the words "KeyPoint defrauded the government," the link that the disclosures forged between KeyPoint and the fraud was even stronger than the one in *Fine,* where we held that the substantially-the-same standard was satisfied. It ineluctably follows that this link was sufficient here to satisfy that standard—that is, to have set the government on the trail of KeyPoint's alleged fraud without Ms. Reed's help.

Ms. Reed's attempts to distinguish *Fine* fall short. For starters, Ms. Reed is mistaken in asserting that "no publicly disclosed˙information prior to [her] lawsuit indicated that KeyPoint was a wrongdoer." Aplt.'s Reply Br. at 10. The news reports linked KeyPoint to the fraud allegations roiling the industry. Even Ms. Reed's statement that "KeyPoint was not investigated for any suspected wrongdoing," *id.,* rings somewhat hollow. After all, the government prosecuted a former KeyPoint employee for lying "about conducting thorough background checks when they were incomplete and rushed." Aplt.'s App. at 410. Even if Ms. Reed's characterization of the absence of a KeyPoint-specific investigation were correct, the fact that KeyPoint was not named as a wrongdoer would not distinguish *Fine*; instead, it would reinforce the parallels with it. And those parallels persist even though—as Ms. Reed points out—unlike the Department of Energy, OPM never "acquiesced to or implicitly approved any fraudulent schemes." Aplt.'s Reply Br. at 10. Ms. Reed overstates the significance of the Department of Energy's acquiescence in *Fine*. We noted this agency conduct there to emphasize that the government knew of the underlying problem at issue in a limited industry; our point was not that the acquiescence itself was independently important. *See Fine,* 70 F.3d at 571. In sum, Ms. Reed errs in suggesting that *Fine* is materially distinguishable. It is not. To the contrary, it bolsters our conclusion that Ms. Reed's allegations are substantially the same as the publicly disclosed allegations.

In re Natural Gas Royalties further supports our view on the substantially-the-same question. The relator there alleged that certain natural gas companies used fraudulent measurement techniques to underpay federal royalties. The relevant public disclosures included (1) congressional documents revealing problems with measurement techniques in the natural-gas industry, (2) an earlier *qui tam* suit against different gas companies for the same fraudulent practices, and (3) press accounts reporting on the earlier suit and "disclos[ing] the industrywide nature of [the suit's] broad allegations." 562 F.3d at 1042. On appeal, the relator argued that these disclosures were not substantially the same as his allegations because the specific "Defendants and techniques were not identified in any public disclosed allegation." *Id.* at 1040. This court disagreed.

Citing *Fine,* we explained in *In re Natural Gas Royalties* that "the public disclosures at issue named a significant percentage of industry participants as wrongdoers and indicated that others in the industry were very likely engaged in the same practices." *Id.* at 1042. These revelations alleviated the burden for the government "to comb through myriad transactions performed by various types of entities in search of potential fraud." *Id.* Rather, the p.751 government needed only to investigate the measurement techniques used by a small pool of actors to ferret out the fraud. For those reasons, we held that, even without naming the specific defendants and techniques identified by the relator, "the allegations of industrywide gas mismeasurment disclosed" in the public documents "were sufficient to set the government on the trail of the fraud as to all Defendants." *Id.* at 1043.

So too here. The allegations in the public disclosures identified pervasive fraud in the background-investigation industry. Recall that in the years before Ms. Reed's suit, the government prosecuted individual investigators for allegedly falsifying information in their reports. Furthermore, a 2013 news article reported that the government was "pursuing suspected fraud in the granting of security clearances" by contractors. Aplt.'s App. at 308. And the USIS suit alleged that one of KeyPoint's two main competitors (i.e., USIS) falsely told OPM that it had provided "accurate and complete investigations." Aplt.'s Reply Br., Addendum A, at 10.

As in *In re Natural Gas Royalties,* the public disclosures here obviated the need for the government "to comb through myriad transactions performed by various types of entities in search of potential fraud." 562 F.3d at 1042. The disclosures identified three main players (including KeyPoint), and generally unearthed the type of fraud—false certifications of accurate and complete investigations—that the government needed to look for. Guided by *In re Natural Gas Royalties,* we conclude that the publicly available information here was more than enough to set the government on the trail of KeyPoint's fraud without Ms. Reed's allegations.

Ms. Reed rejects such a conclusion. She first argues that her allegations "relate to a different entity" than the entities—notably, USIS—accused of wrongdoing in the public disclosures. Aplt.'s Opening Br. at 12. Ms. Reed is quick to point out that the USIS suit made "no allegations against KeyPoint" and that none of the public disclosures expressly accused KeyPoint of defrauding the government. *Id.* at 18. Maybe so. But the substantially-the-same standard does not demand that the disclosures identify the defendant by name as the wrongdoer. *See In re Nat. Gas Royalties,* 562 F.3d at 1039. To the contrary, it is enough that the "public disclosures alleged industry-wide fraud" and "provide[d] enough information" to link the defendant to the scheme.[13] *United States ex rel. Lager v. CSL Behring, L.L.C.,* 855 F.3d 935, 946 (8th Cir. 2017). In a similar way, "the public disclosure bar contains no requirement that a public disclosure use magic words." *Winkelman,* 827 F.3d at 209. Thus, although the public disclosures did not say the magic words "KeyPoint defrauded the government," the disclosures were sufficient to link KeyPoint to fraud in an industry with only three players. No more is required.

p.752 Ms. Reed next argues that her allegations substantially differ from the publicly disclosed allegations because she exposed different schemes. For instance, she maintains that "USIS had a very specific fraudulent scheme that it used to facilitate 'dumping' cases." Aplt.'s Reply Br. at 5. That scheme, Ms. Reed explains, involved representing to OPM that cases were complete when they actually were unfinished or "had not been investigated at all." *Id.* Her complaint, by contrast, describes "several types of fraudulent schemes specific to KeyPoint that are entirely unrelated to the USIS case or any of the other publicly disclosed information." *Id.* at 6.

Ms. Reed is right that some of the schemes she exposed—especially, the scheme involving the TTP—added to the government's knowledge (more on this subject later), but these additions do not alter our substantially-the-same assessment. For now, the relevant question is only whether the public disclosures set the government on the trail of KeyPoint's fraud. As we have explained, this does not require "*complete* identity of allegations." *Boothe,* 496 F.3d at 1174. Rather, it is enough if the relator's complaint is "at least 'in ... part'" substantially the same as "the publicly disclosed information." *Osheroff,* 776 F.3d at 814 (alteration in original) (quoting *Battle v. Bd. of Regents,* 468 F.3d 755, 762 (11th Cir. 2006) (per curiam)).

Moreover, it cannot be gainsaid that in significant, material respects Ms. Reed's complaint averments are substantially the same as the complaint averments in the USIS suit. For instance, Ms. Reed's complaint alleges that KeyPoint conducted "improper, incomplete, and inaccurate investigations." Aplt.'s App. at 33, ¶ 74. The USIS complaint likewise alleges that USIS "failed to provide accurate and complete investigations." Aplt.'s Reply Br., Addendum A, at 10.[14] And there are other substantial similarities between the complaints. *Compare* Aplt.'s App. at 32, ¶ 64 (alleging that KeyPoint "transformed almost every aspect of its investigative processes to maximize profits by hitting deadlines and taking on as much work as possible, without concern for the quality, accuracy, or completeness of its investigations"), *with* Aplt.'s Reply Br., Addendum A, at 5 (alleging that USIS pressured "Field Investigators to submit a large number of [reports of investigations] in a short amount of time in order to meet the revenue goals"). Therefore, given these substantial similarities, that Ms. Reed's complaint revealed one or more KeyPoint fraudulent schemes that are distinct from those alleged in the USIS lawsuit does not dissuade us from the view that the USIS suit helped put the government on the trail of KeyPoint's alleged fraud.

Finally, Ms. Reed argues that the district court erred by not considering 2014 congressional testimony from a KeyPoint executive, Ms. Ordakowski, in its substantially-the-same analysis. In that testimony, Ms. Ordakowski told Congress that KeyPoint met or exceeded OPM standards and had "never wavered from its focus on quality." Aplt.'s Opening Br. at 21. Ms. Reed reasons that "if the government had some suspicions about the quality of KeyPoint's work," this testimony would have "throw[n] the government off the trail of the type of fraud [that Ms. Reed] alleges." *Id.*

p.753 This argument crumbles upon even brief reflection. First of all, Ms. Ordakowski testified months after Ms. Reed communicated her allegations to DOJ and after she sued KeyPoint. So the substance of Ms. Ordakowski's testimony tells us nothing about whether the government would have picked up the trail of fraud at KeyPoint based on the information it already had when Ms. Reed sued KeyPoint. Leaving aside this space-time-continuum problem, Ms. Reed's argument defies common sense. That Congress called a KeyPoint executive to testify about problems with background investigations strongly suggests that Congress thought there *was* a problem and that KeyPoint potentially was among the culprits. *Cf. Fine*, 70 F.3d at 572 ("[T]he public disclosures here were sufficient to put the government on notice as to Sandia's potential for misappropriating nuclear waste funds...."). Simply put, Ms. Ordakowski's testimony supports the district court's (and our) conclusion that the public disclosures were sufficient to have alerted the government to KeyPoint's potential for fraud.

In summary, we agree with the district court that the allegations in Ms. Reed's *qui tam* claims are substantially the same as those in the public disclosures. Thus, *unless* Ms. Reed is an "original source" of the information in her claims, the public disclosure bar prevents those claims from proceeding.

B

We now take up the question of whether Ms. Reed is an original source. Recall that the district court concluded that Ms. Reed was not an original source and therefore dismissed her *qui tam* claims under the public disclosure bar. Ms. Reed argues that in doing so the district court made both a procedural and a substantive error. The court's procedural error, she says, was excluding some of the evidence that she submitted to the court after it converted KeyPoint's motion to dismiss to a summary-judgment motion. As for the alleged substantive error, Ms. Reed contends that the district court erred in concluding that she was not an original source, in particular, because her complaint averments did not materially add to the information in the public disclosures.

As we explain below, Ms. Reed loses the procedural battle but wins the substantive war. That is, we hold that the district court did not err in excluding certain proffered evidence at summary judgment, but we hold that the court did err in concluding that Ms. Reed was not an original source because her complaint averments did not satisfy the materially-adds standard.

1

When a district court relies on material outside the complaint to resolve a Rule 12(b)(6) motion, it ordinarily must convert that motion "into a motion for summary judgment." *Burnham v. Humphrey Hosp. Reit Tr., Inc.,* 403 F.3d 709, 713 (10th Cir. 2005); *see* FED. R. CIV. P. 12(d). If a district court intends to convert a motion, it should inform the parties of this intention and give them "the opportunity to present to the court all material made pertinent to such motion by Rule 56." *Nichols v. United States,* 796 F.2d 361, 364 (10th Cir. 1986) (quoting *Ohio v. Peterson, Lowry, Rall, Barber & Ross,* 585 F.2d 454, 457 (10th Cir. 1978)). Converting a motion "without giving the adverse party an opportunity to present pertinent material is error." *Adams v. Campbell Cty. Sch. Dist.,* 483 F.2d 1351, 1353 (10th Cir. 1973).

We review a district court's choice to exclude evidence at the summary-judgment stage, however, "only for an abuse of discretion." *LifeWise Master* p.754 *Funding v. Telebank,* 374 F.3d 917, 927 (10th Cir. 2004). Without "a definite and firm conviction that the [district] court made a clear error of judgment or exceeded the bounds of permissible choice," we cannot say that the court abused its discretion. *Id.* (quoting *Lantec, Inc. v. Novell, Inc.,* 306 F.3d 1003, 1016 (10th Cir. 2002)).

The district court converted KeyPoint's Rule 12(b)(6) motion into a summary-judgment motion. Before doing so, it allowed the parties to present relevant material. Ms. Reed asked to present three sets of materials: (1) documents that she had given the government both before and after she filed her *qui tam* suit, (2) a declaration in which she attested "to the source of her allegations," and (3) more "briefing on the public disclosure and original source issues." Aplt.'s Opening Br. at 30.

After considering Ms. Reed's proffered materials, the district court allowed her to submit only the documents she gave the government in her pre-filing disclosures: specifically, the court excluded any post-filing disclosures to the government, Ms. Reed's declaration, and the additional briefing. Those other materials, the court reasoned, would not add "any material information" helpful to the public-disclosure-bar inquiry because Ms. Reed's complaint made "clear what the source of [her] knowledge was" and because the parties had fully briefed the applicable legal standards. Aplt.'s App. at 404. Thus, under the court's view, the post-filing documents, declaration, and additional briefing "were not 'made pertinent' by the conversion." *Id.* (quoting *Nichols,* 796 F.2d at 364).

To the extent that Ms. Reed argues that the district court erred by refusing "to allow [her] *the opportunity to provide* all material evidence," Aplt.'s Opening Br. at 30 (emphasis added), the record proves otherwise. The court notified the parties of its intention to convert the motion to a summary-judgment motion, and it gave them time to provide pertinent material. Unlike the parties in the cases she cites,[15] Ms. Reed had ample opportunity to provide the court with "material made pertinent by Rule 56." *Nichols,* 796 F.2d at 364 (quoting *Peterson,* 585 F.2d at 457). Indeed, the court twice permitted Ms. Reed to amend her complaint to include the post-filing information she now complains the court excluded. In the end, the court gave Ms.

Reed notice of the conversion, considered her proffered material, and even accepted some of that evidence.

And the district court's exclusion of the post-filing disclosures, Ms. Reed's declaration, and the added briefing was well within "the bounds of permissible choice." *LifeWise Master Funding,* 374 F.3d at 927 (quoting *Lantec,* 306 F.3d at 1016). Simply put, the court reasonably concluded that none of those items contained material and relevant information that the court did not already possess. Therefore, the excluded materials were not "made pertinent" by the conversion. *Nichols,* 796 F.2d at 364 (quoting *Peterson,* 585 F.2d at 457).

Ms. Reed, however, begs to differ. She says the excluded post-filing disclosure statement and personal declaration were "pertinent" to "establish[ing] her status as an original source." Aplt.'s Opening Br. at 30. These materials, Ms. Reed contends, would have shown "the extent to which [her] allegations materially added to those allegations that had purportedly been publicly disclosed." *Id.* at 33. The problem for Ms. Reed is that—as she admitted—the allegations in her complaint were "based almost entirely upon the documents that p.755 were discussed during the pre-filing meeting with [DOJ]." Aplee.'s Suppl. App., Vol. VII, at 1419 (Ms. Reed's Objs. to R. & R., filed Sept. 12, 2017). And Ms. Reed twice amended her complaint to include the crux of the information from her post-filing disclosures to the government. Ms. Reed's proffered materials, then, would have merely duplicated that existing information in the twice-amended complaint.

In the end, we cannot say that the district court abused its discretion as to this procedural matter. Thus, we leave undisturbed the district court's ruling excluding the post-filing disclosures, Ms. Reed's declaration, and the additional briefing.

2

a

Having resolved the procedural issue, we turn to the substance of the original-source question. The False Claims Act instructs courts to dismiss *qui tam* claims under the public disclosure bar "if substantially the same allegations ... were publicly disclosed"—*unless* the relator is "an original source of the information." 31 U.S.C. § 3730(e)(4)(A). We have already resolved the substantially-the-same question in KeyPoint's favor. We now must decide whether the district court erred in determining that Ms. Reed's *qui tam* claims cannot escape the public disclosure bar through the original-source exception.

Two types of relators qualify as "original sources." The first type is a relator who, "prior to a public disclosure [within the meaning of the Act] ..., has voluntarily disclosed to the Government the information on which allegations or transactions in a claim are based." *Id.* § 3730(e)(4)(B). The second type is a relator with "knowledge that is independent of and materially adds to the publicly disclosed allegations" and who gave the government this information before filing her *qui tam* claims. *Id.*

Before the district court, Ms. Reed argued that she was an original source of the second type. The district court agreed that Ms. Reed had in fact given the government her information before she sued KeyPoint. But the court ruled that Ms. Reed's allegations did not "materially add" to the public disclosures. And so, without addressing whether Ms. Reed's knowledge was "independent of" the public disclosures, the district court concluded that Ms. Reed was not an original source.

On appeal, Ms. Reed argues that the district court erred in concluding that her allegations did not "materially add" to the public disclosures. As for the "independent of" portion of the original-source inquiry, Ms. Reed says in a short footnote that she satisfies that criterion, too. *See* Aplt.'s Opening Br. at 29 n.8. For its part, KeyPoint posits that "regardless of whether her knowledge was 'independent of' the public disclosures," Ms. Reed is not an original source because her allegations "did not materially add to the public disclosures." Aplee.'s Resp. Br. at 34.

Our circuit has yet to expound on the meaning of the "materially adds" language in the original-source exception. Congress added this language in the same 2010 amendment discussed earlier but did not define the term. Since then, however, several other courts of appeals have interpreted the "materially adds" requirement.[16]

p.756 We are particularly persuaded by the First Circuit's analysis in *Winkelman*. There, the court framed the relevant question for the materially-adds inquiry as "whether the relators' allegedly new information is sufficiently significant or essential so as to fall into the narrow category of information that materially adds to what has already been revealed through public disclosures." 827 F.3d at 211. To determine what information falls into the materially-adds bucket, the First Circuit looked to the ordinary legal meaning of "material"—i.e., an addition that "is '[o]f such a nature that knowledge of the item would affect a person's decision-making,' or if it is 'significant,' or if it is 'essential.'" *Id.* (quoting BLACK'S LAW DICTIONARY 1124 (10th ed. 2014) [hereinafter BLACK'S]). In other words, *Winkelman* teaches that a relator "materially adds" to public disclosures if her information "is sufficiently important to influence the behavior of the recipient." *Id.*

The *Winkelman* definition of "materially adds" finds support in the Act's provisions defining the scope of liability, which state that "the term 'material' means having a natural tendency to influence, or be capable of influencing, the payment or receipt of money or property." 31 U.S.C. § 3729(b)(4); *see also* Joel D. Hesch, *Restating the "Original Source Exception" to the False Claims Act's "Public Disclosure Bar" in Light of the 2010 Amendments,* 51 U. OF RICH. L. REV. 991, 1019 (2017) (looking to § 3729(b)(4) in attempting to discern the meaning of "materially adds" and ultimately concluding that it means that "a reasonable person would attach importance to the information"). Furthermore, though they have applied the definition in different ways, a few federal circuit courts have expressly adopted a like definition of "materially adds." *See United States ex rel. Advocates for Basic Legal Equal., Inc. v. U.S. Bank, N.A.,* 816 F.3d 428, 431 (6th Cir. 2016) ("Materiality in this setting requires the claimant to show it had information '[o]f such a nature that knowledge of the item would affect a person's decision-making,' is 'significant,' or is 'essential.'" (quoting BLACK'S, *supra,* at 1124)); *United States ex rel. Moore & Co. v. Majestic Blue Fisheries, LLC,* 812 F.3d 294, 306 (3d Cir. 2016) (concluding based on dictionary definitions of the separate words "materially" and "add" that to "'materially add[ ]'" to "the publicly disclosed allegation or transaction of fraud, a relator must contribute significant additional information to that which has been publicly disclosed so as to improve its quality"); *see also United States ex rel. Paulos v. Stryker Corp.,* 762 F.3d 688, 694-95 (8th Cir. 2014) (relying on dictionary definitions of the separate words "material" and "add" and suggesting that information "materially adds" to something when it "substantially" or "considerably" "improve[s] or alter[s] its quality or nature" (quoting THE NEW OXFORD AMERICAN DICTIONARY 18, 1079 (3d ed. 2010))).

Winkelman also offered several helpful guideposts for how to distinguish between new but immaterial information and material additions. It noted that what is "significant" or "essential" depends in part on "the level of detail in [the] public disclosures." 827 F.3d at 211. That is, the fewer questions the public disclosures answer, p.757 the more room there is for a relator's allegations to add material information. However, the court pointed out that "a relator who merely adds detail or color to previously disclosed elements of an alleged scheme is not materially adding to the public disclosures." *Id.* at 213. *Winkelman* also recognized the potential overlap between the materially-adds inquiry and the inquiry into "whether the relator's allegations are substantially the same as th[e] prior revelations." *Id.* at 211. "Despite this potential for overlap," the First Circuit explained, "the 'materially adds' inquiry must remain conceptually distinct; otherwise, the original source exception would be rendered nugatory." *Id.* at 211-12.

In sum, we find persuasive the materially-adds standard that the First Circuit articulated in *Winkelman.* Under that standard, a relator who discloses new information that is sufficiently significant or important that it would be capable of "influenc[ing] the behavior of the recipient"—i.e., the government—ordinarily will satisfy the materially-adds standard. *Id.* at 211. On the other hand, a relator who merely adds background information or details about a known fraudulent scheme typically will be found not to have materially added to the publicly disclosed information. *See id.* at 213.

We recognize that the Seventh Circuit has taken a different path. For example, in *Cause of Action v. Chicago Transit Authority,* 815 F.3d 267 (7th Cir. 2016), the court held that if a relator's "allegations are substantially similar to those contained in the" public disclosures, her allegations *cannot* "'materially add[ ]' to the public disclosure[s]." *Id.* at 283. This standard, however, has the effect of collapsing the materially-adds inquiry into the substantially-the-same inquiry. As such, we cannot embrace it.

The plain terms of the original-source exception contemplate that some *qui tam* claims involving allegations that are substantially the same as publicly disclosed allegations nevertheless will survive the public disclosure bar because they materially add to the publicly disclosed information. Yet, the Seventh Circuit's view runs counter to this idea. And as a logical matter, its view is simply unpersuasive. After all, what good is an exception (i.e., the original-source exception) that does not actually except anything? *See* Hesch, *supra,* at 1016 (noting that because the materially-adds condition "is designed to be an exception to the public disclosure bar," it "is not meant to block out relators simply because there had been a qualifying public disclosure that contains similar allegations").

Reflecting this sort of reasoning, one commentator observed:

> The addition of the new requirement that the information "materially add" to the publicly disclosed information has caused some confusion. Some courts have required the information to be "qualitatively different" from the

publicly disclosed information or *not substantially the same as the public disclosure.* That approach renders the [materially-adds] requirement the same as the public disclosure question rather than part of an exception to the public disclosure bar. Materially adds connotes the addition of something of significance or import and whether it is substantially the same as the type of information already publicly disclosed should not matter.

Claire M. Sylvia, THE FALSE CLAIMS ACT: FRAUD AGAINST THE GOVERNMENT § 11:68, Westlaw (database updated June 2018) (emphasis added) (footnote omitted); *see also* Hesch, *supra,* at 1017 ("[M]erely because the allegations are substantially the same as a qualifying public disclosure, a p.758 relator still qualifies as an original source if she brings something to the table that adds value."). In sum, we agree with the First Circuit's assessment in *Winkelman:* "[T]he 'materially adds' inquiry must remain conceptually distinct; otherwise, the original source exception would be rendered nugatory." 827 F.3d at 211-12.

The path plotted by the Third Circuit in its noteworthy decision, *Moore,* is less clearly defined. However, in fleshing out our approach, we highlight a possible point of distinction with it. In *Moore,* the Third Circuit looked to "Rule 9(b)'s pleading requirement," 812 F.3d at 306, as "a helpful benchmark for measuring 'materially adds,'" *id.* at 307. Relying on this "standard" from Rule 9(b), the court took the position that "a relator materially adds to the publicly disclosed allegation or transaction of fraud when it contributes information—distinct from what was publicly disclosed—that adds in a significant way to the essential factual background: 'the who, what, when, where and how of the events at issue.'" *Id.* (quoting *In re Rockefeller Ctr. Props., Inc. Sec. Litig.,* 311 F.3d 198, 217 (3d Cir. 2002)).

Perhaps *Moore* is amenable to a narrow interpretation. *Cf. id.* at 307 (noting that the materially-adds standard is not met unless the relator's information "adds *in a significant way* to the essential factual background" and describing the Rule 9(b) factors as only "a helpful benchmark," without expressly saying that the presence of one or more of the factors is always dispositive) (emphasis added). *But see United States v. Medtronic, Inc.,* 327 F.Supp.3d 831, 851 (E.D. Pa. 2018) (contrasting *Moore*'s "relatively broad definition of materiality" with "*Winkelman*['s]... narrower definition"). However, insofar as *Moore* is (reasonably) interpreted as holding that a relator's averments that add a not-insignificant who, what, when, where, or how to a publicly disclosed fraudulent scheme should be uniformly deemed to meet the materially-adds standard, we must disagree.

In our view, the materially-adds analysis must be firmly grounded in the facts and circumstances of a particular case. And those facts and circumstances will guide our determination of whether the who, what, when, where, or how actually should be considered sufficiently significant or important to affect the government's actions regarding the fraudulent scheme. For example, as discussed further below, when, as here, the publicly disclosed fraud exists within an industry with only a few players, a relator who identifies a particular industry actor engaged in the fraud (i.e., the "who") is unlikely to materially add to the information that the public disclosures had already given the government.

We are concerned that *Moore* (as interpreted above) could allow the original-source exception to swallow the public disclosure bar. Specifically, one might read the Third Circuit's approach in that case to permit "a relator who merely adds detail or color to previously disclosed elements of an alleged scheme" to qualify as an original source. *Winkelman,* 827 F.3d at 213; *see Medtronic,* 327 F.Supp.3d at 851 ("*Moore* and *Winkelman* apply two different standards: *Moore* adopted a relatively broad definition of materiality while *Winkelman* adopted the narrower definition from *Universal Health [Services, Inc. v. United States ex rel. Escobar,* 579 U.S. ___, 136 S.Ct. 1989, 195 L.Ed.2d 348 (2016)]." (citation omitted)). Like the First Circuit, we do not think that adding detail or color is enough. *See also United States ex rel. Hastings v. Wells Fargo Bank, NA, Inc.,* 656 F. App'x 328, 331-32 (9th Cir. 2016) (unpublished) (Mem. Op.) ("Allegations do not materially add to public disclosures p.759 when they provide only background information and details relating to the alleged fraud—they must add value to what the government already knew.").

Thus, we are guided here by materially-adds principles that are generally consistent with those the First Circuit articulated in *Winkelman.* We believe that these principles are faithful to the balance struck by Congress, in amending the original-source exception in 2010, between "attracting whistleblowers and not paying rewards" to relators who fail to provide information that "materially adds value." Hesch, *supra,* 1026, 1040.

b

We now turn to the question of whether Ms. Reed satisfies this standard. Although we conclude that most of Ms. Reed's arguments relative to this standard fall short, we are persuaded that her complaint averments regarding the TTP program materially add to the information in the public disclosures. Therefore, she prevails on this component of the original-source inquiry.

Ms. Reed argues that her allegations materially add to the public disclosures in several ways. First, Ms. Reed points out that her complaint identifies "a new defendant" (KeyPoint). Aplt.'s Opening Br. at 25. Second, she reasons that naming individual "investigators who violated OPM requirements" adds to the disclosures. *Id.* Third, Ms. Reed posits that she materially adds to the disclosures because she did her own investigation into KeyPoint. Fourth, she says that her allegations uncovered "new schemes to defraud the government (*e.g.,* the telephone testimony violations)." *Id.*

To begin, we disagree that naming KeyPoint as a wrongdoer materially adds to the public disclosures. After all, the news reports linked KeyPoint to the suspected fraud in the background-investigation industry. And the 2010 OPM audit report revealed that there were "falsification and[ ] integrity issues" with investigations done by USIS, KeyPoint, and CACI. Aplt.'s App. at 261. Consequently, Ms. Reed is mistaken in suggesting that there was "no information concerning KeyPoint specifically in the public domain." Aplt.'s Opening Br. at 28. To be sure, the disclosures did not "use the word 'fraud'" when discussing KeyPoint. *Advocates for Basic Legal Equal.,* 816 F.3d at 432. But that omission is irrelevant because the disclosures "presented enough facts to create an inference of wrongdoing" by KeyPoint. *Id.* at 433 (quoting *United States ex rel. Jones v. Horizon Healthcare Corp.,* 160 F.3d 326, 332 (6th Cir. 1998)).

At bottom, the government already suspected fraud in the background-investigation industry. Counting KeyPoint, that industry only has three main players;

and the disclosures linked KeyPoint to the suspected fraud. We cannot see how naming KeyPoint adds information of sufficient significance or importance "to influence the [government's] behavior." *Winkelman,* 827 F.3d at 211. Put another way, this is an instance in which averments regarding the "who" of a publicly disclosed fraudulent scheme are not a material addition within the meaning of the original-source exception. *Cf. Moore,* 812 F.3d at 307.

Similarly, identifying individual investigators as wrongdoers "merely adds detail or color to previously disclosed elements of an alleged scheme." *Winkelman,* 827 F.3d at 213. The government knew that individual investigators (including a former KeyPoint employee) "lied about conducting thorough background checks when they were incomplete and rushed." Aplt.'s App. at 410. And a September 2013 article reported that the government was "pursuing suspected fraud in granting of p.760 security clearances" and had already convicted at least "19 private and government investigators for submitting fabricated reports." *Id.* at 308. True, Ms. Reed's allegations suggested that the problem was more pervasive at KeyPoint than the public disclosures hinted. But if identifying new employees engaged in fraud were enough, the original-source exception would burst from overbreadth. *Cf. Winkelman,* 827 F.3d at 212 (explaining that giving "specific examples of" publicly known fraud "does not provide any significant new information").

Ms. Reed also is mistaken that her allegations materially add to the public disclosures because she did her own investigation into KeyPoint. For starters, as KeyPoint rightly points out, "the 'materially adds' requirement ... focuses on the *substance* of the allegations, not the *source.*" Aplee.'s Resp. Br. at 37. That Ms. Reed's independent investigation confirmed, as to KeyPoint, some of the allegations floating around the public sphere is arguably relevant to the question of whether her knowledge is independent of the public disclosures, but that question is not presently before us. *See Kennard,* 363 F.3d at 1046-47 (explaining that relators had "direct and independent knowledge" because they did "their own investigation"). In sum, in our view, Ms. Reed's separate investigation is irrelevant to the materially-adds question. *See Winkelman,* 827 F.3d at 212 (rejecting argument that relators materially added to the public disclosures by "trumpet[ing] their personal knowledge of specific instances of alleged [fraud]"). As the Eighth Circuit remarked, "A relator is not an original source of information ... simply because he discovered or suspected it *first*" through his own investigation if that investigation only confirms what was "already thoroughly revealed." *Paulos,* 762 F.3d at 694.

All that said, we ultimately conclude that Ms. Reed does satisfy the materially-adds standard. We reach that conclusion because we determine that Ms. Reed's allegations regarding the TTP materially add to the information available in the public disclosures for two related and intertwined reasons. First, Ms. Reed makes specific allegations of both investigator- and management-level fraud in the distinct context of the TTP. Second, many of Ms. Reed's allegations concerning KeyPoint's responses to her reports of possible fraud in the TTP provide direct evidence of KeyPoint's scienter. Neither the allegations of investigator- and management-level fraud in the TTP context nor the allegations of KeyPoint's scienter were available via the public disclosures. Considered together, these allegations reveal a "new scheme[] to defraud the government" involving repeated violations of the TTP by KeyPoint investigators and management. Aplt.'s Opening Br. at 25. And they offer "[t]rue evidence of intent or guilty knowledge" by KeyPoint, *Hesch, supra,* at 1026, insofar as they aver Ms. Reed's specific knowledge of KeyPoint managers' efforts to knowingly cover up the TTP violations. *Cf. United States ex rel. Ambrosecchia v. Paddock Labs., LLC,* 855 F.3d 949, 955 (8th Cir. 2017) ("[Relator] claims that her information materially adds to the existing information by demonstrating scienter. However, the complaint provides no more than the simple, conclusory allegation that Defendants' actions were knowing .... Accordingly, [relator's] complaint is insufficient to plausibly state that she qualifies as an original source." (citation omitted)).

Ms. Reed's allegations of scienter make us especially confident that her allegations regarding KeyPoint's fraudulent TTP practices satisfy the materially-adds standard. False Claims Act "cases often turn on the issue of scienter." *Hesch, supra,* at 1024. Yet, "the government is never in a p.761 good position to have direct evidence of guilty knowledge." *Id.* Thus, Ms. Reed's allegations that KeyPoint's investigators and managers tried to *knowingly* cover up the TTP violations amplify the materiality of the underlying allegations of TTP fraud. *Cf. Winkelman,* 827 F.3d at 213 ("We do not rule out the possibility that furnishing information that a particular defendant is acting 'knowingly' (as opposed to negligently) sometimes may suffice as a material addition to information already publicly disclosed."); *Hesch, supra,* at 1027 ("[R]egardless of how well defined the fraud allegations are in a qualifying public disclosure, when a relator brings forth knowledge of scienter that is not specifically contained in a qualifying public disclosure it should be presumed to materially add value.").

Now consider those underlying allegations. Recall that investigators were generally required to conduct in-person interviews, but the TTP permitted them to do telephone interviews under some circumstances so long as they kept their total number of telephone interviews below a certain percentage threshold. Each month, OPM would send KeyPoint a list of investigators who exceeded their allotted number of telephone interviews during the last month. KeyPoint then would be obliged to send OPM "corrective action report[s]" explaining each infraction and what it was doing to remedy the problem. Aplt.'s App. at 31, ¶ 54.

Ms. Reed avers that KeyPoint investigators repeatedly violated the TTP and KeyPoint management regularly falsified corrective action reports to cover up the violations. For instance, one corrective action report by a KeyPoint Field Manager justified an investigator's violations by claiming that telephone interviews were "justified due to weather and due 'to the remote and large geographical area [the investigator] work[ed].'" *Id.* at 90, ¶ 262. When Ms. Reed looked into the matter, she discovered that the report was false; the investigator's sources were actually "located in nearby Colorado, well within the territory he was required to cover in person" *Id.* at 90, ¶ 264. When Ms. Reed recommended that the investigator be disciplined for violating the TTP, rather than do so and correct the false corrective action report, a KeyPoint Regional Manager "tried to persuade [Ms.] Reed that [the investigator] was covering remote territory in Wyoming." *Id.* at 90, ¶¶ 265-267.

Similarly, Ms. Reed determined that another investigator was violating the TTP by "not giv[ing] many sources the opportunity for in-person interviews," *id.* at 95 ¶ 298, and that KeyPoint management had falsely "certified that [the investigator] had not conducted the telephonic testimonies that OPM had indicated," *id.* at 96, ¶ 300. Ms. Reed specifically informed identified members of KeyPoint management that the investigator was violating the TTP—which meant that KeyPoint's prior certifications to OPM to the contrary were false. *See id.* But rather than discipline the investigator and correct the false certifications, the investigator's "Field Manager continued to issue Corrective Action Reports to OPM about [the investigator] that claimed geographic distance and source request, when Reed had already shown KeyPoint's management that [the investigator] had conducted phone interviews without attempting to conduct in-person interviews." *Id.* at 96, ¶ 310.

Furthermore, on more than one occasion, in response to Ms. Reed's efforts to correct problems in the TTP, "KeyPoint management told [her] to stop interfering." *Id.* at 95, ¶ 292; *see also id.* at 96, ¶ 308 ("[Ms.] Reed was later told to 'stop interfering.'"). In short, Ms. Reed's complaint offers pages of details describing p.762 how KeyPoint managers knowingly schemed to defraud the government by covering up systemic violations of the TTP.

None of the public disclosures accused KeyPoint—or the industry generally— of fraud relating to a TTP. The news reports, for instance, focused generally on problems in the industry with "investigators who were found to have done substandard work in background checks." *Id.* at 303. The articles do not hint at systemic investigator fraud designed to evade the requirements of a TTP (e.g., its percentage ceiling for conducting telephone interviews), let alone discuss knowing efforts of management personnel to cover up that fraud. Likewise, Congress suspected KeyPoint and its competitors only of using "false, incomplete, or rushed information gathering" in its background investigations but unearthed no evidence that industry management knowingly lied about the circumstances in which they gathered information by telephone. *Id.* at 411 & n.3. The two OPM audits do not even reference a TTP or fraudulent corrective action reports covering up violations of such a program. And the USIS suit alleged that USIS investigators "dumped" incomplete and unreviewed cases to OPM and abused OPM's "Blue Zone software." Aplt.'s Reply Br., Addendum A, at 6-12. But this suit makes no mention of a TTP, corrective action reports, or a scheme by management to cover up deficiencies under that program.

In short, Ms. Reed's allegations regarding KeyPoint's fraudulent practices related to its TTP added material information to the public disclosures that satisfied the Act's materially-adds standard. These allegations had the effect of "expanding the scope of the fraud" revealed in the public disclosures and introducing "knowledge of scienter that is not specifically contained in a qualifying public disclosure." *Hesch, supra,* at 1023, 1027. This is not a case where the relator's allegations contributed nothing more than personal "knowledge (even if gained early and independently)." *Paulos,* 762 F.3d at 694. Nor is it a situation where the allegations of fraud in the public disclosures were so detailed that there was no room for Ms. Reed to materially add to them with her allegations of KeyPoint's fraudulent TTP practices. *Winkelman,* 827 F.3d at 211 ("As the level of detail in public disclosures increases, the universe of potentially material additions shrinks."). Indeed, her allegations about KeyPoint's scheme to evade the TTP did more than "add[] detail or color to previously disclosed elements of an alleged scheme." *Id.* at 213; *see also Hastings,* 656 F. App'x at 331-32 ("Allegations do not materially add to public disclosures when they provide only background information and details relating to the alleged fraud—they must add value to what the government already knew."). Hence, we conclude that Ms. Reed's complaint averments relating to KeyPoint's fraudulent TTP practices reveal information "[o]f such a nature that knowledge of the item would affect [the government's] decision-making." *Winkelman*, 827 F.3d at 211 (first alteration in original) (quoting BLACK's, *supra*, at 1124). In other words, her allegations materially add to the public disclosures.

The soundness of this conclusion is highlighted when one contrasts the materiality of the new fraudulent scheme that Ms. Reed alleges regarding the TTP with the *immateriality* of the added information at issue in *Osheroff*. The relator in *Osheroff* alleged that certain medical clinics were violating the federal anti-kickback law and related government contracts by providing "a variety of free services for patients ..., including transportation, meals, spa and salon services, and entertainment." 776 F.3d at 808. An earlier lawsuit had disclosed a different clinic's similar practices. p.763 And news reports publicized that the defendant-clinics provided "'free lunch' ... and free transportation." *Id.* at 813. In arguing that he was an original source, the relator emphasized that his complaint added to the public disclosures by revealing "the type of food the clinics served ..., the destinations of some of the free transportation, the frequency of salon services, and the price of the substitute services or goods." *Id.* at 815. The Eleventh Circuit, however, was "not persuaded." *Id.* At best, the court explained, the relator's "complaint add[ed] background information and details relating to the value of the services offered, making it somewhat more plain that the clinics' programs could violate the [statute]." *Id.* That was not enough. The court held that under the 2010 version of the False Claims Act, the relator's "information d[id] not materially add to the public disclosures, which were already sufficient to give rise to an inference that the clinics were providing illegal remuneration to patients." *Id.*

Ms. Reed's complaint averments relating to KeyPoint's distinct TTP fraud stand in stark contrast to the general background information regarding an existing fraudulent scheme that the relator delivered in *Osheroff*. Unlike in *Osheroff*, Ms. Reed's allegations do not add a few more breadcrumbs on an existing trail; they blaze a new trail.

We underscore that we do not rest our holding that Ms. Reed has satisfied the materially-adds standard based solely on *either* her allegations concerning specific instances of investigator- and management-level fraud in the TTP *or* her allegations concerning KeyPoint's responses to her reports of possible TTP fraud—notably, to cover up fraud—that evinced KeyPoint's scienter. Instead, we base our holding on the *combined, synergistic effect* of the allegations of distinct misconduct in the TTP *and* the related and intertwined allegations detailing KeyPoint's knowing efforts to cover up TTP violations. The combination of these allegations clearly permit Ms. Reed to satisfy the materially-adds standard. We need not—and thus do not—opine on whether either of the two related and intertwined features of Ms. Reed's TTP allegations, standing alone, would be sufficient to satisfy the materially-adds standard.

* * *

In sum, we agree with the district court that the allegations in Ms. Reed's *qui tam* claims are substantially the same as those in the public disclosures. But we disagree with the court's conclusion that Ms. Reed's allegations do not materially add to the public disclosures, such that she did not qualify as an original source. As a consequence, we vacate the district court's summary-judgment order that dismissed Ms. Reed's *qui tam* claims. However, because the district court did not reach the second part of the original-source standard—i.e., whether Ms. Reed's allegations are "independent of" the public disclosures—we remand the case for the district court to resolve that question in the first instance.[17] *See Tabor v. Hilti, Inc.,* 703 p.764 F.3d 1206, 1227 (10th Cir. 2013) ("Where an issue has not been ruled on by the court below, we generally favor remand for the district court to examine the issue."); *see also Singleton v. Wulff,* 428 U.S. 106, 120, 96 S.Ct. 2868, 49 L.Ed.2d 826 (1976) ("It is the general rule, of course, that a federal appellate court does not consider an issue not passed upon below.").

III

We now turn to Ms. Reed's retaliation claim. The False Claims Act protects whistleblowers from retaliation by their employers. *See Potts,* 908 F.3d at 613-14 (discussing 31 U.S.C. § 3730(h)). To state a claim of retaliation, a plaintiff must meet her "burden of pleading facts" that prove (1) she engaged in protected activity, (2) the defendant "had been put on notice" of that protected activity, and (3) the defendant retaliated against the plaintiff "because of" that activity. *McBride v. Peak Wellness Ctr., Inc.,* 688 F.3d 698, 704 (10th Cir. 2012); *see also* 31 U.S.C. § 3730(h).

Ms. Reed alleges that KeyPoint retaliated against her by firing her for trying to stop it from violating the False Claims Act. The district court granted KeyPoint's Rule 12(b)(6) motion to dismiss this retaliation claim because Ms. Reed had, in the district court's view, inadequately pleaded that KeyPoint was on notice that she was engaging in protected activity.

We review de novo "the district court's dismissal under Rule 12(b)(6)." *United States ex rel. Polukoff v. St. Mark's Hosp.,* 895 F.3d 730, 740 (10th Cir. 2018) (quoting *United States ex rel. Lemmon v. Envirocare of Utah, Inc.,* 614 F.3d 1163, 1167 (10th Cir. 2010)). Dismissal under Rule 12(b)(6) "is appropriate only if the complaint, viewed in the light most favorable to plaintiff, 'lacks "enough facts to state a claim to relief that is plausible on its face."'" *Conner,* 543 F.3d at 1217 (quoting *Trentadue v. Integrity Comm.,* 501 F.3d 1215, 1236 (10th Cir. 2007)).

Applying these standards, we affirm the district court's dismissal of Ms. Reed's retaliation claim. At the outset, we are constrained to point out that the district court relied on a legally erroneous view of what constitutes protected activity. But we "can affirm the district court's dismissal on any ground sufficiently supported by the record." *GF Gaming Corp. v. City of Black Hawk,* 405 F.3d 876, 882 (10th Cir. 2005); *accord George v. Urban Settlement Servs.,* 833 F.3d 1242, 1254 (10th Cir. 2016). And we determine that, under the correct legal understanding of protected activity, Ms. Reed has failed to plead sufficient facts to show that KeyPoint was on notice of her purported protected activity. For that reason, we affirm the district court's order dismissing Ms. Reed's retaliation claim.

A

The False Claims Act protects whistleblowers who engage in "protected activity." *Armstrong,* 897 F.3d at 1286. Until 2009, protected activity included only "lawful acts done by the employee ... in furtherance of an action under this section [i.e., a *qui tam* suit]." 31 U.S.C. § 3730(h) (2008). The circuit courts split over what conduct qualified as "in furtherance of" a *qui tam* action. Our circuit and several others interpreted that language to mean that protected activity encompassed conduct p.765 preparing for "a private *qui tam* action or assisting in an ... action brought by the government." *United States ex rel. Ramseyer v. Century Healthcare Corp.,* 90 F.3d 1514, 1522 (10th Cir. 1996); *accord Robertson v. Bell Helicopter Textron, Inc.,* 32 F.3d 948, 951 (5th Cir. 1994). In these circuits, an employee who, for example, reported a False Claims Act violation to her supervisor but did not pursue a *qui tam* action had not engaged in protected activity. *See, e.g., Zahodnick v. Int'l Bus. Machs. Corp.,* 135 F.3d 911, 914 (4th Cir. 1997). Other circuits, by contrast, read "in furtherance of" more broadly to include protection against "retaliation for filing an internal complaint." *United States ex rel. Grenadyor v. Ukrainian Vill. Pharmacy, Inc.,* 772 F.3d 1102, 1108-09 (7th Cir. 2014) (describing the Seventh Circuit's pre-2009 precedent).

Congress resolved this circuit split in 2009. That year, it amended the False Claims Act's whistleblower protections to protect employees who take "lawful" actions "in furtherance of *other efforts to stop 1 or more violations*" of the False Claims Act. 31 U.S.C. § 3730(h)(1) (2009) (emphasis added). With this amendment, Congress thereby expanded "the universe of protected conduct."[18] *United States ex rel. Chorches v. Am. Med. Response, Inc.,* 865 F.3d 71, 97 (2d Cir. 2017). In this expanded universe, whistleblowers who lawfully try to stop one or more violations of the Act are protected, without regard to whether their conduct advances a private or government lawsuit under the Act.

Congress did amend the whistleblower protections again in 2010. As a consequence, the now-effective protections expressly apply to an employee's "lawful" acts "in furtherance of" *either* "an action" under the Act "or other efforts to stop 1 or more violations of" the Act. 31 U.S.C. § 3730(h)(1); *see also United States ex rel. Grant v. United Airlines Inc.,* 912 F.3d 190, 201 & n.3 (4th Cir. 2018) (noting these two amendments to the Act). But as is evident, the 2010 amendment left intact the 2009 amendment's broad "other efforts to stop" language, which is our focus in this appeal. Thus, Ms. Reed could avail herself of this "other efforts to stop" language in this action.

The district court, however, failed to acknowledge the expanded universe that the 2009 amendment defined. Instead, it assessed the sufficiency of Ms. Reed's averments under the pre-2009 rubric. In this regard, the court wrongly declared that under the False Claims Act "the activity prompting plaintiff's discharge must have been taken 'in furtherance of' a[ ] [*qui tam*] action." Aplt.'s App. at 417 (quoting *McBride,* 688 F.3d at 703-04).[19] p.766 The plain text of the amended whistleblower provisions does not support such a narrow view. Congress added the "other efforts to stop" language for a reason—namely, to stretch the "protected activity" umbrella to cover additional conduct. When "Congress expands the scope of activity protected by a statute, we cannot restrict ourselves to applying a narrower old standard that the expansion ... eschew[ed]." *Grant,* 912 F.3d at 201. The district court mistakenly did just that. Tellingly, the phrase "other efforts to stop" does not appear in the district court's order, and the court fails to cite a single case applying the amended provision. Simply put, the district court applied the wrong version of the statute.

This error necessarily affected the district court's consideration of whether Ms. Reed adequately pleaded notice. To adequately plead a retaliation claim, a plaintiff must aver that the defendant was on notice of her protected activity. *See Armstrong,* 897 F.3d at 1286. Once Congress expanded the scope of protected activity, the universe of conduct that a plaintiff could allege to show notice also necessarily expanded. *See United States ex rel. Smith v. Clark/Smoot/Russell,* 796 F.3d 424, 434 & n.6 (4th Cir. 2015) (explaining that the amendment expanded the boundaries of what constitutes notice of protected activity). But because the district court thought that only conduct *in furtherance* of a *qui tam* lawsuit was properly classified as "protected activity," the court asked the wrong question—an improperly narrow one. It asked only whether Ms. Reed pleaded facts sufficient to show that KeyPoint was on notice that she was "taking action in furtherance of a private *qui tam* action or assisting in an ... action brought by the government." Aplt.'s App. at 417 (quoting *Ramseyer,* 90 F.3d at 1522). And the court answered that question in the negative and, accordingly, dismissed Ms. Reed's claim.

But as framed by Ms. Reed's arguments, the right question regarding the notice element of the retaliation claim centers on the language Congress added to the Act in 2009. The district court should have gone beyond its previous inquiry and asked whether Ms. Reed pleaded facts that plausibly show that KeyPoint was on notice that she had tried to stop its alleged False Claims Act violations. The answer to that question determines whether Ms. Reed's retaliation claim stands or falls. Reviewing her complaint de novo, we answer that question in the negative.

B

Specifically, we hold that Ms. Reed has not pleaded sufficient facts to state a claim of retaliation because she has failed to establish the notice element of that claim. We explain that conclusion in two parts. First, we clarify what kind of facts Ms. Reed must plead to show that KeyPoint knew she was trying to stop its violations of the False Claims Act. Second, we determine that Ms. Reed's complaint averments come up short.

1

Our circuit has yet to begin the work of defining the boundaries of what p.767 constitutes protected efforts to stop a violation of the False Claims Act. Naturally, we cannot narrow our consideration to our pre-2009 view that an employee must prove in every instance that the employer knew that she was acting "in furtherance of" a *qui tam* action. *Ramseyer,* 90 F.3d at 1522. Beginning the outline of those boundaries, we state our agreement with KeyPoint "that a relator's actions still must convey a connection to the [False Claims Act]." Aplee.'s Resp. Br. at 52; *see Grant,* 912 F.3d at 202 (noting that "plaintiff's actions need not lead to a viable" *qui tam* action, but "they must still have a nexus to a[ ] [False Claims Act] violation"); *United*

States ex rel. Booker v. Pfizer, Inc., 847 F.3d 52, 59 n.8 (1st Cir. 2017) (explaining that relator's "activities must pertain to violations" of the Act). After all, the text of the amendment says the "other efforts" must be "to stop 1 or more violations of [the False Claims Act]." 31 U.S.C. § 3730(h)(1).

We also agree with KeyPoint that compliance employees typically must do more than other employees to show that their employer knew of the protected activity. Our cases applying the pre-2009 whistleblower provisions explained that an employee "whose job entails the investigation of fraud .... must make clear" that she engaged in protected activity "to overcome the presumption that [she was] merely acting in accordance with [her] employment obligations." *Ramseyer*, 90 F.3d at 1523 n.7; *accord United States ex rel. Sikkenga v. Regence Bluecross Blueshield of Utah*, 472 F.3d 702, 729 (10th Cir. 2006). In other words, in these decisions, we recognized that an employer might reasonably presume that when a compliance employee reports incidents of fraud she is just doing her job. So to hold an employer liable under the Act's whistleblower provisions, our pre-2009 precedent required a compliance employee to overcome that presumption by showing that she was engaging in protected activity, not just doing her job.

We think this reasoning has survived the 2009 amendment. True, as we have explained above, that amendment expanded the scope of protected activity and thus expanded the universe of conduct that a relator may plead in giving the employer notice of the protected activity. But nothing about the 2009 amendment undercuts the rationale of our precedent addressing compliance officers who are charged by their employer with investigating fraud. *See United States ex rel. Campie v. Gilead Scis., Inc.*, 862 F.3d 890, 908 (9th Cir. 2017) (deeming our pre-2009 *Ramseyer* decision "instructive," in a post-amendment context, on the point that compliance employees must do more to show an employer's knowledge), *cert. denied*, ___ U.S. ___, 139 S.Ct. 783, 202 L.Ed.2d 566 (2019).

In sum, to state a retaliation claim, as relevant here, an employee's complaint must allege facts that show her employer knew of her efforts to stop a False Claims Act violation. The 2009 amendment left intact our precedent requiring compliance employees to do more than other employees to meet the notice element. And so, to adequately plead notice, a compliance employee must allege facts that, viewed in her favor, make clear that her employer had been put on notice that she was trying to stop it from violating the False Claims Act and not merely doing her job.

2

We conclude that Ms. Reed's complaint averments come up short of this standard. To be sure, Ms. Reed is correct that her complaint shows that she voiced objections regarding the alleged fraud "to everyone at KeyPoint who would listen." p.768 Aplt.'s Opening Br. at 41. For instance, the complaint alleges that "she approached KeyPoint's Director of Training" and "raised concerns to her supervisor," the "OPM Contract Director," and "the Regional Managers and certain Field Managers." Aplt.'s App. at 31-32, ¶¶ 59, 65. Indeed, the complaint notes that Ms. Reed brought some of "the most egregious instances" of fraud at the investigator level to the attention of "field managers and ... regional managers." *Id.* at 62, ¶ 172.

Likewise, Ms. Reed allegedly told "her supervisor... on numerous occasions" about violations of the TTP. *Id.* at 89, ¶ 253.

However, Ms. Reed was a "Senior Quality Control Analyst"—that is, a compliance officer. *Id.* at 24, ¶ 3. Thus, under our precedent, we may presume that Ms. Reed—as a compliance officer—was just doing her job in repeatedly reporting fraud internally to employees at KeyPoint. And Ms. Reed's complaint averments do not overcome that presumption—indeed, they tend to underscore the soundness of it. In this regard, Ms. Reed herself links her knowledge of, and efforts to report, the alleged fraud at KeyPoint to her role "as a Senior Quality Control Analyst."[20] *Id.* at 25, ¶ 4. For instance, the complaint notes that Ms. "Reed *and her staff* discover[ed]" fraud. *Id.* at 75, ¶ 201 (emphasis added). And at points, the complaint specifies that Ms. "Reed *and her staff* reported [certain] violations." *Id.* at 78, ¶ 207 (emphasis added); *see also id.* at 76, 80, ¶¶ 203, 210. That her staff was assisting Ms. Reed in fraud detection and reporting activities suggests that such activities fell within the ambit of Ms. Reed's responsibilities as a Senior Quality Control Analyst because one might reasonably infer that Ms. Reed's staff would not be assisting her in off-book operations or matters of personal preference, rather than duty. Even when Ms. Reed acted alone, the complaint suggests that she reported misconduct on a regularized schedule as part of her job—averring that she "regularly reported [certain] infractions to her supervisor ... by submitting and discussing a *monthly spreadsheet.*" *Id.* at 62, ¶ 171 (emphasis added); *see also id.* at 86, ¶ 230. And for investigators who persistently violated policies, Ms. Reed reported them "for disciplinary action by KeyPoint"— which strongly suggests that she had some job-related mandate to do so. *Id.* at 90, ¶ 265; *see also id.* at 36, ¶ 99.

In sum, as the district court correctly observed, "[T]he monitoring and reporting activities described in her Complaint were exactly those activities Ms. Reed was required to undertake ... as a Senior Quality Control Analyst." *Id.* at 418-19. In other words, Ms. Reed's complaint averments do not rebut—and, indeed, tend to highlight the soundness of—the presumption that her conduct was just part of her job.

p.769 Ms. Reed tries to rebut this presumption by showing that she went "outside [her] normal chain of command to report fraudulent conduct." Aplt.'s Opening Br. at 37. In this regard, Ms. Reed conclusorily asserts that she complained about the fraud to "people well outside her chain of command." *Id.* at 41. In particular, Ms. Reed avers that she reported the fraud to "the OPM Contract Director ..., the Regional Managers[,] and certain Field Managers." Aplt.'s App. at 32, ¶ 65. Her complaint also refers to a conversation with "KeyPoint's Director of Training." *Id.* at 31-32, ¶ 59. By reporting fraud to these individuals, Ms. Reed argues that she "acted beyond the scope of her ordinary duties in attempting to stop KeyPoint's false statements" and that "[t]he KeyPoint employees who decided to fire [her] knew" as much. *Id.* at 108, ¶¶ 389, 396. Hence, Ms. Reed reasons, KeyPoint knew that her reports of fraud were not part of her job but, instead, efforts to stop False Claims Act violations.

KeyPoint disagrees. It says that Ms. Reed's actions were exactly what she "was required to undertake in fulfillment of her job duties" as a Senior Quality Control Analyst. Aplee.'s Resp. Br. at 53 (quoting *Ramseyer,* 90 F.3d at 1523). KeyPoint also denies that it was properly put on notice of Ms. Reed's protected activity because she ostensibly "went outside of her usual chain of command." *Id.* at 55. Indeed, KeyPoint notes that Ms. Reed "does not cite any binding authority for the proposition that alleged discussions with individuals inside the company but outside of her normal reporting structure would suffice to overcome the presumption that she was acting within the scope of her ordinary duties." *Id.* at 56. Hence, KeyPoint argues that it "could not have been on notice of [Ms. Reed's] allegedly protected actions." *Id.* at 53.

KeyPoint is correct that our court has never expressly held that a compliance employee may put her employer on notice of her efforts to stop False Claims Act violations by reporting fraud internally but outside her chain of command. But other circuits have. The Ninth and D.C. Circuits, for example, each have held that, under certain circumstances, a compliance employee may meet the notice element of retaliation by pleading that her employer knew that she had reported fraud within the company in a manner that violated or went outside the established chain of command. *See, e.g., Campie,* 862 F.3d at 897, 908 (holding that retaliation complaint by a "Senior Director of Global Quality Assurance" adequately pleaded notice because, *inter alia,* the employer knew the employee had "conversations outside of his chain of command regarding his concerns"); *United States ex rel. Schweizer v. Oce N.V.,* 677 F.3d 1228, 1239-40 (D.C. Cir. 2012) (holding that a compliance employee's retaliation claim survived summary judgment because employer knew she had "ignor[ed] 'the chain of command'" by reporting fraud to her boss's boss); *cf. United States ex rel. Williams v. Martin-Baker Aircraft Co.,* 389 F.3d 1251, 1261 (D.C. Cir. 2004) (stating the general proposition that "when an employee acts outside his normal job responsibilities or alerts a party outside the usual chain of command, such action may suffice to notify the employer that the employee is engaging in protected activity," in a case in which the employee "went outside the company and alerted the government").

We need not definitively opine here, however, on the cogency of this precedent. Even if Ms. Reed could legally overcome the compliance-employee presumption by showing that she went outside of the chain of command to report fraud, her complaint averments do not plausibly establish, p.770 as a factual matter, that she did so. That is, she has not pleaded facts showing that she indeed went outside her ordinary reporting structure as a compliance officer. To be sure, we must "assume the truth of all well-pleaded facts in the complaint[ ] and draw all reasonable inferences" in Ms. Reed's favor. *Leverington v. City of Colorado Springs,* 643 F.3d 719, 723 (10th Cir. 2011) (quoting *Dias v. City & County of Denver,* 567 F.3d 1169, 1178 (10th Cir. 2009)). And Ms. Reed avers that she reported fraud to persons other than her direct supervisor—namely, "the OPM Contract Director ..., Regional Managers[,] and certain Field Managers," as well as the "Director of Training." Aplt.'s App. at 31-32, ¶¶ 59, 65. But Ms. Reed never pleaded facts delineating her specific job description or defining the scope of her duties such that we could discern with some specificity the contours of Ms. Reed's chain of command or ordinary reporting structure related to fraud matters. Without that information, we cannot say, or reasonably infer, that Ms. Reed broke the chain of command or ordinary communication protocol by speaking with the Director of Training, OPM Contract Director, Regional Managers, or Field Managers.

For example, as a compliance officer, Ms. Reed may have been obliged as part of her job duties to communicate with, and seek remedial action from, those at KeyPoint other than her direct supervisor regarding instances of employee fraud—

especially if her supervisor did not adequately respond to her concerns. If so, that Ms. Reed turned to, for example, the Regional Managers or Field Managers to address her fraud concerns could not properly be viewed as an instance of Ms. Reed violating the established communication protocol or chain of command. Ms. Reed's complaint averments shed no appreciable light on whether her job description did in fact contemplate such communications beyond her direct supervisor—much less negate this possibility.

Tellingly, in responding to KeyPoint's similar comments regarding factual gaps in her complaint, the best that Ms. Reed seemingly could muster in her Reply Brief was a plea for merciful forbearance: "With respect to her retaliation claim, [Ms. Reed] is arguing that, at the motion to dismiss stage, she *gets the benefit of the doubt*." Aplt.'s Reply Br. at 22 (emphasis added). But the one case that she cites for support—*Gee v. Pacheco,* 627 F.3d 1178 (10th Cir. 2010)—says no such thing. That case and other controlling decisions make quite clear that, "[t]o survive a motion to dismiss," a plaintiff's complaint averments must be factually plausible. *Id.* at 1184 (quoting *Ashcroft v. Iqbal,* 556 U.S. 662, 678, 129 S.Ct. 1937, 173 L.Ed.2d 868 (2009)). And that plausibility standard is satisfied "when the plaintiff pleads factual content that allows the court to draw the reasonable inference that the defendant is liable for the misconduct alleged." *Id.* (quoting *Iqbal,* 556 U.S. at 678, 129 S.Ct. 1937). As relevant here, Ms. Reed had to plead facts from which we could reasonably infer that she put KeyPoint on notice of her protected activity by going outside the established communication protocol or chain of command. But she has failed to plead such facts.[21]

p.771 The D.C. Circuit's analysis in *Schweizer* offers a useful contrast. Like Ms. Reed, the relator there was responsible for ensuring "compliance with government contracts." 677 F.3d at 1239. Upon uncovering fraud, the relator voiced concerns to her supervisor and then "repeatedly disobeyed the orders of ... her supervisor[ ] to stop investigating" the alleged fraud. *Id.* In fact, the relator went over her boss's head to his supervisor "on two separate occasions." *Id.* In those conversations, "she alleged a variety of specific False Claims Act violations" and "made an emotional plea to 'sav[e] the company' from 'legal trouble.'" *Id.* at 1239-40 (alteration in original). Some weeks later, "[t]he company fired" the relator. *Id.* at 1240. Her termination letter specified that she was fired for "'refusing to follow orders' and ignoring 'the chain of command.'" *Id.* From this evidence, the D.C. Circuit held that the relator's "factual allegations [were] sufficient to overcome 'the presumption that [she was] merely acting in accordance with [her] employment obligations.'" *Id.* (second and third alterations in original) (quoting *Williams,* 389 F.3d at 1261).

Measured against the allegations in *Schweizer,* the paucity of the factual content in Ms. Reed's complaint averments is patent. Unlike in *Schweizer,* we have no specifically pleaded facts here indicating that Ms. Reed violated the chain of command in reporting suspected fraud to KeyPoint officials other than her direct supervisor. Whereas the relator in *Schweizer* was ordered to stop investigating the fraud, Ms. Reed was "tasked with extra audits of investigators." Aplt.'s App. at 61, ¶ 165. And while the employer in *Schweizer* fired the relator for "failing to follow orders and the chain of command," 677 F.3d at 1240, we lack any specific—much less express—basis in Ms. Reed's complaint from which to infer that Ms. Reed's activities in reporting suspected fraud, in her capacity as a compliance officer, violated

KeyPoint's established communication protocols or broke her chain of command. Simply put, Ms. Reed's complaint averments fail to rebut the presumption that her actions were just doing her job.

* * *

In summary, Ms. Reed has the burden of pleading sufficient facts to show that KeyPoint knew of her protected activity. *See McBride*, 688 F.3d at 704. To do so, she must overcome the presumption that her internal reports of fraud were part of her job as a Senior Quality Control Analyst. This she cannot do. Accordingly, we p.772 hold that Ms. Reed has failed to adequately allege that KeyPoint was on notice of her efforts to stop its alleged False Claims Act violations. Consequently, her retaliation claim fails.

IV

For the reasons stated above, we VACATE the district court's judgment and order insofar as it granted summary judgment on Ms. Reed's *qui tam* claims. We AFFIRM the district court's order insofar as it dismissed Ms. Reed's retaliation claim. And we REMAND for further proceedings consistent with this opinion.[22]

[1] Before Congress amended the False Claims Act in 2010, the public disclosure bar was jurisdictional—that is, if the bar applied, courts lacked subject-matter jurisdiction. *See Boothe*, 496 F.3d at 1177 (explaining that, as of 2007, the public disclosure bar was jurisdictional). The pre-2010 provision read: "No court shall have jurisdiction over" a *qui tam* action "based upon the public disclosure of allegations." 31 U.S.C. § 3730(e)(4)(A) (2006). The 2010 amendments removed the reference to jurisdiction, counseling district courts instead to "dismiss an action" if the public disclosure bar applies. 31 U.S.C. § 3730(e)(4)(A) (2010). The federal courts of appeals that have confronted the issue have unanimously held that the 2010 "amendments transformed the public disclosure bar from a jurisdictional bar to an affirmative defense." *United States ex rel. Prather v. AT&T, Inc.*, 847 F.3d 1097, 1102 (9th Cir.), *cert. denied*, ___ U.S. ___, 137 S.Ct. 2309, 198 L.Ed.2d 751 (2017); *see also United States ex rel. Beauchamp v. Academi Training Ctr.*, 816 F.3d 37, 40 (4th Cir. 2016) (holding the amended "public-disclosure bar is ... an affirmative defense," not "a jurisdictional bar"); *United States ex rel. Moore & Co. v. Majestic Blue Fisheries, LLC*, 812 F.3d 294, 300 (3d Cir. 2016) (same); *United States ex rel. Osheroff v. Humana Inc.*, 776 F.3d 805, 810 (11th Cir. 2015) (same).

Our circuit has yet to opine on this issue. And we need not do so today. Let us briefly explain the most salient reasons. KeyPoint properly raised the public disclosure bar as a defense in its motion to dismiss before the district court. As a result, we need not determine the jurisdictional status of the public disclosure bar here. If KeyPoint had failed to raise the bar before the district court and had asserted it for the first time on appeal, we would have been obliged to consider the issue only if it was jurisdictional—that is, if it implicated our jurisdiction to hear the merits of Ms. Reed's *qui tam* claims—not if it was merely an affirmative defense. Therefore, under such hypothetical circumstances, the jurisdictional status of the issue would have been an important question that we needed to resolve. *See Smith v. Cheyenne Ret. Inv'rs L.P.,* 904 F.3d 1159, 1164 (10th Cir. 2018) (noting that "[i]n most cases, including this one, this distinction between a jurisdictional requirement and an affirmative defense is immaterial" because the party has "pled failure to exhaust as an affirmative defense"); *McQueen ex rel. McQueen v. Colo. Springs Sch. Dist.,* 488 F.3d 868, 873 (10th Cir. 2007) (explaining that the distinction between an affirmative defense and a jurisdictional prerequisite "is important ... only when the defendant has waived or forfeited the issue" but because "there is no question of waiver or forfeiture" the court "need not decide whether exhaustion is jurisdictional"); *accord Coleman v. Newburgh Enlarged City Sch. Dist.,* 503 F.3d 198, 204 (2d Cir. 2007) ("[W]e are not forced to decide whether our precedent, which labels the IDEA's exhaustion requirement as a rule affecting subject matter jurisdiction rather than an 'inflexible claim-processing' rule that may be waived or forfeited, remains good law... because there can be no claim of waiver or forfeiture here."); *see also Davoll v. Webb,* 194 F.3d 1116, 1128 (10th Cir. 1999) ("If [an] issue implicates subject matter jurisdiction, we have an obligation to address it 'regardless of normal rules governing the presentation of issues.'" (quoting *Int'l Union of Operating Eng'rs, Local 150 v. Rabine,* 161 F.3d 427, 429 (7th Cir. 1998))). But those hypothetical circumstances are not present here; therefore, we need not consider the jurisdictional status of the public disclosure bar. Furthermore, as we explain later, we conclude that the original-source analysis that the district court used in concluding that the public disclosure bar precludes Ms. Reed's *qui tam* claims is legally flawed. Accordingly, we vacate its judgment and remand for further proceedings. As a product of that disposition, Ms. Reed's *qui tam* claims are not (at least for the time being) subject to the public disclosure bar. Thus, also for this reason, whether that bar is jurisdictional or not is immaterial. Finally, we observe that the parties did not meaningfully address the public disclosure bar's proper characterization—i.e., jurisdictional or an affirmative defense. Although this failure would not obviate the need for us to independently consider that question if our jurisdiction over the merits depended on the answer, the parties' underdeveloped arguments on this score further militate against us trying to answer the question when the answer is *not* material here, let alone determinative of our jurisdiction. *Cf. Hill v. Kemp,* 478 F.3d 1236, 1251 (10th Cir. 2007) ("Our system of justice, after all, is not a self-directed inquisitorial one; to avoid error, we are dependent on the full development of issues through the adversarial process....").

[2] The copy of the audit report included in the record is undated. But a copy of the report that is publicly available via the Internet lists the date the report was published as June 4, 2014. *See* OFFICE OF PERS. MGMT., AUDIT OF THE FEDERAL INVESTIGATIVE SERVICES' CASE REVIEW PROCESS OVER BACKGROUND INVESTIGATIONS (2014), https://www.opm.gov/our-inspector-general/publications/reports/2014/audit-of-the-federal-investigative-services-case-review-process-over-background-investigations.pdf.

[3] Ms. Reed also alleged that KeyPoint violated the Americans with Disabilities Act by retaliating against her because of her disability. The district court granted KeyPoint's motion to dismiss that claim. Ms. Reed does not challenge that ruling on appeal.

[4] For the public disclosure bar to apply, two other conditions must be met. First, "the alleged 'public disclosure'" must "contain[ ] allegations... from one of the listed sources" in the Act. *In re Nat. Gas Royalties,* 562 F.3d 1032, 1039 (10th Cir. 2009) (quoting *United States ex rel. Holmes v. Consumer Ins. Grp.,* 318 F.3d 1199, 1203 (10th Cir. 2003)); *see* 31 U.S.C. § 3730(e)(4)(A)(i)-(iii) (listing, among other things, news reports, congressional hearings, prior lawsuits, and federal audits as "sources"). Second, the disclosure must be "public." *See In re Nat. Gas Royalties,* 562 F.3d at 1039. Because the parties agree that these conditions are met, we need not (and do not) consider them.

[5] We typically answer "only the questions we must, not those we can." *Valley Forge Ins. Co. v. Health Care Mgmt. Partners, Ltd.,* 616 F.3d 1086, 1094 (10th Cir. 2010). Thus, we pause to explain our rationale for resolving the substantially-the-same question even though we ultimately vacate the district court's judgment regarding the *qui tam* claims because of its error in resolving the original-source question. In other words, because the original-source error is ultimately determinative here in our resolution of the public-disclosure-bar issue, some might question the need to first rule on the substantially-the-same component of the public-disclosure-bar issue. But our precedent teaches that application of the public disclosure bar "requires a four-step inquiry." *Kennard v. Comstock Res., Inc.,* 363 F.3d 1039, 1042 (10th Cir. 2004). The first two steps—which are not at issue here—relate to whether the information in question qualifies under the Act as a public disclosure. *See id.* The third step is the substantially-the-same inquiry. These first three steps determine whether, absent an exception, the public disclosure bar applies at all. *See id.* And so our circuit has counseled courts to "address the first three public disclosure issues first." *Id.* (quoting *United States ex rel. Hafter v. Spectrum Emergency Care,* 190 F.3d 1156, 1161 (10th Cir. 1999)). Reaching "the fourth, 'original source' issue is necessary *only if* the court answers the first three questions in the affirmative." *Id.* (emphasis added) (quoting *Hafter,* 190 F.3d at 1161). In *Kennard,* for example, we first concluded that the public disclosure bar's three prerequisites applied. *Id.* Then we held that the relators "qualif[ied] as an original source," thus reversing the district court's order. *Id.* at 1046.

Admittedly, this precedent instructing courts to reach the original-source question only after answering in the affirmative the substantially-the-same question interpreted the pre-2010 version of the public disclosure bar, which was jurisdictional. That said, we see no reason why the 2010 amendment—irrespective of its jurisdictional import—should change our view that the substantially-the-same "analysis is a threshold inquiry" that we should resolve before "reach[ing] the 'original source' analysis." *United States ex rel. Fine v. MK-Ferguson Co.,* 99 F.3d 1538, 1545 (10th Cir. 1996) (quoting *United States ex rel. Precision Co. v. Koch Indus., Inc.,* 971 F.2d 548, 552 (10th Cir. 1992)). After all, as we explain below, the 2010 amendment establishes an analytical rubric consistent with our pre-2010 precedent. Moreover, the structure of the amended provision—like the unamended version—supports the proposition that the substantially-the-same inquiry is a threshold one. That provision instructs courts to dismiss a *qui tam* claim "if substantially the same allegations ... were publicly disclosed .... *unless* ... the person bringing the action is an original source of the information." 31 U.S.C. § 3730(e)(4)(A) (2010) (emphasis added); *see Moore,* 812 F.3d at 297-98 (quoting this amended language and concluding that a relator's allegations were substantially the same as those in the public sphere, "but that [the relator] was nevertheless an original source"). Thus, we adhere to our pre-2010-amendment view that courts should resolve the substantially-the-same question before considering whether a relator's *qui tam* claims may proceed under the original-source exception.

[6] *Accord United States ex rel. Winkelman v. CVS Caremark Corp.*, 827 F.3d 201, 208 n.4 (1st Cir. 2016) ("The revised statutory langauge—'substantially the same'—merely confirms our earlier understanding."); *United States ex rel. Mateski v. Raytheon Co.*, 816 F.3d 565, 569 n.7 (9th Cir. 2016) ("[O]ur analysis of the issue of substantial similarity would be the same under either version [of the public-disclosure-bar provision]."); *Cause of Action v. Chi. Transit Auth.*, 815 F.3d 267, 281 n.20 (7th Cir. 2016) ("Our analysis [of substantial similarity] is therefore the same under either version of the statute."); *see also United States ex rel. Armes v. Garman*, 719 F. App'x 459, 463 n.2 (6th Cir. 2017) (unpublished) ("[T]he 2010 amendment does not affect our public-disclosure analysis ....").

[7] We are aware of scholarly criticism of the on-the-trail-of-fraud standard. *See* Susan Schneider Thomas & Jonathan Z. DeSantis, *Misguided Meanders: The "Trail of Fraud" Under the Public Disclosure Bar of the False Claims Act*, 43 UNIV. OF DAYTON L. REV. 161, 182 (2018) ("[R]ather than using the innately ambiguous assessment of whether the alleged public disclosures *'might have' 'set'* the government on the *'trail'* of fraud, it would be a far more meaningful analysis to examine, as the plain language of the statute commands, whether the potentially disabling public disclosures in fact disclosed allegations or transactions of fraud, or made actual allegations of fraudulent conduct."). However, *Fine* and its progeny are binding precedent in this circuit. Moreover, Ms. Reed does not challenge the propriety of this standard in her Opening Brief.

[8] *See also United States ex rel. Lager v. CSL Behring, L.L.C.*, 855 F.3d 935, 946 (8th Cir. 2017) (concluding that the disclosures "'set the government squarely on the trail' of the defendants'" fraud even though the disclosures did not name defendants (quoting *In re Nat. Gas Royalties*, 562 F.3d at 1041)); *United States ex rel. Zizic v. Q2Administrators, LLC*, 728 F.3d 228, 238 (3d Cir. 2013) (concluding allegations were substantially similar even though defendants "were not actually identified" in the public disclosure).

[9] *See also Lager*, 855 F.3d at 946 (finding substantial similarity when disclosures gave enough information about an industry-scheme to "identify the defendants" without naming them); *cf. United States ex rel. Jamison v. McKesson Corp.*, 649 F.3d 322, 329, 330 (5th Cir. 2011) (observing that "the public disclosures need not name particular defendants so long as they 'alerted the government to the industry-wide nature of the fraud and enabled the government to readily identify wrongdoers through an investigation,'" but reasoning that "the defendants' documents, considered alone, likely are not sufficient publically to disclose allegations specific to" them because their industries "are large" and "[t]he public disclosures do not indicate that fraud is universal or even widespread within them" (quoting *In re Nat. Gas Royalties*, 562 F.3d at 1039)).

[10] *See also Bellevue*, 867 F.3d at 718-19 (noting that the substantially-the-same standard requires only "that the government had enough information" from the public disclosures to infer that the defendant knowingly violated the False Claims Act); *Winkelman*, 827 F.3d at 208 (explaining that it is enough that the public

disclosures "lead to a plausible inference of fraud" (quoting *United States ex rel. Ondis v. City of Woonsocket,* 587 F.3d 49, 54 (1st Cir. 2009))); *Osheroff,* 776 F.3d at 814 (same).

[11] Ms. Reed alleges on appeal that the district court "fail[ed] to do a diligent comparison of the putative public disclosures with [her] allegations." Aplt.'s Opening Br. at 3. Not so. Beyond incorporating the magistrate judge's discussion of the relevant allegations, *see* Aplt.'s App. at 409, the district court dutifully recounted Ms. Reed's allegations and the publicly disclosed allegations in turn, *see id.* at 408-12. From this comparison, the court then concluded that Ms. Reed's allegations were substantially similar to the publicly disclosed allegations. The sufficiency of this analysis cannot be questioned. In any event, our review is de novo, and we have thoroughly compared the averments of Ms. Reed's operative complaint to the identified public disclosures. Accordingly, Ms. Reed's assertion that the district court conducted a faulty analysis of the summary judgment record is ultimately of no moment. *Cf. Rivera v. City & County of Denver,* 365 F.3d 912, 920 (10th Cir. 2004) ("Because our review is de novo, we need not separately address Plaintiff's argument that the district court erred by viewing evidence in the light most favorable to the City and by treating disputed issues of fact as undisputed.").

[12] We, like other circuits, would have reservations about keeping our analysis of Ms. Reed's allegations solely at such a high level of generality. *See Mateski,* 816 F.3d at 578 (agreeing with the "Seventh Circuit's warning against reading *qui tam* complaints at only the 'highest level of generality'" (quoting *Leveski v. ITT Educ. Servs., Inc.,* 719 F.3d 818, 831 (7th Cir. 2013))). But at what precise level of generality we should compare a relator's claims with allegations in public disclosures is a difficult question. The Act tells us to ask if the relator's claims are "substantially the same." 31 U.S.C. § 3730(e)(4)(A). The ordinary meaning of "substantial" is: "concerning the essentials of something." THE NEW OXFORD AMERICAN DICTIONARY 1687 (2d ed. 2005). And the ordinary meaning of "same" is: "identical; not different; unchanged" or "of an identical type." *Id.* at 1498. "Substantially the same," then, connotes a standard that requires only the *essentials* of the relator's allegations to be identical to or of an identical type as those disclosed publicly. This plain-meaning analysis comports with our precedent. *See Boothe,* 496 F.3d at 1174 (noting that "a *complete* identity of allegations" is unnecessary; it is enough for "the essence of" the relator's allegations to be "'derived from' a prior public disclosure"). We need not put a finer point on this issue in this case. That is because it is clear to us that only if we accept Ms. Reed's hyper-specific reading that requires near-complete identity of allegations could we conclude that her allegations are not substantially similar to those in the public disclosures. And our precedent forecloses such a hyper-specific reading. *See id.*

[13] *See also Bellevue,* 867 F.3d at 719 (noting that the substantially-the-same standard requires only "that the government had enough information" from the public disclosures to infer that the defendant knowingly violated the Act); *Osheroff,* 776 F.3d at 814 (same); *Jamison,* 649 F.3d at 329 ("[T]he public disclosures need not name particular defendants so long as they 'alerted the government to the industry-wide nature of the fraud and enabled the government to readily identify wrongdoers through an investigation.'" (quoting *In re Nat. Gas Royalties,* 562 F.3d at 1039)); *United States ex rel. Gear v. Emergency Med. Assocs. of Ill., Inc.,* 436 F.3d 726, 729 (7th Cir. 2006)

(rejecting "argument that for there to be public disclosure, the specific defendants named in the lawsuit must have been identified in the public records").

[14] *Compare also* Aplt.'s App. at 88, ¶ 244 ("Each case was submitted as though it had been properly completed, reviewed, and checked when none had received the required oversight."), *with* Aplt.'s Reply Br., Addendum A, at 6 ("USIS knowingly submitted Cases to OPM for payment that they knew had not been reviewed....").

[15] *See Peterson,* 585 F.2d at 457 (reversing because district court gave party no chance to present material); *Adams,* 483 F.2d at 1353 (same).

[16] Although KeyPoint concedes that the meaning of "materially adds" "is a matter of first impression for the Tenth Circuit," Aplee.'s Resp. Br. at 34, it nonetheless relies on pre-2010-amendment cases to argue that Ms. Reed's allegations do not materially add to the public disclosures, *see id.* at 36-37. Although the 2010 amendment ratified our prior cases by adopting the "substantially the same" language that we already used, the amendment added a new component to the original-source analysis—namely, the materially-adds inquiry. Before the 2010 amendment, our original-source analysis asked whether the relator "had direct and independent knowledge of the information underlying his allegations." *In re Nat. Gas Royalties,* 562 F.3d at 1043. We did not ask whether the relator's knowledge materially added to the public disclosures. Thus, our pre-2010-amendment cases are not germane to the materially-adds inquiry.

[17] We likewise decline KeyPoint's invitation to affirm the district court's judgment on alternative bases not ruled on by the district court. *See* Aplee.'s Resp. Br. at 58-60 (arguing that Ms. Reed's FCA claims fail for want of (1) particularity under Rule 9(b), (2) falsity, (3) materiality, and (4) scienter). Although it is true that we may affirm on any basis finding support in the record, *see Richison v. Ernest Grp., Inc.,* 634 F.3d 1123, 1130 (10th Cir. 2011), we are often "reluctant" to do so when "we are deprived of the benefit of vigorous adversarial testing of the issue, not to mention a reasoned district court decision on the subject." *Abernathy v. Wandes,* 713 F.3d 538, 552 (10th Cir. 2013); *accord Sylvia v. Wisler,* 875 F.3d 1307, 1325 (10th Cir. 2017). KeyPoint offers only brief arguments in support of the alternative bases for affirmance. In these circumstances, the superior course of action is to remand so that district court may decide the issues in the first instance. *See United States v. McLinn,* 896 F.3d 1152, 1157 (10th Cir. 2018) (declining to rule on inadequately briefed issues "not fully addressed by the district court").

[18] *See also United States ex rel. Grant v. United Airlines Inc.,* 912 F.3d 190, 201 (4th Cir. 2018) ("[W]e and other circuits have recognized that the amended language broadens the scope of protected activity."); *Halasa v. ITT Educ. Servs., Inc.,* 690 F.3d 844, 847-48 (7th Cir. 2012) (noting the broader scope of protected activity under the amended provision).

[19] Although we decided *McBride* in 2012, the conduct at issue there occurred in January 2009—before the 2009 amendment took effect in May of that year. *See* Fraud Enforcement and Recovery Act of 2009, Pub. L. No. 111-21, § 4(f), 123 Stat. 1617 (2009) (effective date May 20, 2009). *McBride,* then, had no reason to consider or apply the amended whistleblower provision. Hence, its analysis is inapposite to post-2009 protected conduct. That said, in a 2017 unpublished opinion, a panel of our court quoted *McBride* for the proposition that "without evidence that [plaintiff]

was planning to report [defendant] to the government or file a *qui tam* suit, [plaintiff's] retaliation claim cannot survive summary judgment." *Cash v. Lockheed Martin Corp.*, 684 F. App'x 755, 764 (10th Cir. 2017) (unpublished) (quoting *McBride*, 688 F.3d at 704). That seeming declaration of post-2009-amendment law (embodied in a 2017 decision) is of course not binding on us; *Cash* is not precedential. *See* 10TH CIR. R. 32.1(A). More fundamentally, *Cash* is problematic because (1) it is contrary to the plain text of the current (i.e., post-amendment) whistleblower provisions, (2) contains no analysis of the change in statutory language, and (3) conflicts with the decisions of our sister circuits that have construed the current provisions, *see, e.g., Grant*, 912 F.3d at 201. Accordingly, we decline to follow *Cash*'s lead, and KeyPoint's reliance on *Cash* is unavailing.

[20] *See also* Aplt.'s App. at 28-29, ¶¶ 29, 33 (noting that KeyPoint put Ms. "Reed in charge of the [TTP]," and through these duties, she "uncovered systemic violations" of the OPM contract); *id.* at 31, ¶¶ 52, 55 (noting that Ms. "Reed developed and ran" the TTP, and in that role, she "discovered that KeyPoint management repeatedly falsified corrective action reports by fabricating justifications for the violations"); *id.* at 33, ¶ 78 (explaining that Ms. Reed's job "allowed her to review investigators' work" and "compile[ ] extensive records of [improper] investigations"); *id.* at 61, ¶ 165 (alleging that when extra compliance work was needed, KeyPoint "occasionally tasked [Ms. Reed] with extra audits of investigators"); *id.* at 84, ¶ 228 ("Reed was assigned to determine the nature of the chronic infractions."); *id.* at 86, ¶¶ 231-232 (pointing out that "[i]n the course of her duties, Reed discovered that certain investigators were" circumventing OPM requirements); *id.* at 90, ¶ 260 ("Reed was tasked with investigating ... each investigator's high frequency of telephone testimonies.").

[21] Putting aside Ms. Reed's failure to demonstrate KeyPoint's notice through a chain-of-command theory, Ms. Reed's complaint averments do not provide sufficient facts from which we could conclude that the content of her communications with the identified KeyPoint officials would have put KeyPoint on notice that she was doing something more than her job. For example, regarding Ms. Reed's conversation with the "OPM Contract Director," we do not know which "concerns" she voiced or whether voicing those unspecified concerns was inconsistent with her job duties. Aplt.'s App. at 32, ¶ 65. It is the same story with Ms. Reed's discussions with "the Regional Managers and certain Field Managers." *Id.* And, as to the Director of Training, we are especially hard-pressed to see how Ms. Reed's communications with that official would have alerted KeyPoint to the fact that she was seeking to prevent the company from committing a violation the False Claims Act. Specifically, Ms. Reed's complaint speaks of the problems that the Director of Training brought to Ms. Reed's attention—not the other way around. *See id.* at 32, ¶¶ 60-63. That the Director of Training reported problems to Ms. Reed tells us nothing about whether KeyPoint knew of *Ms. Reed's* efforts to stop a False Claims Act violation. Therefore, her complaint averments regarding the content of her communications with the identified KeyPoint officials do not aid her argument that KeyPoint was on notice of her protected activity. Moreover, lest there be any doubt, Ms. Reed's averments also cannot support a reasonable inference that her reports of fraud to her direct supervisor were outside her ordinary job duties. In fact, the complaint suggests otherwise. Recall that Ms. Reed often reported violations "to her

supervisor ... by submitting and discussing a monthly spreadsheet." *Id.* at 62, ¶ 171. Ms. Reed's descriptions of these meetings with her direct supervisor strongly suggest that she was just doing her "regular monthly duties." *Id.* at 38, ¶ 127.

[22] We also GRANT KeyPoint's unopposed motion to seal Volumes II through VI of its unredacted supplemental appendix. KeyPoint filed two versions of its seven-volume supplemental appendix, one redacted and one unredacted. KeyPoint moves to seal Volumes II through VI of the unredacted materials, which include OPM's contract with KeyPoint and OPM's Investigator's Handbook. The public has a "right of access to judicial records." *Eugene S. v. Horizon Blue Cross Blue Shield of N.J.,* 663 F.3d 1124, 1135 (10th Cir. 2011); 10TH CIR. R. 30.1(D). To seal court records and thus impair that right, a party "must articulate a real and substantial interest that justifies depriving the public of access to the records that inform our decision-making process." *Helm v. Kansas,* 656 F.3d 1277, 1292 (10th Cir. 2011). Three considerations lead us to conclude that sealing is appropriate here. First, KeyPoint has articulated a strong national-security interest in sealing. The OPM contract and handbook contain sensitive materials regarding the techniques used in performing background checks; revealing this information could compromise future background investigations. Second, KeyPoint has preserved the public's right to view judicial records by publicly filing a redacted version of the appendices proffered under seal. This publicly available—albeit redacted—version of the appendices leaves the content of the appendices visible in significant measure. Finally, sealing is appropriate because the documents at issue "play[ed] no role in our resolution of this appeal." *Lenox MacLaren Surgical Corp. v. Medtronic, Inc.,* 847 F.3d 1221, 1246 n.14 (10th Cir. 2017). Although KeyPoint's Response Brief references the unredacted materials, we did not rely on the underlying unredacted documents in deciding this appeal.

895 F.3d 730 (2018)

UNITED STATES of America EX REL. Gerald POLUKOFF, Plaintiff-Appellant,
v.
ST. MARK'S HOSPITAL; Intermountain Healthcare, Inc.; Sherman Sorensen, M.D.; Sorensen Cardiovascular Group; Intermountain Medical Center, Defendants-Appellees, and
HCA, Inc., a/k/a HCA, Defendant.
United States of America, Amicus Curiae and Intervenor.

No. 17-4014.

United States Court of Appeals, Tenth Circuit.

FILED July 9, 2018.

Appeal from the United States District Court for the District of Utah; (D.C. No. 2:16-CV-00304-JNP-EJF).

Tejinder Singh, Goldstein & Russell, P.C., Bethesda, Maryland (Thomas C. Goldstein, Goldstein & Russell, P.C., Bethesda, Maryland; Rand P. Nolen, George M. Fleming, Sylvia Davidow, Gregory D. Brown, David Hobbs, and Jessica A. Kasischke, Fleming, Nolen & Jez, LLP, Houston, Texas, with him on the briefs), appearing for Appellant.

J. Scott Ballenger, Latham & Watkins LLP, Washington DC (Alexandra P. Shechtel, Latham & Watkins LLP, Washington DC; Katherine A. Lauer, Latham & Watkins LLP, San Diego, California; Andrew A. Warth, W. David Bridgers, and Wells Trompeter, Waller Lansden Dortch & Davis LLP, Nashville, Tennessee, with him on the brief), appearing for Appellee St. Mark's Hospital.

Matthew L. Knowles, McDermott Will & Emery LLP, Boston, Massachusetts (M. Miller Baker, McDermott Will & Emery LLP, Washington, DC; Shamis Beckley and Alexander J. Kritikos, McDermott Will & Emery LLP, Boston, Massachusetts; Alan C. Bradshaw, Sammi V. Anderson, and Christopher M. Glauser, Manning Curtis Bradshaw & Bednar, PLLC, Salt Lake City, Utah; Daniel S. Reinberg and Asher D. Funk, Polsinelli PC, Chicago, Illinois, with him on the brief), appearing for Appellee Intermountain Healthcare, Inc. and Intermountain Medical Center.

Blaine J. Benard, Holland & Hart LLP, Salt Lake City, Utah, and Gregory Goldberg, Holland & Hart LLP, Denver, Colorado, on the brief for Appellees Sherman Sorensen M.D., and Sorensen Cardiology Group.

Sarah Carroll, Attorney, Appellate Staff, Civil Division, United States Department of Justice, Washington, DC (Chad A. Readler, Acting Assistant Attorney General, United States Department of Justice, Washington, DC; John W. Huber, United States Attorney for the District of Utah, Salt Lake City, Utah; Douglas N. Letter and Michael S. Raab, Attorneys, Appellate p.734 Staff, Civil Division, United States Department of Justice, Washington, DC), appearing for Intervenor and Amicus Curiae United States of America.

Before TYMKOVICH, Chief Judge, BRISCOE and HARTZ, Circuit Judges.

p.733 BRISCOE, Circuit Judge.

This is a *qui tam* action alleging violations of the False Claims Act ("FCA"), 31 U.S.C. §§ 3729-33, involving fraudulent reimbursements under the Medicare Act, 42 U.S.C. §§ 1395-1395ccc. Plaintiff Gerald Polukoff, M.D., is a doctor who worked with Defendant Sherman Sorensen, M.D. After observing some of Dr. Sorensen's medical practices, Dr. Polukoff brought this FCA action, on behalf of the United States, against Dr. Sorensen and the two hospitals where Dr. Sorensen worked (collectively, "Defendants"). Dr. Polukoff alleges Dr. Sorensen performed thousands of unnecessary heart surgeries and received reimbursement through the Medicare Act by fraudulently certifying that the surgeries were medically necessary. Dr. Polukoff further alleges the hospitals where Dr. Sorensen worked were complicit in and profited from Dr. Sorensen's fraud. The district court granted Defendants' motions to dismiss, reasoning that a medical judgment cannot be false under the FCA. Exercising jurisdiction pursuant to 28 U.S.C. § 1291, we REVERSE and REMAND for further proceedings.

I

A. Statutory Background

"The FCA 'covers all fraudulent attempts to cause the government to pay out sums of money.'" *United States ex rel. Conner v. Salina Regional Health Ctr., Inc.,* 543 F.3d 1211, 1217 (10th Cir. 2008) (quoting *United States ex rel. Boothe v. Sun Healthcare Grp., Inc.,* 496 F.3d 1169, 1172 (10th Cir. 2007)). Specifically, any person who:

(A) knowingly presents, or causes to be presented, a false or fraudulent claim for payment or approval;

(B) knowingly makes, uses, or causes to be made or used, a false record or statement material to a false or fraudulent claim;

(C) conspires to commit a violation of subparagraph (A), (B), (D), (E), (F), or (G); [or]

. . .

(G) knowingly makes, uses, or causes to be made or used, a false record or statement material to an obligation to pay or transmit money or property to the Government, or knowingly conceals or knowingly and improperly avoids or decreases an obligation to pay or transmit money or property to the Government, is liable to the United States Government for a civil penalty [and treble damages].

31 U.S.C. § 3729(a)(1). The FCA defines the "knowingly" scienter requirement as follows:

(A) mean[s] that a person, with respect to information —

(i) has actual knowledge of the information;

(ii) acts in deliberate ignorance of the truth or falsity of the information; or

(iii) acts in reckless disregard of the truth or falsity of the information; and

(B) require[s] no proof of specific intent to defraud....

Id. § 3729(b)(1).

There are two options to remedy a violation of the FCA. "First, the Government itself may bring a civil action against the alleged false claimant." *Vt. Agency of Nat. Res. v. United States ex rel. Stevens,* 529 U.S. 765, 769, 120 S.Ct. 1858, 146 L.Ed.2d p.735 836 (2000). "Second, as is relevant here, a private person (the relator) may bring a *qui tam* civil action 'for the person and for the United States Government' against the alleged false claimant, 'in the name of the Government.'" *Id.* (quoting 31 U.S.C. § 3730(b)(1)). If a relator files a *qui tam* civil action, the government may intervene and take over the case. 31 U.S.C. § 3730(b)(2). "If the government elects not to proceed with the action," the relator "shall have the right to conduct the action." *Id.* § 3730(c)(3). Depending on the specific circumstances of the *qui tam* suit, the government and the relator divide any proceeds derived from the suit. *Id.* § 3730(d).

The FCA is applicable to many statutes that provide for federal reimbursement of expenses. One such statute is the Medicare Act,[1] which imposes requirements for reimbursement of medical expenses. As relevant here, the Medicare Act states that "no payment may be made ... for any expenses incurred for items or services" that "are not *reasonable and necessary* for the diagnosis or treatment of illness or injury or to improve the functioning of a malformed body member." 42 U.S.C. § 1395y(a)(1)(A) (emphasis added). Physicians and medical providers who seek reimbursement under the Medicare Act must "certify the *necessity* of the services and, in some instances, recertify the continued need for those services." 42 C.F.R. 424.10(a) (Oct. 1, 2013) (emphasis added); *see also* 42 U.S.C. §§ 1395f(a), 1395n(a) (listing the various certifications).

The Secretary of Health and Human Services decides "whether a particular medical service is 'reasonable and necessary'... by promulgating a generally applicable rule *or* by allowing individual adjudication." *Heckler v. Ringer,* 466 U.S. 602, 617, 104 S.Ct. 2013, 80 L.Ed.2d 622 (1984) (emphasis added). The *former* course involves a "national coverage determination" that announces "whether or not a particular item or service is covered nationally." 42 U.S.C. § 1395ff(f)(1)(B). In the absence of a national coverage determination, local Medicare contractors may issue a "local coverage determination" that announces "whether or not a particular item or service is covered" by that contractor. *Id.* § 1395ff(f)(2)(B).

The *latter* course allows "contractors [to] make individual claim determinations, even in the absence of [a national or local coverage determination], ... based on the individual's particular factual situation." 68 Fed. Reg. 63,692, 63,693 (Nov. 7, 2003). In making an individual claim determination about whether to reimburse a medical provider, "[c]ontractors shall consider a service to be reasonable and necessary if the contractor determines that the service is: [(1)] Safe and effective; [(2)] Not experimental or investigational ...; and [(3)] Appropriate." Centers for Medicare & Medicaid Services ("CMS"),[2] *Medicare* p.736 *Program Integrity Manual* § 13.5.1 (2015) (describing local coverage determinations); *see also id.* § 13.3 (incorporating § 13.5.1's standards for individual claim determinations). One factor that contractors consider when deciding whether a service is "appropriate" is whether it is "[f]urnished in accordance with accepted standards of medical practice for the diagnosis or treatment of the patient's condition or to improve the function of a malformed body member." *Id.* § 13.5.1.

B. Factual Background

"At the motion-to-dismiss stage, we must accept all the well-pleaded allegations of the complaint as true and must construe them in the light most favorable to the plaintiff." *Albers v. Bd. of Cty. Comm'rs of Jefferson Cty.,* 771 F.3d 697, 700 (10th Cir. 2014) (quotation omitted). As a result, we rely on Dr. Polukoff's amended complaint.[3]

1. The PFO closure procedure

This case involves two very similar cardiac conditions: patent foramen ovale ("PFO") and atrial septal defect ("ASD"). Both PFOs and ASDs involve a hole between the upper two chambers of the heart, but they have different causes. Most people are born with a PFO, as it helps blood circulate throughout the heart while in the womb, but for 75% of the population, the hole closes soon after birth. ASDs, on the other hand, are an abnormality. Regardless, both PFOs and ASDs allow blood to flow in the wrong direction within the upper chambers of the heart. In rare cases, they can lead to a variety of dangerous complications, including stroke. Physicians can "close" ASDs and PFOs through ASD and PFO closures (collectively, "PFO closures"), a percutaneous surgical procedure involving cardiac catheterization. In layman's terms, physicians insert a thin tube into a blood vessel to access the heart, rather than performing open heart surgery.

The amended complaint makes specific reference to industry guidelines published by the American Heart Association and American Stroke Association (the "AHA/ASA Guidelines") in 2006 and 2011, related to PFO closures.[4] The 2006 AHA/ASA Guidelines observed that "[s]tudies have found an association between PFO and cryptogenic stroke."[5] App'x at 2077. They noted "conflicting reports concerning the safety and efficacy of surgical PFO closure" to treat cryptogenic stroke, but after reviewing several studies, also noted that each reported "no major complications." *Id.* The 2006 AHA/ASA Guidelines concluded: "Insufficient data exist to make a recommendation about PFO closures in patients with a first stroke and a PFO. PFO closure may be considered for patients with recurrent cryptogenic stroke despite optimal medical therapy...." *Id.* at 2079. In other words, the 2006 AHA/ASA Guidelines advised that (1) for patients with two or more cryptogenic strokes, PFO closures may be considered; (2) for patients with only one cryptogenic stroke, there was insufficient data to make a recommendation; and (3) for patients without a single cryptogenic stroke, the p.737 AHA/ASA Guidelines did not contemplate the potential for PFO closures.

The 2011 AHA/ASA Guidelines are similarly inconclusive. In a table titled "Recommendations for Stroke Patients With Other Specific Conditions," the guidelines stated: "There are insufficient data to make a recommendation regarding PFO closure in patients with stroke and PFO...." *Id.* at 2125. The 2011 AHA/ASA Guidelines did, however, observe that recent "studies provide[d] new information on options for closure of PFO and generally indicate[d] that short-term complications with these procedures are rare and for the most part minor." *Id.* at 2126.

Relying on the AHA/ASA Guidelines, the amended complaint alleges "[t]here has long been general agreement in the medical community that PFO closure is not medically necessary, except in the limited circumstances where there is a confirmed diagnosis of a recurrent cryptogenic stroke or TIA,[[6]] despite optimum medical management." *Id.* at 524.

2. The Defendants' conduct

Dr. Sorensen practiced medicine as a cardiologist in Salt Lake City, Utah. He was the principal shareholder of Sorensen Cardiovascular Group ("SCG"). Dr. Sorensen, through SCG, provided cardiology services at two hospitals: (1) Intermountain Medical Center and (2) St. Mark's Hospital ("St. Mark's"). Intermountain Medical Center is part of a large network of hospitals in Utah principally owned by Intermountain Healthcare, Inc., a not-for-profit corporation (collectively, with Intermountain Medical Center, "Intermountain"). St. Mark's, on the other hand, is a for-profit corporation owned by HCA, Inc. Dr. Polukoff is a practicing cardiologist who worked with Dr. Sorensen at both St. Mark's and Intermountain.

Dr. Sorensen started providing cardiology services at Intermountain in December 2002. Later, in 2008, he began working at St. Mark's as well. Part of his practice included performing a relatively high number of PFO closures. For example, "[t]he Cleveland Clinic reported that it had performed 37 PFO closures in 2010; during that same time period [Dr.] Sorensen's billing records indicate that he had performed 861." *Id.* at 542. The amended complaint alleges that Dr. Sorensen performed so many PFO closures because of "his medically unsupported belief that PFO closures would cure migraine headaches or prevent strokes." *Id.* In addition, "Dr. Sorensen knew that Medicare and Medicaid would not pay for PFO closures to treat migraines, so he chose to represent that the procedures had been performed based upon indications set forth in the AH[A]/ASA stroke guidelines — the existence of confirmed recurrent cryptogenic stroke." *Id.*

The amended complaint describes Dr. Sorensen's medical notes and reasons for the large number of PFO closures:

> Dr. Sorensen's notes in his patients' medical records indicate that [Dr.] Sorensen fully understands, but rejects, the standard of care for PFO/ASD closures set forth in the [AHA/ASA] Guidelines described above. For example, Dr. Sorensen notes that closures are considered medically necessary only for recurrent cryptogenic strokes or TIA, secondary to paradoxical embolization despite medical therapy, but argues that while "[w]e do have experience with the two strokes first and then closure approach, we p.738 found this very unsatisfactory as a very high number of patients were disabled and disability is not reversed by closure." Dr. Sorensen notes that "[w]e therefore follow a preventative strategy and risk stratify the patient...." Dr. Sorensen notes that he considers waiting for a stroke or TIA to reoccur before proceeding to closure is "unethical."

Id. at 607.

In early 2011, several doctors at Intermountain objected to Dr. Sorensen's approach to PFO closures, claiming Dr. Sorensen was violating Intermountain's internal guidelines for PFO closures. In March 2011, in response to the objections, Intermountain adopted new internal guidelines for PFO closures that mirrored the AHA/ASA Guidelines. In May 2011, Intermountain conducted an investigation into Dr. Sorensen's practice and internally released an audit of the 47 PFO closures Dr. Sorensen performed in April 2011. The audit concluded that "the guidelines had been violated in many of the 47 cases reviewed." *Id.* at 535.

On June 27, 2011, following the internal investigation, Intermountain suspended Dr. Sorensen's cardiac privileges. The suspension was effective until July 11, 2011. On July 12, 2011, Dr. Sorensen returned to Intermountain, but continued to violate the hospital's internal guidelines for PFO closures. Intermountain discovered the continued violations, and subsequently entered into a settlement agreement with Dr. Sorensen to avoid his permanent suspension. Intermountain later found that Dr. Sorensen had violated the terms of the settlement agreement and moved to permanently suspend Dr. Sorensen, but Dr. Sorensen tendered his resignation in September 2011.

After Dr. Sorensen left Intermountain, he moved his entire practice to St. Mark's. St. Mark's knew of Dr. Sorensen's suspension from Intermountain, but courted his moving his practice anyway. St. Mark's allowed Dr. Sorensen to continue his cardiology practice until he retired from medical practice altogether a few months later, on December 9, 2011.

Dr. Polukoff — the relator in this case — worked at both Intermountain and St. Mark's, but not directly for Dr. Sorensen until 2011. On June 11, 2011, Dr. Polukoff signed an employment agreement with SCG to learn PFO closures from Dr. Sorensen, and on August 17, 2011, actually began working for Dr. Sorensen at St. Mark's. While working for Dr. Sorensen, Dr. Polukoff "personally observed [Dr.] Sorensen perform medically unnecessary PFO closures on patients at St. Mark's." *Id.* at 536. He alleges to have "observed [Dr.] Sorensen *create* a PFO by puncture of the atrial septum in patients who were found to have an intact septum during surgery." *Id.*

The amended complaint further alleges that St. Mark's and Intermountain "signed or caused to be executed provider agreements with Medicare that permitted each Defendant to submit claims and accept payment for services." *Id.* at 518. Both hospitals "allowed and encouraged Dr. Sorensen to perform and submit claims to federal health benefit programs for PFO and ASD procedures despite clear compliance red flags, including, but not limited to, the fact that Dr. Sorensen was performing these procedures at a rate that far exceeded that of any other institution or physician." *Id.* at 507.

C. Procedural Background

On December 6, 2012, Dr. Polukoff filed this *qui tam* action under seal in the United States District Court for the Middle District of Tennessee against: (1) Dr. Sorensen; (2) Sorensen Cardiovascular Group; (3) Intermountain Healthcare, Inc.; (4) St. p.739 Mark's Hospital; and (5) HCA, Inc. On June 15, 2015, the government filed its notice of election to decline intervention. On June 19, 2015, the district court unsealed the *qui tam* complaint. All Defendants moved to dismiss the action.

Dr. Polukoff then filed an amended complaint against all Defendants previously named, and added Intermountain Medical Center. The amended complaint alleged four separate violations of the FCA, corresponding to four separate subsections of the FCA. *Id.* at 611-14 (citing 31 U.S.C. § 3729(a)(1)(A)-(C), (G)). All Defendants moved to dismiss the amended complaint. The district court dismissed the claims against HCA, and concluded that, without HCA, venue in the United States District Court for the Middle District of Tennessee was no longer proper. Consequently, the district court transferred the case to the United States District Court for the District of Utah, without ruling on the motions to dismiss as to the remaining Defendants — Dr. Sorensen (both as an individual and the Sorensen Cardiovascular Group); Intermountain (both the individual hospital and the nonprofit that owned it); and St. Mark's.

The remaining Defendants filed renewed motions to dismiss. Oral arguments were scheduled for November 10, 2016. The day before oral arguments, Dr. Polukoff filed a motion for leave to file an amended complaint. The district court heard oral arguments as scheduled. Before the district court ruled on the motions to dismiss, Dr. Polukoff filed an amended motion for leave to file a second amended complaint on January 18, 2017. The next day, the district court granted Defendants' motions to dismiss, with prejudice, and denied Dr. Polukoff's motion for leave to amend.

As relevant to this appeal, the district court first addressed Defendants' Rule 9(b) argument that Dr. Polukoff had failed to plead with particularity. The district court determined that the proper standard was "whether Dr. Polukoff has pled the who, what, when, where and how of a fraudulent scheme perpetrated by each of the defendants." *Id.* at 2519. "In addition, the court must decide whether the operative complaint provides 'an adequate basis for a reasonable inference that false claims were submitted as part of that scheme.'" *Id.* (quoting *United States ex rel. Lemmon v. Envirocare of Utah, Inc.,* 614 F.3d 1163, 1172 (10th Cir. 2010)). The court concluded that Dr. Polukoff had adequately pled his claims against Dr. Sorensen and St. Mark's but not against Intermountain because he failed to identify a "managing agent" involved in the conspiracy at Intermountain. *Id.* at 2519-22.

The court then turned to Defendants' Rule 12(b)(6) argument. Relying on language from this court's unpublished decision in *United States ex rel. Morton v. A Plus Benefits, Inc.,* 139 F. App'x 980 (10th Cir. 2005), the district court concluded that "Dr. Polukoff must show that the defendants knowingly made an objectively false representation to the government that caused the government to remit payment." App'x at 2526. It observed that "Dr. Polukoff's FCA causes of action rest upon his contention that the defendants represented (either explicitly or implicitly) that the PFO closures performed by Dr. Sorensen were medically reasonable and necessary and that this representation was false." *Id.* at 2524. But, because "[o]pinions, medical judgments, and 'conclusions about which reasonable minds may differ cannot be false' for the purposes of an FCA claim," *id.* at 2526 (quoting *Morton,* 139 F. App'x at 983), Dr. Sorensen's representations to the government could not be false absent "a regulation that clarifies the conditions under which it will or will not pay for a PFO closure," *id.* at 2528. Thus, Dr. Polukoff's p.740 "FCA claims fail[ed] as a matter of law and the court dismisse[d] all causes of action asserted against the defendants." *Id.* at 2529. The court further determined that "leave to amend would be futile," *id.,* so it dismissed the amended complaint with prejudice.

Dr. Polukoff timely appealed. The government filed an amicus brief in his support. All three Defendants — Dr. Sorensen, St. Mark's, and Intermountain — filed response briefs. Of particular note, in Intermountain's brief, it argued that the *qui tam* provisions of the FCA violate Article II of the U.S. Constitution. The government intervened thereafter, pursuant to 28 U.S.C. § 2403(a), to respond to Intermountain's constitutional argument in an additional brief as intervenor.

II

The district court relied upon Rules 12(b)(6) and 9(b) to dismiss Dr. Polukoff's amended complaint with prejudice. We address the district court's holdings in turn.[7]

A. Rule 12(b)(6)

We first address the district court's conclusion that, absent a specific regulation addressing the necessity of the treatment, a physician's medical judgment concerning the necessity of a treatment could not be "false or fraudulent" under the FCA. As a result of this conclusion, the district court dismissed Dr. Polukoff's amended complaint under Rule 12(b)(6), believing it failed to state a claim as a matter of law, and then denied leave to amend, believing amendment would have been futile. We disagree.

"We review the district court's dismissal under Rule 12(b)(6) de novo." *Lemmon,* 614 F.3d at 1167. "Although we generally review for abuse of discretion a district court's denial of leave to amend a complaint, when this 'denial is based on a determination that amendment would be futile, our review for abuse of discretion includes de novo review of the legal basis for the finding of futility.'" *Cohen v. Longshore,* 621 F.3d 1311, 1314 (10th Cir. 2010) (quoting *Miller ex. Rel. S.M. v. Bd. of Educ. of Albuquerque Pub. Schs.,* 565 F.3d 1232, 1250 (10th Cir. 2009)).

"Enacted in 1863, the False Claims Act 'was originally aimed principally at stopping the massive frauds perpetrated by large contractors during the Civil War.'" *Universal Health Servs., Inc. v. United States ex rel. Escobar,* ___ U.S. ___, 136 S.Ct. 1989, 1996, 195 L.Ed.2d 348 (2016) (quoting *United States v. Bornstein,* 423 U.S. 303, 309, 96 S.Ct. 523, 46 L.Ed.2d 514 (1976)). "'[A] series of sensational congressional investigations' prompted hearings where witnesses 'painted a sordid picture p.741 of how the United States had been billed for nonexistent or worthless goods, charged exorbitant prices for goods delivered, and generally robbed in purchasing the necessities of war.'" *Id.* (quoting *United States v. McNinch,* 356 U.S. 595, 599, 78 S.Ct. 950, 2 L.Ed.2d 1001 (1958)).

Today, the FCA generally prohibits private parties from "knowingly" submitting "a false or fraudulent claim" for reimbursement. 31 U.S.C. § 3729(a)(1)(A). Unfortunately, "Congress did not define what makes a claim 'false' or 'fraudulent.'" *Escobar,* 136 S.Ct. at 1999. Without a definition from Congress, the Supreme Court has turned to common law. And "common-law fraud has long encompassed ... more than just claims containing express falsehoods." *Id.* Consequently, the Court favors a more expansive view of "false or fraudulent."

As we have held, "false or fraudulent" includes both factually false and legally false requests for payment. *See Lemmon,* 614 F.3d at 1168. "Factually false claims generally require a showing that the payee has submitted an incorrect description of goods or services provided or a request for reimbursement for goods or services never provided." *United States ex rel. Thomas v. Black & Veatch Special Projects Corp.*, 820 F.3d 1162, 1168 (10th Cir. 2016) (quotation omitted). "Claims arising from legally false requests, on the other hand, generally require knowingly false certification of compliance with a regulation or contractual provision as a condition of payment." *Id.* In this case, Dr. Polukoff does not allege Dr. Sorensen submitted *factually* false requests because his claims do not focus on an inaccuracy of the PFO closures performed. Instead, he claims the PFO closures do not comply with Medicare's "reasonable and necessary" requirement, meaning Dr. Sorensen submitted *legally* false requests for payment.

"Such claims of legal falsity can rest on one of two theories — express false certification, and implied false certification." *Id.* at 1169 (quotation and brackets omitted). "An express false certification theory applies when a government payee falsely certifies compliance with a particular statute, regulation or contractual term, where compliance is a prerequisite to payment." *Conner,* 543 F.3d at 1217 (quotation omitted). "By contrast, the pertinent inquiry for implied-false-certification claims is not whether a payee made an affirmative or express false statement, but whether, through the act of submitting a claim, a payee knowingly and falsely implied that it was entitled to payment." *Thomas,* 820 F.3d at 1169 (quotation and brackets omitted).

As relevant here, Dr. Polukoff brings express-false-certification claims against Dr. Sorensen. The amended complaint alleges Dr. Sorensen submitted express false certifications when he signed and submitted CMS Form 1500, which states: "I certify that the services shown on this form were medically indicated and necessary for the health of the patient...." App'x at 518.

The district court concluded that Dr. Polukoff's express-false-certification claims were not legally cognizable under the FCA. First, it held that "medical judgments and 'conclusions about which reasonable minds may differ cannot be false' for the purposes of an FCA claim." App'x at 2526 (quoting *Morton,* 139 F. App'x at 983). Second, the district court determined that a physician's certification that a PFO closure was "reasonable and necessary" could not be false under the FCA — given that it would constitute a medical judgment — absent "a regulation that clarifies the conditions under which [the government] p.742 will or will not pay for a PFO closure." *Id.* at 2528.

Morton is narrower than the district court suggests. First, *Morton* involved the application of the FCA to ERISA, not Medicare. Second, we explicitly cabined *Morton* to the facts in that case:

> We agree that liability under the FCA must be predicated on an objectively verifiable fact. Nonetheless, we are not prepared to conclude that in all instances, merely because the verification of a fact relies upon clinical medical judgments, or involves a decision of coverage under an ERISA plan, the fact cannot form the basis of an FCA claim. In this case, the nature of neither the scientific nor contract determinations inherent in the formation and evaluation of the allegedly "false" statement is susceptible to proof of truth or falsity.

139 F. App'x at 983. We did not create a bright-line rule that a medical judgment can never serve as the basis for an FCA claim.

It is possible for a medical judgment to be "false or fraudulent" as proscribed by the FCA for at least three reasons. First, we read the FCA broadly. *See United States v. Neifert-White Co.,* 390 U.S. 228, 232, 88 S.Ct. 959, 19 L.Ed.2d 1061 (1968) (observing that the FCA "was intended to reach all types of fraud, without qualification, that might result in financial loss to the Government," and "refus[ing] to accept a rigid, restrictive reading"). Second, "the fact that an allegedly false statement constitutes the speaker's opinion does not disqualify it from forming the basis of FCA liability." *United States ex rel. Loughren v. Unum Grp.,* 613 F.3d 300, 310 (1st Cir. 2010) (holding, in the Social Security benefits context, that "an applicant's opinion regarding the date on which he became unable to work" can give rise to FCA liability); *cf. Omnicare, Inc. v. Laborers Dist. Council Constr. Indus. Pension Fund,* ___ U.S. ___, 135 S.Ct. 1318, 1326, 191 L.Ed.2d 253 (2015) (suggesting, in the securities context, that a "false-statement provision ... appl[ies] to expressions of opinion"). Third, "claims for medically unnecessary treatment are actionable under the FCA." *United States ex rel. Riley v. St. Luke's Episcopal Hosp.,* 355 F.3d 370, 376 (5th Cir. 2004) (holding relator's complaint "sufficiently allege[d] that statements were known to be false, rather than just erroneous, because she assert[ed] that Defendants ordered the services knowing they were unnecessary"); *cf. Frazier ex rel. United States v. Iasis Healthcare Corp.,* 392 F. App'x 535, 537 (9th Cir. 2010) (affirming FCA claim was inadequately pled, but suggesting an FCA claim could survive if the relator "provide[s] 'reliable indicia' that [the defendant] submitted claims for medically unnecessary procedures").

As the government states in its amicus brief, "A Medicare claim is false if it is not reimbursable, and a Medicare claim is not reimbursable if the services provided were not medically necessary." Amicus Br. at 14. For a claim to be reimbursable, it must meet the government's definition of "reasonable and necessary," as found in the Medicare Program Integrity Manual. The manual instructs contractors to "consider a service to be reasonable and necessary" if the procedure is:

- Safe and effective;
- Not experimental or investigational...; and
- Appropriate, including the duration and frequency that is considered appropriate for the item or service, in terms of whether it is:

  ○ Furnished in accordance with accepted standards of medical practice for the diagnosis or treatment of the p.743 patient's condition or to improve the function of a malformed body member;

  ○ Furnished in a setting appropriate to the patient's medical needs and condition;

  ○ Ordered and furnished by qualified personnel;

  ○ One that meets, but does not exceed, the patient's medical need; and

  ○ At least as beneficial as an existing and available medically appropriate alternative.

CMS, *Medicare Program Integrity Manual* § 13.5.1; *see also id.* § 13.3 (incorporating § 13.5.1's definition of reasonable and necessary for individual claim determinations).

We thus hold that a doctor's certification to the government that a procedure is "reasonable and necessary" is "false" under the FCA if the procedure was not reasonable and necessary under the government's definition of the phrase. We understand the concerns that a broad definition of "false or fraudulent" might expose doctors to more liability under the FCA, but the Supreme Court has already addressed those concerns: "Instead of adopting a circumscribed view of what it means for a claim to be false or fraudulent, concerns about fair notice and open-ended liability can be effectively addressed through strict enforcement of the [FCA]'s materiality and scienter requirements. Those requirements are rigorous." *Escobar*, 136 S.Ct. at 2002 (quotation marks and some brackets omitted).

In this case, Dr. Polukoff adequately alleges that Dr. Sorensen performed unnecessary PFO closures on patients and then knowingly submitted false certifications to the federal government that the procedures were necessary, all in an effort to obtain federal reimbursement. Specifically, Dr. Polukoff alleges: (1) Dr. Sorensen performed an unusually large number of PFO closures, App'x at 542 ("The Cleveland Clinic reported that it had performed 37 PFO closures in 2010; during that same time period [Dr.] Sorensen's billing records indicate that he had performed 861."); (2) these procedures violated both industry guidelines and hospital guidelines, *id.* at 524-26, 535; (3) other physicians objected to Dr. Sorensen's practice, *id.* at 535; (4) Intermountain eventually audited Dr. Sorensen's practice, and concluded that its "guidelines had been violated in many of the 47 cases reviewed," *id.*; and (5) "Dr. Sorensen knew that Medicare and Medicaid would not pay for PFO closures to treat migraines, so he chose to represent that the procedures had been performed based upon indications set forth in the AH[A]/ASA stroke guidelines — the existence of confirmed recurrent cryptogenic stroke," *id.* at 542. Under these specific factual allegations, Dr. Polukoff has pleaded enough to state a claim as a matter of law and survive Rule 12(b)(6) dismissal against Dr. Sorensen.

We further hold the amended complaint adequately states express-false-certification claims against St. Mark's and Intermountain, both of which allegedly "billed for the hospital charges associated with" PFO closures. *Id.* at 542-43. More specifically, the amended complaint alleges St. Mark's and Intermountain both requested reimbursements for these procedures by submitting annual Hospital Cost Reports. The reports require hospitals to certify: "I further certify that I am familiar with the laws and regulations regarding the provision of health care services, and that the services identified in this cost report were provided in compliance with such laws and regulations." *Id.* at 516. By submitting a Hospital Cost Report, then, St. Mark's and Intermountain p.744 expressly certified that every procedure for which they sought reimbursement complied with Medicare's requirements. Because the complaint adequately alleges that Dr. Sorensen's surgeries and any procedure associated therewith was not, in fact, "reasonable and necessary," the complaint adequately alleges that St. Mark's and Intermountain submitted false claims for reimbursement to the government through their Hospital Cost Reports.

Moreover, Dr. Polukoff adequately alleges St. Mark's and Intermountain submitted these false certifications "knowingly." As to St. Mark's, Dr. Polukoff alleges that he personally told the CEO about the circumstances surrounding Dr. Sorensen's suspension from Intermountain for performing unnecessary PFO closures. Nonetheless, according to Dr. Polukoff, St. Mark's continued to recruit Dr. Sorensen's business:

> Contemporaneously with his suspension from Intermountain, St. Mark's executive management knew that [Dr.] Sorensen had been suspended for performing medically unnecessary PFO closures. Dr. Polukoff personally discussed the suspension with the CEO of St. Mark's Hospital, Steve Bateman, and his physician liaison, Nikki Gledhill. Despite the fact that St. Mark's knew that [Dr.] Sorensen was performing medically unnecessary PFO closures, and knew that [Dr.] Sorensen had been suspended from Intermountain for performing medically unnecessary PFO closures, St. Mark's Hospital continued to court [Dr.] Sorensen's septal closure business and provide a platform and assistance to [Dr.] Sorensen.

Id. at 540-41.

As to Intermountain, Dr. Polukoff alleges that, "at all times relevant to this case, Intermountain knew that septal closures were rarely indicated." *Id.* at 535. This is because, "[f]or years Intermountain ignored the loud objections from its own medical staff and leadership, including the Director of the Catheterization Laboratory, Dr. Revenaugh, and the Medical Director for Cardiovascular Services at Intermountain Healthcare, Dr. Lappe, as well as written warnings and complaints from Professor Andrew Michaels of the University of Utah." *Id.* Because Dr. Sorensen performed an excessively large number of profitable PFO closures for Intermountain, Dr. "Sorensen was given his own catheterization lab room at Intermountain and provided with a handpicked staff of Intermountain employees." *Id.* at 610. "No other cardiologist received this type of special treatment from Intermountain." *Id.*

The FCA requires a defendant submit a false claim "knowingly," which includes the submission of claims by an entity who "acts in deliberate ignorance of the truth or falsity of the information" or "acts in reckless disregard of the truth or falsity of the information." 31 U.S.C. § 3729(b)(1)(A). At a minimum, the amended complaint adequately alleges that St. Mark's and Intermountain acted with reckless disregard as to whether the PFO closures Dr. Sorensen was performing were medically necessary.

B. Rule 9(b)

All Defendants also challenged the amended complaint under Rule 9(b), arguing that Dr. Polukoff had failed to plead his claims with sufficient particularity. The district court denied the motions as to Dr. Sorensen and St. Mark's, but granted the motion as to Intermountain. Dr. Polukoff appeals, arguing his amended complaint pleaded allegations against Intermountain with sufficient particularity to survive a motion to dismiss under Rule 9(b). We agree with Dr. Polukoff.

Rule 9(b) states: "In alleging fraud or mistake, a party must state with particularity the circumstances constituting fraud or mistake. Malice, intent, knowledge, and other conditions of a person's mind may be alleged generally." Fed. R. Civ. P. 9(b). "Concerning the failure to plead fraud with particularity under Rule 9(b), we ... review a dismissal de novo." *Lemmon*, 614 F.3d at 1167.

The purpose of Rule 9(b) is "to afford defendant[s] fair notice of plaintiff's claims and the factual ground upon which [they] are based." *Id.* at 1172 (quotations omitted). "Thus, claims under the FCA need only show the specifics of a fraudulent scheme and provide an adequate basis for a reasonable inference that false claims were submitted as part of that scheme." *Id.* Practically speaking, FCA claims comply with Rule 9(b) when they "provid[e] factual allegations regarding the who, what, when, where and how of the alleged claims." *Id.* But, "in determining whether a plaintiff has satisfied Rule 9(b), courts may consider whether any pleading deficiencies resulted from the plaintiff's inability to obtain information in the defendant's exclusive control." *George v. Urban Settlement Servs.,* 833 F.3d 1242, 1255 (10th Cir. 2016). This reflects the principle that "Rule 9(b) does not require omniscience; rather the Rule requires that the circumstances of the fraud be pled with enough specificity to put defendants on notice as to the nature of the claim." *Williams v. Duke Energy Int'l, Inc.,* 681 F.3d 788, 803 (6th Cir. 2012) (quotation omitted).

The district court dismissed Dr. Polukoff's allegations against Intermountain under Rule 9(b) because "vital information regarding who knew what and when they knew it [was] missing." App'x at 2521-22. But, for many of the same reasons the amended complaint survived Rule 12(b)(6) against all Defendants, it survives Rule 9(b) as well. Rule 9(b) itself states: "Malice, intent, *knowledge,* and other conditions of a person's mind may be alleged *generally.*" Fed. R. Civ. P. 9(b) (emphases added). Moreover, we excuse deficiencies that result from the plaintiff's inability to obtain information within the defendant's exclusive control. *See George,* 833 F.3d at 1255. Intermountain,[8] no doubt, knows which employees handle federal billing for procedures reimbursable under Medicare, and in particular, who reviewed reimbursement claims for Dr. Sorensen during his decade there.[9]

III

Because Dr. Polukoff's amended complaint satisfies the pleading requirements p.746 of Rules 12(b)(6) and 9(b), we REVERSE and REMAND this case for further proceedings.

[1] The amended complaint also references the "TRICARE/CHAMPUS Program." App'x at 521-22. This healthcare program benefits retired military personnel and dependents of both active and retired military personnel. *Id.* at 521; *see also Baptist Physician Hosp. Org., Inc. v. Humana Military Healthcare Servs., Inc.,* 368 F.3d 894, 895 (6th Cir. 2004). The amended complaint alleges that Defendants "submitted Requests for Reimbursement to TRICARE/CHAMPUS that were based on their submissions to Medicare." App'x at 522. We do not distinguish this program from Medicare and Medicaid in our analysis because Defendants failed to argue for any relevant distinction.

[2] CMS is an agency within Health and Human Services, *see Protocols, LLC v. Leavitt,* 549 F.3d 1294, 1295 (10th Cir. 2008), and this agency administers the Medicare Act, *see United States ex rel. Sikkenga v. Regence Bluecross Blueshield of Utah,* 472 F.3d 702, 705 & n.1 (10th Cir. 2006).

[3] Although Dr. Polukoff filed a motion (and later, an amended motion) for leave to file a second amended complaint, the district court denied the amended motion. Thus, Dr. Polukoff's amended complaint is the operative complaint.

[4] The amended complaint also references the 2014 AHA/ASA Guidelines. Those guidelines, however, were published after all relevant conduct occurred in this case, and thus are irrelevant.

[5] A "cryptogenic stroke" describes a stroke for which the cause is unknown.

[6] A "TIA" is a "transient ischemic attack," which is a brief interruption of blood flow to the brain that causes stroke-like symptoms.

[7] Intermountain argues, for the first time on appeal, that "at least where the Government has not intervened, a private relator's prosecution of an FCA case on behalf of the Government violates the separation of powers." Intermountain Br. at 54. Intermountain concedes it "did not assert a constitutional challenge below." *Id.* at 54 n.11. We consider this argument forfeited. "It is the general rule, of course, that a federal appellate court does not consider an issue not passed upon below." *Singleton v. Wulff,* 428 U.S. 106, 120, 96 S.Ct. 2868, 49 L.Ed.2d 826 (1976). "[W]here the ground presented here has not been raised below we exercise this authority [to consider the newly raised argument] 'only in exceptional cases.'" *Heckler v. Campbell,* 461 U.S. 458, 468 n.12, 103 S.Ct. 1952, 76 L.Ed.2d 66 (1983) (quoting *McGoldrick v. Compagnie Generale Transatlantique,* 309 U.S. 430, 434, 60 S.Ct. 670, 84 L.Ed. 849 (1940)). "[T]he decision regarding what issues are appropriate to entertain on appeal in instances of lack of preservation is discretionary." *Abernathy v. Wandes,* 713 F.3d 538, 552 (10th Cir. 2013). We decline to address Intermountain's separation of powers argument.

[8] This applies with equal force to St. Mark's. But, because the district court determined that Dr. Polukoff satisfied Rule 9(b)'s particularity requirements as to St. Mark's, we limit our discussion of Rule 9(b) to Intermountain.

[9] In discussing the legal background of Rule 9(b), the district court stated: "Because both [Intermountain] and St. Mark's are corporations, this knowledge must be held by a managing agent of either of these corporate entities." App'x at 2521. The district court then failed to cite any authority for its "managing agent" theory. To the extent the district court relied upon the "managing agent" theory, we disagree. "It is well established that a corporation is chargeable with the knowledge of its agents and employees acting within the scope of their authority." *W. Diversified Servs., Inc. v. Hyundai Motor Am., Inc.,* 427 F.3d 1269, 1276 (10th Cir. 2005); *see also United States ex rel. Jones v. Brigham & Women's Hosp.,* 678 F.3d 72, 82 n.18 (1st Cir. 2012) ("We have long held that corporate defendants may be subject to FCA liability when the alleged misrepresentations are made while the employee is acting within the scope of his or her employment."). Thus, under Rule 9(b), it suffices that *any* employee, acting within the scope of his or her employment, had knowledge.

ELEVENTH CIRCUIT DECISIONS
Qui Tam Actions

30 F.4th 1035 (2022)

Sheldon CHO, MD, Relators and ON BEHALF OF the STATES of Florida, Colorado, Georgia, North Carolina and Texas, Dawn Baker, Relators and on behalf of the States of Florida, Colorado, Georgia, North Carolina and Texas, Plaintiffs-Appellants-Cross Appellees,

v.

SURGERY PARTNERS, INC., et al., Defendants, H.I.G. Capital, LLC, H.I.G. Surgery Centers, LLC, Defendants-Appellees-Cross Appellants.

No. 20-14109.

United States Court of Appeals, Eleventh Circuit.

Filed: April 1, 2022.

Cho on Behalf of States v. Surgery Partners, Inc., 30 F. 4th 1035 (11th Cir. 2022)

Appeals from the United States District Court for the Middle District of Florida, D.C. Docket No. 8:17-cv-00983-VMC-AEP.

Jennifer Waugh Corinis, Greenberg Traurig, PA, Tampa, FL, Charles Z. Kopel, Lowey Dannenberg, PC, W Conshohocken, PA, Uriel Rabinovitz, Attorney, Peter St. Phillip, Jr., Lowey Dannenberg, PC, White Plains, NY, Alan S. Wachs, Smith Gambrell & Russell, LLP, Jacksonville, FL, Pamela Coyle Brecht, Marc S. Raspanti, Pietragallo Gordon Alfano Bosick & Raspanti, LLP, Philadelphia, PA, Joseph C. Crawford, Dean Mead, Melbourne, FL, John G. Murphy, John G. Murphy Law Office, Baton Rouge, LA, for Plaintiffs-Appellants-Cross Appellees.

Jeffrey J. Bushofsky, Laura G. Hoey, Ropes & Gray, LLP, Chicago, IL, Arthur Lee Bentley, III, Giovanni P. Giarratana, Bradley Arant Boult Cummings, LLP, Tampa, FL, Kathryn M. Roulett, Ropes & Gray, LLP, New York, NY, Christopher J. Walsh, Ropes & Gray, LLP, Boston, MA, for Defendants-Appellees-Cross Appellants.

Before WILSON, LAGOA, Circuit Judges, and MARTINEZ[*], District Judge.

p.1037 WILSON, Circuit Judge:

The False Claims Act (FCA) allows private parties, known as qui tam relators, to bring suit on behalf of the United States against persons who submitted false claims to the government. In this case, Dawn Baker and Dr. Sheldon Cho (the Relators) allege that H.I.G. Capital, LLC and H.I.G. Surgery Centers, LLC (collectively, H.I.G. or the H.I.G. entities) spearheaded a fraudulent enterprise to submit false claims for reimbursement to Medicare and p.1038 other government payors. The district court dismissed the claim without prejudice under the FCA's first-to-file bar, which prohibits relators from bringing a qui tam action while a related action is pending. On appeal, the Relators argue that the district court's first-to-file analysis was flawed because (1) it should have focused on the moment at which they filed their amended complaint rather than their original complaint, and (2) the earlier-filed action the district court relied on is unrelated to this suit. On cross-appeal, H.I.G. argues that we should convert the district court's dismissal without prejudice to a dismissal *with* prejudice for failure to state a claim and for failure to meet the heightened pleading standard required for allegations of fraud— grounds the district court did not address below.

After careful review and with the benefit of oral argument, we hold, first, that the FCA's plain language makes the original complaint—not the amended complaint— the proper point of reference for the first-to-file analysis. Second, we hold that this action is related to an earlier-filed action that alleged the same material elements of fraud. Therefore, we affirm the district court's dismissal of the complaint without prejudice pursuant to the first-to-file bar. Finally, we deny H.I.G.'s cross-appeal. Even assuming we could enlarge H.I.G.'s relief based on grounds the district court did not reach, we decline to do so.

I.

We begin with an overview of the facts and procedural background of this case. Because this is an appeal from a motion to dismiss, we take as true the facts pleaded in the complaint and construe them in the light most favorable to the Relators. *Belanger v. Salvation Army,* 556 F.3d 1153, 1155 (11th Cir. 2009).

In 2009, H.I.G., an international private equity firm, purchased Surgery Partners, Inc., along with its subsidiaries and affiliates (collectively, Surgery Partners). Surgery Partners owned and operated a network of surgery and pain-management centers. At the time of the acquisition, an H.I.G. affiliate entered into a management contract with Surgery Partners, giving H.I.G. control over Surgery Partners' operation. Shortly thereafter, H.I.G. placed three of its representatives on Surgery Partners' Board of Directors. In 2011, H.I.G. and Surgery Partners formed a diagnostic testing business called Logan Laboratories, LLC (Logan Labs), which specialized in urine drug testing (UDT).

There are two types of UDT: qualitative, which can detect the *presence* of drugs in a patient's system, and quantitative, which can detect *how much* of a drug is in a patient's system. While quantitative UDT has the advantage of providing more information, it is often not medically necessary. And because it must be performed in a laboratory, by laboratory professionals, it is more expensive than qualitative UDT.

The Relators allege that Surgery Partners —under H.I.G.'s guidance— consistently and routinely pressured its medical providers to refer patients to Logan Labs for quantitative UDT, regardless of whether qualitative UDT, the cheaper option, would have been sufficient. Making matters worse, the Relators say, Logan Labs would run excessive UDT panels, thus further increasing costs. Based on these UDT panels, Logan Labs then submitted claims for reimbursement to government healthcare programs, generating millions of dollars in payments. The Relators allege that H.I.G. caused this fraudulent overbilling, evidenced by the fact that it controlled Surgery Partners and Logan Labs during the relevant time period. Several H.I.G. executives who sat on Surgery Partners' p.1039 Board of Directors allegedly furthered the fraud by manipulating Surgery Partners' electronic medical records (EMR) software to justify unnecessary UDT.

In April 2017, the Relators—a pain management specialist and a physician recruiter —filed a complaint under the FCA and several state fraud statutes alleging that dozens of defendants had engaged in a fraudulent scheme. The Relators amended their complaint as of right in January 2019. A year later, the United States intervened as to some defendants named in the action, but declined to intervene as to H.I.G.

Importantly, however, a separate group of relators had also filed an FCA action (hereinafter, the Ashton Action) under seal against Surgery Partners and Logan Labs in connection with the same fraudulent scheme, though they did not name the H.I.G. entities as defendants. *See United States ex rel. Ashton v. Logan Laboratories, LLC, et al.,* Case No. 16-4583 (E.D. Pa. 2016). The Ashton Action was filed in August 2016— eight months before the Relators filed their initial complaint. The United States eventually intervened in the Ashton Action and reached a $41 million settlement agreement with four defendants, the Relators in this case, and the Ashton relators. The settlement agreement, announced in April 2020, contained a general release of FCA liability for Logan Labs' "current and former direct and indirect[ ] parent corporations . . . [and] corporate owners" based on the conduct described in the agreement. And specifically as to H.I.G., the agreement included a release of "liability against the H.I.G. Entities. . . for their own independent conduct outside their status as investors in or owners of" Logan Labs. The Ashton Action was then unsealed, and the settlement agreement became public.

Subsequently, the Relators in this case filed a second amended complaint narrowing their allegations to focus on H.I.G.'s conduct. The second amended complaint brought causes of action against the H.I.G. entities for violation of the FCA, 31 U.S.C. § 3729(a)(1)(A) and (B), and for conspiracy to violate the FCA, 31 U.S.C. § 3729(a)(1)(C). H.I.G. moved for dismissal on several grounds, including that (1) the FCA's first-to-file rule barred the claim; (2) the Relators failed to state a claim because they did not sufficiently allege that H.I.G. knowingly caused the submission of false claims; (3) the Relators failed to plead fraud with particularity; and (4) the settlement agreement released H.I.G. from any liability.

The district court granted the motion, finding that the second amended complaint was barred by the FCA's first-to-file rule. Although the Relators filed the second amended complaint at a time when the Ashton Action was no longer pending, the district court held that the relevant question was whether the Ashton Action was pending at the time the Relators filed their *initial* complaint. Because the Ashton Action was pending at that time, the district court concluded that it barred the Relators' action so long as the two actions were related. The district court held next that the two actions were related because "they allege the same essential facts regarding the UDT fraud against the Government committed by Surgery Partners and Logan Labs." Accordingly, the district court dismissed the claim without prejudice.[1] The Relators appealed the district court's grant of the motion to dismiss.

p.1040 **II.**

We review de novo a district court's grant of a motion to dismiss. *Wiersum v. U.S. Bank, N.A.,* 785 F.3d 483, 485 (11th Cir. 2015). Likewise, we review de novo a district court's interpretation of a statute. *Id.*

III.

We split our discussion into two parts. First, we address whether the FCA bars a complaint that is (a) filed while a related action is pending, but (b) amended after the related action is dismissed. Second, we determine the proper standard for analyzing whether a claim is related to a previously-filed action, and we apply that standard to the facts before us.

A.

The Relators' first argument on appeal is that the FCA's first-to-file bar is inapplicable because the Ashton Action was no longer pending at the time the Relators filed the second amended complaint. Under the first-to-file bar, "[w]hen a person brings an action under [the FCA], no person other than the Government may intervene or bring a related action based on the facts underlying the pending action." 31 U.S.C. § 3730(b)(5). As other courts have observed, the first-to-file bar serves two related purposes: "to eliminate parasitic plaintiffs who piggyback off the claims of a prior relator, and to encourage legitimate relators to file quickly by protecting the spoils of the first to bring a claim." *In re Nat. Gas Royalties Qui Tam Litig. (CO2 Appeals),* 566 F.3d 956, 961 (10th Cir. 2009); *see also United States ex rel. Wood v. Allergan, Inc.,* 899 F.3d 163, 169-70 (2d Cir. 2018).

Here, there is no dispute that the Ashton Action was still pending when the Relators filed their original complaint. But when the Relators filed their second amended complaint, the Ashton Action had settled, and therefore was no longer "pending." *See Kellogg Brown & Root Servs., Inc. v. United States, ex rel. Carter,* 575 U.S. 650, 664, 135 S.Ct. 1970, 191 L.Ed.2d 899 (2015). The core issue, then, is whether it is the filing of a relator's original complaint or his amended complaint that informs our analysis of the first-to-file bar. Or, to frame the question another way: Can a first-to-file defect be cured by the filing of an amended complaint?[2]

We begin our analysis, as always, with the statutory text. In this case, it happens to be fairly straightforward: a person may not "bring a related action" while the first-filed action is pending. 31 U.S.C. § 3730(b)(5). We have held several times that the key phrase—to "bring" an "action"—"has a settled customary meaning at law, and refers to the initiation of legal proceedings in a suit." *Harris v. Garner,* 216 F.3d 970, 973 (11th Cir. 2000) (en banc) (quoting Black's Law Dictionary 192 (6th ed. 1990)). Absent any indication to the contrary, "we readily presume that Congress knows the settled legal definition of the words it uses, and uses them in the settled sense." *Id.* at 974.

Applying that settled definition here, the statutory prohibition turns on the moment the Relators *initiated* legal proceedings— not on the moment the Relators amended their complaint. As other circuits have recognized, "an amended . . . pleading cannot p.1041 change the fact that [the relator] *brought* an action while another related action was pending."[3] *Wood,* 899 F.3d at 172 (citing *United States ex rel. Shea v. Cellco P'ship,* 863 F.3d 923 (D.C. Cir. 2017)). Here, the Relators brought this suit while the Ashton Action was pending. Therefore, we hold that the first-to-file bar applies.

The Relators offer two counterarguments. First, they argue that the purpose of the FCA is to encourage more private enforcement, and that we should interpret the first-to-file bar narrowly in furtherance of that purpose. As we have explained, however, "[w]e interpret and apply statutes, not congressional purposes." *In re Hedrick,* 524 F.3d 1175, 1188 (11th Cir. 2008). And in any event, the FCA does not pursue a singular purpose. It pursues the "twin goals" of rewarding whistleblowers for bringing fraud to the government's attention, while seeking to discourage opportunists who would enrich themselves by pursuing fraud the government already knows about. *See United States ex rel. Springfield Terminal Ry. v. Quinn,* 14 F.3d 645, 649-51 (D.C. Cir. 1994). How best to mediate those competing interests is for Congress to decide, and Congress has spoken clearly here.

Second, the Relators argue that their interpretation of the first-to-file bar finds support in Supreme Court precedent and our own precedent. At the Supreme Court level, the Relators point to *Rockwell International Corp. v. United States,* 549 U.S. 457, 127 S.Ct. 1397, 167 L.Ed.2d 190 (2007), a case that involved the FCA's public-disclosure bar and its original-source exception. Under the then-applicable version of the statute, courts lacked jurisdiction over qui tam suits that were "based upon the public disclosure of allegations or transactions 'unless . . . the person bringing the action [was] an original source of the information.'" *Id.* at 460, 127 S.Ct. 1397 (quoting 31 U.S.C. § 3730(e)(4)(A) (1994)). The relator in *Rockwell* amended his complaint but asked the Court to consider only his initial complaint in determining whether he was an original source. *Id.* at 473, 127 S.Ct. 1397. The Supreme Court rejected that argument, holding that the word "allegations," as used in the public-disclosure bar, "includes (at a minimum) the allegations in the original complaint *as amended*." *Id.* (emphasis in original). The Court emphasized that a "demonstration that the original allegations were false will defeat jurisdiction." *Id.*

What we can take from *Rockwell* is that where the analysis turns on the *substance* of a relator's allegations in the public-disclosure context, courts cannot ignore new, relevant allegations that reveal a jurisdictional defect. But the crux of the issue here is *timing*. The temporal question of when an action was brought (i.e., filed) remains unaffected by whatever new allegations a relator brings forward. *See Wood,* 899 F.3d at 172. Therefore, *Rockwell* does not help the Relators.

p.1042 As to our own precedent, the Relators cite to *Makro Capital of America, Inc. v. UBS AG,* 543 F.3d 1254 (11th Cir. 2008), but that decision too is distinguishable. In *Makro,* the original complaint was not a qui tam action under the FCA; it alleged non-FCA fraud and tort claims. *Id.* at 1256. After the plaintiff amended its complaint, restyling it as an FCA qui tam action, the district court granted dismissal based on the then-applicable government knowledge bar, 31 U.S.C. § 3730(b)(4) (1982) (repealed 1986), finding that the suit was based on information that was publicly available at the time of the amended complaint. *Makro,* 543 F.3d at 1256-57. On appeal, we agreed that the filing of the amended complaint was the proper reference point—but only because the original complaint had not been a qui tam action. *Id.* at 1259. We stressed the "disjunction" between the plaintiff's "original claim seeking personal recovery for fraud (and other torts)," and "its *qui tam* claim seeking recovery for fraud committed against the United States." *Id.* at 1259-60. Without that sort of disjunction here, our holding that the Relators first brought an FCA action when they filed their original complaint is not in tension with *Makro*.

As a result, we conclude that the FCA's plain text tethers our analysis to the moment a qui tam action is filed. When the Relators filed this qui tam suit, the Ashton Action was pending. Therefore, the Relators cannot evade the first-to-file bar by amending their pleading after the Ashton Action was dismissed.

B.

Having determined that the first-to-file bar applies to the filing of the original complaint, we now address the Relators' argument that, in any event, their complaint is unrelated to the Ashton Action.

We have not yet adopted a test for determining whether two qui tam actions are related. Both parties suggest that we follow our sister circuits in adopting the "same material elements" test, also called the "same essential elements" test, which the district court applied below. *See United States ex rel. Chovanec v. Apria Healthcare Grp. Inc.,* 606 F.3d 361, 363 (7th Cir. 2010) (collecting cases). Under this test, two actions are related if they "incorporate 'the same material elements of fraud.'" *Wood,* 899 F.3d at 169. That is, "to be related, the cases must rely on the same 'essential facts.'" *Id.* In applying this test, several circuits have compared the two complaints "side-by-side" and asked "whether the later complaint 'alleges a fraudulent scheme the government already would be equipped to investigate based on the first complaint.'" *United States ex rel. Heath v. AT&T, Inc.,* 791 F.3d 112, 121 (D.C. Cir. 2015) (alterations adopted); *see also Wood,* 899 F.3d at 169; *United States ex rel. Carson v. Manor Care, Inc.,* 851 F.3d 293, 303 (4th Cir. 2017).

As these courts have emphasized, this test finds support in the text of the FCA. Under 31 U.S.C. § 3730(b)(5), the first-filed and later-filed claims need not be identical; they need only be "related." Drawing upon this distinction, the same material elements test creates a framework under which § 3730(b)(5) can still bar a later claim, "even if the allegations 'incorporate somewhat different details.'" *Heath,* 791 F.3d at 116. Finding that this test aligns with the FCA's plain text, we adopt it here.

Our next task is to determine whether the district court correctly applied this test to conclude that the Relators' original complaint alleged the same essential facts as did the original complaint in the Ashton Action, which was pending at p.1043 the time.[4] The Relators contend that it did not for two reasons. First, the Relators named the H.I.G. entities as defendants, whereas the Ashton Action did not. Second, in addition to the Relators' substantive FCA claim, they alleged a conspiracy, which the Ashton relators did not allege.

Beginning with the Relators' first contention, we disagree that the first-to-file bar requires a necessarily defendant-specific approach. Though we have no binding precedent on point, we find instructive the view of our sister circuits that adding a new defendant to the mix does not *necessarily* allow a later-filed action to evade the first-to-file bar, particularly where the new defendant is a corporate relative or affiliate of the earlier-named defendants. *See, e.g., Nat. Gas Royalties,* 566 F.3d at 962; *United States ex rel. Hampton v. Columbia/HCA Healthcare Corp.,* 318 F.3d 214, 218 (D.C. Cir. 2003). What we must determine is whether the addition of a new defendant put the government on notice of a broader, more pervasive, or distinct scheme. Two cases from the D.C. Circuit, *Hampton* and *Heath,* serve as useful bookends for this analysis.

In *Hampton,* the earlier-filed action was brought against one corporate entity, HCA, alleging a "corporate-wide" fraudulent scheme that HCA carried out through its subsidiaries in thirty-seven states. 318 F.3d at 218. A later-filed action alleged that an additional HCA subsidiary perpetrated the same fraudulent scheme in six other states. *Id.* The court held that merely adding another corporate subsidiary did not amount to a difference in the material elements of the alleged fraud. *Id.* Therefore, the later-filed action was barred. At the other end of the spectrum is *Heath.* In that case, the earlier-filed action alleged that Wisconsin Bell, Inc., a subsidiary of AT&T, Inc., engaged in a scheme to defraud the government. *Heath,* 791 F.3d at 118. That scheme, according to the earlier-filed action, was "limited" in scope and did not extend beyond Wisconsin. *Id.* at 121-122. The later-filed action, in contrast, "allege[d] a different and more far-reaching scheme to defraud the federal government through service contracts entered into across the Nation." *Id.* at 121. On these facts, the court held that the later-filed action alleged different material elements of fraud. *Id.* at 122-23.

These cases help illustrate that there is no bright-line rule as to whether naming an additional defendant states a different essential claim. We must determine whether the introduction of a new defendant amounts to allegations of a "different" or "more far-reaching scheme" than was alleged in the earlier-filed action. *See id.*

The Relators argue that their allegations are indeed broader than those in the Ashton Action. Specifically, they argue that their complaint puts the government on notice that the scheme "involved a unique breed of healthcare fraud, designed and directed by outside capital." But when comparing the Relators' complaint side-by-side with the Ashton complaint, the Relators' allegations do not meaningfully expand the scope of the UDT scheme or suggest that it was more pervasive than the Ashton Action indicated.[5] *See id.* Both p.1044 complaints allege that: (1) Surgery Partners and Logan Labs were engaged in a scheme to order expensive and unnecessary quantitative UDT panels for patients at Logan Labs; (2) Surgery Partners paid kickbacks to physicians and pain management specialists to entice them to refer patients to Logan Labs for UDT; (3) Surgery Partners' EMR software was manipulated to support orders for unnecessary UDT; (4) Logan Labs ran these UDT panels; and (5) this scheme caused Logan Labs to submit millions of dollars' worth of fraudulent claims for reimbursement to government healthcare programs.

Taken as a whole, both complaints allege the same essential UDT scheme carried out by Surgery Partners and Logan Labs. Based on the Ashton Action, the government was already alerted to that scheme, and would have been equipped to investigate whether any corporate affiliates or investors connected to Surgery Partners and Logan Labs were participants. The Relators did not allege different material facts by naming H.I.G. as a defendant without making any allegations that would meaningfully magnify the scope or pervasiveness of the scheme.

In urging that we reach the contrary conclusion, the Relators analogize a case in the public-disclosure context: *Cooper v. Blue Cross & Blue Shield of Florida, Inc.,* 19 F.3d 562 (11th Cir. 1994) (per curiam). In *Cooper,* the question was whether public disclosure of industry-wide insurance fraud, as well as allegations against Blue Cross Blue Shield of Georgia (BCBSG) amounted to public disclosure of fraud by

BCBSG's sister corporation—Blue Cross Blue Shield of Florida. *Id.* at 566-67. We held that it did not, reasoning in part that "[r]equiring that allegations specific to a particular defendant be publically disclosed before finding the action potentially barred encourages private citizen involvement and increases the chances that every instance of specific fraud will be revealed." *Id.* at 566.

We find, however, that *Cooper* is distinguishable. To be sure, a public disclosure that one of a company's subsidiaries engaged in fraud may not alert the government to a parallel, distinct scheme by another subsidiary. But our facts are different. A comparison of the two complaints at issue here belies any notion that the Relators are alleging a fraudulent scheme distinct from the one alleged in the Ashton Action. The Relators allege that an additional player who was affiliated with Surgery Partners and Logan Labs had its hands in the same fraudulent scheme. The government would have been equipped, based on the Ashton Action, to investigate this matter. Therefore, the Relators' claim is related to the Ashton Action for purposes of the first-to-file bar.

Finally, the Relators' raise a separate argument that their FCA conspiracy claim under 31 U.S.C. § 3729(a)(1)(C) is unrelated to the Ashton Action, which alleged only substantive FCA violations. That argument can be dealt with in short order. Because the Relators' conspiracy claim is based on the same fraudulent scheme that was alleged in the Ashton Action, the government would have been equipped to investigate both substantive FCA violations and any conspiracies stemming from, or derivative to, the same scheme. *See Heath,* 791 F.3d at 121. Therefore, the Relators' conspiracy claim is related to the Ashton Action and is barred by § 3730(b)(5).

IV.

In conclusion, when relators file a qui tam action that is related to an already-pending action, that claim is incurably flawed from the moment it is filed. Here, p.1045 the Relators' claims focus on the same fraudulent scheme at issue in the Ashton Action, which was pending when the Relators brought this action. Therefore, the Relators' claim is barred under the FCA's first-to-file rule. We affirm the district court's dismissal without prejudice.

AFFIRMED.

[*] Honorable Jose E. Martinez, United States District Judge for the Southern District of Florida, sitting by designation.

[1] Because the first-to-file bar precluded the Relators' suit, the district court did not address H.I.G.'s remaining arguments.

[2] We note that, in any event, the first-to-file bar will not prevent relators from bringing a new action once the earlier-filed action is no longer pending. However, other barriers such as the statute of limitations may present an obstacle in that scenario. *See United States ex rel. Wood v. Allergan, Inc.,* 899 F.3d 163, 174 (2d Cir. 2018); *United States ex rel. Shea v. Cellco P'ship,* 863 F.3d 923, 932 (D.C. Cir. 2017).

[3] Nearly every circuit to consider the issue has endorsed this reasoning. *See United States ex rel. Carter v. Halliburton Co.,* 866 F.3d 199, 206-07 (4th Cir. 2017);

Walburn v. Lockheed Martin Corp., 431 F.3d 966, 972 n.5 (6th Cir. 2005); *United States ex rel. Chovanec v. Apria Healthcare Grp. Inc.*, 606 F.3d 361, 362 (7th Cir. 2010); *United States ex rel. Lujan v. Hughes Aircraft Co.*, 243 F.3d 1181, 1188 (9th Cir. 2001); *Grynberg v. Koch Gateway Pipeline Co.*, 390 F.3d 1276, 1279 (10th Cir. 2004). Though we acknowledge that the First Circuit reached the contrary conclusion, it did not explain how its reading comports with the plain language of the first-to-file bar. *See United States ex rel. Gadbois v. PharMerica Corp.*, 809 F.3d 1, 3-4 (1st Cir. 2015). Therefore, we find that decision unpersuasive.

[4] We compare the Ashton complaint to the Relators' original complaint for the reasons we outlined above. But in any event, it does not appear that it would make any difference if we looked to the substance of the second amended complaint, as the Relators concede that the allegations set forth in their initial and second amended complaints are "virtually identical."

[5] The district court properly took judicial notice of the Ashton complaint, which is publicly available, to establish the content of those allegations. *See Bryant v. Avado Brands, Inc.*, 187 F.3d 1271, 1277 (11th Cir. 1999).

21 F.4th 1288 (2021)

Michele YATES, Plaintiff-Appellee,
v.
PINELLAS HEMATOLOGY & ONCOLOGY, P.A., Defendant-Appellant,
Pratibha Desai, an individual, Defendant.

No. 20-10276.

United States Court of Appeals, Eleventh Circuit.

Filed: December 29, 2021.

Yates v. Pinellas Hematology & Oncology, PA, 21 F. 4th 1288 (11th Cir. 2021)

Appeal from the United States District Court for the Middle District of Florida, D.C. Docket No. 8:16-cv-00799-WFJ-CPT.

Christopher David Gray, Scott L. Terry, Florin Gray Bouzas Owens, LLC, Lutz, FL, for Plaintiff-Appellee.

Shyam Dixit, Dixit Law Firm, Edward B. Carlstedt, FordHarrison, LLP, Tampa, FL, for Defendant-Appellant.

Michael Shih, U.S. Department of Justice Civil Division, Appellate Staff, Charles W. Scarborough, U.S. Attorney General's Office, Washington, DC, for Amicus Curiae United States of America.

Before Jordan, Newsom, and Tjoflat, Circuit Judges.

p.1294 Jordan, Circuit Judge.

The jury in this qui tam case found that Pinellas Hematology & Oncology violated p.1295 the False Claims Act, 31 U.S.C. § 3729 et seq., on 214 occasions, and that the United States had sustained $755.54 in damages. Following that verdict, the district court trebled the damages and imposed statutory minimum penalties of $1,177,000 ($5,500 for each of the 214 violations).

On appeal, Pinellas challenges the admission of an exhibit, the jury's verdict on liability and damages, and the monetary award imposed by the district court. After a review of the record, and with the benefit of oral argument, we affirm in part and dismiss in part.

I

We summarize the facts in the light most favorable to the jury's verdict. *See Royal Palm Properties, LLC v. Pink Palm Properties, LLC,* 950 F.3d 776, 782 (11th Cir. 2020).

A

Pinellas was a medical practice owned by Dr. Pratibha Desai. During the relevant period, Pinellas' headquarters and primary office were located on Park Street in Saint Petersburg, Florida. We refer to this location as Park Place.

Park Place had a clinical laboratory at which, among other things, Pinellas would draw blood from patients and run laboratory tests on those blood samples. For patients who had Medicare coverage, Pinellas would seek reimbursement from the federal government for those tests.

In April of 2015, Pinellas purchased an oncology practice that was located at Bayfront Hospital in Saint Petersburg, Florida. We refer to this practice, which also had its own clinical laboratory, as Bayfront.

Under the Clinical Laboratory Improvement Amendments of 1988 and its regulations, no laboratory can conduct tests on materials derived from the human body unless it has the proper CLIA certificate. *See* 42 U.S.C. § 263a(b); 42 C.F.R. §§ 493.1, .3(a), .15, .43-49; Center for Medicare and Medicaid Services, Medicare Claims Processing Manual, § 70.1 (2020). Both Park Place and Bayfront had the appropriate CLIA certificates prior to the purchase of Bayfront, but Bayfront's CLIA certificate did not transfer to Pinellas. Because each laboratory location must have its own CLIA certificate, *see* 42 C.F.R. § 493.43(a), Pinellas could not use either of the preexisting CLIA certificates to perform its laboratory tests at Bayfront. Pinellas instead had to obtain a new CLIA certificate for Bayfront linking the latter to it.[1]

The problem for Pinellas was that it did not have the proper CLIA certificate for Bayfront from April of 2015 until March of 2016, but it still performed tests at Bayfront during that time. The bigger problem for Pinellas was that it then submitted reimbursement claims to Medicare for those tests. And the biggest problem for Pinellas was that when Medicare rejected those claims, it altered the relevant information and resubmitted them—twice.

Michele Yates, Pinellas' billing manager, filed a qui tam action against Pinellas and Dr. Desai. She alleged that they had violated the FCA by defrauding the United States through the submission of the Bayfront reimbursement claims to Medicare p.1296 and by retaliating against her for attempting to stop their fraudulent conduct. The United States chose not to intervene. *See* 31 U.S.C. § 3730(b)(2).

Before trial, Pinellas filed a motion in limine to exclude Exhibit 24, a spreadsheet prepared by Ms. Yates which summarized some of the allegedly fraudulent claims submitted to Medicare. The district court denied Pinellas' motion without prejudice.

At trial, Ms. Yates told the jury that, between April and July of 2015, Pinellas had billed Medicare over 2,000 times for laboratory tests performed at Bayfront. Because Bayfront did not have a CLIA certificate at that time, those initial claims did not include a CLIA certificate number. As a result, Medicare denied those claims.

To have Medicare pay the claims, Pinellas altered the information on the claim forms to make it seem as if the laboratory tests had been conducted at Park Place, which did have a valid CLIA certificate linked to Pinellas. When it first resubmitted the claims, Pinellas added Park Place's CLIA certificate number to the Bayfront claim forms. Medicare, however, also denied that second set of claims. So, Pinellas resubmitted the claims once again, this time changing the location of service from Bayfront's address to Park Place's address. Medicare paid some of the claims from the third set.

Documentary evidence corroborated Ms. Yates' testimony. For instance, a May 9, 2015, internal email from Lia Valentin, a Pinellas billing assistant, to Ms. Yates and others read as follows:

Michel[e], I just wanted to remind you that the claims with medicare that have labs in them the location has to be switched to pinellas park because the claim are denying until we have the clia fixed for the bayfront office location. Im correcting the claims that came back that did not get paid & refiling them.

D.E. 201-3 at 2.

Another email sent by Ms. Valentin, on July 14, 2015, stated:

I verify we have not yet added bayfront office ... to Dr. Desai['s] Clia number. the only two offices that are currently ok with the Clia number is park place & largo. For now any denial we receive we change the place of address to Pinellas park address and refile the claim to medicare. [T]hat way we can get the lab paid.

D.E. 201-4 at 5.

Ms. Yates moved during trial to introduce Exhibit 24—the spreadsheet—into evidence, and Pinellas did not object. She testified that Exhibit 24 showed that Pinellas had submitted 214 claims for Bayfront laboratory tests with Park Place's CLIA certificate number and had changed the location of service to Park Place's address. Out of that total, Medicare paid 64 claims totaling $755.54.[2]

B

The jury found Dr. Desai not liable. As to Pinellas, the jury found it liable for having knowingly submitted 214 materially false claims to Medicare, thereby violating the FCA. The jury also found that the United States had suffered $755.54 in damages.

p.1297 Following the verdict, Pinellas filed a renewed motion for judgment as a matter of law and/or remittitur under Rules 50(b) and 59(e) of the Federal Rules of Civil Procedure. In its motion and subsequent filings, Pinellas argued that the evidence presented at trial was insufficient to support the jury's verdict. Pinellas also asserted that, for various reasons, discrete claim subsets should be deducted from the 214 claims for which the jury had found it liable. In the alternative, Pinellas moved for remittitur, submitting that the damages and statutory penalties mandated by the FCA constituted an excessive fine in violation of the Eighth Amendment.

The district court denied Pinellas' renewed motion. It found that the evidence, though contested, was sufficient to support the jury's verdict. As to the damages and statutory penalties, the FCA mandated the imposition of treble damages and statutory penalties of between $5,500 and $11,000 per false claim. *See* 31 U.S.C § 3729(a)(1); 28 C.F.R. § 85.3(a)(9). Accordingly, the court imposed a total monetary award of $1,179,266.62—composed of (i) treble damages of $2,266.62 (3 × $755.54), and (ii) the lowest permissible statutory penalty of $1,177,000.00 (214 × $5,500). Though noting that the amount was "very harsh," the court ultimately held that it did not violate the Eight Amendment's prohibition on excessive fines. *See* D.E. 227 at 3-4.

On appeal, Pinellas challenges the district court's admission of Exhibit 24, the jury's verdict on liability and damages, and the total monetary award. We address each argument below.

II

Pinellas argues that, for various reasons, the district court abused its discretion in admitting Exhibit 24 at trial. Ms. Yates responds that Pinellas failed to preserve its objection, which in any event lacks merit. We agree with Ms. Yates on the first point.

To preserve a claim that a district court improperly admitted evidence, a party must make a timely objection. *See* Fed. R. Evid. 103(a)(1)(A). That objection can come before or during trial, and once the district "court rules definitively on the record... a party need not renew [its] objection... to preserve a claim of error for appeal." Fed. R. Evid. 103(b). When the objection comes in the form of a motion in limine before trial, a district court makes a definitive ruling if its decision is final or with prejudice; conversely, if the court's ruling is tentative or without prejudice, there is no definitive ruling on the objection. *See Tan Lam v. City of Los Banos,* 976 F.3d 986, 1005 (9th Cir. 2020); 1 Jack B. Weinstein & Margaret A. Berger, Weinstein's Federal Evidence, § 103.11[2][b] (2d ed. 2021). In the latter scenario, the objecting party must renew its objection at trial to preserve a claim of error for appeal. *See United States v. Wilson,* 788 F.3d 1298, 1313 (11th Cir. 2015); *Tan Lam,* 976 F.3d at 1006.

When a party fails to preserve an evidentiary objection, we review the district court's admission of evidence for plain error. *See Wilson,* 788 F.3d at 1313. To reverse under plain error review, we must find an error that is plain and that has affected the objecting party's substantial rights. *See United States v. Olano,* 507 U.S. 725, 733-34, 113 S.Ct. 1770, 123 L.Ed.2d 508 (1993); *United States v. Hesser,* 800 F.3d 1310, 1324 (11th Cir. 2015). "Once those three conditions have been met," we ask whether the forfeited error "seriously affects the fairness, integrity or public reputation of judicial proceedings." *Rosales-Mireles v. United States,* ___ U.S. ___, 138 S. Ct. 1897, 1905, 201 L.Ed.2d 376 (2018) (internal quotation marks omitted). Our ultimate decision under plain error p.1298 review is discretionary. *See* Fed. R. Evid. 103(e) ("A court *may* take notice of a plain error affecting a substantial right, even if the claim of error was not properly preserved.") (emphasis added); *United States v. Marcus,* 560 U.S. 258, 262, 130 S.Ct. 2159, 176 L.Ed.2d 1012 (2010) (explaining that under plain error review, "an appellate court may, in its discretion, correct an error not raised at trial only where the appellant demonstrates" that the required elements are met).

In this case, Pinellas objected to the admission of Exhibit 24 through a motion in limine. The district court denied that motion without prejudice, meaning that its ruling was not definitive. Pinellas was accordingly required to renew its objection to the admission of Exhibit 24 at trial when Ms. Yates moved for its admission. Pinellas did not do so, and thus failed to preserve its claim of error for appeal. *See Wilson,* 788 F.3d at 1313.

As a result, we would generally review the admission of Exhibit 24 for plain error. But, as noted, reversal for plain error is discretionary. And because the onus to demonstrate plain error is on the party challenging the evidentiary ruling, we have in the past declined to conduct a plain error analysis sua sponte when that party makes no effort to satisfy the standard. *See United States v. Gari,* 572 F.3d 1352, 1362 (11th Cir. 2009).

On appeal, Pinellas was put on notice of its failure to preserve its claim of error by Ms. Yates, but it has chosen not to argue in the alternative that the admission of Exhibit 24 constituted plain error. Instead, Pinellas argues (incorrectly) only that it preserved its claim of error below. As Pinellas has not argued that the admission of Exhibit 24 rose to the level of plain error, we decline to construct that argument for Pinellas and then rule on it. We therefore affirm the district court's admission of Exhibit 24.

III

Pinellas' challenge to the jury's verdict comes to us, for the most part, from the district court's denial of the renewed motion for judgment as a matter of law. Therefore, except where otherwise noted, "[w]e review the district court's decision *de novo,* applying the same standard that court applied." *Royal Palm,* 950 F.3d at 782. Under that standard, our task is to determine whether the record—viewed in the light most favorable to Ms. Yates (the prevailing party)—points so overwhelmingly in favor of Pinellas that the jury's verdict cannot stand. *See id.* Stated differently, the verdict will be set aside only if no reasonable jury could have arrived at it. *See id.*

A

Enacted in 1863 to combat fraud perpetrated against the Union Army during the Civil War, the FCA has become the United States' "primary litigative tool for combatting fraud." S. Rep. No. 99-345, at 2, 4 (1986). Before delving into the merits of Pinellas' challenge to the jury's verdict, we provide a brief overview of §§ 3729(a)(1)(A) and (a)(1)(B), the relevant provisions of the FCA.

Through § 3729(a)(1)(A), the FCA imposes liability on any person who "knowingly presents, or causes to be presented, a false or fraudulent claim for payment or approval." And § 3729(a)(1)(B) imposes liability on anyone who "knowingly makes, uses, or causes to be made or used, a false record or statement material to a false or fraudulent claim."

Pinellas' challenge to the jury's verdict on liability takes aim at the three elements shared by both provisions: the existence of a false claim or statement, the materiality of that false claim or statement, and scienter. *See United States ex rel. Phalp v.* p.1299 *Lincare Holdings, Inc.,* 857 F.3d 1148, 1154 (11th Cir. 2017). Pinellas also asks us to overturn the jury's verdict on damages because, it says, the United States suffered no harm.

B

Turning first to Pinellas' argument on the falsity element, we note that the FCA does not define the term "false." Case law, however, has identified various types of false claims and statements. For example, a claim is false when it misrepresents the goods or services provided. *See United States ex rel. Greenfield v. Medco Health Sols., Inc.,* 880 F.3d 89, 94 (3d Cir. 2018); *United States ex rel. Thomas v. Black & Veatch Spec. Projects Corp.,* 820 F.3d 1162, 1168 (10th Cir. 2016); *United States v. Sci. Applications Intern. Corp.,* 626 F.3d 1257, 1266 (D.C. Cir. 2010). A claim is also false when a person or entity fails to comply with statutory, regulatory, or contractual requirements but certifies that it has complied with them. *See Universal Health Services Inc., v. United States ex rel. Escobar,* 579 U.S. 176, 186-88, 136 S. Ct. 1989, 195 L.Ed.2d 348 (2016); *Phalp,* 857 F.3d at 1154.

Ms. Yates based her FCA claims on a false certification theory. She asserted that Pinellas falsely certified that it complied with the CLIA's requirement that a laboratory possess the proper CLIA certificate to conduct, and bill for, laboratory tests. Pinellas, she claimed, did that by adding Park Place's CLIA certificate number and address to Medicare reimbursement claims for laboratory tests conducted at Bayfront.

In its brief on appeal, Pinellas argues that none of the claims it submitted to Medicare is false. According to Pinellas, the unpaid claims are not false because "they did not list any CLIA [certificate] number on the claims form." Appellant's Br. at 37. As to the paid claims, Pinellas contends that they are not false because they are not material. Both arguments fail.

First, Pinellas does not point to any evidence to support its argument that none of the unpaid claims is false. Its single citation is to an explanation of a benefits form that, as best we can tell, was not introduced at trial. Moreover, we see no indication that this form relates to any of the 214 claims on which the jury found Pinellas liable. And even if the form did correspond to one of the claims, the explanation of benefits would tell us nothing about the remaining 213 claims included in Exhibit 24. Finally, the few claim forms that are in the record on appeal all include Park Place's CLIA certificate number.

Indeed, Ms. Yates testified that she created Exhibit 24 with data provided by her expert, Adam Sharp, who converted Pinellas' electronic claims data into a reimbursement form format. According to Ms. Yates, she whittled down the reimbursement claim forms that Mr. Sharp had provided her to 214, all of which included Park Place's CLIA certificate number.

Second, we reject Pinellas' argument that the paid claims are not false because they are not material. The falsity and materiality elements of an FCA claim are distinct and independent requirements. A claim may be material but not false, false but not material, or both material and false. A reasonable jury could have found that the 214 claims included in Exhibit 24 were false.

C

We also disagree with Pinellas' arguments on the FCA's materiality element. Based on our review of the record, a reasonable jury could have found that the 214 claims included in Exhibit 24 were material to the United States' decision to pay.

p.1300 The FCA defines the term "material" as "having a natural tendency to influence, or be capable of influencing, the payment or receipt of money or property." 31 U.S.C. § 3729(b)(4). The materiality element seeks to limit the scope of liability under the FCA to claims for which the government "would have attached importance to the violation in determining whether to pay the claim." *United States ex rel. Marsteller v. Tilton,* 880 F.3d 1302, 1313 (11th Cir. 2018). *See Escobar,* 136 S. Ct. at 2003 ("Materiality ... cannot be found where noncompliance is minor or insubstantial."). Significantly, the materiality analysis is holistic. *See United States ex rel. Bibby v. Mortg. Inv'rs Corp.,* 987 F.3d 1340, 1347 (11th Cir. 2021). Some of the relevant, non-exhaustive factors include whether the matter is an express condition to payment; whether, to the extent the United States had actual knowledge of the misrepresentations, they had an effect on its behavior; and whether the misrepresentations went to the essence of the bargain. *See id.* Pinellas targets those factors in its appeal.

Pinellas first argues that "because the incorrect CLIA number was not a condition to payment," Ms. Yates' claims are not actionable under the FCA. *See* Appellant's Br. at 27. In support, Pinellas relies on *United States ex rel. New Mexico v. Deming Hosp. Corp.*, 992 F. Supp. 2d 1137 (D.N.M. 2013), and *United States ex rel. Hobbs v. MedQuest Associates, Inc.*, 711 F.3d 707 (6th Cir. 2013). But to the extent that Pinellas relies on the labelling of the CLIA certification requirement as one of payment, the Supreme Court in *Escobar* rejected formalism for reality. There, the Court stated that the United States' decision to label a requirement as a condition of payment is relevant but not dispositive. *See Escobar*, 136 S. Ct. at 2003. The materiality inquiry asks whether a misrepresentation would or did influence the United States' decision to pay, and neither *Deming* nor *Hobbs* helps answer that question.[3]

Deming and *Hobbs* dealt with legal requirements different from those at issue here. *Deming* involved regulations requiring hospital laboratories that were already CLIA-certified to remain in compliance with certain standards. *See Deming*, 992 F. Supp. 2d at 1148. And the regulations at issue in *Hobbs* are unrelated to CLIA certification. *See Hobbs*, 711 F.3d at 710-12 (considering an FCA claim based on misstatements regarding supervising physician regulations). Therefore, *Deming* and *Hobbs* tell us little, if anything, about whether falsely stating that tests were conducted in a CLIA-certified laboratory would or did influence the United States' decision to pay Pinellas' claims.

Pinellas next argues that the United States' failure to seek reimbursement or seek sanctions once it had actual knowledge of the misrepresentations indicates that they were not material. We agree with Pinellas that the United States' p.1301 behavior after it has paid a claim, and knows of a violation, may be relevant to the materiality analysis. *See Bibby*, 987 F.3d at 1350-51. Yet that behavior is relevant only to the extent that it helps answer the ultimate question: whether the United States "would have attached importance to the violation in determining whether to pay the claim." *Marsteller*, 880 F.3d at 1313. The record in this case includes other evidence on that question—e.g., Medicare's actions and Pinellas' beliefs at the time of the submission of the false claims—that is more than sufficient to uphold the jury's verdict.

Based on Ms. Yates' testimony, the May 9th and July 14th emails from Ms. Valentin, and Exhibit 24, the jury could reasonably find that the United States denied the initial Bayfront claims that lacked a CLIA certificate number; that Pinellas understood the denial of those claims to be the result of the lack of a CLIA certificate number; that, in response, Pinellas refiled those claims with Park Place's CLIA certificate number; that Pinellas understood the denial of those refiled claims to be due to the mismatch between Park Place's CLIA certificate number and Bayfront's address; that, to obtain payment, Pinellas directed its employees to again refile the claims, this time with the location of service changed to Park Place's address, until the CLIA certificate issue was "fixed"; and that the United States paid some of those refiled claims. That evidence was enough to prove the materiality of the false certification on the 214 claims.

Moreover, Dr. Desai testified that she knew that Pinellas could not bill for Bayfront laboratory tests until the facility was properly licensed (though she claimed to be unsure of the precise type of license required and of the method for obtaining it). It was that knowledge that allegedly led her to order a hold of all Bayfront laboratory test claims. And both Dr. Desai's husband, who helped her run Pinellas, and Pinellas' office manager, Illiana Bolton, testified that they generally knew that a laboratory is required to have a CLIA certificate to bill Medicare. That testimony, though not dispositive, is also relevant to the materiality inquiry. *See Escobar,* 136 S. Ct. at 2003 (explaining that it is relevant that "the defendant knows that the Government consistently refuses to pay claims in the mine run of cases based on noncompliance with the particular statutory, regulatory, or contractual requirement").

Finally, Pinellas contends that its failure to obtain a CLIA certificate for Bayfront was a minor, administrative error. In that vein, one factor in the materiality inquiry is whether the requirement at issue goes to the essence of the bargain with the government—i.e., whether the requirement is a central part of the regulatory program. *See Bibby,* 987 F.3d at 1347-48.

According to Pinellas, what the United States would consider important in determining whether to pay its claims is that Bayfront had a preexisting CLIA certificate, and that it was providing cancer patients with laboratory tests necessary to start chemotherapy. That may be one way of looking at things, but it is not the only way. In our view, there is sufficient evidence in the record for the jury to find that the United States would find a lack of compliance with the CLIA certificate requirement important when deciding whether to pay Pinellas' claims. For example, the United States did not pay Pinellas' initially submitted claims, which lacked a CLIA certificate number, or the second set of claims, which contained Park Place's CLIA certificate number but not its address. Pinellas' internal emails—directing that, to obtain payment from Medicare, the claims would be refiled with Park Place's p.1302 address—are also indicative of the importance of CLIA certification. So too is the fact that the Florida agency that regulated the CLIA program within the state closed Bayfront in October of 2015 upon learning that it had been operating without a CLIA certificate.

Pinellas relies on *United States ex rel. Spay v. CVS Caremark Corp.,* 875 F.3d 746, 764-65 (3d Cir. 2017), in which the Third Circuit held that minor, insubstantial misstatements did not violate the FCA. Pinellas maintains that, as in *Spay,* the United States here paid for services that were in fact provided, and that, like the Third Circuit in *Spay,* we should hold that its misstatements are the type of minor violations that do not give rise to liability under the FCA. Pinellas, however, misreads *Spay.*

The Third Circuit's materiality determination in *Spay* was based on the fact that Medicare knew of the relevant inaccuracies and nevertheless paid the claims. *See id.* at 763-65. More precisely, the defendant in *Spay,* a pharmacy chain, submitted prescription reimbursement claims to Medicare that contained dummy prescriber identification numbers. *See id.* at 750-51. It did so because it often lacked the real, unique identification numbers for prescribing physicians, and the electronic claims system would reject claims submitted without that unique identification number. *See id.* at 750, 764. There was no dispute that the prescriptions filled by the defendant had been issued by properly licensed prescribers. Medicare knew of the difficulties that pharmacies were facing when obtaining prescribers' unique identification numbers, and it knowingly paid claims containing dummy prescriber identification numbers because it did not want the prescriptions of Medicare recipients to be rejected. *See id.* at 764. Based on that evidence, the Third Circuit held that the defendant's violation of the requirement that claims include true, unique prescriber identification numbers was not material to the United States' decision to pay the claims. *See id.* at 763-65. That analysis was, of course, based on the evidence available in the *Spay* record, and there is no similar evidence here.

In sum, there was sufficient evidence for the jury to have found that, had Medicare known of Pinellas' misrepresentations, it would not have paid the refiled reimbursement claims. We therefore reject Pinellas' challenge to the verdict.

D

Pinellas submits that the evidence does not demonstrate that it acted knowingly. According to Pinellas, it was confused about the proper procedure for obtaining a CLIA certificate for Bayfront, and until it cleared up that confusion it was unaware that it could not use Park Place's CLIA certificate number for laboratory tests conducted at Bayfront. As Pinellas sees it, the 214 claims for which it was found liable should be chalked up to "honest mistakes or negligent claims," which is insufficient to satisfy the FCA's scienter element. We disagree with Pinellas' arguments on this point as well.

Liability under the FCA arises only when a defendant acted "knowingly." *See* §§ 3729(a)(1)(A) & (a)(1)(B); *Urquilla-Diaz v. Kaplan Univ.,* 780 F.3d 1039, 1058 (11th Cir. 2015). The FCA defines the term "knowingly" to "mean that a person, with respect to information.... (i) has actual knowledge of the information;.... (ii) acts in deliberate ignorance of the truth or falsity of the information; or.... (iii) acts in reckless disregard of the truth or falsity of the information." § 3729(b)(1)(A). A defendant need not, however, have acted with the specific intent to defraud the United States. *See* § 3729(b)(1)(B).

p.1303 Reckless disregard is the lowest scienter threshold under the FCA. *See Urquilla-Diaz,* 780 F.3d at 1058 n.15. As a result, so long as a reasonable jury could have found that Pinellas acted with reckless disregard of the truth or falsity of the relevant information, we must uphold the verdict.

Under the FCA, reckless disregard is tantamount to gross negligence. *See id.* at 1058. When Congress added reckless disregard to the FCA's scienter element in 1986, it intended to capture "the ostrich type situation where an individual has buried his head in the sand and failed to make simple inquiries which would alert him that false claims are being submitted." *Id.* (internal quotation marks omitted). So, a person acts with reckless disregard—and thus "knowingly"—under the FCA when he "knows or has reason to know of facts that would lead a reasonable person to realize that harm is the likely result of the relevant act." *Id.* (internal quotation marks omitted).

In this case there was sufficient evidence for the jury to find that Pinellas acted with reckless disregard of the truth or falsity of the information it included in the 214 claims for which it was found liable. Take, for example, the testimony of Dr. David

Dresdner, the former owner of Bayfront. He testified that after he sold his practice to Pinellas, his laboratory manager offered Dr. Desai assistance in obtaining a CLIA certificate, but Dr. Desai rejected the offer, stating that she knew the process for obtaining one. Moreover, Ms. Valentin's May 9th email shows that Pinellas was aware that Medicare was denying the claims it submitted with Park Place's CLIA certificate number. The solution provided in that email was to change the location of service to Park Place's address *until* the CLIA certificate issue was "fixed"—i.e., while the issue remained "unfixed" —and to refile the claims. Ms. Valentin's July 14th email acknowledged that Pinellas had not yet obtained the proper CLIA certificate for Bayfront and likewise explained that the solution was to change the location of service to Park Place's address and refile the claims. And Ms. Yates testified on redirect that she heard Dr. Desai and her husband say that they knew that they could not bill Medicare for laboratory tests conducted at an uncertified laboratory.

Broadly speaking, Pinellas presents two arguments on scienter. The first is that it believed that it could transfer Bayfront's CLIA certificate to Park Place. The second is that Dr. Desai had ordered the billing department to hold all Bayfront claims until the transfer was completed.

The first argument misses the point. Whether Pinellas believed (mistakenly or not) that it could transfer Bayfront's pre-existing CLIA certificate does not negate the fact that before Bayfront possessed a valid CLIA certificate (irrespective of the proper method of acquisition) Pinellas filed Medicare claims for laboratory tests conducted there. The question is whether Pinellas acted with, at least, reckless disregard of the truth or falsity of the certification of compliance that the use of Park Place's CLIA certificate number and address entailed. The record evidence is sufficient for the jury to find that it did.

The second argument—that Dr. Desai had ordered the billing department to hold all Medicare claims for Bayfront laboratory tests—fares little better. Though Dr. Desai testified that she issued such a hold, Ms. Yates contradicted that testimony. We recognize that Ms. Bolton corroborated Dr. Desai's testimony, but Dr. Desai was copied on both the May 9th and July 14th emails that explained the procedure for altering the information on the rejected Bayfront reimbursement claims and refiling them, and she never p.1304 objected to those directions. In short, whether a hold was issued, and if so, what the hold said about Pinellas' knowledge, were quintessential jury issues, and "[i]t is for the jury—not for us or the district court—to weigh conflicting evidence and inferences and determine the credibility of witnesses." *Mamani v. Sanchez Bustamante*, 968 F.3d 1216, 1230 (11th Cir. 2020) (internal quotation marks omitted).

Viewed in the light most favorable to the verdict, the evidence on scienter is not overwhelmingly in favor of Pinellas. The jury's decision therefore stands.

E

In addition to challenging the verdict on liability, Pinellas asks us to overturn the jury's finding that the United States suffered $755.54 in damages. According to Pinellas, the measure of damages in an FCA action is the difference between the market value of the product or service that the United States received and the market value of the promised product or service. In this case, there is no dispute that Pinellas conducted the laboratory tests for which it billed Medicare. Therefore, Pinellas says, the United States received the benefit that it bargained for and suffered no damages by paying the fraudulent claims. Though superficially attractive, the argument fails.

A person who violates the FCA is liable to the United States for "3 times the amount of damages which the Government sustains because of the act of that person." § 3729(a)(1). But "there is no set formula for determining the government's actual damages." *United States v. Killough,* 848 F.2d 1523, 1532 (11th Cir. 1988). That is because "'[f]raudulent interference with the government's activities damages the government in numerous ways that vary from case to case.'" *Id.* (quoting S. Rep. No. 96-615, at 4 (1980)).

In the context of a product or service that is provided *to* the United States, courts have indeed measured damages by comparing the market value of the delivered product or service with that of the product or service that was promised. *See, e.g., United States v. Bornstein,* 423 U.S. 303, 316 n.13, 96 S.Ct. 523, 46 L.Ed.2d 514 (1976); *United States ex rel. Wall v. Circle C Constr., LLC,* 868 F.3d 466, 470 (6th Cir. 2017); *Science Applications,* 626 F.3d at 1278. But in the context of Medicare claims, where no product or service is provided *to* the United States, courts have measured damages as the difference between what the government paid and what it would have paid had the defendant's claim been truthful and accurate. *See United States v. Mackby,* 339 F.3d 1013, 1018 (9th Cir. 2003); *United States ex rel. Drakeford v. Tuomey,* 792 F.3d 364, 386 (4th Cir. 2015); *United States v. Rogan,* 517 F.3d 449, 453 (7th Cir. 2008). The rationale is that, had the defendant truthfully admitted that it was non-compliant, the United States would not have paid. *See Rogan,* 517 F.3d at 453. For a number of reasons, we believe that the proper measure of damages here is the difference between what the United States paid and what it would have paid had Pinellas' claims been truthful.

Pinellas' argument that the United States fully received what it bargained for—because the billed-for laboratory tests were conducted—suffers from a conceptual conflict with our *post-Escobar* understanding of materiality. In *Escobar,* the Supreme Court rejected the notion that a false claim is material if the United States merely *could* refuse payment if it were aware of the violation—irrespective of whether it did or would. *See Escobar,* 136 S. Ct. at 2003. Instead, the Court held that "materiality look[s] to the effect on the likely or actual behavior of the recipient of p.1305 the alleged misrepresentation." *See id.* at 2002 (internal quotation marks omitted).

Given what *Escobar* held, ruling that the United States did not incur damages when it in fact paid for claims that it would not have paid had they been truthful is difficult to square with a finding that a false statement or representation is material. Indeed, Pinellas' argument ignores the implicit, necessary conclusion of the jury's materiality finding—that CLIA certification is a considerable part of what the United States expected and bargained for.

In *Killough* we rejected an argument similar to Pinellas'—that outside of the context of the delivery of a product or service to the United States, damages can be determined based on the value purportedly provided to the United States. *Killough* involved a kickback scheme in the awarding of government contracts to build mobile homes in the aftermath of a hurricane. *See Killough,* 848 F.2d at 1525. Officials responsible for awarding contracts would solicit kickbacks and, to generate money for the kickbacks, contractors would submit inflated invoices. *See id.* We held that, though there is no set formula for calculating the United States' damages in an FCA action, the proper measure of damages there was "the difference between what the government actually paid on the fraudulent claim and what it would have paid had there been fair, open and competitive bidding." *Id.* at 1532. We rejected the defendants' argument that because the bids of the contractors who had not participated in the scheme were at least as expensive as those of the corrupt contractors, the United States had suffered no damages when contracts were awarded to the corrupt contractors. *See id.* Hence, instead of ruling that the United States had suffered $0 in damages, we affirmed the jury's finding that it had suffered $633,000 in damages. *See id.*

The similarities between this case and *Mackby, Drakeford,* and *Rogan* persuade us that the damages analysis in those cases fit here. Like this case, *Mackby, Drakeford,* and *Rogan* involved the submission of Medicare reimbursement claims and the false certification of compliance with a condition required for payment. *See Mackby,* 339 F.3d at 1014-15 (compliance with requirement that physical therapy be rendered by a physician, a qualified employee of a physician, a physician-directed clinic, or a qualified physical therapist); *Drakeford,* 792 F.3d at 386 (compliance with the Stark Amendments to the Medicare Act); *Rogan,* 517 F.3d at 452-53 (same). Each case explained that the proper measure of damages is the difference between what the United States paid and what it would have paid had the claims been truthful and accurate. *See Mackby,* 339 F.3d at 1018-19; *Drakeford,* 792 F.3d at 386-87; *Rogan,* 517 F.3d at 453. And each case held that the difference was the full amount that the United States paid because, had the defendants truthfully admitted that they were non-compliant, the United States would not have paid.

As a result, we think that the proper measure of damages in this case is the difference between what the United States paid and what it would have paid had Pinellas' claims been truthful. The jury found that amount to be $755.54, the sum paid by the United States on Pinellas' third set of false claims. Because the jury could have found that the United States would have paid nothing had Pinellas' claims been truthful and accurate, we affirm its finding on damages.

F

We conclude our analysis of Pinellas' challenge to the jury's verdict by addressing one final set of arguments. In addition to its more general challenges, Pinellas p.1306 also contests discrete subsets of the 214 claims on which the jury based its verdict. According to Pinellas, these claim subsets are either not false, not material, or neither false nor material. The parties debated those matters in supplemental briefing on Pinellas' motion for remittitur, and the district court ruled in favor of Ms. Yates. Reviewing for abuse of discretion, *see Moore v. Appliance Direct, Inc.,* 708 F.3d 1233, 1237 (11th Cir. 2013), we affirm the district court's ruling on Pinellas' tailored challenges.

Pinellas first argues that 18 claims should be excised from the verdict because they do not contain Park Place's CLIA certificate number or its address. The factual premise of Pinellas' argument is simply not true—each of those claims includes Park Place's CLIA certificate number and some also include Park Place's address. We know because we looked. Pinellas similarly claims that four claims were not submitted to Medicare. That is also untrue— each one was indeed submitted.

In addition, Pinellas contends that 58 claims did not include charges for one type of laboratory test—a complete blood count test. In the district court, Ms. Yates responded that all but two of those claims included charges for complete blood count tests. Our review of the record convinces us that Ms. Yates was right. The remaining two claims, Ms. Yates explained, included charges for other laboratory tests that also require a CLIA certificate. On appeal, Pinellas does not explain why the district court erred in ruling for Ms. Yates on those two claims. It has therefore abandoned any argument related to them. *See Sapuppo v. Allstate Floridian Ins. Co.,* 739 F.3d 678, 681 (11th Cir. 2014).

Finally, Pinellas identifies 21 claims that were submitted to Medicare more than once and characterizes them as duplicates. What exactly Pinellas argues is unclear. To the extent that Pinellas implies that imposing liability for those claims constitutes double-dipping, Ms. Yates correctly explained below that Pinellas submitted the claims to Medicare more than once, and thus that each claim constitutes a distinct request for payment. Insofar as Pinellas argues that the 21 claims are not material, we disagree for the reasons we have laid out earlier.

IV

Having finished the heavy lift of analyzing Pinellas' challenges to the jury's verdict, we turn to its challenge of the total monetary award. To recall, the monetary award of $1,179,266.62 is comprised of $2,266.62 in treble damages and $1,177,000.00 in statutory penalties ($5,500 per violation).

Whether a particular FCA monetary award violates the Eighth Amendment's Excessive Fines Clause is a legal question subject to plenary review. *See United States v. Bajakajian,* 524 U.S. 321, 336, 118 S.Ct. 2028, 141 L.Ed.2d 314 (1998). The parties dispute whether the Eighth Amendment's Excessive Fines Clause applies to the monetary award, and, if it does, whether the award constitutes an excessive fine. They also disagree about whether Ms. Yates' share of the monetary award should be decreased.

A

There are two civil enforcement mechanisms under the FCA (other than a private right of action for retaliation). The United States can initiate a civil action, *see* § 3730(a), or a private plaintiff (called a relator) can initiate a civil action on behalf of the United States, *see* § 3730(b)(1), in what is referred to as a qui tam suit. There are, in turn, two classes of qui tam actions under the FCA: one in which the United States intervenes and thereby becomes the p.1307 primary party responsible for prosecuting the suit, and one in which the United States chooses to not intervene. *See* §§ 3730(b)(1) & (c)(1). The case before us is a qui tam action filed by Ms. Yates, as the relator, in which the United States chose to not intervene.

The Eighth Amendment provides that: "[e]xcessive bail shall not be required, nor excessive fines imposed, nor cruel and unusual punishments inflicted." U.S. Const., amdt. 8. The Supreme Court has held that "[t]he Excessive Fines Clause limits the government's power to extract payments, whether in cash or in kind, as punishment for some offense." *Austin v. United States,* 509 U.S. 602, 609-10, 113 S.Ct. 2801, 125 L.Ed.2d 488 (1993) (internal quotation marks omitted). So punitive damages awarded in civil disputes between private parties are not subject to the Eighth Amendment's proscription on excessive fines. *See Browning-Ferris Indus. of Vermont, Inc. v. Kelco Disposal, Inc.,* 492 U.S. 257, 260, 268, 275, 109 S.Ct. 2909, 106 L.Ed.2d 219 (1989).[4]

Though the United States is not a formal party in a non-intervened qui tam action, in such a case the relator prosecutes the suit "in the name of the [United States]," *see* § 3730(b)(1), as a partial assignee of the United States' damages claim. *See Vermont Agency of Nat. Res. v. United States ex rel. Stevens,* 529 U.S. 765, 773, 120 S.Ct. 1858, 146 L.Ed.2d 836 (2000). And in a non-intervened qui tam action, the United States generally receives between 70 and 75 percent of the recovery, with the relator receiving the rest. *See* § 3730(d)(2). Non-intervened FCA qui tam actions therefore fall in a grey area between disputes amongst purely private parties and disputes pitting the United States against a private party.

The Supreme Court has left open whether the Excessive Fines Clause applies to non-intervened FCA qui tam actions. *See Browning-Ferris,* 492 U.S. at 275 n.21, 109 S.Ct. 2909; *Austin,* 509 U.S. at 607 n.3, 113 S.Ct. 2801. None of our sister circuits has directly answered that question. *Cf. Hays v. Hoffman,* 325 F.3d 982, 992 (8th Cir. 2003) (stating in dicta, in a qui tam action in which the United States had not intervened at the district court, that FCA penalties are encompassed by the Excessive Fines Clause). At least one district court, however, has provided an affirmative answer. *See United States ex rel. Smith v. Gilbert Realty Co., Inc.,* 840 F. Supp. 71, 74 (E.D. Mich. 1993) (holding that the Excessive Fines Clause applies to a non-intervened qui tam action because it "is brought in the name of the United States by a private party[, and] [t]he Government will share in the proceeds"). We likewise answer the question in the affirmative, and hold that the damages and statutory penalties awarded in a non-intervened FCA qui tam action are subject to the Eighth Amendment's prohibition on excessive fines.

We first explain why an FCA monetary award is a "fine" for purposes of the Eighth Amendment. We then conclude that it is the United States that imposes such a fine in a non-intervened qui tam action.[5]

p.1308 1

The Excessive Fines Clause applies only to "fines," i.e., "payment[s] to a sovereign as punishment for some offense." *Bajakajian,* 524 U.S. at 327, 118 S.Ct. 2028 (internal quotation marks omitted). We must therefore decide whether an FCA monetary award is a fine for the purposes of the Excessive Fines Clause. We conclude that it is.

A payment constitutes a fine so long as "it can only be explained as serving in part to punish." *Austin,* 509 U.S. at 610, 113 S.Ct. 2801. *See also Bajakajian,* 524 U.S. at 328, 118 S.Ct. 2028. In *Stevens,* the Supreme Court explained that the FCA's treble damages and statutory penalties "are essentially punitive in nature." *Stevens,* 529 U.S. at 784-86, 120 S.Ct. 1858. It noted that "[t]he very idea of treble damages reveals an intent to punish past, and to deter future, unlawful conduct, not to ameliorate the liability of wrongdoers." *Id.* at 786, 120 S.Ct. 1858. That is even more true of the FCA's statutory penalties—which are preset by Congress and compulsory irrespective of the magnitude of the financial injury to the United States, if any. *See* § 3279(a)(1); *Killough,* 848 F.2d at 1533. And though FCA treble damages have a compensatory aspect, *see Cook County v. United States ex rel. Chandler,* 538 U.S. 119, 130, 123 S.Ct. 1239, 155 L.Ed.2d 247 (2003), FCA monetary awards are, at least, partially punitive. In fact, the Ninth, Eighth, and Fourth Circuits have all accepted that FCA monetary awards are fines for the purposes of the Excessive Fines Clause, precisely because they are at least in part punitive. *See United States v. Mackby,* 261 F.3d 821, 830-31 (9th Cir. 2001); *United States v. Aleff,* 772 F.3d 508, 512 (8th Cir. 2014); *Drakeford,* 792 F.3d at 387-89. We join those circuits today and hold that FCA monetary awards constitute fines for the purposes of the Excessive Fines Clause.

2

"The Excessive Fines Clause limits the government's power to extract payments, whether in cash or in kind, as punishment for some offense." *Austin,* 509 U.S. at 609-10, 113 S.Ct. 2801 (internal quotation marks omitted). That is because the object of the Eighth Amendment is "to prevent *the government* from abusing its power to punish." *Id.* at 607, 113 S.Ct. 2801. Consequently, the Excessive Fines Clause applies only to payments imposed by the United States (or the States) and payable to it (or them). *See id.* at 606-07, 113 S.Ct. 2801; *Browning-Ferris,* 492 U.S. at 264, 109 S.Ct. 2909.[6]

We have no difficulty concluding that the monetary award in a non-intervened FCA qui tam action meets the second prong of the Supreme Court's Eighth Amendment framework. In a non-intervened action, the United States generally receives between 70 and 75 percent of the recovery, but its share can be even greater in some circumstances. *See* §§ 3730(d)(2) & (3). The question is whether the monetary award in a non-intervened qui tam action is imposed by the United States. *See Austin,* 509 U.S. at 607, 113 S.Ct. 2801. For the following reasons, we conclude that that it is.

First, all monetary awards in FCA qui tam actions are imposed by the United States because they are mandated by the FCA, a federal law enacted by Congress. Ms. Yates argues that the monetary award here was not imposed by the United States p.1309 because it was not a party to the proceedings below. But that argument ignores that the Excessive Fines Clause challenge here is aimed at *the application of the FCA,* and not simply the litigation behavior of a private party. Ms. Yates is correct that the Eighth Amendment serves as a check on the power of the sovereign, but Goliath (to use her term) acted by mandating through federal law—the FCA—the imposition of treble damages and statutory penalties. *See* § 3729(a).

For all the ink spilled on the identity of the formal party in a non-intervened action, this case involves what Chief Justice Marshall called "a proposition too plain to be contested." *Marbury v. Madison,* 5 U.S. (1 Cranch) 137, 177, 2 L.Ed. 60 (1803). The FCA is a federal enactment, and therefore it must comply with the Constitution. *See id.* at 180 ("[A] law repugnant to the constitution is void; and [] courts, *as well as other departments,* are bound by that instrument.") (emphasis altered from original). *See also United States v. Comstock,* 560 U.S. 126, 135, 130 S.Ct. 1949, 176 L.Ed.2d 878

(2010) ("[A] federal statute... must ... not [be] prohibited by the Constitution.") (internal quotation marks omitted). Indeed, the subjection of statutes to the Constitution is the premise that undergirds the doctrine of judicial review. *See Marbury,* 5 U.S. at 176-80. *See also Natl. Fedn. of Indep. Bus. v. Sebelius,* 567 U.S. 519, 538, 132 S.Ct. 2566, 183 L.Ed.2d 450 (2012) (explaining that because the powers of Congress are defined and limited by the Constitution, "it is the responsibility of [the judiciary] to enforce the limits on federal power by striking down acts of Congress that transgress those limits").

As we have explained, FCA monetary awards are fines—i.e., they constitute payment to the United States as punishment (or at least in part as punishment) for an offense. *See Bajakajian,* 524 U.S. at 327, 118 S.Ct. 2028. That conclusion cannot be reconciled with the theory that such fines are not imposed by the United States simply because Congress ordered their imposition irrespective of the Executive's decision whether to intervene. That imposition and the fact that the United States receives the bulk of the monetary award are the direct result of government action. *Cf. Lugar v. Edmondson Oil Co., Inc.,* 457 U.S. 922, 941, 102 S.Ct. 2744, 73 L.Ed.2d 482 (1982) ("[T]he procedural scheme created by the statute obviously is the product of [government] action."). Pinellas' challenge is to the FCA as applied, and accordingly it is a challenge precisely about whether the United States overstepped its constitutional bounds. That claim is fully within the purview of the Excessive Fines Clause.

Second, even if we accept Ms. Yates' premise that we should focus only on the government's lack of formal party status in non-intervened qui tam actions, we conclude that any resulting monetary award is imposed by, and attributable to, the United States. Unlike a traditional private party, a relator does not initiate an FCA action to recover for an injury she herself suffered. She is instead filing suit on behalf of the United States, *see* § 3730(b)(1), for a fraud committed against the United States, *see* § 3730(a), and as a partial assignee of the United States' damages claim. *See Stevens,* 529 U.S. at 773, 120 S.Ct. 1858. Indeed, "[a] qui tam relator has suffered no [] invasion [of a legally protected right]," and it is "the United States' injury [that] suffices to confer standing on [the relator]." *Id.* at 773, 774, 120 S.Ct. 1858. In short, "the private plaintiff is merely acting as a stand-in for the government." *Makro Capital of America, Inc. v. UBS AG,* 543 F.3d 1254, 1260 (11th Cir. 2008). Though the United States is not a formal party to a non-intervened qui tam p.1310 action, it remains a real party in interest. *See United States ex rel. Eisenstein v. City of New York,* 556 U.S. 928, 934-36, 129 S.Ct. 2230, 173 L.Ed.2d 1255 (2009). Consequently, "the fact that the government delegates some portion of [its] power to private litigants does not change the governmental character of the power exercised." *Edmonson v. Leesville Concrete Co., Inc.,* 500 U.S. 614, 626, 111 S.Ct. 2077, 114 L.Ed.2d 660 (1991).

To the extent that an FCA relator must be considered a government actor of some kind to trigger the Eighth Amendment, such a requirement is satisfied here. Courts consider private persons to be government actors when they perform "a function which is traditionally the exclusive prerogative of the state." *Ancata v. Prison Health Servs., Inc.,* 769 F.2d 700, 703 (11th Cir. 1985) (finding state action in the provision of medical services in a prison by a private provider). *See Harper v. Prof. Probation Servs. Inc.,* 976 F.3d 1236, 1240 n.5 (11th Cir. 2020) (finding state action where a private party was delegated the judicial function of the state).

Here, the traditional, exclusive function of the government is the protection of the public fisc. *See United States v. Hughes Properties, Inc.,* 476 U.S. 593, 603, 106 S.Ct. 2092, 90 L.Ed.2d 569 (1986) ("[T]he major responsibility of the Internal Revenue Service is to protect the public fisc."); *Wilkins v. Gaddy,* 734 F.3d 344, 351 (4th Cir. 2013) ("Protection of the public fisc is a core responsibility of the legislative branch."). The FCA's qui tam provisions merely grant the United States the flexibility to do so effectively through an avatar in litigation. *See United States ex rel. Bunk v. Gosselin World Wide Moving, N.V.,* 741 F.3d 390, 406 (4th Cir. 2013) ("[T]he FCA was crafted in acknowledgment of the flexibility typically afforded the government to right a public wrong."); *United States v. Northrop Corp.,* 59 F.3d 953, 968 (9th Cir. 1995) ("The relator's right to recovery exists solely as a mechanism for deterring fraud and returning funds to the federal treasury.") (emphasis omitted). That a private litigant acts as a "collection agent for the government" does not negate the fact that the United States imposes the monetary award for the harm to the public fisc. *See* Nancy J. King, *Portioning Punishment: Constitutional Limits on Successive and Excessive Penalties,* 144 U. Pa. L. Rev. 101, 180 (1995).

Furthermore, the United States exercises sufficient control in non-intervened qui tam actions that it imposes any resulting monetary award. At the beginning of a non-intervened qui tam action, the United States possesses significant procedural rights that allow it to decide whether to intervene. A relator who files a qui tam complaint under the FCA must do so under seal and serve it only on the United States. *See* § 3730(b)(2). While the lawsuit remains under seal, the United States may serve a civil investigative demand upon any person believed to be in possession of documents or information relevant to an investigation of false claims, which would require that person to produce documents, answer interrogatories, or give oral testimony. *See* § 3733(a)(1). And "the United States may meet with the relator and her attorney, giving the government an opportunity to ask questions to assess the strengths and weaknesses of the case and the relator a chance to assist the government's investigation." *United States ex rel. Hunt v. Cochise Consultancy, Inc.,* 887 F.3d 1081, 1086 (11th Cir. 2018). Finally, in non-intervened qui tam actions, the relator has primary responsibility to assert the rights of the United States only because the latter allows it to do so by declining to intervene. *See* §§ 3730(b)(2) & (b)(3).

And "even in cases where the government does not intervene, there are a number p.1311 of control mechanisms present in the qui tam provisions of the FCA so that the Executive nonetheless retains a significant amount of control over the litigation." *Riley v. St. Luke's Episcopal Hosp.,* 252 F.3d 749, 753 (5th Cir. 2001) (en banc) (rejecting an Article II challenge to the FCA's qui tam provisions). The United States retains the right to request to intervene at any time, a request that may be granted for good cause. *See* § 3730(c)(3). It can also request to be served with copies of all pleadings and supplied copies of all deposition transcripts. *See id.* The United States can obtain a stay of discovery if it "would interfere with the Government's investigation or prosecution of a criminal or civil matter arising out of the same facts." § 3730(c)(4). Significantly, the relator cannot dismiss her qui tam action unless the United States consents in writing. *See* § 3730(b)(1).

We have already recognized and relied on the substantial control that the United States possesses over non-intervened FCA qui tam actions in other contexts. In *Hunt,* for example, we held that a subsection of the FCA's statute of limitations provision applies in non-intervened qui tam cases. *See Hunt,* 887 F.3d at 1092. That provision, § 3731(b)(2), limits the time to file suit to "3 years after the date when facts material to the right of action are known or reasonably should have been known by the official of the United States charged with responsibility to act in the circumstances." The appellees in *Hunt* argued that § 3731(b)(2) did not apply in non-intervened actions because it would be absurd to have a knowledge-based limitations period depend on a non-party's knowledge. *See id.* at 1091. We rejected the opinions of courts that had agreed with the appellees' theory, explaining that "[t]hey reflexively applied the general rule that a limitations period is triggered by the knowledge of a party [while] fail[ing] to consider the unique role that the United States plays even in a non-intervened qui tam case." *Id.* at 1092. Instead, we concluded that § 3731(b)(2) applies to non-intervened qui tam suits because "the United States remains the real party in interest and retains significant control over the case." *Id.* at 1091.

The United States maintains this control at the remedy phase of qui tam proceedings. "Any recovery obtained from a defendant in an FCA qui tam action belongs to the United States." *Id.* at 1087. Thus, as noted above, the United States receives the lion's share of the monetary award in a non-intervened qui tam action. *See* § 3730(d)(2). The relator, in contrast, receives a small share of the award as a bounty for prosecuting the action on the United States' behalf. *See Stevens,* 529 U.S. at 772, 120 S.Ct. 1858. In certain instances, the FCA even augments the portion of the monetary award that the United States receives. *See* § 3730(d)(3).

Such is the United States' grip that, subject to court approval, even in a non-intervened action it "may settle the action with the defendant notwithstanding the objections of the person initiating the action [i.e., the relator]." § 3730(c)(2)(B). Our decision in *United States v. Everglades College, Inc.,* 855 F.3d 1279 (11th Cir. 2017), is instructive in this regard. In *Everglades College,* the relators had been successful in a non-intervened action. *See id.* at 1282. Believing that they deserved a larger monetary award, the relators appealed. *See id.* at 1284. During the pendency of the appeal, the United States settled with one of the defendants, securing a larger sum than the one the relators had obtained. *See id.* at 1284-85. But the relators thought that they could obtain an even larger sum, so they also appealed the district court's approval of the settlement. *See id.* at 1285, 1289. We upheld the United States' settlement. *See id.* at 1289. We held that when p.1312 the United States steps in to settle a non-intervened FCA qui tam action after trial, it need not show good cause. *See id.* at 1285. We also noted that its decision to settle could be based on considerations different from a relator's, such as public policy, political ramifications, efficient use of its limited prosecutorial resources, or wariness of the impact of potential adverse appellate decisions. *See id.* at 1288-89. After all, "when the government settles a qui tam case, it is agreeing to compromise with respect to its own injuries only, not those of the relator." *Id.* at 1288. And we held that courts should grant deference to the settlement rationale of the United States because "[its] decision to end a case through settlement is similar enough to a decision to dismiss the case—a choice committed to the discretion of the Executive Branch." *Id.*

Precisely because of the United States' significant control over FCA qui tam actions, our sister circuits have held that they do not violate (i) Article II's Take Care Clause, *see Riley,* 252 F.3d at 753-57; (ii) the principle of separation of powers, *see*

United States ex rel. Kelly v. Boeing Co., 9 F.3d 743, 749-57 (9th Cir. 1993); *United States ex rel. Taxpayers Against Fraud v. Gen. Elec. Co.,* 41 F.3d 1032, 1041 (6th Cir. 1994); *United States ex rel. Kreindler & Kreindler v. United Techs. Corp.,* 985 F.2d 1148, 1154-56 (2d Cir. 1993); or (iii) the States' Eleventh Amendment immunity, *see United States. ex rel. Milam v. U. of Texas M.D. Anderson Cancer Ctr.,* 961 F.2d 46, 48-49 (4th Cir. 1992).[7]

Those constitutional issues are not before us, so we take no position on our sister circuits' ultimate conclusions. We think those cases are nevertheless relevant due to their reliance on the United States' substantial control over FCA qui tam actions. *See Riley,* 252 F.3d at 753 ("[T]hough Congress has historically allowed alternative mechanisms of fraud enforcement against the federal government, this state of affairs does not therefore mean that the Executive's functions to control such litigation are necessarily impinged.... [T]he Executive retains significant control over litigation pursued under the FCA by a qui tam relator."); *Kreindler,* 985 F.2d at 1155 ("[T]he FCA qui tam provisions do not usurp the executive branch's litigating function because the statute gives the executive branch substantial control over the litigation."); *Kelly,* 9 F.3d at 757 (holding that the FCA's qui tam provisions do not "disrupt the proper balance between the branches because ... the FCA permits the Executive Branch to retain sufficient control over prosecutorial functions") (internal quotation marks omitted); *Taxpayers Against Fraud,* 41 F.3d at 1041 (explaining that the FCA's qui tam provisions "have been crafted with particular care to maintain the primacy of the Executive Branch in prosecuting falseclaims") (internal quotation marks omitted); *Milani,* 961 F.2d at 48-49 (ruling that a non-intervened qui tam action "is [] a suit by the United States" in part because of "the extensive power the government has to control the litigation").

The FCA itself, our interpretation of its provisions, and the decisions of our sister circuits all point to the United States' considerable authority over intervened and non-intervened qui tam actions. Given that power, the United States still imposes an FCA monetary award for the purposes of p.1313 the Eighth Amendment, even when it lacks formal party status.

Third, and to conclude, the history and nature of qui tam actions support our understanding that the United States imposes the monetary award in a non-intervened FCA action. Statutory qui tam actions trace back to 14th-century England, when Parliament authorized two types: those that allowed injured parties to sue to vindicate their own interests and those of the Crown, and "those that allowed informers to obtain a portion of the penalty as a bounty for their information, even if they had not suffered an injury themselves." *Stevens,* 529 U.S. at 775, 120 S.Ct. 1858. *See also* 3 William Blackstone, Commentaries *160 (1768). FCA qui tam actions are of the latter type. *See Stevens,* 529 U.S. at 773, 120 S.Ct. 1858 (explaining that "[a] qui tam relator has suffered no ... invasion [of a legally protected] right").

The impetus for the authorization of qui tam actions was the truism that governments have limited resources. *See* J. Randy Beck, *The False Claims Act and the English Eradication of Qui Tam Legislation,* 78 N.C. L. Rev. 539, 568 (2000) ("The King, of course, could not be in all places at all times. Nor did he have an extensive network of paid royal officials whose loyalty to the interests of the Crown could be assumed.... Parliament's solution was to permit qui tam enforcement of the penalty [for statutory violations]."). Providing a share of the recovery to those who initiated qui tam actions incentivized persons with knowledge of violations to come forward (hence the name, "informer"). *See id.* In that way, "the default method of enforcement was to induce the cooperation of local citizens to act as the King's agents." *Id.*

Statutes authorizing qui tam actions were common in the early Republic. *See Stevens,* 529 U.S. at 776, 120 S.Ct. 1858. The First, Second, Third, and Fourth Congresses promulgated numerous statutes authorizing qui tam actions. *See id.* at 776-77 nn.5-7 (listing statutes passed by the First Congress authorizing qui tam actions); *Sierra v. City of Hallandale Beach,* 996 F.3d 1110, 1125 (11th Cir. 2021) (Newsom, J., concurring) (identifying statutes passed by the First, Second, Third, and Fourth Congresses authorizing qui tam actions). Chief Justice Marshall noted in *Adams v. Woods,* 6 U.S. (2 Cranch) 336, 341, 2 L.Ed. 297 (1805), that "[a]lmost every fine or forfeiture under a penal statute, may be recovered by an action of debt, as well as by information." In other words, qui tam actions were viewed as a routine enforcement mechanism in the early Republic. It thus stands to reason that the Eighth Amendment's prohibition on excessive fines would have been considerably circumscribed if it exempted such actions.

FCA qui tam actions serve the same enforcement purpose. The Senate Judiciary Committee's report on the 1986 amendments to the FCA explained that "perhaps the most serious problem plaguing effective enforcement [of the FCA] is a lack of resources on the part of Federal enforcement agencies." S. Rep. 99-345, at 7. That meant that the United States was forced to screen potential cases based on financial considerations and was outmanned by corporate defendants. *See id.* The treble damages and increased statutory penalties "allow and encourage assistance from the private citizenry [who] can make a significant impact on bolstering the Government's fraud enforcement effort." *Id.* at 8. That history "makes clear that the qui tam provisions were intended to expand the government's ability to prosecute wrongdoing directed at the government by rewarding informers; they were not primarily for the benefit of the informer." Michael Waldman, *"Damage Control": A Defendant's Approach to the Damage and Penalty Provisions of the Civil False* p.1314 *Claims Act,* 21 Pub. Contract L.J. 131, 154 (1992).

All of this leads us to conclude that the United States' lack of formal party status in a non-intervened qui tam action is not dispositive. The United States is still imposing and receiving a penalty for an offense committed against it. Given that reality, we will not exalt form over substance. Accordingly, a monetary award in a non-intervened qui tam action is imposed by the United States. *See Austin,* 509 U.S. at 607, 113 S.Ct. 2801.[8]

B   .

A fine "violates the Excessive Fines Clause if it is grossly disproportional to the gravity of a defendant's offense." *Bajakajian,* 524 U.S. at 334, 118 S.Ct. 2028. We hold that the monetary award (i.e., the "fine") imposed in this case does not violate the Excessive Fines Clause.

Before delving in, we address the parties' debate on whether we should consider the amount of the fine cumulatively or per violation. Our answer is that in this case it does not matter. Seeing a judgment of $1.179 million based on $755.54 in actual damages may raise an eyebrow. But whatever optics inure to Pinellas' benefit by that comparison, they are negated when one realizes that this total is the result of Pinellas' repeated (214) instances of fraud against the United States. The district court here imposed the lowest-possible statutory penalty of $5,500 for all of the 214 violations, and treble damages are mandated by the FCA. Therefore, no matter the perspective, the monetary award imposed represents the lowest possible sanction under the FCA.

"Translating the gravity of a crime [or offense] into monetary terms—such that it can be proportioned to the value of [a fine]-is not a simple task." *United States v. 817 N.E. 29th Drive,* 175 F.3d 1304, 1309 (11th Cir. 1999). But we have identified several, non-exhaustive factors that guide an Excessive Fines Clause analysis: (i) whether the defendant is in the class of persons at whom the statute was principally directed; (ii) how the imposed penalties compare to other penalties authorized by the legislature; and (iii) the harm caused by the defendant. *See United States v. Chaplin's, Inc.,* 646 F.3d 846, 851 (11th Cir. 2011). *See also Bajakajian,* 524 U.S. at 338-39, 118 S.Ct. 2028 (considering, among other things, the three factors we identified in *Chaplin's*); *Mackby,* 339 F.3d at 1017-18 (same).

Additionally, we have recognized that "Congress, as a representative body, can distill the monetary value society places on harmful conduct," and thus that "[penalties] falling below the maximum statutory fines for a given offense ... receive a strong presumption of constitutionality." *Chaplin's,* 646 F.3d at 852 (internal quotation marks omitted). *See Bajakajian,* 524 U.S. at 336, 118 S.Ct. 2028 ("[J]udgments about the appropriate punishment for an offense belong in the first instance to the legislature."). Because the monetary award here is at the statutory minimum, we grant it a strong presumption of constitutionality and proceed to determine whether Pinellas has rebutted that presumption. We do not think it has.

For starters, Pinellas is in the class of defendants at whom the FCA is principally directed. The FCA imposes liability on any person who defrauds or conspires to defraud the United States. *See* § 3729(a)(1). It is the United States' "primary litigative tool for combatting fraud" against it and "is intended to reach all fraudulent attempts to cause the Government to pay our [sic] sums of money." S. Rep. No. 99-345, at 2, 9. Pinellas is not in the same position as the defendant in *Bajakajian,* who, by not reporting the removal of legal currency from the United States, was subject to forfeiture under a statute principally targeted at money launderers, drug traffickers, or tax evaders. *See Bajakajian,* 524 U.S. at 338, 118 S.Ct. 2028. Pinellas, by submitting fraudulent claims, is squarely in the FCA's crosshairs. *See Mackby,* 339 F.3d at 1017 (finding that the defendant, who submitted false reimbursement claims to Medicare, fell among the class of persons targeted by the FCA).

Pinellas contends that it merely made an "error" in submitting its claims with Park Place's CLIA certificate number and address, and that this error is not the type of violation at which the FCA is directed. That, however, is merely an attempt to refashion an evidentiary liability challenge into an Excessive Fines Clause argument. To the extent that Pinellas' assertion is that any violations were inadvertent, we have already upheld the jury's finding as to scienter. *See Drakeford,* 792 F.3d at 389 (rejecting an argument that, as the defendant's FCA violations were the result of a "mere accident," damages should be reduced, because the jury had already found that the defendant had acted knowingly). And if Pinellas is trying to diminish the gravity of its violation, our ruling on materiality forecloses that gambit as well. *See Escobar,*

136 S. Ct. at 2003 ("Materiality... cannot be found where noncompliance is minor or insubstantial.").

The treble damages awarded here also compare favorably to other penalties authorized by Congress. Treble damages are authorized by Congress in other statutes. *See, e.g.,* 18 U.S.C. § 1964(c) (authorizing treble damages in a civil RICO suit); 15 U.S.C. § 15(a) (same for violations of the Clayton Act); 35 U.S.C. § 284 (same for patent infringement). Perhaps because of that, and because of the negligible value of the treble damages in this case, Pinellas does not seriously dispute their constitutionality. In any event, we conclude that the treble damages imposed by the district court do not compare unfavorably to other penalties authorized by Congress.

As to the imposed statutory penalties, they are lower than the potential maximum penalties under the FCA and other statutes. At the time of Pinellas' violations, the FCA required the imposition of statutory penalties between $5,500 and $11,000 per violation. *See* § 3729(a)(1); 28 C.F.R. § 85.3(a)(9). The penalties that the district court imposed here, based on the lowest possible statutory assessment of $5,500, were half the potential maximum. *See United States v. Emerson,* 107 F.3d 77, 80-81 (1st Cir. 1997) (holding that a $5,000 per-flight fine on a pilot for not possessing a proper FAA certificate was not excessive, in part because the statutory maximum penalty was $10,000 per flight). Moreover, in 2015 Congress passed the Federal Civil Penalties Inflation Adjustment Act Improvements Act of 2015, which required federal agencies to adjust civil payments to account for inflation. *See* Bipartisan Budget Act of 2015, Pub. L. 114-74, § 701, 129 Stat. 584, 599 (2015) (codified at 28 U.S.C. § 2461 note). As a result of that directive, the FCA's statutory penalties currently stand at between $11,665 and $23,331 per violation. *See* 28 C.F.R. § 85.5. Thus, the statutory penalties imposed on Pinellas are less than half the FCA's lowest, current statutory assessment. And they also compare well to other statutory penalties authorized by Congress. For example, violations of the Anti-Kickback Act are subject to a $23,331 statutory penalty per violation. *See* 41 U.S.C. § 8706(a)(1)(B); 28 C.F.R. § 85.5. These p.1316 comparisons are not determinative, but they are relevant.

The harm caused by Pinellas, moreover, is considerable. On this point, Pinellas tries to equate harm to the $755.54 in damages that the United States suffered. But the harm caused by an FCA violation is not so narrow. Indeed, if Pinellas were correct, then the FCA would not require the imposition of statutory penalties even when the United States does not pay a false claim. *See Killough,* 848 F.2d at 1533. *See also Bunk,* 741 F.3d at 409 (imposing a penalty of $24 million even though the relator did not seek any damages). Nor would the FCA impose statutory penalties on mere conspiracy to submit a false claim. *See* § 3729(a)(1)(C).

Fraud harms the United States in ways untethered to the value of any ultimate payment. For instance, we have explained that when the United States is defrauded, "the government has been damaged to the extent that such corruption causes a diminution of the public's confidence in the government." *Killough,* 848 F.2d at 1532. Our sister circuits have reached similar conclusions. *See, e.g., Mackby,* 339 F.3d at 1019 ("Fraudulent claims make the administration of Medicare more difficult, and widespread fraud would undermine public confidence in the system."); *Bunk,* 741 F.3d at 409 (noting that the prevalence of fraud "shakes the public's faith in the government's competence and may encourage others similarly situated to act in a like fashion"). Fraud imposes costs on the United States in the form of "the expense of the constant Treasury vigil [it] necessitate[s]." *Id.* at 409 (internal quotation marks omitted). *See also* Lani Anne Remick, *Penalty Points, Part Three: Constitutional Defenses,* 41 False Cl. Act and Qui Tam Q. Rev. 118, 131-32 (2006).

In the context of the FCA, we also consider the deterrent effect of a monetary award. *See Mackby,* 339 F.3d at 1019; *Bunk,* 741 F.3d at 409. In this case, the imposition of the lowest-possible monetary award—though, as the district court noted, "very harsh"—properly balances the need to deter potential fraudsters with the gravity of Pinellas' conduct. This is all the more so when one considers that the size of the award is a direct reflection of Pinellas' repeated and knowing submission of false claims to the United States. We agree with the Fourth Circuit that "[s]ubstantial penalties... serve as a powerful mechanism to dissuade" repeated violations of the FCA. *See Drakeford,* 792 F.3d at 389.

On this record, the monetary award imposed does not violate the Excessive Fines Clause. We reject Pinellas' contrary argument.[9]

C

Finally, Pinellas asks us to decrease Ms. Yates' share of the monetary award. Ms. Yates, who received 30 percent of the award pursuant to an agreement with the United States, argues that Pinellas does not have standing to challenge her share because it was allocated between her and the United States. Pinellas responds that it has standing because—unlike in *Taxpayers Against Fraud,* 41 F.3d at 1046, on which Ms. Yates relies—here it is p.1317 not seeking to participate in collateral litigation between the United States and a relator.

In the district court, Pinellas sought a reduction of Ms. Yates' share of the monetary award because she had supposedly planned and initiated the fraudulent scheme. *See* § 3730(d)(3) ("[I]f the court finds that the action was brought by a person who planned and initiated the violation..., then the court may, to the extent the court considers appropriate, reduce the share of the proceeds of the action which the person would otherwise receive."). As best we can tell, Ms. Yates did not challenge Pinellas' standing, and the district court did not rule on Pinellas' request. Given the procedural context, rather than analyze whether the district court lacked jurisdiction to consider Pinellas' argument, we hold that we lack jurisdiction to rule on Pinellas' appeal of the allocation. *See Frulla v. CRA Holdings, Inc.,* 543 F.3d 1247, 1250 (11th Cir. 2008) ("[A]lthough neither party challenges our jurisdiction, we are obligated to address jurisdictional questions *sua sponte.*").

The Constitution grants federal courts the power to decide issues only in the presence of an actual controversy. *See Wittman v. Personhuballah,* 578 U.S. 539, 543-44, 136 S. Ct. 1732, 195 L.Ed.2d 37 (2016); *Hollingsworth v. Perry,* 570 U.S. 693, 705, 133 S.Ct. 2652, 186 L.Ed.2d 768 (2013). Consequently, a party invoking a federal court's jurisdiction must establish that it has standing. *See Wittman,* 136 S. Ct. at 1736. That requires the party to prove that it has suffered an injury in fact, that the injury is fairly traceable to the challenged conduct, and that the injury will likely be redressed by a favorable ruling. *See id.* Because an actual controversy must persist during all stages of a litigation, "standing must be met by persons seeking appellate review, just as it must be met by persons appearing in courts of first instance." *Hollingsworth,* 570 U.S.

at 705, 133 S.Ct. 2652 (internal quotation marks omitted). Accordingly, as in the district court, on appeal "a litigant must seek relief for an injury that affects him in a personal and individual way." *Id.* (internal quotation marks omitted). Moreover, because "standing is not dispensed in gross," a litigant "must demonstrate standing for each claim he seeks to press and for each form of relief that is sought." *Town of Chester v. Laroe Estates, Inc.,* ___ U.S. ___, 137 S. Ct. 1645, 1650, 198 L.Ed.2d 64 (2017).

The amount of the total judgment that Pinellas must pay is independent of its allocation between Ms. Yates and the United States. Pinellas does not argue otherwise. In fact, it admits that a reduction in Ms. Yates' share would not reduce the total judgment amount. As a result, Pinellas has not suffered an injury in fact, let alone one that is fairly traceable to the allocation, and no injury (assuming one existed) would be redressed by a ruling from us altering the allocation. Pinellas therefore lacks standing to appeal the allocation of the monetary award between Ms. Yates and the United States, and we have no jurisdiction to rule on it. *See Wittman,* 136 S. Ct. at 1736-37 (dismissing an appeal by intervenors who could not explain how their alleged injury would be redressed by a favorable judicial decision).

V

We affirm the district court's admission of Exhibit 24, the jury's verdict, and the total monetary award. We dismiss Pinellas' appeal as to the allocation of the monetary award between Ms. Yates and the United States.

AFFIRMED IN PART AND DISMISSED IN PART.

p.1318 Newsom, Circuit Judge, joined by Jordan, Circuit Judge, concurring:

I concur in the Court's opinion and write separately simply to flag an issue that struck me as a little odd while working my way through this case: In determining whether a fine set by Congress is unconstitutionally "excessive" within the meaning of the Eighth Amendment, we give great deference to Congress's judgment about the excessiveness of the fine. *See United States v. Chaplin's, Inc.,* 646 F.3d 846, 852 (11th Cir. 2011). As a result, Congress both levies the fine and, at least as a presumptive matter, determines its constitutionality. Seems a bit like letting the driver set the speed limit.

And it looks to me like our hyper-deferential posture toward Congress's judgments about excessiveness stems from some lingering uncertainty about the basis for our own. In particular, from the premise that the text and history of the Excessive Fines Clause don't shed much useful light on the excessiveness issue, we've reasoned to the conclusion that the issue should be left to Congress. The logic is sound enough—I agree that inherently subjective judgments are often better made elsewhere—but I'm not sure the premise is correct. Based on my own examination, the Excessive Fines Clause, as originally understood, directs our attention to two discernible and instructive guideposts: (1) the proportionality between a fine and an offense, a factor that we have traditionally considered, *and* (2) the relationship between a fine and an offender's ability to pay it, one that we have not. Recovering that second part of the excessiveness inquiry would make our own evaluations of fines more objective and, by extension, alleviate any felt need to be so deferential to Congress's.

Let me unpack that a bit.

I

A

First, a word about the deference that we give Congress in the excessive-fines space. We've held that fines "falling below the maximum statutory fines for a given offense ... receive a 'strong presumption' of constitutionality." *Chaplin's,* 646 F.3d at 852 (quotation marks omitted); *see also United States v. 817 N.E. 29th Drive,* 175 F.3d 1304, 1309 (11th Cir. 1999) ("[I]f the value of forfeited property is within the range of fines prescribed by Congress, a strong presumption arises that the forfeiture is constitutional.").[1] In effect, then, Congress supplies an answer to the questions of what a fine should be *and* whether it's excessive. You might think that dynamic is strange for much the same reason that it would be odd for us to presume that a police officer's use of force wasn't excessive simply because he said so.

After all, we didn't end up with the Bill of Rights because of the founding generation's great faith in the powers that be. Brutus, for one, warned that "[t]hose who have governed have been found in all ages ever active to enlarge their powers and abridge the public liberty." Brutus II (Nov. 1, 1787), *in* 2 The p.1319 *Complete Anti-Federalist* 374 (Herbert J. Storing ed., 1981). For that reason, he argued, the prohibitions against excessive bail, excessive fines, and cruel and unusual punishments were "as necessary under the general government as under that of the individual states." *Id.* at 375. Patrick Henry made much the same point, telling Virginia's ratifying convention that "when we come to punishments, no latitude ought to be left, nor dependence put on the virtue of representatives." *See Timbs v. Indiana,* ___ U.S. ___, 139 S.Ct. 682, 696, 203 L.Ed.2d 11 (2019) (Thomas, J., concurring in the judgment) (quoting 3 *Debates on the Federal Constitution* 447 (J. Elliot, 2d ed. 1854)). Those critics counted. "The concerns voiced by the Antifederalists led to the adoption of the Bill of Rights." *Minneapolis Star & Trib. Co. v. Minn. Comm'r of Revenue,* 460 U.S. 575, 584, 103 S.Ct. 1365, 75 L.Ed.2d 295 (1983). So far as the Eighth Amendment was designed to limit the power of Congress to punish, then, great deference to Congress's judgments about the constitutionality of the punishments it chooses might be precisely the opposite of what the Eighth Amendment prescribes.[2]

Having said that, we've laid out some good reasons for respecting Congress's judgment on these questions. We've recognized, for instance, that "[t]ranslating the gravity of a crime into monetary terms ... is not a simple task." *817 N.E. 29th Drive,* 175 F.3d at 1309. More generally, fitting a punishment to an offense entails some tough judgment calls, the nature of which might lead one to conclude that other branches are better suited to make them: "The question of what acts are 'deserving' of what punishments is bound so tightly with questions of morality and social conditions as to make it, almost by definition, a question for legislative resolution."

Graham v. Florida, 560 U.S. 48, 120, 130 S.Ct. 2011, 176 L.Ed.2d 825 (2010) (Thomas, J., dissenting).

Furthermore, since the "Eighth Amendment does not mandate adoption of any one penological theory," *Graham,* 560 U.S. at 71, 130 S.Ct. 2011 (majority op.) (quotation marks omitted), Congress is generally free to select punishments with an eye to retribution, deterrence, or rehabilitation, *etc.,* or various combinations thereof. And Congress's freedom is our constraint—the Eighth Amendment gives us no power to displace Congress's choices simply because we'd have made different ones. *Cf. Coker v. Georgia,* 433 U.S. 584, 592, 97 S.Ct. 2861, 53 L.Ed.2d 982 (1977) (plurality op.) ("[T]hese Eighth Amendment judgments should not be, or appear to be, merely the subjective views of individual Justices."). Plus, because Congress represents the American people, "its pronouncements regarding the appropriate range of fines for a crime represent the collective opinion of the American people as to what is and is not excessive." *817 N.E. 29th Drive,* 175 F.3d at 1309. To the extent that "excessiveness is a highly subjective p.1320 judgment," *id.,* you can see why courts have largely left that judgment to the people's representatives.

Here's the thing: I'm not sure that excessiveness is *necessarily* a "highly subjective judgment." Because we seem to have reached that conclusion based on the Supreme Court's decision in *United States v. Bajakajian,* 524 U.S. 321, 118 S.Ct. 2028, 141 L.Ed.2d 314 (1998), I'll turn to it now.

B

Before *Bajakajian,* the Excessive Fines Clause had long remained largely unexplored and unexplained. That is, for about two centuries, the Supreme Court had little occasion to apply the Clause. *See Bajakajian,* 524 U.S. at 327, 118 S.Ct. 2028. So it fell to the *Bajakajian* Court to flesh out a standard for determining the excessiveness of fines.

The Court began its work by examining the text and history of the Excessive Fines Clause. *Id.* at 335, 118 S.Ct. 2028. Digging into those sources, the *Bajakajian* Court concluded that both showed "the centrality of proportionality to the excessiveness inquiry." *Id.* In reaching that conclusion, the Court traced the Clause's lineage to the Magna Carta, which required that economic punishments "be proportioned to the offense." *Id.* Crucially for my purposes— for reasons I'll get into—the Court also noted that the Magna Carta mandated that punishments "not deprive a wrongdoer of his livelihood." *Id.* Yet the Court passed over that second consideration, seemingly because Bajakajian hadn't argued "that his wealth or income are relevant to the proportionality determination or that full forfeiture would deprive him of his livelihood, and the District Court made no factual findings in this respect." *Id.* at 340 n.15, 118 S.Ct. 2028 (citation omitted).

As to the question of proportionality, the Court observed that the "text and history of the Excessive Fines Clause ... provide little guidance as to how disproportional a [fine] must be to the gravity of an offense in order to be 'excessive.'" *Id.* at 335, 118 S.Ct. 2028. So, having bracketed what I'll call the deprivation-of-livelihood issue, the Court looked to its Cruel and Unusual Punishments Clause caselaw for help with proportionality. There, it found the principle that "judgments about the appropriate punishment for an offense belong in the first instance to the legislature." *Id.* at 336, 118 S.Ct. 2028. Extending that principle to the context of economic penalties, the Court adopted the same "gross disproportionality" standard for fines that it had used for other punishments. *See id.* Thus, if a fine "is grossly disproportional to the gravity of the defendant's offense, it is unconstitutional." *Id.* at 337, 118 S.Ct. 2028.

Significantly for our jurisprudence in this area, our Court has taken *Bajakajian* to mean that "excessiveness is determined in relation to the characteristics of the offense, *not in relation to the characteristics of the offender." 817 N.E. 29th Drive,* 175 F.3d at 1311 (emphasis added) (citing *Bajakajian,* 524 U.S. at 334, 118 S.Ct. 2028). It's from that premise—and perhaps because the Supreme Court had told us that the text and history of the Excessive Fines Clause have little to say on the question of proportionality—that we concluded "that excessiveness is a highly subjective judgment." *Id.* at 1309. And, again, presumably because such judgments are best left with those who represent the people, we then adopted a "strong presumption" of constitutionality for fines falling within the ranges set by Congress. *Id.*

If, as it seems, an assumption underlying our decision in *817 N.E. 29th Drive* was that *Bajakajian* positively foreclosed the possibility of considering an offender's characteristics in evaluating the excessiveness of a fine, we may have gotten that p.1321 much wrong. To be sure, the *Bajakajian* Court did say that "the test for the excessiveness of a punitive forfeiture involves *solely* a proportionality determination," 524 U.S. at 333-34, 118 S.Ct. 2028 (emphasis added), and it framed that inquiry in terms of "how disproportional to the gravity of an offense a fine must be," *id.* at 336, 118 S.Ct. 2028. Yet in *Timbs v. Indiana,* the Supreme Court characterized *Bajakajian* as having "tak[en] no position on the question whether a person's income and wealth are relevant considerations in judging the excessiveness of a fine." 139 S.Ct. at 688 (majority op.). And even before *Timbs,* other circuits had disagreed with our elision of the deprivation-of-livelihood issue from the excessiveness inquiry. *See, e.g., United States v. Levesque,* 546 F.3d 78, 83 & n.4 (1st Cir. 2008) (holding that courts should consider whether a fine "would deprive the defendant of his or her livelihood"); *United States v. Lippert,* 148 F.3d 974, 978 (8th Cir. 1998) (holding that a "defendant's ability to pay is a factor under the Excessive Fines Clause"); *United States v. Viloski,* 814 F.3d 104, 111 (2d Cir. 2016) (similar).[3] It may be, then, that our excessive-fines jurisprudence rests in part on a misreading of *Bajakajian.*

More importantly to me, blinding ourselves to the effect of a fine on a defendant's livelihood may well contravene the original meaning of the Eighth Amendment's Excessive Fines Clause. So let's get into that.

C

The Eighth Amendment states that "[e]xcessive bail shall not be required, nor excessive fines imposed, nor cruel and unusual punishments inflicted." U.S. Const. amend. VIII. Not exactly self-explanatory. Looking solely at the text of the Excessive Fines Clause, one is left to wonder, excessive in relation to *what?*[4] The answer, history suggests, is not just a *what*—the offense —but also a *whom*—the offender.

Return to the Eighth Amendment's lineage. It descends most directly from the Virginia Declaration of Rights, *see Solem v. Helm,* 463 U.S. 277, 286 n.10, 103 S.Ct. 3001, 77 L.Ed.2d 637 (1983), which provided that "excessive bail ought not to be

required, nor excessive fines imposed, nor cruel and unusual punishments inflicted,"
Va. Declaration of Rights § 9 (1776). That language, in turn, came from the English
Bill of Rights of 1689. *See Timbs,* 139 S.Ct. at 688. And that document's prohibition
on excessive fines drew on and reaffirmed the Magna Carta's guarantees. *Id.*

Among those guarantees was a prohibition on economic sanctions that would
deprive an offender of his livelihood. Where p.1322 the Magna Carta addressed
amercements —a forerunner of fines—it required, among other things, "that the
amount of the amercement be proportioned to the wrong" and "not be so large as
to deprive [an offender] of his livelihood." *Browning-Ferris Indus. of Vt., Inc. v. Kelco
Disposal, Inc.,* 492 U.S. 257, 271, 109 S.Ct. 2909, 106 L.Ed.2d 219 (1989). Translated
from the Latin, the most pertinent provision of the Magna Carta said the following:

> A free man shall be amerced for a small fault only according to the measure
> thereof, and for a great crime according to its magnitude, saving his position;
> and in like manner, a merchant saving his trade, and a villein saving his tillage,
> if they should fall under Our mercy.

Timbs, 139 S. Ct. at 693 (Thomas, J., concurring in the judgment) (quoting Magna
Carta, Ch. 20 (1215), *in* A. Howard, *Magna Carta: Text & Commentary* 42 (rev. ed.
1998)).

To save a free man's "position," a merchant's "trade," and a villein's "tillage"—
all reflect the principle that no offender be "pushed absolutely to the wall: his means
of livelihood must be saved to him." William Sharp McKechnie, *Magna Carta: A
Commentary on the Great Charter of King John* 287 (2d ed. 1914).[5] The Magna Carta also
provided a means to that end. No amercements could be imposed "except by the
oath of honest men of the neighbourhood." Magna Carta, Ch. 20 (1215), *in*
McKechnie, *supra,* at 284. In practice, then, after a judge ensured that sanctions were
"proportionate to the gravity of the offense," 12 members of the offender's
community could reduce the sanctions "in accordance with their knowledge of the
wrong-doer's ability to pay." McKechnie, *supra,* at 288; *see also* 4 William Blackstone's
Commentaries *379 (explaining that "the great charter also directs that the
amercement ... shall be set ... or reduced to a certainty, by oath of good and lawful
men of the neighbourhood"). In both substance and procedure, then, the Magna
Carta protected an offender's livelihood. No wonder one eminent legal historian
thought it "[v]ery likely there was no clause in Magna Carta more grateful to the mass
of the people than that about amercements." F.W. Maitland, *Pleas of the Crown for the
County of Gloucester* xxxiv (1884).

Blackstone confirms that the deprivation-of-livelihood component of the
excessiveness inquiry endured across the centuries. In his discussion of the
prohibition of excessive fines, he observed that the 1689 "bill of rights was only
declaratory of the old constitutional law"—including, of course, the Magna Carta.
Blackstone, *supra,* at *377. So, on Blackstone's account, the 1689 Bill of Rights'
excessive fines clause carried forward the Magna Carta's provision concerning
amercements. *Id.* Hence, the rule was that "no man shall have a larger amercement
imposed upon him than his circumstances or personal estate will bear." *Id.* at *379.
Because Blackstone's "works constituted the preeminent authority on English law

for the founding generation," *Alden v. Maine,* 527 U.S. 706, 715, 119 S.Ct. 2240, 144 L.Ed.2d 636 (1999), his treatment of the English Bill of Rights of 1689—and its renewal of the Magna Carta's protections of an offender's p.1323 livelihood—supports an analogous reading of our Eighth Amendment's Excessive Fines Clause.

What's more, Blackstone's understanding accords with sources from colonial America and the early Republic. *See* Nicholas M. McLean, *Livelihood, Ability to Pay, and the Original Meaning of the Excessive Fines Clause,* 40 Hastings Const. L.Q. 833, 866-68 (2013) (collecting sources); *see also* Beth A. Colgan, *Reviving the Excessive Fines Clause,* 102 Cal. L. Rev. 277, 330 (2014) ("The principle espoused by the Magna Carta and Blackstone that fines should not permanently impoverish defendants is also found in colonial and early American records."). When William Penn set the metes and bounds of colonial Pennsylvania's government, for instance, he echoed the language of the Magna Carta: "[A]ll fines shall be moderate, and saving men's contenements, merchandise, or wainage." Pa. Frame of Government § XVIII (1682). Subsequent legislation in the same colony provided for moderate fines as well, "saving men's contenements, merchandise and wainage, which is to say, their furniture of their calling and means of livelihood." McLean, *supra,* at 866 n.128. A proto-constitutional document from New York likewise echoed the Magna Carta's protections against excessive fines. *See* N.Y. Charter of Privileges and Liberties (1683). A century later, legislation in New York did the same. *See* Colgan, *supra,* at 330 (citing a 1787 law requiring that any fine be proportioned to an offense and save to the offender "his or her contenement; That is to say every freeholder saving his freehold, a merchant saving his merchandize and a mechanick saving the implements of his trade"). Given the importance of Virginia's Declaration of Rights to the Eighth Amendment, it's perhaps especially telling that a decision from that state's apex court explained that the Declaration and ensuing legislation provided that a "fine should be according to the degree of the fault *and the estate of the offender.*" *Jones v. Commonwealth,* 5 Va. (1 Call.) 555, 557 (1799) (Roane, J.) (emphasis added).

There's good reason to think, then, that when the founding generation ratified a prohibition against "excessive fines," the phrase carried with it an understanding that a fine's excessiveness (or lack thereof) depended on *both* the relationship between the fine and the offense *and* that between the fine and the offender. If so, the excessiveness inquiry as it stands—in this Circuit, at least—is incomplete.

* * *

I've written separately to question the degree of deference we give Congress's judgments on the constitutionality of fines it sets. It's not obvious to me that Supreme Court precedent compels, or the Constitution allows, courts to ignore the impact of a fine on an offender's livelihood. And, to the extent that the Excessive Fines Clause requires us to consider precisely that, as I think it well may, returning to the Clause's original meaning would provide a more objective basis for our own judgments—and thereby alleviate any need for undue deference to Congress's.[6]

p.1324 Perhaps another court in another case will answer those questions. As we—by which I mean the three of us—are not that court and this is not that case, I concur in today's fine opinion.

Tjoflat, Circuit Judge, concurring in part and dissenting in part:

I agree that the Excessive Fines Clause is applicable to False Claims Act ("FCA") statutory penalties, but I disagree with the Court's new test for the Excessive Fines Clause as it applies to civil fines.[1] So, I endeavor to lay out, first, why the statute fails to provide a set of standards by which to impose statutory penalties, making an Excessive Fines Clause analysis the only means by which to evaluate the penalty amount. And, second, I will lay out an alternative analysis to the Court's for the Excessive Fines Clause as it applies to civil fines.

I.

I start from the premise that a district court order without reasoning is arbitrary and therefore unreviewable by us because we have no standards by which to evaluate it. *See Danley v. Allen,* 480 F.3d 1090, 1091 (11th Cir. 2007) ("Many times, and in many contexts, this Court has admonished district courts that their orders should contain sufficient explanations of their rulings so as to provide this Court with an opportunity to engage in meaningful appellate review."); *see also Gall v. United States,* 552 U.S. 38, 51, 128 S. Ct. 586, 597, 169 L.Ed.2d 445 (2007) (explaining that a criminal sentence is procedurally unreasonable when the district court "fail[s] to adequately explain the chosen sentence").

The extent of the District Court's reasoning in this case is that it was bound by our decision in *United States v. Killough,* 848 F.2d 1523, 1533-34 (11th Cir. 1988), which held that the statutory violation penalties under the FCA were mandatory and must be stacked for each violation of the statute. But *Killough* said nothing about how district courts should impose fines within the statutory range set by Congress. Beyond requiring the district court to impose at least the statutory minimum amount for every false claim, *Killough* gives no guidance as to what fine is appropriate. At the time of this case, every claim against Pinellas required, in addition to treble damages, a statutory penalty of between $5,500 and $11,000 per violation.[2] Pinellas cost the Government $755.54 in actual damages, and it submitted 214 false claims. So, the District Court imposed $2,266.62 in treble damages plus $1,177,000 in statutory penalties. The District Court imposed the minimum statutory penalty of $5,500 for each of the 214 false claims. But it provided no legal justification as to why it chose $5,500 within the statutory range of $5,500 to $11,000 per false claim penalty. Presumably, the District Court imposed the statutory minimum fine per violation because it thought that even the statutory minimum fine was "quite harsh"; but it grounded this determination in no set of standards.

The District Court's damages order reveals an internal problem within the FCA—the FCA provides no guidance as to what considerations district courts should take into account when imposing a fine within the statutory range. To understand how district courts should evaluate FCA p.1325 fines, we must first turn to the factors district courts must consider in evaluating fines in the criminal context.

II.

In the criminal law, district courts impose fines based on a set of statutory standards, located in 18 U.S.C. §§ 3553(a) and 3572.[3] These standards are Congress's codification of the traditional purposes of sentencing: general deterrence, specific deterrence or incapacitation, and retribution. *United States v. Scroggins,* 880 F.2d 1204, 1206 (11th Cir. 1989) (explaining the development of the common-law purposes of punishment from the time of the American Revolution to the 1800s). Because the traditional purposes of sentencing guide a district court's discretion in imposing criminal penalties, we, as a reviewing court, have standards by which to evaluate a district court's imposition of a sentence of confinement under § 3553(a) or a criminal fine under § 3572.[4]

With that background, I turn to the FCA's statutory scheme. It is a civil penalty system that is "essentially punitive." *Vt. Agency of Nat. Res. v. United States ex rel. Stevens,* 529 U.S. 765, 784, 120 S. Ct. 1858, 1869, 146 L.Ed.2d 836 (2000). Aside from the problems of using a civil lawsuit to effectuate criminal punishment, I have another concern—that essentially criminal penalties are being levied without the protection criminal defendants have when they are being sentenced. What I mean by this is that the FCA does not direct district courts to consider the traditional purposes of punishment as codified in § 3553(a) and § 3572 when imposing FCA penalties *within* the statutory fine range per violation, nor does it offer an alternative set of standards.

So, without a set of standards, the district court has unfettered discretion to impose any fine within the statutory range. And that makes imposition of such fines essentially unreviewable for us, except under the Eighth Amendment.[5] Of course, if a penalty is outside the statutory range, less than the minimum or more than the maximum, we can review that deviation without any governing standards inside the FCA. But that leads to very limited review and defeats the purpose of making a fine within the statutory range reviewable.

The FCA's standardless penalty scheme is like a return to pre-1984 sentencing. Prior to the sentencing reforms codified in the Sentencing Reform Act of 1984, we, as the reviewing court, could only disturb a district court's sentence if it was illegal, meaning that it was outside the statutory range, or if it was in violation of the Eighth Amendment. *See United States v. Irey,* 612 F.3d 1160, 1180 (11th Cir. 2010) (en banc) ("Before the Sentencing Reform Act was enacted in 1984, there was practically no appellate review of federal sentences,... [and] [s]o long as sentencing judges stayed within the statutory boundaries, they had unbridled discretion to arrive at any sentence they pleased."). But p.1326 Congress discarded that approach when it adopted the Sentencing Reform Act. That Act "channeled and cabined the discretion of sentencing judges by establishing the sentencing guidelines (effective in November 1987) and by specifying factors that had to be considered when imposing a sentence." *United States v. Fowler,* 749 F.3d 1010, 1020-21 (11th Cir. 2014). Now, even after *United States v. Booker,* 543 U.S. 220, 125 S. Ct. 738, 160 L.Ed.2d 621 (2005), district courts must use the guidelines range as an "initial benchmark for their sentencing decisions" and then "must consider the factors set forth in § 3553(a) to determine whether to impose a sentence within or without the guidelines range." *Fowler,* 749 F.3d at 1021 (internal citation and quotation marks omitted). This is so because "the guidelines remain the lodestone of sentencing." *Id.* (internal citation and quotation marks omitted).

And now, "post-guidelines sentences are subject to meaningful appellate review for reasonableness." *Id.* (noting that "if a court elects to impose a sentence based on a major variance from the guidelines range, the chances of reversal on appeal increase"). So, the criminal sentencing context allows for appellate review because the district court must apply standards leading to a result that we can review. The chances of such a sentence violating the Eighth Amendment are very low because the sentence should have already accounted for a guidelines computation, derived from empirical studies directed to the need of general deterrence and retribution, and the § 3553(a) factors.

But the imposition of civil fines under the FCA is stuck in pre-1984 sentencing, where, based on the statute, we can only hold that a fine is illegal if it departs from the statutory range. This is certainly at odds with our jurisprudence on review of terms of incarceration and criminal fines, even after *Booker,* and appellate review more generally, which requires standards for evaluation of district court action. And, without any internal standards for review on the amount of the statutory penalty, we must review the present fine under the Eighth Amendment's Excessive Fines Clause.[6]

III.

In reaching the Excessive Fines Clause analysis, I feel compelled to first explain why the Court has erred in applying *United States v. Bajakajian.* Forfeitures in the context of criminal proceedings, as in *Bajakajian,* are vastly different from civil fines, as in the FCA, and to apply the same test to both would be to start our Excessive Fines Clause jurisprudence as it applies to civil fines on the wrong foot from the beginning.

In *Bajakajian,* the defendant pled guilty for his failure to report $357,144 that he was planning to take overseas, and the applicable forfeiture statute for the crime of failing to report traveling out of the p.1327 country with more than $10,000 required that he forfeit the entire amount he was traveling with—all $357,144. 524 U.S. 321, 337-39, 118 S. Ct. 2028, 2038-39, 141 L.Ed.2d 314 (1998). In that case, the Supreme Court held that such a forfeiture would be grossly disproportionate to the simple crime of failing to report, especially since the crime was not related to other illegal activities. *Id.*

In my view, central to *Bajakajian*'s analysis was the common-law roots of forfeiture. At the time of the framing of the Eighth Amendment, three kinds of forfeiture existed in England: 1) deodand, 2) forfeiture upon conviction for a felony or treason, and 3) statutory forfeiture. *Austin v. United States,* 509 U.S. 602, 611-12, 113 S. Ct. 2801, 2806-07, 125 L.Ed.2d 488 (1993). Each of these forms of forfeiture could be used to punish, and in American law, the third category, statutory forfeiture, took the greatest hold. *Id.* In *Bajakajian,* the forfeiture was "imposed at the culmination of a criminal proceeding and require[d] conviction of an underlying felony." *Bajakajian,* 524 U.S. at 328, 118 S. Ct. at 2033. The Court determined that the forfeiture was *in personam,* that is, as a result of an individual's criminal conduct, rather than *in rem,* that is, against guilty property. *Id.* at 331-332, 118 S. Ct. at 2035. This choice was significant because the Court correlated *in personam* forfeiture with punishment, making that particular forfeiture subject to the Excessive Fines Clause.[7] *Id.*

What is key in all the Court's discussion of forfeiture for purposes of our analysis is the fact that the property at issue in any form of forfeiture is related to the criminal offense. If the forfeiture is *in personam,* the property is related to the individual's criminal conduct. If the forfeiture is *in rem* and relates to a criminal matter, the property has been used in a criminal manner, even if the owner of the property is innocent. Either way, the forfeiture is directed at property directly tied to criminal conduct, and the property forfeited is directly correlated to the property that was involved in the criminal offense. *See Austin,* 509 U.S. at 627-28, 113 S. Ct. at 2815 (Scalia, J., concurring) ("But an *in rem* forfeiture goes beyond the traditional limits that the Eighth Amendment permits if it applies to property that cannot properly be regarded as an instrumentality of the offense—the building, for example, in which an isolated drug sale happens to occur. Such a confiscation would be an excessive fine. The question is not *how much* the confiscated property is worth, but *whether* the confiscated property has a close enough relationship to the offense." (emphasis in original)). And, in the case of *in personam* forfeiture, as in *Bajakajian,* the forfeiture was related to a criminal sentence that could include imprisonment and a fine under the applicable statute. *Bajakajian,* 524 U.S. at 338, 118 S. Ct. at 2038.

p.1328 From *Bajakajian,* we derived a three-factor test to determine whether a forfeiture is grossly disproportional to the gravity of a defendant's offense. *See United States v. Browne,* 505 F.3d 1229, 1281 (11th Cir. 2007). We explained that in these cases we examine "(1) whether the defendant falls into the class of persons at whom the criminal statute was principally directed; (2) other penalties authorized by the legislature (or the Sentencing Commission); and (3) the harm caused by the defendant." *Browne,* 505 F.3d at 1281 (internal citation omitted). We later clarified, in *United States v. Chaplin's, Inc.,* that these factors do not represent an "exclusive checklist," 646 F.3d 846, 851 n.16 (11th Cir. 2011), and that we apply a "strong presumption" of constitutionality when the forfeiture is below the maximum criminal statutory fine, *id.* at 852 (citing *United States v. 817 N.E. 29th Drive,* 175 F.3d 1304, 1309 (11th Cir. 1999).

Bajakajian was tailored to the context of forfeiture. Forfeiture's deep common-law roots make it distinct from the FCA's civil fines regime, and I think this difference makes the test we developed in *Browne* (from *Bajakajian*) inapplicable to the present case. *Cf. Austin,* 509 U.S. at 627, 113 S. Ct. at 2814 (Scalia, J., concurring) ("[I] think it worth pointing out that on remand the excessiveness analysis [for *in rem* forfeitures] must be different from that applicable to monetary fines and, perhaps, to *in personam* forfeitures."). Here, in the FCA context, there is no natural limit to the fine extracted, like there is a natural limit to the property forfeited based on its involvement in criminal activity. And, because the criminal fine at issue in *Bajakajian* was *in personam,* that is, based on the defendant's criminal conviction, the Court could compare the forfeiture amount to how culpable Congress thought the conduct was under the criminal scheme. In addition, the Guidelines inherently consider specific deterrence, general deterrence, and retribution. *See Scroggins,* 880 F.2d at 1209 ("Thus, while the guidelines consider evidence of the offender's criminal history for purposes of punishment and general deterrence, its primary importance is to ensure that the specific defendant is deterred from future criminal conduct.").

I take issue with the Court's treatment of both the second *Browne* factor, derived from *Bajakajian,* and the strong presumption of constitutionality because neither has a place in the FCA context. The second *Browne* factor directs the court to analyze "other penalties authorized by the legislature (or the Sentencing Commission)."

Browne, 505 F.3d at 1281. Undoubtedly, the Court today evaluates other penalties authorized by the legislature, but it evaluates the *wrong* penalties. The Court goes outside the FCA statutory scheme to compare the FCA fines to the fines of such statutes as civil RICO, the Clayton Act, federal aviation laws, and the Anti-Kickback Act. *See* Maj. Op. at 1315-16. But that analysis misinterprets the second *Browne* factor. As *Bajakajian's* analysis makes clear, a court must look *within* the statutory scheme in evaluating what other penalties are authorized for the *same* offense. *Bajakajian,* 524 U.S. at 338, 118 S. Ct. at 2038 (focusing on the Sentencing Guidelines (*pre-Booker*) and explaining that while the applicable forfeiture statute required forfeiture of the entire $357,144 the maximum period of incarceration that could have been imposed under the guidelines for the crime of failing to report the currency was six months with a maximum fine of $5,000). The purpose of looking within the statutory scheme is to figure out how culpable Congress considered the conduct at issue to be. *Id.* at 339, 118 S. Ct. at 2038 (explaining that in Bajakajian's case, "such penalties confirm a minimal level of culpability").

p.1329 The Court's method of comparing FCA penalties to other statutory schemes is like comparing apples and oranges. And figuring out how culpable Congress thinks an orange is tells us nothing about how culpable it thinks an apple is. In fact, the Court's method reveals how little room district courts have to maneuver in imposing fines under the FCA. The district court must impose treble damages and statutory penalties, with no discretion to craft a tailor-made sentence. This is not like the flexibility in criminal sentencing afforded to district courts, which often have statutory fines, statutory sentencing ranges, and guidelines ranges as guides when imposing punishment. This difference between the criminal context and FCA fines leads me to believe that the second *Browne* factor is totally inapplicable to the FCA context. Today's decision is precedential because we are deciding to apply the Excessive Fines Clause to FCA fines. On this blank slate, I would hesitate to apply a wooden analysis of the second *Browne* factor without accounting for the differences between forfeitures associated with criminal convictions and civil fines.

Next, I turn to the Court's application of the strong presumption of constitutionality. *Chaplin's* tells us that when a forfeiture is below *the statutory maximum criminal fine,* we give that forfeiture a strong presumption of constitutionality. 646 F.3d at 852. Congress determines how culpable the conduct is, and a comparison of the forfeiture amount to the fine amount allowed by statute is one way of measuring culpability. This is because the criminal fine amount is the product of Congress weighing the traditional purposes of punishment in crafting sentences. "Congress, as a representative body, can distill the monetary value society places on harmful conduct," and "[t]he Sentencing Guidelines reflect institutional expertise and monetize culpability with even greater precision than criminal legislation." *Chaplin's, Inc.,* 646 F.3d at 852 (internal citation and quotation marks omitted). But the strong presumption of constitutionality should only apply when Congress and/or the Sentencing Commission bring their expertise to bear. And, here, there is no indication of how culpable either body thought the false claims were by any other measure than the fine itself, unlike in the forfeiture context, where the criminal fine guides the forfeiture analysis.[8] For sure, the legislative reports surrounding the 1986 amendments to the FCA suggest that the fines were aimed at deterrence. H.R. Rep. No. 99-660, at 20 (1986) ("The Committee recommends this change in order that the False Claims Act penalties will have a strong deterrent effect."). But evaluation of deterrence should be tied to evidence of what will, in fact, most efficiently deter. *See* § 3553(a) ("The court shall impose a sentence sufficient, but not greater than necessary, to comply with the" traditional purposes of punishment."). That is, Congress should want to make the costs of doing the prohibited activity higher than not doing it. But just how much higher the costs should be is a matter of legislative p.1330 determination. The circumstances of the case will have a bearing on efficient deterrence. If a child steals a candy bar, a $100 fine and a $1,000 fine will both deter the child, but the $1,000 fine would probably be disproportionate to the offense. So, the $100 fine is probably more appropriate.

The FCA covers a vast swath of conduct, from solo practice medical clinics sending in false Medicare claims to government contractors defrauding the Government of millions of dollars. *See* S. Rep. No. 110-507, at 3-4 (2008) (discussing the impetus behind the 1986 Amendments to the False Claims Act and "widespread" fraud against the Government (internal citation omitted)). Of course, the commonality is that all False Claims Act cases involve —well—false claims. But the sheer permutations of false claims violations falling under the FCA precluded Congress from "distill[ing] the monetary value society places on harmful conduct"[9] or "monetize[ing] culpability" under the statutory fine scheme.[10] *Chaplin's, Inc.*, 646 F.3d at 852. A solo doctor could submit 50 false claims in Medicare fraud that only cost the Government $500. A Government contractor could submit 50 false claims that cost the Government $5 million. In both cases, the statutory minimum and maximum fine range would be the same, even though the treble damages amounts would be vastly different and the cost to society would likely be much higher in the case of Government contractor fraud. My point is that the statutory fine ranges are not at all tethered to what will efficiently deter a particular defendant based on evidence, so the strong presumption of constitutionality is unwarranted in the FCA fine context.

IV.

Having explained why the *Bajakajian* analysis is inapplicable to the civil fines context, I now turn to what I deem to be a more sensible approach to evaluating civil fines under the Eighth Amendment.

Our Eighth Amendment has a distinguished lineage. In 1215, Magna Carta directed that "[a] Free-man shall not be amerced for a small fault, but after the manner of the fault; and for a great fault after the greatness thereof, saving to him his contenement."[11] § 20, 9 Hen. III, ch. 14, in 1 Eng. Stat. at Large 5 (1225). The p.1331 baseline for amercements and fines under Magna Carta was proportionality to the wrong committed and to the defendant's ability to pay. *See Timbs v. Indiana*, ___ U.S. ___, 139 S. Ct. 682, 688, 203 L.Ed.2d 11 (2019) (citing *Browning-Ferris Indus. v. Kelco Disposal, Inc.*, 492 U.S. 257, 271, 109 S. Ct. 2909, 2918, 106 L.Ed.2d 219 (1989)). Because abuses abounded under the Stuart kings in the seventeenth century, the English Bill of Rights of 1689 picked up on Magna Carta's language and directed that "excessive Bail ought not to be required, nor excessive Fines imposed; nor cruel and unusual Punishments inflicted." 1 Wm. & Mary, ch. 2, § 10, in 3 Eng. Stat. at Large 441 (1689). Ultimately, that language was incorporated into the Virginia Declaration of Rights[12] and then into our Eighth Amendment. *See Timbs,* 139 S. Ct. at 688-89; *see also* Calvin Massey, *The Excessive Fines Clause and Punitive Damages: Some Lessons from History,* 40 Vand. L. Rev. 1233, 1241 (1987) (noting that there was little debate over the Eighth Amendment and explaining that it is likely that the First Congress "uncritically accepted the language [of the Excessive Fines Clause], treating it as a shorthand expression for ancient rights rooted in the soil of English law").

The prohibition of excessive fines "has been a constant shield throughout Anglo-American history." *Timbs,* 139 S. Ct. at 689. One example of the need for the Excessive Fines Clause is that "[e]ven absent a political motive, fines may be employed 'in a measure out of accord with the penal goals of retribution and deterrence,' for 'fines are a source of revenue,' while other forms of punishment 'cost a State money.'" *Id.* (citing *Harmelin v. Michigan,* 501 U.S. 957, 978 n.9, 111 S. Ct. 2680, 2693 n.9 (opinion of Scalia, J.) ("it makes sense to scrutinize governmental action more closely when the State stands to benefit")).[13]

What is key from this statement in *Timbs* is that the Court is looking at the traditional purposes of punishment—retribution and deterrence—in evaluating the Excessive Fines Clause, now codified in § 3553(a). This makes sense because the Eighth Amendment was not written on a blank slate. The venerable history of the Eighth Amendment, tracing back from Magna Carta, should inform how we view the content of the Eighth Amendment.

We know that at common law, "colonial courts fashioned sentences with three basic purposes in mind: to punish the offender for his crime, thereby satisfying society's desire for retribution ('punishment'); to deter others from committing the same crime by demonstrating its disadvantageous consequences ('general deterrence'); and to incapacitate the wrongdoer, so as to protect society from further criminal activity ('specific deterrence' or 'incapacitation')." p.1332 *Scroggins,* 880 F.2d at 1206. In light of these common-law goals and the Eighth Amendment's incorporation of the common law, our first goal should be to figure out how the historical common law—from Magna Carta to our Constitution —viewed the traditional purposes of punishment in the context of excessive fines.

In the 1600s, Sir Edward Coke described Magna Carta as "but a confirmation or restitution of the Common Law." 1 Edward Coke, Institutes of the Lawes of England (1608), *reprinted in* 2 *The Selected Writings and Speeches of Sir Edward Coke* § 108, at 697 (Steve Sheppard ed., 2003); *see generally* Brief of Professor John F. Stinneford as Amicus Curiae in Support of Neither Party, Kahler v. Kansas, ___ U.S. ___, 140 S. Ct. 1021, 206 L.Ed.2d 312 (2019) (No. 18-6135). And the English common law interpreted Magna Carta as requiring that fines be "reasonable and proportional." Brief of Stinneford, at 9; *see Richard Godfrey's Case,* 11 Co. 42a, 44a., 77 Eng. Rep. 1199, 1202 (1615) (explaining that "the reasonableness of the fine shall be adjudged by the justices; and, if it appears to them to be excessive, it is against the law, and shall not bind.").[14] Under Magna Carta, "imprisonment ought always to be according to the quality of the offence." *Hodges v. Humkin,* 2 Bulst. 139, 140, 80 Eng. Rep. 1015 (1615).

Although there is some debate about the impetus for the 1689 English Bill of Rights, most scholars agree that it was necessary because of the Stuart kings' drift away from the principles of Magna Carta during the late 1600s. By this time, the idea of excessive fines had come to incorporate the principle that the punishment imposed should be in keeping with the traditional common-law sentence for that particular crime. *See Harmelin,* 501 U.S. at 973-74, 111 S. Ct. at 2690 (explaining that during the 1600s in England "a punishment [wa]s not considered objectionable because it [wa]s disproportionate, but because it [wa]s out of the Judges' Power, contrary to Law and ancient practice, without Precedents or express Law to warrant, unusual, illegal, or imposed by Pretence to a discretionary Power" (internal quotation marks and citation omitted)). So, during this period, too, the common law was the bedrock of sentencing.[15]

With that background, I turn to Blackstone's Commentaries. The Supreme Court has described Blackstone's Commentaries as "more read in America before the Revolution than any other law book." *C.J. Hendry Co. v. Moore,* 318 U.S. 133, 151, 63 S. Ct. 499, 509, 87 L.Ed. 663 (1943); *see also Schick v. United States,* 195 U.S. 65, 69, 24 S. Ct. 826, 827, 49 L.Ed. 99 (1904) ("Blackstone's Commentaries are accepted as the most satisfactory exposition of the common law of England. At the time of the adoption of the Federal Constitution, it had been published about twenty years, and it has been said that more copies of the work had been sold in this country than in England; so that undoubtedly, the framers of the Constitution were familiar with it.").[16]

Blackstone had much to say about whether a fine is excessive. His commentaries explain that "[t]he reasonableness of fines in criminal cases[17] has also been usually relegated by the determination of Magna Carta, concerning amercements for misbehavior in matters of civil right." Blackstone took his view from the language of the Magna Carta as follows: "Liber homo non amercietur pro parvo delicto, nisi secundum modum ipsius delicti; et pro magno delicto, secundum magnitudinem delicti; salvo contenemento suo: et mercator eodem modo, salva mercandisa sua; et villanus eodem modo amercietur, salvo wainagio suo." 4 William Blackstone's Commentaries *379 (Lewis ed. 1902) (internal quotation marks omitted). Blackstone summarized that "no man shall have a larger amercement imposed upon him, than his circumstances or personal estate will bear: saving to the landholder his contenement, or land; to the trader his merchandise; and to the countryman his wainage, or team and instruments of husbandry." *Id.*

In short, Blackstone's Commentaries look at both the characteristics of the offender and offense in determining the appropriate fine. *Cf.* § 3553(a)(1) (explaining that the court must look at "the nature and circumstances of the offense and the history and circumstances of the defendant" in imposing a sentence). And the principle of proportionality based on the offense and the defendant's ability to pay was embodied in the common law as evidenced by how states interpreted their own excessive fines clauses. *See Steptoe v. The Auditor,* 24 Va. 221, 234 (Va. 1825) (describing a law and explaining that "[i]t would be *excessive,* as bearing no proportion whatever to the nature of the offence, not even graduated by the amount due" (emphasis in original)); *Commonwealth v. Morrison,* 9 Ky. 75, 99 (Ky. 1819) ("The fine imposed should bear a just proportion to the offense committed, the situation, circumstances and character of the offender. That proportion must be ascertained by the sound discretion of the court: a flagrant transcension by the legislature in fixing the fine of that just relative proportion between offense and fine, would be denominated excessive."); *cf.* § 3572 (directing the court to look at the "defendant's income, earning capacity, and financial resources" in determining the appropriate criminal fine).

This proportionality analysis tracks the traditional purposes of punishment of general deterrence, specific deterrence, and retribution. Blackstone, quoting Montesquieu, explained that "excessive severity of laws [out of proportion to the offense] ... hinders their execution." 4 William Blackstone's Commentaries *17; *cf.* § 3553(a) ("The court shall impose a sentence sufficient, but not greater than necessary, to comply with the" traditional purposes of punishment); § 3553(a)(2)(A) (explaining that a sentence should "reflect the seriousness of the offense, [] promote respect for the law, and [] provide just punishment for the offense"). And he defined excessiveness in relation to laws that do not have "due distinctions of severity," with the common law as the baseline. *Id.* American common law, incorporating the traditional purposes of punishment, tracks this reasoning. *See, e.g., Barker v. People,* 3 Cow. 686, 694 (N.Y. 1824) (looking at the common law to determine what kinds of punishment were unusual for purposes of the state's version of the Eighth Amendment); *Jones v. Commonwealth,* 5 Va. 555, 558 (Va. 1799) (determining that a joint fine was excessive because the common law forbade such fines); *see also Johnson v. Tompkins,* 13 F. Cas. 840, 848 (E.D. Pa. 1833) ("Here [in Pennsylvania] punishment is graduated in proportion to the enormity of the offence, and cruel punishments are expressly forbidden by the constitution, as well as excessive fines (article 9, § 13) and by the eighth amendment to the constitution of the United States."); *Ingraham v. Wright,* 430 U.S. 651, 670, 97 S.Ct. 1401, 51 L.Ed.2d 711 (1977) (focusing on the common-law limits to corporal punishment in the Eighth Amendment context).

In other words, at common law, the inquiry into excessiveness hinged on an analysis of an individual defendant with individual characteristics and an individual crime. *Cf.* § 3553(a). The common-law analysis of the Eighth Amendment, therefore, mirrors the evaluation of the traditional purposes of punishment, as they are codified in § 3553(a). So, it makes sense that if the Eighth Amendment incorporates the common law and its traditional purposes of punishment, and the common law performed an individual analysis for excessiveness, that we too should opt for a particularized analysis for excessive fines.

I suggest that district courts should apply the § 3553(a) factors (and thus the § 3572 factors) to the FCA context as the test for excessiveness of civil fines under the Eighth Amendment.[18] To do so would be to create a set of standards for district p.1335 courts to apply that accords with common law, and it would give us something to review on appeal. In practice, district courts would hold evidentiary hearings to allow the defendant, pulling from the §§ 3553(a) and 3572 factors, to explain why the purposes of punishment—i.e., retribution, general deterrence, and specific deterrence —are not served by the penalty the Government (or qui tam relator) seeks to impose.

The constitutional analysis for excessive fines puts the burden on the defendant bringing the constitutional challenge to provide evidence as to how the proposed statutory penalty fails to accord with the traditional purposes of punishment. The defendant's goal would be to show that the fine is disproportionate to the offense. And the Government may respond with evidence of its own to rebut the defendant's challenge. The district court's task is to assess the evidence before it and determine how the characteristics of the offense and the characteristics of the offender correspond to the fine in question. *See* William Blackstone's Commentaries *15-16 ("To kill a man upon sudden and violent resentment is less penal, than upon cool deliberate malice. The age, education, and character of the offender; the repetition (or otherwise) of the offense; the time, the place, the company wherein it was committed; all these, and a thousand other incidents, may aggravate or extenuate the crime."). The best way for the district court to follow the common-law model is to evaluate the § 3553(a) factors.

Section 3572 is simply an explication of the § 3553(a) factors. It directs the district court to look at factors like the defendant's income, the burden the fine would impose on the defendant or his dependents, the harm caused by the defendant, how much restitution is made, the need to take away from the defendant illegal profit, and the costs to the government of the defendant's misconduct. These are exactly the kind of factors that common-law courts considered when imposing a fine, and they serve as the ideal guide for today's district courts when trying to conduct an Eighth Amendment analysis for excessive fines. In other words, the Excessive Fines Clause analysis should be holistic, considering all the individual facts of the case, not a wooden application of *Bajakajian.*

It is worth noting that, in reviewing the evidence, even the statutory minimum penalty is in clear focus, and the district court might find that based on the evidence before it even the statutory minimum range is too high. In the event that the district court finds that the statutory minimum range is excessive in relation to the offense, it may lower the fine amount to correspond to the traditional purposes of punishment and must provide a reasoned explanation as to how it came to that determination.[19] This also goes to reviewability p.1336 because such a reasoned explanation allows us to evaluate the district court's reasoning and usage of the § 3553(a) factors in the constitutional analysis.

And, in 1998, the Supreme Court confirmed that proportionality is the "touchstone" of the Excessive Fines Clause. *Bajakajian,* 524 U.S. at 334, 118 S. Ct. at 2036. And using the traditional purposes of punishment as a set of guideposts honors the tradition of proportionality because it considers the characteristics of the offender and the characteristics of the offense in each case. I would remand so that the District Court could allow the defendant to present evidence on both the characteristics of the offense and the offender. To do otherwise would be to allow an arbitrary fine to stand under the Excessive Fines Clause.

[1] The parties debate whether Bayfront's preexisting CLIA certificate could be transferred to Pinellas or whether Pinellas had to obtain a new CLIA certificate for Bayfront. In our view, the particular method of obtaining a CLIA certificate for Bayfront linked to Pinellas does not matter. Whether through a transfer or a brand-new application, Bayfront was required to have a CLIA certificate linked to Pinellas, and it did not have one from April of 2015 until March of 2016.

[2] Ms. Yates testified that all 214 claims included in Exhibit 24 had the location of service changed to Park Place's address. Our review of the few claim forms that are in the record on appeal, however, confirms that that is not the case. Though all the available claim forms include Park Place's CLIA certificate number, some did not

have the location of service changed to Park Place's address. We note this discrepancy but do not address its implications, if any, because the insertion of Park Place's CLIA certificate number by itself is sufficient to constitute a false certification under the FCA.

[3] We have significant doubts about Pinellas' argument that a CLIA certificate is not a condition of payment. "Conditions of payment are those which, if the government knew they were not being followed, might cause it to actually refuse payment." *United States ex rel. Conner v. Salina Regl. Health Ctr., Inc.,* 543 F.3d 1211, 1220 (10th Cir. 2008). "CMS always cancels a laboratory's approval to receive Medicare payment for its services if CMS suspends or revokes the laboratory's CLIA certificate." 42 C.F.R. § 493.1842(a)(1). And Medicare's claims processing manual indicates that "[t]he CLIA mandates that virtually all laboratories, including physician office laboratories (POLs)... have a CLIA certificate in order to receive reimbursement from Federal programs." *See* CMS, *Medicare Claims Processing Manual,* § 70.1. Because the jury had sufficient evidence otherwise to find that Pinellas' violations were material, however, we need not decide whether CLIA certification is a condition of payment.

[4] Punitive damages awarded in litigation between private parties, however, must satisfy due process standards. *See BMW of N.A., Inc. v. Gore,* 517 U.S. 559, 568-86, 116 S.Ct. 1589, 134 L.Ed.2d 809 (1996).

[5] In addition to the FCA, at least one other federal statute authorizes qui tam actions. *See* 25 U.S.C. § 201 (providing a cause of action and share of recovery against a person who violates Indian protection laws). We do not address that statute today, as it is not before us.

[6] The Excessive Fines Clause has been incorporated, and is thus applicable to the States, through the Due Process Clause of the Fourteenth Amendment. *See Timbs v. Indiana,* ___ U.S. ___, 139 S. Ct. 682, 687, 203 L.Ed.2d 11 (2019).

[7] In *Stevens,* the Supreme Court held that States are not subject to liability under the FCA because they are not "persons" for the purposes of the FCA. *See Stevens,* 529 U.S. at 787, 120 S.Ct. 1858. It left open, however, whether the Eleventh Amendment provides immunity to States from non-intervened qui tam actions. *See id.* at 773 n.4, 120 S.Ct. 1858.

[8] The United States, as amicus curiae, agreed at oral argument that the Excessive Fines Clause applies in this case. *See* Oral Arg. Tr. at 23:43-50. We are not bound by its constitutional position, *see Orloff v. Willoughby,* 345 U.S. 83, 87, 73 S.Ct. 534, 97 L.Ed. 842 (1953), but based on our independent analysis we agree.

[9] In his separate opinion, Judge Tjoflat asserts that the FCA fails to provide standards to guide a district court in choosing the appropriate penalty within the statutory range. We do not address that issue for two reasons. First, Pinellas has not based its Eighth Amendment challenge on the procedural claim that the FCA lacks standards. Second, where—as here—the statutory minimum penalty is imposed, the district court lacks the authority to go below that minimum absent a constitutional violation. In other words, standards do not come into play if the court is imposing only the statutory minimum penalty mandated by Congress.

[1] Some of the caselaw on this subject involves forfeitures, but the Supreme Court has held that a forfeiture can constitute "a 'fine' within the meaning of the

Excessive Fines Clause." *United States v. Bajakajian,* 524 U.S. 321, 334, 118 S.Ct. 2028, 141 L.Ed.2d 314 (1998); *see also Austin v. United States,* 509 U.S. 602, 614 n.7, 113 S.Ct. 2801, 125 L.Ed.2d 488 (1993) (collecting definitions from founding-era dictionaries showing that "'fine' was understood to include 'forfeiture' and vice versa"); *Browning-Ferris Indus. of Vt., Inc. v. Kelco Disposal, Inc.,* 492 U.S. 257, 265, 109 S.Ct. 2909, 106 L.Ed.2d 219 (1989) (explaining "that at the time of the drafting and ratification of the [Eighth] Amendment, the word 'fine' was understood to mean a payment to a sovereign as punishment for some offense").

[2] As an aside, I wonder whether fines might differ from other punishments, such that the degree of deference we give congressional judgments concerning them ought to differ, too:

There is good reason to be concerned that fines, uniquely of all punishments, will be imposed in a measure out of accord with the penal goals of retribution and deterrence. Imprisonment, corporal punishment, and even capital punishment cost a State money; fines are a source of revenue. As we have recognized in the context of other constitutional provisions, it makes sense to scrutinize governmental action more closely when the State stands to benefit.

Harmelin v. Michigan, 501 U.S. 957, 978 n.9, 111 S.Ct. 2680, 115 L.Ed.2d 836 (1991) (opinion of Scalia, J.). I see no reason why that concern should be unique to fines imposed by states. Every government needs revenue, of course.

[3] How exactly the deprivation-of-livelihood issue should be analyzed is the subject of some disagreement. For instance, the First Circuit considers the deprivation-of-livelihood issue to be independent of the question of gross disproportionality, *see Levesque,* 546 F.3d at 84-85, whereas the Second Circuit considers the former as part of its test for the latter, *see Viloski,* 814 F.3d at 111-12 & n.12. The Second Circuit's approach seems easier to reconcile with *Bajakajian's* statement that the test for excessiveness "involves *solely* a proportionality determination," 524 U.S. at 334, 118 S.Ct. 2028 (emphasis added), but the First Circuit's approach may more accurately reflect the historical sources, which appear to treat the proportionality and deprivation-of-livelihood issues separately, *see id.* at 335, 118 S.Ct. 2028 (explaining that the Magna Carta required that economic sanctions "be proportioned to the offense *and* that they should not deprive a wrongdoer of his livelihood" (emphasis added)).

[4] The Framers' debate on the Eighth Amendment, though quite brief, suggests that at least one participant—Samuel Livermore—had basically that question and seemed worried about who would answer it: "What is understood by excessive fines? It lies with the court to determine." 1 Annals of Congress 782 (1789) (Joseph Gales ed., 1834).

[5] The words taken as "position," "trade," and "tillage" in the version of the Magna Carta that I've quoted have elsewhere been rendered "contenement," "merchandize," and "waynage," respectively, and, as that variation suggests, scholars debate the exact contours of those terms. *See generally* Nicholas M. McLean, *Livelihood, Ability to Pay, and the Original Meaning of the Excessive Fines Clause,* 40 Hastings Const. L.Q. 833, 854-56 (2013). But all seem to agree that the Magna Carta forbade an amercement "so large as to deprive [an offender] of his livelihood." *Browning-Ferris Indus.,* 492 U.S. at 271, 109 S.Ct. 2909.

[6] Judge Tjoflat seems to agree with my basic premise. He cites many of the same English, colonial, and Framing-era sources that I do in support of the proposition that an excessive-fines inquiry should account for "both the characteristics of the offender and offense." Tjoflat Concurring and Dissenting Op. at 1333. So far, so good. I can't agree, however, with his further "suggest[ion]" that district courts apply the 18 U.S.C. § 3553(a) sentencing factors as "*the test* for excessiveness of civil fines under the Eighth Amendment." *Id.* at 1334 (emphasis added). Whatever commonsense appeal Judge Tjoflat's proposal may have as a policy matter, it lacks (so far as I can tell) any firm footing in the text or history of the Excessive Fines Clause.

[1] I would not reach whether my proposed Excessive Fines Clause test for civil fines also applies to criminal fines. Unlike civil fines, criminal fines are already governed by the Sentencing Guidelines and the factors laid out in 18 U.S.C. §§ 3553(a) and 3572. So, a different test may be required in the criminal fines context.

[2] This number has skyrocketed. As of June 2020, FCA penalties range from $11,665 to $23,331 per violation. *See* 28 C.F.R. § 85.5.

[3] Section 3572 is an explication of the § 3553(a) factors as they apply to criminal fines. *See* § 3553(a) (explaining that the court must look at the specific characteristics of the offense and offender in determining the appropriate sentence).

[4] In the fines context, the § 3572 factors represent a mix of both general and specific deterrence. Specific deterrence, also known as incapacitation in the incarceration context, merges with general deterrence in the fines context because what will deter the public at large will necessarily deter the individual who has to pay the fine. But the individual is not literally incapacitated when he pays a fine, like he would be if he were incarcerated.

[5] Separately, if a defendant were not allowed by statute to appeal his fine, he would have to collaterally attack the fine under the Eighth Amendment to obtain review.

[6] Judge Jordan misunderstands the purpose of the preceding discussion when he says that "Pinellas has not based its Eighth Amendment Challenge on the procedural claim that the FCA lacks standards." Maj. Op. at 1316 n.9. I am not suggesting that Pinellas's Eighth Amendment challenge is based on the lack of standards in the FCA for review of statutory penalties. Notwithstanding the arguments of the parties in this case, I am only pointing out that, unlike in the criminal context, the only method by which we may evaluate statutory penalties in the FCA is the Constitution itself. That seems like an odd arrangement to me, one I felt was worth noting, before diving into the Eighth Amendment analysis. Judge Jordan's second point in footnote 9, *see id.,* is exactly my own. As I explain later, *see infra* Section IV n.19, as a constitutional matter, even the statutory minimum may be too high, and nothing in our precedent suggests that a district court may not dip below that statutory minimum if a constitutional violation is present.

[7] The Court did note, however, that the inquiry is whether the forfeiture is punitive, not whether the forfeiture is *in personam* or *in rem,* for the purposes of the Excessive Fines Clause analysis. *See Bajakajian,* 524 U.S. at 332 n.6, 118 S. Ct. at 2036 n.6 ("It does not follow, of course, that all modern civil *in rem* forfeitures are nonpunitive and thus beyond the coverage of the Excessive Fines Clause. Because

some recent federal forfeiture laws have blurred the traditional distinction between civil *in rem* and criminal *in personam* forfeiture, we have held that a modern statutory forfeiture is a 'fine' for Eighth Amendment purposes if it constitutes punishment even in part, regardless of whether the proceeding is styled *in rem* or *in personam. See Austin v. United States, supra,* at 621-622, 113 S.Ct. at 2811-2812 (although labeled *in rem,* civil forfeiture of real property used "to facilitate" the commission of drug crimes was punitive in part and thus subject to review under the Excessive Fines Clause).").

[8] The strong presumption of constitutionality is premised on "two very competent bodies," Congress and the Sentencing Commission, "[t]ranslating the gravity of a crime into monetary terms." *817 N.E. 29th Drive,* 175 F.3d at 1309. Specifically, the guidelines "are the product of extensive research, though, input from commentators, and experience," and "[t]hey are designed to proportion punishments to crimes with even greater precision than criminal legislation." *Id.* at 1310; *see also* 28 U.S.C. § 994 (explaining the many considerations, including the § 3553(a) factors, the Commission must take into account when determining guidelines ranges). None of these protections apply in the FCA context, and the need for us to evaluate Congress's work becomes greater in the absence of such protections.

[9] While monetary recoveries "represent a victory for American taxpayers, they are only one measure of the fraud against the Government. As the GAO pointed out, fraud erodes public confidence in the Government's ability to efficiently and effectively manage its programs." S. Rep. No. 110-507, at 8.

[10] "Complexity of subject matter should never preclude the Government from uncovering fraud, but, unfortunately, it is impossible to determine how much fraud goes undetected." S. Rep. No. 110-507, at 8.

[11] "Lord Coke believed that the Magna Charta's protections against excessive amercements were 'made in the affirmance of the common law.'" Calvin Massey, *The Excessive Fines Clause and Punitive Damages: Some Lessons from History,* 40 Vand. L. Rev. 1233, 1251 (1987) (citing 2 E. Coke, The Institutes of the Laws of England *27-28). Prior to Magna Carta, legal writers were espousing the principle of proportionality. *See id.* at 1251 (quoting Glanvill who wrote in the late twelfth century). It is worth noting that Magna Carta only applied to amercements and not fines, but the later 1689 English Bill of Rights applied to both amercements and fines. *See id.* at 1252-53. But, since an amercement "was a financial penalty payable to the crown or its representative," for either a civil or criminal misdeed, *id.* at 1252, it serves as a common-law analog to the modern FCA fine. In contrast, fines at common law were "voluntary offering[s] made to the king to avoid royal displeasure or obtain some favor." By the eighteenth century, the distinction between these two schemes vanished. *Id.* at 1264. For our purposes, common-law amercements serve an important role in deciphering the original meaning of the Excessive Fines Clause because they most closely mirror the civil fines of the FCA.

[12] *See* Allan Nevins, *The American States During and After the Revolution, 1775-1789* 146 (1924) (explaining that the Virginia Declaration of Rights "was a restatement of English principles—the principles of Magna Charta... and the Revolution of 1688"); *see also Solem v. Helm,* 463 U.S. 277, 286, 103 S. Ct. 3001, 3007, 77 L.Ed.2d 637 (1983) ("Although the Framers may have intended the Eighth Amendment to go beyond the scope of its English counterpart, their use of the language of the English Bill of Rights is convincing proof that they intended to

provide at least the same protection—including the right to be free from excessive punishments.").

[13] Because the "Excessive Fines Clause was drafted in an era in which the amount of a fine was determined solely by the judiciary" and "the Clause was thus intended as a limitation on courts, not legislatures," it falls on us to scrutinize fine schemes, especially where there is no indication that Congress filtered these fines through the § 3553(a) factors as it would have done in the criminal context. *United States v. 817 N.E. 29th Drive,* 175 F.3d at 1309 n.8.

[14] *Godfrey's Case* draws from both the law of amercements and fines in determining whether the particular fine in that case was excessive. *See* 77 Eng. Rep. at 1202.

[15] *Harmelin* seems to question whether the historical Excessive Fines Clause analysis more properly looks at proportionality or legality. In other words, *Harmelin* creates a distinction as to whether the common-law excessive fines analysis would have looked at a sentence's departure from the common-law sentence or a sentence's lack of proportionality to an offense for determining excessiveness. 501 U.S. at 973, 111 S. Ct. at 2690. I believe this is a false dichotomy. Presumably, the common-law sentencing regime naturally incorporated proportionality and the traditional purposes of punishment. So, a departure from the common-law regime would necessarily be a departure from proportionality. There may be a time when we think a common-law punishment is disproportionate to an offense, and thus applying the legality test for excessiveness may yield a different outcome from the proportionality test. But I think such an instance would be rare and would only reflect that the common law itself has departed from the traditional purposes of punishment. *Cf. Graham v. Florida,* 560 U.S. 48, 59, 130 S. Ct. 2011, 2021, 176 L.Ed.2d 825 (2010) ("For the most part, however, the Court's precedents consider punishments challenged not as inherently barbaric but as disproportionate to the crime. The concept of proportionality is central to the Eighth Amendment.").

[16] And from its inception to the present, the Supreme Court has relied on Blackstone to understand how the framers viewed the common law. *See, e.g., Chisholm v. Georgia,* 2 U.S. (2 Dall.) 419, 442-43, 1 L.Ed. 440 (1793) (extensively quoting Blackstone to determine the contours of sovereign immunity prior to the enactment of the Eleventh Amendment); *Marbury v. Madison,* 5 U.S. (1 Cranch) 137, 147-48, 2 L.Ed. 60 (1803) (looking to Blackstone to define a writ of mandamus); *United States v. Wong Kim Ark,* 169 U.S. 649, 659, 18 S. Ct. 456, 461, 42 L.Ed. 890 (1898) (using Blackstone to define the right of citizenship in the United States under the Citizenship Clause); *C.J. Hendry Co. v. Moore,* 318 U.S. 133, 151, 63 S. Ct. 499, 509, 87 L.Ed. 663 (1943) (calling on Blackstone to carve out the contours of admiralty jurisdiction); *United States v. Hayman,* 342 U.S. 205, 221 n.35, 72 S. Ct. 263, 273 n.35, 96 L.Ed. 232 (1952) (using Blackstone to expound on the meaning and breadth of habeas corpus); *Morissette v. United States,* 342 U.S. 246, 251, 72 S. Ct. 240, 244, 96 L.Ed. 288 (1952) (equating Blackstone's view of intent with the English common law and American common law); *Bucklew v. Precythe,* ___ U.S. ___, 139 S. Ct. 1112, 1123, 203 L.Ed.2d 521 (2019) (turning to Blackstone to explicate the original meaning of the Eighth Amendment's Cruel and Unusual Punishments Clause).

[17] Although Blackstone singles out criminal cases, the protection against excessive fines in the English Bill of Rights of 1689 "included more than protection

from criminal fines; it also provided a great deal of protection with respect to civil fines [i.e., amercements]." Calvin Massey, *The Excessive Fines Clause and Punitive Damages: Some Lessons from History,* 40 Vand. L. Rev. 1233, 1275 (1987). And since FCA fines are essentially punitive in nature, serving the same purpose as criminal fines at common law, I do not hesitate to apply Blackstone's analysis here.

[18] Judge Newsom takes issue with my suggestion that the § 3553(a) factors be used as a way of implementing the constitutional standard for excessiveness because this approach "lacks (so far as [he] can tell) any firm footing in the text or history of the Excessive Fines Clause." Newsom Op. at 1323 n.6. I find this criticism unavailing. Judge Newsom signs on to the Court's opinion applying the *Browne* factors (derived from *Bajakajian*) to the civil fines context. The *Browne* factors, by that name, are nowhere in the common-law history of the Excessive Fines Clause, so the same critique could be leveled against them. But their goal is to distill the common-law purposes of punishment into a test that respects the original meaning of the Eighth Amendment. Both the Court's opinion today and my own approach are simply implementing doctrines, not the Constitution itself, based on the common law. My approach, the application of the § 3553(a) factors as the Excessive Fines Clause test for civil fines, takes account of the fact that the § 3553(a) factors are just an adoption of the common-law purposes of sentencing and reflect the policy underpinnings of punishment throughout our nation's history.

[19] The District Court seemed to believe that *Killough* prevented it from making the fine less than the minimum statutory fine per claim. *See also United States v. Bornstein,* 423 U.S. 303, 313, 96 S. Ct. 523, 529, 46 L.Ed.2d 514 (1976) (assuming that statutory fines would be stacked outside the Eighth Amendment context). But *Killough* only clarified how statutory fines should be assessed under the FCA. *See Killough,* 848 F.2d at 1533. It did not say anything about how the Excessive Fines Clause interacts with the statutory scheme. *Killough* does not prevent a defendant from bringing an as-applied constitutional challenge to even the minimum statutory fine amount based on Excessive Fines Clause grounds. On a separate note, *Killough* adopted the Seventh Circuit view that "imposition of forfeitures under the Act is not discretionary, but is mandatory for each claim found to be false." *Id.* (citing *United States v. Hughes,* 585 F.2d 284, 286 (7th Cir. 1978)). That is, according to *Killough,* penalties must be stacked as a statutory matter. However, *Killough* was not considering stacking based on a constitutional challenge, and I suggest that in another case stacking could be challenged on Eighth Amendment as-applied grounds in the same way that the amount per violation could be challenged.

987 F.3d 1340 (2021)

UNITED STATES of America EX REL., Plaintiff,
Victor E. Bibby, Brian J. Donnelly, Plaintiffs-Appellants Cross-Appellees,
v.
MORTGAGE INVESTORS CORPORATION, William L. Edwards, "Bill",
Defendants-Appellees Cross-Appellants,
William L. Edwards, as Trustee of William L. Edwards Revocable Trust, Defendant.

No. 19-12736.

United States Court of Appeals, Eleventh Circuit.

February 17, 2021.

United States v. Mortgage Investors Corporation, 987 F. 3d 1340 (11th Cir. 2021)

Appeal from the United States District Court for the Northern District of Georgia, D.C. Docket No. 1:12-cv-04020-AT.

James Edward Butler, Jr., Joseph Colwell, Brandon Lee Peak, Ramsey B. Prather, Joel Orba Wooten, Jr., Butler Wooten & Peak, LLP, Columbus, GA, Robert Henry Snyder, Jr., Butler Wooten & Peak, Atlanta, GA, for Plaintiffs-Appellants Cross-Appellees.

Lesli Christine Esposito, Brian J. Boyle, Ben Fabens-Lassen, John D. Huh, DLA Piper LLP (US), Philadelphia, PA, Raanon Gal, Matthew Robert Rosenkoff, Taylor English Duma, LLP, Atlanta, GA, John Kenneth Lisman, Hoegen & Associates, PC, Wilkes-Barre, PA, for Defendant-Appellee Cross-Appellant Mortgage Investors Corporation.

Michael James King, Jeffrey Michael Smith, Greenberg Traurig, LLP, Matthew Robert Rosenkoff, Taylor English Duma, LLP, Atlanta, GA, for Defendant-Appellee Cross-Appellant William L. Edwards.

Charles W. Scarborough, Michael Raab, U.S. Attorney General's Office, Washington, DC, for Amicus Curiae United States of America.

Before WILSON, NEWSOM, and ED CARNES, Circuit Judges.

p.1343 WILSON, Circuit Judge:

We vacate our previous opinion published at 985 F.3d 825 and replace it with the following opinion.

More than 14 years ago, Appellants Victor Bibby and Brian Donnelly (Relators) brought this qui tam action against Mortgage Investors Corporation (MIC) under the False Claims Act (FCA).

The FCA imposes liability on any person who "knowingly presents, or causes to be presented, a false or fraudulent claim for payment or approval," or "knowingly makes, uses, or causes to be made or used, a false record or statement material to a false or fraudulent claim." 31 U.S.C. § 3729(a)(1)(A)-(B). As an enforcement mechanism, the FCA includes a qui tam provision under which private individuals, known as relators, can sue "in the name of the [United States] Government" to recover money obtained in violation of § 3729. *Id.* § 3730(b)(1).[1] If the relators prevail, they are entitled to retain a percentage of any proceeds as a reward for their efforts. *Id.* § 3730(d).

The Relators in this case are mortgage brokers. For years, they specialized in originating United States Department of Veterans Affairs (VA) mortgage loans, particularly Interest Rate Reduction Refinance Loans (IRRRL). Relators learned through their work with IRRRLs that lenders often charged veterans fees that were prohibited by VA regulations, while p.1344 falsely certifying to the VA that they were charging only permissible fees. In doing so, these lenders allegedly induced the VA to insure the IRRRLs, thereby reducing the lenders' risk of loss in the event a borrower defaults.

On March 3, 2006, Relators filed this qui tam action under the FCA against MIC to recover the money the VA had paid when borrowers defaulted on MIC-originated loans.[2] Relators later amended their complaint to add a state law fraudulent transfer claim against MIC executive William L. Edwards and to add a corporate veil-piercing theory of liability, which made Edwards a defendant to the FCA claim. The district court granted Edwards's motion to dismiss the fraudulent transfer claim for lack of standing. And it granted MIC's motion for summary judgment on the FCA claim, holding that no reasonable jury could find MIC's alleged fraud was material. Relators now appeal. In conditional cross-appeals, Edwards argues that the district court lacks personal jurisdiction over him, while MIC argues that if we reverse the district court's ruling on materiality, the FCA claim is nonetheless barred by previous public disclosure.

We conclude that summary judgment was improper on Relators' FCA claim because genuine issues of material fact remain as to whether MIC's alleged false certifications were material. Next, we agree with the district court that Relators' claim is not barred by previous public disclosure. Further, we hold that the district court has personal jurisdiction over Edwards. Finally, we hold that Relators lack standing on the fraudulent transfer claim because their pre judgment interest in preventing a fraudulent transfer is a mere byproduct of their FCA claim and cannot give rise to an Article III injury in fact.

I. BACKGROUND

A. IRRRL Program Background

An overview of the IRRRL program is necessary to understand Relators' claims on appeal. The program seeks to help veterans stay in their homes by allowing them to refinance existing VA-backed mortgages at more favorable terms. In keeping with the program's goal of helping veterans, VA regulations restrict the fees and charges that participating lenders can collect from veterans. 38 C.F.R. § 36.4313(a). And to hold lenders accountable, the regulations require lenders to certify their compliance as a prerequisite to obtaining a VA loan guaranty. *Id.* Specifically, § 36.4313(a) permits lenders to collect only those fees and charges that are "expressly permitted under paragraph (d) or (e) of this section...." *Id.* Relevant to this appeal, paragraph (d) allows veterans to pay "reasonable and customary" charges for "[t]itle examination and title insurance," as well as various other itemized fees. *Id.* § 36.4313(d)(1).[3] Attorney fees are not among the permitted fees and charges. *Id.* § 36.4313(d).

The mechanics of the loan certification process work like this. Once a lender has approved an IRRRL, it "gives closing instructions to the attorney or title company handling the closing for the lender."[4] The p.1345 lender or its agent then prepares a statement, known as a HUD-1, listing all the closing costs and fees. The HUD-1 requires lenders to break out the costs they incurred and the amounts they are collecting for various charges and fees, such as title search and title examination. Before closing, the lender is to review the HUD-1 for accuracy. Then, after the lender's agent closes the loan, the lender sends the HUD-1 to the VA along with a certification that it has not imposed impermissible fees on the veteran borrower. Only upon this certification does the VA issue a guaranty to the lender.

Complicating matters, once lenders such as MIC obtain VA loan guaranties on IRRRLs, they sell those loans on the secondary market to holders in due course. This is an important wrinkle because when a holder in due course holds the IRRRLs, the VA is required by statute and regulation to honor the guaranties corresponding to those loans. *See* 38 U.S.C. § 3721 (the Incontestability Statute) ("Any evidence of guaranty or insurance issued by the Secretary shall be conclusive evidence of the eligibility of the loan for guaranty or insurance under the provisions of this chapter and of the amount of such guaranty or insurance."); 38 C.F.R. § 36.4328(a)(1) (providing that misrepresentation or fraud by the lender shall not constitute a defense against liability as to a holder in due course). In other words, the guaranties are incontestable vis-à-vis holders in due course. The VA must turn to the originating lender to seek a remedy for that lender's fraud or material misrepresentation— it cannot simply refuse to honor the guaranties. *See id.*

B. Procedural Background

Relators filed suit under the FCA's qui tam provision in 2006, alleging the following facts. MIC charged veterans impermissible closing fees and attempted to cover its tracks by "bundling" the unallowable charges with allowable charges, listing them together as one line-item on HUD-1 forms. For example, MIC would collect prohibited attorney fees from veterans and bundle those fees with allowable title examination and title insurance fees, so that the attorney fees were concealed. By doing so, and by falsely certifying its compliance with VA regulations, MIC induced the VA to guaranty IRRRLs and to ultimately honor those guaranties when borrowers defaulted. MIC countered, in relevant part, that the FCA claim is barred because a 2002 court filing had already publicly disclosed Relators' allegations.

In late 2011, as Relators' case against MIC proceeded, MIC began to distribute assets to its shareholders—in large part to Edwards, MIC's majority shareholder and chairman of its Board of Directors. This trend escalated in 2012 and 2013. During that two-year period, MIC allegedly transferred a whopping $242,006,838 to Edwards and MSP (Edwards's wholly-owned entity), leaving MIC insolvent. According to Relators, MIC then shut down its operation to prevent Relators from collecting any judgment they might obtain in this FCA action. MIC initially insisted that it remained solvent and was "here for the long haul." But by May 2015, when the district court inquired about MIC's continued solvency, counsel for MIC responded that "it's not a secret that my client stopped making loans some time ago, but that's it." And in June 2015, MIC's counsel could not "make any representation about the financial state of the company." Relators amended their complaint in January 2016 to add a state law fraudulent transfer claim against Edwards and to plead a corporate veil-piercing theory.

In a series of orders, the district court first found that it had personal jurisdiction p.1346 over Edwards but dismissed Relators' fraudulent transfer claim for lack of standing. It then found that Relators' FCA claim was not barred by public disclosure but ultimately granted MIC summary judgment on the ground that Relators provided insufficient evidence to create a genuine issue of material fact on the element of materiality.

II. STANDARD OF REVIEW

We review de novo the district court's grant of summary judgment on the FCA claim, applying the same standard applied by the district court. *Urquilla-Diaz v. Kaplan Univ.,* 780 F.3d 1039, 1050 (11th Cir. 2015). Under this standard, summary judgment is appropriate only if the record shows "that there is no genuine dispute as to any material fact and the movant is entitled to judgment as a matter of law." Fed. R. Civ. P. 56(a). Even self-serving and uncorroborated statements can create an issue of material fact. *United States v. Stein,* 881 F.3d 853, 856 (11th Cir. 2018) (en banc). And all reasonable inferences from the evidence are to be drawn in favor of the non-moving party; the court may not resolve factual disputes by weighing conflicting evidence. *Ryder Int'l Corp. v. First Am. Nat. Bank,* 943 F.2d 1521, 1523 (11th Cir. 1991).

We also review de novo the dismissal of Relators' fraudulent transfer claim for lack of standing and the denial of Edwards's motion to dismiss for lack of personal jurisdiction. *Ga. State Conf. of NAACP Branches v. Cox,* 183 F.3d 1259, 1262 (11th Cir. 1999); *United States v. Elmes,* 532 F.3d 1138, 1141 (11th Cir. 2008).

III. DISCUSSION

First, we address the district court's grant of summary judgment on Relators' FCA claim. After careful review, we reverse the district court because it impermissibly resolved factual disputes by weighing conflicting evidence, a task that should have been left to the factfinder. Because genuine issues of material fact remain on the element of materiality, MIC is not entitled to summary judgment.[5]

Second, we affirm the district court's finding that Relators' FCA claim is not barred by previous public disclosure. The previous court filings at issue did not disclose the allegations on which Relators' claim is based.

Third, we affirm the district court's ruling that Edwards is subject to personal jurisdiction. Because Relators sufficiently alleged that MIC was Edwards's alter ego, MIC's suit-related forum contacts can be imputed to Edwards for the purposes of the personal jurisdiction analysis.

Fourth, we affirm the district court's finding that Relators lack standing to bring the fraudulent transfer claim. Relators have standing to pursue an FCA action only through the government's assignment of its damages claim. And because the FCA does not assign the right to bring additional causes of action related to the FCA claim, Relators lack Article III standing to assert this claim.

A. The FCA's Materiality Standard

To prevail on their FCA claim, Relators must prove: "(1) a false statement or fraudulent course of conduct, (2) made with scienter, (3) that was material, causing (4) the government to pay out money or forfeit moneys due." *Urquilla-Diaz,* 780 p.1347 F.3d at 1045. In a comprehensive 83-page order, the district court granted MIC summary judgment, finding that Relators failed to provide sufficient evidence to create a genuine issue of material fact on the third element—materiality.

The Supreme Court recently addressed materiality under the FCA in a landmark decision. *Universal Health Servs., Inc. v. United States ex rel. Escobar,* ___ U.S. ___, 136 S. Ct. 1989, 195 L.Ed.2d 348 (2016). In *Escobar,* the Court emphasized that the FCA's "materiality standard is demanding." *Id.* at 2003. The FCA is not "an all-purpose antifraud statute," nor is it "a vehicle for punishing garden-variety breaches of contract or regulatory violations." *Id.* Therefore, "noncompliance [that] is minor or insubstantial" will not satisfy the FCA's materiality requirement. *Id.*

Materiality is defined as "having a natural tendency to influence, or be capable of influencing, the payment or receipt of money or property." *Id.* at 2002. And while several factors can be relevant to the analysis, "materiality cannot rest on a 'single fact or occurrence as always determinative.'" *Id.* at 2001 (quoting *Matrixx Initiatives, Inc. v. Siracusano,* 563 U.S. 27, 39, 131 S.Ct. 1309, 179 L.Ed.2d 398 (2011)). Accordingly, several of our sister circuits have described the test as "holistic." *United States ex rel. Escobar v. Universal Health Servs., Inc.,* 842 F.3d 103, 109 (1st Cir. 2016) *(Escobar II); United States ex rel. Harman v. Trinity Indus. Inc.,* 872 F.3d 645, 661 (5th Cir. 2017); *United States v. Brookdale Senior Living Cmtys., Inc.,* 892 F.3d 822, 831 (6th Cir. 2018), *cert. denied sub nom. Brookdale Senior Living Cmtys., Inc. v. United States ex rel. Prather,* ___ U.S. ___, 139 S. Ct. 1323, 203 L.Ed.2d 565 (2019); *United States ex rel. Janssen v. Lawrence Mem'l Hosp.,* 949 F.3d 533, 541 (10th Cir. 2020), *cert. denied sub nom. United States, ex rel. Janssen v. Lawrence Mem'l Hosp.,* ___ U.S. ___, 141 S.Ct. 376, 208 L.Ed.2d 98 (2020).

While no single factor is dispositive, some factors that are relevant to the materiality analysis include: (1) whether the requirement is a condition of the government's payment, (2) whether the misrepresentations went to the essence of the bargain with the government, and (3) to the extent the government had actual knowledge of the misrepresentations, the effect on the government's behavior.[6] *Escobar,* 136 S. Ct. at 2003 & n.5, 2004. We address these factors in turn.

1. Condition of Payment

"[T]he Government's decision to expressly identify a provision as a condition of payment is relevant, but not automatically dispositive" to the materiality analysis. *Id.* at 2003. Here, we agree with the district court's conclusion that a lender's truthful certification that it charged only permissible fees was a condition of the government's payment on IRRRL guaranties. The relevant VA regulation clearly designates that requirement a condition to payment: "no loan shall be guaranteed or insured unless the lender certifies ... that it has not imposed and will not impose any [impermissible] charges or fees...." 38 C.F.R. § 36.4313(a). Therefore, this factor weighs in favor of materiality.

2. Essence of the Bargain

We also consider the extent to which the requirement that was violated is central to, or goes "to the very essence of[,] the bargain." *Escobar,* 136 S. Ct. at 2003 n.5; *see also Escobar II,* 842 F.3d at 110 (considering p.1348 "the centrality of the ... requirements" in the context of the regulatory program); *John T. Boese, Civil False Claims and* Qui Tam *Actions* 2-268-69 (5th ed. 2020) (explaining that it is *Escobar*'s "basic requirement" to show that the "misrepresentation [went] to the very essence of the bargain") (internal quotation mark omitted).

When viewing the evidence in the light most favorable to Relators, a reasonable factfinder could conclude that the VA's fee regulations were essential to the bargain with IRRRL lenders. The central aim of the IRRRL program was to help veterans stay in their homes, and fee regulations contributed to that goal. VA Pamphlet 26-7 draws this connection neatly, summarizing the purpose of the IRRRL program as follows: "The VA home loan program involves a veteran's benefit. VA policy has evolved around the objective of helping the veteran to use his or her home loan benefit. Therefore, VA regulations limit the fees that the veteran can pay to obtain a loan." The Pamphlet further provides:

> The limitations imposed upon the types of charges and fees which can be paid by veteran borrowers and the concomitant certification by the lender as to its compliance with this requirement furthers the purpose of "limit[ing] the fees that the veteran can pay to obtain a loan" which, in turn, ensures that a veteran borrower can effectively "use his or her home loan benefit."

These excerpts suggest that fee compliance was essential to the bargain, rather than an ancillary requirement that the government labeled a condition of payment. Therefore, a reasonable factfinder could conclude that the requirement went to the essence of the bargain.

3. Effect on the VA's Behavior

The government's reaction to the defendant's violations is also a factor in the materiality inquiry. *Escobar,* 136 S. Ct. at 2003-04. *Escobar* discusses three ways the government might behave upon learning of noncompliance and instructs us on how that behavior factors into the materiality analysis.

First, the government might refuse to pay claims. *Id.* at 2003. If "the defendant knows that the Government consistently refuses to pay claims in the mine run of cases based on noncompliance," that is evidence of materiality. *Id.* Second, and "[c]onversely, if the Government pays a particular claim in full despite its actual knowledge that certain requirements were violated, that is *very strong evidence* that those requirements are not material." *Id.* (emphasis added). And third is a middle possibility: "if the Government regularly pays a particular *type* of claim in full despite actual knowledge that certain requirements were violated, and has signaled no change in position, that is *strong evidence* that the requirements are not material." *Id.* at 2003-04 (emphases added).

Because these three possibilities each hinge on the government discovering the defendant's violations, the logical first step in this analysis is to determine what the government actually knew.

a. The VA's Actual Knowledge

Assessing the government's actual knowledge requires that we drill down to when that knowledge was acquired, and what exactly the government learned. *See Harman,* 872 F.3d at 668 (finding no materiality as a matter of law only after determining that there was "no question about 'what the government knew and when'"). Here, the district court determined that the VA had gained "the requisite knowledge of the alleged fraud" by 2009, largely through communication with Relators p.1349 about their allegations and through the VA's own investigatory audits.

As to the first of these two sources, Relators' counsel discussed Relators' allegations with the government in February 2006, shortly before filing the initial complaint. Then, after filing the complaint, Relators' counsel engaged in discussions with the Department of Justice, the United States Attorney's Office, and the VA Office of Inspector General. And for the next several years, Relators continued to correspond with the government. Therefore, the VA was aware of Relators' allegations since 2006.

MIC argues that this knowledge of Relators' allegations is sufficient to establish the VA's actual knowledge of noncompliance during the relevant timeframe. We have not previously addressed whether the government's knowledge of *allegations* is tantamount to knowledge of *violations* for purposes of the materiality analysis. And decisions by our sister circuits have varied in their treatment of this issue. *Compare Escobar II,* 842 F.3d at 112 ("[M]ere awareness of allegations concerning noncompliance with regulations is different from knowledge of actual noncompliance."); *with United States ex rel. Nargol v. DePuy Orthopaedics, Inc.,* 865 F.3d 29, 34 (1st Cir. 2017) (holding that government inaction "in the wake of Relators' allegations... renders a claim of materiality implausible").

Yet we need not answer this question here because, in any event, the VA had actual knowledge of MIC's noncompliance through another source—the VA audit findings. VA investigatory audits came in two varieties: (1) ongoing spot audits of loan samples by the VA's Regional Loan Centers (RLC Audits); and (2) periodic onsite audits by the Loan Guarantee Service Monitoring Unit (LGSMU Audits). The RLC Audits, which reviewed ten percent of all IRRRLs, revealed instances of MIC and other lenders violating fee regulations. In fact, according to VA representative Jeffrey London, lenders collecting impermissible fees and charges was "one of the most common loan deficiencies" identified in the RLC Audits. As a result, the VA sent MIC post-audit deficiency letters between 2009 and 2011, indicating that MIC had charged veteran borrowers unallowable fees and that those fees should be refunded. Likewise, the LGSMU Audits in both 2010 and 2012 identified noncompliant fees and charges by MIC. The VA subsequently directed MIC to "review the VA *Lender's Handbook* and make the necessary adjustments to ensure future compliance." Based on these audit findings, it is undisputed that the VA was aware of MIC's violation of fee regulations.

Relators contend, however, that the VA believed that any noncompliance was the result of inadvertent, good faith mistakes. Relators urge us to draw a distinction between the VA's knowledge of inadvertent violations based on audit findings and its knowledge of actual fraud. Specifically, Relators point to the testimony of London and former VA employee William White that the VA would have investigated further if it had been aware of IRRRL lenders intentionally bundling fees and knowingly submitting false certifications of compliance. Relators argue that the district court erred when it discounted that testimony as "speculative and seemingly self-serving."

We agree that to the extent the testimony was self-serving, it must nevertheless be credited as true at this stage. *See Stein,* 881 F.3d at 856. But even taking that testimony as true, *Escobar* does not distinguish between inadvertent mistakes and intentional violations. What matters is simply whether the government knew "that certain requirements were violated." *Escobar,* p.1350 136 S. Ct. at 2003-04. For this reason, our sister circuits have declined to explain away the government's actual knowledge of violations based on post hoc rationalizations that the government *might* have done more if it had investigated further. *See United States ex rel. McBride v. Halliburton Co.,* 848 F.3d 1027, 1034 (D.C. Cir. 2017) (explaining that the analysis should remain focused on "what actually occurred" rather than on testimony that hypothesizes what might have occurred). Here, regardless of whether the VA assumed MIC's noncompliance was inadvertent, it is undisputed that VA audits had revealed MIC's violations of IRRRL fee requirements by 2009. Therefore, the VA had actual knowledge of MIC's noncompliance during the relevant time frame.

b. The VA's Reaction

Having considered the VA's actual knowledge of MIC's violations, we now consider the VA's reaction in the wake of discovering those violations. *Escobar,* 136 S. Ct. at 2003-04. But before proceeding, we must address a threshold question: Which government action is relevant to the materiality inquiry in this case? MIC argues that what matters is the government's decision to continue paying claims, despite knowledge of noncompliance. In support of its position, MIC points to language in *Escobar* that appears to link materiality to the government's *payment* decision. *Id.; see also id.* at 2002 (looking to whether noncompliance has a "natural tendency to influence, or be capable of influencing, the payment or receipt of money or property"). Relators, along with the government as amicus curiae, contend that the VA's continued payment merits little weight because the payments were required by law, regardless of any fraud by the originating lender.

While we agree with MIC that, under *Escobar,* the government action relevant to the materiality inquiry is typically the payment decision, the significance of continued payment may vary depending on the circumstances. *See United States ex rel. Campie v. Gilead Scis., Inc.,* 862 F.3d 890, 906 (9th Cir. 2017) (cautioning that "to read too much into the FDA's continued approval—and its effect on the government's payment decision—would be a mistake" where there were other reasons for that approval). Here, there was a reason for the VA's continued payment of IRRRLs other than violations of fee regulations being immaterial. Once the VA issues guaranties, it is required by law to honor those guaranties and to pay holders in due course in possession of the IRRRLs, regardless of any fraud by the original lender. 38 U.S.C. §

3721. Given this constraint, we disagree with the district court that much can be drawn from Relators' failure to submit "any evidence that ... noncompliance would have a palpable and concrete effect on the VA's *decision to honor the loan guarantees....*" (emphasis added). The VA was bound to honor the guaranties. Consequently, the facts of this case require that we cast our materiality inquiry more broadly to consider "the full array of tools" at the VA's disposal "for detecting, deterring, and punishing false statements," and which of those it employed. *See Nargol,* 865 F.3d at 34 (internal quotation mark omitted).

With that in mind, we return to the framework *Escobar* provides. In order to find "very strong evidence" that MIC's conduct was *not* material, we would need to find that the VA paid particular claims—or as relevant here, took comparable action—despite its actual knowledge of violations. *Escobar,* 136 S. Ct. at 2003. That is, while the Incontestability Statute rendered the VA's *payment* decision less probative, MIC might have established p.1351 "very strong evidence" of materiality by showing, for example, that the VA agreed to *guaranty* a particular loan despite actual knowledge that MIC had falsely certified fee compliance on that loan.[7] But on the quite voluminous record before us, MIC has not pointed to a single such instance. *See* Oral Argument Recording at 32:43-33:15 (Oct. 21, 2020).

Next, in order to find even "strong evidence" that the requirements were not material, we would need to find that the VA paid a particular *type* of claim—or took comparable action—despite its "actual knowledge" of violations. *Escobar,* 136 S. Ct. at 2003-04. Here, MIC fares better if we consider the VA's issuance of a guaranty to be the relevant government action. Although the VA never issued a guaranty with knowledge that improper fees were collected on that particular loan, it did issue loan guaranties related to a "particular type of claim," despite its knowledge of audit findings that MIC imposed impermissible fees on a certain percentage of its loans.[8] *Id.*

But once we divorce our analysis from a strict focus on the government's payment decision, we see no reason to limit our view only to the VA's issuance of guaranties. Looking at the VA's behavior holistically, the record shows that the VA took a number of actions to address noncompliance with fee regulations. First, the VA released Circular 26-10-01 on January 7, 2010, reminding lenders of the applicable fee regulations and warning of the consequences of noncompliance. Citing VA regulations, the Circular reminded lenders that they are to charge only the "reasonable and customary amount for certain itemized fees," and that "[t]he lender may NOT charge the veteran for attorney's fees associated with settlement." The Circular further stated: "Lenders must comply with these policies when making VA loans. Any lender who does not comply with these policies is subject to removal from the program, fines by the VA, government-wide debarment, and other civil and criminal penalties that may be applicable."

Second, after learning of Relators' allegations, the VA implemented more frequent and more rigorous audits in 2010 and 2011 to root out improper fees and charges. The change in audit methodology incorporated data from a website, Bankrate.com, that surveys lenders and provides information on average fees and charges in the mortgage industry. By comparing actual fees and charges imposed by IRRRL lenders with industry averages, the VA hoped to identify fraudulent fee bundling more effectively. Although the change in methodology apparently proved ineffective, it is nonetheless evidence of the VA attempting to use tools at its disposal to detect and address false statements.

Third, the VA consistently required lenders to refund any improperly charged fees that they discovered. Both London and White offered testimony to that effect in their depositions.

MIC argues that the VA could have pursued more severe remedies such as recoupment, debarment, or suspension p.1352 from the IRRRL program. Certainly, imposing such remedies would have been evidence of materiality. *See United States v. Luce,* 873 F.3d 999, 1007 (7th Cir. 2017) (finding materiality as a matter of law where the government debarred the defendant from the relevant government program upon discovering its noncompliance). But these were not the only tools in the VA's toolbox. The bottom line is that, because the Incontestability Statute precludes us from focusing narrowly on the VA's payment decision, we must broaden our view to consider the VA's pattern of behavior as a whole. And while the VA did not take the strongest possible action against MIC, it did take some enforcement actions.

To recap, we have thus far considered the following indicators of materiality: (1) whether the requirement is a condition of payment, (2) whether the misrepresentation was essential to the bargain, and (3) the VA's relevant actions based on its actual knowledge of violations. On the first point, the VA's fee requirements are a condition of payment. That is indicative of materiality but does not, by itself, "automatically" establish materiality. *Escobar,* 136 S. Ct. at 2003. The *Escobar* Court drove home that the government cannot take "insignificant regulatory or contractual violations" and imbue them with materiality simply by labeling them as such. *Id.* at 2004.

But here, the requirement's centrality within the regulatory scheme also points toward materiality. As the district court found, "the [VA's] charges and fees regulation is ... more than an insignificant regulatory requirement." The requirement promoted the IRRRL program's central purpose, and a reasonable factfinder could have found that it was essential to the bargain between the VA and MIC. So both the requirement's designation as a condition of payment and its centrality to the government program favor materiality.

The district court, however, weighed this evidence against countervailing evidence of the VA's knowledge and its reaction to noncompliance. This countervailing evidence, the court found, "significantly belie[d] the notion that the VA characterized the alleged noncompliance in this case as material." The court thus held that the "sheer weight" of the evidence militated against materiality.

To resolve the issue by weighing conflicting evidence was error. *See Ryder,* 943 F.2d at 1523. The materiality test is holistic, with no single element—including the government's knowledge and its enforcement action—being dispositive. To be sure, the materiality standard is "demanding," and courts may dismiss FCA cases at summary judgment where relators fail to create a genuine issue of material fact on that element. *Escobar,* 136 S. Ct. at 2003, 2004 n.6. That is particularly true where "'very strong evidence' ... of ... continued payment remains unrebutted." *See Harman,* 872 F.3d at 665. But here, we do not have "very strong evidence" of immateriality. *Escobar,* 136 S. Ct. at 2003. And even if we viewed the VA's continued issuance of guaranties as "strong evidence" of immateriality, that evidence is not unrebutted. *Id.*

at 2004. A factfinder would still have to weigh that factor against others, including, as relevant here, the fee and charges requirement being a condition to payment and essential to the IRRRL program. Because there is sufficient evidence to support a finding of materiality, we must leave that determination to the fact-finder. We therefore reverse the district court's grant of summary judgment.

B. The FCA's Public Disclosure Bar

Because we reverse the district court's grant of summary judgment on the issue p.1353 of materiality, we must address MIC's conditional cross-appeal arguing that Relators' FCA claim is barred by previous public disclosure. An FCA action cannot be based on allegations that are already publicly disclosed. 31 U.S.C. § 3730 (2006).[9] The relevant provision of the FCA provides that:

> No court shall have jurisdiction over an action under this section based upon the public disclosure of allegations or transactions in a criminal, civil, or administrative hearing, in a congressional, administrative, or Government Accounting Office report, hearing, audit, or investigation, or from the news media, unless the action is brought by the Attorney General or the person bringing the action is an original source of the information.

Id. § 3730(e)(4)(A).

The reason for the public disclosure bar is fairly obvious. Without it, opportunistic relators—with nothing new to contribute—could exploit the FCA's qui tam provisions for their personal benefit. *See United States ex rel. Springfield Terminal Ry. Co. v. Quinn,* 14 F.3d 645, 649 (D.C. Cir. 1994) (recalling the "notorious plaintiff who copied the information on which his *qui tam* suit was based from the government's own criminal indictment"). Here, MIC argues that Relators' allegations had already been publicly disclosed in a 2002 South Carolina consumer protection case, *Cox v. Mortgage Investors Corp. d/b/a Amerigroup Mortgage Corp.,* in which a solitary MIC HUD-1 (the Cox HUD-1) was filed on the docket—first in state court and later in federal court. Case No. 2:02-cv-3883-DCN (D.S.C. Nov. 15, 2002). At his deposition, Relator Donnelly admitted that the Cox HUD-1 appears to reflect fee bundling. MIC argues that if fee bundling is apparent on the face of the Cox HUD-1—based on inflated fees listed on a particular line-item—then the filing of that form in 2002 was a previous public disclosure of Relators' allegations.

We have framed the public disclosure inquiry as a three-part test: "(1) have the allegations made by the plaintiff been publically disclosed; (2) if so, is the disclosed information the basis of the plaintiff's suit; (3) if yes, is the plaintiff an 'original source' of that information." *Cooper v. Blue Cross & Blue Shield of Fla., Inc.,* 19 F.3d 562, 565 n.4 (11th Cir. 1994) (per curiam). So, under the *Cooper* framework, the first prong becomes dispositive where the plaintiff's allegations have not been publicly disclosed.

Here, on the first *Cooper* prong, we must determine whether the Cox HUD-1 publicly disclosed the "allegations" on which Relators' claim is based. *Id.* Because the *Cooper* test does not further define "allegations," we have found instructive the D.C. Circuit's *Springfield* formula. Under that formula, "one generally must present a submitted statement or claim (X) and the true set of facts (Y), which shows that X is untrue. These two things together allow the conclusion (Z) that fraud has occurred."

United States ex rel. Saldivar v. Fresenius Med. Care Holdings, Inc., 841 F.3d 927, 935 (11th Cir. 2016) (citing *Springfield,* 14 F.3d at 654). There is no allegation of fraud under this p.1354 formula unless each variable is present. "[W]here only one element of the fraudulent transaction is in the public domain (*e.g.,* X), the *qui tam* plaintiff may mount a case by coming forward with either the additional elements necessary to state a case of fraud (*e.g.,* Y) *or* allegations of fraud itself (*e.g.,* Z)." *Springfield,* 14 F.3d at 655.

The Cox HUD-1 is not an "allegation" under the *Springfield* test. Even if we were to view the form as presenting the "statement or claim" that MIC did not impose excess fees and charges on veterans, it would set forth only the (X) variable. *Id.* at 654. To be an allegation of fraud, the Cox HUD-1 would also have to reveal the true set of facts (Y): that MIC actually collected impermissible fees and bundled those fees on the same line-item as permissible fees.

As the district court found, the Cox HUD-1, standing alone, does not do so. True, Donnelly was able to combine his industry knowledge with the information presented on the Cox HUD-1 to surmise that the form reflected bundled fees. But putting aside Donnelly's knowledge about fee bundling in the IRRRL industry, the information on the face of the HUD-1 alone does not disclose that MIC concealed impermissible fees. To the contrary, the form purports to show that MIC collected only permissible fees. As such, Relators were not barred from using their industry knowledge to "mount a case by coming forward" with allegations that MIC fraudulently bundled fees on HUD-1s to conceal violations of VA regulations. *Id.* at 655.

So, in conclusion, the Cox HUD-1 is not an allegation of fraud under the *Springfield* formula, and, accordingly, it fails the first prong of the *Cooper* test. Therefore, we affirm the district court's finding on MIC's conditional cross-appeal that Relators' FCA claim is not barred by previous public disclosure.

C. Personal Jurisdiction

Next, we address Edwards's conditional cross-appeal challenging personal jurisdiction. The Due Process Clause of the Fourteenth Amendment "protects an individual's liberty interest in not being subject to the binding judgments of a forum with which he has established no meaningful 'contacts, ties, or relations.'" *Burger King Corp. v. Rudzewicz,* 471 U.S. 462, 471-72, 105 S.Ct. 2174, 85 L.Ed.2d 528 (1985) (quoting *Int'l Shoe Co. v. Washington,* 326 U.S. 310, 319, 66 S.Ct. 154, 90 L.Ed. 95 (1945)). "Due process requires that a non-resident defendant have certain minimum contacts with the forum so that the exercise of jurisdiction does not offend traditional notions of fair play and substantial justice." *Meier ex rel. Meier v. Sun Int'l Hotels, Ltd.,* 288 F.3d 1264, 1274 (11th Cir. 2002). Specific jurisdiction may be exercised "over a defendant in a suit arising out of or related to the defendant's contacts with the forum," whereas general jurisdiction may be exercised "over a defendant in a suit not arising out of or related to the defendant's contacts with the forum." *Helicopteros Nacionales de Colombia v. Hall,* 466 U.S. 408, 414 n.8-9, 104 S.Ct. 1868, 80 L.Ed.2d 404 (1984).

The district court found that Edwards would not ordinarily have been subject to personal jurisdiction in Georgia based on his own contacts. However, the court held that it could exercise specific jurisdiction over Edwards based on MIC's suit-related forum contacts—which satisfy the minimum contacts test—because Relators sufficiently alleged that MIC was Edwards's alter ego under a corporate veil-piercing theory. Edwards argues that this approach is inconsistent with basic concepts of due process under the Fourteenth Amendment. p.1355 He cites *Walden v. Fiore* for the proposition that minimum contacts cannot be merely attributable to the defendant— they must be "contacts that the 'defendant *himself*' creates." 571 U.S. 277, 284, 134 S.Ct. 1115, 188 L.Ed.2d 12 (2014) (quoting *Burger King,* 471 U.S. at 475, 105 S.Ct. 2174). Edwards argues that, while it is true that a nonresident defendant's relationship with an entity may be relevant to the minimum contacts analysis, courts should not categorically impute all of the entity's forum contacts to the defendant.

Edwards's criticism of veil piercing as a basis for personal jurisdiction runs up against circuit precedent. *Meier,* 288 F.3d at 1272; *see also Stubbs v. Wyndham Nassau Resort & Crystal Palace Casino,* 447 F.3d 1357, 1361 (11th Cir. 2006). In *Meier,* the district court determined that due process prevented the exercise of personal jurisdiction based on the imputation of a subsidiary's forum contacts to a parent company. 288 F.3d at 1268. We reversed the district court, holding that "if the subsidiary is merely an agent through which the parent company conducts business in a particular jurisdiction or its separate corporate status is formal only and without any semblance of individual identity, then... the [parent] will be said to be doing business in the jurisdiction through the subsidiary for purposes of asserting personal jurisdiction." *Id.* at 1272 (quoting Wright & Miller, Fed. Prac. & Proc. § 1069.4 (3d ed. 2002)).

Under the prior panel precedent rule, "a prior panel's holding is binding on all subsequent panels unless and until it is overruled or undermined to the point of abrogation by the Supreme Court or by this court sitting *en banc.*" *United States v. Archer,* 531 F.3d 1347, 1352 (11th Cir. 2008). *Meier* is binding here. While we recognize that *Meier* involved a subsidiary and a parent company—instead of a corporation and an individual shareholder—that distinction is not meaningful for the purposes of this analysis. The Fifth Circuit's discussion of the issue helps illustrate this point:

> [F]ederal courts have consistently acknowledged that it is compatible with due process for a court to exercise personal jurisdiction over an individual or a corporation that would not ordinarily be subject to personal jurisdiction in that court when the individual or corporation is an alter ego or successor of a corporation that would be subject to personal jurisdiction in that court. The theory underlying these cases is that, because the two corporations (or the corporation and its individual alter ego) are the *same entity,* the jurisdictional contacts of one *are* the jurisdictional contacts of the other for the purposes of the *International Shoe* due process analysis.

Patin v. Thoroughbred Power Boats Inc., 294 F.3d 640, 653 (5th Cir. 2002). Regardless of whether the actors are two companies, or a company and an individual, the rule from *Meier* is that where the apparent forum contacts of one actor are really the forum contacts of another, it is consistent with due process to impute those contacts for personal jurisdiction purposes. 288 F.3d at 1272.

And the Supreme Court's decision in *Walden v. Fiore* did not abrogate our precedent. In fact, it did not even mention veil piercing. True, *Walden* emphasized that personal jurisdiction must be based on "contacts that the 'defendant *himself*' creates with the forum." 571 U.S. at 284, 134 S.Ct. 1115 (quoting *Burger King,* 471 U.S. at 475, 105 S.Ct. 2174). But the jurisdictional veil piercing we endorsed in *Meier* is based on the rationale that when a defendant exerts a high degree of control over an entity, the contacts created by the entity are, in reality, created by the defendant. p.1356 *See Patin,* 294 F.3d at 653. We do not find that proposition to be irreconcilable with *Walden.*[10] So, under *Meier,* Relators could establish that the court had personal jurisdiction over Edwards by sufficiently pleading that it could pierce MIC's corporate veil and impute MIC's forum contacts to Edwards.

Relators did so. To establish personal jurisdiction over a nonresident defendant, the plaintiff has the burden of establishing a prima facie case by presenting enough evidence to withstand a motion for directed verdict. *Meier,* 288 F.3d at 1268-69. The defendant must then submit affidavits to the contrary in order to shift the burden back to the plaintiff. *Id.* at 1269. To the extent the allegations in the complaint are uncontroverted by the defendant's evidence, the court construes the allegations as true. *Morris v. SSE, Inc.,* 843 F.2d 489, 492 (11th Cir. 1988). And "where the evidence presented by the parties' affidavits and deposition testimony conflicts," the court must draw all reasonable inferences in the plaintiff's favor. *Id.*

The Fourth Amended Complaint includes allegations that Edwards unilaterally controlled MIC, ignored corporate formalities, and commingled his personal assets with corporate assets. The result, Relators allege, was that "MIC was a corporation in name only" and that "Edwards is, legally, MIC." Based on these allegations, Relators established a prima facie case that MIC was Edwards's alter ego, so that MIC's suit-related forum contacts were really Edwards's.

To rebut Relators' prima facie case, Edwards testified by affidavit that he had never personally originated loans on behalf of MIC in the state of Georgia, and that he had never personally attested to the legality of fees charged by MIC on the Georgia loans at issue in this FCA case. He further testified that "[d]ecisions about distributions from MIC to its shareholders are made by and among the officers and directors of MIC in Florida." But as the district court's thorough analysis demonstrates, deposition testimony from MIC employees supported Relators' contention that Edwards dominated decision making, and that corporate formalities were often not observed. To the extent Edwards's affidavit testimony conflicted with other evidence, all reasonable inferences must be made in Relators' favor. *Morris,* 843 F.2d at 492. Therefore, Edwards's testimony did not rebut Relators' prima facie case for piercing MIC's veil and imputing its forum contacts to Edwards. As a result, we affirm the district court's ruling that Edwards is subject to personal jurisdiction in Georgia.

D. Fraudulent Transfer

Finally, we turn to the second issue Relators appeal: whether the district court correctly held that Relators lack Article III standing to pursue a state law claim against Edwards under Georgia's Uniform Voidable Transfers Act (UVTA). After careful review, we affirm.

It is well-established that a plaintiff must satisfy three requirements to establish Article III standing. *See Lujan v. Defs. of Wildlife,* 504 U.S. 555, 560, 112 S.Ct. 2130, 119 L.Ed.2d 351 (1992). First, there must be an "injury in fact" that is p.1357 both "concrete and particularized," as well as "actual or imminent, not conjectural or hypothetical." *Id.* (internal quotation marks omitted). "Second, there must be a causal connection between the injury and the conduct complained of—the injury has to be fairly ... trace[able] to the challenged action of the defendant." *Id.* (alteration in original) (internal quotation mark omitted). "Third, it must be likely, as opposed to merely speculative, that the injury will be redressed by a favorable decision." *Id.* at 561, 112 S.Ct. 2130 (internal quotation marks omitted).

The Supreme Court has addressed the first of those requirements—injury in fact—in the context of relators bringing qui tam actions under the FCA. *See Vt. Agency of Nat. Res. v. United States ex rel. Stevens,* 529 U.S. 765, 120 S.Ct. 1858, 146 L.Ed.2d 836 (2000). There, the Court explained that a relator does not have standing to pursue a qui tam action based on his *own* injury in fact. *Id.* at 772-73, 120 S.Ct. 1858. Before obtaining a judgment, a relator's interest is comparable to that of a person "who has placed a wager upon the outcome" of a case. *Id.* at 772, 120 S.Ct. 1858. So how, then, do relators have standing to bring qui tam actions? The answer, *Stevens* tells us, is found in the common law doctrine of assignment: an assignee has standing to vindicate the rights of an assignor. *Id.* at 773, 120 S.Ct. 1858. As the doctrine of assignment applies in this context, the FCA's qui tam provision "effect[s] a partial assignment" of the government's claim to the relator. *Id.* And only as an assignee does the relator have standing to pursue the qui tam action. *Id.*

But because the assignment to relators is "partial" rather than total, relators are not assigned *all* of the government's rights associated with a particular action. *Id.* The FCA assigns the narrow right to "bring a civil action for a violation of section 3729 for the person and for the United States Government." 31 U.S.C. § 3730(b)(1). It does not assign relators the right to pursue additional claims that arise from, or are related to, the qui tam action. Indeed, *Stevens* states that "an interest that is merely a 'byproduct' of the [FCA] suit itself cannot give rise to a cognizable injury in fact for Article III standing purposes." 529 U.S. at 773, 120 S.Ct. 1858. As Relators conceded at oral argument, that is what we have here. *See* Oral Argument Recording at 22:52-23:11 (Oct. 21, 2020). Therefore, the FCA itself does not confer standing on Relators to pursue the fraudulent transfer claim.

Relators argue, however, that they can show an injury in fact, notwithstanding *Stevens,* because they base their fraudulent transfer claim on their own injury in fact suffered as creditors under Georgia's UVTA. *See* O.C.G.A. § 18-2-70, *et seq.* That statute gives creditors the right to avoid fraudulent transfers and to obtain an injunction against the debtor to prevent further disposition of property. *Id.* § 18-2-77(a). And because the UVTA applies pre-judgment, Relators argue that they have standing under that statute as pre-judgment creditors of Edwards. *See id.* § 18-2-71(3) ("'Claim' means a right to payment, whether or not the right is reduced to judgment....").

At oral argument in this case, Relators argued that the *Stevens* Court envisioned this scenario when it noted that Congress could "define new legal rights, which in turn will confer standing to vindicate an injury caused to the claimant." 529 U.S. at 773, 120 S.Ct. 1858. Picking up on that language, Relators argue that, through the UVTA, the Georgia legislature conferred a new legal right to assert a pre-judgment claim that is contingent upon the underlying FCA claim.

p.1358 It is true that Congress can take "concrete, *de facto* injuries that were previously inadequate in law" and "elevat[e] [them] to the status of legally cognizable injuries." *Spokeo, Inc. v. Robins,* ___ U.S. ___, 136 S. Ct. 1540, 1549, 194 L.Ed.2d 635 (2016) (citing *Lujan,* 504 U.S. at 578, 112 S.Ct. 2130) (first alteration in original). We can assume for purposes of our decision (without deciding) that a state legislature can do the same. And when courts analyze what "constitutes injury in fact," legislative judgment can play an "important role[]" in that determination. *Id.* at 1547-48. But legislatures cannot simply create an injury in fact where there is no concrete injury. "Injury in fact is a constitutional requirement, and 'it is settled that Congress cannot erase Article III's standing requirements by statutorily granting the right to sue to a plaintiff who would not otherwise have standing.'" *Id.* (internal citation and brackets omitted).

This means (on our assumption) that the Georgia legislature could give relators the right to pursue a fraudulent transfer claim only if relators have a concrete interest in a claim that is a byproduct of the underlying suit. *Stevens* makes clear that they do not.[11] 529 U.S. at 773, 120 S.Ct. 1858. Consequently, it would be inconsistent with *Spokeo* to hold that the UVTA can create a concrete injury where none existed. To do so would be to "erase Article III's standing requirements" by finding that the Georgia legislature "statutorily grant[ed] the right to sue to a plaintiff who would not otherwise have standing." *Spokeo,* 136 S. Ct. at 1547-48. Accordingly, Relators cannot establish standing under Georgia's UVTA. Therefore, we affirm the district court's holding that Relators lack standing to assert a fraudulent transfer claim against Edwards.

AFFIRMED IN PART, REVERSED IN PART, AND REMANDED.

[1] The government has the option to intervene in the action, either within 60 days after receiving the complaint or upon a later showing of good cause. 31 U.S.C. § 3730(b)(2), (b)(4), (c)(3). In this case, the government communicated with Relators about their allegations but eventually decided not to intervene.

[2] Relators originally filed suit against 27 other mortgage lenders, but MIC is the only remaining defendant.

[3] Paragraph (d) further provides that "[a] lender may charge ... a flat charge not exceeding 1 percent of the amount of the loan, provided that such flat charge shall be in lieu of all other charges relating to costs of origination not expressly specified and allowed in this schedule." 38 C.F.R. § 36.4313(d)(2).

[4] In outlining the loan certification process, we rely in part on allegations in Relators' Fourth Amended Complaint that MIC does not appear to contest.

[5] MIC also asserts that it is entitled to summary judgment because Relators failed to establish causation. Because the district court has not yet addressed that issue, we remand to give the district court an opportunity to do so.

[6] While *Escobar* does not impose a rigid three-part test or an exhaustive list of factors, it gives guidance on factors that can be relevant to the materiality inquiry.

[7] We find support for looking to the government's guaranty decision in a post-*Escobar* FCA case from the Fifth Circuit. *United States v. Hodge,* 933 F.3d 468 (5th Cir. 2019). In *Hodge,* lenders were accused of "fraudulently obtaining FHA insurance for

loans that later defaulted." *Id.* at 472. The Fifth Circuit said that the "gist of this [materiality] inquiry is whether false representations ... *induced HUD to issue insurance.*" *Id.* at 474 (emphasis added).

[8] London testified that, based on the VA's audit findings, the VA "infer[red] that there were fee issues with other loans" that had not been audited.

[9] Congress amended this section in 2010. The pre-2010 version categorized documents as "public" if they were filed on the publicly available docket. In the post-2010 version, Congress significantly narrowed the scope of a public disclosure, making it easier for relators to clear the public disclosure hurdle. While the facts of our case straddle the pre- and post-amendment timeframes, the district court reasoned that it need not determine which version applied because there was no public disclosure even under the broader pre-2010 version. Our analysis follows the same trajectory.

[10] Our conclusion is reinforced by the fact that the rule Edwards cites from *Walden* was already well-established at the time we decided *Meier. See Rush v. Savchuk,* 444 U.S. 320, 332, 100 S.Ct. 571, 62 L.Ed.2d 516 (1980) ("The requirements of *International Shoe* ... must be met as to each defendant over whom a state court exercises jurisdiction."); *Keeton v. Hustler Magazine, Inc.,* 465 U.S. 770, 781 n.13, 104 S.Ct. 1473, 79 L.Ed.2d 790 (1984) ("Each defendant's contacts with the forum State must be assessed individually.").

[11] This is not to say, of course, that pre-judgment creditors cannot establish Article III standing based on their *own* damages claim. For example, in *Enterprise Financial Group, Inc. v. Podhorn,* 930 F.3d 946 (8th Cir. 2019), cited by Relators, a pre-judgment creditor had Article III standing based on its own damages claim, rather than a damages claim that the government had partially assigned to it.

963 F.3d 1089 (2020)

Angela RUCKH, Relator, Plaintiff-Appellant,
v.
SALUS REHABILITATION, LLC, d.b.a. La Vie Rehab, 207 Marshall Drive Operations, LLC, d.b.a. Marshall Health and Rehabilitation Center, et al., Defendants - Appellees.

No. 18-10500.

United States Court of Appeals, Eleventh Circuit.

June 25, 2020.

Ruckh v. Salus Rehabilitation, LLC, 963 F. 3d 1089 (11th Cir. 2020)

Appeal from the United States District Court for the Middle District of Florida, D.C. Docket No. 8:11-cv-01303-SDM-TBM.

Derek T. Ho, Rebecca A. Beynon, Joseph Solomon Hall, Bradley E. Oppenheimer, Silvija Anna Strikis, James McCormick Webster, III, Kellogg Hansen Todd Figel & Frederick, PLLC, Washington, DC, Kevin John Darken, The Barry A. Cohen Legal Team, Tampa, FL, Royston Delaney, Boston, MA, Charles F. Kester, Calabasas, CA, Delaney Kester, LLP, for Plaintiff-Appellant.

Gregory M. Luce, John Anthony James Barkmeyer, Jonathan L. Marcus, Skadden Arps Slate Meagher & Flom, LLP, Washington, DC, Catherine E. Creely, Robert S. Salcido, Carroll Skehan, Stanley E. Woodward, Akin Gump Strauss Hauer & Feld, LLP, Washington, DC, Jason Alex Watson, Office of Corporate Counsel, TAMPA, FL, Defendants-Appellees

Benjamin M. Shultz, Charles W. Scarborough, Kathleen M. Von Hoene, Associate Deputy Attorney General, Washington, DC, Jill Marie Bennett, Tallahassee, FL, Pam Bondi, Tampa, FL, U.S. Attorney General's Office, Peter John Grilli, Peter J. Grilli, PA, Paul Andrew McDermott, Holland & Knight, LLP, Tampa, FL, for Amicus Curiae.

Henry C. Su, Constantine Cannon LLP, Washington, DC, for Amicus Curiae.

Colette G. Matzzie, Phillips & Cohen, LLP, Washington, DC, for Amicus Curiae.

Peter Douglas Keisler, Sidley Austin, LLP, Washington, DC, for Amicus Curiae.

Scott D. Stein, Sidley Austin, LLP, Chicago, IL, for Amicus Curiae.

Cory L. Andrews, Washington Legal Foundation, Washington, DC, for Amicus Curiae.

James F. Segroves, Reed Smith, LLP, Washington, DC, for Amicus Curiae.

Before BRANCH and MARCUS, Circuit Judges, and UNGARO,[*] District Judge.

p.1093 UNGARO, District Judge:

Relator Angela Ruckh, a registered nurse, brought this *qui tam* action alleging violations of the False Claims Act, 31 U.S.C. §§ 3729 *et seq.* (the "FCA"), and the p.1094 Florida False Claims Act, Fla. Stat. §§ 68.081 *et seq.* (the "Florida FCA"), against two skilled nursing home facilities, two related entities that provided management services at those and 51 other facilities in the state, and an affiliated company that provided rehabilitation services. The relator appeals the district court's grant, after jury trial, of the defendants' renewed motion for judgment as a matter of law or, in the alternative, for a new trial.

The jury found the defendants liable for the submission of 420 fraudulent Medicare claims and 26 fraudulent Medicaid claims and awarded $115,137,095 in damages. After applying statutory trebling and penalties, the district court entered judgment in favor of the relator, the United States, and the State of Florida in the total amount of $347,864,285. After judgment was entered, the defendants timely renewed their motion for judgment as a matter of law or, in the alternative, for a new trial. The district court ultimately set aside the jury's verdict as unsupported by the evidence and granted judgment as a matter of law. In the alternative, the district court conditionally granted the defendants' request for a new trial.

After thorough consideration, and with the benefit of oral argument, we affirm in part and reverse in part. We remand with instructions for the district court to reinstate the jury's verdict in favor of the relator, the United States, and the State of Florida and against the defendants on the Medicare claims in the amount of $85,137,095, and to enter judgment on those claims after applying trebling and statutory penalties.

I.

We begin with an overview of the Medicare and Medicaid programs in the skilled nursing home context, the relevant statutory and regulatory requirements that skilled nursing facilities, like the defendants, must satisfy to obtain Medicare and Medicaid reimbursement, and the consequences for failing to comply with these requirements.

The Medicare Program

The Social Security Amendments of 1965 established the Medicare program, which provides federally funded health insurance to eligible elderly and disabled persons. *See* 42 U.S.C. §§ 1395 *et seq.* Medicare Part A pays skilled nursing facilities, or "SNFs," a daily rate for the routine services they provide to each resident. 42 U.S.C. § 1395yy; 42 C.F.R. § 413.335. Medicare bases its payment amount in part on information provided to it by SNFs. 42 C.F.R. § 413.343. Specifically, Medicare requires SNFs to "conduct initially and periodically a comprehensive, accurate, standardized, reproducible assessment of each resident's functional capacity." *Id.* § 483.20; *see also* 42 U.S.C. § 1395i-3(b)(3). The assessments must be made using the resident assessment instrument ("RAI") specified by Centers for Medicare & Medicaid Services ("CMS") and must address several factors, including each resident's cognitive patterns, psychological well-being, disease diagnoses and health conditions, medications, and special treatments or procedures. 42 C.F.R. § 483.20(b)(1).

Medicare regulations require SNFs to complete these evaluations, known as Minimum Data Set ("MDS") assessments, at regular intervals.[1] 42 U.S.C. § 1395i-

3(b)(3)(C); 42 C.F.R. §§ 413.343, 483.20(b)(2). The final day of the assessment interval is referred to as the "assessment reference date," or "ARD." Medicare's p.1095 assessment schedule includes 5-day, 14-day, 30-day, 60-day, and 90-day scheduled assessments. The assessment looks back over a 7-day period, and Medicare also reserves for the SNFs a grace period during which SNFs have discretion to set the precise ARD.

MDS assessments are designed to be comprehensive, accurate, standardized, and reproducible. *See* 42 U.S.C. § 1395i-3(b)(3)(A); 42 C.F.R. § 483.20(g). Each assessment must be conducted or coordinated and certified as complete by a registered professional nurse ("RN"). 42 U.S.C. § 1395i-3(b)(3)(B)(i); 42 C.F.R. § 483.20(h), (i)(1). Each individual who completes a portion of the assessment must sign and certify the accuracy of that portion. 42 U.S.C. § 1395i-3(b)(3)(B)(i); 42 C.F.R. § 483.20(h), (i)(2). RNs are guided in completing the assessments by the Resident Assessment Instrument Manual ("RAI Manual"), which is promulgated and regularly updated by CMS. The RAI Manual facilitates accurate, effective, and uniform resident assessment practices by SNFs and fosters a holistic approach to optimizing resident care, well-being, and outcomes.

The accuracy of MDS assessments is critical because under the Resource Utilization Group ("RUG") model, which governed at the time of this lawsuit, CMS tied the amount of its payments to SNFs in part to RUG codes derived from MDS assessments.[2] Medicare used SNFs' self-reported RUG codes during assessment periods to set payment rates on a forward-looking basis, and the RUG codes governed payment until the next assessment period. The RUG codes were divided among eight classification groups. The relevant RUG codes began with the letter "R," as they were classified as rehabilitation services. The RUG codes were further divided based on each resident's "activities of daily living" ("ADL") needs. Residents with more specialized nursing needs and with greater ADL dependency were assigned to higher groups in the RUG hierarchy. Because providing care to these residents was more costly, CMS reimbursed SNFs for this care at a higher daily rate. *See* Medicare Program; Prospective Payment System and Consolidated Billing for Skilled Nursing Facilities, 63 Fed. Reg. 26252, 26261-65 (May 12, 1998). The second letter of the RUG codes reflected the number of minutes of therapy services provided to residents, and the third letter indicated the level of nursing assistance provided to the residents. Therapy codes ranged from "Low" ("L") to "Ultra High" ("U"). Nursing codes "A," "B," and "C" generally reflected increasing levels of nursing services and greater ADL dependency, with additional codes "L" and "X" reflecting more extensive services.

To receive Medicare reimbursement, SNFs must electronically transmit the MDS assessment to CMS within 14 days of completing it. 42 C.F.R. § 483.20(f)(3).

The Medicaid Program

The Social Security Amendments of 1965 established the Medicaid program. *See* 42 U.S.C. §§ 1396 *et seq.* Medicaid, which is jointly financed by the federal and state governments and administered by the states, helps states provide medical assistance to low-income persons. 42 C.F.R. § 430.0. States pay service providers directly, subject to broad federal rules, and receive partial reimbursement from p.1096 the federal government for their Medicaid expenses. *Id.*; 42 U.S.C. §§ 1396b(a), 1396d(b). Unlike Medicare's fee-for-service model, Florida Medicaid reimburses SNFs for resident care at a flat daily rate. *See*Fla. Stat. § 409.908(1)(f).

Under Florida's Medicaid program, SNFs are required to present claims that "[a]re documented by records made at the time the goods or services were provided, demonstrating the medical necessity for the goods or services rendered." Fla. Stat. § 409.913(7)(f). "Medicaid goods or services are excessive or not medically necessary unless both the medical basis and the specific need for them are fully and properly documented in the recipient's medical record." *Id.*

SNFs are required by federal law and Florida administrative law to "provide services and activities to attain or maintain the highest practicable physical, mental, and psychosocial well-being of each resident in accordance with a written plan of care." 42 U.S.C. § 1396r(b)(2); *see also*Fla. Admin. Code Ann. r. 59A-4.109(2). The written plan of care must:

(A) describe[ ] the medical, nursing, and psychosocial needs of the resident and how such needs will be met;

(B) [be] initially prepared, with the participation to the extent practicable of the resident or the resident's family or legal representative, by a team which includes the resident's attending physician and a registered professional nurse with responsibility for the resident; and

(C) [be] periodically reviewed and revised by such team after each assessment under paragraph (3).

42 U.S.C. § 1396r(b)(2); *see also* Fla. Admin. Code Ann. r. 59A-4.109(2) (requiring SNFs to develop a "comprehensive care plan for each resident").

The Florida Medicaid Nursing Facility Services Coverage and Limitations Handbook, with which SNFs must comply under Florida's Medicaid regulations, elaborates on this requirement. *See* Fla. Admin. Code Ann. r. 59G-4.200 (July 23, 2006). This handbook states that SNFs are "responsible for developing a comprehensive plan of care for each resident." It further states that the care plan is to be developed based on resident evaluations conducted in connection with the MDS assessment process. Additionally, the Florida Medicaid Provider General Handbook puts SNFs on notice that "Medicaid payments for services that lack required documentation or appropriate signatures will be recouped." *See also* Fla. Admin. Code Ann. r. 59G-5.020 (requiring compliance with the Florida Medicaid Provider General Handbook). It cautions that providers are responsible for presenting claims that are "true and accurate" and that are for "goods and services" that "[a]re provided in accord with applicable provisions of all Medicaid rules, regulations, handbooks, and policies and in accordance with federal, state and local law."

Florida's Medicaid regulations require SNFs to submit billing forms known as UB-04s to receive Medicaid reimbursement. *See*Fla. Admin. Code Ann. r. 59G-4.003. The back of the UB-04 contains several representations, including:

• The submitter of this form understands that misrepresentation or falsification of essential information as requested by this form, may serve as the basis for civil monetary penalties and assessments and may upon conviction include fines and/or imprisonment under federal and/or state law(s).

• Submission of this claim constitutes certification that the billing information as shown on the face hereof is true, accurate and complete. That the submitter did not knowingly or recklessly disregard or misrepresent or conceal material facts.

p.1097 • For Medicaid Purposes: The submitter understands that because payment and satisfaction of this claim will be from Federal and State funds, any false statements, documents, or concealment of a material fact are subject to prosecution under applicable Federal or State Laws.

Procedural History

The relator, Ruckh, is a registered nurse certified in preparing MDS assessments. From January 2011 until May 2011, she worked at Marshall Health and Rehabilitation Center ("Marshall") and Governor's Creek Health and Rehabilitation Center ("Governor's Creek") as an interim MDS coordinator preparing RUG assessments. She claimed that over the course of these five months, she discovered that the defendants were misrepresenting the services they provided to Medicare beneficiaries and failing to comply with certain Medicaid requirements in three ways: first, the defendants routinely engaged in "upcoding," or the artificial inflation of RUG codes; second, the defendants engaged in "ramping," or the timing of spikes in treatment to coincide with the ARD, which exaggerated the required payment levels; and third, the defendants submitted claims for Medicaid reimbursement without creating or maintaining comprehensive care plans.

On June 10, 2011, Ruckh filed suit against five defendants: (i) Sea Crest Health Care Management, LLC, which did business under the name La Vie Management Services of Florida ("LVMSF"); (ii) CMC II, LLC, LVMSF's successor-in-interest (together with LVMSF, "La Vie Management"); (iii) Salus Rehabilitation, LLC, which provided rehabilitation therapy services at Marshall; (iv) 207 Marshall Drive Operations, LLC, which did business under the name Marshall Health and Rehabilitation Center; and (v) 803 Oak Street Operations, LLC, which did business under the name Governor's Creek Health and Rehabilitation Center. La Vie Management provided management services to a network of 53 SNFs throughout Florida, including Marshall and Governor's Creek.

In the *qui tam* complaint, Ruckh alleged that the defendants violated 31 U.S.C. § 3729(a)(1)(A), (B), and (G), along with parallel provisions of the Florida FCA. The FCA subjects to liability any person who, in relevant part:

> (A) knowingly presents, or causes to be presented, a false or fraudulent claim for payment or approval;

> (B) knowingly makes, uses, or causes to be made or used, a false record or statement material to a false or fraudulent claim; or

> ....

> (G) knowingly makes, uses, or causes to be made or used, a false record or statement material to an obligation to pay or transmit money or property to the Government, or knowingly conceals or knowingly and improperly avoids

or decreases an obligation to pay or transmit money or property to the Government.

31 U.S.C. § 3729(a)(*l*)(A)-(B), (G).[3]

After both the United States and the State of Florida declined to intervene, p.1098 Ruckh prosecuted the action on her own as a *qui tam* relator. On January 17, 2017, following several years of motions and discovery, the case proceeded to a month-long trial.

At the conclusion of the relator's case-in-chief, the defendants moved for judgment as a matter of law under Federal Rule of Civil Procedure 50(a), which the district court denied. The defendants raised four grounds in support of their motion: first, the relator failed to prove a corporate scheme to knowingly cause the submission of false claims; second, the relator failed to present sufficient evidence of materiality as to the allegedly fraudulent Medicaid claims; third, the relator failed to present sufficient evidence of materiality and scienter as to the allegedly fraudulent Medicare claims; and fourth, the relator's use of statistical sampling and extrapolation to establish damages was impermissible.

On February 13, 2017, the case was submitted to the jury. After two days of deliberation, the jury returned its verdict finding the defendants liable under § 3729(a)(1)(A) and (B) for the submission of 420 fraudulent Medicare claims and 26 fraudulent Medicaid claims and awarded $115,137,095 in damages.[4],[5] After trebling and the application of statutory penalties, the district court entered judgment in favor of the relator, the United States, and the State of Florida totaling $347,864,285.

On March 29, 2017, following entry of judgment, the defendants renewed their motion for judgment as a matter of law under Federal Rule of Civil Procedure 50(b). Defendants advanced three arguments in support of their motion: first, that the alleged Medicaid-related fraud was unsupported by evidence of materiality; second, that the relator failed to prove the materiality of the alleged Medicare-related fraud; and third, that no evidence supported any allegation of fraud on the part of La Vie Management. In the alternative, the defendants moved the court to grant a new trial, arguing the verdict was "excessive and against the weight of the evidence." In the event the court viewed a new trial as unnecessary, the defendants alternatively sought remittitur.

On January 11, 2018, the district court granted the motion for judgment as a matter of law and set aside the jury's verdict. In the alternative, the district court conditionally granted the defendants' request for a new trial and denied the request for remittitur as moot. In granting the defendants' motion for judgment as a matter of law, the district court relied mainly on its assessment that the relator failed to introduce evidence of materiality and scienter at trial. The district court held that "the p.1099 relator failed to offer competent evidence that defendants knew that the governments regarded the disputed practices as material" and would have refused to pay the claims had they known about the disputed practices. The district court concluded that the evidence was insufficient to support any theory of FCA liability against La Vie Management, as the evidence did not show that the management entity "presented" or "caused to be presented" a false claim or "produced" or "caused the production" of a "'false record or statement' material to a false claim." As to the existence of a "corporate scheme," the district court agreed with the defendants that "the relator fail[ed] entirely to connect the testimony about 'RUG budgets,' 'LaVie meetings,' and 'corporate profits' to any particular claim 'actually submitted' to the government." In alternatively granting the defendants' motion for a new trial, the district court did not explain its reasoning except to state that it was conditionally granted "for the reasons explained above and for the reasons identified and satisfactorily explained in the defendants' motion."

The relator filed the instant appeal on February 8, 2018. Before the parties submitted their respective briefs on the merits, the defendants moved to dismiss the appeal for lack of jurisdiction. The defendants' motion to dismiss this appeal was carried with the case. We deny the motion to dismiss. We affirm as to the Medicaid claims. We reverse as to the Medicare claims and remand with instructions for the district court to reinstate the jury's verdict on those claims.

II.

"[T]he decision to grant or deny a motion to dismiss is within the discretion of the Court of Appeals." *Showtime/The Movie Channel, Inc. v. Covered Bridge Condo. Ass'n,* 895 F.2d 711, 713 (11th Cir. 1990) (quoting *Brookhaven Landscape & Grading Co. v. J. F. Barton Contracting Co.,* 681 F.2d 734, 736 (11th Cir. 1982)).

"We review de novo a district judge's granting judgment as a matter of law under Federal Rule of Civil Procedure 50(b) and apply the same standard as the trial judge. In reviewing the record evidence, we draw all inferences in favor of the nonmoving party." *Cadle v. GEICO Gen. Ins. Co.,* 838 F.3d 1113, 1121 (11th Cir. 2016) (citing *Collado v. United Parcel Serv., Co.,* 419 F.3d 1143, 1149 (11th Cir. 2005)). "In considering a Rule 50(b) motion after the jury verdict, 'only the sufficiency of the evidence matters. The jury's findings are irrelevant.'" *Id.* (quoting *Connelly v. Metro. Atlanta Rapid Transit Auth.,* 764 F.3d 1358, 1363 (11th Cir. 2014)). "Judgment as a matter of law for a defendant is appropriate, 'when there is insufficient evidence to prove an element of the claim, which means that no jury reasonably could have reached a verdict for the plaintiff on that claim.'" *Id.* (quoting *Collado,* 419 F.3d at 1149); *see also Munoz v. Oceanside Resorts, Inc.,* 223 F.3d 1340, 1344-45 (11th Cir. 2000) ("A Rule 50(b) motion should only be granted where reasonable jurors could not arrive at a contrary verdict." (citation, internal quotation marks, and alteration omitted)).

"We review the grant of a new trial pursuant to Rule 59 [of the Federal Rules of Civil Procedure] for abuse of discretion. Our review for abuse of discretion is 'more rigorous when the basis' of the grant was the weight of the evidence." *Aronowitz v. Health-Chem Corp.,* 513 F.3d 1229, 1242 (11th Cir. 2008) (internal citation omitted) (quoting *Williams v. City of Valdosta,* 689 F.2d 964, 974 (11th Cir. 1982)). We nevertheless give deference to "the trial court's first-hand experience of the witnesses, their demeanor and a context of the trial." *MacPherson v. Univ. of Montevallo,* 922 F.2d 766, 777 (11th Cir. p.1100 1991). Further, the district court is allowed wide discretion when it grants a new trial and "evidentiary weight is merely one of numerous factors cited in support" thereof. *J.A. Jones Constr. Co v. Steel Erectors, Inc.,* 901 F.2d 943, 944 (11th Cir. 1990).

III.

A.

We first consider the defendants' claim that the relator's entry into a litigation funding agreement (the "Agreement") dated October 17, 2017 with ARUS 1705-556 LLC ("ARUS") vitiates her standing to pursue this appeal.[6] The relator agreed to sell ARUS less than 4% of her share of the judgment originally entered by the district court, if the jury verdict were upheld on appeal, assuming a 30% share to the relator.[7] According to the relator, the Agreement is explicit that ARUS has no power to influence or control this litigation.[8]

In moving to dismiss the present appeal, the defendants argue that the relator's entry into the Agreement is a partial reassignment of her interest in the action to ARUS, which precludes her from continuing as a relator and requires this Court to dismiss her appeal. Specifically, the defendants argue that this partial reassignment violates the Constitution and the text and structure of the FCA.[9] The defendants urge this Court to conclude that because the relator has reassigned her interest in this action, she has forfeited her standing to represent the interests of the United States.

p.1101 Article III Standing

The defendants contend that the relator has forfeited standing to pursue the appeal because she no longer belongs to the class of *qui tam* plaintiffs authorized to bring suit under the FCA and, therefore, the appeal must be dismissed. For the reasons discussed below, we find that the relator's standing is unaffected by the Agreement and that this case is justiciable.

Article III extends "'the judicial power of the United States' ... only to 'Cases' and 'Controversies.'" *Spokeo, Inc. v. Robins,* 578 U.S. ___, ___, 136 S. Ct. 1540, 1547, 194 L. Ed. 2d 635, 643 (2016) (quoting U.S. Const. art. III, §§ 1, 2). The Supreme Court has explained that the doctrine of standing to sue is "rooted in the traditional understanding of a case or controversy" and "limits the category of litigants empowered to maintain a lawsuit in federal court to seek redress for a legal wrong." *Id.* (citations omitted). "'The law of Article III standing serves to prevent the judicial process from being used to usurp the powers of the political branches' and confines the federal courts to a properly judicial role." *Id.* (quoting *Clapper v. Amnesty Int'l USA,* 568 U.S. 398, 408, 133 S. Ct. 1138, 1146, 185 L. Ed. 2d 264, 275 (2013)) (citations, alterations and ellipsis omitted). To establish standing, a plaintiff must show that: (i) she suffered an "injury in fact" that is "concrete and particularized" and "actual or imminent," not "conjectural or hypothetical"; (ii) the injury complained of is "fairly traceable to the challenged action of the defendant"; and (iii) it is "likely," not "merely speculative," that the injury will be "redressed by a favorable decision." *Lujan v. Defs. of Wildlife,* 504 U.S. 555, 560-61, 112 S. Ct. 2130, 2136, 119 L. Ed. 2d 351, 364 (1992) (quotations omitted and alterations adopted).

In *Vermont Agency of Natural Resources v. United States ex rel. Stevens,* 529 U.S. 765, 120 S. Ct. 1858, 146 L. Ed. 2d 836 (2000), the Supreme Court affirmed that *qui tam* relators have Article III standing to pursue actions on behalf of the federal government. The Court held that *qui tam* relators have standing as partial assignees of the United States. *Id.* at 773, 120 S.Ct. 1858. In *qui tam* actions, the injury suffered by the United States "suffices to confer standing on" the relator. *Id.* at 774, 120 S.Ct. 1858.

In this case, the relator sought to remedy an injury in fact suffered by the United States fairly traceable to the defendants' conduct and likely redressable by a favorable decision under the FCA. *See Lujan,* 504 U.S. at 560-61, 112 S.Ct. 2130. For us to hold that relator lacks standing would require a showing that she is no longer the assignee of the United States, or that the United States in fact suffered no injury. The defendants do not assert the latter. Instead, they argue that by entering into a litigation funding agreement, the relator disqualified herself from serving as the government's assignee.

We find the defendants' argument unavailing. The relator has given only a small interest—less than 4% of her share of the potential recovery in this case—to ARUS in exchange for immediate liquidity. *Cf. Aaron Ferer & Sons Ltd. v. Chase Manhattan Bank, N.A.,* 731 F.2d 112, 125 (2d Cir. 1984) (explaining that "[a]n unequivocal and complete assignment extinguishes the assignor's rights against the obligor and leaves the assignor without standing to sue the obligor"). And, as the relator acknowledged, the Agreement is clear that the relator retains sole authority over the litigation and ARUS has no power to control or influence it. Thus, although she has now entered into the litigation funding agreement, these facts remain essentially unchanged: the relator retains sufficient interest to meet the "irreducible constitutional minimum" of standing under Article p.1102 III. *Id.* at 560, 112 S. Ct. 2130. Consequently, she has constitutional standing to pursue this appeal.

FCA

The defendants' position on standing is better understood as an argument that the relator cannot pursue a claim under the FCA once she has assigned even a small portion of any possible recovery to ARUS, because the litigation funding agreement violates the text and structure of the FCA.[10] We recognize that the statute does not expressly authorize relators to reassign their right to represent the interests of the United States in *qui tam* actions. However, we are not persuaded that the FCA proscribes such assignment.

The FCA includes a number of restrictions, including on the conduct of *qui tam* actions and who may serve as a relator. *See* 31 U.S.C. § 3730. It does not, however, prohibit the relator's entry into the litigation funding agreement. Indeed, the statute is silent as to this point. It also does not require a court to dismiss a *qui tam* action upon learning of such an agreement. The defendants nonetheless persist in arguing that the assignment is proscribed because the statute does not affirmatively authorize it.

The text of 31 U.S.C. § 3730(b)(1) provides that "[a] person" may bring a suit under the FCA. From this general grant of power, Congress specifically excludes a person from bringing suit in three situations: where a person serves in the armed forces (under certain circumstances), § 3730(e)(1); where a person seeks to sue certain government officials, § 3730(e)(2); and where the person suing was involved in the very fraud at issue in the claim, § 3730(d)(3). Because the FCA "explicitly enumerates certain exceptions to a general grant of power, courts should be reluctant to imply additional exceptions in the absence of clear legislative intent to the contrary." *United States ex rel. Williams v. NEC Corp.,* 931 F.2d 1493, 1502 (11th Cir. 1991) (citation omitted); *see also* ANTONIN SCALIA & BRYAN A. GARNER, READING LAW 107-11 (2012) (summarizing the "Negative-Implication Canon" as "[t]he expression of one thing implies the exclusion of others").

We decline to interfere in Congress's legislative prerogatives by engrafting any further limitations onto the statute; that task is appropriately left for Congress. *See State Farm Fire & Cas. Co. v. United States ex rel. Rigsby,* ___ U.S. ___, 137 S. Ct. 436, 443, 196 L. Ed. 2d 340, 349 (2016) (declining to read a mandatory dismissal rule into the statute for failure to comply with the statute's seal requirement); *United States v. Florida,* 938 F.3d 1221, 1253 (11th Cir. 2019) ("It is not our function to engraft on a statute additions which we think the legislature logically might or should have made." (Branch, J., dissenting) (quoting *United States v. Cooper Corp.,* 312 U.S. 600, 605, 61 S. Ct. 742, 744, 85 L. Ed. 1071, 1075 (1941))).

Furthermore, we find no basis in the record suggesting that the relator has not complied with all requirements of the FCA to maintain the action and reject the defendants' characterization of ARUS as an unqualified relator. ARUS may fail to meet every requirement imposed by the FCA for serving as a relator, but it is Ruckh— p.1103 not ARUS—who is pursuing the claim as relator. We therefore reject the defendants' contention that the relator's relationship with ARUS disqualifies her as a relator under the FCA and that dismissal is warranted.

We conclude the relator has sufficiently demonstrated she has constitutional standing and, therefore, the case or controversy requirement is satisfied. We further conclude that the relator's entry into the litigation funding agreement does not violate the FCA. Accordingly, we deny the motion to dismiss.

B.

"The FCA is designed to protect the Government from fraud by imposing civil liability and penalties upon those who seek federal funds under false pretenses." *United States ex rel. Lesinski v. S. Fla. Water Mgmt. Dist.,* 739 F.3d 598, 600 (11th Cir. 2014). "Liability under the [FCA] arises from the submission of a fraudulent claim to the government, not the disregard of government regulations or failure to maintain proper internal procedures." *Urquilla-Diaz v. Kaplan Univ.,* 780 F.3d 1039, 1045 (11th Cir. 2015) (quoting *Corsello v. Lincare, Inc.,* 428 F.3d 1008, 1012 (11th Cir. 2005)); *see also McNutt ex rel. United States v. Haleyville Med. Supplies, Inc.,* 423 F.3d 1256, 1259 (11th Cir. 2005) ("The [FCA] does not create liability merely for a health care provider's disregard of Government regulations or improper internal policies unless, as a result of such acts, the provider knowingly asks the Government to pay amounts it does not owe.") (quoting *United States ex rel. Clausen v. Lab. Corp. of Am., Inc.,* 290 F.3d 1301, 1311 (11th Cir. 2002)). "Simply put, the '*sine qua non* of [an FCA] violation' is the submission of a false claim to the government." *Urquilla-Diaz,* 780 F.3d at 1045 (quoting *Corsello,* 428 F.3d at 1012).

Our circuit has expressly adopted a false certification theory of liability under the FCA. *See id.* Under this theory, a defendant may be found liable for falsely certifying its compliance with applicable laws and regulations. *Id.* To prevail, a relator must prove "(1) a false statement or fraudulent course of conduct, (2) made with scienter, (3) that was material, causing (4) the government to pay out money or forfeit moneys due." *Id.* (quoting *United States ex rel. Hendow v. Univ. of Phx.*, 461 F.3d 1166, 1174 (9th Cir. 2006)).

The Supreme Court upheld and clarified the contours of the implied false certification theory of liability in *Universal Health Services, Inc. v. United States ex rel. Escobar*, 579 U.S. ___, ___, 136 S. Ct. 1989, 195 L. Ed. 2d 348 (2016). The Court first held that "the implied false certification theory can, at least in some circumstances, provide a basis for [FCA] liability." *Escobar*, 136 S. Ct. at 1999. The Court explained that the FCA's prohibition against the submission of "false or fraudulent claims" is broad enough to "encompass[ ] claims that make fraudulent misrepresentations, which include certain misleading omissions." *Id.* "When ... a defendant makes representations in submitting a claim but omits its violations of statutory, regulatory, or contractual requirements, those omissions can be a basis for liability if they render the defendant's representations misleading with respect to the goods or services provided." *Id.* Accordingly, the Court held that the implied certification theory can serve as a basis for FCA liability where at least two conditions are satisfied: (1) "the claim does not merely request payment, but also makes specific representations about the goods or services provided" and (2) "the defendant's failure to disclose noncompliance with material statutory, regulatory, or contractual p.1104 requirements makes those representations misleading half-truths." *Id.* at 2001.

The Court also addressed a second, related question: whether FCA liability attaches only if a defendant's failure to disclose noncompliance with a contractual, statutory, or regulatory provision has been expressly designated by the Government a condition of payment. *Id.* The Court declined to so cabin liability but added that only misrepresentations that are "material to the Government's payment decision" are actionable under the FCA. *Id.* at 2002. The Court further emphasized that this materiality standard is "demanding."[11] *Id.* at 2003. The concept of materiality "looks to the effect on the likely or actual behavior of the recipient of the alleged misrepresentation." *Id.* at 2002 (internal quotation and alteration omitted). Ultimately, "the Government's decision to expressly identify a provision as a condition of payment is relevant, but not automatically dispositive." *Id.* at 2003. The Court explained further that "proof of materiality can include, but is not necessarily limited to, evidence that the defendant knows that the Government consistently refuses to pay claims in the mine run of cases based on noncompliance with the particular statutory, regulatory, or contractual requirement." *Id.* On the other hand, the Court noted:

> [I]f the Government pays a particular claim in full despite its actual knowledge that certain requirements were violated, that is very strong evidence that those requirements are not material. Or, if the Government regularly pays a particular type of claim in full despite actual knowledge that certain requirements were violated, and has signaled no change in position, that is strong evidence that the requirements are not material.

Id. at 2003-04.

C.

Medicare Fraud

Drawing all inferences in favor of the relator, as we must when considering a Rule 50(b) motion, we conclude that the evidence at trial permitted a reasonable jury to find that the defendants committed Medicare-related fraud. In this case, the relator alleged that defendants defrauded Medicare through the use of two improper practices: upcoding and ramping. The Court addresses each in turn.

In the context of this case, upcoding involves submitting bills to Medicare with elevated RUG codes. Evidence presented at trial indicated the defendants inflated their RUG codes in two ways. First, the defendants exaggerated the second letter of the code, representing to Medicare that they provided a greater number of therapy minutes than were reflected in their residents' medical records. And second, the defendants elevated the third letter of the code, indicating they provided more extensive nursing services than reflected in their residents' medical records.

Shirley Bradley is a registered nurse who testified as an expert on the relator's behalf at trial. Bradley conducted an audit of 300 Medicare claims and 300 Medicaid claims submitted across the 53 SNFs. Bradley's audit of the Medicare claims revealed evidence of upcoding, which fit into three categories. First, Bradley found evidence that the number of therapy minutes that the defendants reported to the government for billing purposes was higher than those reflected in contemporaneous p.1105 medical records. Bradley concluded that in 56 of the 300 claims she reviewed, the defendants inflated the number of therapy minutes actually provided to residents.

Second, the relator alleged that the defendants inflated the nursing services they provided to residents. Bradley found evidence that the level of nursing services that the defendants reported to Medicare was higher than those reflected in contemporaneous medical records. Bradley testified that 45 of the 300 claims she reviewed contained higher levels of nursing services than actually provided to residents. And third, the relator alleged that the defendants billed for certain complex nursing services when contemporaneous medical records did not include any such services. As an example, Bradley testified she reviewed the file of one patient whose claim was billed at a level reflecting extensive nursing services, but a review of the patient's medical records revealed no such services had been provided. Based upon her audit, Bradley testified that 50 of the 300 claims she reviewed included this type of extensive nursing services upcoding.

Contrary to the district court's decision, these types of affirmative misrepresentations are material. At the time, Medicare reimbursement rates were tied in part to RUG codes. The district court dismissed the relator's upcoding theory as "a handful of paperwork defects." That characterization misses the mark. The defendants' theory at trial was that the RUG codes were accurate and that the entries in the corresponding patient files supporting the RUG codes were either missing or never recorded essentially due to clerical error, and that is the type of recordkeeping mistake the FCA does not punish. But the jury was not required to believe the defendants' position. Rather, a jury could reasonably find mistake to be an implausible explanation for the defendants' upcoding.

At its core, the concept of upcoding is a simple and direct theory of fraud. SNFs receive money from Medicare based on the services they provide. In this case, the SNFs indicated they had provided more services—in quantity and quality—than they, in fact, provided. Therefore, Medicare paid the SNFs higher amounts than they were truly owed. This plain and obvious materiality went to the heart of the SNFs' ability to obtain reimbursement from Medicare.

Like upcoding, ramping presents a fairly straightforward case. Ramping is the impermissible, artificial timing of services to coincide with Medicare's regularly scheduled assessment periods and thereby maximize reimbursements. Because Medicare uses the level of services provided during the assessment reference period to set reimbursement levels on a forward-looking basis, it is possible for SNFs to manipulate this system by providing more extensive services during the look-back period than medically necessary to address patients' needs. An SNF thereby causes Medicare to reimburse at a higher level than it would had the SNF reported the appropriate level of services. Like upcoding, ramping is material, as it goes to the essence of the parties' economic relationship.

We find that the relator presented sufficient evidence to permit a jury to conclude that the defendants engaged in ramping. At trial, the relator testified that she personally witnessed ramping while working at Marshall and Governor's Creek. For instance, she testified that she was transferred to Governor's Creek because she brought up ramping at Marshall by "complaining about the grace days being used on every single assessment and that the patients weren't getting therapy after the [ARDs] or the MDS." Moreover, Bradley testified that she found 112 instances of p.1106 ramping in her audit. Bradley explained the case of one patient, Jean H., in which the defendants billed Medicare for providing the Ultra High level of therapy. Bradley explained that in each week used to set the payment level, the defendants reported providing the patient with 720 minutes of therapy—the minimum amount needed to qualify for the Ultra High level. Bradley further noted that in the weeks between assessment periods, the patient routinely received far fewer than 720 minutes of therapy. In addition, La Vie Management's former chief compliance officer, Stephanie Griffin, confirmed through video testimony at trial that an SNF is not allowed to engage in the practice of ramping: "If you're asking me if you can manipulate grace days in order to maximize reimbursement, that is not allowed. But it's not allowed anywhere in the system. It's not just about grace days, it's any manipulation of a particular aspect of coding and billing that the sole purpose of, unrelated to care, is to impact reimbursement is a problem."

In sum, drawing all inferences in favor of the relator's testimony, as we must, a jury could reasonably conclude the defendants engaged in ramping. And ramping is material, as it directly affects the payments Medicare makes to SNFs. Had the defendants provided only the necessary services to their residents during assessment windows, Medicare would have reimbursed the defendants at a lower level. Instead, the defendants artificially and impermissibly inflated the level of services they provided. Medicare, therefore, paid the defendants more for their services than it owed.

La Vie Management's Liability as to Medicare Fraud

Lastly, the Court addresses the relator's separate contention that the district court erred in concluding as a matter of law that she failed to establish liability with respect to La Vie Management, the entity that provided management services to the defendant facilities.

"To prevail on an FCA claim, the plaintiff must prove that the defendant (1) made a false statement, (2) with scienter, (3) that was material, (4) causing the Government to make a payment." *See United States v. AseraCare, Inc.,* 938 F.3d 1278, 1284 (11th Cir. 2019) (citing *Urquilla-Diaz,* 780 F.3d at 1045). Section 3729(a)(1)(A) prohibits knowingly presenting or causing to be presented a false claim. This creates two theories of liability: (1) a presentment theory and (2) a cause to be presented theory.

At trial, the jury returned a general verdict that La Vie Management knowingly presented or caused to be presented false and fraudulent claims to Medicare. The district court disagreed, citing the absence of any evidence that La Vie Management submitted any claims at all and insufficient evidence to establish the type of "massive, authorized, cohesive, concerted, enduring, top-down" corporate scheme necessary to show that La Vie Management caused the presentation of false Medicare claims. We understand from its words that the district court found the relator's proof lacking as to scienter and causation under either theory. Because on appeal relator argues only that the evidence was sufficient to establish that La Vie Management caused the presentment of false Medicare claims, we confine our discussion to the sufficiency of the evidence in respect of the "cause to be presented" theory.

We begin by noting that this Court has not previously addressed the appropriate standard to prove causation in FCA "cause to be presented" actions. Relator points to two persuasive precedents which use traditional proximate cause tests: *United States ex rel. Sikkenga v. Regence Bluecross* p.1107 *BlueShield of Utah,* 472 F.3d 702, 714-15 (10th Cir. 2006) (adopting a proximate cause test "to determine whether there is a sufficient nexus between the conduct of the party and the ultimate presentation of the false claim to support liability under the FCA"), *abrogated on other grounds by Cochise Consultancy, Inc. v. United States ex rel. Hunt,* ___ U.S. ___, 139 S. Ct. 1507, 203 L. Ed. 2d 791 (2019), and *United States ex rel. Schiff v. Marder,* 208 F. Supp. 3d 1296, 1312 (S.D. Fla. 2016) (noting that "courts have applied traditional concepts of proximate causation to determine whether there is a sufficient nexus between the Defendants' conduct and the ultimate presentation of the allegedly false claim") (internal quotation omitted).

We find that for "cause to be presented" claims, proximate causation is a useful and appropriate standard by which to determine whether there is a sufficient nexus between the defendant's conduct and the submission of a false claim. It has the advantage of familiarity and serves to cull those claims with only attenuated links between the defendant's conduct and the presentation of the false claim. "Under this analysis, a defendant's conduct may be found to have caused the submission of a claim for Medicare reimbursement if the conduct was (1) a substantial factor in inducing providers to submit claims for reimbursement, and (2) if the submission of claims for reimbursement was reasonably foreseeable or anticipated as a natural consequence of defendants' conduct." *Marder,* 208 F. Supp. 3d at 1312-13. (internal quotation and alteration omitted).

We find that the relator introduced sufficient evidence to permit a jury to reasonably conclude that La Vie Management caused the submission of false claims. For example, Pamela Horn, a former investigator with the State of Florida, testified to a conversation she had with Carolyn Packer, another registered nurse who worked at Governor's Creek:

> Q: And did Ms. Packer say anything about what [Lee] Juliano [La Vie Management's regional reimbursement specialist] did with the RUG rate information that she received?
>
> A: Yes, sir.
>
> Q: What did she say?
>
> A: Ms. Juliano reported that to her boss at corporate.
>
> Q: And did Ms. Packer indicate what this all came down to, this focus on the RUG levels?
>
> A: Yes, sir.
>
> Q: What did she say?
>
> A: It was to have the RUG levels as high as possible so that the revenue, the reimbursement, was high.

The relator also introduced evidence that the defendants' employees were pressured routinely to elevate RUG scores irrespective of the services provided. The relator testified:

> Q: What was the focus of the discussion about UH RUG groups in these meetings?
>
> A: That we needed to get the RUGs higher. There was a lot of criticism of the rehab director. Every day he would read off the minutes that he delivered to the patient the previous day. He would have a lot of criticism from the administrator and the business office manager. And the goal was always the 720 minutes for the date of the MDS assessment, when it was due, so that the patient would be a rehab ultra.
>
> Q: And in these — in these daily meetings, was there any discussion about financial targets and financial goals?
>
> A: Yes, they had a Medicare budget, a RUG budget, and so it must be met or exceeded and you were criticized if it wasn't and you were pretty much directed to make that happen.
>
> p.1108 Q: Were these RUG budgets that were set by the company or by the patients, the residents?
>
> A: They were RUG budgets set by the company. I guess, you know — yeah, without any clinical knowledge of the patient whatsoever.

The relator further testified that La Vie Management would reprimand employees constantly for failing to meet RUG budgets. The relator explained that the focus of weekly calls with La Vie Management, including regional coordinators for multiple facilities including Marshall and Governor's Creek, was on "[r]ehab ultra opportunities, how to get the RUGs higher, criticism if you weren't meeting or exceeding their RUG budget for the facility, criticism if you weren't, but really praising the facilities that were above budget for their region." Moreover, the relator introduced into evidence a La Vie Management presentation to SNFs that referred to its one goal as "RUG enhancement" and indicated that the employees should focus on "maximizing therapy minutes." The evidence also suggested La Vie Management had a policy of prohibiting the submission of claims at the lowest RUG code without management approval.

In light of this evidence, a jury could reasonably conclude that La Vie Management's conduct was "(1) a substantial factor in inducing providers to submit claims for reimbursement," and that (2) "the submission of claims for reimbursement was reasonably foreseeable or anticipated as a natural consequence of defendants' conduct." *Id.* at 1313 (internal quotation and alteration omitted).

This same evidence supports an inference that La Vie Management acted knowingly. The scienter requirement in FCA actions is rigorous and must be strictly enforced. *See Escobar,* 136 S. Ct. at 2002. Under the rigorous standard, the evidence reasonably permitted the jury to conclude that La Vie Management acted knowingly under the FCA.

Therefore, with respect to the allegations of Medicare fraud, we conclude that the relator presented sufficient evidence to permit a reasonable jury to conclude that the defendants violated the FCA when they submitted the claims. Further, we find that the district court erred in holding that La Vie Management did not cause the submission of false claims. Accordingly, we reverse the district court's grant of judgment as a matter of law to the defendants as to the Medicare-related fraud claims.

Medicaid Fraud

For the reasons discussed below, we hold that the district court correctly granted the defendants' motion for judgment as a matter of law as to the alleged false Medicaid claims. Specifically, we conclude that based on the evidence presented at trial, no jury could have reasonably concluded that the defendants defrauded Medicaid.

At trial, the relator introduced evidence that the defendants routinely submitted claims for Medicaid reimbursement without preparing and maintaining comprehensive care plans. The relator testified that while working at Governor's Creek and Marshall, there were few, if any, care plans in the patient files. An email introduced into evidence from Juliano confirmed care plans were "a mess." And Bradley testified her audit revealed missing care plans for approximately 52 residents.

The relator's sole allegation as to Medicaid fraud consists of the defendants' failure to prepare and maintain comprehensive care plans for their residents. Even if we accept this allegation as true, we hold that the failure to do so cannot establish Medicaid fraud as a matter of law. Under *Escobar,* the relator was required to prove not only that the defendants failed to comply p.1109 with this requirement, but that their failure to do so was material. Again, this materiality standard sets a "demanding" bar. *Escobar,* 136 S. Ct. at 2003.

The relator contends she met the standard, pointing to evidence at trial that indicated Florida would or could automatically deny payment if the state were to discover care plans are missing. The district court rejected this argument and granted judgment as a matter of law because the relator did not introduce evidence that the state in fact declines to pay claims when it learns SNFs have failed to prepare and maintain comprehensive care plans. We note that the relator introduced evidence at trial of the opposite. The relator testified that when she informed her direct supervisors at La Vie Management that her patient files lacked care plans, they self-reported the deficiencies to the state. There was no evidence, however, that the state refused reimbursement or sought recoupment after this self-reporting. And there was no evidence that the state ever declines payment for, or otherwise enforces, these types of violations. As the Supreme Court stated in *Escobar*, "if the Government pays a particular claim in full despite its actual knowledge that certain requirements were violated, that is very strong evidence that those requirements are not material." *Id.* at 2003-04.

We acknowledge that the absence of evidence that the state declines payment when an SNF fails to comply with the care plans requirement, alone, is not fatal to the relator's case. Rather, this evidence is a useful, but not necessary, indicator of materiality. *See id.* (describing evidence of materiality but noting evidence need not be limited to the examples given). However, we find in this case that the relator's scant evidence supported only the conclusion that care plans are, at most, labeled as conditions of payment under Medicaid regulations. This evidence, without more, is insufficient to establish materiality. Thus, we agree with the district court's conclusion that the relator failed to prove the materiality of the absence of care plans.

Additionally, we conclude that the lack of care plans fails to establish Medicaid fraud for an entirely separate reason under the analysis in *Escobar*. The relator relied on the implied certification theory of liability in alleging Medicaid fraud. That theory can support a jury verdict only where the relevant claim not only requests payment but also "makes specific representations about the goods or services provided." *Id.* at 2001. Here, the relator failed to connect the absence of care plans to specific representations regarding the services provided. Moreover, the relator did not allege, let alone prove, any deficiencies in the Medicaid services provided.

Without more, the failure to create and maintain care plans cannot serve as a basis for FCA liability. The FCA is not a wide-ranging tool to combat failures to comply with even important government regulations. *See Clausen*, 290 F.3d at 1311 ("[W]hile the practices of an entity that provides services to the Government may be unwise or improper, there is simply no actionable damage to the public fisc as required under the [FCA]."); *see also Escobar*, 136 S. Ct. at 2003 ("The [FCA] is not an all-purpose antifraud statute... or a vehicle for punishing garden-variety breaches of contract or regulatory violations." (internal quotation omitted)).[12]

p.1110 D.

Because we affirm the district court's judgment as a matter of law on the Medicaid claims, we need only address the district court's grant of a conditional new trial with respect to our reversal of the judgment as a matter of law on the Medicare claims. The district judge's reasoning for granting a new trial is not evident— he wrote only that "the request for a new trial is conditionally GRANTED for the reasons explained above and for the reasons identified and satisfactorily explained in the defendants' motion."

We perceive no need for a new trial on liability.[13] Our reasons for reversing the judgment as a matter of law on the Medicare claims also support the conclusion that the jury verdict finding the defendants liable with respect to the Medicare claims was not contrary to the weight of the evidence. *Lipphardt v. Durango Steakhouse of Brandon, Inc.,* 267 F.3d 1183, 1186, 1189 (11th Cir. 2001) ("[N]ew trials should not be granted on evidentiary grounds unless, at a minimum, the verdict is against the great—not merely the greater—weight of the evidence." (quoting *Hewitt v. B.F. Goodrich Co.,* 732 F.2d 1554, 1556 (11th Cir. 1984))); *see also McGinnis v. Am. Home Mortg. Servicing, Inc.,* 817 F.3d 1241, 1257 (11th Cir. 2016) (new trial not appropriate where "the verdict was not against the clear weight of the evidence") (quotation omitted). Having held that the relator introduced sufficient evidence to permit a reasonable jury to find the defendants liable for Medicare-related fraud, and not for Medicaid-related fraud, we hold that the district court abused its discretion in conditionally granting the defendants' request for a new trial as to liability on the Medicare claims.

Defendants contend on appeal that a new trial is appropriate because the Medicare-related damages are excessive. We decline to entertain the defendants' arguments because they are conclusory and were not adequately developed in the district court. "As a general principle, this court will not address an argument that has not been raised in the district court." *Stewart v. Dep't of Health & Human Servs.,* 26 F.3d 115, 115 (11th Cir. 1994) p.1111 (citing *Baumann v. Savers Fed. Sav. & Loan Ass'n,* 934 F.2d 1506, 1510 (11th Cir. 1991)).[14] "The corollary of this rule is that, if a party hopes to preserve a claim, argument, theory, or defense on appeal, she must first clearly present it to the district court, that is, in such a way as to afford the district court an opportunity to recognize and rule on it." *Juris v. Inamed Corp.,* 685 F.3d 1294, 1325 (11th Cir. 2012) (quoting *Leonard v. Pan Am. World Airways, Inc. (In re Pan Am. World Airways, Inc., Maternity Leave Practices & Flight Attendant Weight Program Litig.),* 905 F.2d 1457, 1462 (11th Cir. 1990)). The defendants' argument to the district court in their Rule 50(b) motion consisted of one sentence: "The jury's single damages award of over $115 million is excessive and against the weight of the evidence in light of all the deficiencies in Relator's proof discussed above." To the extent the defendants elaborated on their assertion, they pointed only to evidentiary deficiencies with respect to the Medicaid-related damages. These superficial assertions were insufficient to permit reasoned consideration by the district court and were an inadequate justification for the district court's conditional grant of a new trial.

The defendants insist in their Response Brief that their one-sentence argument to the district court was sufficient to preserve on appeal the issue of the excessiveness of the Medicare-related damages because their argument "was not limited to Medicaid, although Defendants highlighted the Medicaid verdict as the '[m]ost egregious' example of this excess." And for the first time on appeal, the defendants offer new arguments as to why the Medicare-related damages award allegedly is excessive. However, having failed to articulate the fact-based reasons for its contentions in the district court, the defendants cannot raise them for the first time on appeal for the purpose of salvaging the erroneous decision of the district court to conditionally grant a new trial. *See Stewart,* 26 F.3d 115 ("Judicial economy is served and prejudice is avoided by binding the parties to the facts presented and the theories argued below." (quoting *Bliss v. Equitable Life Assurance Soc'y of U.S.*, 620 F.2d 65, 70 (5th Cir. 1980))).

IV.

For the foregoing reasons, the motion to dismiss is denied. We affirm in part and reverse in part the district court's grant of the defendants' renewed motion for judgment as a matter of law or, alternatively, for a new trial, and affirm in part and reverse and vacate in part the judgment. Specifically, we affirm the district court's grant of judgment notwithstanding the verdict as to the Medicaid claims. With respect to the Medicare claims, we reverse the district court's grant of judgment notwithstanding p.1112 the verdict and vacate that part of its opinion. In light of our reversal on the Medicare claims, we remand with instructions for the district court to reinstate the jury's verdict in favor of the relator, the United States, and the State of Florida and against the defendants on the Medicare claims in the amount of $85,137,095, and to enter judgment on those claims after applying trebling and statutory penalties. We also reverse and vacate the district court's grant of a conditional new trial.

AFFIRMED in part, REVERSED in part and REMANDED for reinstatement of the jury's verdict consistent with this opinion.

[*] Honorable Ursula Ungaro, United States District Judge for the Southern District of Florida, sitting by designation.

[1] Failure to comply with the assessment schedule carries consequences: "CMS pays a default rate for the Federal rate ... for the days of a patient's care for which the SNF is not in compliance with the assessment schedule." 42 C.F.R. § 413.343(c).

[2] In October 2019, CMS shifted from the RUG model to a patient-driven payment model. *See* Ctrs. for Medicare & Medicaid Servs., Long-Term Care Facility Resident Assessment Instrument 3.0 User's Manual ch. 6-2 (Oct. 2019), https://downloads.cms.gov/files/mds-3.0-rai-manual-v1.17.1_october_2019.pdf. Our opinion in this appeal is limited to the RUG model, which governed at the time of this lawsuit.

[3] The term "claim" includes "direct requests to the Government for payment as well as reimbursement requests made to the recipients of federal funds under federal benefits programs." *See Universal Health Servs., Inc. v. United States ex rel. Escobar,* 579 U.S. ___, ___, 136 S. Ct. 1989, 1996, 195 L. Ed. 2d 348, 358 (2016) (citing § 3729(b)(2)(A)). The statute specifies that a person acts "knowingly" with respect to information when she has "actual knowledge," "acts in deliberate ignorance of the truth or falsity," or "acts in reckless disregard of the truth or falsity" of the information. 31 U.S.C. § 3729(b)(*l*)(A). The statute further defines "material" as "having a natural tendency to influence, or be capable of influencing, the payment or receipt of money or property." *Id.* § 3729(b)(4).

[4] The jury also found the defendants liable under § 3729(a)(1)(G) but calculated damages as $0. The jury's finding in this regard is not before this Court on appeal.

[5] The district court, in its order, did not address whether the methodology employed by the relator's expert to calculate damages was flawed either because the sample size was too small or improvidently drawn and the defendants have abandoned any argument regarding the admission of the expert testimony on appeal. "[T]he law is by now well settled in this Circuit that a legal claim or argument that has not been briefed before the court is deemed abandoned and its merits will not be addressed." *Holland v. Gee,* 677 F.3d 1047, 1066 (11th Cir. 2012) (quoting *Access Now, Inc. v. Sw. Airlines Co.,* 385 F.3d 1324, 1330 (11th Cir. 2004)). Accordingly, we do not address whether the sampling method and extrapolation employed by the relator's expert was reliable and otherwise admissible pursuant to Federal Rule of Evidence 701 and *Daubert v. Merrell Dow Pharmaceuticals, Inc.,* 509 U.S. 579, 113 S. Ct. 2786, 125 L. Ed. 2d 469 (1993).

[6] The relator entered into the Agreement with ARUS during the pendency of the defendants' renewed motion for judgment as a matter of law in the court below. However, the defendants discovered this financing arrangement upon reviewing the relator's Certificate of Interested Persons filed in this Court. The Certificate of Interested Persons describes ARUS as a "privately owned limited liability company focused on litigation funding."

[7] The relator's counsel represented that the Agreement contains a confidentiality provision that precludes its public filing but offered to provide a copy to the Court for an *in camera* review to aid in our consideration of its relevant provisions. At oral argument, the Court informed the parties that we would consider the Agreement only if the relator provided a copy to the defendants. Subsequently, the relator notified the Court that it declined to share the Agreement with the defendants. Nevertheless, at oral argument, the parties acknowledged that the Agreement assigned to ARUS less than 4% of the relator's share of the recovery. Additionally, the relator's counsel submitted a declaration attached to the response in opposition to the motion to dismiss the appeal, stating: "The Agreement is a purchase agreement for less than 4% of Relator's share of the $347 million judgment..., assuming Relator were to receive a 30% relator's share."

[8] The relator represents in opposition to the motion to dismiss and the relator's counsel averred in her declaration that the Agreement provides that ARUS shall not become a party to the litigation, the relator will retain sole authority over the litigation (including settlement authority), and ARUS will offer no advice, issue no instructions, and exercise no influence over the litigation. In the motion to dismiss, the defendants argue that it is unrealistic to conclude that a relator or her counsel would give no consideration to the views of a litigation funding entity, which has powerful incentives to participate in the management of the litigation. The defendants' position at oral argument was that even if this Court accepts as true the relator's contention that she assigned less than 4% of her share of the recovery and maintained complete control of the litigation, the partial assignment nonetheless violates the FCA.

[9] Defendants also argue that relator's entry into the litigation funding agreement violates Article II. We decline to address the issue because it is not jurisdictional. *See Vt. Agency of Nat. Res. v. United States ex rel. Stevens,* 529 U.S. 765, 778 n.8, 120 S.Ct. 1858, 146 L.Ed.2d 836 (2000) (declining to reach the validity of

qui tam suits under Article II because it is not "a jurisdictional issue that we must resolve here").

[10] Courts have referred to this inquiry as one of "statutory standing." However, the Supreme Court has cautioned against use of the phrase, because "the absence of a valid ... cause of action does not implicate subject-matter jurisdiction, *i.e.,* the court's statutory or constitutional *power* to adjudicate the case." *Lexmark Int'l, Inc. v. Static Control Components, Inc.,* 572 U.S. 118, 128 n.4, 134 S. Ct. 1377, 1388 n.4, 188 L. Ed. 2d 392, 404 n.4 (2014). (emphasis omitted) (quoting *Verizon Md. Inc. v. Pub. Serv. Comm'n of Md.,* 535 U.S. 635, 642-43, 122 S. Ct. 1753, 1758, 152 L. Ed. 2d 871, 880 (2002)).

[11] The Court declined to address whether the materiality requirement under § 3729(a)(*1*)(A) is governed by the definition of "materiality" in § 3729(b)(4) or by common law principles. *See Escobar,* 136 S. Ct. at 2002.

[12] In arguing that the district court erred in granting the defendants' renewed motion for judgment as a matter of law, the relator also contends that the district court impermissibly considered two grounds that the defendants waived by not raising them in their Rule 50(a) motion: the sufficiency of evidence as to (1) Medicare fraud and (2) the defendants' knowledge of the materiality of their claims. Rule 50 is designed to protect a plaintiff's Seventh Amendment right to cure evidentiary deficiencies before a case is submitted to the jury. *See Ross v. Rhodes Furniture, Inc.,* 146 F.3d 1286, 1289 (11th Cir. 1998). To determine whether the district court improperly considered arguments waived by defendants, we compare the grounds originally argued in defendants' Rule 50(a) motion with those cited by the court in granting judgment as a matter of law. *See id.* (citing *Nat'l Indus., Inc. v. Sharon Steel Corp.,* 781 F.2d 1545 (11th Cir. 1986)). We do not require complete identity of issues; instead, we consider whether the Rule 50(a) and Rule 50(b) issues are "closely related." *Id.* Only if the old and new grounds "vary greatly" is the district court prohibited from relying on those new grounds in setting aside the jury's verdict. *Id.* (citing *Sulmeyer v. Coca Cola Co.,* 515 F.2d 835, 845-46 (5th Cir. 1975)). The purpose of this waiver rule is to avoid ambush; setting aside a jury's verdict cannot come as a surprise to the non-movant. *Id.* (citing *Sharon Steel,* 781 F.2d at 1549-50).

Here, in granting the defendants' Rule 50(b) motion, the district court cited the defendants' arguments as to materiality and scienter. Since these issues are closely related to the arguments the defendants made in their Rule 50(a) motion, the relator cannot argue she has been ambushed. Further, the district court criticized the sufficiency of evidence as to materiality during the proceeding. Thus, the relator cannot argue that the district court's order came as a surprise. We therefore reject the relator's procedural waiver argument.

[13] Because the district court's order did not expressly discuss the excessiveness of the verdict, "the reasons explained above" could have referred only to the court's determination that the verdict was contrary to the weight of the evidence.

[14] We have permitted issues to be raised for the first time on appeal in five limited circumstances:

First, an appellate court will consider an issue not raised in the district court if it involves a pure question of law, and if refusal to consider it would result in a miscarriage of justice. Second, the rule may be relaxed where the appellant raises an objection to an order which he had no opportunity to raise at the district court level. Third, the rule does not bar consideration by the appellate court in the first instance where the interest of substantial justice is at stake. Fourth, a federal appellate court is justified in resolving an issue not passed on below ... where the proper resolution is beyond any doubt. Finally, it may be appropriate to consider an issue first raised on appeal if that issue presents significant questions of general impact or of great public concern.

Cita Tr. Co. AG v. Fifth Third Bank, 879 F.3d 1151, 1156 (11th Cir. 2018) (quoting *Access Now, Inc. v. Sw. Airlines Co.,* 385 F.3d 1324, 1332 (11th Cir. 2004)). None of these circumstances apply to this case.

938 F.3d 1278 (2019)

UNITED STATES of America, Plaintiff-Appellant,

v.

ASERACARE, INC., GGNSC Administrative Services, d.b.a. Golden Living, f.k.a. Beverly Enterprises, Inc., Hospice Preferred Choice, Inc., Hospice of Eastern Carolina, Inc., Defendants-Appellees.

No. 16-13004.

United States Court of Appeals, Eleventh Circuit.

September 9, 2019.

US v. AseraCare, Inc., 938 F. 3d 1278 (11th Cir. 2019)

Appeal from the United States District Court for the Northern District of Alabama, D.C. Docket No. 2:12-cv-00245-KOB.

Abby Christine Wright, U.S. Attorney General's Office, WASHINGTON, DC, Michael B. Billingsley, Erin Massey Everitt, Don Boyden Long, III, Mary Lester Marshall, Jenny Lynn Smith, Lane H. Woodke, U.S. Attorney's Office, BIRMINGHAM, AL, Stacy C. Gerber Ward, U.S. Attorney's Office, MILWAUKEE, WI, Renee Brooker, Christina Davis, William Edward Olson, Holly H. Snow, Carolyn B. Tapie, Jeffrey Wertkin, U.S. Department of Justice, Civil Division, WASHINGTON, DC, Eva U. Gunasekera, U.S. Department of Justice, WASHINGTON, DC, Joyce White Vance, University of Alabama School of Law, BIRMINGHAM, AL, for Plaintiff-Appellant.

Matthew Howard Lembke, R. Aaron Chastain, Nicholas Adam Danella, Cameron W. Ellis, Jack W. Selden, Tiffany J. deGruy, Bradley Arant Boult Cummings, LLP, BIRMINGHAM, Kimberly Bessiere Martin, Bradley Arant Boult Cummings, LLP, HUNTSVILLE, AL, for Defendants-Appellees.

Colette G. Matzzie, Phillips & Cohen, LLP, WASHINGTON, DC, for Amicus p.1281 Curiae TAXPAYERS AGAINST FRAUD EDUCATION FUND.

Maame Gyamfi, AARP Foundation Litigation, WASHINGTON, DC, for Amici Curiae AARP, AARP FOUNDATION LITIGATION.

James F. Segroves, Reed Smith, LLP, WASHINGTON, DC, for SAVASENIORCARE ADMINISTRATIVE SERVICES, LLC.

Catherine Emily Stetson, Hogan Lovells US, LLP, WASHINGTON, DC, for AMERICAN MEDICAL ASSOCIATION, NATIONAL HOSPICE AND PALLIATIVE CARE ORGANIZATION, NATIONAL ASSOCIATION FOR HOME CARE AND HOSPICE, AMERICAN ACADEMY OF HOSPICE AND PALLIATIVE MEDICINE, HOSPICE AND PALLIATIVE NURSES ASSOCIATION.

Before ROSENBAUM and JULIE CARNES, Circuit Judges, and SCHLESINGER,[*] District Judge.

p.1280 JULIE CARNES, Circuit Judge:

This case requires us to consider the circumstances under which a claim for hospice treatment under Medicare may be deemed "false" for purposes of the federal False Claims Act. Defendants comprise a network of hospice facilities that routinely bill Medicare for end-of-life care provided to elderly patients. In the underlying civil suit, the Government alleged that Defendants had certified patients as eligible for Medicare's hospice benefit, and billed Medicare accordingly, on the basis of erroneous clinical judgments that those patients were terminally ill. Based on the opinion of its expert witness, the Government contends that the patients at issue were not, in fact, terminally ill at the time of certification, meaning that AseraCare's claims to the contrary were false under the False Claims Act.

As the case proceeded through discovery and a partial trial on the merits, the district court confronted the following question: Can a medical provider's clinical judgment that a patient is terminally ill be deemed false based merely on the existence of a reasonable difference of opinion between experts as to the accuracy of that prognosis? The district court ultimately answered this question in the negative and therefore granted summary judgment to AseraCare on the issue of falsity.

Upon careful review of the record and the relevant law, and with the benefit of oral argument, we concur with the district court's ultimate determination that a clinical judgment of terminal illness warranting hospice benefits under Medicare cannot be deemed false, for purposes of the False Claims Act, when there is only a reasonable disagreement between medical experts as to the accuracy of that conclusion, with no other evidence to prove the falsity of the assessment. We do, however, think that the Government should have been allowed to rely on the entire record, not just the trial record, in making its case that disputed issues of fact, beyond just the difference of opinion between experts, existed sufficient to warrant denial of the district court's post-verdict *sua sponte* reconsideration of summary judgment on the falsity question. We therefore affirm in part and remand in part.

p.1282 I. BACKGROUND[1]

Each year, more than a million Americans make the difficult decision to forgo curative care and turn instead to end-of-life hospice care, which is designed to relieve the pain and symptoms associated with terminal illness. *See* 79 Fed. Reg. 50452, 50454-55 (Aug. 22, 2014). The federal government's Medicare program makes such care affordable for a significant number of terminally ill individuals. Defendants, collectively referred to as AseraCare, operate approximately sixty hospice facilities across nineteen states and admit around 10,000 patients each year. Most of AseraCare's patients are enrolled in Medicare. In fact, from 2007 to 2012, Medicare payments composed approximately ninetyfive percent of AseraCare's revenues. As such, AseraCare routinely prepares and submits claims for reimbursement under Medicare.

This case began when three former AseraCare employees alleged that AseraCare had a practice of knowingly submitting unsubstantiated Medicare claims in violation of the federal False Claims Act. We begin by setting out the requirements hospice providers like AseraCare must meet in order to be entitled to hospice reimbursement and identifying the tools the Government uses to police compliance with these requirements.

A. The Medicare Hospice Benefit

In order for a hospice claim to be eligible for Medicare reimbursement, the patient's attending physician, if there is one, and the medical director of the hospice provider must "each certify in writing at the beginning of [each] period, that the individual is terminally ill ... based on the physician's or medical director's clinical judgment regarding the normal course of the individual's illness." 42 U.S.C. § 1395f(7)(A). "Terminally ill" means that the individual "has a medical prognosis that the individual's life expectancy is 6 months or less." 42 U.S.C. § 1395x(dd)(3)(A). Under the statute's implementing regulations, a claim for hospice reimbursement must conform to several requirements in order to be payable. Most notably for purposes of this appeal, the certification must be accompanied by "[c]linical information and other documentation that support the medical prognosis," and such support "must be filed in the medical record with the written certification." 42 C.F.R. § 418.22(b)(2).

An initial certification conforming to these requirements is valid for a period of ninety days. 42 U.S.C. § 1395f(7)(A). The patient must be recertified in a similar manner for each additional sixty- or ninety-day period during which he or she remains in hospice. *Id.* While a life-expectancy prognosis of six months or less is a necessary condition for reimbursement, regulators recognize that "[p]redicting life expectancy is not an exact science." 75 Fed. Reg. 70372, 70488 (Nov. 17, 2010). Accordingly, the Medicare framework does not preclude reimbursement for periods of hospice care that extend beyond six months, as long as the patient's eligibility is continually recertified. This framework also recognizes that, in some cases, patients with an initial prognosis of terminality can improve over time, and it allows such patients to exit hospice without losing their right to Medicare coverage to treat illness. *Id.* Thus, there is no statutory limit p.1283 to the number of periods for which a patient may be properly certified. 42 U.S.C. § 1395d(d)(1) (establishing that hospice providers may collect reimbursement for an unlimited number of recertification periods).

The Medicare program is overseen by the Centers for Medicare and Medicaid Services ("CMS"), a division of the Department of Health and Human Services. CMS operates locally through so-called Medicare Administrative Contractors ("MACs"), which process claims from healthcare providers and make payment for eligible services. A majority of AseraCare's Medicare claims are processed by a MAC called Palmetto GBA ("Palmetto"), which operates in the southeast United States.

In preparing its claims for hospice reimbursement, AseraCare employs interdisciplinary teams of skilled staff—including physicians, nurses, psychologists, social workers, and chaplains—that render services directly to patients and collectively make eligibility determinations. To guide this review, AseraCare professionals rely in part on documents called Local Coverage Determinations ("LCDs"), which are issued by Palmetto's medical directors. LCDs provide detailed lists of diagnostic guidance and clinical information that, if documented in a patient's medical record, suggest that the patient has a life expectancy of six months or less.

LCDs are not clinical benchmarks or mandatory requirements for hospice eligibility, however. Rather, they are designed to help clinical staff understand the type of information that should be considered prior to concluding that a patient is terminally ill. The LCDs themselves explicitly state that they are non-binding.

Once AseraCare physicians reach a clinical judgment that a patient is eligible for hospice care, AseraCare may begin providing treatment. It submits claims to Palmetto for reimbursement only after care has been rendered. The trial testimony of Mary Jane Schultz, a registered nurse and former director of Palmetto's medical review team, clarified at trial the process by which Palmetto reviewed and paid claims for hospice coverage during the relevant time period of 2007 to 2012. As Ms. Schultz described, the first round of claim review was conducted by an automated claim-processing system designed to ensure that no critical information, such as a patient's Medicare identification number, was missing or invalid. If no critical information was missing, the system would then check for any "red flags" that might require further review of the claim—such as the involvement of a particular provider, patient, or type of care that Palmetto staff believed may pose heightened eligibility risks. For instance, if Palmetto wished to conduct a targeted audit of claims submitted by a particular provider, it could program the automated system to pull all or a portion of those claims for additional review before payment.

If automated review uncovered no missing information or red flags, the system would process the claim directly for payment. As a result, Palmetto paid many claims without directly reviewing the medical documentation underpinning them. Where, on the other hand, a claim was flagged for heightened medical review, Palmetto would immediately issue a request to the provider for medical documentation substantiating the patient's terminal prognosis, such as notes from physicians, nurses, and social workers and records of medications and treatments prescribed. A trained medical review team would then review the supporting documentation before determining whether the claim should be paid in full, paid in part, or denied. Like p.1284 AseraCare's medical staff, the medical review team commonly uses the LCDs as guidelines in its assessment, but it is not required to rigidly apply their criteria. Instead, the review team also looks at the "whole picture" of information submitted with the claim.

B. The False Claims Act

The False Claims Act ("FCA") serves as a mechanism by which the Government may police noncompliance with Medicare reimbursement standards after payment has been made. The Act imposes civil liability—including treble damages— on "any person who ... knowingly presents, or causes to be presented, a false or fraudulent claim for payment" to the federal government or who "knowingly makes, uses, or causes to be made or used, a false record or statement material to a false or fraudulent claim." 31 U.S.C. § 3729(a)(1)(A)-(B). To prevail on an FCA claim, the plaintiff must prove that the defendant (1) made a false statement, (2) with scienter, (3) that was material, (4) causing the Government to make a payment. *Urquilla-Diaz v. Kaplan Univ.,* 780 F.3d 1039, 1045 (11th Cir. 2015).

Private citizens, called *qui tam* relators, are authorized to bring FCA suits on behalf of the United States. 31 U.S.C. § 3730(b). The United States can, and frequently does, intervene in *qui tam* suits to develop the civil case itself. Thus, to the extent the Government concludes that it has reimbursed a hospice provider that knowingly submitted deficient claims, the Government can use the FCA cause of action to recoup payments and to penalize the provider.

II. PROCEDURAL HISTORY

A. Suit Against AseraCare Under the FCA

The underlying case began in 2008, when three former AseraCare employees, acting as *qui tam* relators, filed a complaint against AseraCare alleging submission of unsubstantiated hospice claims. Following a transfer of venue from the Eastern District of Wisconsin to the Northern District of Alabama, the Government intervened and filed the operative complaint. In its complaint, the Government alleged that AseraCare knowingly employed reckless business practices that enabled it to admit, and receive reimbursement for, patients who were not eligible for the Medicare hospice benefit "because it was financially lucrative," thus "misspending" millions of Medicare dollars. The Government's complaint described a corporate climate that pressured sales and clinical staff to meet aggressive monthly quotas for patient intake and, in so doing, discouraged meaningful physician involvement in eligibility determinations. More specifically, the Government alleged that AseraCare "submitted documentation that falsely represented that certain Medicare recipients were 'terminally ill'" when, in the Government's view, they were not.

In light of these allegations, the Government's case falls under the "false certification" theory of FCA liability. Under this theory, FCA liability may arise where a defendant falsely asserts or implies that it has complied with a statutory or regulatory requirement when, in actuality, it has not so complied. *See Universal Health Servs., Inc. v. United States ex rel. Escobar,* ___ U.S. ___, 136 S. Ct. 1989, 1999, 195 L.Ed.2d 348 (2016).

In developing its case, the Government began by identifying a universe of approximately 2,180 patients for whom AseraCare had billed Medicare for at least 365 continuous days of hospice care. The Government then focused its attention on a sample of 223 patients from within that p.1285 universe. Through direct review of these patients' medical records and clinical histories, the Government's primary expert witness, Dr. Solomon Liao, identified 123 patients from the sample pool who were, in Dr. Liao's view, ineligible for the hospice benefit at the time AseraCare received reimbursement for their care. Should it prevail as to this group, the Government intended to extrapolate from the sample to impose further liability on AseraCare for a statistically valid set of additional claims within the broader universe of hospice patients for whom AseraCare received Medicare payments.

To supplement the testimony of Dr. Liao, the Government also sought to develop evidence that AseraCare's broader business practices fostered and promoted improper certification procedures while deemphasizing clinical training on terminal-illness prognostication. Several former AseraCare employees, including the *qui tam* relators, supported the Government's narrative by describing a process in which physicians merely rubber-stamped terminal-illness certifications without thoroughly examining the relevant medical records underlying them.

Importantly, though, the Government's false-claims allegations in this case were narrowly circumscribed. There were no allegations that AseraCare billed for phantom patients, that certifications or medical documentation were forged, or that AseraCare employees lied to certifying physicians or withheld critical information regarding patient conditions. Indeed, there was no doubt in the proceeding below that AseraCare possessed accurate and comprehensive documentation of each patient's medical condition and that its certifications of terminal illness were signed by the appropriate medical personnel. Rather, the Government asserted that its expert testimony —contextualized by broad evidence of AseraCare's improper business practices —would demonstrate that the patients in the sample pool were not, as a medical fact, terminally ill at the time AseraCare collected reimbursement for their hospice care. The sole question related to the sufficiency of the clinical judgments on which the claims were based.

On this theory, the Government sought to recover damages under two subsections of the FCA, 31 U.S.C. § 3729(a)(1)(A)[2] and 31 U.S.C. § 3729(a)(1)(B),[3] and on claims of common-law unjust enrichment and mistaken payment.

B. First Motion for Summary Judgment

Following extensive discovery and expert analysis of relevant patient records, AseraCare moved for summary judgment on the ground that the Government failed to adduce evidence of the falsity of any disputed claims and failed to show that AseraCare had any knowledge of the alleged falsity. Most notably for purposes of this appeal, AseraCare put squarely before the district court the question whether the Government's medical-opinion evidence was sufficient to establish the threshold element of falsity. To that point, AseraCare p.1286 urged the district court to embrace a "reasonable doctor" standard for the assessment of falsity, which would state that, to avoid summary judgment in an action involving false claims for hospice reimbursement, the Government must show that a reasonable physician applying his or her clinical judgment could not have held the opinion that the patient at issue was terminally ill at the time of certification.[4]

The district court found the "reasonable doctor" standard "appealing and logical," but noted that it had not been adopted by the Eleventh Circuit and declined to apply it. The court ultimately denied AseraCare's motion for summary judgment, concluding that fact questions remained regarding whether clinical information and other documentation in the relevant medical records supported the certifications of terminal illness on which AseraCare's claims were based.

Following the denial of its motion for summary judgment, AseraCare moved to certify the following question for interlocutory appeal before this Court under 28 U.S.C. § 1292(b):

> In a False Claims Act case against a hospice provider relating to the eligibility of a patient for the Medicare hospice benefit, for the Government to establish the falsity element under 31 U.S.C. § 3729(a)(1), must it show that, in light of the patient's clinical information and other documentation, no reasonable physician could have believed, based on his or her clinical judgment, that the patient was eligible for the Medicare hospice benefit?

The district court certified the question for interlocutory appeal. We considered AseraCare's motion for review but declined to consider the question at that stage of the proceeding.

C. Bifurcation of Trial

Subsequent to the denial of summary judgment, AseraCare moved the district court to bifurcate trial under Federal Rule of Civil Procedure 42(b) into two phases: one phase on the falsity element of the FCA and a second phase on the FCA's remaining elements and the Government's common-law claims. The Government vehemently opposed the motion. It argued that the proposed bifurcation was "extraordinary," requiring the Government "to jump over an arbitrary hurdle that is without precedent" because "the elements of 'falsity' and 'knowledge of falsity' are not so distinct and separable that they may be tried separately without injustice." Indeed, the Government noted, the elements of FCA liability had "never before been bifurcated by a federal district court." The Government further argued that bifurcation was unworkable because documentary and testimonial evidence that was probative in the falsity phase—"because it undermines the reliability of the [certifications of terminal illness]"—was "also probative in the 'knowledge of falsity' phase because it shows AseraCare knew or should have known that it was submitting false claims for non-terminally [*sic*] patients."

p.1287 Nonetheless, the district court granted the motion in light of its concern that evidence pertinent to the knowledge element of the FCA would confuse the jury's analysis of the threshold question of whether the claims at issue were "false" in the first instance. The court noted that, while "pattern and practice" evidence showing deficiencies in AseraCare's admission and certification procedures could help establish AseraCare's *knowledge* of the alleged scheme to submit false claims— the second element of the Government's case—the *falsity* of the claims "cannot be inferred by reference to AseraCare's general corporate practices unrelated to specific patients." In the court's view, allowing the Government to present knowledge evidence before falsity was determined would be unduly prejudicial to AseraCare, thus warranting separation of the knowledge and falsity elements.

In accordance with this rationale, the district court "drew the line of admissibility" in Phase One of trial "at anecdotal evidence about a specific, but unidentified, patient or event that would be impossible for the Defense to rebut." The court did, however, allow in Phase One anecdotal testimony regarding improper clinical or corporate practices that "had a time and place nexus with the 123 allegedly ineligible patients at issue." Such testimony, in the court's view, would have been "highly probative and admissible in Phase One." Indeed, in bifurcating trial, the court presumed —based on the Government's own representations—that the Government possessed and would present such evidence in Phase One. The court did allow in Phase One general testimony regarding AseraCare's business practices and claim-submission process during the relevant time period, but only to contextualize the falsity analysis and "afford[] the jury an opportunity to more fully understand the hospice process within AseraCare." Such evidence was not, however, admissible to prove the falsity of the claims at issue.[5]

D. Phase One of Trial

The first phase of the trial lasted approximately eight weeks and proceeded to a jury verdict largely against AseraCare on the question of falsity. During its case in chief, the Government presented several days of testimony from Dr. Liao, who explained that, in his expert opinion, the medical records of the patients at issue did not support AseraCare's "terminal illness" certifications because they did not reveal a life expectancy of six months or less. Dr. Liao made clear that his testimony was a reflection of only his own clinical judgment based on his after-the-fact review of the supporting documentation he had reviewed. He conceded that he was "not in a position to discuss whether another physician [was] wrong about a particular patient's eligibility. Nor could he say that AseraCare's medical expert, who disagreed with him concerning the accuracy of the prognoses at issue, was necessarily 'wrong.' Notably, Dr. Liao never testified that, in his opinion, no reasonable doctor could have concluded that the identified patients were terminally ill at the time of certification. Instead, he only testified that, in his opinion, the patients were not terminally ill. Even more notable is the fact that Dr. Liao himself changed his opinion concerning the eligibility of certain patients p.1288 over the course of the proceeding—deciding that some of the patients he had earlier concluded were not terminally ill were in fact terminally ill. Nevertheless, he testified at trial that both sets of contradictory opinions remained "accurate to a reasonable degree of certainty." To explain these reversals, Dr. Liao stated that he "was not the same physician in 2013 as [he] was in 2010."

The Government also presented testimony of the relators and other AseraCare employees regarding AseraCare's certification procedures, but, as discussed *supra,* this testimony was characterized as being offered solely to show context, not falsity. In rebuttal, AseraCare offered expert testimony that directly contradicted Dr. Liao's opinions.

The parties' expert witnesses disagreed along two lines. First and foremost, they fundamentally differed as to how a doctor should analyze a patient's life expectancy for Medicare reimbursement purposes. The Government's Dr. Liao applied what might be called a "checkbox approach" to assessing terminal illness: He examined the patients' records and compared them against Palmetto's LCDs (and other, similar medical guidelines) for specific diagnoses, including Alzheimer's, heart disease, cardiopulmonary disease, and "adult failure to thrive." By contrast, AseraCare's experts considered but did not formulaically apply the LCD guidance in making their assessments. Instead, they took a "whole patient" approach, making prognoses based on the entirety of the patient's history, the confluence of ailments from which a patient may be suffering, and their own experience with end-of-life care. AseraCare's experts did not discount the LCD "criteria," but—as the latter instruct— these experts did not consider themselves compelled to conclude that a patient was ineligible merely because the patient had failed to meet one of those indicia.

The district court correctly stated in its instructions to the jury that the LCDs are "eligibility guidelines" that are not binding and should not be considered "the exact criteria used for determining" terminal illness. As such, the jury was not permitted to conclude that Dr. Liao's testimony was more credible because he made reference to the LCD criteria, or that AseraCare's claims were false if they failed to conform to those criteria. Nonetheless, the experts' disagreement as to the proper analytical approach impacted their ultimate judgments as to each patient's terminality.

Because neither the checkbox approach nor the holistic approach to making terminal-illness prognoses is contrary to the law, the jury's sole job at trial was to review the medical records of each patient and decide which experts' testimony seemed more persuasive on the question whether a particular patient should be characterized as "terminally ill" at the time of certification. To be clear, the Government never alleged that AseraCare's doctors relied on medical documentation that was too thin, vague, or lacking in detail to reasonably substantiate their "clinical judgments" of terminal illness. Indeed, there is no dispute that each patient certification was supported by a meaningful set of medical records evidencing various serious and chronic ailments for which the patient was entitled to some level of treatment. The question before the jury was instead which doctor's interpretation of those medical records sounded more correct. In other words, in this battle of experts, the jury was to decide which expert it thought to be more persuasive, with the less persuasive opinion being deemed p.1289 to be false. To guide that assessment, the district court provided the following instruction on falsity: "A claim is 'false' if it is an assertion that is untrue when made or used. Claims to Medicare may be false if the provider seeks payment, or reimbursement, for health care that is not reimbursable."

Ultimately, the expert testimony in this case revealed a fundamental difference of professional opinion regarding the manner in which each patient's complete medical picture contributed to his or her life expectancy at the time he or she received hospice care. Both sets of experts looked at the same medical documentation, considered the same medical standards for the terminal-illness determination (even while differing as to the weight such standards should be given), and relied on their own experience as seasoned physicians specializing in end-of-life care. Dr. Liao testified that, in his professional opinion, the patients at issue were not likely to die within six months of the date on which they were certified for hospice care. AseraCare's experts arrived at opposite conclusions.

As an illustration of this disagreement, consider the testimony of the Government's Dr. Liao and AseraCare's Dr. Gail Cooney regarding the patient Elsin K., who was an AseraCare hospice patient for over a year and who ultimately died in an AseraCare facility. Elsin was first admitted to hospice upon her physician's diagnosis of "debility," also called "adult failure to thrive," in which a patient experiences a general decline in health due to old age. Elsin experienced subsequent periods of improvement and decline; she left hospice care and was recertified on at least two occasions before her death.

As with each patient at issue in this case, Dr. Liao's assessment of Elsin's hospice eligibility contrasted starkly with Dr. Cooney's, even though there was no dispute as to Elsin's underlying diagnoses. Dr. Liao noted that many of Elsin's ailments, including severe infections arising from a joint replacement, were chronic and had recurred for many years. He also noted that she did not demonstrate the level of physical debility that published medical criteria typically associate with terminal patients. On the basis of his medical review, he described Elsin as struggling with chronic illness but "overall rather stable, if not improving," and thus lacking a prognosis of six months or less to live at the time of her certifications and recertifications. Dr. Cooney, the defense expert, also recognized that Elsin "had been sick for a long time," but she saw in the medical records a trend of steady physical and mental decline, decreased mobility, and increasing pain. Elsin's physical and psychological ailments, viewed in combination with one another, complicated the picture of Elsin's overall health and contributed to Dr. Cooney's judgment that Elsin was terminally ill during each relevant time period. In the Government's view, it was properly within the purview of the jury to decide which doctor's judgment was correct and, to the extent the jury found Dr. Liao's prognosis to be more persuasive, to find that AseraCare had thereby submitted a false statement when it filed a claim based on a prognosis that differed from Dr. Liao's.

At the conclusion of the parties' cases, the court instructed the jury to answer special interrogatories regarding the prognoses of each of the 123 patients at issue. The jury ultimately found that AseraCare had submitted false claims for 104 patients of the 123 patients at issue during the relevant time periods.

E. Grant of New Trial and Second Motion for Summary Judgment

Following the partial verdict in this first phase of trial, AseraCare moved for judgment p.1290 as a matter of law, arguing that the court had articulated the wrong legal standard in its instructions to the jury. The district court agreed. In the court's own words, "[a]s the court worked through AseraCare's challenges," it "became convinced that it had committed reversible error in the instructions it provided to the jury." It ultimately concluded that proper jury instructions would have advised the jury of two "key points of law" that the court had not previously acknowledged: (1) that the FCA's falsity element requires proof of an objective falsehood; and (2) that a mere difference of opinion between physicians, *without more,* is not enough to show falsity. AseraCare had advocated for this legal standard since the start of trial, but only after hearing all the evidence had the court become "convinced" that "a difference of opinion is not enough." The court ultimately concluded that the failure to instruct the jury on these points was reversible error and that the only way to cure the prejudice caused thereby was to order a new trial.

The court then went one step further, deciding to consider summary judgment *sua sponte* under Federal Rule of Civil Procedure 56(f)(3). Specifically, it informed the parties that it intended to consider "whether the Government, under the correct legal standard, has sufficient admissible evidence of more than just a difference of opinion to show that the claims at issue are objectively false as a matter of law." The court gave the parties an opportunity to brief the issue, advising that:

> The Government's proof under the FCA for the falsity element would fail as a matter of law if all the Government has as evidence of falsity in the second trial is Dr. Liao's opinion based on his *clinical judgment* and the medical records that he contends do not support the prognoses for the 123 patients at issue in Phase One.

In its summary-judgment briefing, the Government argued that it was procedurally improper for the court to raise summary judgment *sua sponte* after already deciding to grant a new trial. The district court rejected this argument, and the Government does not revive the challenge on appeal.

Following briefing and a hearing, the court granted summary judgment in AseraCare's favor on the basis of the court's newly adopted legal standard. The court concluded, "[a]fter careful review of all [the parties'] submissions and the Phase One [trial] record, ... that the Government has failed to point the court to any admissible evidence to prove falsity other than Dr. Liao's opinion that the medical records for the 123 patients at issue did not support the Certifications of Terminal Illness" that were submitted for Medicare reimbursement. Because "[t]he Government [] presented no evidence of an objective falsehood for any of the patients at issue," it could not prove the falsity element of its FCA claim as a matter of law. The court thus granted summary judgment in AseraCare's favor.

The Government appeals the district court's summary judgment order and its grant of a new trial, contending that the legal standard the court ultimately adopted reflected a "deeply flawed" understanding of the falsity element of an FCA claim. The Government thus asks this Court to reject the legal standard for falsity that the district court adopted, reverse the district court's grant of summary judgment and order of a new trial, and reinstate the jury's Phase One findings: namely, that the Government successfully p.1291 proved falsity as to several of the claims at issue.

III. STANDARD OF REVIEW

This Court reviews the district court's grant of summary judgment *de novo*, viewing all the evidence and drawing all reasonable inferences in favor of the non-moving party. *Vessels v. Atlanta Indep. Sch. Sys.*, 408 F.3d 763, 767 (11th Cir. 2005). By contrast, we review a district court's ruling on a motion for a new trial for abuse of discretion. *Hewitt v. B.F. Goodrich Co.*, 732 F.2d 1554, 1556 (11th Cir. 1984).

IV. DISCUSSION

This appeal requires us to consider how Medicare's requirements for hospice eligibility —which are centered on the subjective "clinical judgment" of a physician as to a patient's life expectancy—intersect with the FCA's falsity element. Under this Court's precedent, "Medicare claims may be false if they claim reimbursement for services or costs that either are not reimbursable or were not rendered as claimed." *United States ex rel. Walker v. R&F Props. of Lake Cty., Inc.*, 433 F.3d 1349, 1356 (11th Cir. 2005). There is no allegation that the hospice services AseraCare provided were not rendered as claimed. Thus, the sole question is whether the claims AseraCare submitted were reimbursable under the Medicare framework for hospice care—that is, whether AseraCare's certifications that patients were terminally ill satisfied Medicare's statutory and regulatory requirements for reimbursement. If not, the claims are capable of being "false" for FCA purposes.

Thus framed, our primary task on appeal is to clarify the scope of the hospice eligibility requirements, which are set out in the federal Medicare statute, 42 U.S.C. § 1395f, and its implementing regulation, 42 C.F.R. § 418.22. Our secondary task is to determine whether the district court's formulation of the falsity standard was consistent with the law and properly applied. Neither this Court nor any of our sister circuits has considered the standard for falsity in the context of the Medicare hospice benefit, where the controlling condition of reimbursement is a matter of clinical judgment. After careful review of the relevant law, the underlying record, and the considerations raised by the parties and the amici curiae, we agree that the instruction given to the jury was inadequate and agree with the general sense of the legal standard embraced by the district court after the verdict.

A. Legal Standard for Falsity of Hospice Claims

The Government argues that the district court's initial jury instructions—that "[a] claim is 'false' if it is an assertion that is untrue when made or used" and that "[c]laims to Medicare may be false if the provider seeks payment, or reimbursement, for health care that is not reimbursable" —comprised a complete and correct statement of the legal standard for falsity. As applied to this case, the Government argues that it can show falsity by producing expert testimony that a patient's medical records do not support a terminalillness prognosis as a factual matter. Where the parties present competing expert views on a patient's prognosis, the "falsity" of the defendant's prognosis is put to a jury.

AseraCare contests the Government's characterization of the statutory and regulatory framework, arguing that the determinative p.1292 inquiry in an eligibility analysis is whether the certifying physician exercised genuine clinical judgment regarding a patient's prognosis and further arguing that the accuracy of such judgment is not susceptible to being proven true or false as a factual matter.

Given the dearth of controlling case law regarding the intersection of the FCA and the Medicare hospice benefit and the parties' vigorous disagreement on the fundamental points of law, we begin by defining the contours of the hospice-eligibility framework and clarifying the circumstances under which a claim violates the requirements for reimbursement. We then consider the ways in which a hospice claim might be deemed "false" for purposes of the FCA.

1. Hospice Eligibility Framework

Our analysis begins with the language of the relevant statute and regulations. *See United States v. Aldrich,* 566 F.3d 976, 978 (11th Cir. 2009) ("[T]he 'starting point' of statutory interpretation is 'the language of the statute itself.'") (citing *Randall v. Loftsgaarden,* 478 U.S. 647, 656, 106 S.Ct. 3143, 92 L.Ed.2d 525 (1986)). "To determine the plain meaning of a statute or regulation, we do not look at one word or term in isolation, but rather look to the entire statutory or regulatory context." *Sec. & Exch. Comm'n v. Levin,* 849 F.3d 995, 1003 (11th Cir. 2017).

In relevant part, the statute states that payment for hospice care provided to an individual may be made only if:

> (i) in the first 90-day period ... (I) the individual's attending physician ... and (II) the medical director (or physician member of the interdisciplinary group described in [42 U.S.C. § 1395x(dd)(2)(B)]) of the hospice program providing ... the care, *each certify in writing at the beginning of the period, that the individual is terminally ill* (as defined in [42 U.S.C. § 1395x(dd)(3)(A)]) *based on the physician's or medical director's clinical judgment regarding the normal course of the individual's illness,* [and]

(ii) in a subsequent 90- or 60-day period, the medical director or physician... recertifies at the beginning of the period that the individual is terminally ill based on such clinical judgment.

42 U.S.C. § 1395f(a)(7)(A) (emphasis added).[6] "Terminally ill" means that the individual "has a medical prognosis that the individual's life expectancy is 6 months or less." 42 U.S.C. § 1395x(dd)(3)(A). In any p.1293 case, "no payment may be made ... for any expenses incurred ... which are not reasonable and necessary for the palliation or management of terminal illness." 42 U.S.C. § 1395y(a)(1)(C).

The implementing regulations echo the language of the statute, reiterating that each written certification of terminal illness "will be based on the physician's or medical director's clinical judgment regarding the normal course of the individual's illness." 42 C.F.R. § 418.22(b). *See also* 42 C.F.R. § 418.22(a)(1) (stating "general rule" that hospice provider "must obtain written certification of terminal illness" for each claimed period of care).

The regulations go on to identify several requirements for the submission of claims. First, and most significant to this appeal, "[c]linical information and other documentation that support the medical prognosis must accompany the certification and must be filed in the medical record with the written certification." 42 C.F.R. § 418.22(b)(2). Second, the certifying physician must include with the certification "a brief narrative explanation of the clinical findings that supports a life expectancy of 6 months or less." 42 C.F.R. § 418.22(b)(3). This narrative explanation "must reflect the patient's individual clinical circumstances and cannot contain check boxes or standard language used for all patients." 42 C.F.R. § 418.22(b)(3)(iv).[7] And third, in deciding whether to certify a patient as terminally ill, a physician is obligated to consider several factors: the patient's primary terminal condition and related diagnoses; current subjective and objective medical findings; current medication and treatment orders; and information about the medical management of any conditions unrelated to the terminal illness. 42 C.F.R. § 418.102(b); 42 C.F.R. § 418.25(b) (establishing that, "[i]n reaching a decision to certify that the patient is terminally ill, the hospice medical direct must consider at least" the diagnosis of the patient, other health conditions, and "[c]urrent clinically relevant information supporting all diagnoses"). *See also* 78 Fed. Reg. 48234, 48247 (Aug. 7, 2013) ("[T]he certification of terminal illness is based in the unique clinical picture of the individual that is reflected in the comprehensive assessment and other clinical records and documentation...."); 79 Fed. Reg. 50452, 50471 (Aug. 22, 2014) (noting that, in deciding whether to recertify a patient who has not shown measurable decline, the physician "must assess and evaluate the full clinical picture" of the patient).

The language of the statute and implementing regulations makes plain that the clinical judgment of the patient's attending physician (or the provider's medical director, as the case may be) lies at the center of the eligibility inquiry. Under this language, a patient is eligible for the Medicare hospice benefit if the appropriate physician makes a clinical judgment that the patient is terminally ill in light of the patient's complete medical picture, as evidenced by the patient's medical records.

Importantly, none of the relevant language states that the documentary record underpinning a physician's clinical judgment must prove the prognosis as a matter of medical fact. Indeed, CMS has recognized in crafting the implementing regulations that "[p]redicting life expectancy is not an exact science." 75 Fed. Reg. 70372, p.1294

70448 (Nov. 17, 2010). *See also* 79 Fed. Reg. at 50470 ("[W]e also have recognized the challenges in prognostication" and therefore expect "that the certifying physicians will use their best clinical judgment.").[8] Nor does this framework state or imply that the patient's medical records must unequivocally demonstrate to an unaffiliated physician, reviewing the records after the fact, that the patient was likely to die within six months of the time the certifying physician's clinical judgment was made. Rather, the framework asks a physician responsible for the patient's care to exercise his or her judgment as to the proper interpretation of the patient's medical records.

The Government seeks to elevate the significance of the regulation's supporting-documentation requirement, asserting that eligibility "turns on" whether the clinical information and other documentation accompanying a certification of terminal illness support, as a factual matter, the physician's certification. Specifically, the Government maintains that the testimony of Dr. Liao, which "was designed to assist the jury in understanding the medical records" for each patient, created "a factual dispute as to whether '[c]linical information and other documentation' in the medical record 'support[ed] the medical prognosis' of a life expectancy of six months or less." (Citing 42 C.F.R. § 418.22(b)(2).)

We conclude that the Government's framing of the eligibility inquiry is not consistent with the text or design of the law. The relevant regulation requires only that "clinical information and other documentation that support the medical prognosis... *accompany the certification*" and "*be filed in the medical record*." 42 C.F.R. § 418.22(b)(2) (emphases added). This "medical prognosis" is, itself, "based on the physician's ... clinical judgment." 42 C.F.R. § 418.22(b). To conclude that the supporting documentation must, standing alone, prove the validity of the physician's initial clinical judgment would read more into the legal framework than its language allows. Read in the context of the statute and regulations, the requirement that supporting documentation "accompany" the claim is designed to address CMS's mandate that "there must be a clinical basis for a certification." 79 Fed. Reg. at 50470 (noting that, although "certification is based on a clinical judgment," this "does not negate the fact that there must be a clinical basis for a certification"). That is, the physician's clinical judgment dictates eligibility as long as it represents a reasonable interpretation of the relevant medical records.

We also note that, had Congress or CMS intended the patient's medical records to objectively demonstrate terminal illness, it could have said so. Yet, Congress said nothing to indicate that the medical documentation presented with a claim must prove the veracity of the clinical judgment on an after-the-fact review. And CMS's own choice of the word "support"— instead of, for example, "demonstrate" or "prove"—does not imply the level of certitude the Government wishes to attribute to it. *Cf. Davidson v. Capital One Bank (USA), N.A.,* 797 F.3d 1309, 1316 (11th Cir. 2015) (We "presume that Congress p.1295 said what it meant and meant what it said.") (quotation marks omitted).

More broadly, CMS's rulemaking commentary signals that well-founded clinical judgments should be granted deference. As noted *supra,* CMS has repeatedly emphasized that "[p]redicting life expectancy is not an exact science." 75 Fed. Reg. at 70448. *See also* 79 Fed. Reg. at 50470 (same). And in clarifying the process for reporting a patient's "principal hospice diagnosis" on a hospice claim, CMS stated:

"We believe that the certifying physicians have the best clinical experience, competence and judgment to make the determination that an individual is terminally ill." 78 Fed. Reg. at 48247. Furthermore, in response to public comment, CMS removed the term "criteria" from a proposed regulation defining the certification requirements, wishing "to remove any implication that there are specific CMS clinical benchmarks in this rule that must be met in order to certify terminal illness." 73 Fed. Reg. 32088, 32138 (June 5, 2008). While there is no question that clinical judgments must be tethered to a patient's valid medical records, it is equally clear that the law is designed to give physicians meaningful latitude to make informed judgments without fear that those judgments will be second-guessed after the fact by laymen in a liability proceeding.

The Government cautions that a narrow reading of the eligibility framework "would entitle hospice providers to reimbursement for services provided to *any* individual, regardless of medical condition, assuming the provider could find a physician willing to sign the certification." This point again ignores that the physician's clinical judgment, informed by the patient's medical records, is the threshold requirement for eligibility. A physician cannot, as the Government suggests, hold a clinical judgment under the eligibility framework that disregards the patient's underlying medical condition. *See, e.g.,* 42 C.F.R. § 418.102(b) (identifying factors physicians must consider when arriving at clinical judgments regarding terminal illness, including "subjective and objective medical findings" regarding the patient's condition). Such a clinical judgment would clearly be illegitimate under the law.

The Government further warns that, under our reading of the framework, "if a physician certifies a patient as terminally ill, CMS is *required* to reimburse the hospice care provider unless it can determine that *no* other reviewer of the patient's medical records could possibly conclude the patient was terminally ill." But, as the Government elsewhere notes, CMS is statutorily prohibited from reimbursing providers for services "which are not reasonable and necessary for the palliation or management of terminal illness." 42 U.S.C. § 1395y(a)(1)(C). *See also* 79 Fed Reg. 50452, 50470 (Aug. 22, 2014) (explaining that CMS retains a well-established right to review claims for hospice reimbursement and to deny claims that it does not consider to be "reasonable and necessary" under the statutory standard). The Government's argument that our reading of the eligibility framework would "tie CMS's hands" and "requir[e] improper reimbursements" is contrary to the plain design of the law.

2. Falsity in this case under the FCA

Having identified the contours of the Medicare framework, it becomes clear that there are two separate representations embedded in each claim for hospice reimbursement: a representation by a physician to AseraCare that the patient is p.1296 terminally ill in the physician's clinical judgment and a representation by AseraCare to Medicare that such clinical judgment has been obtained and that the patient is therefore eligible. As such, this case requires us to distinguish between two possible species of "falsity." The first relates to the legitimacy of a physician's clinical judgment. The second relates to the legitimacy of AseraCare's statement that a clinical judgment has been properly made.

Under the Government's false-certification theory in this case, AseraCare "submitted documentation that falsely represented that certain Medicare recipients were 'terminally ill'" when, in the Government's view, they were not. There is no allegation that AseraCare submitted claims that were not, in fact, based on a physician's properly formed clinical judgment, nor is there an allegation that AseraCare failed to abide by each component of the claim requirements.[9] The Government's allegations focus solely on the accuracy of the physician's clinical judgment regarding terminality. If, the theory goes, AseraCare represented to Medicare that a patient was "terminally ill" based on a physician's clinical judgment, and the Government later persuades a jury that this clinical judgment was wrong, then AseraCare's representation was, in turn, "false." This "falsity" opens the door to FCA liability. Thus, the Government's FCA case hangs entirely on the following question: When can a physician's clinical judgment regarding a patient's prognosis be deemed "false"?

In light of our foregoing discussion, we concur with the district court's post-verdict conclusion that "physicians applying their clinical judgment about a patient's projected life expectancy could disagree, and neither physician [] be wrong." Indeed, the Government's own witness—Mary Jane Schultz, the former head of Palmetto's medical review department—conceded at trial that "two doctors using their clinical judgment could come to different conclusions about a patient's prognosis and neither be right or wrong." Nothing in the statutory or regulatory framework suggests that a clinical judgment regarding a patient's prognosis is invalid or illegitimate merely because an unaffiliated physician reviewing the relevant records after the fact disagrees with that clinical judgment. Nor does the law suggest that a hospice provider has failed to comply with Medicare's requirements for hospice reimbursement if the only flaw in its claim is an absence of certitude that, in light of the relevant medical records, the patient will die within six months. The legal framework signals, and CMS itself has acknowledged, that no such certitude can be expected of physicians in the practice of treating end-of-life illness. All the legal framework asks is that physicians exercise their best judgment in light of the facts at hand and that they document their rationale.

It follows that when a hospice provider submits a claim that certifies that a patient is terminally ill "based on the physician's or medical director's clinical judgment regarding the normal course of the individual's illness," 42 U.S.C. § 1395f(7), 42 C.F.R. § 418.22(b), the claim cannot be "false"—and thus cannot trigger FCA liability p.1297 —if the underlying clinical judgment does not reflect an objective falsehood.

Objective falsehood can be shown in a variety of ways. Where, for instance, a certifying physician fails to review a patient's medical records or otherwise familiarize himself with the patient's condition before asserting that the patient is terminal, his ill-formed "clinical judgment" reflects an objective falsehood. The same is true where a plaintiff proves that a physician did not, in fact, subjectively believe that his patient was terminally ill at the time of certification. A claim may also reflect an objective falsehood when expert evidence proves that no reasonable physician could have concluded that a patient was terminally ill given the relevant medical records. In each of these examples, the clinical judgment on which the claim is based contains a flaw that can be demonstrated through verifiable facts.

By contrast, a reasonable difference of opinion among physicians reviewing medical documentation *ex post* is not sufficient on its own to suggest that those judgments—or any claims based on them—are false under the FCA. A properly formed and sincerely held clinical judgment is not untrue even if a different physician later contends that the judgment is wrong. *Cf. Omnicare, Inc. v. Laborers Dist. Council Const. Indus. Pension Fund,* ___ U.S. ___, 135 S. Ct. 1318, 1327, 191 L.Ed.2d 253 (2015) (holding that "a sincere statement of pure opinion is not an 'untrue statement of material fact'" under the Securities Act of 1933, "regardless whether an investor can ultimately prove the belief wrong").

Accordingly, in order to properly state a claim under the FCA in the context of hospice reimbursement, a plaintiff alleging that a patient was falsely certified for hospice care must identify facts and circumstances surrounding the patient's certification that are inconsistent with the proper exercise of a physician's clinical judgment. Where no such facts or circumstances are shown, the FCA claim fails as a matter of law.

In so holding, we agree with the district court's conclusion that, in order to show objective falsity as to a claim for hospice benefits, the Government must show something more than the mere difference of reasonable opinion concerning the prognosis of a patient's likely longevity.[10] And although we appear to be the first circuit court to consider the precise p.1298 question at issue here, a number of opinions from our sister circuits lends support to our conclusion that the Government must show an objective falsity.[11]

The Government urges that the standard we adopt today improperly "usurp[s] the role of the jury" by precluding the jury from determining, based on expert testimony, the accuracy of the clinical judgments at issue. In support of this contention, the Government relies heavily on this Court's reasoning in *United States ex rel. Walker v. R&F Properties of Lake County, Inc.,* 433 F.3d 1349 (11th Cir. 2005). But *Walker* is clearly distinguishable and does not control our analysis.

In *Walker,* an FCA relator contended that her employer, a medical-clinic operator, billed Medicare for services rendered by non-physicians as if those services had been rendered "incident to the service of a physician," as the relevant statute required. *See id.* at 1353. In reality, the relator alleged, services had been provided by nurse practitioners or physician assistants without any physician involvement. *Id.* The defendant-clinic did not dispute that physicians were not present in the clinic when services were rendered. *Id.* at 1354. It argued instead that these claims could not have been false as a matter of law because the meaning of "incident to the service of a physician" was "vague and subject to reasonable interpretations other than that championed by Walker." *Id.* Specifically, the clinic argued that it interpreted "incident to the service of a physician" to cover services that were rendered by non-physicians as long as a physician was available by pager or telephone, even if not actually physically present in the office. *Id.* The district court agreed, finding the statute ambiguous and defendant's interpretation of the statute reasonable. *Id.*

This Court reversed. *Walker,* 433 F.3d at 1356. The question presented was whether a claim based on a reasonable interpretation of an ambiguous statutory term could never be deemed "false," or whether instead the meaning of the ambiguous term—and the corresponding falsity p.1299 of the claims made thereunder—could potentially pose factual questions that should be put to a factfinder. *Id.* Given the particular facts of the case before us, our Court adopted the latter approach. Specifically, the relator presented evidence from the Medicare Carrier's manual, Medicare bulletins, and seminar programs to "support a finding that, in the Medicare community, the language of the statute was understood to mean that a physician had to be physically present in the office suite" in order to justify reimbursement for the medical service provided by a non-physician. *Id.* at 1356-57. We concluded that this evidence created a jury question as to both whether the Medicare regulation required more physician involvement with a patient than the defendant clinic had provided and whether the defendant knew of this requirement. *Id.* at 1358.

In *Walker,* the eligibility criterion at issue was subject to multiple interpretations because its language was ambiguous, yet ultimately only one of the two possible interpretations could be deemed correct. By contrast, the key eligibility criterion at issue here—"terminally ill"—presents, by design, a question of debatable clinical judgment that may not, in all circumstances, lend itself to just one determination as to the proper exercise of that judgment. As the district court noted below, asking the jury to decide whether medical records supported a finding of "terminal illness" put the jury in the position of evaluating, and second-guessing, the clinical judgment of the certifying physician. This is not the role the factfinder was playing in *Walker;* indeed, it is a role requiring medical knowledge and expertise that Congress has clearly reserved for physicians in the hospice-benefit context. *Walker* therefore does not compel the conclusion that eligibility requirements that hinge on clinical judgment present jury questions simply because they are susceptible to differing opinions, each of which could be reasonable.

The Government has also filed supplemental authority, citing to out-of-circuit appellate cases that it says establish that a mere difference of medical opinion can be sufficient to show that a statement is false. We find these cases distinguishable. In *United States v. Paulus,* 894 F.3d 267 (6th Cir. 2018), the physician-defendant had been convicted of healthcare fraud based on his performance of allegedly unnecessary coronary stent procedures. In arguing for reversal of his conviction, the defendant contended that he based his decision to perform the procedures on his interpretation of angiogram tests showing a high degree of blockage in the patients' arteries, and thus his medical judgment on this point represented merely an opinion that could neither be truthful nor false. The Government contended that, to the contrary, the defendant had lied when he said that he interpreted the angiograms as showing a level of coronary blockage that would warrant inserting a stent into the heart, and it offered substantial expert testimony disputing that the level of blockage shown on the angiogram test was at the level the defendant asserted it was.

The Sixth Circuit[12] agreed with the defendant that "[o]rdinarily, facts are the only item that fits in [the false statement] category; opinions—when given honestly— are almost never false.... There is no p.1300 such thing as a false idea." *Id.* at 275 (citations and internal quotation marks omitted). Nevertheless, the court continued, opinions have "never been completely insulated from scrutiny. At the very least, opinions may trigger liability for fraud when they are not honestly held by their maker, or when the speaker knows of facts that are fundamentally incompatible with his opinion." *Id.* The court then cited with apparent approval the district court opinion in the present case for the proposition that "certain good-faith medical diagnoses by a doctor cannot be false."[13] *Id.* In the case before it, however, the *Paulus* court noted that "coronary artery blockage actually exists as an aspect of reality," meaning that an assertion about the degree of blockage can be objectively true or false. *Id.* at 276 (quotation marks omitted). And it concluded that the Government's expert testimony was sufficient to support an inference that the defendant had lied when he reported readings of the angiograms that the experts said were simply not true: "[W]e think it is clear that Paulus was convicted for misrepresenting facts, not giving opinions." *Id.*

Moreover, whereas in the present case the Government's expert witness declined to conclude that AseraCare's physicians had lied about their clinical judgment or even that their judgments were unreasonable or wrong[14]—as opposed to just different from what the Government's expert opined—in *Paulus,* it appears clear that the Government's experts there were not so charitable. The *Paulus* court noted that the Government had claimed that "Paulus repeatedly and systematically saw one thing on the angiogram and consciously wrote down another, and then used that misinformation to perform and bill unnecessary procedures," and it explained that "[h]owever difficult it might be for a cardiology expert to prove that his colleague was lying about what he saw on a scan," it was up to the jury to decide the reliability of that testimony. *Id.* at 267-77. In short, the Government's expert testimony in *Paulus* appeared to suggest that no reasonable doctor could interpret the scan as had Paulus and that Paulus was actually lying. Thus, *Paulus* is not supportive of the Government's contentions here.[15]

The Government expresses concern that a requirement of objective falsehood will p.1301 produce a troubling under-inclusion problem: that is, by holding that an FCA claim fails as a matter of law if the plaintiff proves nothing more than a reasonable difference of opinion as to the patient's prognosis, hospice providers with sloppy or improper admission practices may evade FCA liability so long as they can argue after the fact that their physicians' clinical judgments were justifiable. That may well be. To be sure, it will likely prove more challenging for an FCA plaintiff to present evidence of an objective falsehood than to find an expert witness willing to testify to a contrasting clinical judgment regarding cold medical records.

But if this is a problem, it is one for Congress or CMS to solve. In deciding how to craft the hospice eligibility requirements, Congress and CMS could have imposed a more rigid set of criteria for eligibility determinations that would have minimized the role of clinical judgment. Instead, they were careful to place the physician's clinical judgment at the center of the inquiry. Indeed, CMS has considered and expressly declined to impose defined criteria that would govern the physician's exercise of judgment. *See* 73 Fed. Reg. 32088, 32138 (June 5, 2008).

In any event, absent a showing of an objective and knowing falsehood, the FCA is an inappropriate instrument to serve as the Government's primary line of defense against questionable claims for reimbursement of hospice benefits. For the above reasons, we agree that the district court's jury instruction concerning falsity was lacking and that a new trial was warranted to allow the giving of a more complete charge: specifically, a charge that would convey that the mere difference of reasonable opinion between physicians, without more,[16] as to the prognosis for a patient seeking hospice benefits does not constitute an objective falsehood. We therefore AFFIRM the district court's grant of a new trial.

B. Grant of Summary Judgment

Deciding that the district court acted correctly in determining that a new trial was warranted—with a revised instruction to the jury concerning falsity—does not end our review of this case. Instead, as noted in the procedural discussion above, the district court went further and, after granting a new trial, it then *sua sponte* granted summary judgment to AseraCare. p.1302 The court reasoned as follows. Given its new position on the standard for determining falsity—that falsity cannot be established based merely on a reasonable disagreement between experts as to whether clinical records in a patient's file warranted a prognosis of a terminal illness that would likely result in the patient's death within six months—the district court indicated that it would hear from the Government whether the court record contained any other evidence sufficient to create a jury question as to whether AseraCare had made an objectively false representation when claiming reimbursement for hospice benefits it had provided. Following that response and concluding that the Government's evidence of falsity consisted only of Dr. Liao's testimony indicating his disagreement with the prognosis arrived at by AseraCare for most of the patient files he reviewed, the district court found that the Government's evidence of falsity was insufficient to allow it to proceed further. For that reason, the court granted summary judgment.

Leaving aside the question whether the substance of an opinion, by itself, can ever be deemed to constitute an objective falsity, the parties agree that an opinion can be considered objectively false if the speaker does not actually hold that opinion. *See Omnicare, Inc. v. Laborers Dist. Council Const. Indus. Pension Fund,* ___ U.S. ___, 135 S. Ct. 1318, 1323, 1326-27, 191 L.Ed.2d 253 (2015) (holding in the context of securities fraud statutes that a statement of opinion can be "false" if the opinion did not reflect the speaker's actual belief at the time it was given). Further, in examining whether a physician's clinical judgment was truly communicated, the latter must first have actually exercised such judgment. If it can be shown that the physician never considered the underlying records supporting the prognosis at issue, but instead rubber-stamped whatever file was put in front of him, then the physician has offered no clinical judgment. Moreover, an opinion can enter falsifiable territory when it is based on information that the physician knew, or had reason to know, was incorrect. Finally, if no reasonable physician would think that a patient had a terminal illness based on the evidence before that physician, then falsity can be inferred, as well as the existence of a knowing violation.

With the above thoughts in mind, the Government argues that the district court took too constricted a view of the evidence upon which a determination of falsity could be made by a jury when it refused to consider other evidence from the first phase of the trial that the Government asserts tended to show knowledge of the falsity of the claim, as well as evidence that the Government intended to present in the second phase of the trial to further show AseraCare's alleged awareness[17] that it was submitting claims that did not reflect a physician's good faith clinical judgment and prognosis for each patient. In its opposition to the *sua sponte* grant of summary judgment, the Government stated:

> It is indefensible for the Court to grant summary judgment on the grounds that this case is just about a good faith disagreement p.1303 between

experts—and that the United States failed to present evidence that AseraCare knew or recklessly disregarded that its claims were false—when the Court bifurcated the trial and expressly excluded from Phase One any evidence of AseraCare's knowledge of falsity.

We agree with the Government that before granting summary judgment, the district court should have considered all the evidence, both in the trial record and the summary judgment record, to determine whether a triable issue existed regarding falsity. Here is why we reach that conclusion.

The Government had been prepared to introduce evidence to show AseraCare's knowledge at trial, but was prevented from doing so by the district court's decision, over the Government's strong objections, to bifurcate the trial and preclude introduction of any evidence showing knowledge of falsity in Phase I. The Government did, however, introduce evidence in that first phase that seems to offer some potential basis for inferring knowledge. Specifically, nine witnesses, whose testimony was purportedly connected in time and location to the patients at issue, testified that AseraCare had a deliberate practice of not giving physicians relevant, accurate, and complete information about patients whose certifications for hospice the doctors were being asked to sign. For example, one former director of clinical services in Decatur, Alabama, testified that when she declined to admit ineligible patients to hospice, she was instructed to go back and find whatever she needed to admit the patient. Further, she typically did not provide the certifying physician with any clinical information, but usually just gave him a stack of papers to sign. Indeed, each of the nine former-employee witnesses reiterated these themes in their testimony. In large part, because the Government had not denominated this evidence as proof of falsity during this first phase—but instead as evidence of context—the district court refused to consider it as evidence of falsity in this post-verdict summary judgment phase.

The Government also intended to offer at the second phase evidence from AseraCare's internal and external auditors criticizing the company because the certifying medical directors were not adequately involved in making initial eligibility determinations and did not consistently receive medical information prior to the initial certification. In addition to the testimony of other former employees, the Government also planned to offer testimony from a former AseraCare physician that employees did not defer to his clinical judgment that certain patients were unentitled to hospice benefits, but instead proceeded to file the claims. The district court declined to factor the above evidence into its evaluation of whether a jury question still remained concerning AseraCare's knowledge that it was submitting claims that did not warrant the reimbursement of hospice benefits.

The district court's refusal to consider any of the above-described additional evidence on the question of falsity was largely based on the Government's response to AseraCare's discovery interrogatories inquiring what evidence the Government would offer on that issue. The district court emphasized that the Government had "painted itself into a corner by failing to disclose during discovery that it would use anything other than the testimony of Dr. Liao and medical records to prove the falsity of the claims."

p.1304 It is true that the Government denominated only the Liao testimony as evidence of falsity during the discovery period. But, in fairness to the Government, it disclosed all the above evidence in question during discovery, including the evidence that the district court declined to consider for post-verdict summary judgment purposes. At the time of disclosure, the Government had no idea that the district court would later order the bifurcation of trial between falsity and knowledge phases, and it clearly assumed that all of its evidence would be heard by the jury in one proceeding, with no need to so starkly pigeon-hole the category into which a given piece of evidence might fit. As the Government noted in its opposition to bifurcation, with no contradiction by AseraCare, the elements of an FCA liability claim had "never been before been bifurcated by a federal district court." Nor had the Government ever anticipated such a decision, because, according to it, such an order was "extraordinary, requiring the United States to jump over an arbitrary hurdle that is without precedent ... [because] [t]he elements of 'falsity' and 'knowledge of falsity' are not so distinct and separable that they may be tried separately without injustice."

Moreover, the district court had rejected AseraCare's initial motion for summary judgment based on the latter's argument that the mere disagreement of experts is insufficient to imply falsity. At the time of trial, the court had already declined to apply this "reasonable physician" standard to the falsity analysis, despite granting AseraCare's § 1292(b) motion for review. As such, the Government's failure to present its case in a manner consistent with such a standard is understandable. Moreover, the court declined to give the instructions requested by AseraCare to that effect and instead gave only the charge requested by the Government: "Claims to Medicare may be false if the provider seeks payment, or reimbursement, for health care that is not reimbursable. For a hospice provider's claims to Medicare to be reimbursable, the patient must be eligible for the Medicare hospice benefit."

Accordingly, the Government, which had prepared and presented its case based on all the above information, was never alerted to the possibility that the conceptual underpinnings of its case would shift so dramatically once it had won a jury verdict on that theory. We emphasize that we do not criticize the district court for its post-verdict change of mind about the appropriate standard for proving falsity. To the contrary, this district court judge was diligent, conscientious, and thoughtful throughout the long and complex pre-trial proceedings and the eight-week trial whose verdict she ultimately vacated. Given that expenditure of time and energy, it is commendable that the district court would consider starting over once she became convinced that she had made a legal error.

Nonetheless, under all these unusual circumstances, it is only fair that the Government be allowed to have summary judgment considered based on all the evidence presented at both the summary judgment and trial stages, and we direct that this occur. When the goalpost gets moved in the final seconds of a game, the team with the ball should, at the least, have one more opportunity to punch it into the endzone.

Having given the Government the green light to once again try to persuade the district court that a triable issue exists on both falsity and knowledge, we emphasize that we do not know that this effort will succeed. For sure, to the extent that a reasonable jury might credit the Government's p.1305 proffered evidence regarding AseraCare's practices, that evidence suggests that AseraCare's certification procedures were seriously flawed. As noted, a former Director of Clinical Services testified that one physician she worked with was in the habit of signing certifications before reviewing any medical documentation whatsoever; clinical staff typically "just gave him ... a stack of papers to sign, [and] he just signed the papers." Another former employee testified that signing certifications had become so rote for one physician that he "would nod off" while signing. This testimony certainly raises questions regarding AseraCare's certification process writ large. But crucially, on remand the Government must be able to link this evidence of improper certification practices to the specific 123 claims at issue in its case. Such linkage is necessary to demonstrate both falsehood and knowledge.[18] *See Urquilla-Diaz v. Kaplan Univ.,* 780 F.3d 1039, 1045 (11th Cir. 2015) ("disregard of government regulations or failure to maintain proper internal procedures" are not sufficient to demonstrate FCA violation); *Carrel v. AIDS Healthcare Foundation, Inc.,* 898 F.3d 1267, 1277-78 (11th Cir. 2018) (a relator cannot prove that an actual false claim was filed based only on a showing of general practices untethered to that claim).

For the above reasons, we VACATE the district court's post-verdict grant of summary judgment to AseraCare and REMAND for the court to reconsider that matter based on the entirety of the evidence, not just that evidence presented at trial nor just the evidence denominated as being offered to prove falsity.

V. CONCLUSION

For the reasons explained above, we AFFIRM the district court's grant of a new trial. We, however, VACATE the post-verdict grant of summary judgment to AseraCare and REMAND for the district court to reconsider that decision in light of all the relevant evidence proffered by the Government.

[*] The Honorable Harvey E. Schlesinger, United States District Judge for the Middle District of Florida, sitting by designation.

[1] We derive the pertinent facts from the parties' submissions, the summary judgment record, and the trial testimony presented in the proceeding below.

[2] "[A]ny person who ... knowingly presents, or causes to be presented, a false or fraudulent claim for payment or approval ... is liable to the United States Government...." 31 U.S.C. § 3729(a)(1)(A).

[3] "[A]ny person who ... knowingly makes, uses, or causes to be made or used, a false record or statement material to a false or fraudulent claim ... is liable to the United States Government...." 31 U.S.C. § 3729(a)(1)(B).

[4] AseraCare asked the district court to adopt the standard for falsity established by the Northern District of Illinois in a case with a similar fact pattern and posture. The court in that case dismissed FCA claims against a for-profit hospice facility because relators failed to allege facts "demonstrating that the certifying physician did not or could not have believed, based on his or her clinical judgment, that the patient was eligible for hospice care." *United States ex rel. Geschrey v. Generations Healthcare, LLC,* 922 F. Supp. 2d 695, 703 (N.D. Ill. 2012).

[5] The Government continues to complain on appeal that bifurcation of the trial was "fundamentally unfair" and confused the issues, albeit it does not expressly challenge on appeal the district court's decision.

[6] The statute contains three additional requirements, each of which was in place during the relevant time period of 2007 through 2012:

(B) a written plan for providing hospice care with respect to such individual has been established ... and is periodically reviewed by the individual's attending physician and by the medical director (and the interdisciplinary group described in 42 U.S.C. § 1395x(dd)(2)(B)]) of the hospice program;

(C) such care is being or was provided pursuant to such plan of care; [and]

(D) on and after January 1, 2011 ... a hospice physician or nurse practitioner has a face-to-face encounter with the individual to determine continued eligibility ... prior to the 180th-day recertification and each subsequent recertification ... and attests that such visit took place....

42 U.S.C. § 1395f(a)(7). The Government does not allege that AseraCare failed to meet any of these additional requirements.

[7] The requirement of a brief narrative explanation accompanying the certification was added to the regulations on October 1, 2009. *See* 74 Fed. Reg. 39384, XXXXX-XXX, 39413 (Aug. 6, 2009).

[8] We have held in the context of FCA proceedings that "guidance issued by the governmental agency charged with administrating the regulatory scheme," including the Medicare regulatory scheme, "can be consulted to understand the meaning of that regulation." *United States ex rel. Walker v. R&F Props. of Lake Cty., Inc.,* 433 F.3d 1349, 1357 (11th Cir. 2005).

[9] We might, for instance, envision a viable FCA suit alleging that a hospice provider failed to obtain any clinical judgment at all, or obtained a clinical judgment from someone other than the patient's attending physician or the provider's medical director, or fabricated the certification itself. No such facts are alleged here.

[10] Several district courts within and outside the Eleventh Circuit have embraced comparable reasoning in cases alleging FCA liability on the basis of clinical judgments of terminal illness. *See, e.g., United States ex rel. Wall v. Vista Hospice Care, Inc.,* 2016 WL 3449833, at *17 (N.D. Tex. June 20, 2016) ("Because a physician must use his or her clinical judgment to determine hospice eligibility, an FCA claim about the exercise of that judgment must be predicated on the presence of an objectively verifiable fact at odds with the exercise of that judgment, not a matter of questioning subjective clinical analysis."); *United States ex rel. Fowler v. Evercare Hospice, Inc.,* 2015 WL 5568614, at *9 (D. Colo. Sept. 21, 2015) (observing that, if Government's complaint had been "based entirely on disagreements with [the provider's] certifying physicians," the complaint "would be insufficient to state a claim"); *United States ex rel. Geschrey v. Generations Healthcare, LLC,* 922 F. Supp. 2d 695, 703 (N.D. Ill. 2012) (dismissing FCA claims because "[r]elators have not alleged facts demonstrating that the certifying physician did not or could not have believed, based on his or her clinical judgment, that the patient was eligible for hospice care"). *But see Druding v. Care Alternatives, Inc.,* 164 F. Supp. 3d 621, 623 (D.N.J. 2016) (holding that where plaintiffs alleged that patients were ineligible for hospice because they did not meet LCD

criteria, claims were "legally false ... because the claim[s] did not include sufficient clinical facts in the patient's medical records to justify a terminal prognosis").

[11] *See United States ex rel. Yannacopoulos v. General Dynamics,* 652 F.3d 818, 836 (7th Cir. 2011) (stating that "[a] statement may be deemed 'false' for purposes of the False Claims Act only if the statement presents 'an objective falsehood'") (citing *United States ex rel. Wilson v. Kellogg Brown & Root, Inc.,* 525 F.3d 370, 376 (4th Cir. 2008)); *United States ex rel. Loughren v. Unum Grp.,* 613 F.3d 300, 310 (1st Cir. 2010), (explaining that an opinion may qualify as a false statement for purposes of the FCA where the speaker "knows facts 'which would preclude such an opinion'") (quoting *United States ex rel. Siewick v. Jamieson Science and Engineering, Inc.,* 214 F.3d 1372, 1378 (D.C. Cir. 2000)); *Wilson,* 525 F.3d at 376-77 (holding that "[t]o satisfy [the] first element of an FCA claim, the statement or conduct alleged must represent an objective falsehood" and "imprecise statements or differences in interpretation growing out of a disputed legal question are [] not false under the FCA") (quotation omitted); *United States ex rel. Burlbaw v. Orenduff,* 548 F.3d 931, 959 (10th Cir. 2008) ("At a minimum the FCA requires proof of an objective falsehood."); *Harrison v. Westinghouse Savannah River Co.,* 176 F.3d 776, 792 (4th Cir. 1999) (noting that opinions or estimates can be "false" under the FCA if their speaker knows they are not supported by the facts); *Hooper v. Lockheed Martin Corp.,* 688 F.3d 1037, 1047-49 (9th Cir. 2012) (same). *Cf. Omnicare, Inc. v. Laborers Dist. Council Const. Indus. Pension Fund,* ___ U.S. ___, 135 S. Ct. 1318, 1323, 1326-27, 191 L.Ed.2d 253 (2015) (holding in the context of securities fraud statutes that a statement of opinion can be "false" if the opinion did not reflect the speaker's actual belief at the time it was given).

[12] The *Paulus* court indicated its intention to clarify the standard underlying its earlier decision in *United States v. Persaud,* 866 F.3d 371 (6th Cir. 2017), which the Government has also cited in the present case. *Paulus,* 894 F.3d at 275.

[13] The court stated, "*see also United States v. AseraCare, Inc.,* 176 F. Supp. 3d 1282 (N.D. Ala. 2016) (holding that certain good-faith medical diagnoses by a doctor cannot be false.") *Paulus,* 894 F.3d at 275.

[14] As noted *supra,* the former head of the Palmetto medical review team, called as a Government witness, also conceded at trial that "two doctors using their clinical judgment could come to different conclusions about a patient's prognosis and neither be right or wrong."

[15] The Government here also cites *United States ex rel. Polukoff v. St. Mark's Hospital,* 895 F.3d 730 (10th Cir. 2018), an FCA case in which the district court had granted the defendant's motion to dismiss on the ground that his medical judgment about the need for cardiac PFO closure procedures to prevent future strokes in his patients was an opinion that was not subject to being deemed true or false. The Tenth Circuit reversed, found a plausible allegation of falsity, and directed that the case proceed to discovery. The circuit court noted that the Government had alleged that the applicable Medicare statute authorized reimbursement only when the he PFO procedure was reasonable and necessary for the treatment of an illness; that there is agreement in the medical community that a PFO closure is not medically necessary except where there is a confirmed diagnosis of a recurrent stroke; that the applicable guidelines allow for consideration of the procedure only when the patient has had two or more strokes and that the guidelines do not "contemplate the potential for PFO closures" if the patient has not had a prior stroke; that the defendant claimed

to believe that the procedure should be performed prophylactically to cure migraine headaches or to prevent strokes even if the patient had never before had a stroke; and, knowing that Medicare would not pay on that basis, the defendant falsely represented that the procedure was being performed based on the indications set forth in the guidelines. *Id.* at 736, 737. In addition, a fellow physician alleged that he had witnessed the defendant perform an unnecessary procedure and actually *create* the problem the surgery was intended to remedy by puncturing intact septa in the patients. *Id.* at 738.

Obviously, the above facts are quite different from those alleged in this case. It is true that the Tenth Circuit opinion held that regardless of the physician's opinion to the contrary, he will be deemed to have made a false statement when claiming reimbursement if the medical procedure is determined to have not been reasonable or necessary. "We thus hold that a doctor's certification to the government that a procedure is 'reasonable and necessary' is 'false' under the FCA if the procedure was not reasonable and necessary under the government's definition of the phrase." *Id.* at 742. As set out in text, however, the hospice-benefit provision at issue here, by design, looks to whether a physician has based a recommendation for hospice treatment on a genuinely-held clinical opinion as to a patient's likely longevity.

[16] Should there be another trial on this matter, we leave to the district court and the parties the task of fleshing out just what that "more" needs to include.

[17] For purposes of the FCA, "the terms 'knowing' and 'knowingly' (A) mean that a person, with respect to information—(i) has actual knowledge of the information; (ii) acts in deliberate ignorance of the truth or falsity of the information; or (iii) acts in reckless disregard of the truth or falsity of the information, and (B) no proof of specific intent to defraud is required." 31 U.S.C. § 3729(b).

[18] Alternatively, the Government could meet its burden under the falsity standard now adopted by the district court, and endorsed by this Court, if it could establish through expert testimony that no reasonable physician reviewing the medical records at issue could have concluded that a particular patient was terminally ill. The Court, however, is unaware that any such evidence exists. Indeed, as noted, Mary Jane Schultz, the former head of Palmetto's medical review department, testified that "two doctors using their clinical judgment could come to different conclusions about a patient's prognosis and neither be right or wrong." Also, as noted, Dr. Liao himself changed his opinion concerning the eligibility of certain patients over the course of the proceeding but testified at trial that both sets of opinions remained "accurate to a reasonable degree of certainty." To explain these reversals, Dr. Liao stated that he "was not the same physician in 2013 as [he] was in 2010." As the district court observed, if Dr. Liao can form contradictory opinions based on the same medical records and yet claim not to have been wrong on either occasion, then it is difficult to explain how his difference of opinion with AseraCare's physicians concerning other patients would demonstrate that no reasonable physician could agree with AseraCare, absent some additional evidence to warrant that inference.

887 F.3d 1081 (2018)

UNITED STATES of America, EX REL. Billy Joe HUNT, Plaintiff-Appellant,
v.
COCHISE CONSULTANCY, INC., doing business as Cochise Security, The
Parsons Corporation, doing business as Parsons Infrastructure & Technology,
Defendants-Appellees.

No. 16-12836.

United States Court of Appeals, Eleventh Circuit.

April 11, 2018.

US ex rel. Hunt v. Cochise Consultancy, Inc., 887 F. 3d 1081 (11th Cir. 2018)

Appeal from the United States District Court for the Northern District of Alabama, D.C. Docket No. 5:13-cv-02168-RDP.

Gary Vestal Conchin, Conchin Cloud & Cole, LLC, HUNTSVILLE, AL, Earl N. Mayfield, Christopher Day, JurisDay, PLLC, FAIRFAX, VA, for Plaintiff-Appellant.

Duane Allan Daiker, Robert R. Warchola, Jr., Shumaker Loop & Kendrick, LLP, TAMPA, FL, for Defendant-Appellee Cochise Consultancy, Inc., doing business as Cochise Security.

Aaron S. Dyer, James M. Carter, Michael Robert Rizzo, Pillsbury Winthrop Shaw Pittman, LLP, LOS ANGELES, CA, Jeffrey Paul Doss, Jackson Roger Sharman, III, Lightfoot Franklin & White, LLC, BIRMINGHAM, AL, Kevin M. Fong, Pillsbury Winthrop Shaw Pittman, LLP, SAN FRANCISCO, CA, for Defendant-Appellee The Parsons Corporation, p.1083 doing business as Parsons Infrastructure & Technology.

Before WILSON and JILL PRYOR, Circuit Judges, and BARTLE,[*] District Judge.

p.1082 JILL PRYOR, Circuit Judge:

Relator Billy Joe Hunt filed a *qui tam* action alleging that his employer The Parsons Corporation and another entity, Cochise Consultancy, Inc., violated the False Claims Act ("FCA"), 31 U.S.C. §§ 3729-33, by submitting to the United States false or fraudulent claims for payment. Hunt filed his action more than six years after the alleged fraud occurred but within three years of when he disclosed the fraud to the government. In this appeal, we are called upon to decide whether Hunt's FCA claim is time barred. To answer this question, we must construe the FCA's statutory provision that requires a civil action alleging an FCA violation to be brought within the later of:

- "6 years after the date on which the violation ... is committed," 31 U.S.C. § 3731(b)(1), or
- "3 years after the date when facts material to the right of action are known or reasonably should have been known by the official of the United States charged with responsibility to act in the circumstances, but in no event more

than 10 years after the date on which the violation is committed," *id.* §
3731(b)(2).

The question we answer today, which is one of first impression, is whether §
3731(b)(2)'s three year limitations period applies to a relator's FCA claim when the
United States declines to intervene in the *qui tam* action.

The district court concluded that the limitations period in § 3731(b)(2) is
inapplicable in such cases and thus Hunt's claim is time barred. After careful
consideration of the statutory scheme, we hold that § 3731(b)(2)'s three year
limitations period applies to an FCA claim brought by a relator even when the United
States declines to intervene. Further, because the FCA provides that this period
begins to run when the relevant federal government official learns of the facts giving
rise to the claim, when the relator learned of the fraud is immaterial for statute of
limitations purposes. Here, it is not apparent from the face of Hunt's complaint that
his claim is untimely because his allegations show that he filed suit within three years
of the date when he disclosed facts material to the right of action to United States
officials and within ten years of when the fraud occurred. The district court therefore
erred in dismissing his complaint. We reverse and remand to the district court for
further proceedings.

I. FACTUAL BACKGROUND

A. The Fraudulent Scheme

Hunt alleges that Parsons and Cochise (the "contractors") defrauded the United
States Department of Defense for work they performed as defense contractors in
Iraq.[1] The Department of Defense awarded Parsons a $60 million contract to clean
up excess munitions in Iraq left behind by retreating or defeated enemy forces. Hunt
worked for Parsons in Iraq p.1084 on the munitions clearing contract, managing the
project's day-to-day operations. One facet of the contract required Parsons to
provide adequate security to its employees, its subcontractors, and others who were
working on the munitions clearing project. Parsons relied on a subcontractor to
provide the security services.

After seeking bids for the security subcontract, a Parsons committee awarded it
to ArmorGroup. But an Army Corps of Engineers contracting officer in Iraq whom
Cochise had bribed with trips and gifts, Wayne Shaw, was determined to override
this decision and have the subcontract awarded to Cochise. Shaw directed Hunt to
have Hoyt Runnels, another Parsons employee who served on the committee that
selected ArmorGroup, issue a directive awarding Cochise the subcontract. When
Hunt did so, Runnels refused to issue the directive, explaining that such a directive
had to come from the Corps.

Shaw then created a forged directive rescinding the award to ArmorGroup and
awarding the subcontract to Cochise. The directive had to be signed by Steven
Hamilton, another Corps contracting officer. Hamilton, who was legally blind, relied
on Shaw to describe the document he was signing. Shaw did not disclose that the
directive rescinded the award to Armor-Group so that the subcontract could be
awarded to Cochise.

After Hamilton signed the directive, Shaw directed Runnels to execute it. Runnels again refused because he believed the award to Cochise had been made in violation of government regulations. Shaw threated to have Runnels fired. Two days later, Hamilton learned that the directive Shaw had him sign rescinded the award to ArmorGroup and awarded Cochise the subcontract. Hamilton immediately rescinded his directive awarding the subcontract to Cochise.

After Runnels refused to follow Shaw's directive to award the subcontract to Cochise, another Parsons employee, Dwight Hill, replaced Runnels and was given responsibility for awarding the security subcontract. Rather than give the subcontract to ArmorGroup, Hill awarded it to Cochise through a no-bid process. Hill justified using a no-bid process by claiming there was an urgent and immediate need for convoy services and then defended the choice of Cochise to fill this immediate need by asserting that Cochise had experience that other security providers lacked. But Hunt alleges that Hill selected Cochise because he was its partner in the fraudulent scheme.

From February through September 2006, Cochise provided security services under the subcontract. Each month the United States government paid Cochise at least $1 million more than it would have paid ArmorGroup had ArmorGroup been awarded the subcontract. The government incurred other additional expenses as well. For example, armored vehicles were needed to provide the security services, and because Cochise had no such vehicles, the government paid more than $2.9 million to secure the vehicles. In contrast, Armor-Group would have supplied its own armored vehicles, saving the government millions of dollars. In September 2006, when Shaw rotated out of Iraq, Parsons immediately reopened the subcontract for bidding and awarded it to ArmorGroup.

Several years later, Hunt reported the fraud to the United States government. On November 30, 2010, FBI agents interviewed Hunt about his role in a separate kickback scheme. During the interview, Hunt told the agents about the contractors' fraudulent scheme involving the subcontract for security services. For his role in the separate kickback scheme, Hunt was charged with federal crimes, pled p.1085 guilty, and served ten months in federal prison.

B. Procedural History

After his release from prison, on November 27, 2013, Hunt filed under seal in federal district court an FCA complaint against the contractors. Hunt set forth two theories why the claims the contractors submitted for payment qualified as false claims under the FCA. First, he alleged that Cochise fraudulently induced the government to enter into the subcontract to purchase Cochise's services by providing illegal gifts to Shaw and his team. He alleged that Parsons, through Hill, conspired with Cochise and Shaw to rig the bidding process for the subcontract. Second, Hunt alleged that the contractors had a legal obligation to disclose credible evidence of improper conflicts of interest and payment of illegal gratuities to the United States but failed to do so.

After the United States declined to intervene, Hunt's complaint was unsealed. The contractors moved to dismiss, arguing that the claim was time barred under the six year limitations period in 31 U.S.C. § 3731(b)(1), and Hunt had waited more than seven years after the fraud occurred to file suit. Hunt responded that his claim was timely under the limitations period in § 3731(b)(2) because he had filed suit within three years of when the government learned of the fraud at his FBI interview and ten years of when the fraud occurred. The district court disagreed, concluding that § 3731(b)(2)'s limitations period was either (1) unavailable to Hunt because the United States had declined to intervene or (2) expired because it began to run when Hunt learned of the fraud. The district court then granted the motions to dismiss, finding Hunt's claim untimely under § 3731(b)(1)'s limitation period because it was apparent from the face of Hunt's complaint that he failed to file suit within six years of when the fraud occurred. This is Hunt's appeal.

II. STANDARD OF REVIEW

We review *de novo* a district court's dismissal of a complaint for failure to state a claim upon which relief can be granted. *Am. Dental Ass'n v. Cigna Corp.,* 605 F.3d 1283, 1288 (11th Cir. 2010). A dismissal for failure to state a claim on statute of limitations grounds is appropriate "only if it is apparent from the face of the complaint that the claim is time-barred." *La Grasta v. First Union Sec., Inc.,* 358 F.3d 840, 845 (11th Cir. 2004) (internal quotation marks omitted). "We review the district court's interpretation and application of statutes of limitations *de novo.*" *Ctr. for Biological Diversity v. Hamilton,* 453 F.3d 1331, 1334 (11th Cir. 2006).

III. BACKGROUND ON THE FCA

Before addressing whether Hunt's claim is timely, we pause to provide some necessary background information about the roles of the government and the private plaintiff in a *qui tam* suit and to discuss the relevant FCA provisions. The FCA was enacted in 1863 to "stop[] the massive frauds perpetrated by large contractors during the Civil War." *Universal Health Servs., Inc. v. United States ex rel. Escobar,* ___ U.S. ___, 136 S.Ct. 1989, 1996, 195 L.Ed.2d 348 (2016) (internal quotation marks omitted). These contractors billed the United States "for nonexistent or worthless goods, charged exorbitant prices for goods delivered, and generally robbed in purchasing the necessities of war." *Id.* (internal quotation marks omitted). In response, Congress passed the original FCA, which imposed civil and criminal liability for fraud on the government, subjecting p.1086 violators to double damages, forfeiture, and imprisonment. *Id.*

Since 1863, Congress repeatedly has amended the FCA. Today, the FCA continues to prohibit making false claims for payment to the United States. *See* 31 U.S.C. § 3729(a). But unlike the original FCA that provided for both civil and criminal liability, violators today face only civil liability, which subjects them to treble damages and civil penalties.[2] *Id.*

Section 3730 of the FCA sets forth three different enforcement mechanisms for a violation of the Act. Section 3730(a) provides that the Attorney General may sue a violator in a civil lawsuit. Section 3730(b) allows a private plaintiff, known as a relator, to bring a *qui tam* action in the name of the United States against a violator. Section 3730(h) creates a private right of action for an individual whose employer retaliated against him for assisting an FCA investigation or proceeding.

This appeal concerns the second mechanism, a *qui tam* action brought by a relator under § 3730(b). In a *qui tam* action, the relator "pursues the government's claim against the defendant, and asserts the injury in fact suffered by the government." *Stalley ex rel. United States v. Orlando Reg'l Healthcare Sys., Inc.,* 524 F.3d 1229, 1233 (11th Cir. 2008).[3] In bringing a *qui tam* action, the relator "in effect, su[es] as a partial assignee of the United States." *Vt. Agency of Nat. Res. v. United States ex rel. Stevens,* 529 U.S. 765, 773 n.4, 120 S.Ct. 1858, 146 L.Ed.2d 836 (2000) (emphasis omitted).

Special procedures apply when a relator brings an FCA action; these procedures afford the government the opportunity to intervene and assume primary control over the litigation. A relator who initiates an FCA action must file her complaint under seal and serve it only on the United States. 31 U.S.C. § 3730(b)(2). While the lawsuit remains under seal, the United States has the opportunity to investigate and decide whether to intervene as a party.[4] *Id.* During this period, the United States may serve a civil investigative demand upon any person believed to be in possession of documents or information relevant to an investigation of false claims, requiring that person to produce documents, answer interrogatories, or give oral testimony. *Id.* § 3733(a)(1). In addition, the United States may meet with the relator and her attorney, giving the government an opportunity to ask questions to assess the strengths and weaknesses of the case and the relator a chance to assist the government's investigation.[5]

p.1087 If the United States decides to intervene, the government acquires "primary responsibility for prosecuting the action," although the relator remains a party. *Id.* § 3730(c)(1). In contrast, if the United States declines to intervene, the relator may proceed with the action alone on behalf of the government, but the United States is not a party to the action. *Id.* § 3730(c)(3).

Although the United States is not a party to a non-intervened case, it nevertheless retains a significant role in the litigation. The government may request to be served with copies of all pleadings and deposition transcripts, seek to stay discovery if it "would interfere with the Government's investigation or prosecution of a criminal or civil matter arising out of the same facts," and veto a relator's decision to voluntarily dismiss the action. *Id.* § 3730(b)(1), (c)(3), (c)(4). Additionally, the court may permit the government to intervene later "upon a showing of good cause." *Id.* § 3730(c)(3).

Any recovery obtained from a defendant in an FCA *qui tam* action belongs to the United States, regardless of whether the government has intervened. The relator is entitled to a portion of the recovery, however. *Id.* § 3730(d). Because the relator receives a share of the government's proceeds, he "is essentially a self-appointed private attorney general, and his recovery is analogous to a lawyer's contingent fee." *United States ex rel. Milam v. Univ. of Tex. M.D. Anderson Cancer Ctr.,* 961 F.2d 46, 49 (4th Cir. 1992); *see Cook Cty. v. United States ex rel. Chandler,* 538 U.S. 119, 122, 123 S.Ct. 1239, 155 L.Ed.2d 247 (2003) (explaining that a relator sues in the name of the government "with the hope of sharing in any recovery"). By allowing a relator to bring a *qui tam* action and share in the government's recovery, the FCA creates an economic incentive to encourage "citizens to come forward with knowledge of frauds against the government." *Milam,* 961 F.2d at 49.

484   *Qui Tam Actions*

The size of the relator's share depends upon whether the United States intervenes. In an intervened case, the relator usually is entitled to between 15 and 25 percent of the proceeds, as well as reasonable expenses, attorney's fees, and costs. 31 U.S.C. § 3730(d)(1). In a non-intervened case, the relator's share usually is greater: between 25 and 30 percent of the proceeds, as well as reasonable expenses, attorney's fees, and costs. *Id.* § 3730(d)(2).

Even though the relator receives a smaller share in an intervened case, relators generally try to persuade the United States to intervene because the government's intervention makes it far more likely that there will be a recovery. When the United States elects to intervene, about 90 percent of the time the case generates a recovery, either through settlement or a final judgment. But only about 10 percent of non-intervened cases result in recovery.[6] p.1088 *See* David Freeman Engstrom, *Public Regulation of Private Enforcement: Empirical Analysis of DOJ Oversight of Qui Tam Litigation Under the False Claims Act,* 107 Nw. U. L. Rev. 1689, 1720-21 (2013). Indeed, when the government declines to intervene, more than 50 percent of the time the relator decides not to proceed and voluntarily dismisses the action. *See id.* at 1717-18.

IV. ANALYSIS

With this general background in mind, we now turn to the issue in this case: whether it is apparent from the face of Hunt's complaint that his FCA claim is time barred. To answer this question, we must interpret the FCA's statute of limitations provision, which creates two limitations periods that potentially apply:

(b) A civil action under section 3730 may not be brought —

(1) more than 6 years after the date on which the violation of section 3729 is committed, or

(2) more than 3 years after the date when facts material to the right of action are known or reasonably should have been known by the official of the United States charged with responsibility to act in the circumstances, but in no event more than 10 years after the date on which the violation is committed,

whichever occurs last.

31 U.S.C. § 3731(b). Because it *is* apparent from the face of Hunt's complaint that he failed to file his action within the six year limitations period of § 3731(b)(1), this case turns on whether Hunt can avail himself of § 3731(b)(2). To determine whether § 3731(b)(2) applies, we must address whether its limitations period is available when the United States declines to intervene and, if so, whether the limitations period is triggered when the relator knew or should have known facts material to his claim.

A. Section 3731(b)(2) Applies When the United States Declines to Intervene.

The primary question before us is whether Congress intended to allow relators in non-intervened cases to rely on § 3731(b)(2)'s limitations period. We must begin "where courts should always begin the process of legislative interpretation, and where they often should end it as well, which is with the words of the statutory provision."

Harris v. Garner, 216 F.3d 970, 972 (11th Cir. 2000) (en banc). In considering the text, we bear in mind that "[a] provision that may seem ambiguous in isolation is often clarified by the remainder of the statutory scheme." *Koons Buick Pontiac GMC, Inc. v. Nigh,* 543 U.S. 50, 60, 125 S.Ct. 460, 160 L.Ed.2d 389 (2004) (internal quotation marks omitted). We look to "the whole statutory text, considering the purpose and context of the statute, and consulting any precedents or authorities p.1089 that inform the analysis." *Dolan v. U.S. Postal Serv.,* 546 U.S. 481, 486, 126 S.Ct. 1252, 163 L.Ed.2d 1079 (2006). As part of this inquiry, we also consider the canons of statutory construction. *CBS Inc. v. Prime-Time 24 Joint Venture,* 245 F.3d 1217, 1225 (11th Cir. 2001). Legislative history may prove helpful when the statutory language remains ambiguous after considering "the language itself, the specific context in which that language is used, and the broader context of the statute as a whole." *Robinson v. Shell Oil Co.,* 519 U.S. 337, 341, 117 S.Ct. 843, 136 L.Ed.2d 808 (1997).

We conclude that the phrase "civil action under section 3730" in § 3731(b) refers to civil actions brought under § 3730 that have as an element a violation of § 3729, which includes § 3730(b) *qui tam* actions when the government declines to intervene. Section § 3731(b) begins by providing that its limitations periods apply to "[a] civil action under section 3730." 31 U.S.C. § 3731(b). A non-intervened cases is a type of civil action under § 3730. *See id.* § 3730(b)(1) (permitting any person to bring a civil action alleging a violation of § 3729); *id.* § 3730(c)(3) (allowing a relator to continue to conduct a *qui tam* action after the United States declines to intervene). And nothing in § 3731(b)(2) says that its limitations period is unavailable to relators when the government declines to intervene. In the absence of such language, we conclude that the text supports allowing relators in non-intervened cases to rely on § 3731(b)(2)'s limitations period.

To ascertain its meaning, we must, of course, view § 3731(b)(2) in the broader statutory context. Looking to the statutory context, the Supreme Court has recognized that the phrase "[a] civil action under section 3730" did not refer to *all* types of § 3730 civil actions because it excluded retaliation actions brought under § 3730(h). *Graham Cty. Soil & Water Conservation Dist. v. United States ex rel. Wilson,* 545 U.S. 409, 415, 125 S.Ct. 2444, 162 L.Ed.2d 390 (2005).[7] In *Graham County,* the Supreme Court considered whether § 3731(b)(1)'s six year limitations period — which begins to run when the defendant submits a false claim — applied to an employee's § 3730(h) retaliation claim alleging that her employer forced her to resign after she assisted federal officials investigating her employer for submitting false claims to the United States. *Id.* at 413-14, 125 S.Ct. 2444. On its face, § 3731(b) appeared to apply to § 3730(h) retaliation actions, which were a type of civil action under § 3730. *Id.* at 415, 125 S.Ct. 2444. Relying on statutory context, the Court nonetheless concluded that § 3731(b)'s literal text was ambiguous as to whether the phrase "[a] civil action under section 3730" included § 3730(h) retaliation actions. *Id.* at 417, 125 S.Ct. 2444. The Court observed that § 3731(b)(1)'s limitations period was triggered by the defendant's submission of a false claim. *Id.* at 415, 125 S.Ct. 2444. But a plaintiff bringing a retaliation claim under § 3730(h) did not need to allege or prove that the defendant actually submitted a false claim because an employer can be liable for retaliating against an employee p.1090 who assists with an investigation or civil action even if the employer is innocent. *Id.* at 416, 125 S.Ct. 2444. This tension in applying § 3731(b)(1)'s limitation period to retaliation actions led the Court to find the statute ambiguous as to whether "action under section 3730" referred to "all actions under § 3730, or only §§ 3730(a) and (b) actions." *Id.*

The Supreme Court resolved this ambiguity by concluding that § 3731(b)(1)'s limitations period did not apply to retaliation claims under § 3730(h). The Court recognized that Congress generally drafted statutes of limitations to begin to run when a cause of action accrues. *Id.* at 418, 125 S.Ct. 2444. Applying § 3731(b)(1)'s limitations period to an FCA retaliation action would violate this general rule because the limitations period would begin to run when the employer committed the actual or suspected FCA violation, not when it retaliated against the employee. This interpretation could lead to the odd result that a plaintiff's retaliation claim was time barred before the employer took any retaliatory action. *Id.* at 420-21, 125 S.Ct. 2444. To "avoid[] these counterintuitive results," the Court construed "civil action under section 3730" to "mean[] only those civil actions under § 3730 that have as an element a violation of section 3729, that is, §§ 3730(a) and (b) actions." *Id.* at 421-22, 125 S.Ct. 2444 (internal quotation marks omitted).[8] *Graham County* thus made clear that to determine whether § 3731(b)(2) includes *qui tam* actions where the United States declines to intervene, we must consider the text of § 3731(b)(2) in the relevant statutory context. But nothing in *Graham County* directly addressed whether the statutory context shows that § 3731(b)(2)'s limitations period is available only when the government is a party.

Here, the contractors raise several arguments contending that the statutory context and the canons of statutory construction show that Congress intended for § 3731(b)(2) to be unavailable to relators in non-intervened cases. They claim that allowing a relator in a non-intervened action to rely on a limitations period that is triggered by a government official's knowledge would lead to absurd results and render a portion of § 3731(b) superfluous. We reject each of these arguments. The text of § 3731(b)(2), when viewed in context, shows that § 3731(b)(2) is available to relators when the government declines to intervene. But even if we were to conclude that § 3731(b)(2) is ambiguous making it p.1091 appropriate to consider legislative history, as the contractors urge us to do, we still would conclude that § 3731(b)(2) is available to relators when the government declines to intervene.

1. We Reject that Allowing a Relator in a Non-Intervened Case to Rely on § 3731(b)(2)'s Limitations Period Is Absurd.

The contractors' primary argument is that the statutory context shows that § 3731(b)(2) is available only when the United States is a party to the case because the limitations period is triggered by a federal official's knowledge. They argue that Congress must have intended such a limitations period to be available only when the government is a party to the case because to apply a limitations period triggered by a federal official's knowledge when the United States is not a party would create a "bizarre scenario." Parsons' Br. at 12 (quoting *United States ex rel. Sanders v. N. Am. Bus Indus., Inc.,* 546 F.3d 288, 293 (4th Cir. 2008)). Put differently, they argue that reading § 3731(b)(2) to apply to non-intervened actions would lead to an absurd result. Of course, we should refrain from interpreting a statute in a way that "produces a result that is not just unwise but is clearly absurd." *CBS,* 245 F.3d at 1228 (internal quotation marks omitted). But we have cautioned that the absurdity doctrine is "rarely applied" to avoid having "clearly expressed legislative decisions ... be subject to the policy predilections of judges." *Id.* (internal quotation marks omitted).

This case presents no such rare instance when the absurdity doctrine applies. Certainly, it is generally the case that a discovery-based limitations period begins to run when a *party* — the plaintiff — knew or should have known about the fraud or claim. *See, e.g., Merck & Co. v. Reynolds,* 559 U.S. 633, 637, 130 S.Ct. 1784, 176 L.Ed.2d 582 (2010) (recognizing that a securities fraud claim accrued when the plaintiff knew or should have known the facts constituting the violation); *see also* Restatement (Second) of Torts § 899(e) (statute of limitations begins to run when "the injured person has knowledge or reason to know of the facts"). We cannot say that in the unique context of an FCA *qui tam* action,[9] however, it would be absurd to peg a limitations period to a federal official's knowledge unless the United States brings the action or chooses to intervene. We reject the contractors' absurdity argument because even though the United States is not a party to a non-intervened *qui tam* action, the United States remains the real party in interest and retains significant control over the case.

Even in a non-intervened case, the relator brings the suit as the partial assignee of the United States and asserts a claim based on injury suffered by the United States as the victim of the fraud. *United States ex rel. Eisenstein v. City of New York,* 556 U.S. 928, 934-35, 129 S.Ct. 2230, 173 L.Ed.2d 1255 (2009). Importantly, as the victim of the fraud, the United States — not the relator — is entitled to the bulk of the recovery. *See* 31 U.S.C. § 3730(d)(2). Given the government's primary interest in a non-intervened *qui tam* action, Congress carved out for it a formal role, allowing it to intervene at any time upon a showing of good cause, request service of pleadings and deposition transcripts, seek to stay discovery if it "would interfere with the Government's investigation or prosecution of a criminal or civil matter arising out of the same facts," and p.1092 veto a relator's decision to voluntarily dismiss the action. *Id.* § 3730(b)(1), (c)(3), (c)(4). Given this unique role, we cannot say that it would be absurd for Congress to peg the start of the limitations period to the knowledge of a government official even when the United States declines to intervene.

The contractors argue that allowing a relator in a non-intervened case to rely on § 3731(b)(2)'s limitations period conflicts with the Supreme Court's decision in *Eisenstein.* In *Eisenstein,* the relators in a non-intervened case filed a notice of appeal 54 days after the district court entered a final judgment dismissing their claims. 556 U.S. at 930, 129 S.Ct. 2230. Although parties normally have 30 days to file a notice of appeal, the relators argued that they could avail themselves of the 60 day deadline that applies when the United States is a party to the action. *Id.* at 930-31, 129 S.Ct. 2230. The Supreme Court rejected this argument and affirmed the dismissal of the appeal, holding that the United States is not a party to a *qui tam* action when it declines to intervene. *Id.* at 937, 129 S.Ct. 2230. But our decision today in no way relies on the United States being a party to the non-intervened case, and nothing in *Eisenstein* addressed whether the United States' non-party status means that the limitations period in § 3731(b)(2) is unavailable to relators in non-intervened cases.

We recognize that our decision to reject the absurdity doctrine is at odds with the published decisions of two other circuits. *See Sanders,* 546 F.3d at 293 ("Congress intended Section 3731(b)(2) to extend the FCA's default six-year period only in cases in which the government is a party, rather than to produce the bizarre scenario in which the limitations period in a relator's action depends on the knowledge of a non-party to the action."); *United States ex rel. Sikkenga v. Regence Bluecross Blueshield of Utah,* 472 F.3d 702, 726 (10th Cir. 2006) ("Surely, Congress could not have intended to base a statute of limitations on the knowledge of a non-party.").

These cases do not persuade us. They reflexively applied the general rule that a limitations period is triggered by the knowledge of a party. They failed to consider the unique role that the United States plays even in a non-intervened *qui tam* case. In light of this role, we cannot say that it would be absurd or "bizarre" to peg the limitations period to the knowledge of a government official when the government declines to intervene. We disagree that Congress, by specifying that § 3731(b)(2)'s limitations period is triggered by the knowledge of a United States official, necessarily intended that this limitations period be available only in § 3730 civil actions where the United States is a party and not in non-intervened *qui tam* actions.[10] We thus cannot say that the statutory p.1093 context shows that § 3731(b)(2)'s limitations period is unavailable to relators in non-intervened *qui tam* actions.

2. Our Interpretation Does Not Render a Portion of § 3731(b) Superfluous.

The contractors, relying on a canon of construction, next argue that to give meaning to the entirety of § 3731(b), we must construe § 3731(b)(2) to exclude non-intervened cases. Certainly, "a statute ought, upon the whole, to be so construed that, if it can be prevented, no clause, sentence, or word shall be superfluous, void, or insignificant." *TRW Inc. v. Andrews,* 534 U.S. 19, 31, 122 S.Ct. 441, 151 L.Ed.2d 339 (2001) (internal quotation marks omitted). But this canon does not apply when a statutory provision would remain operative under the interpretation in question in at least some situations. *See Black Warrior Riverkeeper, Inc. v. Black Warrior Minerals, Inc.,* 734 F.3d 1297, 1304 (11th Cir. 2013).

The contractors assert that if relators have three years from the date when the government learned of the fraud to file suit under § 3731(b)(2), relators will always delay telling the government about the fraud to increase the damages in the case. Therefore, they say, the limitations period in § 3731(b)(1), which expires six years after the date when the violation occurred, will never apply, rendering the provision meaningless. We disagree. The contractors overlook that other provisions of the FCA create strong incentives to ensure that relators promptly report fraud.

A relator who waits to report a fraud risks recovering nothing or having his relator's share decreased. The relator's claim may be barred if another relator beats him to the courthouse with an FCA claim based on the same facts, 31 U.S.C. § 3730(b)(5), or if the allegations or transactions are publicly disclosed either in a federal hearing where the government was a party or in a news report, unless the relator was the original source of the information, *id.* § 3730(e)(4). And because § 3731(b)(2)'s limitations period begins to run when the relevant government officials learns about the fraud from any source, a relator who delays reporting the fraud to the government also runs the risk that the government will learn about the fraud from another source and thus that § 3731(b)(2)'s three year period will expire before the relator files suit. But even if there were no risk that the government could learn of the fraud from another source, a relator still would have an incentive to report fraud promptly because the court in setting the relator's share may consider whether he "substantially delayed in reporting the fraud or filing the complaint." *United States ex rel. Shea v. Verizon* p.1094 *Commc'ns, Inc.,* 844 F.Supp.2d 78, 89 (D.D.C. 2012).

Looking at the FCA as a whole, we conclude that relators who can rely on the limitations period in § 3731(b)(2) will still have sufficient incentive to report fraud promptly. Because relators will continue to report fraud promptly and under § 3731(b)(2) suit must be filed within three years of the fraud being reported, there will be cases in which § 3731(b)(1)'s six year limitations period will expire later. We thus reject the contractors' argument that our reading of the FCA would render superfluous one of its provisions.

3. To the Extent that Legislative History is Relevant, It Bolsters Our Conclusion.

The contractors argue that the legislative history shows that § 3731(b)(2)'s limitations period is unavailable to a relator when the United States declines to intervene. Assuming that the statutory language, after viewing it in light of the statutory context and the canons of construction, remains ambiguous such that a resort to legislative history is appropriate, *see United States v. Alabama,* 778 F.3d 926, 939 (11th Cir. 2015), we cannot agree that the relevant Congressional records undermine our interpretation of § 3731(b)(2).

Congress added the limitations period in § 3731(b)(2) to the FCA in 1986. False Claims Amendments Act of 1986 ("1986 FCA Amendments"), Pub. L. No. 99-562, 100 Stat. 3153 (1986). The legislative history reveals that one of the broad purposes of the 1986 FCA Amendments was to "encourage more private enforcement suits." S. Rep. No. 99-345 at 23-24 (1986). This purpose is consistent with Congress's historical use of *qui tam* rights of action to create incentives for private individuals to help root out fraud against the government. *See United States ex rel. Williams v. NEC Corp.,* 931 F.2d 1493, 1497 (11th Cir. 1991). Allowing relators to continue to pursue FCA claims even after the government declines to intervene is consistent with the broad underlying purpose of the FCA because it creates the potential for "more fraud [to] be discovered, more litigation [to] be maintained, and more funds [to] flow back into the Treasury." *Milam,* 961 F.2d at 49.

The contractors argue that we should not infer Congressional intent to extend the limitations period for non-intervened cases because in the legislative history for the 1986 FCA Amendments Congress indicated that *qui tam* actions must be brought shortly after the fraud occurred. To support their position, the contractors point to the following portion of the Senate Committee Report, which quotes from the reasoning in a Supreme Court decision:

> [The FCA] is intended to protect the Treasury against the hungry and unscrupulous host that encompasses it on every side, and should be construed accordingly. It was passed upon the theory, based on experience as old as modern civilization, that one of the least expensive and most effective means of preventing frauds on the Treasury is to make the perpetrators of them liable to actions by private persons acting, if you please, under the strong stimulus of personal ill will or the hope of gain.

Prosecutions conducted by such means compare with the ordinary methods as the enterprising privateer does to the slow-going public vessel.

S. Rep. No. 99-345, at 11 (quoting *United States ex rel. Marcus v. Hess,* 317 U.S. 537, 541 n.5, 63 S.Ct. 379, 87 L.Ed. 443 (1943)).

The contractors argue this language shows that Congress allowed relators to bring *qui tam* actions under the FCA because p.1095 relators are able to expose fraud more rapidly than the United States can discover it, from which they infer that Congress intended for a shorter limitations period to apply when the United States was not a party to the case. But nothing in this statement addresses the length of time that a relator should have to bring a *qui tam* action or whether the limitations period should depend on the government's decision to intervene. And so we fail to see how this legislative history supports the contractors' position that a shorter limitations period should apply when the government declines to intervene.

All told, there is little legislative history for § 3731(b)(2). And the few references there are do not directly address the question before us. The contractors point to a floor statement from Senator Charles Grassley and testimony from Assistant Attorney General Richard K. Willard before a House subcommittee. But neither piece of legislative history is particularly helpful.

Senator Grassley said in a floor statement that Congress borrowed the language in § 3731(b)(2) from 28 U.S.C. § 2416, which sets forth the limitations period that generally applies to other actions brought by the United States. *See* 132 Cong. Rec. 20,536 (1986) (statement of Sen. Grassley). Senator Grassley's statement reflects that Congress borrowed the language "facts material to the right of action are known or reasonably should have been known by the official of the United States charged with responsibility to act" from 28 U.S.C. § 2416. *See* 28 U.S.C. § 2416(c); 31 U.S.C. § 3731(b)(2). But we disagree with the inference the contractors draw from this fact: that Congress intended to make the statute of limitations in § 3731(b) available only when the United States was a party.

To understand 28 U.S.C. § 2416, we must also look to § 2415. Section 2415 establishes various limitations periods for certain categories of claims "brought by the United States or an officer or agency thereof," such as contract or tort claims. 28 U.S.C. § 2415(a), (b). Section 2416 tolls the limitations period for the United States to bring such claims when "facts material to the right of action are not known and reasonably could not be known by an official of the United States charged with the responsibility to act in the circumstances." *Id.* § 2416(c). The duplicate language in § 2416 is not what specifies that a limitations period in § 2415 applies only when the United States is a party. Instead, § 2415 itself dictates that the United States must be a party for its limitations period to apply. *See id.* § 2415(a), (b) (stating limitations period applies only to claims "brought by the United States or an officer or agency thereof"). There is no similar language in any FCA provision expressly restricting § 3731(b)(2)'s limitations period to actions where the United States is a party. So we cannot say that by borrowing the description of the trigger for the limitations period from § 2416 Congress evinced an intent that the United States must be a party for the limitations period in § 3731(b)(2) to apply.

Turning to the committee testimony from Assistant Attorney General Willard, he explained that the purpose of § 3731(b)(2)'s limitations period was to give "us a little more flexibility in bringing some cases that otherwise would be barred."[11] The contractors construe Willard's testimony to mean that § 3731(b)(2) was intended to give the government — but p.1096 not relators — more flexibility to bring FCA claims. Certainly, Willard testified that § 3731(b)(2) would extend the time period for the Attorney General to sue under the FCA. But Willard offered nothing about the intended effect of § 3731(b)(2) on *qui tam* actions or, more specifically, whether § 3731(b)(2) was intended to apply to *qui tam* actions when the government declined to intervene. Willard's testimony does not advance the ball for the contractors. *See also Regan v. Wald,* 468 U.S. 222, 237, 104 S.Ct. 3026, 82 L.Ed.2d 171 (1984) (discussing limited usefulness of testimony of witnesses to ascertain meaning of statutory language given the risk that relying on such colloquies "would open the door to the inadvertent, or perhaps even planned, undermining of the language actually voted on by Congress and signed into law by the President"). Because the legislative history does not squarely address whether Congress intended to make § 3731(b)(2)'s limitations period available to relators in non-intervened cases, we cannot agree with the contractors that the legislative history undermines our interpretation.

To wrap up, we conclude that Congress intended for § 3731(b)(2)'s limitations period to be available to relators even when the United States declines to intervene. The statutory text reflects that this limitations period applies to "[a] civil action under section 3730," and nothing in § 3731(b)(2) makes the limitations period unavailable in *qui tam* actions under § 3730 simply because the United States decides not to intervene. The contractors argue that because § 3731(b)(2)'s limitations period is triggered by government knowledge, Congress must have intended for it to apply only when the United States is a party to avoid absurd results. But in the unique context of a non-intervened *qui tam* action, we cannot say that it is absurd to apply a limitations period triggered by government knowledge. And even if the contractors are correct that we may consider legislative history, the legislative history provides no convincing support for their position.

B. The Statute of Limitations in § 3731(b)(2) Depends on the Government's Knowledge, Not the Relator's Knowledge.

Having concluded that the statute of limitations in § 3731(b)(2) is available to a relator in a non-intervened case, we must now address whether that limitations period is triggered by the knowledge of a government official or of the relator. We hold that it is the knowledge of a government official, not the relator, that triggers the limitations period.

Section 3731(b)(2) is clear that the time period begins to run when "the official of the United States charged with responsibility to act in the circumstances" knew or reasonably should have known the material facts about the fraud. 31 U.S.C. § 3731(b)(2). Nothing in the statutory text or broader context suggests that the limitations period is triggered by the relator's knowledge. Given that the language is plain, we cannot rewrite the statute to say that the limitations period is triggered when the *relator* knew or should have known about the facts material to the fraud.

The Ninth Circuit nonetheless adopted such an approach, concluding that the statute of limitations is triggered by the relator's knowledge. *See United States ex rel.*

Hyatt v. Northrop Corp., 91 F.3d 1211, 1217 (9th Cir. 1996). The Ninth Circuit created a new legal fiction that because the relator "sue[d] on behalf of the government," the relator became a government agent and the government official charged with responsibility to act. *Id.* at 1217 n.8. p.1097 Again, we find nothing in the text of § 3731(b)(2) or the statutory context to support this legal fiction. Because the text unambiguously identifies a particular official of the United States as the relevant person whose knowledge causes the limitations period to begin to run, we must reject the Ninth Circuit's interpretation as inconsistent with that text.

Applying our conclusions that § 3731(b)(2) applies in non-intervened cases and is triggered by the knowledge of a government official, not of the relator, we hold that it is not apparent from the face of Hunt's complaint that his FCA claim is untimely. Hunt alleged that the relevant government official learned the material facts on November 30, 2010 when he disclosed the fraudulent scheme to FBI agents, and he filed suit within three years of this disclosure.[12] The district court therefore erred in dismissing his complaint on statute of limitations grounds.

V. CONCLUSION

For the reasons set forth above, we reverse the district court's order dismissing Hunt's FCA claim as time barred and remand the case for further proceedings consistent with this opinion.

REVERSED AND REMANDED.

[*] Honorable Harvey Bartle III, United States District Judge for the Eastern District of Pennsylvania, sitting by designation.

[1] In deciding whether the district court erroneously dismissed the complaint as untimely, we accept as true the well-pleaded allegations in the complaint. *See Ashcroft v. Iqbal,* 556 U.S. 662, 678, 129 S.Ct. 1937, 173 L.Ed.2d 868 (2009); *La Grasta v. First Union Sec., Inc.,* 358 F.3d 840, 845 (11th Cir. 2004). We thus recite the facts as Hunt has alleged them.

[2] The FCA imposes a civil penalty of up to $11,000 for each violation occurring on or before November 2, 2015 and up to $21,563 for each violation occurring after that date. *See* 31 U.S.C. § 3729(a); 28 C.F.R. §§ 85.3(a)(9), 85.5.

[3] The FCA is one of only a handful of federal laws still in effect that may be enforced through a *qui tam* action. *See Vt. Agency of Nat. Res. v. United States ex rel. Stevens,* 529 U.S. 765, 768 n.1, 120 S.Ct. 1858, 146 L.Ed.2d 836 (2000) (identifying four federal statutes that authorize *qui tam* actions).

[4] The United States intervenes in approximately 25 percent of FCA *qui tam* actions. David Freeman Engstrom, *Public Regulation of Private Enforcement: Empirical Analysis of DOJ Oversight of Qui Tam Litigation Under the False Claims Act,* 107 Nw. U. L. Rev. 1689, 1719 (2013).

[5] Relators often provide such assistance while the government is deciding whether to intervene. *See, e.g., United States ex rel. Shea v. Verizon Commc'ns, Inc.,* 844 F.Supp.2d 78, 86-87 (D.D.C. 2012) (explaining that the relator worked closely with the government while the case was under seal by identifying potential witnesses,

proposing categories of documents to be subpoenaed, and making presentations about the merits of the case); *United States ex rel. Rille v. Hewlett-Packard Co.,* 784 F.Supp.2d 1097, 1099 (E.D. Ark. 2011) (discussing actions taken by the relator while the case was under seal including meeting with government lawyers, reviewing documents for the government, and maintaining a database of subpoenaed documents); *United States ex rel. Alderson v. Quorum Health Grp., Inc.,* 171 F.Supp.2d 1323, 1326 (M.D. Fla. 2001) (explaining that while the complaint was under seal the relator was interviewed by the government multiple times, identified categories of documents for the government to subpoena, and reviewed subpoenaed documents for the government); *see also* Robert Fabrikant & Nkechinyem Nwabuzor, *In the Shadow of the False Claims Act: "Outsourcing" the Investigation by Government Counsel to Relator Counsel During the Seal Period,* 83 N.D. L. Rev. 837, 843 (2007) (summarizing the types of support a relator's counsel may give to the government while a complaint is under seal).

[6] To be clear, we do not take the dramatically different success rates for intervened cases and non-intervened cases to mean that if the government declines to intervene, the case necessarily is meritless. The government may decline to intervene based on its evaluation of factors other than the merits of the claim, such as the likely size of the recovery, available agency resources, or whether the relator and his counsel have resources to prosecute the action on their own. *See* Engstrom, *supra,* at 1714. Conversely, the fact that most intervened cases generate a recovery does not necessarily mean that every intervened case has merit. The involvement of the Department of Justice in an intervened case may create a strong incentive for a defendant to settle an FCA claim regardless of its relative merit to avoid things like increased publicity of the fraud because the defendant cannot cast the litigation solely as the product of an overzealous relator; the disadvantages of litigating against the government with its considerable resources and ability to coordinate with officials at the affected agency; or the risk that the defendant may be barred from federal contracting, a sanction that is unavailable in non-intervened cases. *Id.* at 1713.

[7] Section 3730(h) creates a cause of action for an employee, contractor, or agent who "is discharged, demoted, suspended, threatened, harassed, or in any other manner discriminated against in the terms and condition of employment because of lawful acts done by the employee, contractor, agent or associated others in furtherance of an action under this section or other efforts to stop 1 or more violations of this subchapter." 31 U.S.C. § 3730(h)(1). Although the FCA now expressly provides a three year statute of limitations for retaliation claims, *id.* § 3730(h)(3), this provision was added after the Supreme Court decided *Graham County. See* Dodd-Frank Wall Street Reform and Consumer Protection Act, Pub. L. No. 111-203, § 1079A(c), 124 Stat. 1376, 2079 (2010).

[8] The Court also considered that Congress used the phrase "action under section 3730" imprecisely throughout § 3731 "to refer only to a subset of § 3730 actions." *Graham Cty.,* 545 U.S. at 417-18, 125 S.Ct. 2444. In § 3731(d), Congress used similar language to provide that "[i]n any action brought under section 3730, the United States shall be required to prove all essential elements of the cause of action, including damages, by a preponderance of the evidence." 31 U.S.C. § 3731(d). Despite the broad reference to civil actions under § 3730, the Court explained that Congress intended for this provision to apply only to § 3730(a) actions brought by

the United States or § 3730(b) actions when the United States intervened because Congress could not have intended for the United States to bear the burden of proof when it was not participating in the action. *Graham Cty.*, 545 U.S. at 417-18, 125 S.Ct. 2444.

Acknowledging that imprecision permeates § 3731, the Court in *Graham County* accepted that the similar language in § 3731(b) and § 3731(d) referred to different categories of § 3730 actions. That is, the phrase "[a] civil action under section 3730" as used in § 3731(b) referred to any civil action that has an element a violation of § 3729, including non-intervened actions brought under § 3730(b), while the phrase "action brought under section 3730" as used in § 3731(d) referred only to those civil actions where the United States was a party. *Id.* at 421-22, 125 S.Ct. 2444.

[9] *See Stevens*, 529 U.S. at 768 n.1, 120 S.Ct. 1858 (explaining that the FCA is one of only four statutes authorizing *qui tam* action that remain in effect).

[10] In *Sanders*, the Fourth Circuit also asserted that allowing a relator in a non-intervened case to rely on the limitations period in § 3731(b)(2) would place an inappropriate burden on the defendant and government by expanding the litigation into the issue of government knowledge. 546 F.3d at 295. The Fourth Circuit was concerned about allowing discovery into government knowledge when the United States declined to intervene as a party. *Id.* We agree that allowing a relator to rely on § 3731(b)(2)'s limitations period means that the parties may engage in discovery about government knowledge, but we think the Fourth Circuit's concerns about the burden associated with this discovery were overstated because the court ignored that government knowledge may be relevant to the merits of the relator's FCA claim even in a non-intervened *qui tam* action.

To prevail on the merits of her FCA claim, the relator must show, among other things, that the defendant made a misstatement that was material and that the defendant "knowingly" submitted a false claim. *See* 31 U.S.C. § 3729(a)(1); *Universal Health*, 136 S.Ct. at 2003. A defendant may rely on evidence of government knowledge to negate both of these elements. Government knowledge may disprove materiality because "if the Government pays a particular claim in full despite its actual knowledge that certain requirements were violated, that is very strong evidence that those requirements are not material." *Universal Health*, 136 S.Ct. at 2003. Evidence that the government knew the relevant facts at the time that the defendant submitted its claim may also show that the defendant understood its conduct to be lawful. *See Hooper v. Lockheed Martin Corp.*, 688 F.3d 1037, 1051 (9th Cir. 2012) ("[T]he extent and the nature of government knowledge may show that the defendant did not 'knowingly' submit a false claim and so did not have the intent required by the ... FCA." (internal quotation marks omitted)); *United States ex rel. Becker v. Westinghouse Savannah River Co.*, 305 F.3d 284, 289 (4th Cir. 2002) ("[T]he government's knowledge of the facts underlying an allegedly false record or statement can negate the scienter required for an FCA violation.").

[11] False Claims Act Amendments: Hearings Before the Subcomm. on Admin. Law & Governmental Relations of the Comm. on the Judiciary H.R., *99th Cong. 159 (1986) (statement of Richard K. Willard, Assistant Att'y Gen.).*

[12] To be clear, if facts developed in discovery show that the relevant government official knew or should have known the material facts about the fraud

at an earlier date, Hunt's claims could still be barred by the statute of limitations. We hold only that at the motion to dismiss stage it was error to dismiss the complaint on statute of limitations grounds.

906 F.3d 1223 (2018)

UNITED STATES of America, Plaintiff - Appellee,
Lori L. Carver, Interested Party - Appellant,
v.
John Patrick COUCH, M.D., Xiulu Ruan, M.D., Defendants - Appellees.

No. 17-13402.

United States Court of Appeals, Eleventh Circuit.

October 17, 2018.

US v. Couch, 906 F. 3d 1223 (11th Cir. 2018)

Appeal from the United States District Court for the Southern District of Alabama, D.C. Docket No. 1:15-cr-00088-CG-B-1.

Christopher John Bodnar, Deborah A. Griffin, Adam W. Overstreet, U.S. Attorney Service — Southern District of Alabama, U.S. Attorney's Office, Mobile, AL, Steven Butler, U.S. Attorney's Office, Pensacola, FL, William Ernest Havemann, U.S. Department of Justice, Civil Rights Division, Appellate Section, Washington, DC, Charles W. Scarborough, U.S. Attorney General's Office, Washington, DC, for Plaintiff - Appellee.

Jeffrey Paul Doss, Brandon K. Essig, Robert Jackson Sewell, Jackson Roger Sharman, III, Benjamin Sanders Willson, Lightfoot Franklin & White, LLC, Birmingham, AL, Arthur T. Powell, III, Arthur T Powell III, PC, Mobile, AL, for Defendant - Appellee JOHN PATRICK COUCH.

Gordon G. Armstrong, III, Gordon G. Armstrong, III, PC, Mobile, AL, Jason Darley, Jason Darley Law Office, Mobile, AL, Steve Martinie, Steve Martinie Law Office, Whitefish Bay, WI, Page Anthony Pate, Pate & Johnson, LLC, Atlanta, GA, for Defendant - Appellee XIULU RUAN.

Peter Scott Mackey, Peter F. Burns, William M. Cunningham, Jr., Troy Thomas Schwant, Burns Cunningham & Mackey, PC, Mobile, AL, Richard Hamner Holston, Freman & Kaoui, LLC, Mobile, AL, Gregory Vaughan, Holston, Vaughan & Rosenthal, LLC, Mobile, AL, for Interested Party - Appellant LORI L. CARVER.

Before WILLIAM PRYOR, MARTIN, and BALDOCK,[*] Circuit Judges.

p.1224 MARTIN, Circuit Judge:

When a private person brings a False Claims Act suit — known as a qui tam action — the government may choose to intervene and take over the action. 31 U.S.C. § 3730(b)(2). It may also choose to pursue "any alternate remedy available." Id. § 3730(c)(5). If it pursues an "alternate remedy," the False Claims Act gives the qui tam plaintiff the "same rights" in the "alternate" proceeding as she would have had if the qui tam action "had continued." Id. Presented here is the question of whether this statute allows a qui tam plaintiff to intervene in criminal forfeiture proceedings when the government chooses to prosecute fraud rather than to intervene in the qui tam plaintiff's action.

Even if the False Claims Act could be read to allow intervention, the statutes p.1225 governing criminal forfeiture specifically bar it, with exceptions that do not apply here. We conclude that the criminal forfeiture statutes control, and we agree with the District Court's denial of Lori Carver's motion to intervene for that reason.

Our Circuit precedent does not permit us to affirm, however. On appeal of denial of a motion to intervene, our precedent provides for "provisional jurisdiction" to determine whether the District Court properly denied intervention. EEOC v. E. Airlines, Inc., 736 F.2d 635, 637 (11th Cir. 1984). If, as here, denial was proper, "jurisdiction evaporates because the proper denial of leave to intervene is not a final decision." Id. For the reasons that follow, we will therefore dismiss this appeal for lack of jurisdiction.

I. FALSE CLAIMS ACT BACKGROUND

The False Claims Act imposes civil liability on any person who "knowingly presents... a false or fraudulent claim for payment or approval" to the federal government. 31 U.S.C. § 3729(a). It allows the Attorney General to sue for violations. Id. § 3730(a). A private person, called a relator, may bring a False Claims Act action "in the name of the Government," which is known as a qui tam action. Id. § 3730(b)(1). The government may intervene to take over a qui tam action from the relator, id. § 3730(b)(2), but the relator "shall have the right to conduct the action" if the government opts not to intervene, id. § 3730(b)(4), (c)(3). Most of the recovery in a qui tam action goes to the government, to remedy the fraud. See id. § 3730(d). But whether the government intervenes or not, a relator in a successful qui tam action is typically entitled to a share of the recovery. Id. This incentivizes people to come forward from the private sector with evidence of fraud perpetrated on the government. See United States ex rel. Williams v. NEC Corp., 931 F.2d 1493, 1496-97 (11th Cir. 1991).

The government has options other than intervention when a private person brings a qui tam action. The False Claims Act expressly allows the government to pursue remedies besides the qui tam action: "[T]he Government may elect to pursue its claim through any alternate remedy available to the Government, including any administrative proceeding to determine a civil money penalty." 31 U.S.C. § 3730(c)(5). If the government opts for an "alternate remedy," the False Claims Act gives the relator "the same rights in such proceeding as such person would have had if the action had continued under this section." Id. We will call this the alternate-remedy provision.

With this statutory background in mind, we turn to the facts of this case.

II. FACTUAL AND PROCEDURAL BACKGROUND

Lori Carver worked at Physicians Pain Specialists of Alabama, P.C., a pain management clinic in Mobile, Alabama. Two doctors, John Patrick Couch and Xiulu Ruan, ran the clinic. Ms. Carver discovered Dr. Couch and Dr. Ruan submitted fraudulent claims for payment to federal healthcare programs. She took this information to the U.S. Attorney's office, which encouraged her to bring a qui tam action against the clinic and doctors.

Ms. Carver brought the suggested qui tam action in 2013. See Dkt. No. 1, United States ex rel. Carver v. Physician Pain Specialists of Ala., P.C., Case No. 1:13cv392-JB-N (S.D. Ala. Aug. 1, 2013). That case remains pending. See Dkt. No. 208, Carver, Case No. 1:13cv392-JB-N (setting pretrial conference for January 2019). She is litigating it herself, since the government chose not to intervene. Dkt. No. 24, Carver, Case No. 1:13cv392-JB-N p.1226 (notice of non-intervention); see 31 U.S.C. § 3730(b), (c)(3).

The government did not disregard Ms. Carver's allegations, however. With Ms. Carver's information, the government began investigating Dr. Couch and Dr. Ruan. In April 2015, almost two years after Ms. Carver brought her qui tam action, the government criminally charged both doctors with conspiracy to distribute controlled substances and conspiracy to commit healthcare fraud. The charges in the indictment partially overlapped with the allegations in Ms. Carver's qui tam complaint.

After further investigation, the government issued a superseding indictment in October 2015 and a second superseding indictment in April 2016. The first superseding indictment added new defendants (who later pled guilty) and new charges: racketeering, Anti-Kickback Statute violations, wire fraud, and drug distribution offenses. The second superseding indictment further fleshed out the factual basis for the charges. The superseding indictments, like the first, also partially overlapped with the allegations in Ms. Carver's qui tam action. However, the indictments also included charges based on unlawful prescribing practices, which were not alleged in the initial qui tam complaint. All three indictments included forfeiture counts.

The criminal case went to trial, and the jury convicted Dr. Couch of all charges, and Dr. Ruan of all but one. The District Court promptly entered a preliminary forfeiture order.

Ms. Carver moved to intervene in the forfeiture proceedings, asserting a right to some of the forfeited assets. She primarily argued the alternate-remedy provision permits her to intervene to claim the share of the assets she would have been entitled to if the government had intervened in her qui tam action. In the alternative, she petitioned to assert an interest in the forfeited property under 21 U.S.C. § 853 and Federal Rule of Criminal Procedure 32.2. This statute and rule permit a third party to assert an interest in criminally forfeited property if the third party either had a legal interest in the property prior to the crime or is a bona fide purchaser for value of the property. See 31 U.S.C. § 853(n); Fed. R. Crim. P. 32.2. Ms. Carver has conceded she meets neither criterion.

The government argued Ms. Carver has no right to intervene under the alternate-remedy provision because her qui tam case remains pending — meaning she has not yet established a right to a relator's share. It further asserted the False Claims Act does not permit intervention in criminal cases.

The district court denied Ms. Carver's motion to intervene. It ruled that the alternate-remedy provision does not permit intervention in criminal cases. It also ruled Ms. Carver had no right to intervene under 21 U.S.C. § 853(n) and Rule 32.2. This appeal followed.

III. STANDING

Before getting to the merits, we stop to address Ms. Carver's standing to intervene, which the government challenges. We are aware of the recent ruling of the Ninth Circuit that a qui tam plaintiff lacked standing to intervene in criminal forfeiture proceedings. See United States v. Van Dyck, 866 F.3d 1130, 1133-34 (9th Cir. 2017). We do not join in the rationale of our sister Circuit. Rather, we conclude Ms. Carver does have standing to assert that the alternate-remedy provision gives her a right to intervene in criminal forfeiture proceedings so as to claim an interest in the forfeited property.

Ms. Carver asserts a statutory procedural right — specifically, a right under the alternate-remedy provision to have her p.1227 relator's share adjudicated in the criminal forfeiture proceeding. A "person who has been accorded a procedural right [by statute] to protect his concrete interests can assert that right." Lujan v. Defs. of Wildlife, 504 U.S. 555, 572 n.7, 112 S.Ct. 2130, 2142 n.7, 119 L.Ed.2d 351 (1992) (emphasis added); see also Spokeo, Inc. v. Robins, 578 U.S. ___, 136 S.Ct. 1540, 1549-50, 194 L.Ed.2d 635 (2016) (discussing standing in context of statutory procedural rights). Ms. Carver asserts an interest in property forfeited to the government. This Court has said a party claiming an interest in such property has suffered a concrete injury. See, e.g., Via Mat Int'l S. Am. Ltd. v. United States, 446 F.3d 1258, 1262-63 (11th Cir. 2006). Ms. Carver reads the alternate-remedy provision to create a procedure for her to protect this concrete interest. We have jurisdiction to decide whether her reading is correct.

We are not persuaded by the government's contention that Ms. Carver's property interest is so "speculative" as to deprive us of jurisdiction. It is true that no court has yet adjudicated whether she is entitled to a relator's share. Yet if this were enough to deprive us of jurisdiction, no person claiming a property interest would ever get into federal court. Federal courts resolve property disputes every day. Indeed, criminal forfeiture courts routinely "determine whether any third parties have an interest in the forfeited property." United States v. Davenport, 668 F.3d 1316, 1320 (11th Cir. 2012) (emphasis added). That is, courts adjudicate third-party property interests, subject to the limitations set forth in the criminal forfeiture statutes. We have never doubted that courts have jurisdiction to adjudicate these interests, and this case raises no new doubts on the issue.

Finally, the general principle that private parties lack standing to intervene in criminal proceedings has no application here. See Linda R.S. v. Richard D., 410 U.S. 614, 619, 93 S.Ct. 1146, 1149, 35 L.Ed.2d 536 (1973); United States v. Alcatel-Lucent France, SA, 688 F.3d 1301, 1307 (11th Cir. 2012) (per curiam) (holding a third party lacked standing to appeal a sentence). Linda R.S. concerned Texas's discriminatory application of a statute criminalizing the refusal to provide child support, where Texas prosecuted only parents of legitimate children. 410 U.S. at 615, 93 S.Ct. at 1147. The mother of an illegitimate child sued to have her child's father prosecuted. Id. at 614-15, 93 S.Ct. at 1147. The Supreme Court held she had no interest in the enforcement of Texas's criminal laws and thus lacked standing. Id. at 619, 93 S.Ct. at 1149. In Alcatel-Lucent, our Court held an alleged victim of a crime had no standing to appeal a sentence that did not include a restitution award. 688 F.3d at 1306-07. Ms. Caver's case is distinguishable from Linda R.S. and from Alcatel-Lucent. Ms.

Carver's motion to intervene in a forfeiture proceeding to enforce an alleged property interest is materially different from an attempt to compel a criminal prosecution or alter a sentence.

Thus, we have jurisdiction to decide whether the alternate-remedy provision confers a procedural right on Ms. Carver to have her relator's share adjudicated in the forfeiture proceeding.

IV. INTERPRETING THE ALTERNATE-REMEDY PROVISION

That brings us to the merits of whether the alternate-remedy provision allows qui tam plaintiffs like Ms. Carver to intervene in criminal forfeiture proceedings. As relevant here, the alternate remedy provision reads:

> [T]he Government may elect to pursue its claim through any alternate remedy available to the Government, including p.1228 any administrative proceeding to determine a civil money penalty. If any such alternate remedy is pursued in another proceeding, the person initiating the [qui tam] action shall have the same rights in such proceeding as such person would have had if the [qui tam] action had continued under this section.

31 U.S.C. § 3730(c)(5).

Whether a criminal fraud prosecution is an "alternate remedy" is an open question.[1] See Van Dyck, 866 F.3d at 1135; see also United States ex rel. Babalola v. Sharma, 746 F.3d 157, 160-63 (5th Cir. 2014) (concluding a criminal fraud prosecution brought before a qui tam action was not an alternate remedy). Insofar as Ms. Carver asks us to read the alternate-remedy provision to allow her to intervene in the criminal forfeiture proceedings, we will interpret the alternate-remedy provision by reference to the "commonplace of statutory construction that the specific governs the general." NLRB v. SW Gen., Inc., 580 U.S. ___, 137 S.Ct. 929, 941, 197 L.Ed.2d 263 (2017) (quotation marks omitted); see also Morton v. Mancari, 417 U.S. 535, 550-51, 94 S.Ct. 2474, 2483, 41 L.Ed.2d 290 (1974) ("When there is no clear intention otherwise, a specific statute will not be controlled or nullified by a general one, regardless of priority of enactment.").

Three criminal forfeiture statutes apply in this case, and each expressly bars third parties from intervening in forfeiture proceedings to claim an interest in property subject to forfeiture. See 18 U.S.C. § 982(b)(1) (incorporating forfeiture procedures from 21 U.S.C. § 853); 18 U.S.C. § 1963(i); 21 U.S.C. § 853(k); see also Van Dyck, 866 F.3d at 1133 (noting that 21 U.S.C. § 853 "imposes a general bar on parties intervening in the criminal case"). Each of the three statutes has exceptions to allow third parties to petition a court for the forfeited property if they either had a legal right to the property before the defendant committed the offense or are bona fide purchasers for value. See 18 U.S.C. § 1963(*l*); 21 U.S.C. § 853(n); see also 18 U.S.C. § 982(b)(1) (incorporating forfeiture procedures from 21 U.S.C. § 853). But Ms. Carver has conceded neither of these exceptions applies to her. These criminal forfeiture statutes speak to the precise issue raised in this appeal, and they make plain that Ms. Carver has no right to intervene.

In contrast to the precision of the forfeiture statutes, the alternate-remedy provision does not expressly provide a right of intervention in an "alternate proceeding." Neither does it define "alternate remedy" to include criminal fraud prosecutions. The specific bar on intervention in the criminal forfeiture provisions controls our interpretation of the alternate-remedy provision's general terms here. That being the case, we need not pass on whether the alternate-remedy provision would entitle qui tam plaintiffs to intervene in other "alternate remedy" proceedings.

A final word. Our ruling will not disable Ms. Carver from getting her relator's share. The government assured us in its brief that a ruling against intervention "will not necessarily prevent a future recovery." It continued:

> Where a defendant is found civilly liable for damages in a False Claims Act suit after being found criminally liable for the same fraud, the defendant may deduct restitution paid to the United States in the criminal proceedings as a credit against the False Claims Act damages award. In such circumstances, a qualified relator is entitled to a share of the full amount of the damages p.1229 award, including restitution previously paid.

We understand this to mean a relator is entitled to a share of the forfeited property to the extent the qui tam defendant can deduct any forfeiture from the qui tam award. It appears the government gave the Ninth Circuit the same assurance in Van Dyck. See 866 F.3d at 1135 n.3. We expect the government will honor it.

V. CONCLUSION

The District Court properly denied Ms. Carver's motion to intervene. Under this Circuit's "anomalous rule," our jurisdiction "evaporates" with this conclusion "because the proper denial of leave to intervene is not a final decision." E. Airlines, Inc., 736 F.2d at 637. We therefore DISMISS this appeal for lack of jurisdiction.

[*] Honorable Bobby R. Baldock, Senior United States Circuit Judge for the Tenth Circuit, sitting by designation.

[1] The question has divided federal District Courts. Compare United States v. Kurlander, 24 F.Supp.3d 417, 424 (D.N.J. 2014), with United States v. Bisig, Case No. 100cv335JDTWTL, 2005 WL 3532554, at *2-6 (S.D. Ind. Dec. 21, 2005).

880 F.3d 1302 (2018)

Philip MARSTELLER, for the use and benefit of the United States of America, Robert Swisher, for the use and benefit of the United States of America, Plaintiffs-Appellants,
v.
Lynn TILTON, Patriarch Partners, LLC, MD Helicopters, Inc., Norbert Vergez, Defendants-Appellees.

No. 16-11997.

United States Court of Appeals, Eleventh Circuit.

January 26, 2018.

Marsteller v. Tilton, 880 F. 3d 1302 (11th Cir. 2018)

Appeal from the United States District Court for the Northern District of Alabama, D.C. Docket No. 5:13-cv-00830-AKK.

Phillip Eugene Benson, Warren-Benson Law Group, MINNETONKA, MN, Lisa Rosano, Phillip Paul Weidner & Associates, ANCHORAGE, AK, for Plaintiffs-Appellants.

Christopher Nicholas Manning, Alexis A. Lien, Edward Charles Reddington, Kristin Ann Shapiro, U.S. House of Representatives, Office of General Counsel, WASHINGTON, DC, Anthony Aaron Joseph, Ralph Harrison Smith, III, Maynard Cooper & Gale, PC, BIRMINGHAM, AL, for Defendants-Appellees LYNN TILTON, PATRIARCH PARTNERS, LLC, MD HELICOPTERS, INC.

Anne M. Chapman, Lee Stein, Anna H. Finn, Mitchell Stein Carey, PC, PHOENIX, AZ, Stephanie Fleischman Cherny, SCOTTSDALE, AZ, for Defendant-Appellee NORBERT VERGEZ.

Benjamin M. Shultz, U.S. Attorney General's Office, WASHINGTON, DC, Amicus Curiae for UNITED STATES OF AMERICA.

Before WILLIAM PRYOR, JORDAN, and RIPPLE,[*] Circuit Judges.

p.1304 RIPPLE, Circuit Judge:

Relators Philip Marsteller and Robert Swisher brought this action against their former employer, MD Helicopters ("MD"), and codefendants Patriarch Partners ("Patriarch"), Lynn Tilton, and Colonel Norbert Vergez, under the *qui tam* provision of the False Claims Act ("FCA" or "Act"), 31 U.S.C. §§ 3729-30.[1] The allegations of the complaint concern a series of contracts between the United States Army ("the Army") and MD for the purchase and support of military helicopters. The complaint alleges that the defendants misled the Government by providing material false or incomplete information at two points in the transactional relationship, MD's pre-contract representations to the Government to enter the contracts and MD's submission of claims for payment. The complaint also describes other improprieties between Col. Vergez, then a representative of the Army, and the remaining defendants. These alleged improprieties included gifts and an offer of prospective employment.

In the district court, the defendants moved under Federal Rules of Civil Procedure 12(b)(6) and 9(b) for dismissal for failure to state a claim. They asserted that the complaint failed the specificity requirements applicable to allegations of fraud and that, in any event, the claims did not adequately state a case for liability. The district court granted the motion. It concluded that the complaint failed to establish liability under the implied certification theory, because the relators had not alleged adequately that a defendant had violated an express condition of payment or a material contractual requirement. The district court also concluded that the relators did not plead a fraud in the inducement theory, but that, if they had, it would have failed for the same reasons as the implied certification theory.

The relators have appealed. During the pendency of this appeal, the Supreme Court has examined the implied certification theory in *Universal Health Services, Inc. v. United States ex rel. Escobar,* ___ U.S. ___, 136 S.Ct. 1989, 195 L.Ed.2d 348 (2016). We conclude that the district court must revisit whether the relators alleged facts sufficient to support a theory of implied certification as articulated in *Escobar.* We also conclude that the complaint did plead fraud in the inducement, and we therefore remand so that the district court can reexamine the allegations relating to that theory.

Accordingly, we vacate the judgment of the district court and remand for further proceedings consistent with this opinion.

I

BACKGROUND

A.

The allegations of the complaint concern a series of specific contracts between MD, an Arizona corporation that manufacturers high-performance helicopters, and the Army. The relators, Mr. Marsteller and Mr. Swisher, are the former Director of Sales and Marketing and the former Director of Military Business Development, respectively, for MD. Both are also Army veterans; indeed, Mr. Swisher remains a Major in the Army Individual Ready Reserve. At all times relevant to this action, Ms. Tilton has been CEO of MD and of Patriarch. Patriarch, which was founded and is wholly owned by Ms. Tilton, is a debt and equity investment and management p.1305 company and performs services for MD.

From 2010 to 2012, Col. Vergez was a project manager at the Army's Non-Standard Rotary Wing Aircraft Office ("NSRWA") in Huntsville, Alabama. NSRWA is responsible for the procurement and support of non-standard rotorcraft, including procurement for the foreign military sales program ("FMS") of the Department of Defense. In his role at NSRWA, Col. Vergez was personally and substantially involved in issuing, selecting, negotiating, pricing, and awarding FMS contracts.

The core of the complaint addresses five contracts between MD and the Army in 2011 and 2012. Under these agreements MD provided: (1) six helicopters to the Afghan Air Force, (2) logistical support to the Afghan Air Force, (3) three helicopters to the El Salvador Air Force, (4) two helicopters to the Government of Costa Rica, and (5) twelve helicopters to the Saudi Arabian National Guard. The forty-five-page complaint describes the interactions between MD and NSRWA on each of these bids and contracts. In describing several of the bid processes, the complaint alleges that the Army requested pricing data, presumably to establish the commercial reasonableness of the price proposed in MD's bid. The complaint alleges that MD cherry-picked the highest priced prior sales and omitted lower-dollar sales. With respect to one such contract, for example, the complaint asserts that, in response to the Army's request for a sales history,

> MD only provided the Army information regarding the October 11, 2011 sale of an MD 500E to the Columbus, Ohio Police Department for the base price of $1,802,282, but did not disclose any other prior sales, including the May 20, 2011 sale of a new MD 500E helicopter to Fuchs Helikopter for the base price of $1,550,000. The Army relied on MD's incomplete disclosure and was deprived of its ability to effectively negotiate a reasonable and lower price which caused the agreed base price for each aircraft to be higher than it would have been if MD had fully complied with the Army's request for pricing data.[2]

With respect to another contract for helicopters for the Saudi Arabian National Guard, the complaint alleges that MD's Chief Operations Officer sent a draft bid to Ms. Tilton that included a price of $2,178,000 and noted that the base price for the aircraft was $2,150,000.[3] In replying to the email, Ms. Tilton asked, "Why is this not Army pricing?"[4] The COO then recommended raising the bid to $2,300,000, and Ms. Tilton immediately approved it. Mr. Marsteller, one of the relators in this action, alerted Ben Weiser, an executive vice president at MD, that he believed that the pricing was "criminal."[5] Weiser then contacted Ms. Tilton and asked her to "reconsider" the pricing, given that it was $150,000 more than the commercial list price that MD had published two-and-a-half months earlier.[6] Ms. Tilton declined to lower the price, explaining that her decision was "not about the money but about consistency with the Army."[7]

The complaint also contains allegations about Col. Vergez's relationship with MD and his dealings with Ms. Tilton. According to the allegations, although he previously had met other MD employees, Col. p.1306 Vergez first met Ms. Tilton at an industry event in March 2011, and informed her then that MD had won the bid to supply helicopters to the Afghan military. Ms. Tilton was impressed with Col. Vergez and began grooming him for a future role at MD; she also began traveling regularly to Huntsville to meet with him. She told MD's employees that he "got us this Afghan contract, he has great connections and he will drive our Army business."[8] From shortly after they met through early 2012, Col. Vergez brought Ms. Tilton or other MD employees into numerous conversations with Army personnel, including a meeting at the Pentagon with a Deputy Assistant Secretary of Defense. He also facilitated conversations with foreign officials and with private sector companies for MD. On Col. Vergez's recommendation, MD hired several staff people, including employees of other contractors and other retiring Army officers.[9] On one occasion, he provided Ms. Tilton with competition-sensitive information about forthcoming solicitations and leaked requests from a foreign government to NSRWA.

The complaint also alleges that Col. Vergez anticipated retirement from active service in late 2012. While his actions for MD's benefit were ongoing, Ms. Tilton and Col. Vergez discussed, over the course of approximately a year, his own future employment at MD or at Patriarch. In February 2012, Col. Vergez notified the Army of his disqualification from engaging in procurement activities involving MD because he had an offer of future employment from the company. During the following month, Col. Vergez participated in talks with MD and a private helicopter vendor, toured an MD facility with them, and signed in as a representative of the Army. In summer 2012, Col. Vergez signed a written employment contract with Patriarch to direct, at a salary more than double his military base pay, MD's Civil and Military Programs. Mr. Marsteller had a conversation with an MD manager during this period in which both agreed that the employment relationship was illegal.[10]

Col. Vergez took terminal leave status in November 2012, but remained on active duty until May 2013. In December 2012, during a plant-wide meeting, Ms. Tilton introduced him to MD employees as "a very special person who had been very influential in MD's receipt of Army contracts."[11] On February 1, 2013, the Colonel assumed a position as head of all of MD's programs, reporting directly to the COO, Schopfer. An internal organizational chart disclosed this arrangement, but to disguise the relationship, Col. Vergez was, on paper, a Patriarch employee with a Patriarch phone and email and receiving a Patriarch salary. In April 2013, Col. Vergez told one of the relators, Mr. Swisher, then an MD employee, that all military submissions were to go through him first. This directive provoked Mr. Swisher to resign over the improper relationship.[12]

p.1307 In its prayer for relief, the complaint also specifically alleges that, in submitting a bid and later in submitting invoices for payment, MD certified that it had complied with certain requirements applicable to government contractors, but that the company had no intention of complying with these requirements. Several of the counts also assert that, through lack of candor regarding both ethics and price disclosure requirements, MD deprived the Army of its ability to negotiate a reasonable price and, consequently, the Army agreed to terms it otherwise would not have.

B.

In 2013, relators brought this *qui tam* action in the Northern District of Alabama. The United States declined to intervene. The defendants filed a motion to dismiss, and, prior to a ruling on that motion, the relators filed an amended complaint. The amended complaint sets forth the facts as we have just described them. It then set forth six claims for relief: five FCA claims, one for each of the contracts, and one additional conspiracy claim. The relators claimed that the defendants had not complied, nor intended to comply, with the Contractor Code of Business Ethics and Conduct ("Contractor Code of Ethics"), see 48 C.F.R. § 52.203-13, or with the Truth in Negotiations Act, 10 U.S.C. § 2306a. They also alleged that the defendants' implicit promise of compliance had influenced the Government's initial decision to enter into the contracts and its later decision to pay out claims. The Defendants again moved to dismiss.

In ruling on the motion to dismiss the first amended complaint, the district court had to rule on the viability and possible scope of the implied certification theory. Under this theory, a party "impliedly certifies compliance with underlying contractual or statutory duties when submitting claims to the government" such that "[a] violation of those duties thus renders the claims false for purposes of the FCA." *United States ex rel. Osheroff v. Humana, Inc.,* 776 F.3d 805, 808 n.1 (11th Cir. 2015). In undertaking this task, the district court faced a daunting legal landscape. Our published cases "express[ed] no opinion as to the viability" of the implied certification theory. *Id.* To compound the district court's dilemma, our sister circuits disagreed on the validity and scope of the implied certification theory. The Seventh Circuit had rejected the theory entirely. *See United States v. Sanford-Brown, Ltd.,* 788 F.3d 696, 711-12 (7th Cir. 2015), *vacated sub nom. United States ex rel. Nelson v. Sanford-Brown, Ltd.,* ___ U.S. ___, 136 S.Ct. 2506, 195 L.Ed.2d 836 (2016) (remanding for reconsideration in light of *Escobar*), *aff'd,* 840 F.3d 445 (7th Cir. 2016). Other courts, including the Second Circuit, had accepted it, but had cabined its application to "cases where defendants fail to disclose violations of expressly designated conditions of payment." *Escobar,* 136 S.Ct. at 1999 (citing *Mikes v. Straus,* 274 F.3d 687, 700 (2d Cir. 2001)). Still others, including the District of Columbia Circuit, had p.1308 held "that conditions of payment need not be expressly designated as such to be a basis for False Claims Act liability." *Id.* (citing *United States v. Sci. Applications Int'l Corp.,* 626 F.3d 1257, 1269 (D.C. Cir. 2010)).

Because these pre-*Escobar* cases shed an important cross-light on the district court's decision and therefore aid substantially in our understanding of the course it chose, we pause briefly to review in somewhat more detail the different perspectives that formed the legal landscape at that time. We begin with the Second Circuit's decision in *Mikes v. Straus,* 274 F.3d 687 (2d Cir. 2001). *Mikes* involved an FCA claim by a dismissed employee of a pulmonology practice. She charged that her former employers did not maintain their equipment or perform certain tests consistent with industry-standard guidelines. She alleged that the defendants had expressly and impliedly certified compliance with these standards when submitting claims for reimbursement to the Medicare and Medicaid programs. The Second Circuit concluded that although the claims for payment certified that the tests were "medically necessary," that certification did not equate to an *express* certification that the tests were performed in compliance with industry standards. *Id.* at 698. While accepting the implied certification theory, the Second Circuit saw a danger in its being read "expansively and out of context." *Id.* at 699. In particular, the court believed the theory was a poor fit in the medical context; it saw a risk of "federaliz[ing]... medical malpractice." *Id.* at 700. Accordingly, it decided to apply the theory "only when the underlying statute or regulation upon which the plaintiff relies *expressly* states the provider must comply in order to be paid." *Id.* (emphasis in original).

The District of Columbia Circuit took a different approach to implied certification. In *United States v. Science Applications International Corp.,* 626 F.3d 1257 (D.C. Cir. 2010), the underlying contract was between the Nuclear Regulatory Commission and the defendant, "a scientific, engineering, and technology applications company." *Id.* at 1261. The contract was "to provide technical assistance and expert analysis to support the agency's potential rulemaking" on the release of radioactive waste at a contamination level that was "below 'regulatory concern.'" *Id.* The contractual arrangement included "provisions designed to identify and prevent potential conflicts of interest," including requiring the defendant to forego outside contracts that created a conflict and to disclose any potential conflicts. *Id.* at 1262. Regulations defined these conflicts. In executing the contract, the defendant had certified compliance with the requirements, which the contract did not identify as conditions of payment. The defendant did not include an express certification of compliance when it later requested payment. In a subsequent FCA action alleging conflicts of interest involving the defendant's business, the District of Columbia Circuit rejected the *Mikes* approach. Instead, it adopted a rule that an FCA plaintiff may state a cause of action against a federal contractor who "withheld information about its noncompliance with material contractual requirements" and that "express contractual language specifically linking compliance to eligibility for payment" is not "a necessary condition." *Id.* at 1269.

The District of Columbia Circuit thereafter acknowledged that although the implied certification theory could be prone to abuse, any "concern can be effectively addressed through strict enforcement of the Act's materiality and scienter requirements." *Id.* at 1270.[13] Referring to the p.1309 facts before it and to the issue of materiality, the court distinguished the conflict of interest rules from "any of 'potentially hundreds of legal requirements established by contract'" which were "minor" or "merely ancillary to the parties' bargain." *Id.* at 1271. It then cited record evidence that the conflict of interest obligations "were important to the overall purpose of the contract." *Id.* (quoting *United States v. Sci. Applications Int'l Corp.,* 653 F.Supp.2d 87, 103 (D.D.C. 2009), *aff'd in part and vacated in part,* 626 F.3d 1257 (D.C.Cir. 2010)).

Operating within this legal backdrop, the district court granted the motion. It decided that the amended complaint failed to state a claim under the general pleading standards of Rule 8 and, because the complaint alleged fraud, under the particularity requirements of Rule 9(b). Turning to the relators' implied certification theory of liability, the court considered the defendants' contention that "noncompliance with [a] statute or regulation may form the basis of an FCA claim under an implied certification theory only where the government expressly conditioned payment on compliance."[14] The Government, in its statement of interest filed in the district court, noted a recent trend away from the *Mikes* line of cases and urged the district court to follow those more recent authorities.[15]

The court declined the Government's suggestion to limit the restrictive reading of the implied certification theory found in *Mikes.* Instead, it relied on an unpublished decision of this court where we had described the implied certification theory as recognizing "that the FCA is violated where compliance with a law, rule, or regulation *is a prerequisite to payment*" and a participant makes a claim for payment despite a knowing failure to comply with that p.1310 condition.[16] The district court next inquired whether either the Contractor Code of Ethics or the Truth in Negotiations Act was an express condition of payment and concluded that they were not. The court found "no provision" in any of the relevant contracts "that prohibits payment in the event of noncompliance" with either requirement.[17]

The court then stated that even if the express condition of payment approach embodied in *Mikes* were incorrect, the relators' claim would still fail under the more generous standards of *Science Applications International Corp.,* 626 F.3d at 1269. The district court could find no "'objective requirements' in the contract that MD 'failed to provide,' or that MD 'continued to bill the Government with the knowledge that it was not providing the contract's requirements.'"[18]

The court noted in a footnote that, although the response to the motion to dismiss had argued a fraud in the inducement theory of liability as well, it was absent from the pleadings. It further determined, without elaboration, that such a claim would "fail for the same reasons" as the implied certification claims and because it failed to meet the particularity standards of Rule 9(b).[19] Finally, the court held that in light of the dismissals of all substantive claims, the conspiracy claim also must fail.

The relators now appeal. They submit that the district court erred in rejecting their fraud in the inducement and implied certification theories of FCA liability. The Government has declined to intervene, but has filed a brief as amicus curiae. Although it takes no position on the sufficiency of the complaint, it contends that contractors who engage in the type of behavior alleged here can be liable under either an implied certification theory or a fraud in the inducement theory. MD, Patriarch, and Ms. Tilton have filed a brief addressing all of the relators' claims. Col. Vergez, named in the conspiracy count, has filed a separate brief focusing primarily on that count.

II

DISCUSSION

The basic standards that must guide our analysis are well established. "We review *de novo* the district court's grant of a motion to dismiss for failure to state a claim under Fed. R. Civ. P. 12(b)(6), accepting the allegations in the complaint as true and construing them in the light most favorable to the plaintiff." *Timson v. Sampson,* 518 F.3d 870, 872 (11th Cir. 2008) (per curiam). Generally, "[t]o survive a motion to dismiss, a complaint need only present sufficient facts, accepted as true, to 'state a claim to relief that is plausible on its face.'" *Renfroe v. Nationstar Mortg., LLC,* 822 F.3d 1241, 1243 (11th Cir. 2016) (quoting *Bell Atl. Corp. v. Twombly,* 550 U.S. 544, 570, 127 S.Ct. 1955, 167 L.Ed.2d 929 (2007)). However, we also have stated clearly that, in a *qui tam* action, the enhanced pleading requirements of Rule 9(b) apply. *See United States ex rel. Clausen v. Lab. Corp. of Am., Inc.,* 290 F.3d 1301, 1309-10 (11th Cir. 2002). "[U]nder Rule 9(b) allegations of fraud 'must include facts as to time, place, and substance of the defendant's alleged fraud.'" *Id.* at 1308 (quoting *United States ex rel. Cooper v. Blue Cross &* p.1311 *Blue Shield of Fla., Inc.,* 19 F.3d 562, 567 (11th Cir. 1994) (per curiam)).

The relators submit that the district court erred in dismissing claims based on an implied certification theory and based on a fraud in the inducement theory. We will address in turn each of these contentions. Before we focus on these particular contentions, however, we will set forth the governing statutory language and examine the Supreme Court's holding in *Escobar,* 136 S.Ct. 1989, which, as we have noted earlier, was decided after the district court rendered its decision in this case.

A.

The FCA imposes significant financial liability on any person who "knowingly presents, or causes to be presented, a false or fraudulent claim for payment or approval," or "knowingly makes, uses, or causes to be made or used, a false record or statement material to a false or fraudulent claim." 31 U.S.C. § 3729(a)(1)(A)-(B).

Following the district court's dismissal of relators' first amended complaint, the Supreme Court decided *Escobar*. This decision examines a claim of FCA liability based on the implied certification theory. It is also helpful in assessing the relators' fraud in the inducement theory. In *Escobar,* the relators were the parents of a disabled teenager who died from an adverse reaction to medication provided to treat a diagnosis of bipolar disorder. A mental health facility operated by Universal Health had treated their daughter prior to her death and then had sought reimbursement for her treatment through the Medicaid program. The parents alleged in their complaint that Universal Health submitted its itemized claims to Medicaid by employing standard reimbursement codes. These codes, continued the complaint, "made representations about the specific services provided by specific types of professionals," but "failed to disclose serious violations of regulations pertaining to staff qualifications and licensing requirements for these services." *Id.* at 1998.

The rules of the Massachusetts Medicaid program, which paid the claims, required "satellite facilities to have specific types of clinicians on staff, delineate[d] licensing requirements for particular positions (like psychiatrists, social workers, and nurses), and detail[ed] supervision requirements for other staff." *Id.* Although five separate practitioners treated the relators' daughter, only one of the five had a license. Another who held herself out as a psychologist with a Ph.D. had received her degree from an unaccredited institution, and the state licensing board had rejected her credentials. The prescriber of the medication that prompted the fatal reaction held herself out as a psychiatrist, but "was in fact a nurse who lacked authority to prescribe medication absent supervision." *Id.* at 1997. The relators' complaint alleged that the requests for payment constituted a false claim because inherent in the use of the codes was a certification that the care provided satisfied the requirements for payment set by the Medicaid program.

The Court held "that the implied false certification theory can, at least in some circumstances, provide a basis for liability." *Id.* at 1999. Specifically, "[w]hen, as here, a defendant makes representations in submitting a claim but omits its violations of statutory, regulatory, or contractual requirements, those omissions can be a basis for liability if they render the defendant's representations misleading with respect to the goods or services provided." *Id.* Because the statutory text does not include an independent definition of "false or fraudulent," the Court applied the usual interpretive principle that Congress intended to incorporate settled common law meanings. *Id.* At common law, "fraud has long encompassed certain misrepresentations by omission." *Id.* The Court declined p.1312 to "resolve whether all claims for payment implicitly represent that the billing party is legally entitled to payment." *Id.* at 2000. But it held that Universal Health's claims "fall squarely within the rule that half-truths — representations that state the truth only so far as it goes, while omitting critical qualifying information — can be actionable misrepresentations." *Id.* In its view,

> the implied certification theory can be a basis for liability, at least where two conditions are satisfied: first, the claim does not merely request payment, but also makes specific representations about the goods or services provided; and second, the defendant's failure to disclose noncompliance with material

statutory, regulatory, or contractual requirements makes those representations misleading half-truths.

Id. at 2001. In so holding, the Court explicitly noted the *Mikes v. Straus* line of cases, relied upon by the district court in this case, and rejected its approach.

The Court went on to emphasize that, "[u]nder the Act, the misrepresentation must be material to the other party's course of action" and that the Act's scienter requirement means that a plaintiff must show that the defendant had actual knowledge of or recklessly disregarded a condition's materiality. *Id.* The statutory definition of materiality, "having a natural tendency to influence, or be capable of influencing, the payment or receipt of money," *id.* at 2002 (quoting 31 U.S.C. § 3729(b)(4)), focuses the inquiry on "the *effect* on the likely or actual behavior of the recipient of the alleged misrepresentation." *Id.* (emphasis added). The designation of a statutory, regulatory, or contractual provision as a condition of payment is "relevant, but not automatically dispositive," because the FCA "is not 'an all-purpose antifraud statute'" which "punish[es] garden-variety breaches of contract or regulatory violations." *Id.* at 2003 (quoting *Allison Engine Co. v. United States ex rel. Sanders,* 553 U.S. 662, 672, 128 S.Ct. 2123, 170 L.Ed.2d 1030 (2008)). Materiality therefore is not established by showing "that the Government would have the option to decline to pay if it knew of the defendant's noncompliance" or where noncompliance "is minor or insubstantial." *Id.* The materiality standard is "demanding," *id.,* and "rigorous," *id.* at 1996, 2002. The Court concluded,

> In sum, when evaluating materiality under the False Claims Act, the Government's decision to expressly identify a provision as a condition of payment is relevant, but not automatically dispositive. Likewise, proof of materiality can include, but is not necessarily limited to, evidence that the defendant knows that the Government consistently refuses to pay claims in the mine run of cases based on noncompliance with the particular statutory, regulatory, or contractual requirement. Conversely, if the Government pays a particular claim in full despite its actual knowledge that certain requirements were violated, that is very strong evidence that those requirements are not material. Or, if the Government regularly pays a particular type of claim in full despite actual knowledge that certain requirements were violated, and has signaled no change in position, that is strong evidence that the requirements are not material.

Id. at 2003-04.[20]

Escobar therefore clarified two central and interrelated principles of FCA p.1313 liability. First, the implied certification theory can be a premise of liability at least where a party, in requesting payment, makes certain representations which are misleading because of the omission of violations of statutory, regulatory, or contractual requirements; any such requirement need not be an express condition of payment for liability to attach. Second, such an omission, to be actionable, must be material.

We now apply these principles to the complaint before us. The relators allege a series of improprieties in the relationship between Ms. Tilton, MD, and Patriarch, on the one hand, and Col. Vergez, an officer with authority in the NSRWA contracting office on the other. Those improprieties, they contend, amount to potential violations of criminal law involving fraud, conflict of interest, bribery, or gratuity violations. The Contractor Code of Ethics, which is part of the Federal Acquisitions Regulations and is a mandatory term of acquisitions contracts, requires disclosure of any credible evidence of such conduct. The Truth in Negotiations Act sets forth certain disclosure requirements that assist the Government in determining the market value of the products it purchases, which the relators submit, "naturally affect[s] the government's negotiation posture."[21] The relators contend, at some length in their brief, that the Government considers these terms essential and that compliance goes directly to the integrity of the contracting process.

We believe it is appropriate to afford the district court the opportunity to reconsider the allegations in light of the changed legal landscape. *Escobar* makes clear that the district court's principal method for evaluating implied certification claims, under *Mikes,* is no longer appropriate. The Supreme Court explicitly rejected a standard for implied certification claims that focuses exclusively on whether the Government expressly designates a contractual, statutory, or regulatory obligation as a condition of payment. Whether a condition is so designated is "relevant to but not dispositive of the *materiality* inquiry," but not a precondition to the theory of liability itself. *Id.* at 2001 (emphasis added).

Escobar now provides the district court with a more refined framework to address the questions before it. The definition of "material" contained within the statute considers whether the misrepresentation had "a natural tendency to influence, or be capable of influencing, the payment or receipt of money or property," 31 U.S.C. § 3729(b)(4), a definition "descend[ed] from 'common-law antecedents,'" *Escobar,* 136 S.Ct. at 2002 (quoting *Kungys v. United States,* 485 U.S. 759, 769, 108 S.Ct. 1537, 99 L.Ed.2d 839 (1988)). *Escobar* instructs courts to consider whether noncompliance is "minor or insubstantial" and amounts to "garden-variety breaches of contract or regulatory violations," or, conversely, whether the Government would have attached importance to the violation in determining whether to pay the claim. *Id.* at 2002-03 (citing 26 Richard A. Lord, Williston on Contracts § 69:12 (4th ed. 2003); Restatement (Second) of Torts § 538 (Am. Law Inst. 1977)).

We believe that the district court ought to reconsider this case for another reason: given the advent of *Escobar,* the district court may decide that, in fairness to the relators, they should have an opportunity p.1314 to replead their allegations in light of the Supreme Court's guidance.[22]

B.

The relators also challenge the district court's conclusion, expressed in a footnote, that the complaint failed to allege fraud in the inducement. The district court did not discern that theory to be in the complaint. If it were in the complaint, continued the court, it failed "for the same reasons" as the implied certification theory, and because the allegations were insufficient under the particularity standards for fraud of Rule 9(b).[23]

Claims alleging fraudulent inducement to support an FCA action derive from *United States ex rel. Marcus v. Hess,* 317 U.S. 537, 63 S.Ct. 379, 87 L.Ed. 443 (1943), *superseded in part on other grounds as noted in Schindler Elevator Corp. v. United States ex rel. Kirk,* 563 U.S. 401, 412, 131 S.Ct. 1885, 179 L.Ed.2d 825 (2011). *Marcus* involved a request for competitive bids for Public Works Administration projects. Electrical contractors colluded to ensure that there would be no price competition. The Court found that the collusion was a "fraud" that satisfied the Act and that the "fraud did not spend itself with the execution of the contract." *Id.* at 543, 63 S.Ct. 379. That is, the original fraud that influenced the Government's decision to enter into a particular contract at a particular price "pressed ever to the ultimate goal — payment of government money to persons who had caused it to be defrauded." *Id.* at 543-44, 63 S.Ct. 379. The contractor's ultimate claims for payment were "grounded in fraud" when the Government paid them, even though the "fraud" occurred prior to the execution of the contract itself. *Id.* at 544, 63 S.Ct. 379. As one of our sister circuits has recognized, subsequent claims are false "because of an *original fraud* (whether a certification or otherwise)." *United States ex rel. Hendow v. Univ. of Phoenix,* 461 F.3d 1166, 1173 (9th Cir. 2006) (emphasis in original).[24]

We agree with Government as amicus curiae that the allegations of the relators' complaint could support multiple theories of fraud in the inducement. First, the allegations can be read to support the view that the prospective promise to comply with various provisions of law, including the Contractor Code of Ethics and the Truth in Negotiations Act, were false when made. The Government would not have p.1315 entered into those had it known of the defendants' unwillingness to comply with these rules. The allegations also support the view that, on at least some occasions, MD provided incomplete pricing data to the Government. This incomplete data induced the Government to enter contracts on terms more favorable to MD than it would have had the pricing data been complete. Indeed, the complaint is explicit on this point. With respect to several of the contracts, the relators allege that the Army requested pricing data, that MD provided misleadingly incomplete data to support an inflated price, and that the Government relied on the data in awarding the contract.[25] The Government also asserts that the undisclosed conflicts of interest while MD and Col. Vergez were negotiating their future relationship might have caused the Army to accept an inflated contract price. MD's response to these allegations, that the Government is not necessarily entitled to the best price commercially available, is unavailing. Here, the concern is whether the pricing data was misleadingly incomplete such that it amounted to fraud, and whether that data was material to the Government's decisions on the contracts. As *Escobar* reminds us, "fraud" at common law has long included "misrepresentations by omission" such as the above. 136 S.Ct. at 1999.

The district court also concluded that, even if the complaint did include a fraudulent inducement theory, such a claim would fail for the "same reasons" as the implied certification claims. We have concluded that, in light of *Escobar,* the district court should evaluate anew the implied certification claims, both with respect to the fraudulent statements and with respect to materiality. More fundamentally, it is far from self-evident that the court's assessment of the implied certification theory should control its disposition of the fraudulent inducement theory. Each theory of liability rests on different factual allegations. Finally, we are not convinced that the court's brief mention of a failure under Rule 9(b)'s specificity requirement accurately assesses the relators' detailed forty-five-page complaint.

Conclusion

The district court decided the motion to dismiss in a profoundly uncertain legal environment. The Supreme Court now has provided significant guidance. The correct course is to allow the district court to consider this matter in light of that guidance. On remand, the district court also should consider whether to allow the plaintiffs to file a second amended complaint that conforms its allegations to the requirements of *Escobar*. We also conclude that the complaint did plead fraud in the inducement, and we therefore remand so that the district court can reexamine the allegations relating to that theory.

VACATED and REMANDED.

[*] Honorable Kenneth F. Ripple, United States Circuit Judge for the Seventh Circuit, sitting by designation.

[1] The complaint also alleged a conspiracy count, which was the only count to name Col. Vergez.

[2] R.57 at 18-19, ¶ 33.

[3] The complaint alleges that MD did not disclose a sale for $1,900,000 during the prior year. *Id.* at 23, ¶ 50.

[4] Id.

[5] *Id.* at 24, ¶ 51.

[6] Id.

[7] Id.

[8] *Id.* at 15, ¶ 25.

[9] Among those recommended by Col. Vergez was Ben Weiser, the executive vice president who challenged Ms. Tilton on the Saudi Arabian National Guard contract.

[10] It appears that the MD employees were concerned about the provisions of federal ethics laws applying to procurement officials and post-government employment with contractors. *See generally* 41 U.S.C. § 2104.

[11] R.57 at 29, ¶ 66.

[12] Subsequent to the filing of the complaint, Col. Vergez pleaded guilty to two counts of making false statements, in violation of 18 U.S.C. § 1001, and one count of conflict of interest, in violation of 18 U.S.C. §§ 208, 216(a)(2). Col. Vergez disputes the relevance of his guilty plea, which the relators submitted in the district court as an attachment to their brief in opposition to his motion to dismiss. Col. Vergez's brief on appeal discusses the circumstances of his conviction at some length. One of the convictions related to a failure to disclose his employment with MD on an ethics disclosure form and to disclose $30,000 in relocation expenses received from MD. Another of his convictions, for conflict of interest, relates to his involvement in negotiating favorable payment terms for MD in the Saudi Arabian National Guard contract after he had accepted an offer with an MD affiliate. The remaining count was unrelated to MD and this action. Following oral argument, the parties also

submitted judicial orders disposing of various other unrelated claims involving Ms. Tilton and her investment practices, including an SEC action resolved in her favor and a state court decision in Delaware resolved against her. None of these facts bears on our current assessment of the legal sufficiency of the complaint.

[13] The court provided an example to illustrate "[t]he logic of [its] conclusion" that the express condition approach was too restrictive, in a way that was "freed from the complexities" and "intricacies" of the case before it. *United States v. Sci. Applications Int'l Corp.,* 626 F.3d 1257, 1269 (D.C. Cir. 2010). The court surmised that the Government enters into a contract with a company that will provide gasoline with an octane rating of ninety-one or higher. The company provides noncompliant lower octane gasoline and seeks reimbursement on a form that nowhere requires certification of the octane level. An appropriate plaintiff could bring an FCA claim on these facts, the court noted, as the octane rating would be material to the contract even if not an express condition of payment, and even if the company did not separately certify that it satisfied that requirement. Importantly, the discussion was not defining the outer limits of materiality, but merely demonstrating that an FCA action is available on an implied certification theory even absent an express designation as a condition of payment, where the requirement plainly satisfies materiality.

[14] R.77 at 9.

[15] Specifically, the Government noted that several circuits had concluded that *Mikes* involved Medicare-specific considerations and should not be applied to all contexts, or that the express condition rule did not have a basis in the text of the Act. *See* R.70 at 5-7 (citing *United States ex rel. Badr v. Triple Canopy, Inc.,* 775 F.3d 628, 637 n.5 (4th Cir. 2015), *vacated by* ___ U.S. ___, 136 S.Ct. 2504, 195 L.Ed.2d 836 (2016) (remanding for reconsideration in light of *Escobar*), *remanded to* 857 F.3d 174 (4th Cir. 2017) (affirming the prior opinion applying the standards of *Escobar*); *United States ex rel. Hutcheson v. Blackstone Med., Inc.,* 647 F.3d 377, 388 (1st Cir. 2011); *Sci. Applications Int'l Corp.,* 626 F.3d 1257; *United States ex rel. Hendow v. Univ. of Phoenix,* 461 F.3d 1166, 1177 (9th Cir. 2006)). Although the Government took no position on the viability of the complaint itself, it "respectfully urge[d] the Court not to adopt the atextual position that implied certification False Claims Act liability for noncompliance with a contract provision (including regulatory or statutory provisions incorporated therein) necessarily hinges on the presence of an express statement within that provision that payment is conditioned on its compliance." *Id.* at 7.

[16] R.77 at 10-11 (emphasis in original); *United States ex rel. Keeler v. Eisai, Inc.,* 568 Fed.Appx. 783, 799 (11th Cir. 2014) (unpublished).

[17] R.77 at 11; *see also id.* at 17-18.

[18] *Id.* at 13 (quoting *Triple Canopy,* 775 F.3d at 638).

[19] *Id.* at 7 n.2.

[20] To illustrate its point about the limits of materiality, the Court hypothesized a contract for health services that required providers to use American-made staplers. If the Government routinely paid claims, irrespective of whether it knew of the use of foreign staplers and even though it had the right to withhold payment, the provision would not be material; False Claims Act liability would not attach. A contrary rule would be "an extraordinarily expansive view" of fraud liability not

justified by the statute. *Universal Health Services, Inc. v. United States ex rel. Escobar,* ___ U.S. ___, 136 S.Ct. 1989, 2004, 195 L.Ed.2d 348 (2016).

[21] Appellants' Amended Br. 42-43.

[22] Our resolution of the substantive claims equally affects the allegations concerning the conspiracy count.

[23] R.77 at 7 n.2. Although the label of fraudulent inducement does not appear on the face of the complaint, neither does the label of implied certification. Nor does a plaintiff's labeling of their complaint bind us. *See Johnson v. City of Shelby,* ___ U.S. ___, 135 S.Ct. 346, 346, 190 L.Ed.2d 309 (2014) (per curiam) (noting that federal pleading rules "do not countenance dismissal of a complaint for imperfect statement of the legal theory supporting the claim asserted").

[24] Other circuits have conceptualized such claims somewhat differently under this statute, although still acknowledging their validity:

The False Claims Act covers anyone who "knowingly makes, uses, or causes to be made or used, a false record or statement to get a false or fraudulent claim paid or approved by the Government[."] 31 U.S.C. § 3729(a)(2). The [defendant] "uses" its [initial fraudulent statement] when it makes... [an] application for payment. No more is required under the statute.... The statute requires a causal rather than a temporal connection between fraud and payment. If a false statement is integral to a causal chain leading to payment, it is irrelevant how the federal bureaucracy has apportioned the statements among layers of paperwork.

United States ex rel. Main v. Oakland City Univ., 426 F.3d 914, 916 (7th Cir. 2005) (citation omitted).

[25] *See, e.g.,* R.57 at 18-19, ¶ 33; 35, ¶ 91 (relating to the El Salvador contract).

898 F.3d 1267 (2018)

Jack CARREL, Mauricio Ferrer, Shawn Loftis, Plaintiffs-Appellants,

v.

AIDS HEALTHCARE FOUNDATION, INC., Defendant-Appellee.

No. 17-13185.

United States Court of Appeals, Eleventh Circuit.

August 7, 2018.

Carrel v. AIDS Healthcare Foundation, Inc., 898 F. 3d 1267 (11th Cir. 2018)

Appeal from the United States District Court for the Southern District of Florida, D.C. Docket No. 0:14-cv-61301-KMW.

Geoffrey R. Kaiser, Kaiser Law Firm, PLLC, 926 RXR PLZ, UNIONDALE, NY 11556-0926, Diana L. Martin, Cohen Milstein Sellers & Toll, PLLC, 2925 PGA BLVD., STE. 200, PALM BEACH GARDENS, FL 33410-2909, for Plaintiffs-Appellants.

Jay L. Bhimani, Gavin C.P. Campbell, David Horowitz, Kirkland & Ellis, LLP, 333 S HOPE ST., ste. 2900, LOS ANGELES, CA 90071, Arti Bhimani, Courtney Conner, Thomas A. Myers, Aids Healthcare Foundation, 6255 W SUNSET BLVD., FL 21, LOS ANGELES, CA 90028-7403, Jeffrey Marcus, Michael Anthony Pineiro, Marcus Neiman & Rashbaum, LLP, 2 S BISCAYNE BLVD., STE. 1750, MIAMI, FL 33131, Erin E. Murphy, Kirkland & Ellis, LLP, 655 15TH ST., NW p.1269 STE. 1200, WASHINGTON, DC 20005-5793, Jeffrey A. Neiman, Marcus Neiman & Rashbaum LLP, 100 SE 3RD AVE., STE. 805, FORT LAUDERDALE, FL 33394, for Defendant-Appellee.

Before WILLIAM PRYOR and MARTIN, Circuit Judges, and HALL,[*] District Judge.

p.1268 WILLIAM PRYOR, Circuit Judge:

This appeal requires us to decide whether the employee exemption to the Anti-Kickback Statute, 42 U.S.C. §§ 1320a-7b(b)(3)(B), applies to payments that AIDS Healthcare Foundation, Inc., made to an employee tasked with referring HIV-positive patients to healthcare services offered by the Foundation. The Foundation is a nonprofit group that contracts with the State of Florida to provide an extensive array of medical services to patients with HIV/AIDS. The contracts require the Foundation to match patients who test positive for the disease with suitable providers of care. The Foundation offers financial incentives to some employees who refer patients to other healthcare services operated by the Foundation, and it offers incentives to patients who use its services. The costs of these services often are reimbursed by federal healthcare programs, such as Medicare, Medicaid, and programs funded by the Ryan White Comprehensive AIDS Resources Emergency Act. Three former employees sued the Foundation under the False Claims Act, 31 U.S.C. § 3729 *et seq.*, alleging that the incentives offered to employees and patients are unlawful kickbacks that render false any claims for federal reimbursement. The district court dismissed all but two of the claims for lack of particularity. And it later granted summary judgment in favor of the Foundation on the remaining claims based on the employee exemption to the Anti-Kickback Statute. The district court also denied the relators leave to file a fourth amended complaint. We affirm.

I. BACKGROUND

We divide this section in two parts. First, we describe the facts, as we must, in the light most favorable to the relators. *See Chaparro v. Carnival Corp.,* 693 F.3d 1333, 1335 (11th Cir. 2012); *Jones v. UPS Ground Freight,* 683 F.3d 1283, 1291-92 (11th Cir. 2012). Second, we describe the proceedings in the district court.

A. The Facts

AIDS Healthcare Foundation, Inc., is a national nonprofit that provides a variety of medical services to individuals with HIV/AIDS. It has contracts with the State of Florida that require it to conduct HIV testing and to match clients with positive test results to healthcare providers. To promote this goal, the Foundation offers financial incentives to certain employees who refer individuals who test positive for HIV/AIDS to other medical offerings provided by the Foundation, such as its clinic and pharmacy services. For example, the Foundation employs "Linkage Coordinators" who earn a $100 bonus for every referred patient who completes certain follow-up procedures at Foundation clinics. It also provides small incentives, such as nutrient shakes and vitamins, to patients who use its services. The Foundation receives approximately half of its revenue from federal healthcare programs, including Medicare, Medicaid, and programs established by the Ryan White Comprehensive AIDS Resources Emergency Act.

p.1270 Three former employees of the Foundation, Jack Carrel, Mauricio Ferrer, and Shawn Loftis, sued the Foundation under the False Claims Act, 31 U.S.C. § 3729 *et seq.* They alleged that the incentives provided to employees and patients violated the Anti-Kickback Statute, 42 U.S.C. § 1320a-7b, and rendered false any claims for public reimbursement for the treatment of these patients, *see id.* § 1320a-7b(g). And the relators later filed a third amended complaint that alleged that the Foundation engaged in a widespread practice of submitting claims for services tainted by unlawful payments to employees and patients.

In their effort to satisfy the particularity requirement for allegations of fraud, *see* Fed. R. Civ. P. 9(b), the relators identified several pieces of evidence. They asserted that Foundation policies provide for incentive payments to Linkage Coordinators and employees who administer HIV tests, that the President of the Foundation has admitted to offering incentives to patients, and that the Foundation has aggressive policies for recruiting patients. The relators also pointed to a spreadsheet created by the Foundation that lists hundreds of patients, employees, test dates, and potential sources of insurance coverage, including federal healthcare programs. And they alleged that because public funds account for almost 50 percent of Foundation revenue, mathematical probability suggests that the Foundation submitted claims for unlawfully referred patients.

The relators also highlighted their positions at the Foundation. Carrel was "the Director of Public Health" for the Southern Bureau of the Foundation between August 2012 and August 2013, Ferrer was a "Senior Program Manager" from May 2011 to August 2012, and Loftis was a "Grants Manager" from January 2013 to August 2013. They asserted that their jobs gave them insight into the "standard operating procedure at [the Foundation]" where "patients ... were referred to and received health services from [the Foundation], which included services paid for by Federal Health Care Programs." And they described various meetings with other officials where they observed discussions of financial data and incentives.

With two exceptions, the relators failed to identify specific claims submitted to the federal government that involved incentives given to patients or employees. On the contrary, the complaint conceded that "[t]he precise number of illegally referred HIV-positive patients cannot be known with certainty at this time," and it primarily relied on allegations about "the regular course of business at [the Foundation]."

The two exceptions involved "representative false claims" where the government was actually billed for services provided to referred patients. The first concerned a patient, John Doe #1, who "tested positive for HIV at [a Foundation] facility in January 2013" and was "assigned to [a Foundation] Linkage Coordinator named Julio Rodriguez who referred him to [the Foundation] for clinical services." John Doe #1 completed his follow-up visits at a Foundation clinic, and in February 2013 the Foundation "directed its accounts payable department to pay ... Rodriguez a commission for successfully linking [the] patient... to treatment with [the Foundation]." The Foundation then informed John Doe #1 that "it was billing [the] Ryan White [Program] for his treatment," and "the Broward County Health Services Planning Council [told him] that it was paying [the Foundation] for his treatment with Ryan White funds." And the relators made parallel allegations about another patient, John Doe #2, who received health care funded by the Ryan White Program p.1271 after he was referred to Foundation services by Rodriguez.

B. The Proceedings in the District Court

After the United States and Florida declined to intervene, the Foundation moved to dismiss the complaint. It argued that the complaint failed to plead the actual submission of false claims with particularity. *See* Fed. R. Civ. P. 9(b). And it contended that the referral fees fell within a statutory exemption to the Anti-Kickback Statute that excludes "any amount paid by an employer to an employee ... for employment in the provision of covered items or services." 42 U.S.C. § 1320a-7b(b)(3)(B).

The district court granted the motion in part and dismissed all claims except the representative claims about the John Does. It ruled that the combination of allegations that the Foundation relied on public money, that the "kickback schemes were pervasive," and that the relators had some insider knowledge about Foundation funding were insufficient to establish that the Foundation "actually submitted false claims or received payment on such claims." It also highlighted that the spreadsheet that listed patient data failed to establish that the Foundation submitted false claims because this document did "not memorialize any *actual claims* [the Foundation] submitted to government programs for services provided to illegally referred patients."

After discovery, the Foundation moved for summary judgment against the two remaining claims based on the employee exemption to the Anti-Kickback Statute. *See id.* The Foundation underscored that this exemption applies to "any amount paid by an employer to an employee ... for employment in the provision of covered items or services," *id.,* and that the Ryan White Act specifically provides that "referrals" are covered "services," *id.* § 300ff-51(e)(1)-(2); *see also id.* §§ 300ff-14(c)(3)(E) & (e)(1), 300ff-22(b)(3)(E) & (d)(1), 300ff-51(c)(3)(e). It concluded that this exemption applied because Rodriguez was an employee providing a statutory service when he referred the John Does to other Foundation offerings. And it highlighted that contracts with Florida required the Foundation to refer patients to medical care.

The relators then moved for leave to file a fourth amended complaint. They stated that the amended complaint had the benefit of new information gleaned from discovery and that these new findings warranted "broaden[ing] the scope of th[e] action." But the motion failed to state exactly what new information the revised 64-page complaint included or to explain how these facts could satisfy the particularity requirement.

The United States filed a statement of interest in support of the Foundation. It explained that it had "a significant interest in the proper interpretation and correct application of the False Claims Act ... and the Anti-Kickback Statute" and that the Foundation had correctly interpreted the law. It maintained that "the Ryan White Program ... explicitly includes referrals to appropriate providers as covered services," and that the relevant "statutes and regulations do not restrict grant recipients... from paying employees to refer patients needing medical care to *that same grant recipient* if, as here, it is an otherwise appropriate Ryan White provider."

The district court granted summary judgment in favor of the Foundation. It ruled that the employee exemption applied because Rodriguez was an employee and the referrals were covered "services." 42 U.S.C. § 1320a-7b(b)(3)(B). And it denied the motion to amend as moot.

p.1272 II. STANDARD OF REVIEW

Two standards govern our review. We review *de novo* both the dismissal of a complaint, *Access Now, Inc. v. Sw. Airlines Co.,* 385 F.3d 1324, 1326 (11th Cir. 2004), and a summary judgment, *Ellis v. England,* 432 F.3d 1321, 1325 (11th Cir. 2005). And we review a denial of leave to amend a complaint for abuse of discretion. *Carruthers v. BSA Advertising, Inc.,* 357 F.3d 1213, 1217 (11th Cir. 2004).

III. DISCUSSION

We divide our discussion in three parts. First, we explain that the payments to Rodriguez fell within the employee exemption to the Anti-Kickback Statute. Second, we explain that the district court correctly dismissed the relators' other claims for lack of particularity. Third, we explain that the relators waived their argument about amendment.

A. The Referral Payments to Rodriguez Fell Within the Employee Exemption.

To determine whether the Foundation was entitled to pay Rodriguez for referring patients to other Foundation services, we must consider the texts of three statutes: the False Claims Act, the Anti-Kickback Statute, and the Ryan White Act. A careful review of their relevant provisions and related regulations establishes that the Foundation was entitled to pay its employee for referring patients to its services. And the relators' arguments about congressional intent fail.

The False Claims Act, 31 U.S.C. § 3729 *et seq.*, creates liability for individuals "who present or directly induce the submission of false or fraudulent claims" to the government, *Universal Health Servs., Inc. v. United States ex rel. Escobar*, ___ U.S. ___, 136 S.Ct. 1989, 1996, 195 L.Ed.2d 348 (2016); *see also* 31 U.S.C. § 3729(a)(1)(A), (B), (G) (forbidding specific fraudulent acts). It also "permits, in certain circumstances, suits by private parties on behalf of the United States against [violators]." *Hughes Aircraft Co. v. United States ex rel. Schumer*, 520 U.S. 939, 941, 117 S.Ct. 1871, 138 L.Ed.2d 135 (1997) (citing 31 U.S.C. § 3730(b)). Florida has enacted a parallel statutory scheme with similar provisions. *See* Fla. Stat. §§ 68.082(2)(a), (b), (g), 68.083(2).

The Anti-Kickback Statute, which broadly forbids kickbacks, bribes, and rebates in the administration of government healthcare programs, *see* 42 U.S.C. § 1320a-7b(b), provides that "a claim that includes items or services resulting from a violation of [the Anti-Kickback Statute] constitutes a false or fraudulent claim for purposes of [the False Claims Act]," *id.* § 1320a-7b(g). The Anti-Kickback Statute creates liability for anyone who "knowingly and willfully offers or pays any remuneration... to any person to induce such person ... *to refer an individual* to a person for the furnishing ... of any item or service for which payment may be made in whole or in part under a Federal health care program." *Id.* § 1320a-7b(b)(2) (emphasis added). Notwithstanding its general prohibition on paying for "refer[rals]," *id.*, the Anti-Kickback Statute exempts "any amount paid by an employer to an employee (who has a bona fide employment relationship with such employer) for employment in *the provision of covered items or services*," *id.* § 1320a-7b(b)(3)(B) (emphasis added). And the statute exempts "any payment practice specified by the Secretary [of the Department of Health and Human Services] in regulations." *Id.* § 1320a-7b(b)(3)(E). A regulation provides a parallel exemption for "any amount paid by an employer to a[] [bona fide] employee... for employment in the furnishing of any item or service for which payment p.1273 may be made in whole or in part under Medicare, Medicaid, or other Federal health care programs." 42 C.F.R. § 1001.952(i).

The Ryan White Act establishes that the referral of patients with HIV/AIDS is a standalone compensable "service." The Act permits funding of "core medical services," 42 U.S.C. § 300ff-14(a)(2)(A); *see also id.* § 300ff-22(a)(1), a definition that includes "[e]arly intervention services," *id.* § 300ff-14(c)(3)(E); *see also id.* §§ 300ff-14(e)(1), 300ff-22(b)(3)(E) & (d)(1). In turn, the Act explains that these early intervention services include "referrals of individuals with HIV/AIDS to appropriate providers of health and support services, including ... to entities receiving [funding under the Ryan White Act] for the provision of such services." *Id.* § 300ff-51(e)(2); *see also id.* § 300ff-51(e)(1)(C).

The texts of these laws make clear that the Foundation was entitled to pay Rodriguez for referring the John Doe patients. As the district court ruled and the relators concede, Rodriguez was an employee of the Foundation. The Anti-Kickback Statute permits payments to employees for their "employment in the provision of covered items or services." *Id.* § 1320a-7b(b)(3)(B). And the Ryan White Act defines "[c]ore medical services," *id.* § 300ff-51(c)(3), to include "referrals of individuals with HIV/AIDS to appropriate providers of health ... services," *id.* § 300ff-51(e)(2); *see also id.* §§ 300ff-14(c)(3)(E) & (e)(1), 300ff-22(b)(3)(E) & (d)(1), 300ff-51(c)(3)(e). The relators do not dispute that the Foundation is an "appropriate provider." And they admit that contracts between the Foundation and Florida "required [the Foundation] to refer HIV [positive] patients into medical care." Because referrals are compensable medical services under the Ryan White Act, the Foundation was entitled to pay Rodriguez for referring the John Does.

Despite the plain text of the statutes and regulation, the relators contend that Congress and the agency did not really mean what they wrote. Instead, they assert that drafting history, policy concerns, and tangentially related regulations and caselaw implicitly bar the Foundation from "buying" referrals on a per-capita basis. They also suggest that, even if certain kinds of referral arrangements are covered by the exemption, the exemption implicitly excludes the "purchase" of referrals that direct patients to a *particular* provider instead of to *any* provider in a nondiscriminatory fashion. And they colorfully argue that there is a "yawning difference between the appropriate provision of referral services to people with HIV/AIDS and the corrupt purchase of patient referrals."

The relators cite the drafting history and general purpose of the Anti-Kickback Statute and its regulatory exceptions for the proposition that "buy[ing]" referrals categorically violates the principle of honesty in medical services. They assert that Congress intended for the statute to prohibit "financial incentives to induce referrals of program business" and the "steering of patients to particular providers, thus violating the policy of freedom of choice." The relators also underscore that the statute requires the agency to consider factors such as "patient freedom" and "competition among health care providers" when it promulgates safe harbors, *id.* § 1320a-7d(a)(2), and that the agency consequently stated in a proposed rule that safe harbors should "encourage competition, innovation[,] and economy." The relators maintain that these general principles of freedom and neutrality establish that referral programs — particularly those that pay on a per-capita basis and those that pay employees only when they refer patients to a p.1274 medical program run by the payor — are unlawful.

We lack the authority to ignore the texts of these laws in the service of general purposes and selective legislative history. Although the relators complain that paid referrals threaten "freedom of choice" and introduce market inefficiencies, the employee exemption plainly covers the payments to Rodriguez. And the relevant statutes say nothing to forbid payment on a per-capita basis or to require nondiscriminatory referrals to any available healthcare provider. Indeed, the employee exemption covers "*any amount* paid by an employer to an employee" without specifying the terms, method, or frequency of payment, *id.* § 1320a-7b(b)(3)(B) (emphasis added), and the Ryan White Act requires only that referrals be made to an "appropriate provider[]," *id.* § 300ff-51(e)(2). And that *another* regulatory exemption to the Anti-Kickback Statute specifically excludes the kind of "volume"-based compensation that the relators complain about, 42 C.F.R. § 100.952(f)(2), implies the lack of similar language in the regulation about the employee exemption permits payment on a per-capita basis, *see id.* § 100.952(i).

The relators cannot complain that this interpretation of the exemption is absurd. On the contrary, incentive-based referral arrangements are logical in the light of the urgent need to ensure that people with HIV/AIDS receive prompt care before their conditions worsen. Congress may well have concluded that it preferred that patients receive any care — even if not from the optimal provider — as quickly as possible. And paid incentives logically further this goal. Indeed, the statement of interest submitted by the government in the district court states "that Congress embraced the notion of 'one stop shopping' for patients with HIV/AIDS."

The relators next cite a variety of unrelated regulatory exemptions to the Anti-Kickback Statute for the same proposition that pay-per-referral arrangements are inherently abusive and implicitly excluded from the employee exemption. For example, they point out that different exemptions for referral arrangements may not apply if compensation is "based ... on the *volume* or value of any referrals ... or [the] business otherwise generated," 42 C.F.R. § 1001.952(f)(2) (emphasis added), or if the referrals are not accompanied by disclosures, *see id.* § 1001.952(f)(4); *see also generally id.* § 1001.952 (outlining other regulatory exemptions). The relators conclude that because these other safe harbors were promulgated "after enactment of the Ryan White Program," their principles of fairness and disclosure somehow implicitly limit the scope of the employee exemption.

We disagree. That *other* exemptions to the Anti-Kickback Statute may not apply to the payments that the Foundation made to Rodriguez is irrelevant to whether the John Doe referrals were statutorily exempted "covered items or services," 42 U.S.C. § 1320a-7b(b)(3)(B), under the plain terms of the Ryan White Act, *see id.* § 300ff-51(e). Indeed, many of the other regulatory exemptions cited by the relators apply to business relationships that are completely different from an employee-employer relationship. *See, e.g.,* 42 C.F.R. § 1001.952(b) (concerning "payment[s] made by a lessee to a lessor"); *id.* § 1001.952(c) (concerning "[e]quipment rental"); *id.* § 1001.952(d) (concerning "[p]ersonal services and management contracts"). In short, unrelated regulatory provisions cannot eviscerate a distinct statutory exemption that plainly applies to the actions of the Foundation.

The relators also cherry-pick statements from caselaw to suggest that paid referrals p.1275 are inherently unlawful. For example, they cite *United States v. Starks,* where we held that the Anti-Kickback Statute reached a scheme where a publicly-funded drug-treatment program paid unaffiliated public-health workers tasked with "advis[ing] pregnant women about possible treatment for drug abuse" to refer these women to the drug-treatment program. 157 F.3d 833, 836 (11th Cir. 1998); *see also id.* at 835-36. In upholding the convictions against a void-for-vagueness challenge to the statute, we explained that "even if [the defendants] believed that [the workers] were bona fide employees [of the program], they were not providing 'covered items or services.'" We explained that one of the workers "received payment ... only for referrals and not for any legitimate service for which the Hospital received any Medicare reimbursement." *Id.* at 839. And we pointed out that the program "did not at any time pay [the workers] for any of their time, effort, or business expenses, or for any covered Medicare service." *Id.* at 836. The relators contend that the employee exemption categorically "does not protect payments made only for referrals."

The relators' argument misses the mark. Unlike the payments in *Starks* that were made to non-employees in exchange for referrals not contemplated by a healthcare program, the payments that the Foundation made to Rodriguez were in exchange for referrals that were both a standalone compensable service under the Ryan White Act and demanded by its contracts with Florida. The relators cannot avoid the plain text of the statutory exemption.

B. The Relators' Other Allegations Fail for Lack of Particularity.

Federal Rule of Civil Procedure 9(b) requires a party "alleging fraud or mistake ... [to] state with particularity the circumstances constituting fraud or mistake." To satisfy this particularity standard in a *qui tam* action, a relator must allege the actual "submission of a [false] claim" because "[t]he False Claims Act does not create liability merely for a health care provider's disregard of [g]overnment regulations or improper internal policies unless ... the provider ... asks the [g]overnment to pay amounts it does not owe." *United States ex rel. Clausen v. Lab. Corp. of Am.,* 290 F.3d 1301, 1311 (11th Cir. 2002). The complaint also must offer "some indicia of reliability ... to support the allegation of *an actual false claim* for payment being made to the [g]overnment." *Id.* It is not enough that a relator "merely ... describe[s] a private scheme in detail [and] then ... allege[s] simply and without any stated reason ... his belief that claims requesting illegal payments must have been submitted, were likely submitted[,] or should have been submitted." *Id.* Nor may he point to "improper practices of the defendant[]" to support "the inference that fraudulent claims were submitted" because "submission ... [can]not [be] inferred from the circumstances." *Corsello v. Lincare, Inc.,* 428 F.3d 1008, 1013 (11th Cir. 2005). Indeed, even if the relator is an insider who alleges awareness of general billing practices, an accusation of "[u]nderlying improper practices alone [is] insufficient... absent allegations that a *specific fraudulent claim was in fact submitted* to the government." *Id.* at 1014 (emphasis added); *see also United States ex rel. Sanchez v. Lymphatx, Inc.,* 596 F.3d 1300, 1302 (11th Cir. 2010). In short, he must "allege the 'who,' 'what,' 'where,' 'when,' and 'how' of fraudulent submissions." *Corsello,* 428 F.3d at 1014.

For example, in *Clausen* we held that the relator's "descri[ptions of] the various schemes [the defendant company] allegedly implemented to generate unneeded or duplicative medical tests on unsuspecting... patients" were insufficient because he p.1276 "merely offer[ed] conclusory statements... and d[id] not adequately allege when — or even if — the schemes were brought to fruition" by the actual submission of false claims. 290 F.3d at 1312. Although the relator generally alleged that false bills were submitted for unnecessary tests, "[n]o amounts of charges were identified," "[n]o actual dates were alleged," "[almost no] policies about billing or even second-hand information about billing practices were described," and "[n]o copy of a single bill or payment was provided." *Id.* And in *United States ex rel. Atkins v. McInteer,* we held that "detail[ed]" allegations of "an elaborate scheme for defrauding the government by submitting false claims" were insufficient when the relator failed to "show[] that the defendants *actually submitted* reimbursement claims for the services he describe[d]." 470 F.3d 1350, 1359 (11th Cir. 2006). Although the relator was an insider "psychiatrist responsible for the provision of medical care," we explained that he lacked "firsthand knowledge of the defendants' submission of false claims" because he was "not a billing and coding administrator responsible for filing and submitting the ... claims" and relied instead on "rumors from staff and observ[ations of] records of what he believed to be the shoddy medical and business practices of two other psychiatrists." *Id.; see also Sanchez,* 596 F.3d at 1302.

To be sure, "we are more tolerant toward complaints that leave out some particularities of the submissions of a false claim if the complaint also alleges personal knowledge or participation in the fraudulent conduct." *United States ex rel. Matheny v. Medco Health Solutions, Inc.,* 671 F.3d 1217, 1230 (11th Cir. 2012). For example, in *Matheny* we held sufficient allegations that the defendant had submitted false "[d]iscovery [s]amples" when the relator "allege[d] personal involvement in... the creation of [an] actual [d]iscovery [s]ample," alleged when the discovery sample was submitted, *id.* at 1230, and "allege[d] in detail who made the [d]iscovery [s]amples ..., who approved and directed the process ..., and how various employees, including [the] [r]elator ..., altered the patient accounts to produce a false [d]iscovery [s]ample," *id.* at 1229. And in *United States ex rel. Walker v. R&F Properties of Lake County, Inc.,* we held sufficient allegations of fraudulent billing when the realtor was a nurse practitioner who had personally used incorrect billing codes on a consistent basis and had been told by the "office administrator" that the defendant healthcare provider "'*never*' billed [these fraudulent services] in another manner." 433 F.3d 1349, 1360 (11th Cir. 2005) (emphasis added). Although the relator failed to specify when the defendant actually submitted the false claims that were based on the fraudulent billing methods, we held that her pertinent insider information was "sufficient to explain why [she] believed [that the defendant] submitted false or fraudulent claims." *Id.* at 1360. Nonetheless, we have made clear that even if a relator "assert[s] ... direct knowledge of [a] defendant['s] billing and patient records," she still must allege "specific details" about false claims to establish "the indicia of reliability necessary under Rule 9(b)." *Sanchez,* 596 F.3d at 1302 (internal quotation marks omitted).

The relators contend that the district court erred when it dismissed their broad allegations of widespread misconduct. They maintain that they pleaded with sufficient particularity their sweeping claims that the Foundation sought reimbursement after it paid employees for unlawful referrals and enticed patients with free food, gift cards, cash, and other perks. Although they admit ignorance of "the exact number of illegally referred patients for whom [the Foundation] submitted p.1277 claims for payment with government funds," they assert "direct knowledge that [the Foundation] does so." We disagree.

The complaint failed to allege fraud with particularity. Most importantly, the relators failed to offer sufficient "indicia of reliability ... to support the allegation [that] *actual false claim*[*s*] for payment [were] made to the [g]overnment." *Clausen,* 290 F.3d at 1311. Although the relators allege a mosaic of circumstances that are perhaps consistent with their accusations that the Foundation made false claims — such as that the Foundation provided incentives to certain patients and employees, that the Foundation frequently requested reimbursement from federal healthcare programs, and that Foundation policies focused on aggressive patient recruitment — the relators fail to allege with particularity that these background factors ever converged and produced an actual false claim where the Foundation both violated the Anti-

Kickback Statute when it unlawfully recruited a patient and then billed the government for the services provided to that patient. Indeed, the relators conceded in their complaint that "[t]he precise number of illegally referred HIV-positive patients cannot be known with certainty at this time."

To be sure, the relators made particular allegations about the John Doe representative claims, but these claims cannot help the relators because they involved no fraud. As explained above, the payments to Rodriguez fell squarely within the employee exemption, so these defective allegations hardly suggest other instances of actual fraud. Indeed, that the referrals cited by the relators were covered "services" under the Ryan White Act only undercuts the notion that the Foundation was engaged in rampant illegal conduct in other transactions that the relators failed to identify with specificity. We will not infer fraud from instances of perfectly lawful conduct.

Nor can the relators rely on mathematical probability to conclude that the Foundation surely must have submitted a false claim at some point. Again, a relator must allege an "*actual false claim* for payment" that was presented to the government. *Id.* Speculation that false claims "must have been submitted" is insufficient. *Id.* If anything, the relators' mathematical guesswork cuts the other way. They concede that less than 50 percent of Foundation funding comes from public coffers, so it is entirely possible that even if certain patients and employees received incentives, the ensuing treatment was untethered from government funding. *Cf. Matheny,* 671 F.3d at 1227 (explaining that "the [r]elators... alleged the existence of federal funds with particularity" when the "[c]omplaint specifie[d] the Medicare or Medicaid invoice number or reimbursement check and the [billing] code for accounts alleged to contain [o]verpayments" and included exhibits that "identif[ied] the Medicare or Medicaid claim invoice number ... or the government reimbursement check number" (internal quotation marks omitted)). The relators failed to establish that the Foundation ever submitted a claim for an unlawfully referred patient.

The relators also cannot rely on their "personal knowledge or participation" in the alleged fraud. *Id.* at 1230. Carrel pointed to his position as a "Director of Public Health" and his attendance at "monthly financial review meetings with the ... Finance Manager." And Ferrer and Loftis highlighted their managerial positions and possession of nondescript information that "patients who were illegally referred ... would, as a matter of course, receive various [reimbursed] health services from the [F]oundation" and that public "funding was used in [Foundation] operations." p.1278 But the relators failed to explain how their access to possibly relevant information translated to knowledge of actual tainted claims presented to the government. Indeed, that the relators supposedly had access to pertinent data and still were unable to pinpoint specific false claims other than meritless accusations about the John Does suggests that they lack any meaningful "personal knowledge or participation in the fraudulent conduct." *Id.* To be sure, Ferrer asserted that he personally saw Foundation workers offer gift cards to "employees who secured and referred clients" and that he knew that the Foundation gave incentives like "milkshakes and vitamins" to patients. But these allegations about exchanges at unspecified times are untethered to any particular transaction or claim that actually involved government funding. In short, the relators' general allegations of "standard operating procedure[s]," "standard business practice[s]," and the "course of ... operations" at the Foundation hardly establish that the Foundation ever "ask[ed] the [g]overnment to pay amounts it [did] not owe." *Clausen,* 290 F.3d at 1311.

The relators also unpersuasively point to a Foundation spreadsheet that lists various patients, employees, test dates, and other medical and referral information, and they highlight that this sheet identifies public healthcare programs — such as Medicaid and the Ryan White program — as funding sources for some of these patients. According to the relators, this document suggests that the Foundation unlawfully claimed government funding for these patients. But the notations on the spreadsheet about *possible* sources of funding fail to establish that the relevant claims "*actual[ly]*... [were] made to the [g]overnment." *Id.* Indeed, the relators admit that the spreadsheet reflects "what *potential* governmental sources of funding were available for medical care." As the district court explained, the "[s]preadsheet is neither a billing form nor a record of actual reimbursements" and it "does not memorialize any actual claims [the Foundation] submitted to government programs for services provided to illegally referred patients." And again, that the Foundation was entitled to pay for at least some referrals covered by the Ryan White Act dilutes any inference of fraud from this record.

The relators also cite statements made by Foundation executives and excerpts of company documents that suggest that the Foundation took an aggressive approach to patient recruitment, but this evidence fails to identify actual false claims. For example, the president of the Foundation allegedly has admitted to "[t]he provision of small incentives to patients" and the payment of referral fees to employees. But that the Foundation supposedly made such expenditures at unknown times and places again fails to establish specific instances where the Foundation wrongfully demanded payment from the government. The relators also point to an internal financial presentation where the Foundation listed referral figures, which they conclude "evidences [the Foundation's] intense interest in tracking its success in channeling patient referrals." But this information again fails to tie the referral program to specific, fraudulent claims submitted to the government.

In sum, the general allegations that the Foundation sometimes claimed public reimbursement for services, sometimes offered incentives to employees and patients, and sometimes served patients eligible for government programs is not a specific allegation of the "*presentment* of [a false] claim." *Id.* Absent more exact allegations that these factors converged into actual false claims, even accusations that "the practices of [the Foundation were] unwise or improper ... [do not establish] actionable damage to the public fisc as required under the False Claims Act." *Id.* The relators p.1279 cannot rely on their sweeping accusations that lack the "'who,' 'what,' 'where,' 'when,' and 'how'" of the supposedly fraudulent submissions. *Corsello,* 428 F.3d at 1014.

C. The Relators Waived Their Argument About Amendment.

The relators briefly argue that the district court abused its discretion when it denied as moot their motion to file a fourth amended complaint. They allege that the new complaint contained unspecified "additional details of the organization-wide kickback scheme," and they argue that the employee exemption does not bar amendment because Medicare and Medicaid, unlike the Ryan White Act, "do not reimburse for referral services." We are unpersuaded.

The relators' opening brief contains only a single paragraph of abstract arguments about why they should be permitted to amend, and we have consistently explained that "argument[s] ... briefed in the most cursory fashion ... [are] waived." *In re Globe Mfg. Corp.,* 567 F.3d 1291, 1297 n.3 (11th Cir. 2009). This failure to clearly identify relevant arguments and supporting factual allegations is particularly significant in the light of the heightened pleading requirement of Rule 9(b). More specifically, the relators are demanding that we comb through the 64-page fourth amended complaint, identify new allegations, and determine *sua sponte* whether these accusations are sufficiently particular. We reject this invitation to do the relators' work for them.

IV. CONCLUSION

We AFFIRM.

[*] Honorable James Randal Hall, United States District Judge for the Southern District of Georgia, sitting by designation.